Crisis and Recovery

Learning from the Asian Experience

Crisis and Recovery

Learning from the Asian Experience

Jong-Wha Lee

Korea University, South Korea

World Scientific

NEW JERSEY • LONDON • SINGAPORE • BEIJING • SHANGHAI • HONG KONG • TAIPEI • CHENNAI • TOKYO

Published by

World Scientific Publishing Co. Pte. Ltd.
5 Toh Tuck Link, Singapore 596224
USA office: 27 Warren Street, Suite 401-402, Hackensack, NJ 07601
UK office: 57 Shelton Street, Covent Garden, London WC2H 9HE

British Library Cataloguing-in-Publication Data
A catalogue record for this book is available from the British Library.

CRISIS AND RECOVERY
Learning from the Asian Experience

ISBN 978-981-4749-63-3

Desk Editors: Li Hongyan/Jiang Yulin

Typeset by Stallion Press
Email: enquiries@stallionpress.com

To my dearest wife, Kyunghee Kim

About the Author

Jong-Wha Lee is a professor of economics and director of the Asiatic Research Institute at Korea University. He was previously Chief Economist and Head of the Office of Regional Economic Integration at the Asian Development Bank and an economist at the International Monetary Fund. He also served as a senior adviser for international economic affairs to former President of the Republic of Korea. He has taught at Australian National University, Harvard University and Peking University and served as a consultant to the Harvard Institute for International Development, the Inter-American Development Bank, the International Monetary Fund, the United Nations Development Programme, and the World Bank.

Lee has written and published extensively on topics relating to growth, human capital, financial crises, and economic integration in leading academic journals such as American Economic Review, Journal of Monetary Economics, Journal of International Economics, Journal of Development Economics, Journal of Economic Growth, and Review of Economics and Statistics. His most recent books include *Education Matters: Global Schooling Gains from the 19th to the 21st Century*, coauthored with R. J. Barro (Oxford University Press, 2015) and *Rebalancing for Sustainable Growth: Asia's Postcrisis Challenge*, co-edited with M. Kawai (Springer, 2015). He is a regular columnist for Project Syndicate.

A citizen of the Republic of Korea, Lee obtained his Ph.D. and Master's degree in Economics from Harvard University, and his Master's and Bachelor's degrees in economics from Korea University in Seoul.

Acknowledgements

First of all, I would like to express my sincere gratitude to the original publishers for their permissions of reprinting the following articles in the current book.

Chapter 1. Determinants and Prospects of Economic Growth in Asia (co-authored with Steven Radelet and Jeffrey Sachs) was originally published in *International Economic Journal*, Vol. 15, No. 3 (Autumn 2001), pp. 1–19;

Chapter 2. Overinvestment, Collateral Lending, and Economic Crisis (co-authored with Yong Jin Kim) was originally published in *Japan and the World Economy*, Vol. 14, No. 2 (April 2002), pp. 181–201;

Chapter 3. Financial Reform and the Efficiency of Credit Allocation in Korea (co-authored with Eduardo Borensztein) was originally published in *The Journal of Policy Reform*, Vol. 8, No. 1 (March 2005), pp. 55–68;

Chapter 4. Growth and Investment in East Asia Before and After the Financial Crisis (co-authored with Robert J. Barro) was originally published in *Seoul Journal of Economics*, Vol. 16, No. 2 (Summer 2003), pp. 83–118;

Chapter 5. Recovery and Sustainability in East Asia (co-authored with Yung Chul Park) was originally published in Michael P. Dooley and Jeffrey A. Frankel eds., *Managing Currency Crises in Emerging Markets*, Chicago: University of Chicago Press, 2003, pp. 275–316;

Chapter 6. Crisis and Recovery: What We Have Learned from the Korean Experience? (co-authored with Changyong Rhee) was published in *Asian Economic Policy Review*, Vol. 2, No. 1 (June 2007), pp. 146–164;

Chapter 7. Financial Crisis and Credit Crunch: Evidence from the Korean Firm Level Data (co-authored with Eduardo Borensztein) was originally published in *Journal of Monetary Economics*, Vol. 49, No. 5 (May 2002), pp. 853–875;

Chapter 8. IMF Programs: Who Is Chosen and What Are the Effects (co-authored with Robert J. Barro) was originally published in *Journal of Monetary Economics*, Vol. 52, No. 7 (October 2005), pp. 1245–1269;

Chapter 9. Exchange Rate Regime and Monetary Policy Independence in East Asia (co-authored with Chang Jin Kim) was originally published in *Pacific Economic Review*, Vol. 13, No. 2 (May 2008), pp. 155–170;

Chapter 10. Crises in Asia: Historical Perspectives and Implications (co-authored with Kiseok Hong and Hsiao Chink Tang) was originally published in *Journal of Asian Economics*, Vol. 21, No. 3 (June 2010), pp. 265–279;

Chapter 11. Global Financial Turmoil: Impact and Challenges for Asia's Financial Systems (co-authored with Cyn-Young Park) was originally published in *Asian Economic Papers*, Vol. 8, No. 1 (April 2009), pp. 9–40;

Chapter 12. Real and Financial Integration in East Asia (co-authored with Soyoung Kim) was originally published in *Review of International Economics*, Vol. 20, No. 2 (May 2012), pp. 332–349;

Chapter 13. Emerging Asia: Decoupling or Recoupling (co-authored with Soyoung Kim and Cyn-Young Park) was originally published in *The World Economy*, Vol. 34, No. 1 (January 2011), pp. 23–53;

Chapter 14. Financial Integration in Emerging Asia: Challenges and Prospects (co-authored with Cyn-Young Park) was published in *Asian Economic Policy Review*, Vol. 6, No. 2 (December 2011), pp. 176–198;

Chapter 15. Will Renminbi Emerge as an International Reserve Currency was originally published in *The World Economy*, Vol. 37, No. 1 (January 2014), pp. 42–62;

Chapter 16. Economic Growth in Asia: Determinants and Prospects (co-authored with Kiseok Hong) was originally published in *Japan and World Economy*, Vol. 24, No. 2 (March 2012), pp. 101–113.

I have been privileged to do research collaborations with numerous colleagues and friends. I want to thank my co-authors for their contributions to the relevant chapters and their kind permissions for the inclusion of the articles in this individual collection. These co-authors are Robert J. Barro, Eduardo Borensztein, Kiseok Hong, Chang Jin Kim, Soyoung Kim,

Yong Jin Kim, Steven Radelet, Changyong Rhee, Cyn-Young Park, Yung Chul Park, Jeffrey Sachs, and Hsiao Chink Tang. While writing the articles, I have also benefitted a great deal from valuable comments and discussions from my colleagues and participants in the workshops and seminars. Special thanks go to my students and research assistants for their excellent help. I have acknowledged all of the contributors in individual chapters. Of course, all remaining errors and mistakes are mine.

During my research career, I have received a variety of support and assistance from numerous institutions. Deep appreciation goes to Korea University, the ADB, Asian Development Bank Institute, Australian National University, Center for International Development at Harvard University, and the IMF.

I am very grateful to Eunbi Song, Hanol Lee and Donghan Ryu for their extensive assistance in preparing the manuscript. I also appreciate the work of Jiang Yulin, Li Hongyan and the editors of World Scientific who professionally managed the production and editing processes and expedited the publication of this book.

This book is dedicated to my wife, Kyunghee Kim. Her sacrifices and support always encourage me to continue my research. This book is the product of her love and understanding for over 28 years.

Seoul
May 2016

Contents

List of Tables

List of Figures

Introduction

The Asian financial crisis (AFC) in 1997–98 was a surprising event. Since East Asian economies had been growing rapidly, serving as a growth model for the late-coming developing countries, their sudden collapse was the least expected. The crisis had a devastating effect on the five Asian economies — Indonesia, South Korea, Thailand, Malaysia, and the Philippines — causing unprecedented economic and social distress. Within a few years after the crisis, these economies managed impressive recoveries. The recoveries were faster than anyone had expected. The startling experience of the five economies presented many intellectually challenging questions as well as useful lessons for the late-comers.

The outbreak of the AFC inspired me to begin research on economic crisis. As a Korean researcher who had conducted research on economic growth, international economics, economic integration, and human capital, I naturally paid attention to the crisis and expanded my research scope.

I have been involved with the research that examined the experience of the Asian economies' growth and financial crises. I had a deep intellectual curiosity about the fundamental factors that contributed to East Asia's 'growth miracle' from the 1960s through the mid-1990s and those that made Asia's strong growth succumb to the AFC. An important question was whether the East Asia's development strategies made the Asian economies inevitably lead to the financial crisis. I assessed the experiences of Asian financial crisis — its causes, the desirability of IMF programs, the progress of recovery and structural reforms, and post-crisis prospects.

When I joined the Asian Development Bank (ADB) as Head of the Office of Regional Economic Integration in 2007, it happened to be the 10th year anniversary of the AFC. By recalling and looking for an appropriate response to the AFC, the Asian economies came up with regional cooperation and integration. It was considered an effective mechanism for Asia to prevent and to cope with future crises should they appear. This motivated the establishment of a regional financial mechanism among the ASEAN+3 economies, which included the 10 members of the Association of Southeast Asian Nations (ASEAN) plus Japan, the People's Republic of China (China), and the Republic of Korea (Korea). It resulted in a "self-managed" reserve polling mechanism, called as the Chiang Mai Initiative Multilateralization (CMIM), whose key elements were determined in May 2008 and which has been in effect since March 2010.

The wake of US subprime crisis in mid–2007 aroused fears of the possible spillover effects in the Asian economies. These fears had a solid foundation. The crisis eventually evolved into the global financial crisis (GFC) that deteriorated the world economy beyond everyone's imagination. Asia was not an exception. The region was seriously affected by the spillovers. While serving as Chief Economist at ADB at that time, I turned my research focus to the evolution of the GFC — its causes and effects, and the processes and drivers that led to its spillovers to the Asian economies — and to the need for Asia to find alternative sources of growth, including domestic and regional demand.

My discussions on the crisis highlight the policy implications for Asian economies. Beyond the GFC, the Asian economies must improve their resilience to external shocks, strengthen their own macroeconomic management system and implement reforms to reduce the disruptive impact of volatile short-term capital flows, and create opportunities for medium- and long-term sustained growth.

This book, *Crisis and Recovery: Learning from the Asian Experience*, is a collection of selected articles related to the Asian experience with two crises — AFC and GFC, which I have published since 2000. The 16 articles are grouped into three broad topics:

- Part 1: Anatomy of Asian Growth and Crises
- Part 2: Asian Financial Crises: Responses and Lessons
- Part 3: Global Financial Crisis and Challenges to Asia's Sustained Growth.

In Part 1, Chapters 1–4 discuss the characteristics of Asian growth model and the causes and impacts of the AFC in 1997–98.

Chapter 1, "Determinants and Prospects of Economic Growth in Asia," analyzes Asia's growth experience in a broad historical and international context. East Asian countries grew faster than the rest of the world for four key reasons: they had substantial potential for catching up; their geography and structural characteristics were, by and large, favorable; demographic changes worked in favor of more rapid growth; and their economic policies and strategy were conducive to sustained growth. This essay asserts that the major cause of the AFC was too much short-term capital flowing into weak and under-supervised financial systems, suggesting that with better financial management and a return to the core policies that resulted in the rapid growth that they achieved, the East Asian economies can again return to sustained growth.

As stated in Chapter 1, the essence of the AFC was a huge sudden reversal of capital flows triggered by investor panic. However, structural problems underlying the Asian economies, including under-supervised financial systems and over-leveraged corporate sectors, led to the accumulation of vulnerabilities that set the stage for the crisis and amplified its shock to the economy. The discussions in Chapters 2 and 3 focus more on structural factors as the possible sources of the AFC.

Chapter 2, "Overinvestment, Collateral Lending, and Economic Crisis," explores in greater detail the mechanism through which a high-growth economy becomes susceptible to a sudden financial crisis. In the model, firms are motivated to over-invest because of government subsidies, and bear the burden of the tax or other costs caused by government subsidies. A higher government subsidy generates higher investment and gross domestic product (GDP) growth rates, a higher level and growth of real estate price, and a higher level of current account deficits. On the other hand, the rapid growth induced by government subsidies makes the economy very vulnerable to adverse shocks. When adverse shocks hit the economy and the expected loan-to-collateral value ratio rapidly increases, foreign investors become suspicious about the safety of domestic banks and begin to withdraw their loans. Subsequently, financial panic ensues and an economic crisis suddenly occurs.

Chapter 3, "Financial Reform and the Efficiency of Credit Allocation in Korea," investigates some of the structural problems associated with the Korean financial sector and the efficiency of credit allocation by the financial system over the period from 1970 to 1996. This paper finds no evidence that credit flows were directed to sectors that were more profitable, either before or after financial reforms were initiated in the 1980s. It also shows that the financial support did not contribute to improving the performance of the favored industries over time.

The focal point of Chapter 4, "Growth and Investment in East Asia Before and After the Financial Crisis," turns to analyzing both the immediate and long-term impacts of the AFC on economic performance in East Asia. This paper argues that in 1997–98, five East Asian countries — namely Indonesia, Korea, Malaysia, the Philippines, and Thailand — experienced both sharp currency and banking crises. It also shows that the contraction of real GDP was severe in relation to other instances in the past. It is unclear whether the pre-crisis growth rates will be re-attained. Indications for permanently depressed prospects come from the sharp reductions in investment ratios, which have recovered only slightly, and the lowered stock market prices. A panel analysis for a broad group of economies in this essay presents evidence that a combined currency and banking crisis, such as the AFC, typically reduced economic growth over a five-year period by 2% per year, but it had no effect on growth that persisted beyond a five-year period.

Chapters from 5 to 9 in Part 2 are devoted to exploring the evolution of the AFC.

In Chapter 5, "Recovery and Sustainability in East Asia," the macroeconomic adjustment from the crisis in East Asia is examined in a broad international prospective. The stylized pattern from the previous 160 episodes of currency crisis over the period shows a V-type adjustment of real GDP growth in the years prior to and following a crisis. Cross-country regressions show that depreciation of real exchange rate, expansionary macroeconomic policies and favorable global environments are critical for the speedy post-crisis recovery. In this sense, the East Asian process of adjustment can be argued as not being all that different from the stylized pattern from the previous episodes of currency crisis. However, the degree of initial contraction and following recovery has been far greater in East Asia than what the cross-country evidence predicts. This chapter argues that the sharper adjustment pattern in East Asia can be attributed to the severe liquidity crisis that was triggered by investor panic and then amplified by the weak corporate and bank balance sheet.

Chapter 6, "Crisis and Recovery: What We Have Learned from the Korean Experience?" draws lessons from Korea's crisis adjustment and management experience. The rapid restoration of financial stability due to the early closure of non-viable financial institutions and quick resolution of non-performing loans was critical for the speedy recovery of the Korean economy. The swift adjustment in fiscal and monetary policies in addition to the large depreciation of real exchange rates also bolstered the fast recovery. Corporate and government bond markets played an important role in the financial restructuring and macroeconomic adjustment process. Structural reforms helped to alleviate the weaknesses in the corporate sector, particularly in chaebol groups. Thanks to structural reform, corporate and financial sectors began to recognize the importance of micro risk management, but increased risk aversion contributed to the slowdown of corporate investment and, therefore, reduced long-run growth perspective in Korea.

The Korean experience in the financial sector reform is analyzed in greater detail in Chapter 7, "Financial Crisis and Credit Crunch: Evidence from the Korean Firm Level Data." The analysis shows that there were big differences in the magnitude of the credit contraction across different types of firms during the financial crisis. In particular, chaebol (conglomerate)-affiliated firms appeared to have lost the preferential access to credit that they had enjoyed in the pre-crisis period, and credit appears to have been reallocated in favor of more efficient firms. This suggests that the credit crunch suffered by certain sectors can be attributed to the adjustment by banks and enterprises to the restructuring of the financial sector, rather than tight monetary policy or an external credit constraint.

In Chapter 8, "IMF Programs: Who is Chosen and What are the Effects," the economic effects of the IMF loan programs are examined. The essay provides empirical evidence that IMF loans react to economic conditions but are also sensitive to politico-economic variables. Loans tend to be larger and more frequent when a country has a bigger quota and more professional staff at the IMF and when a country is more connected politically and economically to the United States and major European countries. The results provide instrumental variables for estimating the effects of IMF loan programs on economic growth and other variables. This instrumental estimation, which allows us to sort out the economic effects of the loan programs from the responses of IMF lending to economic conditions, shows that a higher IMF loan-participation rate reduces economic growth. IMF lending does not have significant effects on investment, inflation, government consumption, and international openness. However, IMF loan participation has small negative effects on democracy and the rule of law.

Following the AFC, most crisis-affected Asian economies such as Indonesia, Korea, the Philippines, and Thailand shifted their exchange rate regimes from *de facto* US dollar pegs to floating ones. In Chapter 9, "Exchange Rate Regime and Monetary Policy Independence in East Asia," whether the choice of exchange rate regimes influences the sensitivity of domestic interest rates to international interest rates is investigated. The estimation using a regime switching model presents that the sensitivity of local interest rates to international interest rates declined in Korea and Thailand after their adoption of floating exchange rate regimes. The Asian economy with a floating exchange regime has greater independence in monetary policy than a pegged economy, suggesting that exchange rate flexibility provides greater monetary independence.

Part 3 turns to the GFC — its causes and consequences, including its spillovers to the Asian economies, and its implications to Asia's pursuit of more balanced and sustained growth strategies.

Chapter 10, "Crises in Asia: Historical Perspectives and Implications," analyzes the stylized features of historical crisis episodes for 21 developing Asian economies over the period from 1961–2007. While there was substantial diversity, on average, recessions and financial downturns were more frequent, longer lasting, and more severe in Asia than in the Organisation for Economic Co-operation and Development (OECD) countries. The findings of the papers show that the likelihood and severity of a recession were likely to increase when it was associated with credit crunches or stock market crashes. They also indicate that severe financial downturns or recessions in the global economy are often coupled with financial crises or recessions in Asia.

Chapter 11, "Global Financial Turmoil: Impact and Challenges for Asia's Financial Systems," examines the unfolding of the U.S. sub-prime generated turmoil and its spillover effects on Asia's emerging financial systems. Emerging Asian financial markets remained open to contagion given underlying weaknesses in the region's financial systems. Rapid financial globalization also posed new challenges as the region's largely unsophisticated banking and financial systems strived to keep up with the evolving financial environment. It suggests policy priorities to foster regional financial stability, such as enhancing transparency and governance, improving risk management, strengthening regulation and supervision, and deepening and broadening financial systems, especially by developing local currency bond markets.

The following three chapters, Chapters 12 to 14, empirically analyze the extent, nature, and consequences of East Asia's real and financial integration and macroeconomic interdependence.

Chapter 12, "Real and Financial Integration in East Asia," examines the real and financial integration of East Asian economies, by comparing the degree of real vs financial and global vs regional integration, before vs after the AFC. The empirical analyses show that the degree of real integration significantly increased after the crisis, both regionally and globally; and quantity and price measures such as cross-border financial assets, stock return correlation, and interest rate differentials show an increased financial integration after the crisis. The findings also show that the degree of regional financial integration was smaller than that of global financial integration, based on the consumption relation; and financial integration lags real integration, especially for regional integration.

Chapter 13, "Emerging Asia: Decoupling or Recoupling," investigates the degree of real economic interdependence between emerging East Asian and major industrial countries to shed light on the heated debate over the 'decoupling' of emerging East Asia. Empirical findings show that real economic interdependence increased significantly in the post-crisis period, suggesting 'recoupling', rather than decoupling, in recent years. Output shocks from major industrial countries had a significant positive effect on emerging East Asian economies. More interestingly, the reverse was also true. Output shocks from emerging East Asia (and China) had a significant positive effect on output in major industrial countries. The result suggests that macroeconomic interdependence between emerging East Asia and industrial countries became 'bi-directional', defying the traditional notion of the 'North–South relationship' as one of 'uni-directional' dependence.

Chapter 14, "Financial Integration in Emerging Asia: Challenges and Prospects," examines the impact of a regional shock relative to a global shock on local equity and bond markets. The findings suggest that the region's equity markets were integrated more globally than regionally, although the degrees of both regional and global integration had increased significantly since the 1997/1998 AFC. However, emerging Asia's local currency bond markets remained generally segmented, being neither regionally nor globally integrated. This paper argues for potential benefits from increased regional integration of financial markets. Financial integration at the regional level would allow for the region's economies to benefit from allocation efficiency and risk diversification.

From the AFC and GFC, Asian economies have learned the importance of well-constructed responses at the national level as well as regional and global levels in order to effectively manage the cross-border capital flows. They have actively pursued regional currency swap arrangements such as the CMIM to secure more international liquidity. Moreover, China has taken a number of new initiatives that are critically important for the future of regional and global financial architecture.

Chapter 15, "Will the Renminbi Emerge as an International Reserve Currency," assesses the emergence of Chinese renminbi as a new international currency and its implications to the global reserve system. Given China's strong economic growth over the last 35 years and its growing influence on the world economy, the renminbi certainly emerges as a new international currency, contributing to the creation of a more stable and efficient global reserve system. However, the renminbi's emergence as a new international reserve currency would likely be a gradual and drawn-out process, contingent on the China accepting a more convertible capital account and developing an efficient financial system. Simulations show that, with greater convertibility, the renminbi could gradually become an international currency within Asia and beyond — sharing from 3 to 12% of international reserves by 2035.

Can Asia continue to achieve more sustainable growth? How Asia will look like over the next two decades? In Chapter 16, "Economic Growth in Asia: Determinants and Prospects," long-run growth projections for 12 developing Asian economies are made up to 2030 by combining the growth accounting framework with growth regression approach. The baseline projections based on the model of conditional convergence show that the GDP growth rates of the 12 economies will be consistently lower for the next two decades than their historical performance. However, policy reforms in education, property rights, and research and development can substantially raise GDP growth in the region and partly offset the slowdown in growth caused by the convergence phenomenon. China's average GDP growth over the period from 2011 to 2030 is projected to decline to about 5.5% per year under the baseline scenario, and 6.5% under the reform scenario.

Based on my previous works, I am still conducting research on the topics related to growth and crises and trying to deliver policy implications for Asia's more balanced and sustained growth in the coming decade through journal articles and columns to the public and policymakers.

As an author, I hope the research collected in this book can contribute to ongoing research and policy debates on the future of Asian economies and provide useful lessons for the policymakers who want to learn from the Asian experience with the crises.

To strengthen the financial environment against the volatile external shocks, the Asian economies need to strengthen domestic weaknesses while maintaining the responsiveness of macroeconomic and foreign exchange policies. In addition, they must continue to strengthen effective financial supervision and regulation and develop more effective macroeconomic frameworks at the national and regional levels.

Rebalancing the sources of growth towards own domestic demand is necessary for the Asian economies to overcome uncertain global environments and to pursue further sustainable growth. A higher priority must be given to structural supply-side policies to improve productivity growth that requires improvements in the elements including infrastructure, human capital, technological investment, and institutional quality.

Asia has raised its economic power in global production, trade and investment, and contributed to major parts of global growth during the crisis. With regard to its increasing stature, Asia's pursuit of stable and strong growth must be accomplished, serving as a key element for the global economy.

Part 1

Anatomy of Asian Financial Crises

Chapter 1

The Determinants and Prospects of Economic Growth in Asia*

1.1. Introduction

The countries of East and Southeast Asia grew extremely rapidly from the 1960s through the mid-l990s. The eight best performers — Hong Kong, Singapore, Taiwan, Korea, China, Malaysia, Thailand, and Indonesia — grew at an average of over 5.5% per year in per capita terms between 1965 and 1995. With the exception of several European countries in the immediate post-World War II period, growth rates of this magnitude and duration are apparently unprecedented in history. Although Asia's period of rapid economic growth has come to an end, at least temporarily, with the Asian financial crisis, the region's rapid economic growth during the past three decades continues to fuel an intense debate among economists and policymakers. Was the rapid growth the result of a unique model of economic development? Are there lessons from the East Asian experience that are applicable to other developing countries? Did the strategies that led to

---

*This chapter is co-authored with Steven Radelet and Jeffrey Sachs and was originally published in *International Economic Journal*, Vol. 15, No. 3 (Autumn 2001), pp. 1–19.

This paper was written while Steven Radelet was at Harvard University and before he joined the U.S. Treasury. Part of this work is based on our earlier paper "Economic Growth in Asia." We received helpful comments and insights from David Bloom, David Canning, Francis Harrigan, Changyong Rhee, Andrew Warner, Jeffrey Williamson, and staff of the ADB. We are grateful for excellent research assistance from Mumtaz Hussain, Staci Warden, Dilip Parajuli, Hui Pan, Matt MaGuire and Sarmila Nanda. The views expressed are the authors' alone and should not be attributed to the organizations that the authors are affiliated with. This work was supported by Korea Research Foundation Grant.

Asia's rapid growth inevitably lead to the financial crisis? Can the East Asian countries resume robust long-term growth?

This paper begins to address these critical questions by placing Asia's growth experience in a broad historical and international context. We explore Asian growth patterns by quantifying the empirical relationships between long-term growth and various structural and policy variables. Our objective is to understand the critical dimensions in which the East Asian countries differed from other countries that allowed them to achieve rapid growth, and to explore the extent to which those dimensions are unique to these fast-growing economies. Our basic conclusion is that East Asia's growth record can indeed be understood according to the patterns of global growth.[1] We also explore the extent to which East Asia's rapid growth can be emulated by other Asian countries, particularly the slower growing countries of South Asia. We believe that the East Asian record is broadly transferable to many other countries of Asia, and especially to the countries of South Asia. At the same time, we stress that parts of Asia have physical constraints that will limit their dynamism. For example, the mountainous, landlocked countries of Central Asia and the distant, lightly populated states of the Pacific Islands will have a difficult time generating the same success in export-led growth as the fast-growing East Asian economies.

The financial crisis that began in the middle of 1997 abruptly brought a halt to Asia's period of robust growth. In our interpretation, the crisis was at least as much due to weaknesses in global capital markets and policy mismanagement in the early stages of the crisis, as to fundamental problems in the crisis economies. Our conclusion is that there was little in Asia's fundamental growth strategy that inevitably led to the crisis, with one key exception: the Asian countries most adversely affected by the crisis mismanaged the process of financial liberalization in the early 1990s. The

[1] Throughout this paper, "East Asia" refers to the ten countries for which we have complete data in the region: the PRC, Hong Kong, Indonesia, Korea, Malaysia, Papua New Guinea, the Philippines, Singapore, Taipei, China, and Thailand. The "Four Tigers" include Hong Kong, Korea, Singapore and Taipei, China. "Southeast Asia" refers to Indonesia, Malaysia, the Philippines, and Thailand; and "South Asia" includes Bangladesh, India, Pakistan, and Sri Lanka.

key to the crisis was too much short-term capital flowing into weak and under-supervised financial systems. This suggests that with better financial management and a return to the core policies that resulted in rapid growth, the East Asian economies can again return to sustained growth. As these economies become richer, and the population ages, growth rates will gradually slow over time. Nevertheless, most Asian countries continue to have the capacity for sustained long-term growth.

We should be clear at the outset that the cross-country growth framework that we follow is not designed to answer all of the many questions about the process of long-term growth. The approach does not identify all of the specific factors associated with economic growth across countries, nor does it in every case clarify the precise channels through which certain variables affect growth. Rather, it is an attempt to distill the vast amounts of information available on dozens of countries into a tractable, parsimonious framework that identifies a small set of variables that stand out as the factors most strongly associated with rates of growth around the world. This approach allows us to discern broad trends across countries that illuminate some of the key differences between fast and slow growing economies. It also provides a foundation to consider the prospects for long-run growth in the future in Asia and other developing regions.

Our analysis proceeds as follows. In Section 1.2, we outline the basic cross country growth framework. Section 1.3 discusses the empirical results from estimating the model for a large sample of countries. Section 1.4 estimates the quantitative importance of various policy, structural, and demographic factors in accounting for the differences in growth rates between East Asia and other developing regions. Section 1.5 briefly discusses the East Asian financial crisis and its implications for long-term growth. Section 1.6 provides some concluding observations.

1.2. The Basic Growth Framework

The basic empirical framework is based on an extended version of the neoclassical growth model, as described by Barro (1991), Barro and Lee (1994), and Sachs and Warner (1995a and 1995b). This model predicts conditional convergence of income: a country with a low initial income relative to its own long-run (or steady-state) potential level of income will grow faster than a country that is already closer to its long-run potential level of income. The fundamental idea is that the farther an economy is located from its steady-state income level, the greater is the gap of reproducible (physical and human) capital and technical efficiency from their long-run levels. The gap of existing capital and technology from steady-state levels offers the chance for rapid "catching up," via high rates of capital accumulation as well as the diffusion of technology from more technically advanced economies. Hence the lower is the initial level of per capita income relative to steady state, the higher will tend to be the subsequent growth. This framework presumably helps to explain why wealthier countries, with relatively large capital stocks and already operating near the world's technological frontier, tend to grow more slowly than some lower-income countries that are catching up with the leaders.

If we could presume that all countries have the same steady-state income levels, then the neoclassical approach would imply, simply, that poorer countries would grow faster than richer countries. In fact, such a pattern is not generally observed. The cross-country growth framework therefore builds in a crucial assumption, that countries have distinctive long-term levels of per capita income to which each is converging. The long-term levels depend on two main kinds of variables: economic policies and economic structure. Countries with favorable economic policies and economic structure (as identified below) tend to have a higher steady state level of income, and therefore faster growth at any given initial level of income.

We should stress the precise meaning of "long-term" or "steady-state" as used in this analysis. In our interpretation, the steady state to which an economy is converging at any time t is conditional on the actual policies in place at time t. For example, an economy that is closed to international trade at time t is found to have a lower "steady-state" income level than an open economy. Strictly speaking, we are measuring the "steady state" on the assumption of no future changes in the explanatory (policy and structural) variables. If a closed economy subsequently opens to trade, then we interpret this as raising the steady-state level of income to which the country tends to converge.

The basic model is summarized in two equations:

$$\log\left(QL_t^i\right) = a + bZ_t^i \tag{1}$$

$$d\log\left(Q_t^i\right)/dt = c[\log\left(QL_t^i\right) - \log\left(Q_t^i\right) \tag{2}$$

According to Equation (1), the logarithm of the long-run steady-state level of output per worker in country i, denoted QL_t^i, is a function of a vector of variables Z_t^i, which includes both policy and structural variables as of time t. According to Equation (2), the instantaneous proportionate growth rate of output per worker, $d\log\left(Q_t^i\right)/dt$, is proportional to the gap between the long-run level and the current level of output. By combining (1) and (2), we arrive at:

$$d\log\left(Q_t^i\right)/dt = a' + b'Z_t^i - c\log\left(Q_t^i\right) \tag{3}$$

where $a' = ac$ and $b' = bc$

This equation describes current economic growth per worker as a function of structural and policy variables as well as current income. Of course, current output, all other things equal, has a negative effect on growth: countries with higher output have less chance to "catch up" with their own potential. The next step in getting an estimated cross-country equation is to integrate the differential equation in (3) between time periods 0 (the initial year) and T (the final year). Simple manipulation of (3) gives:

$$(1/T)\log\left(Q_T^i/Q_o^i\right) = a'' + b'Za^i - c''\log\left(Q_o^i\right) \tag{4}$$

Where $a'' = a\left(1 - e^{-cT}\right)/T$, $Za'' = \left(e^{-cT}\right)/T\int\left(e^{ct}Z_t^i\right)dt$, $c'' = \left(1 - e^{-cT}\right)/T$

Note that Za^i is, essentially, an average value of Z^i during the period of observation. Note that in a growth equation estimated over the time period 0 to T, we use initial income at time 0 rather than average income during 0 to T, as the level of "current" income which determines the growth over the period of observation. Finally, consistent with most other growth studies, we would like to express the dependent variable as the growth in income per capita (rather than per worker). We note that:

$$Q_T^i / Q_0^i = Y_T^i / Y_0^i * N_T^i / N_0^i * W_0^i / W_T^i \tag{5}$$

where Y_T^i, N_T^i, and W_T^i; denote per capita income, population, and labor force, respectively, in country i at time T. Substituting Equation (5) into (4) and rearranging yields:

$$\begin{aligned}(1/T)\log\left(Y_T^i / Y_0^i\right) = a'' + b'Za^i - c''\log\left(Q_o^i\right) + (1/T)\log\left(W_T^i / W_0^i\right) \\ -(1/T)\log\left(N_T^i / N_0^i\right)\end{aligned} \tag{6}$$

The two final terms in Equation (6) are the instantaneous growth rate of the labor force and the total population, respectively. Equation (6) is the key equation for estimation.

In order to account for cross-country difference in growth rates, we consider a wide variety of policy and structural variables Z^i that have been proposed by earlier studies as important determinants of long-run income, and therefore current economic growth. We categorize these explanatory variables into four broad dimensions: (1) initial conditions (initial per capita GDP and initial human capital stock); (2) natural resources and geography, including natural resource intensity, land-lockedness, location in the tropics, and the ratio of coastline distance to land area; (3) policy variables (government savings, quality of institutions, and openness); and (4) demographic variables (growth of the working age population, growth of the total population, and initial life expectancy at birth). A summary of the variables, grouped by regions, is presented in Table 1.1.

1.2.1. *Initial Conditions*

In the basic framework, for given values of the other explanatory variables, the model predicts that a country with a lower initial per capita GDP is in a more favorable position for future growth. However, it is well-known that, without controlling for other factors, poor countries do not generally grow faster than rich countries. Empirical evidence shows that without

Table 1.1. Summary of key variables by region (unweighted averages)

	All Countries (N = 78)	Four Tigers (N = 4)	South Asia (N = 4)	Southeast Asia (N = 4)	Sub-Saharan Africa (N = 17)	Latin America (N = 21)
Growth rate of per capita GDP (1965–90, %)[a]	1.9	6.7	1.7	3.8	0.6	0.8
Initial Conditions						
Real GDP per capita in 1965 (1985 prices, '000)[a]	3,163	2,010	996	1,161	826	2,611
Average Years of Secondary Schooling in 1965	0.8	1.5	0.5	0.5	0.2	0.6
Resources and Geography						
Natural Resource Intensity (primary exports/GDP, 1971)	0.11	0.01	0.05	0.17	0.16	0.16
Tropics	0.53	0.63	0.40	1	0.91	0.79
Landlocked	0.17	0	0	0	0.47	0.10
Coastline distance/land area	0.29	2.83	0.07	0.43	0.02	0.17
Policy and Choice Variables						
Openness (0 to 1; 1 = most open)[b]	0.43	0.97	0.06	0.73	0.08	0.17
Government Savings Rate (% of GDP)	1.6	5.6	1.0	3.5	3.0	1.2
Quality of Institutions (1 to 10; 10=best)[c]	5.99	7.79	4.23	4.95	4.72	4.37

(Continued)

Table 1.1. (*Continued*)

	All Countries (N = 78)	Four Tigers (N = 4)	South Asia (N = 4)	Southeast Asia (N = 4)	Sub-Saharan Africa (N = 17)	Latin America (N = 21)
Demography						
Life Expectancy in 1965 (years)	57	63	49	52	41	56
Growth of Working Age Population (annual avg., 1965–90, %)	2.23	2.68	2.51	2.90	2.85	2.60
Growth of Total Population (annual avg., 1965–90, %)	1.96	1.68	2.26	2.35	2.92	2.20

Notes: [a] GDP growth rates and levels are on a purchasing power parity basis, and are taken from the Penn World Tables version 5.6. [b] The openness index is the share of years between 1965–90 that a country is considered to be open to world markets. To be considered open in any year, average tariffs must be lower than 40 percent; quotas and licensing must cover less than 40 percent of total imports; the black market premium must be less than 20 percent; and export taxes must be moderate. [c] The institutional quality index was created by Knack and Keefer (1995), and is the average of five indicators of quality in (i) government bureaucracy, (ii) corruption (iii) rule of law, (iv) expropriation risk, and (v) repudiation of contracts by government.

controlling for other variables, there is no simple relationship between income levels and growth rates (Barro, 1991). However, a considerable body of empirical evidence has shown that once important structural and policy variables are taken into account, poor countries indeed grow faster than rich countries (Barro, 1991, Mankiw, Romer, and Weil, 1992, Barro and Sala-i-Martin, 1992, Barro and Lee, 1994, Sachs and Warner, 1995a). This outcome has become known as conditional convergence. Sachs and Warner (1995a), for example, found that poor but open economies tend to grow faster than rich open countries. Countries that isolate themselves from the global economy are in a much weaker position to take advantage of new technologies, or to develop as extensive a division of labor, and therefore show less tendency to catch up. For the group of countries that have been most open to the global economy, there is a strong negative relationship between the initial level of income and the subsequent rate of economic growth.

The tendency for poor countries to grow faster than rich countries has two important implications in the Asian context. First, it provides one piece to the puzzle of explaining East Asia's rapid growth during the last thirty years. Low levels of income in the 1960s provided the potential for rapid growth. Importantly, this reasoning also implies that some of the other, slow-growing Asian countries have the capacity for more rapid growth in the future. Second, as East Asian countries become wealthier, their growth rates are likely to slow. Japan is a clear example of this pattern; its expansion slowed considerably during the 1980s as it narrowed the gap in per capita income with Europe and the United States (Figure 1.1). When income per capita in Japan was less than 50% of the U.S. average in the 1960s, annual growth exceeded 9%. By the time Japan had reached 70% of U.S. income, its annual growth rate had slowed to 4%, and now that its income is about 90% of the U.S. level, its growth rate is closer to 2%.

The data on 1965 income in Table 1.1 indicate that all three groups of Asian countries were well placed for rapid growth, based on their relatively low levels of income. But obviously there is more to the story — sub-Saharan Africa and South Asia had the lowest initial income levels, and therefore had the potential, all other things equal, to grow more rapidly than the East Asian countries. Clearly, differences in long-term potential income, as conditioned by policies, structure, and demography,

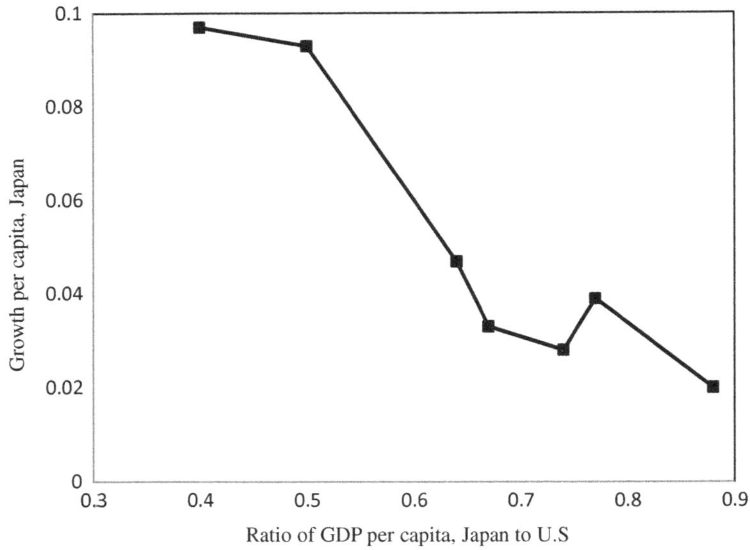

Figure 1.1 Japan's relative income level and growth rates (5-year averages, 1960–94)

have played a role in the differences in growth within Asia and between East Asia and the rest of the world.

Human capital, measured in terms of levels of education and health, is often suggested as a possible source of growth. A better educated, more skilled workforce is likely to be able to produce more from a given resource base than less-skilled workers. Following Barro and Lee (1996), we use the average years of secondary schooling for the working-age population at the start of the period of observation (1965) as our primary measure of the initial skill level of the population. The Four Tigers' average of 1.5 years of secondary schooling was the highest of the developing country regions in our sample.

1.2.2. *Natural Resources and Geography*

We examine four kinds of structural variables that may represent natural barriers to economic growth. The first variable measures natural resource abundance, and is calculated as the ratio of primary-product exports to GDP in 1971 (the earliest year in which data are available for all countries).

Sachs and Warner (1995b) observe that natural resource-abundant economies have tended to grow more slowly than resource-rich economies during the past twenty years. For example, countries with primary product exports valued at between 0 and 5 percent of GDP recorded growth per person of over 3.2 percent between 1965 and 1990, whereas countries with primary product exports equivalent to over 20 percent of GDP grew just 0.8 percent per person per year. This pattern continues to hold once other variables, including initial income, geography, government policies, are taken into account.

The reasons for this negative relationship remain unclear. After all, natural resource exports can provide foreign exchange earnings and finance investments in infrastructure, health, and education. Indonesia and Malaysia are examples of how governments can use the revenues earned from natural resource exports to boost incomes and improve welfare. During the last century, exports of natural resources also played a critical role in supporting sustained growth and development in several countries, including the United States and Argentina.

Over the last thirty years, however, many countries with abundant natural resources have performed poorly. In Mexico, Venezuela, Nigeria, Zambia, and a host of other countries, the initial fillip to income from natural resource exports was followed by long periods of stagnation or even decline. There are several possible explanations for this poor performance. First, natural resource abundance tends to produce a "Dutch Disease" phenomenon, in which a strong resource base causes an appreciation of the real exchange rate, and thereby renders unprofitable an export-oriented or import-competing manufacturing sector. Second, profitable investments in the resource sector itself tend to be limited in scope, so that after the resource sector is developed, it usually does not generate continuing marked improvements in technology and job growth. Third, it is possible that resource-abundant economies may provide greater opportunity and incentive for rent seeking and corruption, particularly if the resources are government owned, or heavily taxed. Fourth, resource abundant countries tend to follow boom-and-bust cycles in line with sharply fluctuating prices of their export commodities, complicating macroeconomic management, creating uncertainty, and undermining long-term investment. Fifth, long-term structural trends in commodity markets may have put primary producers at a disadvantage, as was argued long ago by Raul Prebisch (1950, 1959) and Ragnar Nurske (1961). Although there is much debate on these trends, the evidence appears to support both a gradual decline in commodity prices and slower growth in demand for primary products, especially since 1970.[2]

The second structural variable we examine is access to the sea, as indicated by whether or not a country is landlocked. Landlocked countries have enormous cost and risk disadvantages that they must overcome to compete on world markets. Shipping costs for all imported goods are much higher, as landlocked countries must pay for transport by road and rail, as well as the costs associated with crossing at least one additional international border. The cost of extra shipping is magnified by the uncertainty of inland road conditions and customs clearance, which lead to higher insurance costs for each shipment. Their only alternative is to ship by air, which can be prohibitively expensive for many goods.

A third, and closely related structural variable is the ratio of a country's coastline distance to its total land area. This indicator gives a rough measure of the share of the population with relatively easy access to the sea. In countries where this ratio is relatively high (such as island economies), a larger share of the population is likely to be engaged in activities grounded in international trade. Adam Smith, who pointed out in The Wealth of Nations the difficulties facing landlocked countries, also discussed the importance of access to the sea within countries. He predicted that an extensive division of labor would develop mainly where sea-based trade was feasible. "[S]o it is upon the sea-coast, and along the banks of navigable rivers, that industry of every kind naturally begins to sub divide and improve itself, and it is frequently not till a long time after that those improvements extend themselves to the inland part of the country." China represents an excellent example of this phenomenon, with basically all of its fast growing economy activity located along the Southeast coastline, and little dynamism in its more inland regions. Smith's example was England, where he attributed the economy's relatively high productivity to, in part, its access to the sea. "England, on account of the natural fertility

[2] For summaries of these studies, see Sapsford and Balasubramanyam (1994) and Balassa (1989).

of the soil, of the great extent of the sea-coast in proportion to that of the whole country, and of the many navigable rivers which run through it, and afford the convenience of water carriage to some of the most inland parts of it, is perhaps as well fitted by nature as any large country in Europe, to be the seat of foreign commerce, of manufactures for distant sale, and of all of the improvements which these can occasion." Our variable, the ratio of coastline distance to total land area, is Smith's suggested specification. In the terminology of the neoclassical model, we expect higher values of this indicator to be associated with higher steady state levels of GDP, and therefore higher growth rates. The Four Tigers' ratio of coastline to land area was by far the highest of any region in the world, with Southeast Asia's the second highest.

Our fourth structural variable is location in the tropics. Very few countries located in the tropics have achieved sustained economic success. Tropical countries face several important disadvantages. The prevalence and burden of infectious diseases in much higher in the tropics than in more temperate climates. Malaria, schistosomiasis, and many other debilitating maladies are most prominent in tropic climates. These diseases reduce worker productivity and add to the cost of health care. In additional, tropical agriculture is hindered by warmer temperatures and torrential rains (which tend to leech soils of important nutrients). There are some exceptions — such as the richly fertile volcanic soils of Java — but such cases are relatively rare. As a result of these influences, tropical climates tend to support much lower population densities and thereby a less extensive division of labor than more temperate climates. Singapore and Hong Kong have been much less affected by their location in the tropics, probably because as city states, they have always had a relatively large share of manufacturing and small share of agriculture in GDP. The tropics are likely to have a far smaller deleterious impact on manufacturing firms in the tropics than on agriculture. In the closed space of a factory, air conditioning can compensate for hot, humid weather, putting tropical manufacturing on a par with factories in more temperate climes. This reasoning suggests the possibility of a tropical poverty trap. Agricultural-based economies will have great difficulty in generating sustained growth and affecting the transformation to a manufacturing-based economy. The few economies that are able to make the jump to manufacturing — like

Singapore and Hong Kong — are in a much better position for rapid growth and catching-up with the world economic leaders.

1.2.3. *Policy Variables*

The first policy variable we consider is openness to international trade. Open countries have greater access to new technologies, larger markets, and improved management techniques. They also tend to have fewer distortions and better resource allocation, and their firms are more likely to be competitive on world markets. We use the openness measure constructed by Sachs and Warner (1995a).

This index is the fraction of years between 1965 and 1990 that the country was considered to be open to trade. The judgement on the country's openness is made on the basis of four policy dimensions: (i) average tariff rates, (ii) extent of imports governed by quotas and licensing, (iii) average export taxes, and (iv) the size of the black market premium on the exchange rate. A country is considered to be open if it meets minimum criteria on all four aspects of trade policy: average tariffs must be lower than 40 percent; quotas and licensing must cover less than 40 percent of total imports; the black market premium must be less than 20 percent; and export taxes should be moderate.

Second, neoclassical growth theory suggests that an increase in the national saving rate will raise the growth rate associated with any level of income. However, there is a strong simultaneous relationship between aggregate saving and growth — growth may influence saving as much or more than saving affects growth. The precise nature of the saving-growth relationship remains unclear.[3] As an alternative, we explore the relationship between government saving (defined as the difference between current government revenues and current government expenditures) and economic growth. There are two distinct channels through which government budget policies are likely to influence growth. First, the more governments save, the more the nation as a whole saves (though the relationship is not one to one). This adds to the pool of finances available for investment. Second, higher government saving tends to be indicative of sounder overall

[3] See Radelet, Sachs, and Lee (1997) for more discussion of these issues.

macroeconomic management, including lower rates of inflation, prudent exchange rate policies, and capable monetary management. Stable economies, in turn, lower the risks for investors and therefore lower the cost of capital for long-term investments. Government savings in the Four Tigers were far higher than any other region of the world between 1965–90, averaging 5.6 percent of GDP, whereas governments in the four Southeast Asian countries saved 3.5 percent of GDP. By comparison, government savings in South Asia averaged just 1 percent of GDP during the period.

A third policy indicator is a measure of the quality of public-sector institutions and their relationship to the functioning of markets. We use the index from Knack and Keefer (1995), which is based on data compiled in the International Country Risk Guide (1995). The overall index is itself an average of five indicators of the quality of public institutions, including: (i) the perceived efficiency of the government bureaucracy; (ii) the extent of governmental corruption; (iii) efficacy of the rule of law; (iv) the presence or absence of expropriation risk; and (v) the perceived risk of repudiation of contracts by the government. Each country is scored on these five dimensions on the basis of surveys of business attitudes within the countries. The sub-indexes on the five measures are then averaged to produce a single, overall index that is scaled between 0 and 10. The overall index therefore aims to measure the security of property and contractual rights, the efficiency of the government's intervention in markets, and the allocation of public goods. A lower index indicates poorer quality institutions, and thus higher investment risks and production costs. The Four Tigers' institutions score very high, registering 7.8 on a scale of 1 to 10.

For all the other developing regions, the average index ranges between 4.3–4.9. Malaysia and Thailand both score above 6.0, and India records 5.8. The lowest institutional scores in Asia were recorded by Bangladesh (2.7), the Philippines (3.0), and Indonesia (3.7). These scores compare with an average score of 4.5 for both Latin American and sub-Saharan African countries included in the International Country Risk Guide data.

1.2.4. *Demographic Variables*

Economists have generally given scant attention to the relationship between demographic change and economic growth. Explorations of the role of demography are usually limited to aggregate population growth, which has yielded mixed results. In this paper, we explore the role of changes in the structure of the population, as well as its size, in economic growth. We do so by including the growth rates of both the working-age population (aged 15–64) and the total population in the growth equation.[4] For a given population growth rate, faster growth in the working-age population increases the size of the workforce, which should be positively related to output growth. At the same time, for a given growth rate of the working-age population, faster overall population growth implies an increase in the relative size of the dependent population. Therefore, the growth of GDP per capita is favored when the growth of the working-age population outpaces overall population growth; and GDP growth per capita is reduced in the opposite case, when population growth outpaces the growth of the working-age population.

Our basic growth specification in Equation (6) stipulates a precise relationship between income growth, population growth, and labor force growth. It predicts that for a given population growth rate, a one percentage point increase in the growth rate of the labor force should lead to a one percentage point increase in the growth rate of per capita income. Similarly, for a given growth rate of the labor force, a one percentage point increase in the growth rate of the total population should lead to a one percentage point decrease in the growth rate of per capita income. In the four fast-growing East Asian economies, between 1965–90 the working age population grew one percentage point faster than the total population. In Southeast and South Asia, the differences were 0.55 and 0.25 percentage points, respectively. This suggests that the Four Tigers were given an important demographic boost which raised growth rates.

Our final demographic variable is Life Expectancy at Birth (LEB), measured in the initial year of the growth period. LEB can be viewed as a broad measure of the overall health of the population, encompassing the prevalence of disease and illness of the workforce. A higher life expectancy would tend to indicate a healthier, more productive workforce. LEB also measures changes in population structure, with a higher LEB associated with lower mortality rates and a longer life span for older workers

---

[4] We are grateful to David Bloom and Jeffrey Williamson for suggesting this specification.

and retirees. In the data, East Asia recorded a much higher level of life expectancy than the other developing countries in 1965. Life expectancy at birth was already 63 years in the Four Tigers in 1965, whereas it was only 49 years and 52 years, respectively in South and Southeast Asia. These lower levels presumably reflect both inherent geographic deficits (i.e. a tropic climate, prone to microparasitism) and lags in public health as of 1965.

1.3. Estimation Results

In Table 1.2, we present the results of our regression estimates, using the framework of Equation (6) and the explanatory variables just described. The dependent variable is the annual growth rate of real GDP per capita between 1965–90, as measured by the Penn World Tables, version 5.6.[5] The regressions apply to a data set for 78 countries, including all countries for which we could obtain a complete data set for all variables. Column (1) of Table 1.2 shows the results of the basic regression.

1.3.1. *Basic Results*

The results show strong evidence for conditional convergence. For the basic set of results in column 1, the coefficient on the log value of initial GDP is highly significant, and the estimated coefficient is −1.98 (t = −9.42). Countries with lower incomes in 1965 grew faster than countries that began with higher incomes, after controlling for the other variables that influence the steady-state level of income. Specifically, a country at half the income level of another country tends to grow by 1.4 percentage points (= 1.98 x ln(2)) faster than the richer country, assuming the same level of long-term income. Much of the variation in cross country growth is the result of poorer countries catching up with richer countries. For example, since average income in the Four Tigers was one-sixth the U.S. level in 1965, the catch-up factor boosted their growth rates by 3.5 percentage points a year relative to the U.S. between 1965 and 1990.

[5] The PPP-adjusted income data from the Penn World Tables for China differ widely from other sources. Therefore, we used the growth rate data in Gang, Perkins, and Sabin (1997).

Table 1.2. Cross country growth regressions, basic specification.
Dependent variable: Growth of real per capita GDP, 1965–90 (78 countries)

Independent Variable	Coefficients (t-statistics)		
Initial Output	−1.978	−1.975	−2.137
Per worker (log)	(−9.42)	(−8.78)	(−8.34)
Schooling (log)	0.208	0.200	0.205
	(1.53)	(1.43)	(1.43)
Natural Resource Abundance	−2.430	−2.439	−2.217
	(−2.36)	(−2.31)	(−2.04)
Landlocked	−0.605	−0.613	−0.548
	(−2.28)	(−2.27)	(−2.01)
Tropics	−1.263	−1.337	−1.118
	(−4.29)	(−4.42)	(−3.03)
Coast/Land area	0.262	0.249	0.269
	(2.37)	(2.18)	(2.30)
Government Savings Rate	0.123	0.122	0.123
	(4.94)	(4.81)	(4.83)
Openness	1.965	1.871	1.669
	(6.20)	(5.61)	(4.58)
Quality of Institutions	0.248	0.238	0.285
	(3.47)	(3.28)	(3.22)
Life Expectancy	0.336	0.329	0.313
	(2.81)	(2.72)	(2.55)
Life Expectancy Squared	−0.002	−0.002	−0.002
	(−2.23)	(−2.14)	(−2.01)
Growth of Working Age Population	1.129	1.082	0.977
	(2.86)	(2.61)	(2.20)
Growth of Total Population	−0.774	−0.731	−0.596
	(−1.83)	(−1.64)	(−1.22)
East/Southeast Asia		0.197	−0.209
		(0.51)	(−0.42)
South Asia		−0.395	−0.824
		(−0.95)	(−1.58)
Latin America			−0.348
			(−0.82)
Sub-Saharan Africa			−0.840
			(−1.59)
Adjusted R^2	0.87	0.86	0.86

Note: Constant term not reported.

The estimated coefficient on the initial educational attainment variable (the log value of mean years of secondary schooling) is positive, but is not statistically significant. This result is consistent with other studies that have found a weak direct link between education and growth. One possible explanation is measurement problems. For example, available data do not make any adjustment for the quality of schooling, which arguably is a key determinant of human capital accumulation. It is also possible that low levels of schooling in 1965 implied faster increases in schooling after 1965, and therefore a faster improvement in human capital in the subsequent 25 years.

The estimated coefficient for the natural resource abundance variable is −2.43 (t = −2.36), indicating that during the period 1965–90, countries with abundant natural resources grew more slowly than other countries. This result is consistent with that of Sachs and Warner (1995b). The finding suggests that one reason the Four Tigers grew rapidly was that they were resource poor, which may have induced them to turn to manufacturing more quickly and vigorously than other countries. Of course, there were exceptions to the general correlation of natural resource abundance and slow growth: resource-poor India grew slowly while resource-rich Malaysia and Indonesia both recorded strong growth rates. The negative relationship between resource abundance and growth is a tendency, not a straightjacket. Natural resource abundance is not necessarily an impediment to growth, but it creates challenges in economic management with which many countries have had difficulty coping. As a result, resource abundant countries have tended to grow more slowly than others.

The regression results confirm our hypotheses about geography: countries that were landlocked, or whose populations had relatively little access to the sea, or that were located in the tropics all recorded lower growth rates between 1965–90. Landlocked countries grew on average six-tenths of a percentage point more slowly than other countries between 1965 and 1990, accounting for a cumulative 14 percent lower level of income by the end of the period. Similarly, countries with less coastline relative to their total area grew significantly more slowly than other countries, after controlling for other variables.

Location in the tropics had a very strong, negative impact on growth. We find that countries located in the tropics grew 1.26 (t = −4.29) percentage points slower than countries located in more temperate zones. More specifically, the estimated coefficient on tropics (−1.26), together with the estimated coefficient on initial income (−1.98), imply that the long-run level of income in countries in the tropics only 53% ($1/e^{-1.26/-1.98}$) of the long-run level for countries outside of the tropics. Only eight countries in the tropics (out of sixty tropical countries for which we have data) recorded growth rates in per capita GDP in excess of 3 percent between 1965–90. Five were in East Asia (Singapore, Hong Kong, Malaysia, Indonesia, and Thailand), and the other three were very small island economies (Cape Verde, Barbados, and the Seychelles), which because of their geographic separation may have been spared some of the worst effects of endemic tropical diseases.

The regression results forcefully point to the role of policy variables in determining the rate of economic growth. We find that openness to international trade is very strongly and positively associated with long-term growth, as much theory and previous evidence has indicated. We find that an economy open to trade during the entire period 1965–90 grew 1.97 percentage points faster per year ($t = 6.20$) compared with an economy that was completely closed throughout the period. This result is consistent with Sachs and Warner (1995a), and indeed a long tradition of studies of growth and trade, which have shown that integration with the global economy is associated with faster growth. Trade openness conveys a variety of advantages to a developing economy: it allows countries to undertake more specialized production processes, provides a means to earn foreign exchange to purchase capital goods imports, facilitates inflows of technology from more advanced economies, and provides competitive pressures necessary to increase efficiency and productivity.

The East Asian countries were among the most open of all developing countries between 1965 and 1990. Following an initial stage of modest import substitution, most of the fast-growing Asian countries lowered import tariffs and export taxes, removed quantity restrictions on trade, and reduced the barriers to international flows of capital. Although import barriers remained high in some sectors in certain countries, each of the successful East Asian countries took steps to ensure high profitability for manufactured exporters. Although to some degree Asia's success in manufactured exports can be understood as the outcome of market forces, more than markets were required. The successful Asian economies introduced measures to link multinational production enterprises and their technologies to domestic production processes. The precise strategies varied by country, and included facilitating foreign direct investment, joint ventures, own-equipment manufacturing (OEM) arrangements, licensing agreements, duty exemption systems, export processing zones, and bonded warehouses. These various systems gave exporters easy access to inputs at world market prices, allowed them to overcome the inefficiencies that plagued the rest of the domestic economy, and facilitated direct relationships with leading-edge, competitive firms. In a nutshell, Asia's successful industrial policy was the promotion of labor intensive manufactured exports, not "picking winners" in heavy industry, as is sometimes argued.[6]

The results show that other policies also supported rapid growth. Government saving has a positive and statistically significant impact on growth. The estimated coefficient implies that a 10 percentage point increase in the government saving-GDP ratio is associated with higher growth of 1.2 percentage points per year. Countries in which governments kept spending programs under control and realized larger surpluses on their current budget grew substantially faster than those with smaller surpluses or deficits. Such surpluses financed government investment programs, and had a net positive impact on total national saving.

Our third policy related variable is the quality of government institutions vis-à-vis market regulation. As expected, countries with more constructive interactions between the government and the market tended to record faster economic growth. According to our estimation results, each increment of 1.0 in this index (which is measured on a scale from a low of 0 to a high of 10) is associated with an increase in the growth rate of 0.25 percentage points. Thus, the difference between the Philippines' relatively poor score on institutional quality (2.97) and Singapore's high rating (8.56) accounts for a 1.4 percentage point difference in their average annual growth rates.

Finally, demographic variables are strongly associated with differences in growth rates. Both of the population change variables are of the

---

[6] See Radelet, Sachs and Lee (1997) for a more complete discussion on the relationships between manufactured exports, industrial policies, and economic growth in Asia.

expected sign and approximately the expected magnitude. As we discussed previously, in theory, the estimated coefficients for the growth rates of the working-age population and the total population should be 1 and −1, respectively. The empirical results do not permit rejection of these hypotheses, since the estimated coefficients (1.13 and −0.77) are not significantly different from 1 and −1, respectively. Bloom and Williamson (1997) explore these issues in much more depth. The important, and usually unrecognized point, is that part of East Asia's rapid growth in income is simply due to the rising share of the working age population among the total population between 1965–90. In South Asia, the share of the working age population increased much more slowly, partly accounting for that region's slower growth performance. These patterns are likely to change in the near future, as we discuss later in the paper.

We find evidence for a non-linear relationship between life expectancy at birth and economic growth. At low levels of life expectancy, further increases are strongly associated with more rapid economic growth. In this range, higher life expectancy probably boosts growth by increasing the supply of working-age labor (as a result of lower morbidity); by raising labor productivity (as a healthier population is also a more productive one); by raising the rates of human capital accumulation (as people are more likely to invest in skills and education if they live longer); and by promoting more saving for retirement. Higher life expectancy in East Asia in 1965 (63 years) gave the sub-region a higher growth potential than South Asia, where life expectancy was just 49 years. But the positive effect on growth diminishes as life expectancy increases, and once it passes 68 years, further increases actually have a negative effect on growth. The most plausible explanation for this shift is that after 68 years, further increases in life expectancy indicate that the retired age population is living longer and consuming out of their lifetime savings, with a negative impact on aggregate growth.

Columns 2 and 3 show the results after adding regional dummy variables for East and Southeast Asia (combined), South Asia, Latin America, and sub-Saharan Africa. In each case, these regional variables are insignificant, and there is little change in the estimated coefficients of the other explanatory variables. This result indicates that the basic set of explanatory variables account for most of the differences in growth rates between these regions and the full sample.

Of course, these results represent the "average" relationships across countries, rather than a precise recipe applicable to all countries across time. Some individual countries undoubtedly differ in terms of the magnitude of the relationships, and in terms of the list of the most important variables affecting growth. Nevertheless, the basic specification captures the broad relationships influencing economic growth across countries very well. The adjusted R2 for our base specification is 0.87, indicating that this set of variables explain about 87 percent of the variation in growth rates across the sample, a strong result for this kind of analysis.

In particular, the basic specification tracks the actual growth performance of Asian countries very well. The "fitted" growth rates for each country (calculated by multiplying the estimated coefficients by the actual value for each variable for each country, and adding these terms together) correspond closely with the actual growth rates in most cases. For example, the fitted growth rate for India for 1965–90 is 2.16 percent, compared to the actual rate of 2.03 percent. China's fitted growth rate is 5.30 percent, compared to the actual rate of 5.09 percent. The largest Asian outlier is Malaysia, for which the fitted growth rate (3.53 percent) fell below the actual rate (4.49 percent) by about one percentage point. Indonesia was also a relatively large outlier. These differences are most likely due to Malaysia's and Indonesia's ability to deftly manage the challenges that accompany natural resource abundance. Malaysia and Indonesia managed to avoid the most deleterious effects of the Dutch disease and disruptive terms of trade shocks by diversifying their economies (exploiting a wide range of natural resources as well as encouraging manufactured exports) and reacting quickly to changing international circumstances.

On a regional basis, the basic regression accounts for 6.6 percent growth for the "Four Tigers," very close to the actual rate of 6.7 percent during the period. Similarly, the fitted growth rates are close to the actuals for Southeast Asia (3.4 percent fitted versus 3.8 actual), South Asia (2.1 percent fitted versus 1.7 actual), and almost exactly the same for sub-Saharan Africa (0.7 percent fitted versus 0.6 actual) and Latin America (0.8 percent fitted versus 0.8 actual).

1.3.2. *Variations in Sample Size and Specification*

To test the robustness of these results, we re-estimated the equation in a variety of ways. The full results of these tests are reported in detail in Radelet, Sachs, and Lee (1997). First, we reduced the sample size in two separate ways: by randomly dropping one-fourth of the countries, and by dropping all the Asian countries. In both cases, the estimation results were broadly similar to those from the full sample. We then used these new results to estimate fitted values for the countries that we omitted. In both cases, the fitted values for the out-ofsample countries matched the actual values with a correlation of over 92 percent. These results suggest that our basic results are not particularly sensitive to the sample. Second, we substituted national savings for government savings, and re-estimated the equation using both OLS and a two-stage estimation procedure. Once again, the results did not differ substantially from our basic results.

Finally, we re-estimated the regression with a variety of alternative specifications and explanatory variables. For example, we explored many alternative measures of education and human capital accumulation, with little success in strengthening the results. We substituted government consumption and total government expenditures, respectively, for the government saving rate. The results are similar to, but weaker than, our basic results. We examined the impact of inflation, the initial distribution of income political stability, and political rights. Each of these variables turned out to have a statistically insignificant impact on growth in our sample once all the other explanatory variables are included. The same was true of levels of foreign debt, financial depth (proxied by M2/GDP), prevalence of malaria, components of government spending, and so on. Note that these results do not necessarily mean that these variables are unimportant, especially in some countries. In some cases, it indicates that some of the effects of these variables on growth are captured by the variables already included in the regressions. For instance, inflation rates are closely related to openness and government saving, and the effects of political instability are at least partially captured by the index of institutional quality and the government saving rate.

1.4. Economic Growth of the Asian Countries in Comparative Perspective

These results also allow us to undertake a simple "growth accounting" exercise that explores the relative contribution of each of the explanatory variables in the basic regression to differences in growth rates across regions. Table 1.3 presents the results. For ease of presentation, and because of the strong interest in explaining the very rapid growth of most of the countries of East and Southeast Asia, we use the ten countries in this geographic region[7] as the benchmark, and account for the differences in growth rates between this group of countries and the other regions. Average per capita growth for the four South Asian countries was 2.9 percentage points lower than the average for East/Southeast Asia, and the basic regression can account for a difference of 2.5 percentage points. South Asia started with a lower per capita income in 1965, which, all else being equal, should have led to a growth rate 0.5 percentage points higher than in East Asia. However, the positive effect on growth from low initial income was partially offset by the negative effect from low secondary school attainment. Similarly, natural resources and geography had little net effect on South Asia's performance. South Asian countries have fewer natural resources and are located in more temperate climates, on average, than the nine East/Southeast Asian countries, giving them additional potential for faster growth. The net effects of initial income, education, geography and natural resources are relatively small, and suggest the potential for faster growth in South Asia by 0.5 percentage points relative to East/Southeast Asia.

By contrast, policy choices had a relatively large effect on differences in growth rates. The combined effect of differences in government saving, openness, and the quality of institutions reduced South Asia's growth rate by 2.1 percentage points relative to its East/Southeast Asian neighbors. Openness was by far the most important variable: South Asia's inward-oriented trade strategy accounted for slower growth of 1.2 percentage

[7]The ten economies in our sample from the East/Southeast Asia geographical region include the PRC, Hong Kong, Singapore, Korea, Taiwan, Thailand, Malaysia, Indonesia, the Philippines, and Papua New Guinea.

Table 1.3. Contributions to growth differentials between East/Southeast Asia and various regions, 1965–90 (percent, annual average)

	Contribution of Each Variable to the Difference in per Capita Growth Relative to East/Southeast Asia		
	South Asia	Sub-Saharan Africa	Latin America
Initial Conditions	0.3	0.7	−1.2
Initial GDP per capita	0.5	1.0	−1.2
Schooling	−0.2	−0.4	−0.1
Resources and Geography	0.2	−1.0	−0.6
Natural Resource	0.1	−0.2	−0.2
Landlocked	0.0	−0.3	−0.1
Tropics	0.5	−0.2	−0.0
Coastline /land area	−0.3	−0.3	−0.3
Policy Variables	−2.1	−1.7	−1.8
Government Saving	−0.4	−0.1	−0.3
Openness	−1.2	−1.2	−1.0
Quality of Institutions	−0.5	−0.4	−0.5
Demography	−0.9	−1.9	−0.2
Life Expectancy	−0.5	−1.3	0.1
Growth of Working Age Population	−0.3	0.1	−0.2
Growth of Total Population	−0.2	−0.7	−0.1
Difference in			
Predicted Growth	−2.5	−3.9	−3.8
Actual Growth	−2.9	−4.0	−3.9

Note: The ten economies in our sample from the East/Southeast Asia region are Hong Kong, PRC, Singapore, Korea, Taipei, China, Thailand, Malaysia, Indonesia, the Philippines and Papua New Guinea.

points. Finally, South Asia received less of a boost from demographic change than did East/Southeast Asia. South Asia had lower life expectancy, slower growth in its working age population, and faster overall population growth. These three factors accounted for 0.9 percentage points slower growth in South Asia relative to East/Southeast Asia.

The strong relationship between policies and economic growth is also visible in the comparison between East/Southeast Asia and sub-Saharan Africa (SSA). Between these regions, 1.7 percentage points of the predicted difference in growth rates is due to policy variables, with differences in openness again explaining the bulk of the difference. The demographic variables also explain much of the difference in growth rates. SSA's lower life expectancy and more rapid population growth (relative to growth of the working-age population) accounted for slower growth of 1.9 percentage points. In addition, all of the geography and natural resource variables worked against countries in SSA. There are more landlocked countries in SSA than any other region in the world, and countries in the region, on average, have more natural resources, are more tropical, and have less coastline relative to their area than the countries of East/Southeast Asia. These four variables combined accounted for 1.0 slower growth in SSA relative to East/Southeast Asia.

With respect to Latin America, initial conditions play a more prominent role, mainly because Latin America started with higher income per capita, which reduced its relative growth potential. However, the largest difference between Latin America and East/Southeast Asia lies with the policy variables, which together account for 1.8 percentage points slower annual growth in per capita incomes.

The key lesson from the growth accounting exercise is that initial and resource conditions account for only moderate differences in growth rates. The major role is played by policy variables: high rates of government saving, trade openness, and maintenance of good institutions have been the most important factors behind East Asia's rapid growth during the last three decades. In particular, integration of domestic manufacturing with global production systems (through OEM agreements, EPZs, licensing, and other arrangements) stands out as a key dimension of Asia's success.

The cross-country growth regressions provide a useful starting point for exploring the performance of the Asian developing economies by furnishing a framework which identifies many of the most critical factors that distinguish growth performances across regions and countries. Of course, this framework by itself obviously does not fully explain the process of economic growth. It does not wholly capture the relationships between policy choices, institutional settings, and economic outcomes, nor does it shed light on the important role of economic leadership and skillful policy making. Many of the relationships are explored more fully in our earlier paper (Radelet, Sachs, and Lee 1997). While this framework clearly does not explain everything, it does highlight, at a very broad level, several important common elements within the most successful Asian economies that contributed to robust economic growth.

1.5. The East Asian Financial Crisis

East and Southeast Asia's long period of robust economic growth abruptly came to a halt in the middle of 1997 with the outbreak of the Asian financial crisis. Foreign capital that had been flowing into the Asian economies in large quantities suddenly fled, especially from Indonesia, Korea, Malaysia, the Philippines, and Thailand. The capital withdrawal quickly turned into a financial panic. The panic and its aftermath have had devastating impacts on these economies, with severe economic contraction, rising unemployment, and widespread increases in poverty expected in 1998. Although a full analysis of the crisis is beyond the scope of this paper here we briefly review the most salient points, and the relationships between the crisis and Asia's long-term growth.[8]

At the heart of the crisis was the buildup during the early 1990s of large, short-maturing capital inflows into weak financial and corporate systems. Net private capital inflows into Indonesia, Korea, Malaysia, the Philippines, and Thailand were enormous, reaching $97 billion in 1996. Many factors contributed to this buildup in capital inflows, including financial deregulation in the industrialized countries, low interest rates in Japan and the United States, and the rapid growth and long success of the Asian economies themselves. In addition, each of the crisis economies maintained fixed or very predictable exchange rates, which reduced borrowers' perceived exchange rate risk, and encouraged greater capital inflows. Perhaps most importantly, each of the severely affected economies had undertaken partial financial sector reforms in the late 1980s and early

[8] For analyses of the crisis, see Radelet and Sachs (1998a and 1998b); Borensztein and Lee (l998); Park (1998); Krugman (1998); Goldstein (1998); and Roubini, Corsetti and Pesenti (1998).

1990s that gave banks, financial institutions, and private corporations much greater latitude to borrow abroad.

A critical feature of the capital inflows was that a growing share was short-term, with maturity structures of one year or less. In Indonesia, Korea, and Thailand, over 60 percent of funds owed to foreign banks in mid-1997 were short-term loans. As long as these economies kept growing, these short-term debts posed no problem, since foreign creditors would simply roll them over. But the buildup in short-term debt left these countries vulnerable to rapid credit withdrawals and financial panic. In the three worst hit economies (Indonesia, Korea, and Thailand), short-term debt liabilities exceeded foreign exchange reserves, implying that there was not enough foreign exchange on hand to repay everyone at once.

The capital inflows, while financing new investments, had several adverse consequences. Exchanges rates appreciated in real terms, and a greater share of investment was directed towards non-tradable activities such as real estate and property. The appreciating real exchange rate, together with a glut in global electronics production, the slowdown in the Japanese economy, and perhaps the rise in exports from China all contributed to a dramatic slowdown in export growth in 1996. In most of the crisis economies, a substantial share of the capital inflows were channeled through the domestic banking systems (Indonesia, however, is an important exception, where funds were borrowed mainly by private corporations). Bank lending expanded rapidly, reaching the equivalent of over 140% of GDP in Thailand, Korea, and Malaysia by the end of 1996. This expansion strained the capacity of the commercial banks, financial institutions, and the central banks. Generally speaking, bank regulation and supervision were inadequate to keep up with the rapid expansion in activity.[9]

There is little question that these growing weaknesses in the Asian economies required adjustments and that they contributed to the crisis. These problems alone, however, cannot explain the speed, severity and

---

[9] Radelet and Sachs (1998b) analyze a range of possible explanatory factors for financial crises in emerging markets in the early 1990s. The two factors that emerge as the most important are the buildup of short term foreign debt (relative to foreign exchange reserves), and the rapid expansion in bank lending.

depth of the financial crisis. Several other factors combined to create a full-fledged financial panic, making the crisis much deeper than was either necessary or inevitable.

First, the crisis was in large measure due to the inherent instability in global capital markets. Crises develop when global capital markets first pour large amounts of capital into an emerging market, then suddenly demand repayment when sentiment sours. Developing countries have seen a long succession of sensational international financial crises in this century, including the Latin American debt default in 1929 and 1930, the global debt crisis of the 1980s, and financial crises in the 1990s in Mexico, Argentina, Venezuela, and Turkey. More industrialized countries are not immune, as illustrated most recently in Finland, Sweden, and Norway.[10]

Asia was no exception, with creditors — both foreign and domestic — first providing extraordinarily large amounts of foreign-currency financing when these economies were growing quickly, then overreacting with panicked withdrawals in the early stages of the crisis.

Second, Asian governments made some critical mistakes along the way that added to the withdrawals. Thailand took little action in late 1996 when property and equity prices fell and its financial institutions and banks came under heavy pressure. Had Thailand acted earlier, the worst of the crisis could have been avoided. Korea and Thailand used up substantial portions of their liquid reserves trying to defend their currencies, and Indonesia gave contradicting signals about its approach to addressing the crisis. Inflammatory statements by government officials and market participants (such as the interchanges between the Malaysian Prime Minister and financier George Soros) fanned the flames and added to the withdrawals.

Third, poorly designed IMF programs by some extent added to the rapid withdrawal of funds, and led to a much deeper economic contraction than was necessary. The IMF's ill-conceived approach to financial restructuring and its heavy reliance on strongly contractionary fiscal and monetary policies made a bad situation worse in the early stages of the

---

[10] A growing number of observers point to global capital market instability as a key part of the explanation of financial crises, including Kaminsky and Reinhart (1996) and Eichengreen *et al.* (1997).

crisis. Its failure to include debt restructuring or rescheduling in its original programs deepened the panic and the resulting economic recession (debt rescheduling was central to Korea's second program, included on the insistence of the US government after the IMF's first program had failed).

Fourth, the economic crisis soon evolved into a political crisis in several countries. Thailand and Korea both brought in new governments in late 1997. In Indonesia, political protests led to violent riots and the eventual resignation of President Suharto after three decades in power. In each case, political uncertainty added to the negative sentiment and the capital withdrawals.

By mid-1998, the crisis had devolved into a deep recession, with output contracted in 1998 by 6.7% in Korea, 7.5% in Malaysia, 10.4% in Thailand and an incredible 13.2% in Indonesia. Financial systems were moribund, and even the best firms were unable to obtain credit. Many corporations, including a large number of normally well-run, viable firms, were facing bankruptcy. Unemployment and poverty were rising quickly.

Asia's long period of rapid growth, followed by the deep contraction in some of the same economies, begs a question: was there something in Asia's growth strategy that inevitably led to the crisis? Many analysts, with a strong air of vindication for western economies, have confidently argued that it was precisely Asia's growth strategy that led to the crisis. The argument is based on the idea that Asia's rapid growth was due to strong authoritarian governments, a close-knit relationship between government and business, and selected government subsidies in "picking winners." According to this view, the government-led model led to massive inefficiencies, and ultimately to the financial crisis.

Although there is a grain of truth in these arguments (in that weak investments contributed to the buildup of bad debts in Asian banks), the argument is easily pushed too far. At one level, since the depth of the crisis was in large measure due to instabilities in global financial markets and mismanagement of the early stages of the crisis, Asia's long-term growth strategy clearly does not bear all of the blame. More to the point, in the results from our growth model, and the more complete analysis of Asia's growth in our earlier paper (Radelet, Sachs, and Lee, 1997), we found little evidence to support the claims that authoritarian governments and selected investments in heavy industries were the key to Asia's success in the first place. Instead, the critical elements of Asia's growth were prudent macroeconomic policies (reflected by high government savings rates), openness to the world economy, and relatively high quality institutions compared to other developing countries. If anything, the crisis would seem to strengthen the case for prudent macroeconomic policies and strong institutions.

However, there are some who now question the wisdom of openness and integration with the world economy. In this vein, an important distinction should be made between Asia's success in global integration in manufactured products, and its failure (at least in the crisis economies) to effectively manage integration in world financial markets. As we have shown, at the core of Asia's sustained growth was its success in linking up with global markets through the manufacture of labor-intensive exports. There is little evidence that Asia's export industries were the weak link that led to the crisis.[11] In fact, almost everyone now argues that export industries hold the key to Asia's recovery.

The critical error in the evolution of the crisis economies seems to have been mismanagement of the process of financial liberalization in the early 1990s, in combination with weaknesses in international capital markets which lead to herd behavior among foreign investors. The crisis does suggest some dangers in integrating too rapidly with global financial markets. In particular, rapidly opening up domestic financial markets to foreign capital inflows — especially allowing domestic banks to borrow heavily from abroad — without introducing the appropriate legal and regulatory framework, tends to expose emerging economies to the instabilities of global financial markets. It is important to recognize at this juncture that the hardest hit Asian economies were those that had started, but not fully completed, the process of financial liberalization. Not all of the successful Asian economies succumbed equally to the crisis. At one end of the spectrum, Singapore (and to a lesser extent Hong Kong), with well-developed regulatory and legal systems, avoided the rapid expansion of the

[11] Overcapacity and weak prices for some export products — especially in semiconductors — probably contributed to the crisis, but appear to have played a relatively minor role in comparison with other factors. See Radelet and Sachs (1998b) for a more thorough analysis.

banking system and the build-up of bad loans that characterized the crisis economies. At the other end of the spectrum, Asian countries that had barely begun the process of financial liberalization in earnest (such as China and Vietnam) avoided the crisis because they had not received large capital inflows in recent years. Many analysts believe that the Philippines was affected less than other ASEAN countries simply because it started the process of financial liberalization later than the other economies, and therefore had received less capital inflow in the years before 1997. Perhaps the clearest lesson of the crisis is the need to rethink the pace and sequencing of financial liberalization in emerging markets, especially in reforms affecting short term capital flows.

The growth model used earlier in the paper could not have predicted the crisis and the sharp economic contraction which will follow. At a technical level, the model is intended to capture long-term growth trends and capacities, not short or medium-term variations in these trends. In the 1965–90 period covered by our earlier analysis, many of the Asian economies went through episodes of both relatively fast and slow growth that were not captured by the growth model. Korea's growth slowed markedly in the 1980s, for example. Indonesia started the 1965–90 period with an economic collapse, followed by strong growth in the 1970s when oil prices were high, a dramatic slowdown in the mid-1980s when oil prices plunged, and renewed growth in the late 1980s and early 1990s. The growth model is not designed to capture these kinds of short and medium term variations due to business cycles, terms of trade shocks, or political upheaval and change. The financial crisis is a similar kind of episode, albeit of a much larger magnitude, that is not captured in this kind of long-run model of economic growth.

1.6. Conclusions

Asia's episode of rapid economic growth since the 1960s, as remarkable as it was by historical standards, can be explained in an international comparative context. East Asian countries grew faster than the rest of the world for four key reasons: they had substantial potential for catching up (since the entered the 1960s with relatively low incomes), their geography and structural characteristics were by-and-large favorable, demographic changes following World War II worked in favor of more rapid growth, and their economic policies and strategy were conducive to sustained growth.

At the core of East Asia's success was the recognition of the importance of joining the world economy through the promotion of labor-intensive manufactured exports. Rapid growth was supported by key demographic developments, favorable trends in literacy and education, public health policies which raised life expectancy, government attention to the agricultural sector, high levels of budgetary saving, and the protection of private property rights. Even salutary geographic considerations, such as favorable natural harbors and proximity to major sea lanes have played a role. Quantitatively, however, it seems clear that economic institutions and policies have been the most important factors differentiating the performance of fast-growing and slow-growing nations.

East Asia's policies, however, were far from perfect. The weakest link, at least in several of the East Asian economies, was a haphazard approach to financial liberalization in the early 1990s. A very rapid opening to world financial markets, coupled with an equally rapid and under-supervised expansion of the domestic financial system, created vulnerabilities that led to widespread financial crisis in mid-1997.

It takes several years for the crisis economies to recover. Other Asian economies, notably China, may become vulnerable to a financial crisis at some point in the future, as have nearly all market economies. But, throughout much of Asia, in the long run there will be a continuing opportunity for sustained growth and development. In the richer economies (such as Singapore and Hong Kong), the rates of growth are likely to be somewhat slower than in the past, precisely because the process of catching up has been so successful to date. The middle income economies, with appropriate economic and financial management, have the potential and capacity to return to rapid growth over the long run, once the financial crisis comes to end.

Of course, future growth, even in the long run, is far from guaranteed. It will require successful institutional adaptations to new challenges, including: the pressures related to increasing integration of the global economy (especially the inherent instabilities of the world financial markets); an aging population; increasing urbanization and political participation. As a result, these countries will face increased stresses on public-sector budgets, pressures for continued reforms of the legal system, and the need for flexibility and adjustment of political institutions, including the allocation of powers between central and local governments. For countries that grew more slowly during the past thirty years, the main message is that faster growth is possible, and indeed likely, as these countries adopt market-based strategies, increased openness to world markets, and stronger institutions to support economic growth.

References

Barro Robert J. 1991. "Economic Growth in a Cross Section of Countries," *Quarterly Journal of Economics*, 106, 407–443.

Barro Robert J. and Jong-Wha Lee. 1994. "Sources of Economic Growth," *Carnegie Rochester Conference Series on Public Policy*, 40 (June), 1–46.

Barro Robert J. and Jong-Wha Lee. 1996. "International Measures of Schooling Years and Schooling Quality," *American Economic Review, Papers and Proceedings*, 86 (May) 218–223.

Barro, Robert J. and Xavier Sala-i-Martin. 1992. "Convergence," *Journal of Political Economy*, 100(2), 223–251.

Borensztein, Eduardo and Jong-Wha Lee. 1999. "Credit Allocation and Financial Crisis in Korea." IMF working paper WP/99/20, February 1999.

Coale, Ansley J. and Edgar M. Hoover. 1958. *Population Growth and Economic Development in Low-Income Countries.* Princeton: Princeton University Press.

Eichengreen, Barry, Andrew Rose, and Charles Wyplosz, 1997, "Contagious Currency Crises: First Tests," *Scandinavian Journal of Economics*, 98, 1–22.

Gang, Fan, Dwight Perkins, and Lora Sabin. 1997. "China's Economic Performance and Prospects." Background paper to Emerging Asia: Changes and Challenges. Manila: ADB.

Goldstein, Morris. 1998. The Asian Financial Crisis: Causes, Cures, and Systemic Implications. Policy Analyses in International Economics No. 55, Institute for International Economics (June).

Institute of International Finance. 1998. "Capital Flows to Emerging Market Economies." Report available on the IIF website (www.iif.com). April.

Kaminsky, Graciela, and Carmen Reinhart. 1996, "The Twin Crises: The Causes of Banking and Balance of Payments Problems," International Finance Discussion Paper No. 544. Board of Governors.

Knack, Stephen and Philip Keefer. 1995. "Institutions and Economic Performance: Cross Country Tests Using Alternative Institutional Measures." *Economics and Politics*, 7(3) (November), 207–227.

Krugman, Paul. 1998. "What Happened to Asia?" Unpublished paper (January).

Maddison, Angus. 1995. *Monitoring the World Economy, 1820–1992.* Paris: Organization for Economic Cooperation and Development.

Mankiw, N. Gregory, David Romer, and David N. Weil. 1992. "A Contribution to the Empirics of Economic Growth," *Quarterly Journal of Economics*, 107(2), 407–437.

Nurkse, Rangar. 1961. *Equilibrium Growth in the World Economy.* Cambridge MA: Harvard University Press.

Park, Yung Chul. 1998. "Financial Crisis and Macroeconomic Adjustments in Korea, 1997–98." Mimeo (March)

Political Risk Services, International Country Risk Guide. Political Risk Services (Syracuse, NY), various years.

Prebisch, Raul. 1950. *The Economic Development of Latin America and Its Principal Problems.* New York: United Nations.

Prebisch, Raul. 1959. "Commercial Policy in the Underdeveloped Countries," *American Economic Review*, 49, 251–273.

Radelet, Steven and Jeffrey Sachs. 1998a. "The Onset of the East Asian Financial Crisis." Unpublished manuscript, Harvard Institute for International Development.

Radelet, Steven and Jeffrey Sachs. 1998b. "The East Asian Currency Crisis: Diagnosis, Remedies, Prospects." Brookings Papers on Economic Activity, 1998:1.

Radelet, Steven, Jeffrey Sachs, and Jong-Wha Lee. 1997. "Economic Growth in Asia." Background paper for the Asian Development Bank's Emerging Asia (Manila).

Romer, Paul M. 1986. "Increasing Returns and Long-Run Growth," *Journal of Political Economy*, 99(3), 500–521.

Roubini, Nouriel, Giancarlo Corsetti and Paolo Pesenti. 1998. "What Caused the Asian Currency and Financial Crisis?" Unpublished paper (March).

Sachs, Jeffrey D. and Andrew Warner. 1995a. "Economic Reform and the Process of Global Integration." Brookings Papers on Economic Activity, 1995:1, 1–117.

Sachs, Jeffrey D. and Andrew Warner. 1995b. "Natural Resource Abundance and Economic Growth." Harvard Institute for International Development Discussion Paper No. 517A (October).

Sapsford, David and V. N. Balasubramanyam. 1994. "The Long-Run Behavior of the Relative Price of Primary Commodities: Statistical Evidence and Policy Implications." *World Development*, 22(11) (November), 1737–1745.
Singer, Hans W. 1950. "The Distribution of Trade between Investing and Borrowing Countries." *American Economic Review*, 40 (May), 470–485.
Summers, Robert and Alan Heston. 1994. Penn World Table (Mark 5.6) (website version). Philadelphia: University of Pennsylvania.

Chapter 2

Overinvestment, Collateral Lending, and Economic Crisis*

2.1. Introduction

The financial crises that erupted in the rapidly growing east Asian economies in 1997 brought about unprecedented economic and social distresses on the economies involved. Since the outbreak of the crises, the causes of these crises have been the topic of a hot debate not only because east Asian economies had been growing rapidly, serving as a growth model that many developing countries have tried to emulate, but also because their sudden collapse was the least anticipated. Krugman (1998) and Corsetti *et al.* (1999a) argue that the Asian crisis is a moral hazard crisis as a consequence of poorly regulated and over-guaranteed banks that have recklessly extended credit to risky projects. Radelet and Sachs (1998) regard the crisis in essence as a financial panic triggered by a sudden withdrawal of foreign capital. IMF (1997) and World Bank (1998) attribute the crisis to a combination of factors, including a boom in international lending caused by

---

* Reprinted from *Japan and the World Economy*, Vol. 14, No. 2, Yong Jin Kim and Jong-Wha Lee, Overinvestment, Collateral Lending, and Economic Crisis, pp. 181–201, Copyright (2002), with permission from Elsevier.
The authors would like to thank Ronald Findlay, Se-Jik Kim, Changyong Rhee and participants at the 57th Japan Society of International Economics Conference, the Korea Econometric Society Macroeconomics Workshop, and the University of Washington at Seattle Conference on the Asian Crisis for helpful comments on earlier versions of the paper. Part of this work was undertaken while Jong-Wha Lee was visiting the Center for International Development at Harvard University. This work was supported by Korea Research Foundation Grant.

high growth performance, adverse external shocks, mismanagement of macroeconomic and exchange rate policies, and weak financial sector.

The purpose of this paper is to present a model that explains some salient features of the east Asian crises. The growth process of the east Asian economies is typically characterized by high investment and economic growth, high real estate prices, current account deficits, and then a sudden financial crisis. Until recently, the east Asian economies displayed high saving and investment rates, and rapid GDP growth. Along with these positive signs were a few negative ones such as declines in productivity, increases in current account deficits, and accumulation of corporate and foreign debts. Then, suddenly, financial crises swept through these countries. This paper attempts to show that a fast growing country becomes extremely vulnerable to financial crises.

Because east Asian crises exhibit a complex mixture of currency crisis, banking crisis, and foreign debt crisis, it is hard to single out any one factor as the sole cause of the crises. Recent empirical studies that have examined a large sample of countries for the determinants of the crises could not come up with a clear answer.[1] Theoretical models are still very much sought, although a number of 'third generation' crisis models are competing each other to explain the Asian crises.[2] In this paper, thus, we do not attempt to provide one single answer to the question of why the crises took place in those specific countries in that specific year. Yet, we sketch out another candidate for the third generation crisis models. The basic natures of our model presented here are in line with those of the recent models such as McKinnon and Phil (1997), Krugman (1998), and Corsetti *et al.* (1999b) that focus on 'overinvestment' of the firms caused by the moral hazard behavior of firms and banks. In our model, government subsidies, which motivate the moral hazard behavior of firms and banks, cause the overinvestment of the firms. But, our model also emphasizes the role of the collateral lending practices of banks, which lead to asset bubbles and bust in the economy, in financial crises. The model also shows the feature

---

[1] See Demirguc-Kunt and Detragiache (1997), Eichengreen and Rose (1998), and Kaminsky and Reinhart (1999).

[2] See, for example Krugman (1999) for the discussion of the 'third-generation' crisis models that can explain the Asian crises.

of self-fulfilling prophecy of crises which has been emphasized by another line of work in the third generation crisis models such as Chang and Yelasco (2001), and Aghion *et al.* (2000).

The model presented in the paper describes an economy in which firms, because of a government subsidy, are motivated to invest excessively. We assume that firms bear the burden of paying taxes (or cost of briberies to obtain more subsidies), resulting in making losses. Then, these firms compensate for their losses by obtaining bank loans. We also assume that domestic banks borrow from foreign investors up to the amount of the current account deficit, and lend the money to the firms. Through this process, the foreign borrowing will continue to accumulate, as long as domestic banks and foreign investors continue to provide funds for the firms. One of the critical assumptions of the model is that domestic banks will continue lending money to firms as long as the value of the firms' real estate collateral covers the accumulated loans.

The model explains that a high growth economy caused by a high government subsidy can have a higher price for real estate, higher investment and GDP growth rates, a higher current account deficit, and a higher ratio of debt-to-collateral value. Thus, this model shows that a high growth economy is more likely to be subject to a crisis. It also shows that the underlying financial fragility renders the whole economy extremely vulnerable to adverse shocks. When the adverse shocks hit the economy and foreign investors decide domestic banks are too risky, financial panic and economic crises can suddenly occur. In another words, as soon as foreign investors start to doubt the safety of domestic banks, real estate prices fall to such a level that the market value of real estate can no longer cover the loans which were based on their pre-fall value. As a result, firms and banks become bankrupt. Banking and foreign debt crises suddenly arise. This model also shows that a liberalization of the capital market increases the possibility of crisis and amplifies the scale of crisis due to huge foreign capital inflows and outflows.

The rest of the paper is organized as follows. Section 2.2 describes the basic setup of the model and characterizes its equilibrium. Section 2.3 derives several implications related to the question previously posed, and Section 2.4 analyzes the effect of opening financial markets on the economy. Based on the implications of the model, Section 2.5 presents interpretation and discussion of the Asian crises. Concluding remarks follow in Section 2.6.

2.2. The Model

The model economy consists of identical households, firms and banks. The agent (household) owns a firm through holding shares in the competitive financial markets. The agent consumes one type of commodity and housing service.

The firm produces a commodity with an AK type production technology (Rebelo, 1991 and Barro and Sala-i-Martin, 1995, Chapter 4). The firm owns a house as real estate and uses it as collateral to borrow money from foreign investors. The foreign investors are assumed to lend money to the firm as long as the accumulated loss of the firm remains within the market value of the real estate. In this section, we assume that the government restricts the foreign capital inflow to the extent of current account deficit, while Section 2.4 assumes full capital account liberalization.

2.2.1. *Firm's Maximization*

The firm produces an output Y_t by employing capital k_t. We assume that the firm receives a government subsidy sY_t proportional to the firm's output. The subsidy causes the firm to over-invest.[3] The firm bears the burden of the distortions incurred by the overinvestment in the economy. We simply express the firm's burden by a lump-sum tax of T_t which is imposed to finance the government subsidy. Here, T_t can also include other costs incurring to the firm such as bribes to politicians to get more subsidies or the agency cost due to owner-manager's moral hazard behavior. Each firm owns the fixed $\bar{h}$ units of real estate and rents it to households. Hence, the firm is conducting two businesses — a production business and a real estate business. Or the firm can be considered as a business group (like a Chaebol in South Korea or Keiretsu in Japan) that consists of two subsidiaries.

[3] The government subsidy plays a key role in this model. Due to the government subsidy firms invest in projects that are continuously making losses. We call this 'overinvestment'.

The firm knows the current period's productivity of A_t in the beginning of each period but cannot observe the next period's productivity (A_{t+1}). A change in A_t can represent a productivity shock, a terms-of-trade shock, or other shocks affecting the firm's revenue. Then, the firm owned by the household maximizes its expected discounted profit[4] with respect to the capital stock (k_t) as:

$$\max E_t\left[\sum_{k=0}^{\infty}\left(\prod_{i=1}^{k}\frac{1}{r_{t+i}}\right)\left\{(1+s)A_{t+k}k_{t+k}+q_{t+k}\bar{h}-r_{t+k}k_{t+k}-T_{t+k}\right\}\right] \quad (1)$$

where r_t represents a gross interest rate at time t greater than 1, $q_t\bar{h}$ a rental revenue from a household, and s the government subsidy. Here, we assume that capital depreciates by 100 percent at the end of the period for simplicity. The first order condition (FOC) with respect to kt yields an equilibrium interest rate as:[5]

$$r_t = A_t(1 + S) \quad (2)$$

The government balanced budget constraint produces the relationship of:

$$sA_tk_t = Tt \quad (3)$$

We assume that the firm pays d_t a dividend to stockholders and the dividend equals the rental revenue, because the firm's capital that stockholders own is the real estate. That is, stockholders are being paid the market equilibrium yield for owning the real estate:

$$d_t = q_t\bar{h} \quad (4)$$

From Eqs. (1)–(4), the firm's profit after dividends will be:[6]

$$\pi_t = -T_t = -sA_tk_t \quad (5)$$

---

[4] This profit is an operating profit, which does not include capital gains from holding real estate.

[5] The firm's investment is financed through domestic savings at the domestic equilibrium rate.

[6] We discuss about the reality of this assumption in detail in Section 2.5.

We assume that the firm will compensate for the loss by borrowing foreign capital from banks.[7] The loss will be accumulated as long as the firm continues to borrow.

2.2.2 Household's Maximization

The representative household lives in the house that she rents from the firm. The agent living an infinity life maximizes the preference of:

$$\max U = E_t\left[\sum_{k=0}^{\infty} \beta^{t+j}\left\{\log\left(c_{t+j}\right)+\theta\log\left(h_{t+j}\right)\right\}\right] \tag{6}$$

where $E_t\,[\cdot]$ represents an expectation operator conditional on the information set of time t, c_t the consumption of the commodity at time t, h_t the consumption of housing service and β the time discount rate.

The agent maximizes her discounted utility with the budget constraint of:

$$c_t + q_t h_t + k_{t+1} = r_t k_t + d_t \tag{7}$$

where q_t denotes the price of one unit of housing service, K_{t+1} the saving, r_t the gross interest rate on the saving of k_t observable at time t in the competitive financial market, and d_t the dividend from the holding shares at time t.[8] The budget constraint shows that the household does not bear the burden of the tax at all.[9]

---

[7] Without capital market liberalization, as we assume in this section, the government allows domestic banks to borrow foreign capital only up to the extent of the current account deficit that amounts to the firm's loss each period in this economy. And then domestic banks lend the money to the firms. Section 2.4 will provide implications for the case of full capital market liberalization.

[8] The household owns the firm by holding its shares. The profit the household obtains through dividends cannot be negative due to its limited liability. To simplify the problem, we assume that the dividend equals the rent $q_t h_t$.

[9] If the household bears the full burden of the tax, firms will not suffer losses since the tax is completely internalized by the household. However, even in this case, firms bear some losses, for example due to other costs such as bribes caused by the distortions, as stated before.

We can easily calculate the equilibrium of the aforementioned economy. The equilibrium paths of income, consumption, investment, rental prices of capital and real estate, and dividends of the competitive economy described by Eqs. (1)–(7) are exactly identical to those of another competitive economy that has the production technology of $(1 + s)A_k$, instead of A_k, and has no government intervention (setting T_i equal to zero in Eq. (1)). Then, the equilibrium of the latter competitive economy can be obtained by solving a Pareto optimal problem of this economy due to the fact that it does not have any friction. The Pareto optimal problem without considering the government sector will be solved next.

This Pareto optimal problem has two resource constraints. One is the limited supply of real estate described by $h = \bar{h}$, and the other one is imposed on the goods supply. The latter constraint is derived as follows. Using Eqs. (2) and (4), Eq. (7) can be transformed as:

$$c_t + k_{t+1} = I_t = (1+s)A_t k_t \tag{8}$$

where I_t represents the household's disposable income after paying rents at time t.

The Pareto optimal problem of the economy can be solved by setting up the value function as follows, neglecting the utility from housing service consumption.[10] Here, time subscripts are omitted and the prime on variables represents 'the next period':

$$\mathrm{V}((1 + s)\mathrm{A}k) = \max_{k'} \log((1 + s)Ak - k') + \beta \int V((1 + s)\mathrm{A}'k')dP(A'|A) \tag{9}$$

where $P(A'|A)$ is the cumulative distribution function of A' conditional on the realized value of A.

After positing the value function as:

$$\mathrm{V}(1) = \mathrm{a} + \mathrm{b}\log(I) \tag{10}$$

---

[10] To solve the representative consumer's maximization problem of the economy, we resort to the Pareto optimal problem solving (6) subject to (8) and $h_t = \bar{h}$ as stated before. Then, by substituting $\bar{h}$ for h_t in Eq. (6), we can neglect this variable in the value function and solve for the other decision variable of the consumer.

we can solve Eq. (9) using an envelope theorem and the FOC.

First, we obtain the following relationship by applying an envelope theorem to Eq. (9) and combining it with Eq. (10) as:

$$\frac{b}{(1+s)Ak}=\frac{1}{(1+s)Ak-k'}\Rightarrow k'=\frac{b-1}{b}=(1+s)Ak \quad (11)$$

Additionally, Eq. (11) and the FOC with respect to k' yield:

$$\frac{1}{(1+s)Ak-k'}\beta\int\frac{b(1+s)A'}{(1+s)A'k'}dP(A'|A)=\beta\int\frac{b^2}{(b-1)(1+s)Ak}dP(A'|A) \quad (12)$$

Eq. (12) yields a solution for b as:

$$b=\frac{1}{1-\beta} \quad (13)$$

Thus, Eq. (11) produces a solution for k' as:

$$k'=\beta(1+s)Ak \quad (14)$$

Also, from Eqs. (8) and (14), we can solve for an optimal consumption decision as:

$$c=\frac{I}{b}(1-\beta)(1+s)Ak \quad (15)$$

Note that consumption and investment decisions do not depend on the probability distribution of A'.

Eqs. (14) and (15) produce optimal growth rates of consumption and capital stock as:

$$\frac{k'}{k}=\beta(1+s)A,\ \frac{c'}{c}=\beta(1+s)A \quad (16)$$

Eqs. (15) and (16) show that the household in this economy with a positive government subsidy, $s>0$, enjoys higher consumption-income ratios and higher consumption growth rates over the period.

Utilizing the properties of a logarithmic utility function, we can solve for the price of one unit of the housing service with a general equilibrium condition $h_t = \bar{h}$ as:

$$q_t = \frac{\theta c_t}{\bar{h}} \tag{17}$$

2.2.3. *The Equilibrium*

Eq. (16) shows that consumption and capital grow at the rate $\beta(1 + s)A_t$. Consumption and investment ratios to income stay constant over time, as we can see from Eqs. (11) and (15).

Eq. (8) implies that excess demand for goods over GNP leads to a current account deficit because the tax burden imposed on firms is not internalized in the household's budget constraint. As indicated in Eq. (8), the household budget exceeds the general equilibrium condition for a commodity market by sA_tk_t, because the economy produces only A_tk_t. However, in an open economy, which we assume here, the excess demand of sA_tk_t will be financed by the current account deficit. Note that an economy with $s = 0$ satisfies the general equilibrium condition with a current account balance (see Table 2.1).

Table 2.1. Comparison between an economy characterised by overinvestment and a normal economy

	Over-Investing Economy	Normal Economy
Growth rate of GNP and real estate prices	$\beta A_t(1+s)$	βA_t
Consumption/GNP	$(1-\beta)(1+s)$	$1-\beta$
Investment/GNP	$\beta(1+s)$	β
Land value/GNP	$\theta(1+s)$	θ
Trade deficits/GNP	s	0
National debt/GNP	Less than $\frac{s(1+s)\beta\underline{A}}{\left((1+s)\beta\underline{A}-r^f\right)}$	0
Interest rates	$A_t(1+s)$	A_t

2.2.4. Bank's Behavior

We assumed that the government allows domestic banks to borrow from foreign investors to the extent of the current account deficit, and lend the money to firms at foreign interest rates.[11] Further we assume that the banks will continue lending to the firms as long as the collateral value of real estate covers the accumulated bank loan (the firm's accumulated loss). We discuss more on this assumption in Section 2.5.

We also assume that domestic banks and foreign investors are risk neutral. In other words, they are concerned solely with their expected return. Therefore, if the expected return of loans falls below a certain threshold level, they will stop providing funds for the firms. When the expected ratio of the collateral value to loans falls below a certain threshold level, foreign investors will not continue to lend money to domestic banks. Domestic banks are also assumed to behave as foreign investors do by lending money to the firms until the expected ratio of collateral value to loans falls below the threshold level.[12]

Using Eqs. (2), (16) and (17), the price of one unit of real estate will be calculated as:

$$
\begin{aligned}
p_{ht} &= E_t\left[\sum_{j=0}^{\infty}\left(\Pi_{k=1}^{j}\frac{1}{r_{t+k}}\right)q_{t+j}\right] = E_t\left[\sum_{j=0}^{\infty}\left(\Pi_{k=1}^{j}\frac{1}{r_{t+k}}\right)\frac{\theta}{\bar{h}}c_{t+j}\right] = \\
&E_t\left[\sum_{j=0}^{\infty}\left(\Pi_{k=1}^{j}\frac{g_{t+k}}{r_{t+k}}\right)\frac{\theta}{\bar{h}}c_t\right] = \frac{\theta}{\bar{h}}c_t(1-\beta)^{-1} = A_t k_t\frac{\theta(1+s)}{\bar{h}}
\end{aligned} \tag{18}
$$

Where g_t represents the gross growth rate of income at time t. Eq. (18) says that real estate prices in an overinvesting economy with positive

[11] We consider domestic banks and foreign investors as different economic agents despite their similar roles in the economy in order to focus on the role of weak domestic financial sector in the occurrence of Asian financial crises.

[12] Even though the foreign investor's threshold level can be much lower than the domestic bank's, we simply assume that these threshold levels are identical. This assumption does not influence the main implication because, as long as the foreigner's threshold level is lower than or equal to the domestic bank's, the crisis depends only on the foreign investor's, not on the domestic bank's.

government subsidies $s > 0$ are higher and grow faster than in an economy with $s = 0$.

Then, the ratio of real estate value to GNP will be:

$$\frac{P_{ht}\bar{h}}{A_t k_t} = \theta(1+s) \tag{19}$$

Eq. (19) implies that an increase in s raises this ratio.[13]

Now, recall that domestic banks provide loans for firms by borrowing money from foreign investors as long as the total amount of loans to the firms does not exceed the collateral value of the real estate. To simplify the analysis, we further assume that the lending rate to firms to compensate for their losses is the foreign gross interest rate r^f.[14]

From Eq. (5), the firm's accumulated bank loan to bear its losses at time t can be calculated to be:

$$\begin{aligned} L_t &= s\left(A_t k_t + r^f A_{t-1}k_{t-1} + r^{f^2} A_{t-2}k_{t-2} + \cdots + r^{f^t} A_0 k_0\right) \\ &= sA_t k_t \left(1 + \frac{r^f}{\beta r_t} + \frac{r^f}{\beta r_t}\frac{r^f}{\beta r_{t-1}} + \frac{r^f}{\beta r_t}\frac{r^f}{\beta r_{t-1}}\frac{r^f}{\beta r_{t-2}} + \cdots + \frac{r^f}{\beta r_t}\frac{r^f}{\beta r_{t-1}}\cdots\frac{r^f}{\beta r_1}\right) \end{aligned} \tag{20}$$

Eq. (20) implies that the total amount of bank loans can remain within the collateral value at any point in time, if the inequality of $r^f/\beta r_i \leq \varepsilon < 1$ holds for each period and for a certain constant ε. In the discussion given next, we assume that this inequality holds true. This inequality implies the following. If we define the smallest value in the support of the distribution of A_t as $\underline{A}$, then $\varepsilon = r^f/\beta\underline{A}(1+s)$ and the inequality $r^f/\beta r_i \leq \varepsilon < 1$ implies that $r^f/\beta\underline{A}(1+s) < 1$. Thus, the higher the domestic productivity (A) and the subsidy (s) are and the lower the foreign interest rate (r^f) is, the more probably this relationship holds.

[13] This partly explains why Japan and Korea show very high values of this ratio. One study shows that Japan has a ratio of 2–3, Korea of 4–5, compared to US of 0.6.

[14] The result will not change qualitatively when banks are allowed to charge firms a lending rate higher than the foreign rate, as long as this rate is smaller than β_{ri}. We can assume that the domestic lending rate will fall to the level of the foreign rate through competition among banks.

2.2.5. *Collateral Lending Condition*

Eqs. (2), (18) and (20) yield the expected ratio of bank loan to collateral value to be:

$$E_t\left[\frac{L_{t+1}}{P_{ht+1}\bar{h}}\right]=E_t\left[\frac{s\left(A_{t+1}k_{t+1}+r^f A_t k_t+r^{f^2}A_{t-1}k_{t-1}+\cdots r^{f^t}A_0k_0\right)}{L_{t+1}k_{t+1}\theta(1+s)}\right]$$

$$=E\left[\frac{s}{(1+s)\theta}\left(1+\frac{r^f}{\beta(1+s)A_{t+1}}+\frac{r^{f^2}}{\beta^2(1+s)^2A_{t+1}A_t}+\cdots+\frac{r^{f^{2+1}}}{\beta^{t+1}(1+s)^{t+1}A_{t+1}A_t\cdots A_1}\right)\right] \quad (21)$$

Note that a decrease in the expected A_{t+1} increases this ratio, as we can see from Eq. (21), by lowering the land price more than the accumulated amount of the loan. Thus, for example a negative shock to terms of trade, which lowers A_{t+1}, raises this ratio.

We call the condition of the expected ratio, as expressed by Eq. (21), being less than 1 as the collateral lending condition.[15] We assume that domestic banks will continue to lend money to firms as long as this collateral lending condition holds. At this point, we further assume that foreign investors will also lend money to domestic banks as long as the collateral lending condition is satisfied, just as domestic banks will lend to domestic firms.

With an additional assumption, to get steady state implications, that foreign debt starts from $-\infty$ time, Eqs. (20) and (21) give the collateral lending condition that makes this ratio less than 1 at any time and for any realization of A_t as:

$$Et\frac{L_{t+1}}{P_{ht+1}\bar{h}}\leq\frac{s}{\theta(1-\varepsilon)(1+s)}\leq 1 \quad (22)$$

Substituting $\varepsilon = r^f/\beta\underline{A}(1+s)$ into Eq. (22), the inequality of (22) can be transformed as:

$$\frac{s(1-\theta)}{\theta}\leq\frac{\beta\underline{A}-r^f}{\beta\underline{A}} \quad (23)$$

[15] The condition that the debt to asset value ratio is less than one is commonly used to describe the bank's behavior of collateral lending as in Kiyotaki and Moore (1997) and Schneider and Tornell (1999).

This inequality can be interpreted differently depending on the value of θ. First, if θ is greater than or equal to 1, then inequality of (23) always holds true only if the foreign rate is lower than $\beta\underline{A}$. In other words, irrespective of any realization of A_i the collateral lending condition will be satisfied for any positive value of s. Second, if θ is less than 1, and if the foreign rate is lower than $\beta\underline{A}$, then Eq. (23) gives the inequality on s as:

$$s \leq \frac{\theta}{1-\theta}\frac{\beta\underline{A}-r^f}{\beta\underline{A}} \tag{24}$$

This equation and Eq. (21) imply that if θ is less than 1, the lower the foreign interest rate and the government subsidy are, the more probable the collateral lending condition and (22) hold. In other words, if the government subsidy is too high, then the collateral lending condition will not hold. We consider that this case of θ less than 1 is more plausible. Eqs. (6) and (17) imply that the housing rental expenditure is greater than the sum of other consumption expenditures, if θ is greater than 1. This is very unrealistic. Thus, we will focus on the case of $\theta < 1$.

2.3. Implications

2.3.1. *Welfare Maximizing Government Policy*

In this subsection, we will explore the welfare implications of a government subsidy (s).

Eqs. (15) and (16) imply that an increase in s raises the household consumption in any period $t \geq t_0$ given a fixed capital stock of k_{t0}. Also, note that the government subsidy (s) should satisfy Eq. (23). Thus, we can guess that the welfare maximizing government subsidy plan will be to set s to the maximum value of s subject to Eq. (23), if the cost of violating the collateral lending condition is huge.

Using Eqs. (13) and (15), the expected welfare function (the discounted utility) at time t of a representative agent given the capital stock k_t can be described by:

$$\sum_{i=0}^{\infty}\beta^i E_t\left[\log c_{t+i}\right]=\sum_{i=0}^{\infty}\beta^i E_t\left[\log\left(c_t\,\Pi_{j=1}^{i} g_{t+i}\right)\right]=\frac{1}{1-\beta}\log c_t+\frac{Et\left[\sum_{i=1}^{\infty}\beta^i g_{t+1}\right]}{1-\beta}=$$
$$\frac{1}{1-\beta}\log(1-\beta)(1+s)A_t k_t+\frac{\sum_{i=1}^{\infty}\beta^i(\log\beta(1+s))E_t[A_{t+i}]}{1-\beta} \tag{25}$$

where g_t represents gross growth rate at time t.[16]

Thus, the optimal policy of s will be determined by solving the maximization problem of (25) subject to (23). Eq. (25) implies that an increase in s increases the welfare. In addition, Eq. (23) implies that, in the realistic case of $\theta<1$, the maximum possible value of s is constrained by Eq. (24). Thus, we can easily infer that the maximum value of s (s^*) will depend on the value θ. If the cost of violating the collateral lending condition (22) is large enough, then s^* will be the government's optimal policy. Thus, a lemma follows.

Lemma 1. *If $\theta<1$ and the cost of violating the collateral lending condition is very large, the government's optimal subsidy will be:* $s^*=\frac{\theta(\beta\underline{A}-r^f)}{(\theta-1)\beta\underline{A}}$.

This lemma says that if the government's subsidy to induce a firm's overinvestment is larger than a certain threshold value of $s\left(s\geq\frac{\theta(\beta\underline{A}-r^f)}{(\theta-1)\beta\underline{A}}\right)$ and $\theta<1$, then the collateral lending condition will not hold. In other words, an excessive government subsidy will hurt the economy by incurring a financial crisis. On the contrary, if $\theta>1$, the debt to real estate value ratio decreases in s, because the real estate value increases faster than the accumulated loans to firms as s increases. And, if θ is equal to 1, Eq. (23) holds irrespective of the value of s. Therefore, if $\theta\geq1$, then the government

[16] This welfare function is calculated under the assumptions that foreign investors will continue to lend money to domestic banks, as long as the collateral lending condition is satisfied, and that all agents do not consider the possibility of a crisis. When the possibility of bankruptcy is considered by the foreign investor's behavior, foreign lending rates increase to cover the risk of a crisis.

optimal subsidy will be the infnite value of *s*. However, as stated before, this case is not very probable in the real world.

2.3.2. *Overinvestment, High Growth, and Current Account Deficit*

The following proposition summarizes the results described previously.

Proposition 1. *An increase in the government subsidy (s), which induces overinvestment in the economy, raises income growth rates, the ratio of consumption to income, welfare, real estate prices, and current account deficits as long as* $s \leq \frac{\theta(\beta \underline{A} - r^f)}{(\theta - 1)\beta \underline{A}}$ *an* $\theta < 1$. *If* $\theta \geq 1$, *this always holds true for any positive value of s, as long as the domestic interest rate is higher than the foreign rate.*

Proof. Refer to Table 2.1 in which an over-investing economy is compared to a normal.

This proposition characterizes one example of a Ponzi game equilibrium initiated by a government policy leading to overinvestment. This Ponzi game equilibrium with a higher *s* shares many features with a certain set of developing economies such as Thailand, Indonesia, and other east Asian countries having experienced economic crises in the 1990s. These features include higher growth rates of GNP and investment, higher levels of trade deficit, asset prices, and government intervention, and so on.

2.3.3. *Financial Crisis*

The continuous accumulation of high corporate and foreign debts arising from the collateral lending practices of domestic banks makes this economy very fragile. Whenever the confidence of foreign investors starts to falter, the high debt economy can then collapse easily. As soon as the foreign investors think that the collateral lending conditions will not be likely to hold, they start to recall their loans, which immediately lead to a financial crisis in the country.

A financial crisis occurs if $E_t(L_{t+1}/P_{ht+1}\bar{h} > 1)$. That is, when this collateral lending condition is violated, foreign investors would not lend money to domestic banks nor would domestic banks to firms. Then, firms cannot borrow from domestic banks to compensate for their losses, nor can rollover their previous loans. Subsequently, they are forced to declare insolvency with the accumulated loans that cannot be rolled over. Also they cannot pay for taxes, and thus the government cannot provide the subsidy to firms. In addition to this, the crisis will incur various costs to the economy including restructuring costs of firms and financial institutions. However, for simplicity we postulate that a crisis will lower growth rates of income, by shifting a high growth economy with $s > 0$ to a low growth normal economy with $s = 0$.[17]

Now, we illustrate the eruption of a financial crisis by the following lemma and propositions.

Lemma 2. *In an economy where overinvestment and debt accumulation exist, adverse shocks that lower productivity (A) or raise foreign interest rates* (r^f) *can increase the expected debt-to-collateral value ratio so that the collateral lending condition of both domestic and foreign banks does not continue to be satisfied. This will be more likely to happen in a higher growth economy with a higher level of government subsidy.*

Proof. In Eq. (21), a decrease in the expected A_{t+1} or an increase in r^f can increase the debt-to-collateral value ratio above 1 by lowering the land price more than the accumulated amount of the loan. Also, in Eqs. (20) and (22), it is clear that if a permanent adverse shock forces $r^f/\beta r_i > 1$ for each $i > t$, the total expected value of growing loans will exceed the value of real estate collateral in a finite time. Eq. (21) shows that a decrease in the expected A_{t+1} or an increase in r^f is more likely to cause the debt-to-collateral value ratio to exceed 1 when the level of government subsidy s is higher.

When adverse shocks hit the economy and foreign investors expect the ratio of debt-to-collateral value to rise above 1, the foreign investors will not lend money to domestic banks. As a result, this country with an

[17] This implies that the accumulated loans and other restructuring costs involved with a crisis are paid off in a lump-sum transfer through foreign aids (e.g. IMF bailouts) right after the crisis. We may assume that when a crisis takes place, the loans and other costs are paid by selling off assets. Then, GNP after a crisis will shrink further to a certain fraction of the GNP with the foreign aids. In this case, the real estate price will fall down more with the further decline of GNP.

over-investment policy can easily become a hostage to a foreign debt and banking crisis. The following proposition summarizes these results.

Proposition 2. *Negative shocks such as negative terms-of-trade shocks can push a higher growth country with higher government subsidies into a financial crisis by raising the debt-to-collateral value ratio above 1.*

2.3.4. *Self-fulfilling Feature of the Crisis*

Additionally, this economic crisis possesses a feature of the self-fulfilling prophecy of the bank run model of Diamond and Dybvig (1983). In other words, if foreign investors start to regard domestic banks as risky (even if the ratio of debt-to-collateral value is slightly less than 1), then it will surely become risky, because the gloomy prospect among foreign investors raises this ratio above 1. To explain this feature, we introduce two more equations.

Using Eq. (16), Eq. (21) can be transformed into:

$$E_t\left[\frac{L_{t+1}}{P_{ht+1}\bar{h}}\right] = E_t\left[\frac{s(A_{t+1}k_{t+1} + r^f A_t k_t + r^{f^2} A_{t-1}k_{t-1} + \cdots r^{f^t} A_0 k_0)}{A_{t+1}A_t k_t \beta\theta(1+s)^2}\right] \tag{26}$$

If each foreign investor expects that all other foreign investors will not lend money to the domestic banks, the collateral value will also fall. The reasoning goes as follows. If economic agents realize that borrowing cannot continue due to the behavior of foreign investors, then they will infer that the economy will shift to an economy with $s = 0$. In this case, Eq. (18) implies that real estate prices will fall with $s = 0$.[18] Since the high growth of the economy cannot be sustained without foreign borrowing, economic agents assume that the future expected rents will drop and then the real estate price, the expected summation of future rent flows, will fall. During this period with a given amount of the firm's bank loan, the collateral lending condition (22) with a proper inequality may not be satisfied. When the condition is not satisfied, firms and banks go bankrupt.

---

[18] Without the foreign aids that we assumed, then the land price will fall down more, as we noted in the previous footnote. Then, the self-fulfilling crisis can happen more easily.

Thus, considering that government subsidy is forced to discontinue as foreign investors stop lending, the expected debt-to-collateral value ratio rises as follows:

$$E_t\left[\frac{L_{t+1}}{P_{ht+1}\bar{h}}\right] = E_t\left[\frac{s(A_{t+1}k_{t+1} + r^f A_t k_t + r^{f^2} A_{t-1}k_{t-1} + \cdots r^{f^t} A_0 k_0)}{A_{t+1}A_t k_t \beta\theta}\right] \tag{27}$$

From Eqs. (26) and (27), we can derive an additional proposition related to a self-fulfilling prophecy.

Proposition 3. *If* $1/(1+s)^2 < E_t\left[\frac{L_{t+1}}{P_{ht+1}\bar{h}}\right] < 1$ *with s positive valued, then merely the belief of a bad prospect in the domestic economic condition among foreign investors can push the economy with a positive s into a lower growth economy with* $s = 0$. *It can also trigger bankruptcies of banks and firms in the country.*

Proof. Comparing Eq. (26) with Eq. (27), we can infer that a foreign investor will not invest when the other investors do not invest, because she expects the collateral lending condition will no longer be satisfied. In other words, if a country's debt is in such a risky position as $(1/(1+s)^2 < E_t\left[\frac{L_{t+1}}{P_{ht+1}\bar{h}}\right] < 1)$ and if some foreign investors stop lending money to domestic banks, then other foreign investors will also stop lending. The mechanism of this investors' herd behavior is identical to that of the bank run model of Diamond and Dybvig (1983). Specifically, for an individual foreign investor, it is a Nash equilibrium to stop lending money, when other investors stop lending. If the investor continues lending money to domestic banks whereas others do not, then she suffers losses. This is because the collateral value cannot cover the total value of debt and thereby domestic firms and banks go bankrupt, as we can see from Eqs. (26) and (27) under the condition that $1/(1+s)^2 < E_t\left[\frac{L_{t+1}}{P_{ht+1}\bar{h}}\right] < 1$. So, the proof of the second part of the proposition is followed by the fact that if the debt-to-collateral value ratio exceeds 1 without further foreign investment, then domestic banks and firms will go bankrupt.

In a word, if the fear of the domestic country going bankrupt becomes prevalent among foreign investors, then it can turn into a self-fulfilling prophecy.[19]

Even when the economy is hit by a temporary adverse shock, in terms of trade for example, the vulnerability of the financial system can result in a crisis. Even a little doubt concerning the economy's capability for future debt service can make a foreign investor run to a domestic bank and recall the loan, which can easily trigger other investors' runs on all the other banks. Cole and Kehoe (1996), Radelet and Sachs (1998), and Chang and Yelasco (2001) among others explain the recent financial crises by this self-fulfilling bank run à la Diamond and Dybvig.

A myopic or a more cautious behavior of foreign investors can easily invite a financial crisis. In the real world foreign investors are less tolerant and more cautious than domestic banks in evaluating the situation of the debtor economy because they do not hold collateral directly, nor do they have the loan guarantee, explicit or implicit, which domestic financial institutions obtain from the government. Consequently, foreign investors may have threshold levels lower than one, or different expected ratios in the collateral lending condition, which will make the economy further vulnerable to even smaller shocks.

2.4. Capital Market Liberalization

In previous sections, we assume that foreign capital inflow is allowed only to compensate for the trade deficit (the loss of the firm) indirectly through bank financing. This section considers the impact of financial opening on prompting banking and economic crises. This consideration is important because capital market liberalization and consequent asset price boom and bust often preceded banking and economic crises in most of the countries

[19] This self-fulfilling prophecy is further strengthened with an additional assumption that land price possesses a positive bubble term that will vanish as soon as foreign investors stop lending: if foreign investors stop lending, the land price will drop to such a level that the probability of violating the collateral lending condition becomes much higher.

having experienced recent economic crises (Kaminsky and Reinhart, 1999 and Goldstein, 1998).

We assume that domestic firms and financial institutions are allowed to borrow foreign capital freely at the world interest rate r^f as long as the collateral lending constraint is satisfied. The other assumptions are identical to those in the previous sections.

2.4.1. *Firm's Maximization*

The firm maximizes its expected discounted profit under financial liberalization as

$$\max E_t\left[\sum_{k=0}^{\infty}\frac{1}{(r^f)^k}\left\{(1+s)A_{t+k}(k_{t+k}+k_{t+k}^f)+q_{t+k}\bar{h}-r^f(k_{t+k}+k_{t+k}^f)-T_{t+k}\right\}\right] \tag{28}$$

subject to satisfying the collateral lending constraint, where k_{t+k} indicates the amount of the equilibrium capital stock when the capital market is closed.

We assume that $A_t < r^f < (1+s)A_t$. Then, the firm's objective function implies that an additional unit of foreign capital increases the profit (hence, dividend) by $(1+s)A_t - r^f$. Thus, after the opening, the entrepreneur borrows additional foreign capital (k_t^f) as much as the maximum allowed by the collateral lending constraint. However, this borrowing decreases the GNP by $r^f - A_t$, because we assume that the marginal productivity of capital is lower than the cost of foreign capital.[20] The aforementioned maximization problem with a control variable ($k_t + k_t^f$), will produce the relationships identical to those in the previous sections with some exceptions as shown in the equations given next.

Now, the government balanced budget implies:

$$sA_t(k_t + k_t^f) = T_t \tag{29}$$

This also implies that the trade deficit is $sA_t(k_t + k_t^f) = T_t$.

[20] This assumption is necessary to make 'overinvestment' occur in this economy.

Considering that the profit increases by $[A_t(1+s)-r^f(k_t+k_t^f)]$ owing to the lowering borrowing cost and the additional foreign capital inflow caused by the capital market opening, the dividend will increase as:

$$d_t = q_t\bar{h}+[(A_t(1+s)-r^f)(k_t+k_t^f)] \tag{30}$$

From the aforementioned relationships, the firm's profit after dividends will be:

$$\pi_t = -T_t = -sA_t(k_t+k_t^f) \tag{31}$$

Recall that the firm will compensate for this loss by borrowing foreign capital through the domestic bank. The firm will do business even while accumulating losses as long as the firm can continue to borrow from the bank.

2.4.2. *Household's Maximization*

The maximization becomes very complicated mainly because financial liberalization increases the consumer's disposable income from $A_t(1+s)k_t$ to $A_t(1+s)(k_t+k_t^f)-r^f k_t^f$, and because foreign capital flows into the economy until the collateral lending condition binds in each period.

To simplify the problem, we additionally assume that $A_i = A$, and that capital liberalization started from $-\infty$ time to get steady state implications. Then, we can easily posit that consumption, domestic capital and foreign capital grow at a rate of $\beta A(1+s)$ with the collateral lending condition binding in each period. This will be verified in the next subsection.

Thus, we will have the following modified relationships:

$$(k+k^f)' = \beta A(1+s)(k+k^f) \tag{32}$$

$$c = (1-\beta)\{A(1+s)(k+k^f) - r^f k^f\} \tag{33}$$

The optimal growth rates of consumption and capital stock are identical to those in the pre-liberalization case. And Eq. (17) implies that the housing rental cost will rise because financial market liberalization increases

Table 2.2. Comparison between two economies — with and without capital market liberalization

	No Liberalization	Liberalization
GDP	$A_t k_t$	$A_t (k_t + k_t^f)$
GNP	$A_t k_t$	$A_t (k_t + k_t^f) - r^f k_t^f$
Trade deficit	$sA_t k_t$	$sA_t (k_t + k_t^f)$
Interest rate	$(1 + s)A_t$	r^f
Growth rate	$\beta(1+s)A_t$	$\beta(1+s)A_t$
Real estate prices	P_{ht}	$P_{ht}^f = P_{ht}\left\{((1-\beta))r^f / \left(r^f - \beta(1+s)A\right)\right\} \times\left\{\left(A(1+s)\left(k+k^f\right)-r^f k^f\right)/\left(A(1+s)k\right)\right\}$

the household's income. Two economies-one with financial liberalization and one without-are compared in Table 2.2.

2.4.3. *Bank's Behavior and Implications*

Assuming that $A_t = A$, the price of one unit of real estate is calculated as:

$$P_{ht}^0 = E_t\left[\sum_{j=0}^{\infty} \frac{q_{t+j}}{(r^f)^j}\right] = E_t\left[\sum_{j=0}^{\infty} \frac{\theta c_{t+j}}{(r^f)^j \bar{h}}\right] = \sum_{j=0}^{\infty} \frac{(\beta(1+s)A)^j \theta c_t}{(r^f)^j \bar{h}}$$
$$= \frac{r^f}{r^f - \beta(1+s)A} \frac{\theta}{\bar{h}} c_t \tag{34}$$

where we assume that $A < r^f < (1 + s)A$ and that $r^f > \beta(1 + s)A$.

Eq. (34) implies that the capital market liberalization increases the real estate price through two channels: by lowering the discount rate from the higher domestic interest rate to the lower world interest rate, and by increasing the level of consumption.

Now, let us calculate the collateral lending condition. Using Eqs. (31) and (34), and the fact that the foreign capital inflow to compensate for the current account deficit at time t is $sA(k_t + k_t^f)$, we can explicitly calculate the collateral lending condition. The expected ratio of the bank loan to collateral is less than 1, starting from the time of $-\infty$, as:

$$E_t\left[\frac{L_{t+1}}{P_{ht+1}\bar{h}}\right] = E_t\left[\frac{F_{t+1} + r^f F_t + r^{f^2} F_{t-1} + \cdots + r^{f^{t+i+1}} F_{-i} + \cdots}{P_{ht+1}^0}\right] \leq 1 \quad (35)$$

where $F_t = sA(k_t + k_t^f)$

Right after the financial opening, a huge amount of foreign capital will flow into the country up to the limit in which Eq. (35) binds. As a result, the real estate price will soar as stated. This also greatly increases consumption, investment, and income level. This equilibrium will converge to the steady state in which domestic and foreign capital as well as income and real estate price increase at the constant growth rate of $\beta A(1 + s)$. Eqs. (32)–(35) can easily verify this in that the growth rate of domestic and foreign capital does not violate these conditions in the steady state.

However, if A_t changes over time as in the real world, then the magnitude of foreign capital inflow and outflow also fluctuates depending on the value of A_t.[21] Thus, the growth rates of income, consumption, and investment change as well because the foreign capital flows into the country continuously to the limit of the credit, which depends on the value of A_t, as Eq. (35) implies.

Thus, this model explains the observed empirical fact: capital market liberalization leads to huge foreign capital inflows, which in turn increases income, consumption, and asset prices. This asset bubble induces a boom in lending to risky projects. Sooner or later, the asset bubble bursts at the expense of the banking sector. Then, it drives foreign investors to panic and to withdraw their loans all at once. Subsequently,

[21] It is an interesting fact that due to the credit constraints imposed by collateral lending conditions macroeconomic variables change considerably as productivity changes. See Kiyotaki and Moore (1997) for a model in which a dynamic interaction between credit limits and asset prices makes the effects of productivity shocks persist in the economy.

banking and economic crises follow. The model provides the causal links as follows: financial opening leads to a huge foreign capital inflow, because firms want to maximize their profit by employing cheaper foreign capital within the collateral lending constraint. Then, the lower world interest rate and the higher consumption, caused by the huge inflow of cheaper foreign capital, will hike the real estate prices up, encouraging more foreign capital to flow in again by lowering the debt-to-collateral value ratio. This process brings about a lending boom, increasing the real estate price, income, investment and consumption levels. This lending boom can accelerate the growth of income if it allows firms to speculate in more risky projects with a higher s. This will raise the real estate price even further. Then, finally the bubble bursts and economic crisis sets in.

The capital market liberalization can push the debt-to-collateral value ratio, which was below the self-fulfilling prophecy range before the liberalization, into the self-fulfilling prophecy range presented in Proposition 3.[22] Then, the self-fulfilling prophecy of banking and economic crises will occur. The crisis with capital market liberalization will be much more severe than the one without capital market liberalization, because the huge outflows of foreign capital make income, investment, consumption levels and real estate prices plummet more than in the pre-liberalization case.

2.5. Interpretation and Discussion of the Asian Crisis

In this section, we attempt to interpret and discuss the Asian financial crisis based on the implications of the model.

The Asian financial crisis, which erupted in Thailand and then spread to Indonesia, Malaysia and Korea in 1997 brought about many questions on its causes and its impacts on the economies. Quite a few researches investigate on the unexpected nature of the crisis and the depth of the

[22] Another crisis-triggering mechanism can occur as follows. As more foreign capital flows in, current account deficits and foreign debts increase as implied by Eq. (29). If the increase in foreign debt (particularly, short-term) hits a triggering point of the minimum level of foreign reserves, then foreign investors will panic and make sudden withdrawals of their capital. In Corsetti *et al.* (1999b), the triggering base is the minimum level of reserves.

initial output collapse. Despite all these studies, one important, but still unresolved, question is what are the common elements in the development strategies of Thailand, Indonesia, Malaysia, and Korea that rendered them vulnerable to sudden financial crisis. Before the crisis, these countries had shown a remarkable performance for decades, often lauded as a 'miracle' (World Bank, 1993).

This paper stresses poor corporate governance system, and inefficient management and imprudent lending among financial institutions as main features that rendered the Asian economies vulnerable to the crisis. Clearly, the Asian financial crises had features of a more general financial crisis. Financial crises were common phenomena in global capital markets for a long period. The spread of Asian crises to Russia and Latin America in 1998 confirmed that financial crises were in fact contagious. The quick rebounding of the crisis-hit economies was often interpreted as evidence supporting that the crises were primarily due to the panic of foreign creditors. As in all emerging market financial crises, the Asian crisis is also characterized by a large-scale capital inflow followed by a panicked outflow by foreign creditors holding short-term claims. It is, however, important to understand that although the Asian crisis were sparked off by a rapid and ferocious withdrawal of credits by foreign investors, the countries themselves had some severe institutional weaknesses that made them unusually fragile financially.

We construct a simple model to show that the over-guaranteed and poorly regulated corporate and financial system leads to over-lending and over-investment into risky projects, and thereby makes the Asian economies susceptible to the sudden crisis. The main features of the model are summarized by Propositions 1–3 in the previous sections. As we claimed in Proposition 1, government intervention policies played a key role in the high growth as well as the subsequent crisis in the Asian countries. The governments of those crisis-hit Asian countries have intervened extensively in the economy, mainly pursuing industrial policy objectives. The governments were not 'neutral' nor 'market-friendly'. In the model, we simplified all the various types of government intervention by a single subsidy-cum-tax scheme on producers. The governments provided producers with subsidies to promote investment and exports, thus pursuing high growth strategies (World Bank, 1993, and Rodrik, 1995). Subsidies include various export promoting schemes, such as export financing with low interest rates, tax incentives on investment and export, providing factory sites, and so on. The government industrial policies promote investment and output growth as summarized in Proposition 1. However, the government intervention did not contribute to productivity growth. In contrast, it induced firms to invest excessively in risky and unprofitable projects and lowered the overall efficiency of the investment. Some empirical studies support that government industrial policies led to over-investment and inefficiency. Lee (1996), for example shows that, based on the manufacturing industries of Korea, tax incentives increased output growth rates by stimulating capital accumulation, but did not affect total factor productivity (TFP). The industries that were protected by non-tariff barriers showed lower output and TFP growth rates. Moreover, it is well known that government-led intervention such as allocation of credit at preferential lending rates led to corruption. For example, they induce firms to bribe politicians to obtain more access to subsidized loans.[23] In this context, our model postulated that government subsidies incur firms costs proportional to the size of the subsidies.

Overinvestment in risky projects and high corporate leverage would not cause any serious economic troubles as long as the economies kept growing fast and market perceptions continued to be favorable. But when the economy was hit very hard by unfavorable external shocks, the vulnerability of the system became exposed. Asian countries were hit by significant price declines of their major exports. The largest declines occurred in the electronics industry, in which east Asia specializes in. For example the price of the 16MB DRAM chips fell from a peak of about US$ 150 per unit in 1993 to less than US$ 10 in 1997 (World Bank, 1998, p. 20). The depreciation of the Yen and the Chinese RMB also contributed to the deterioration of export competitiveness in those crisis-hit economies. In 1996 and 1997 export growth abruptly slowed down. Compared to average annual growth rate of 19.6 percent in early 1990s, the export

[23] Among many incidents, one typical case is the scandal with Hanbo group, the 18th largest group in Korea, which collapsed in January 1997 after spending more than US$ 3 billion in a questionable steel-mill project. Indictments for bribery included the President's son, several politicians, bankers and the owner of the group (Borensztein and Lee, 1998).

growth rate in 1996 was −1.3 percent in Thailand. In the same year, Korea's exports grew by just 3.7 percent and Malaysia's by 5.8 percent (Hussain and Radelet, 2000).

The model, by incorporating these features, shows that negative shocks such as adverse terms-of-trade shocks, productivity declines, and high foreign lending rates can cause a financial crisis in the economy. As depicted in Lemma 2 and Proposition 2, the adverse shocks amplify the financial fragility of the economy and thereby cause a crisis. We elaborate this mechanism by focusing on the imprudent lending behavior of financial institutions. Banks made loans on a collateral basis, not a cash-flow basis, thus obfuscating the need for appropriate credit and risk assessment. This collateral lending is well-known business practice adopted by financial institutions in the crisis-hit Asian countries (World Bank, 1998). Because of the poor risk evaluation of projects and the government's implicit loan guarantees, banks were overly optimistic in estimating the value of the loans' collateral. In four Asian countries including Korea, Indonesia, Malaysia, and Philippines, the official collateral valuations were in the range of 80–100 percent of assets (Corsetti *et al.*, 1999a). Thus, the banking institutions of the Asian economies were subject to an excessive exposure to the risk. Our model emphasized that adverse external shocks trigger asset deflation and a sharp drop of the value of the collateral, especially real estate, and then lead to the withdrawal of loans by foreign investors. In east Asian economies, the foreign creditors became skeptical about the future safety of the domestic banks when adverse shocks were likely to raise the ratio of debt-to-collateral value above 1 and increase non-performing loans. In those economies, the panic of foreign creditors became more intensified when they found the economies had the maturity mismatch of external liabilities as the short-term foreign liabilities exceeded the foreign reserve holdings. As we discussed in Section 2.4, the crisis can occur more easily with capital market liberalization. Since interest differentials were substantial and exchange rate risk expectations were very low, financial opening invited huge capital inflows to Asian economies (IMF, 1997, and Corsetti *et al.*, 1999a). Large capital inflows into the Asian economies induced asset bubble and lending boom. In those economies, loans were directed more and more towards risky and unprofitable projects. In Korea and Thailand, the incremental capital-output ratios (ICOR) declined continuously over the 1990s (World Bank, 1998, p. 7). Evidence shows that corporate profitability declined sharply. In Korea, before the onset of the crisis many Chaebol firms' net profits were negative (Corsetti *et al.*, 1999a).

Finally we will briefly comment on the reality of key assumptions of the model in the context of Asian economies. The model presented here is built on a few strong assumptions. First, we assume that the firm pays a dividend (which equals to rental revenue) despite the negative profits. This assumption can be rationalized by considering the poor corporate governance system in east Asia. In Asian countries where the accounting as well as the corporate governance system is under-developed, it is often the case that the owner of the firm, even a loss-making one, extorts a portion of profits. Or as we motivated the model, the firm can represent one business group which controls two subsidiaries. A real estate business subsidiary owns houses through equity financing and rents them to households at market rates. The rents are distributed to shareholders. And the other subsidiary, which produces goods, incurs losses but covers them through loans. The real estate subsidiary guarantees these loans for the production subsidiary by using the real estate as collateral. This situation implies that the group as a whole making losses provides shareholders with positive dividends. The cross-subsidiary debt guarantee is one of the well-known business practices among conglomerates in east Asia (see Classens *et al.*, 1999). World Bank (1998) and Johnson *et al.*, (2000) discuss the role of the weak institutions for corporate governance in Asian crises.

Another strong assumption of the model is that all agents make decisions without considering the possibility of the occurrence of a crisis. This assumption of the myopic behavior of the agents may not be very strong because many studies show that the east Asian financial crises were least anticipated. Few empirical papers that attempted to predict the occurrence of Asian crisis ex post based on multi-country panel data were successful. Perhaps, Thailand could be an exception. It can be argued that the Thailand economy became unsustainable because of the continuous current account deficits (Sachs and Woo, 2000). But, clearly the spread of the crisis to Korea was least anticipated.

2.6. Concluding Remarks

This paper provides a model that can explain the recent experience of east Asian economies characterized by high growth and sudden financial crisis.

The model describes an economy in which firms, subsidized by the government, are motivated to over-invest and banks recklessly lend money to the firms. The model shows that the high growth economy caused by high government subsidies becomes more vulnerable to adverse shocks and more likely to be hostage to bank and foreign exchange crises when foreign investors stop lending money to domestic banks. This paper also demonstrates that capital market liberalization augments the likelihood of an even more severe crisis, especially in a high growth economy.

Recent models on the emerging market crises such as McKinnon and Phil (1997), Krugman (1998), Schneider and Tornell (1999), Corsetti *et al.*, (1999b) and others focus on 'overinvestment' caused by the moral hazard behavior of firms and banks. Our model is observationally equivalent to this kind of moral hazard model. But, we consider our model differs from the others by fully capturing the role of asset bubble and bust in the financial crises within the framework of a simple general equilibrium model. The model also emphasizes the self-fulfilling prophecy of financial crises. When foreign banks or foreign investors start to regard the economies as risky, then it will surely become risky. One foreign investor's run on a domestic bank can trigger other investors' run on banks. The bank run feature of the model implies that financial crises can be contagious among similar countries with high debts. Once foreign investors have experienced a crisis in one country, they will become more cautious in making investments in economies with similar financial systems. The recent Asian financial crises showed this self-fulfilling feature across the countries.

The analysis of this paper shows that an increase in the government subsidy can promote income growth and, under some conditions, consumer welfare as well. But, considering that the government distortions can lead the economy to structural weaknesses and thereby financial crises, the net effect of government industrial policies on welfare is not clear. In most cases, government interventions create distortions in resource allocation and make the economy bear the cost of the inefficiencies in the long-run. The degree of the desirable interventions is a difficult question and must be an important agenda for future research.

References

Aghion, P., Bacchetta, P., Banerjee, A., 2000. A simple model of monetary policy and currency crises. *European Economic Review* 44, 728–738.

Barro, R., Sala-i-Martin, X., 1995. *Economic Growth.* McGraw-Hill, Cambridge, MA.

Borensztein, E., Lee, J.-W., 1998. Credit allocation and financial crisis in Korea. International Monetary Fund Working Paper WP/99/20.

Chang, R., Velasco, A., 2001. A model of financial crises in emerging markets. *Quarterly Journal of Economics* 116, 489–517.

Classens, S., Djankov, S., Fan, J.P.H., Lang, L.H.P., 1999. Corporate diversification in East Asia: the role of ultimate ownership and group affiliation. Policy Research Working Paper, World Bank.

Cole, H.L., Kehoe, T.J., 1996. A self-fulfilling model of Mexico's 1994–1995 debt crisis. *European Economic Review* 41, 309–330.

Corsetti, G., Pesenti, P., Roubini, N., 1999a. What caused the Asian currency and financial crisis? *Japan and the World Economy* 11, 305–373.

Corsetti, G., Pesenti, P., Roubini, N., 1999b. Paper tigers? A model of the Asian crisis. *European Economic Review* 43, 1211–1236.

Demirguc-Kunt, A., Detragiache, E., 1997. The determinants of banking crises: Evidence from developing and developed countries. IMF Working Paper 97/106.

Diamond, D., Dybvig, P., 1983. Bank runs, deposit insurance, and liquidity. *Journal of Political Economy* 91, 401–419.

Eichengreen, B., Rose, A., 1998. Staying afloat when the wind shifts: External factors and emerging-market banking crises. NBER Working Paper No. 6370.

Goldstein, M., 1998. *The Asian Financial Crisis: Causes, Cures and Systematic Implications.* Washington, DC: Institute for International Economics.

Hussain, M., Radelet, S., 2000. Export competitiveness in Asia. In: Woo, W.T., Sachs, J. D., Schwab, K. (Eds.), *The Asian Financial Crisis: Lessons for a Resilient Asia.* Cambridge, MA: MIT Press, pp. 71–90.

International Monetary Fund, 1997. World economic outlook, interim assessment.

Johnson, S., Boone, P., Breach, A., Friedman, E., 2000. Corporate governance in the Asian financial crisis, 1997–1998. *Journal of Financial Economics* 58, 141–186.

Kaminsky, G., Reinhart, C., 1999. The twin crises: The causes of banking and balance of payments problems. *American Economic Review* 89, 473–500.

Kiyotaki, N., Moore, J., 1997. Credit cycles. *Journal of Political Economy* 105, 211–248.

Krugman, P., 1998. What Happened to Asia? Manuscript. MIT Press, Cambridge, MA.

Krugman, P., 1999. Balance Sheets, Financial Crises, and the Transfer Problem. Manuscript. MIT Press, Cambridge, MA.

Lee, J.-W., 1996. Government interventions and productivity growth. *Journal of Economic Growth* 1, 391–414.

McKinnon, R., Phil, H., 1997. Credible economic liberalization and overborrowing. *American Economic Review Papers and Proceedings* 97, 189–193.

Radelet, S., Sachs, J., 1998. On the onset of the East Asian financial crisis. Development Discussion Paper. Harvard Institute for International Development.

Rebelo, S., 1991. Long-run policy analysis and long-run growth. *Journal of Political Economy* 99, 500–521.

Rodrik, D., 1995. Getting interventions right: How South Korea and Taiwan grew rich. *Economic Policy* 20, 55–107.

Sachs, J.D., Woo, W.T., 2000. A reform agenda for a resilient Asia. In: Woo, W.T., Sachs, J.D., Schwab, K. (Eds.), *The Asian Financial Crisis: Lessons for a Resilient Asia.* Cambridge, MA: MIT Press.

Schneider, M., Tornell, A., 1999. Lending Booms and Asset Price Bubbles. Mimeo. Harvard University Press, New York.

World Bank, 1993. East Asian miracle: Economic growth and public policy.

World Bank, 1998. East Asia: The road to recovery.

Chapter 3

Financial Reform and the Efficiency of Credit Allocation in Korea*

3.1. Introduction

The spread of the East Asian crisis to Korea in late 1997 was perhaps one of the most surprising developments in the regional debacle. A member of the original 'four Asian tigers' (the other three being Hong Kong SAR, Singapore and Taiwan Province of China), and a recent addition to the OECD club, Korea had shown a remarkable economic performance for decades. Korea's economic situation clearly did not fit the mold of the typical configuration of a balance of payments crisis. Foreign debt was low, the fiscal position was quite strong, and the exchange rate was hardly overvalued. Moreover, notwithstanding the large terms of trade deterioration of 1996–97, the current account deficit had remained modest and export growth continued at a remarkable pace.

While a healthy debate on many aspects of the Asian crisis is likely to continue for a long time, there will surely be a consensus on the fact that

---

* This chapter is co-authored with Eduardo Borensztein and was originally published in *the Journal of Policy Reform*, Vol. 8, No. 1 (March 2005), pp. 55–68.

This research has been supported in part by a Korea University grant. We should like to thank an anonymous referee, James Gordon, Sung In Jun, Se-Jik Kim and participants at the Korean Econometric Society workshop for helpful comments and suggestions. Part of this work was prepared while Jong-Wha Lee was visiting the Research Department of the International Monetary Fund. The views expressed are the authors' and do not necessarily represent those of the IMF.

the financial sector was the Achilles heel of the Korean economy.[1] However, it was paradoxical that the crisis arose when Korea was trying to accelerate a process of financial reforms that, albeit in a gradual and piecemeal way, had started as long as one decade earlier. How far had these reforms gone in correcting distortions in a system that was characterized as over-guaranteed and poorly regulated (Krugman, 1998).

The purpose of this study is to look for evidence that the pre-1997 reforms had yielded discernible results, in particular in improving the efficiency of credit allocation. The structural problems that affected the Korean financial sector were not unlike those that have been stressed in the recent literature on banking crisis more generally, such as government intervention, connected lending, and deficient prudential regulation and supervision (see Goldstein and Turner, 1996; Demirguc-Kunt and Detragiache, 1998). In Korea, the government had traditionally used the banking sector as the instrument of choice for industrial policy initiatives. Furthermore, the influence and sheer economic power of a few large conglomerates (the chaebols) dominated credit allocation and nearly obviated the need for project evaluation and monitoring by banks. In spite of the general move to a more market-oriented system, explicit or implicit government interventions had not disappeared, and the influence of the chaebols had hardly declined by 1997.

The paper evaluates whether the financial system has allocated credit in an efficient way, before and after the start of the process of financial reform.[2] Using data at the level of 32 industrial branches over the past 30 years, we test whether credit flows were directed to relatively more profitable activities, and we find no evidence to support this proposition, either before or after the financial reforms. We also examine the converse proposition, namely, whether the flow of credits contributed to improve the performance of the favored industries over time. Again, we find no evidence to support this proposition both before and after the reforms.

---

[1] See, for example, IMF (1997), World Bank (1998), Goldstein (1998), Krugman (1998), Corsetti *et al.* (1999), and Radelet and Sachs (2000).

[2] In Borensztein and Lee (2002), we look at the evidence immediately after the crisis.

3.2. Financial Sector and Financial Reform in Korea

In this section, we describe briefly the main features of the Korean financial sector and the financial reforms implemented since the mid-1980s. The Korean financial sector had grown dramatically in the three decades prior to the crisis of 1997.[3] The ratio of M3 to GDP, which is the sum of M2 plus deposits in all non-bank financial institutions (NBFIs), tripled from 48% in 1980 to 146% in 1996. The structure of the financial sector changed significantly too, with non-bank financial institutions (NBFIs) growing fast and reaching a market share of about 68% of deposits in 1996, thanks to a relatively free regulatory environment. Stock markets had also grown impressively, with market capitalization increasing from 7% of GNP in 1980 to approximately 30% of GNP in 1996.

This expansion took place under close control by the Korean government, which intervened extensively in the financial sector, mainly in pursuit of industrial policy objectives. The government was a major stockholder of the five nationwide commercial banks until 1983 and it still operates a number of specialized banks. The government used allocation of credit with preferential interest rates as a powerful tool to promote the development of targeted industries. For most of the period since 1970, the nominal interest rates on deposits and loans were kept low relative to the inflation rate, which created a chronic excess demand for credit. In addition to the interest rate ceilings, the government sponsored various types of policy loans, such as export loans, national investment funds, and special loans for agriculture and fisheries, which received preferential interest rates lower than the general lending rates. By contrast, firms that were not favored by official policies had to resort to the informal, 'curb' market, where interest rates were much higher than both bank lending rates and corporate bond rates.[4]

---

[3] See Cole and Park (1983), Nam (1994), and Park (1994, 1998) for comprehensive discussion of the Korean financial sector.

[4] The exact volume of the curb market has not been known, although it is regarded as having shrunk significantly after deregulation allowed non-bank financial institutions to expand.

Government intervention in the financial system intensified during the period of the heavy and chemical industries (HCI) drive in the 1970s.[5] Over-investment in the HCI sector left a sequel of non-performing loans in the commercial banks' portfolio. At the end of 1986, according to Bank of Korea's estimates, nonperforming loans at the five largest commercial banks amounted to over 11% of total credit and to three times the banks' total net worth (Park and Kim, 1994). Under market principles, most of the largest banks would have been considered insolvent. During 1985 and 1987, the government initiated several programs aimed at restructuring troubled or insolvent firms, and relieving banks of the financial burden they had incurred because of the policy lending programs. This resulted in more subsidized loans by the Bank of Korea carrying interest rates of 3–6% per annum in the unit of domestic currency (Nam, 1994).

The government also controlled the allocation of foreign loans tightly, again with industrial policy goals in mind. All foreign loans had to be officially authorized and nearly all of them were guaranteed by the government either directly or by financial institutions that were owned or controlled by the government. Since the cost of borrowing abroad (adjusted for exchange rate depreciation) was generally lower than the cost of borrowing from domestic sources, the allocation of foreign loans provided the government with the opportunity to subsidize strategic industries.

3.2.1. *Chaebols and Corporate Debts*

Korea's industrial structure in which large conglomerates (chaebols) dominate has influenced many aspects of credit policy. In 1995, for instance, the valued added of the largest 30 groups (excluding the valued added created by their financial affiliates) accounted for 16% of GNP and for 41% of value added in the manufacturing sector (Choi, 1996). The 30 largest chaebols received 18.3% of total bank credit and 42.1% of total non-bank credit in 1989 (BOK data reported by Park and Kim, 1994).

Government policy toward chaebols has been somewhat ambivalent over time (see Leipziger and Petri, 1993; Yoo, 1999). While the government

[5] See Stern *et al.* (1995) for the detailed analysis of heavy and chemical industry drive in Korea.

initially encouraged the formation and growth of chaebols in the belief that large-scale firms were necessary to compete effectively in global markets, it later became concerned about an excessive concentration of power in the Korean society, and tried to check the growth of the chaebols. For instance, to prevent chaebols from owning financial institutions, the government limited bank shareholdings by a single owner to 4% of capital. Yet the government continued, until the 1997 crisis, its policy of supporting financially distressed chaebols. The view that chaebols were 'too big to fail' had become pervasive by the time events started to unfold, and had contributed to the crisis of the financial sector in Korea.

3.2.2. *Liberalization and Deregulation*

Realizing that government intervention had resulted in a backward financial system, the Korean authorities embarked in a gradual process of financial liberalization and deregulation in the 1980s. The major elements of the financial reform were the elimination of many administrative controls, decontrol of interest rates, privatization of major commercial banks, diversification of financial services, and a reduction of entry barriers.[6] In December 1988, the government announced that direct government controls on the allocation of loans would be abolished and most bank and non-bank lending rates and some long-term deposit rates would be decontrolled. However, implicit and indirect controls continued even after the announcement because of the opposition from firms that depended heavily on bank loans (Chung, 1994). In 1993, a wide range of lending interest rates was liberalized, followed by a liberalization of interest rates on deposits in 1994 and 1995.

The reforms also partially opened domestic financial markets to foreign investors. Branches of foreign commercial banks were allowed to offer a broad range of banking services and were given national treatment in 1986. However, foreign banks were not allowed to acquire Korean commercial banks or to name foreign senior managers for their local branches. In 1992, foreign investors were allowed to purchase Korean stocks, but

[6]Nam (1994) and Park (1994, 1998) provide details on Korea's financial reform since the 1980s.

their holdings were subject to an overall ceiling of 10% of the shares and some companies remained off-limits.

Notwithstanding the significant measures undertaken since the 1980s toward a liberalization of the financial sector, Korea's financial sector continued to be subject to considerable government intervention and influence. The share of subsidized, policy-directed loans, which had reached about 50% of total domestic credit by financial institutions in the 1970s, decreased only gradually, and still accounted for about 30% of total credit in 1990. It is still believed that the government maintains a close relation and may directly influence important decisions of financial institutions.

Despite those limitations, financial liberalization helped to strengthen competitive forces and to eliminate some distortions in the Korean financial sector. The government's direct control of the financial system was replaced by market forces to a certain degree. In principle, in a more competitive market environment, financial intermediaries are free and motivated to apply lending policies that were more selective. It seemed, however, that bank management that was accustomed to the earlier repressed environment did not adapt quickly to acquire the requisite expertise to monitor and evaluate projects on a market basis. Furthermore, liberalization appeared to induce some financial institutions — smaller ones in particular — to undertake excessively risky positions, further affecting the overall soundness of financial institutions (Park and Kim, 1994). The pursuit of profit margins that was not possible through domestic lending, and the evasion of domestic controls also encouraged risky strategies in foreign borrowing by financial institutions. As a result of the web of existing regulations, banks relied in foreign currency-denominated short-term borrowing to fund long-term domestic currency-denominated loans. With inadequate prudential regulation, the partial capital market liberalization left the financial sector highly exposed to external shocks.

To summarize, although financial markets had been liberalized and deregulated to some extent, government intervention in financial markets remained substantial, and the environment faced by financial institutions still did not provide the most adequate incentives. The next section investigates the extent to which these financial reforms resulted in a measurable improvement in credit allocation practices by financial institutions.

3.3. Testing the Efficiency of the Financial System

To what extent did the financial reform that started in the mid-1980s reduce distortions and improved the allocation of financial resources in Korea? We approach this question by looking for changes in two dimensions: the relationship between access to credit and the profitability of the industry, and the impact of access to credit on economic performance in later years.

Some previous studies, including Leipziger (1987) and Chung (1994), argued that the financial sector in Korea was not efficient in allocating savings among investment projects but their conclusions are not based on a formal empirical analysis. In contrast, World Bank (1993) and Cho and Kim (1995) make a generally positive evaluation of credit policies in Korea. Dailami and Kim (1994), based on firm-level data for the period 1984–86, show that subsidized credit did not stimulate business investment in productive assets, but instead encouraged corporations to hold more financial assets and increase their investment in real estate operations.

3.3.1. *A Look at the Data*

Table 3.1 summarizes the distribution of bank loans and foreign loans across sectors for two sub periods: before financial reforms (1970–1984), and from the start of reforms until the financial crisis (1985–1996).[7] The data show that there has been some convergence in the access to bank and foreign loans among different sectors, as indicated by the decline in the standard deviation of the ratio of loans (total loans, bank loans and foreign loans) to the (accounting measure of) capital stock. This, in principle, suggests the emergence of a more level playing field among Korean industries. Table 3.1 also shows that the standard deviation of average borrowing costs

[7] All data come from the Bank of Korea, Financial Statement Analysis, issued annually since 1969, which reports aggregate balance sheets and income statements by industry branch. For 1996, the publication covered 41% of all firms and 91% of total corporate sales. The manufacturing sector is disaggregated into 32 sectors based on the classification of the Korea Standard Industry Classification (KSIC).

Table 3.1. Capital structure and profitability in 32 Korean manufacturing industries (averages, in percent)[a]

	Period 1 (1970–84)		Period 2 (1985–96)	
Variable	Average (Percent)	Standard Deviation	Average (Percent)	Standard Deviation
Total loans/capital	35.3	7.9	28.6	3.7
Bank loans/total capital	28.3	7.8	26.8	3.8
Foreign loans/total capital	7.0	6.8	1.8	1.5
Average borrowing cost[b]	20.3[c]	6.5	16.4	4.4
Profit rate[d]	4.0	3.1	2.8	1.4
Productivity of capital[e]	15.4	4.5	12.9	2.1
Debt/total capital	75.8	8.5	76.2	6.5

Notes:
[a] All figures are constructed from the original data available in domestic currency.
[b] The share of financial expenses in total borrowing.
[c] Average over the period from 1979 to 1984.
[d] The share of normal profit (ordinary income) in total capital stock.
[e] The ratio of capital's share of valued added in total capital stock.
Source: Authors' estimates from Bank of Korea, *Financial Statement Analysis*, various issues.

has declined, although slightly, suggesting that access to subsidized credit may have been equal across sectors.[8]

Furthermore, note that remaining differences in the cost of credit and level of access to financing across sectors do not necessarily imply the existence of financial distortions. In a perfectly competitive and efficient financial market, financial intermediaries would normally charge different interest rates to different borrowers and cap their credit exposure to different industries at different levels, based on economic criteria. However, the presence of large disparities in the marginal return to capital among different sectors is an indicator of distortions in the allocation of investment. Abstracting from risk and transaction costs; when resources are allocated efficiently, the marginal return to capital should be equalized

[8] Cho (1988) argues that financial liberalization in Korea led to more efficiency in the allocation of credit by showing that the variance of borrowing costs for the 68 four-digit manufacturing industries declined significantly over the period from 1972 to 1984.

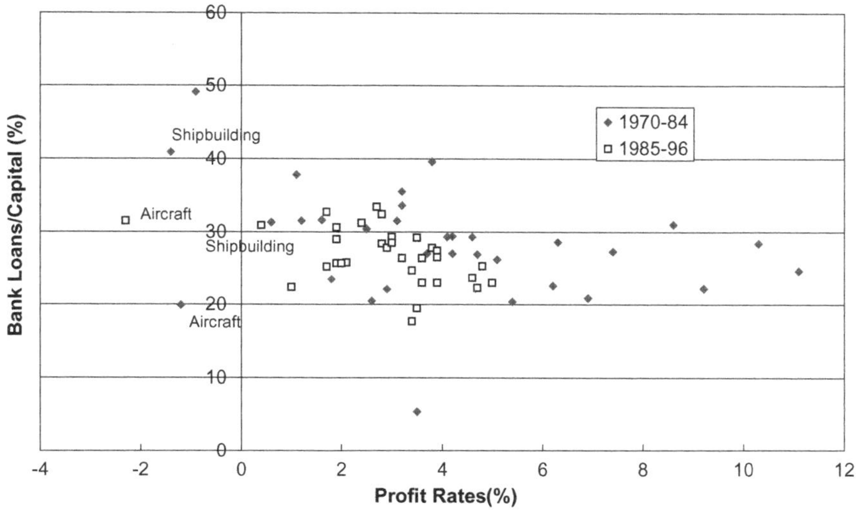

Figure 3.1 Bank loans and profit rates in 32 manufacturing industries

across different industries. Although this proposition applies to ex ante rates of return, and we observe only their ex-post values, it is still a valid test of efficiency if ex-post rates of return are unbiased estimates of the ex-ante rates, and an assumption we see no reason to dispute.

The standard deviations of profit rate and marginal efficiency of capital have also declined, which suggests an improvement in the efficiency in credit allocation. A closer look, however, is less sanguine. Figure 3.1 shows a scatter plot of the allocation of bank loans against the average industry profitability for the two sub-sample periods.[9] The plot suggests a negative correlation between the allocation of loans and the average profitability in the corresponding manufacturing sector over both sample periods. While other factors may have contributed to this unflattering result, the extremely weak performance of sectors that were prime targets of industrial policy, such as aircraft and shipbuilding is certainly suggestive. Figure 3.2, shows that access to foreign loans has been even more concentrated on favored sectors, in particular in the earlier years. Again, higher access to foreign loans does not correlate with stronger economic performance.

[9] The pictures are very similar when we replace the profit rate with the marginal product of capital.

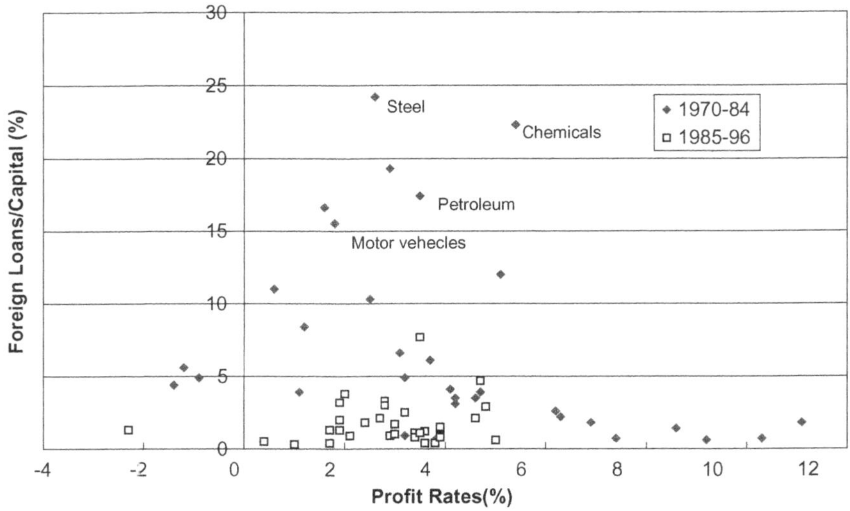

Figure 3.2 Foreign loans and profit rates in 32 manufacturing industries

3.3.2. *Econometric Evidence on the Efficiency of Credit Allocation*

We assess more formally, whether credit allocation was efficient in the Korean manufacturing sector using an industry-level panel of 32 manufacturing sectors for the period from 1969 to 1996. The specific question we pose is whether financial resources have been directed to more (ex-post) efficient sectors after the financial reform process got started.

We first test whether access to credit improved for sectors that had been more profitable in the previous year. In the regressions, the dependent variable is the net flow of total loans as a proportion of the total capital stock over one year in each sector. We measure the efficiency of investment by the accounting profit rate or the marginal productivity of capital in alternative specifications.[10] In addition to the efficiency variable, we include other control variables (mainly industry characteristics) that

[10] Another test in the same spirit was conducted by Jaramillo *et al.* (1993) with reference to financial reforms in Ecuador. See also Schiantarelli (1994) for a survey of empirical studies on the effects of financial liberalization on credit allocation, and Galindo *et al.* (2001) for an empirical test based on data for 12 developing countries.

Table 3.2. Determinants of credit allocation in 32 manufacturing sectors

	Increase in (Total Loans/Capital)					
	1970–96		1970–84		1985–96	
Dependent Variable	**(2.1)**	**(2.2)**	**(2.3)**	**(2.4)**	**(2.5)**	**(2.6)**
Loans/capital (t−1)	−0.522	−0.519	−0.489	−0.480	−0.619	−0.628
	(−16.3)	(−16.4)	(−11.0)	(−11.0)	(−13.3)	(−13.6)
Log(fixed capital) (t−1)	0.648	0.622	0.543	0.514	0.642	0.658
	(3.06)	(2.94)	(1.61)	(1.51)	(2.64)	(2.78)
Debt/capital (t−1)	0.089	0.091	0.096	0.100	0.087	0.078
	(2.44)	(2.70)	(1.84)	(1.97)	(1.70)	(1.90)
Export/output (t−1)	0.034	0.029	0.043	0.038	0.024	0.021
	(2.83)	(2.38)	(2.30)	(2.01)	(1.75)	(1.50)
Profit rate (t−1)	−0.160		−0.157		−0.116	
	(−1.91)		(−1.45)		(−0.81)	
Productivity of capital (t−1)		−0.147		−0.110		−0.247
		(−2.54)		(−1.45)		(−2.47)
R^2	0.34	0.35	0.32	0.32	0.42	0.43
No. of observations	850	850	470	470	380	380

Notes: The dependent variable is the change in the ratio of total loans to the capital stock over a year in each of 32 manufacturing industries. The term (t−1) denotes that the variable corresponds to the previous year. The estimation is by random effect GLS. Year dummies are included but not reported. Z-statistics are reported in parentheses. A value of the Z-statistics greater than 1.96 implies the coefficient is significant at the 5 percent significance level.

may help explain the allocation of credit. These additional explanatory variables are the lagged value of total loans as a ratio to the total capital stock, the logarithm of the fixed capital, the average debt-capital ratio, and the export-output ratio. In order to minimize endogeneity problems, we entered all the efficiency measures and the industry characteristic variables lagged by one year. In the equations we also add year dummies (not reported in the table.) The model was estimated applying the random effects GLS method.[11]

The results, reported in Table 3.2, show that the profitability of investment did not play an important role in the allocation of credit. In fact,

[11] The estimation results, reported in Tables 3.2–3.4, do not change qualitatively when we adopt the fixed effects technique to control for unobserved industry-specific factors.

given other industry characteristics and year dummies, the previous year's profit rate turns out to have a negative effect (although sometimes not a statistically significant one) on the current year's flow of credit. Similarly, the marginal productivity of capital also has a negative effect on credit flows. These results certainly do not suggest that credit was efficiently allocated among Korean manufacturing industries.

The coefficient on total fixed capital is generally positive, which implies that the probability of obtaining credit is higher in industries with larger firms. The positive effect of the fixed capital variable could also capture the greater availability of collateral, although it is likely that it is capturing the power of larger firms to access to credit. The coefficient on the previous year's debt ratio is positive and significant, suggesting that the alleged 'evergreening' of loans to struggling firms did in fact take place.

The coefficient on export-output ratio comes out significantly positive, confirming that the broad targeting of credit to export-oriented firms. In Korea, exporters from all industries had access to subsidized credits and the firm's export performance was a key criterion in allocating credit (World Bank, 1993, p. 281; Hong, 1998).

We tested the impact of the financial liberalization and deregulation that started in the 1980s by dividing the sample into two periods: before and after 1985. Regressions (2.3–2.6) show that the profitability of investment still appears to have negative effects on credit in either sub sample, which does not indicate an improvement in efficiency allocation. This could result from the burden of past debts, and because bank/client relationships continued to be a strong determinant of credit decisions.

We conducted the same test for a breakdown of total loans in domestic bank loans and foreign loans (Table 3.3). We still find negative, although less significant, effects of the efficiency variables on credit flows in Korea for the period 1969 to 1996.[12] There is a difference, however, in the effects of total fixed capital and debt ratios on credit allocation. Total fixed capital is positively related to foreign loans but negatively related to bank loans. Conversely, the debt ratio is positively related to bank loans but negatively, though statistically insignificantly, related to foreign

[12] The impacts of the efficiency variables on credit flows remain either negative or insignificant in the regressions based on the sub samples before and after 1985.

Table 3.3. Determinants of the allocation of bank and foreign loans in 32 manufacturing sectors, 1970–1996

	Increase in Bank Loans/ Capital		Increase in Foreign Loans/Capital	
Dependent Variable	**(3.1)**	**(3.2)**	**(3.3)**	**(3.4)**
Lagged dependent	−0.488	−0.486	−0.244	−0.246
Variable	(−15.6)	(−15.6)	(−11.6)	(−11.7)
Log (fixed capital) (t − 1)	−0.369	−0.384	0.386	0.380
	(−1.87)	(−1.95)	(3.48)	(3.43)
Debt/capital (t − 1)	0.101	0.098	−0.016	−0.020
	(2.91)	(3.03)	(−0.99)	(−1.32)
Export/output (t − 1)	0.048	0.046	−0.006	−0.007
	(4.15)	(3.92)	(−1.11)	(−1.28)
Profit rate (t − 1)	−0.047		−0.017	
	(−0.61)		(−0.44)	
Productivity of capital (t − 1)		−0.060		−0.030
		(−1.10)		(−1.09)
R^2	0.32	0.32	0.21	0.21
No. of observations	850	850	850	850

Notes: The dependent variable is the change in the ratio of either bank loans to capital stock (for regressions 3.1 and 3.2) or foreign loans to capital stock (for regressions 3.3 and 3.4) over a year in each of 32 manufacturing industries. The term (t−1) denotes that the variable corresponds to the previous year. The estimation is by the random effect GLS. Z-statistics are reported in parentheses.

loans. This suggests that evergreening was more widespread in domestic bank credit than in foreign loans, and that firm size may have been an important requirement to gain access to foreign loans.

3.3.3. *Effects of Credit Allocation on Productivity Growth*

The results of the previous section indicate that credit was allocated preferentially to the less profitable sectors of Korean manufacturing. This credit allocation may have been motivated by strategic objectives, 'infant' industry considerations, or to help industries which faced temporary difficulties. However, whether one agrees with those objectives or not, if the economic performance of the beneficiary sectors does not improve over time, such policies will eventually compromise the soundness of the financial system. We tested the effects of access to credit on the subsequent evolution of the industry.

The test uses two economic performance measures: the profit rate and the marginal productivity of capital. In order to capture a possible long-run effect of credit allocation on an industry's performance, we constructed the data as a nine three-year periods panel of 32 sectors from 1970 to 1996 (1970–72, 1973–75, 1976–78, 1979–81, 1982–84, 1985–87, 1988–1990, 1991–93, 1994–96). On this panel, we tested if the previous period's independent variables had any effect on this period's profit rate or productivity of capital. Since all the regressors are included as one-period lagged values, endogeneity problems are minimized.[13]

The regression results indicate that, although the level of significance of the coefficient varies across specifications, credit availability is never found to have served to improve the productivity of the chosen sectors (Table 3.4). In regressions (4.1) and (4.2), there are strong negative effects from total credit to future profit rates. Bank loans or foreign loans have also negative coefficients. In regressions (4.3) and (4.4) in which the productivity of capital is the dependent variable, either total loans, bank loans or foreign loans have negative, though not statistically significant, effects on the productivity of capital. The other clear result is that the sectors with higher debt have been less productive than other sectors.

3.4. Concluding Remarks

Although Korea presented none of the traditional imbalances that make debtor countries vulnerable to balance of payments crisis, it still fell into a deep foreign exchange and financial crisis at the end of 1997. Korea had a

[13]While this seems a reasonable test, we recognize that this empirical framework does not capture externalities, if any, which may radiate from a favored sector to other sectors. Additionally, it is possible that the subsidized credit granted to a specific sector generates productivity gains after a period substantially longer than three years. However, when we have included two-period (six years) lagged values of the credit variables in the regressions, the results change little.

Table 3.4. Effect of credit allocation on performance in 32 manufacturing sectors (9 sub-periods, averaged over three-years from 1970 to 1996)

	Profit Rate (Avg. t to t + 2)		**Productivity of Capital (Avg. t to t + 2)**	
Dependent Variable	**(4.1)**	**(4.2)**	**(4.3)**	**(4.4)**
Lagged dependent Variable	0.360 (5.58)	0.351 (5.38)	0.477 (9.68)	0.475 (5.38)
Debt/capital (avg. t − 1 to t − 3)	−0.058 (−2.26)	−0.064 (−2.42)	−0.056 (−1.92)	−0.058 (−1.95)
Total loans/capital (avg. t − 1 to t − 3)	−0.047 (−2.19)		−0.020 (−0.74)	
Bank loans/capital (avg. t − 1 to t − 3)		−0.038 (−1.54)		−0.015 (−0.47)
Foreign loans/capital (avg. t − 1 to t − 3)		−0.060 (−2.28)		−0.026 (−0.81)
R^2	0.54	0.54	0.54	0.54
No of observations	285	285	285	285

Notes: The dependent variable is profit rate (for regressions 4.1 and 4.2) or productivity of capital (for regressions 4.3 and 4.4), averaged over three years from the period 1970–1996 in each of 32 manufacturing industries. All independent variables are one period lagged (i.e. an average of one to three years lagged values). The estimation is by the random effect GLS. Period dummies are included but not reported. Z-statistics are reported in parentheses.

moderate level of external debt, a non-overvalued exchange rate, and (at least) balanced budgets. Yet the weak position of the financial sector made Korea vulnerable to the regional turbulence. It is paradoxical that, by the time the crisis hit, Korea had already broken away from a strategy of industrial development supported by directed lending and had been taking steps to liberalize financial markets for several years. However, the strategy for financial reform had been timid and slow, and had not encouraged sufficient competition, with the result that financial institutions had taken hardly any action to restructure their loan portfolios and avoid questionable but traditional clients. The empirical results in this paper show, in fact, that it is difficult to discern any change in lending policies of financial institutions after the financial reforms were put under way.

Although government intervention in financial markets may be justified by the existence of externalities and information asymmetries, the degree and nature of the desirable interventions is a difficult question. In most cases, government interventions in financial markets do not remedy market distortions and instead cause different new distortions in credit allocation and pricing. The history of Korea seems to suggest that the costs of heavy controls and repression exceeded the benefits, as for example in the HCI drive of the 1970s. On average, government failure seems to have been greater than market failure in Korea. Therefore, the aim for the Korean financial reform should be on strengthening the autonomy of the financial institutions and insulating them from government intervention.

References

Borensztein, E. & Lee, J.-W. (2002) Financial crisis and credit crunch in Korea: Evidence from firm-level data, *Journal of Monetary Economics*, 49, pp. 853–875.

Cho, Y. J. (1988) The effect of financial liberalization on the efficiency of credit allocation: Some evidence from Korea, *Journal of Development Economics*, 29(July), pp. 101–110.

Cho, Y. J. and Kim, J.-K. (1995) Credit policies and the industrialization of Korea, World Bank Discussion Papers 286, World Bank.

Choi, S.-N. (1996) Analysis of the 30 Korean Big Business Group for 1996 (in Korean) (Seoul: Korea Economic Research Institute).

Chung, U. C. (1994) Is financial deregulation a panacea?, in: S. Y. Kwack (Ed.), Korean Economy at a Crossroad, pp. 105–122 (Westport, CT: Praeger).

Cole, D. C. & Park, Y. C. (1983) Financial Development in the Republic of Korea 1945–78. (Cambridge, MA: Harvard University).

Corsetti, G. *et al.* (1999) What caused the Asian currency and financial crisis?, *Japan and the World Economy*, 11, pp. 305–373.

Dailami, M. & Kim, E. H. (1994) Effects of debt subsidies on corporate investment behavior: The Korean experience, *Pacific-Basin Finance Journal*, 2, pp. 1–21.

Demirguc-Kunt, A. & Detragiache, E. (1998) The determinants of banking crises: Evidence from developing and developed countries, *IMF Staff Papers*, 45, 81–109.

Galindo, A. *et al.* (2001) Does financial liberalization improve the allocation of investment? Micro evidence from developing countries. Working paper, Inter-American Development Bank.

Goldstein, M. & Turner, P. (1996) Banking crises in emerging economies: Origins and policy options, BIS Economic Papers, 46, Bank for International Settlements.

Goldstein, M. (1998) The Asian Financial Crisis: Causes, Cures, and Systemic Implications (Washington, DC: Institute for International Economics).

Hong, W. (1998) Financing export-oriented catching-up in Korea: Credit rationing, sustained high growth and financial chaos, *International Economic Journal*, 12(Spring), pp. 141–153.

International Monetary Fund (1997) World Economic Outlook, Interim Assessment, December.

Jaramillo, F. *et al.* (1993) The effect of financial liberalization on the allocation of credit: Panel data evidence for Ecuador. World Bank Policy Research Working Paper, 1092(February), World Bank.

Kim, K. S. & Hong, S. D. (1997) Accounting for Rapid Economic Growth in Korea, 1963–1995 (Seoul: Korea Development Institute).

Krugman, P. (1998) What Happened to Asia? Mimeo, MIT, January.

Leipziger, D. M. (1987) *Korea: Managing the Industrial Transition.* A World Bank country study, 2 volumes, World Bank.

Leipziger, D. M & Petri, P. A. (1993) Korean industrial policy: Legacies of the past and directions for the future. World Bank discussion papers 197, World Bank.

Nam S.-W. (1994) Korea's financial reform since early 1980s, in: G. Caprio Jr *et al.* (Eds), *Financial Reform: Theory and Experience*, pp. 184–222 (New York: Cambridge University Press).

Park, Y. C. (1994) Korea: Development and structural change of the financial system, in: H. T. Patrick & Y. C. Park (Eds), *The Financial Development of Japan, Korea, and Taiwan: Growth, Repression, and Liberalization*, pp. 165–187 (New York: Oxford University Press).

Park, Y. C. (1998) *Financial Liberalization and Opening in East Asia: Issues and Policy Challenges* (Seoul: Korea Institute of Finance).

Park, Y. C. & Kim, D. W. (1994) Korea: Development and structural change of the banking system, in: H. T. Patrick & Y. C. Park (Eds), *The Financial Development of Japan, Korea, and Taiwan: Growth, Repression, and Liberalization*, pp. 188–221 (New York: Oxford University Press).

Radelet S. & Sachs, J. (2000) On the onset of East Asian financial crisis, in: P. Krugman (Ed.), *Currency Crisis*, pp. 105–162 (Chicago, IL: Chicago University Press).

Schiantarelli, F. *et al.* (1994) Credit where it is due? A review of the macro and micro evidence on the real effects of financial reform, in: G. Caprio Jr *et al.* (Eds), *Financial Reform: Theory and Experience*, pp. 64–84 (New York: Cambridge University Press).

Stern J. J. *et al.* (1995) *Industrialization and the State: The Korean Heavy and Chemical Industry Drive* (Harvard Institute for International Development and Korea Development Institute).

World Bank (1993) *East Asian Miracle: Economic Growth and Public Policy* (New York: Oxford University Press).

World Bank (1998) *East Asia: The Road to Recovery* (New York: Oxford University Press).

Yoo, S. M. (1999) Corporate restructuring in Korea: policy issues before and during the crisis, *Joint U.S.-Korea Academic Studies*, 9, pp. 131–200.

Chapter 4

Growth and Investment in East Asia Before and After the Financial Crisis*

4.1. Introduction

The Asian financial crisis began with the floating of the Thai baht in July 1997. The crisis then spread rapidly to the Philippine peso and the Malaysian ringgit. In August, the Indonesian rupiah devalued, ultimately by more than any other Asian currency. Relatively small depreciations occurred in the Singaporean dollar, starting in August, and the New Taiwan dollar, starting in October. The South Korean won depreciated substantially starting in November. Japan also had a moderate devaluation between July 1997 and January 1998. No significant devaluations took place in China, which has remained relatively insulated from world financial markets, and Hong Kong, which maintained a currency board linked to the U.S. dollar.

This study focuses on the immediate and long-term effects of the Asian financial crisis on economic performance in east Asia. Specifically, we consider the behavior of economic growth and investment in China, Hong Kong, Indonesia, Japan, South Korea, Malaysia, the Philippines, Singapore, Taiwan, and Thailand.

---

*This chapter is co-authored with Robert J. Barro and was originally published in *Seoul Journal of Economics*, Vol. 16, No. 2 (Summer 2003), pp. 83–118 Copyright (2003), with permission from *Seoul Journal Economics*.
We are grateful to John Fernald, Keunkwan Ryu, and participants at the Eleventh Seoul Journal of Economics International Symposium for helpful comments.

These ten economies break down naturally into two groups depending on the extent to which they were impacted by the financial crisis of 1997–8. The first group of five countries — Indonesia, South Korea, Malaysia, the Philippines, and Thailand — experienced nominal currency depreciations of more than 50 percent from July 1997 to early 1998. In these countries, offshore nominal interest rates (determined primarily by forward exchange rates) or onshore rates reached at least 25 percent at some point between June 1997 and January 1998. Subsequently, we refer to this group as Asian-crisis countries. The other five east Asian economies experienced nominal depreciations of less than 25 percent, and nominal interest rates remained below 20 percent.[1]

One objective is to assess whether the Asian financial crisis had a long lasting effect on growth prospects and other dimensions of economic performance for the two groups of Asian economies. This task is difficult because only limited data are available after the ends of the financial crises in 1998. However, we get some information first by looking at post-crisis behavior within the group of east Asian economies, second by imbedding this behavior within a panel analysis of a large number of economies, and finally by using the panel to take a broader view of the impact of currency crises.

4.2. Recent Economic Performance in the East Asian Economies

4.2.1. *Economic Growth*

Figure 4.1 shows the annual growth rate of real per capita GDP for each of the east Asian economies from 1960 to 2002.[2] The sharp economic contractions in 1998 for the five Asian-crisis countries are evident: real per

[1] Offshore interest rates in late 1997 reached 18 percent in Hong Kong and 17 percent in Singapore. Meaningful data on interest rates are unavailable for China, but the official exchange rate remained virtually unchanged.

[2] The underlying GDP data are the purchasing power adjusted values from Penn-World Tables 6.1, as described in Summers and Heston (1991) and Heston, Summers, and Aten (2002). We updated the Summers–Heston data for 2001 and 2002 by using information on real GDP from the International Monetary Fund, World Economic Outlook.

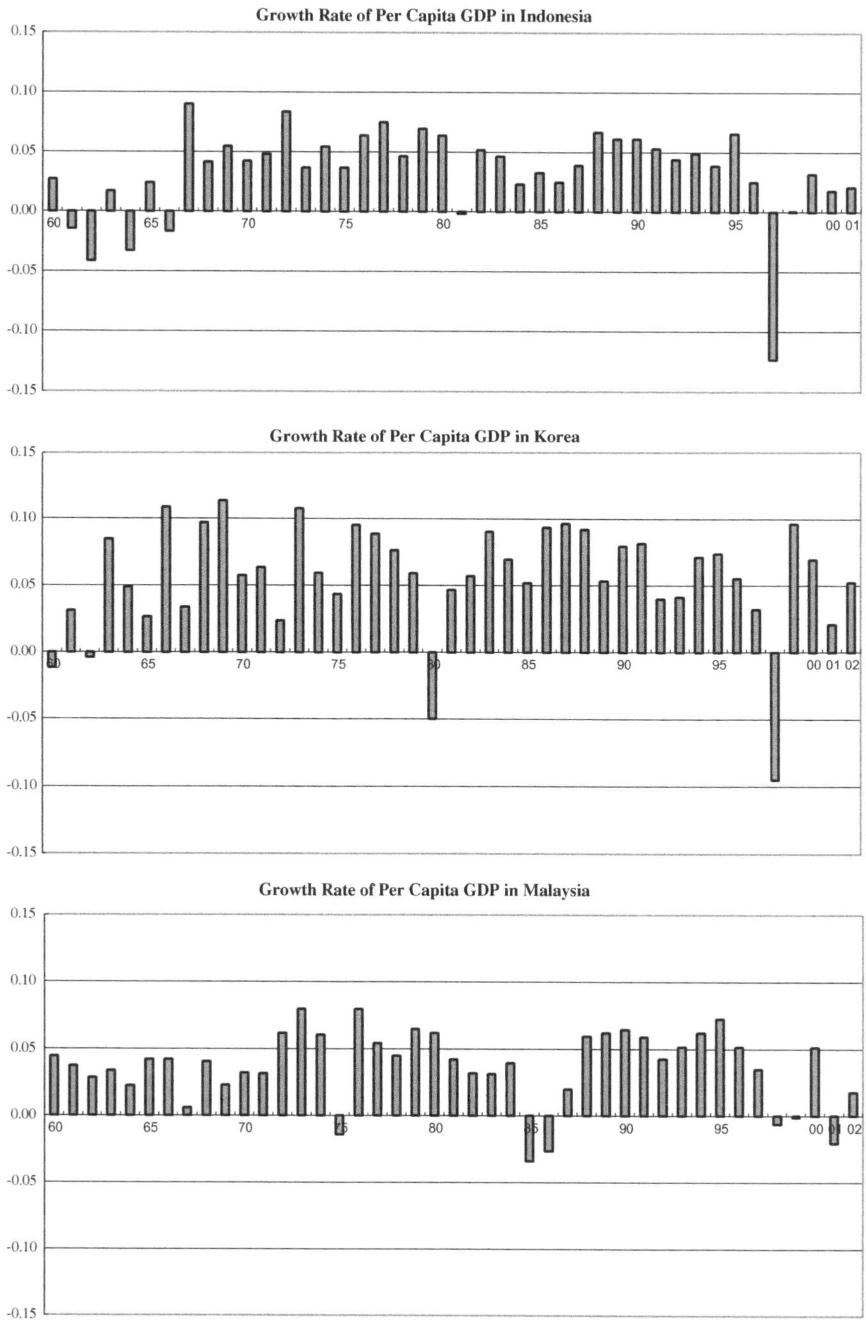

Figure 4.1 Growth rates of per capita GDP

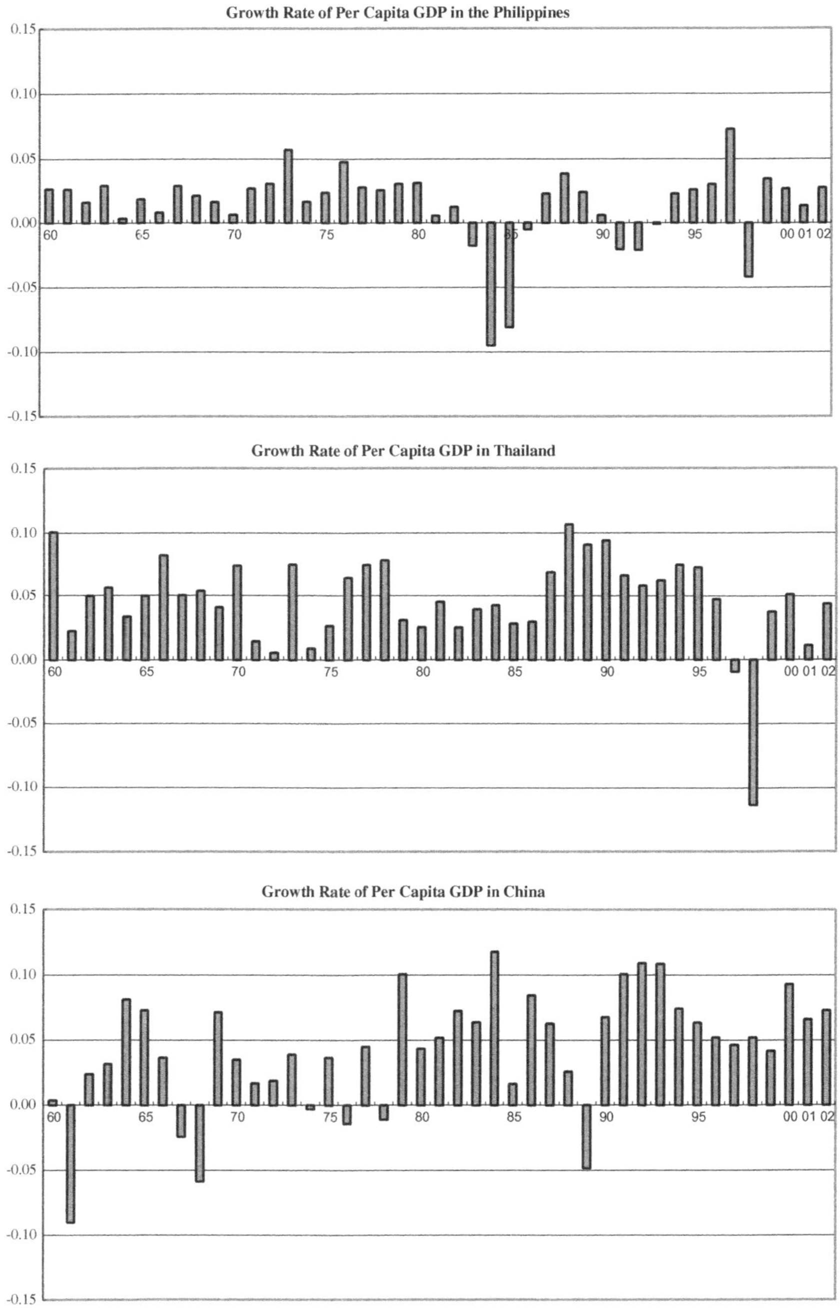

Figure 4.1 (*Continued*)

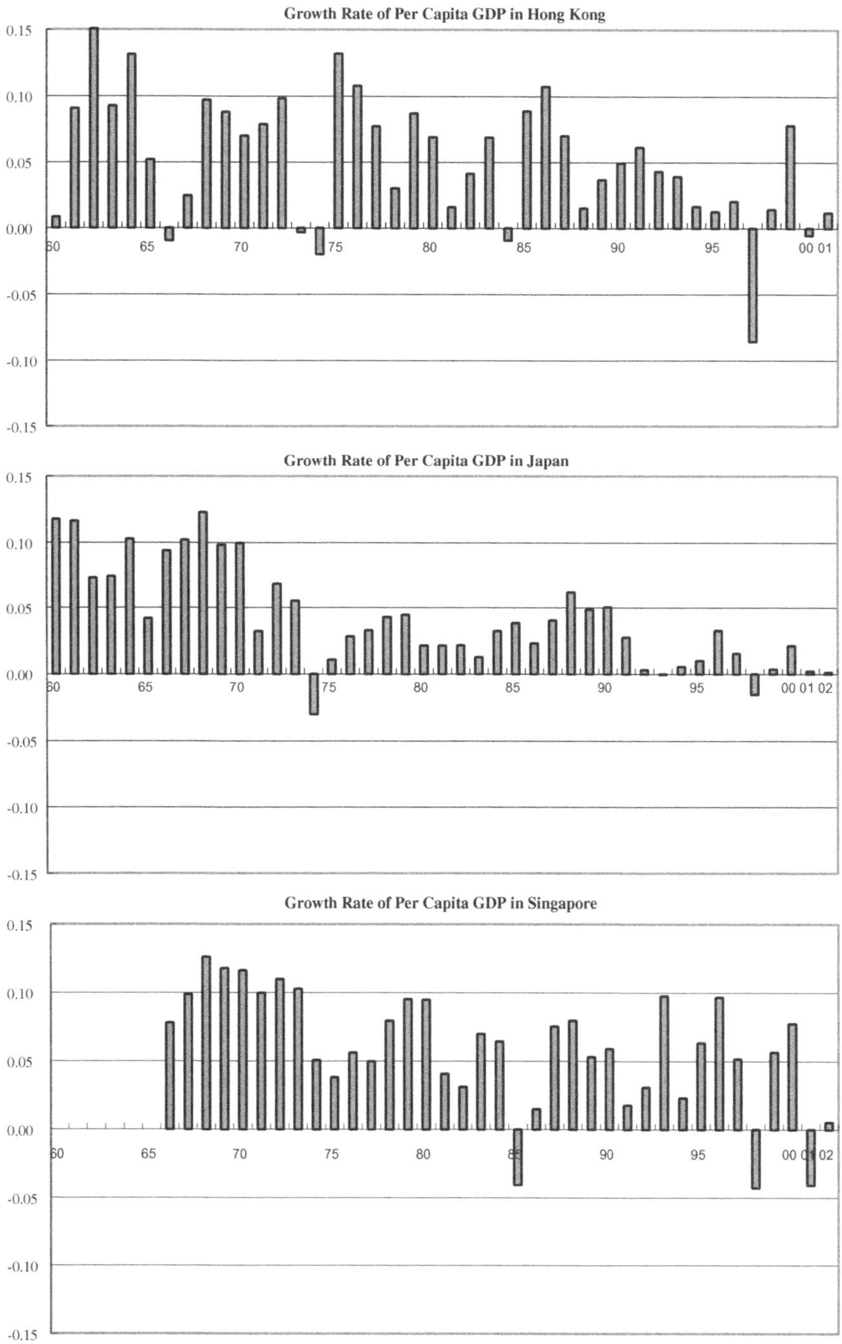

Figure 4.1 *(Continued)*

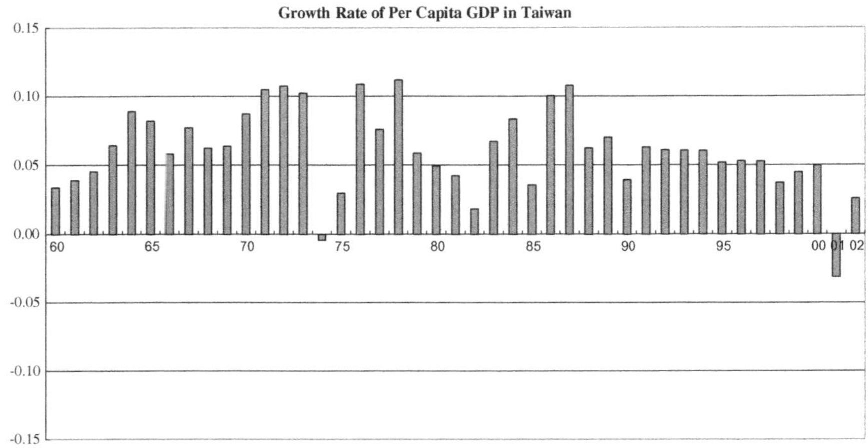

Figure 4.1 (*Continued*)

capita GDP (as the purchasing-power adjusted value) fell by 12 percent in Indonesia, 11 percent in Thailand, and 10 percent in South Korea, but only 3 percent in the Philippines and 1 percent in Malaysia.[3] The other five east Asian economies were less affected: per capita growth during 1998 was −9 percent in Hong Kong, −4 percent in Singapore, −2 percent in Japan, 4 percent in Taiwan, and 5 percent in China.

In 1999–2000, economic recoveries occurred, and the per capita growth rates were positive in all ten economies. Among the five crisis countries, the annualized per capita growth rates were 8 percent in South Korea, 4 percent in Thailand, 3 percent in Malaysia and the Philippines, and 2 percent in Indonesia. For the other five economies, the rates were 7 percent in China and Singapore, 5 percent in Hong Kong and Taiwan, and 1 percent in Japan.

A central issue is whether the east Asian economies will be able to return to the pre-crisis trend rate of growth. It is not clear if the recoveries in the post-crisis period signal a return to the previous patterns of

[3] According to the Penn-World Tables 6.1, per capita GDP growth rate in 1998 was −0.6% for Malaysia. This estimate based on the PPP adjusted GDP series seems too low. For instance, the conventional national account data from the IMF source was −9.7%. For other east Asian countries, the discrepancies between two sources are less significant.

growth for the crisis-hit east Asian economies. In fact, the rebound of growth for 1999–2000 slowed down in the subsequent period. In 2001–2, the annualized per capita growth rates were 4 percent in South Korea, 3 percent in Thailand, 2 percent in Indonesia and the Philippines, and 0 percent in Malaysia.

Thus, it looks likely that the financial crisis in 1997–8 had persisting effects on growth. However, the subsequent downturn over the period 2001–2 may have come from the global recession. During the same period, the non-crisis east Asian economies also experienced a drastic fall in per capita growth rates: the annualized per capita growth rates were –2 percent in Singapore and 0 percent in Hong Kong and Taiwan. Furthermore, even without the Asian financial crisis, projected growth rates in east Asia would have differed from historical ones, partly because the various economies had become so much richer than they were in 1960. Therefore, the question is whether growth forecasts would revert to those that would have been made before the Asian financial crisis. The subsequent analysis quantifies these growth projections and tries to reach some conclusions about the long-term outlook.

4.2.2. *Investment Ratios*

Figure 4.2 depicts the investment ratios for the east Asian economies from 1960 to 2002.[4] Four of the Asian-crisis countries — Indonesia, South Korea, Malaysia, and Thailand — showed dramatic declines in 1998, by well over ten percentage points. For the Philippines, which historically had a low investment ratio, the reduction in 1998 was comparatively small, amounting to about 2 percentage points. For the four countries in which investment declined sharply, the failure to see substantial recoveries in

---

[4]The ratios are for real investment (private plus public) relative to real GDP. The underlying data are the purchasing-power adjusted values from the Penn-World Table 6.1. For 2001 and 2002, the values were estimated from information on real investment and real GDP from the International Monetary Fund, World Economic Outlook and the Asian Development Bank. Key Indicators of Developing Asian and Pacific Countries. These numbers were linked to the Penn-World Tables values based on a comparison in the overlapping year 2000 (1996 for Singapore, 1998 for Taiwan).

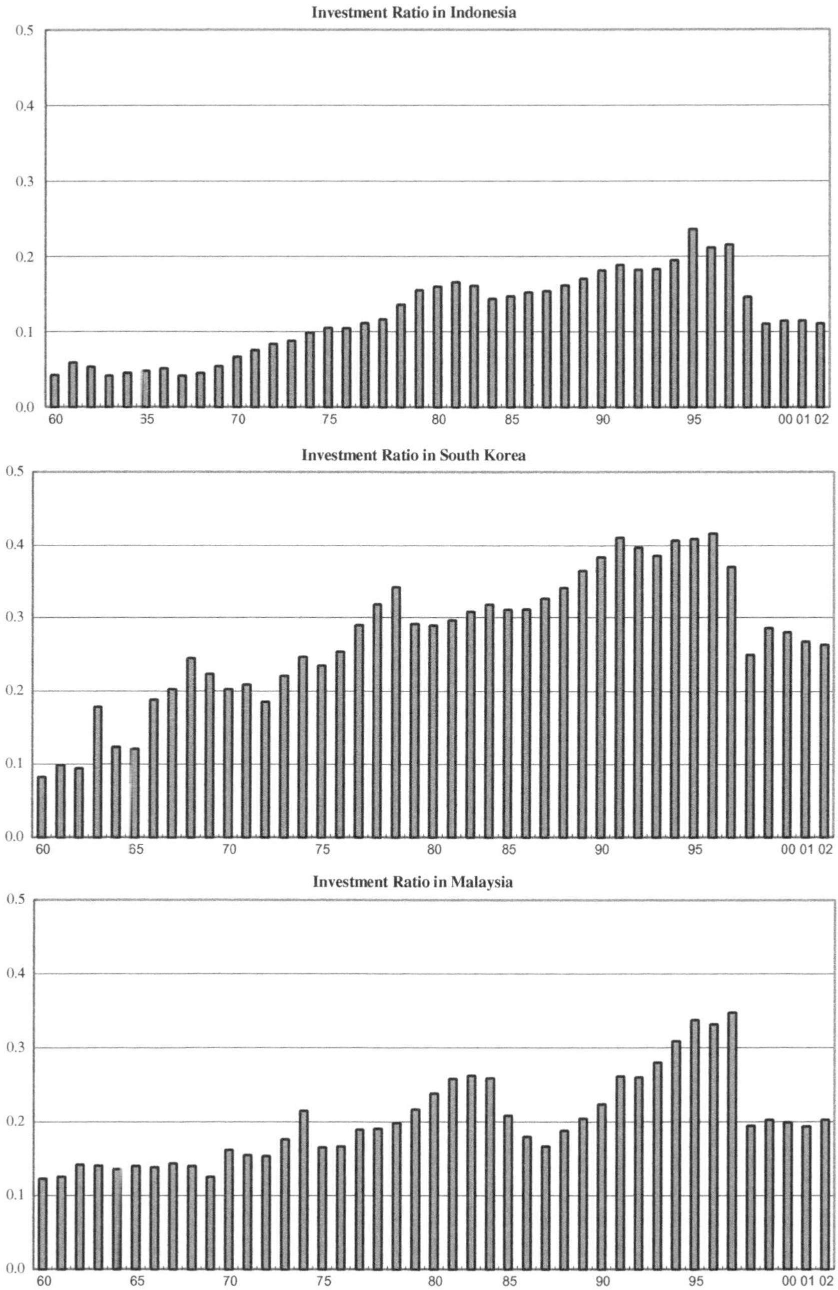

Figure 4.2 Investment ratios

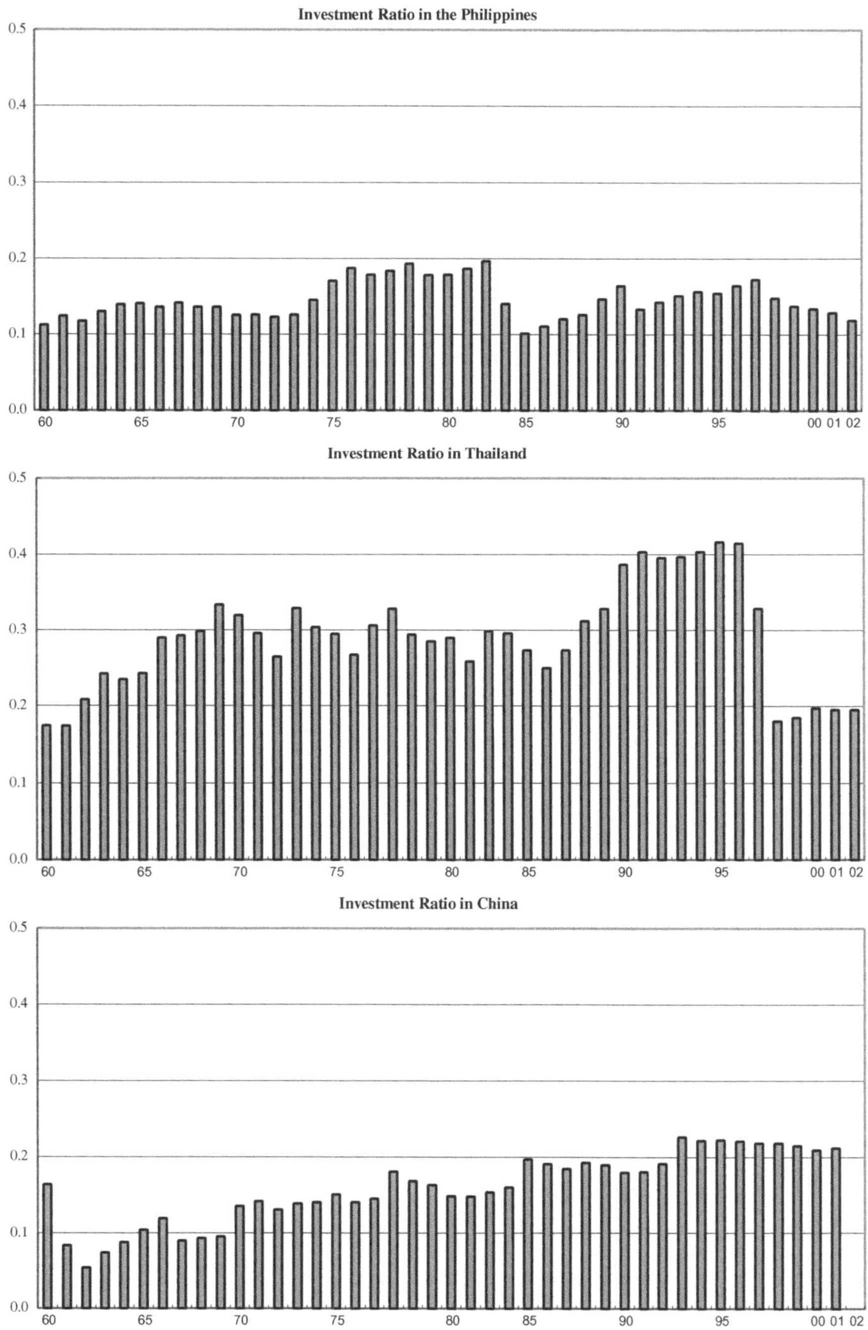

Figure 4.2 *(Continued)*

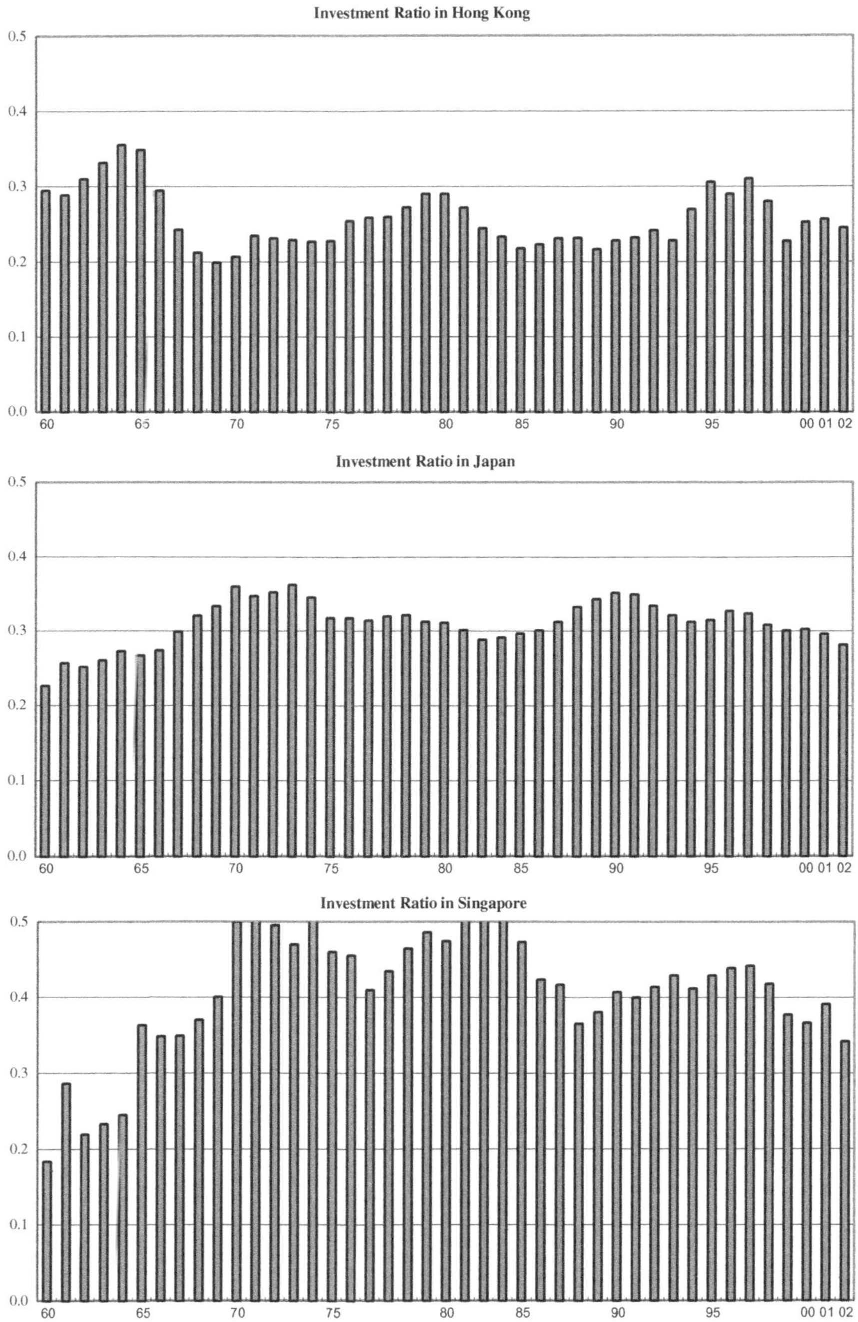

Figure 4.2 *(Continued)*

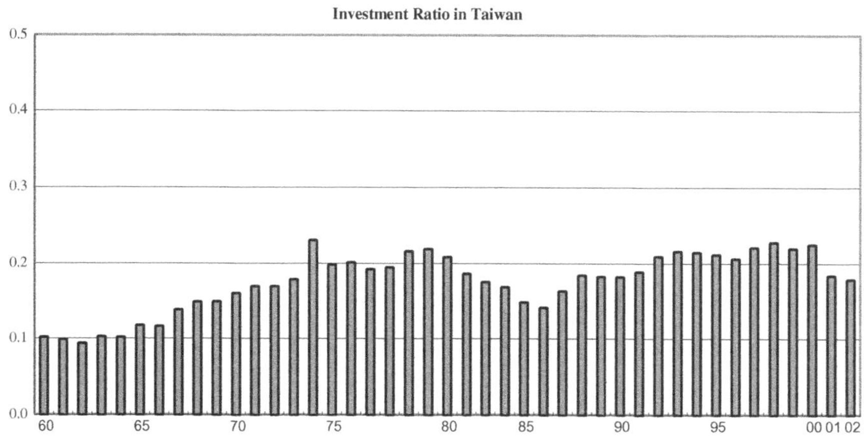

Figure 4.2 *(Continued)*

1999–2002 suggests that something permanent may have occurred.[5] However, it is also possible that investment ratios tend generally to recover more slowly than rates of economic growth, and the subsequent cross-country analysis supports this viewpoint.

The other five east Asian economies exhibited milder decreases or no decreases in investment ratios during 1998. Hong Kong, Japan and Singapore had small reductions from their peak ratios, ranging from 2 to 3 percentage points. There was little or no decline for China and Taiwan. Thus, there is reason to believe that the dramatic falls in the investment ratios in Indonesia, South Korea, Malaysia, and Thailand were specifically related to the Asian financial crisis.

4.2.3. *Stock-market Prices*

Figure 4.3 examines patterns in real stock-market prices. The general idea is that a fall in an economy's stock market likely reflects the market's belief

[5]Although parts of the sharp declines in real investments are attributed to the increase in investment prices due to currency crashes, there must be other factors that have caused the permanent slump of investment. In Korea, for example, after the nominal exchange depreciation of 40% in 1997, domestic price of investment goods on average increased by 19% in 1998. However, since then the price continue to have dropped by 13% over the period of 1999–2002.

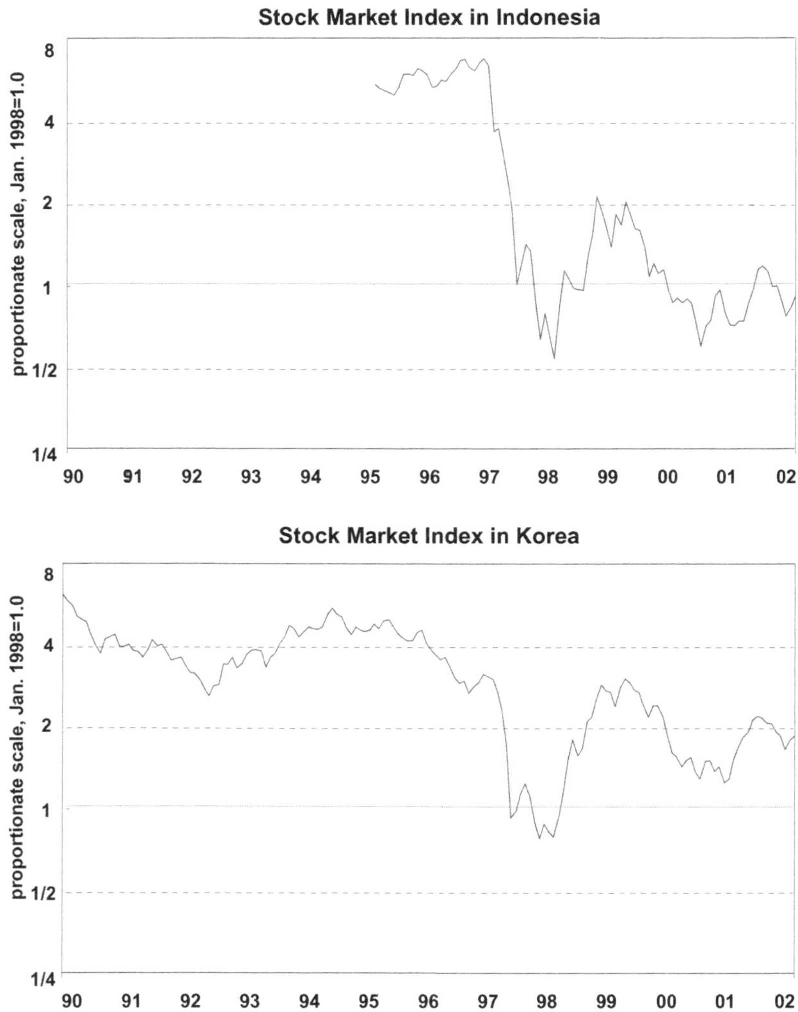

Figure 4.3 Stock market indices

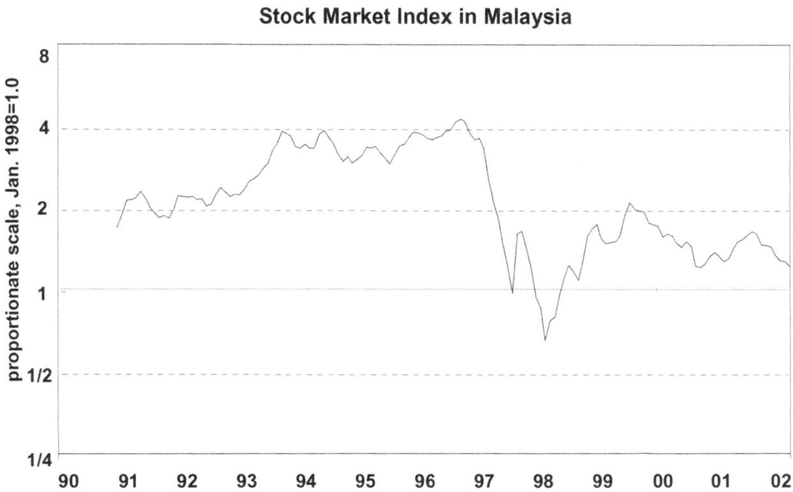

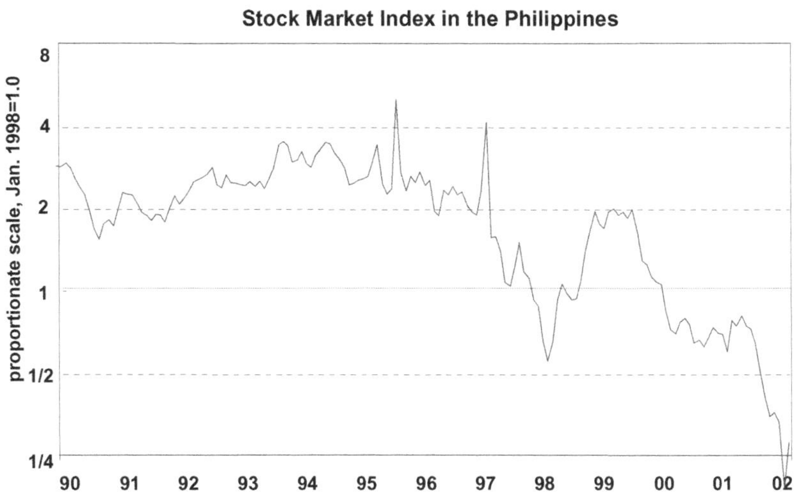

Figure 4.3 (*Continued*)

Figure 4.3 (*Continued*)

Figure 4.3 (*Continued*)

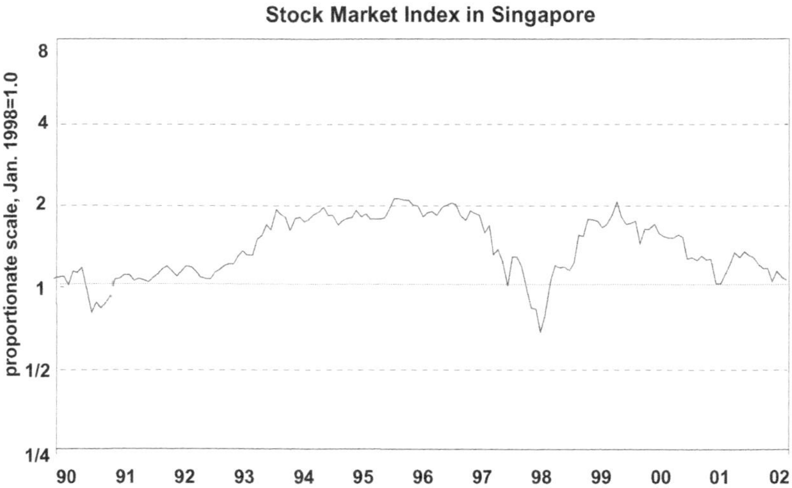

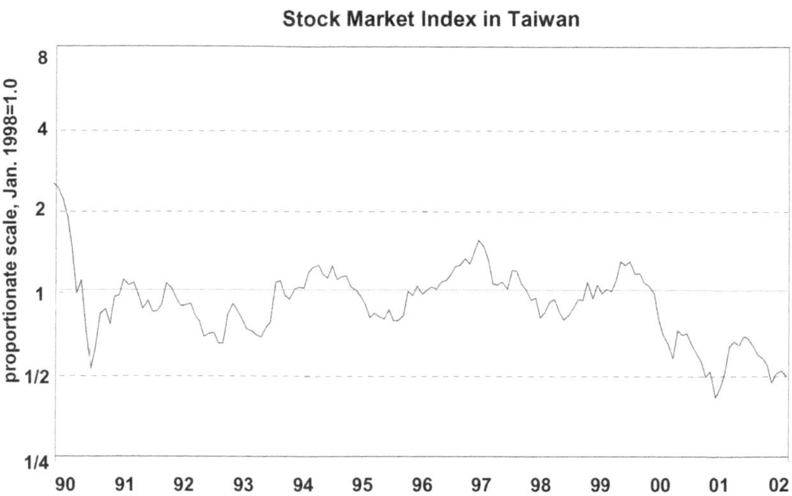

Figure 4.3 (*Continued*)

that long-term growth prospects have diminished. In the figures, the real stock-market values are computed by converting local currency values of stock-market indexes to U.S. dollars and then dividing by a measure of the U.S. price level.[6] An alternative procedure would deflate the local currency

[6]The stock market indexes, reported in domestic currency units, were converted into U.S. dollars using market exchange rates. These values were converted into real terms by

stock-market indexes by measures of local prices. Shifts in real exchange rates cause the two concepts to diverge.

The five Asian-crisis countries saw sharp declines in real stock-market valuations from the start of the financial crisis in summer 1997 until the fall of 1998 (For Thailand, the drop in the stock market clearly precedes the financial crisis). For present purposes, an important observation is that valuations at the end of 2002 fall far short of those from early 1997. The ratios of values for December 2002 to those for January 1997 are 0.10 for the Philippines, 0.14 for Indonesia, 0.31 for Malaysia, 0.43 for Thailand, and 0.65 for South Korea. For the five other east Asian economies, the declines in stock-market valuation are less dramatic. The ratios of values for December 2002 to those for January 1997 are 0.42 for Taiwan, 0.51 for Singapore, 0.55 for Japan, 0.63 for Hong Kong, and 1.24 for China.

Parts of these declines reflect the weak overall stock-market performance during 2000–2. The ratios of real stock prices index for January 2000 to those for January 1997 are 0.28 for Indonesia, 0.57 for Thailand, 0.82 for the Philippines, 0.46 for Malaysia, and 1.01 for South Korea. For the five other east Asian economies, the ratios for January 2000 relative to January 1997 are 1.12 for Taiwan, 0.88 for Singapore, 1.29 for Japan, 1.10 for Hong Kong, and 1.59 for China. It seems reasonable to infer that the most parts of the sharper declines in real stock market valuation for the Asian-crisis countries after the financial crisis of 1997 reflect effects from the financial crisis itself.[7]

The main conclusion from the analysis of stock-market data is that, from the perspective of the financial markets, events from 1997 through 2002 had permanent negative consequences for the economic outlook of the five Asian-crisis countries. The adverse impacts were less significant

---

dividing by the U.S. CPI. The natural logs of these values were calculated, the values in January 1998 were normalized to zero, and all values were divided by the natural log of two (to obtain convenient units for the graph). The resulting numbers are plotted in Figure 4.3, with the values for January 1998 labeled as 1.

[7] Parts of the declines in real stock-market values, as measured, reflect depreciations of real exchange rates. If the real stock-market values are calculated by dividing nominal stock-market indexes by local consumer price indexes, then the ratios for December 2000 to those for January 1997 are 0.31 for Indonesia, 0.32 for Thailand, 0.34 for the Philippines, 0.52 for Malaysia, and 0.69 for South Korea. For the other non-crisis Asian countries, the ratios are 0.68 for Taiwan, 0.93 for Singapore, 0.76 for Japan, 1.10 for Hong Kong, and 2.40 for China.

for the five other east Asian economies and were not present for China. The financial crises that began in summer 1997 were part of the environment that would be reflected in stock-market prices but were, of course, not the entire story. However, the differential market responses in the two groups of economies suggest that the financial crises — and, more specifically, changing perceptions about the long-term consequences of these crises — were significant parts of the story.

4.3. Cross-Country Analyses of Economic Outcomes

The general approach in this section is to modify existing work on cross-country analyses of economic growth and investment to assess the effects of the Asian financial crisis. We begin with a study of economic growth, using an empirical framework that has been widely used in previous studies. See, for example, Barro and Lee (1994), Barro (1997), and Barro and Sala-i-Martin (2004, Ch. 12). Our regression applies to a panel data set of 85 countries over seven five-year periods from 1965 to 2000, corresponding to the periods 1965–70, . . . , and 1995–2000. We include in this analysis a representative set of the explanatory variables that have been used in previous work. Thus, controlling for other important explanatory variables, any effects of the Asian financial crisis would show up as deviations of economic performance during the final five-year interval from those observed in the earlier intervals. When the data are available, it will be interesting to assess persisting effects on performance in the next five-year period, 2000–5.

4.3.1. *Economic Growth*

The framework for determining the growth rate of real per capita GDP is indicated by the baseline system, shown in column 1 of Table 4.1. Since the general approach has been described elsewhere and is likely to be familiar, we include here only a brief discussion.

The dependent variables are the five-year growth rates of real per capita GDP. Estimation is by three-stage least squares, using mostly lagged values of the independent variables as instruments — see the notes to Table 4.1. Individual constant terms are included for each period; hence,

Table 4.1. Cross-country panel regressions for growth rates

Explanatory Variables	(1)	(2)	(3)	(4)	(5)
Log (per capita GDP)	−0.0233	−0.0242	−0.0240	−0.0227	−0.0207
	(0.0030)	(0.0030)	(0.0030)	(0.0030)	(0.0031)
Log (total fertility rate)	−0.0178	−0.0167	−0.0166	−0.0168	−0.0157
	(0.0050)	(0.0050)	(0.0050)	(0.0049)	(0.0049)
Male upper-level schooling	0.0018	0.0064	0.0026	0.0017	0.0015
	(0.0016)	(0.0042)	(0.0016)	(0.0015)	(0.0015)
Log (life expectancy)	0.0633	0.0651	0.0649	0.0636	0.0587
	(0.0168)	(0.0167)	(0.0167)	(0.0165)	(0.0165)
Government consumption/GDP	−0.057	−0.060	−0.058	−0.054	−0.047
	(0.022)	(0.022)	(0.023)	(0.021)	(0.021)
Rule-of-law index	0.0183	0.0177	0.0169	0.0191	0.0165
	(0.0062)	(0.0061)	(0.0061)	(0.0061)	(0.0060)
Inflation rate	−0.0297	−0.0258	−0.0247	−0.0280	−0.0277
	(0.0070)	(0.0069)	(0.0069)	(0.0067)	(0.0067)
Democracy index	0.0460	0.0482	0.0470	0.0452	0.0415
	(0.0162)	(0.0161)	(0.0161)	(0.0161)	(0.0161)
Democracy index Squared	−0.0407	−0.0423	−0.0418	−0.0403	−0.0366
	(0.0149)	(0.0148)	(0.0148)	(0.0148)	(0.0149)

(*Continued*)

Table 4.1. *(Continued)*

Explanatory Variables	(1)	(2)	(3)	(4)	(5)
Openness measure	0.0049	0.0064	0.0071	0.0052	0.0031
	(0.0041)	(0.0042)	(0.0042)	(0.0041)	(0.0043)
Investment/GDP	0.079	0.087	0.089	0.083	0.084
	(0.022)	(0.022)	(0.022)	(0.022)	(0.023)
Growth rate of terms of trade	0.033	0.036	0.037	0.033	0.032
	(0.021)	(0.021)	(0.021)	(0.021)	(0.021)
Group of 5 Asian financial crisis countries (dummy for 95–00)	—	−0.0234	−0.0254	−0.0166	−0.0158
		(0.0091)	(0.0090)	z(0.0095)	(0.0095)
Group of 5 Other East Asian economies (dummy for 95–00)	—	—	−0.0121	—	−0.0048
			(0.0091)		(0.0099)
Group of 5 Asian fin'l crisis countries (dummy for other periods)	—	—	—	0.0114	0.0132
				(0.0056)	(0.0056)

Group of 5 Other East Asian economies (dummy for other periods)	—	—	—	—	0.0105 (0.0068)
Number of countries, observations	85 535	85 535	85 535	85 535	85 535

Notes:

Dependent variables: The dependent variable is the growth rate of real per capita GDP. Data are from the World Tables 6.1, as described in Summers and Heston (1991) and Heston, Summers, and Aten (2002). The growth rate is the average for each of the seven five-year periods 1965–1970, …, 1995–2000.

Independent variables: Individual constants (not shown) are included for each period. The log of real per capita GDP and the average years of male secondary and higher schooling are measured at the beginning of each period. The log of life expectancy at birth is an average for the previous five years. The ratios of government consumption (exclusive of spending on education and defense) and investment (private plus public) to GDP, the inflation rate, the total fertility rate, the democracy index, and the growth rate of the terms of trade (export over import prices) are period averages. The rule-of-law index is the earliest value available (for 1982 or 1985) in the first four equations and the period average for the other equations. The openness measure is the ratio of exports plus imports to GDP, filtered for the estimated effects on this measure of the logs of population and area. The ten east Asian economies are China, Hong Kong SAR, Indonesia, Japan, South Korea, Malaysia, the Philippines, Singapore, Taiwan, and Thailand. (China is omitted because of missing data.) The five Asian-crisis countries are Indonesia, South Korea, Malaysia, the Philippines, and Thailand.

Estimation: Estimation is by three-stage least squares. Instruments are the actual values of the schooling, life-expectancy, openness, and terms-of-trade variables; dummy variables for prior colonial status (which have substantial explanatory power for inflation); lagged values of the log of per capita GDP, the government consumption ratio, and the investment ratio; and the initial values for each period of the rule-of-law index and democracy index. The earliest value available for the rule-of-law index (for 1982 or 1985) is included as an instrument for the first four equations, and the value at the start of each period is included for the other equations. Standard errors are shown in parentheses.

the system does not explain the evolution of world economic growth over time. No country fixed effects are introduced, because this procedure tends to eliminate the bulk of the information in the data, that is, the cross-sectional dimension of the panel. The first explanatory variable, the log of per capita GDP at the start of each period, reveals the familiar conditional convergence effect: the estimated coefficient is –0.023 (s.e. = 0.003).[8] The log of the total fertility rate is significantly negative: –0.018 (0.005). Also included are two measures of initial human capital, each of which has a positive effect on growth. The coefficient on the log of life expectancy at birth is significant, 0.063 (0.017). However, the educational attainment variable, which is measured by the average years of school attainment of males aged 25 and over at the secondary and higher levels is statistically insignificant, 0.0018 (0.0016).[9]

The next five variables capture aspects of government policies and institutions. The ratio of government consumption (measured exclusively of outlays on education and defense) to GDP is significantly negative, –0.057 (0.022). A subjective measure of the extent of maintenance of the rule of law (an indicator of property rights enforcement) is significantly positive, 0.018 (0.006). Higher inflation, an indicator of macroeconomic instability, is significantly negative for growth, –0.027 (0.008).[10]

The regression results confirm the non-linear relationship between democracy and growth, as found by Barro (1997). The coefficients on the indicator of democracy and its square terms are positive and negative respectively and both coefficients are statistically significant. The pattern

[8]The instrument list excludes the log of per capita GDP at the start of each period but includes earlier values of the log of per capita GDP. If the square of the log of per capita GDP is added as an explanatory variable, there is some indication that the rate of convergence (the magnitude of the marginal effect of the log of per capita GDP on the growth rate) increases as an economy gets richer.

[9]Other measures of school attainment lack significant explanatory power for economic growth. Barro and Sala-i-Martin (2004) show that the quality of schooling — measured by scores on internationally comparable tests of educational achievement in the subjects of science and mathematics — is statistically significant. However, data on the quality of schooling cover only about 40 countries.

[10]The instrument list excludes inflation but includes measures of colonial heritage. These colony variables have substantial explanatory power for inflation.

of coefficients indicates that the growth rate increases with political freedom at low levels of democracy but decreases with democracy once the society has attained a certain level of political freedom.

Increased openness to international trade has a positive effect on growth, but the estimated coefficient, 0.005 (0.004) is not statistically significant.[11]

Many of the variables just discussed also affect an economy's propensity to invest, as discussed below. However, given the other explanatory variables, a higher ratio of real investment to real GDP still has a significantly positive effect on growth, as indicated by the coefficient 0.079 (0.022). The inclusion of the lagged, but not contemporaneous, investment ratio in the instrument list may allow a causal interpretation of this effect. A higher growth rate of the terms or trade (export relative to import prices) has also an expansionary effect on growth, but the estimated coefficient, 0.033 (0.020), is not statistically significant.

Columns 2–5 of Table 4.1 show the effects on growth in the period 1995–2000 from dummy variables for being one of the five Asian financial crisis countries and from being one of the five other east Asian economies. In column 2, the estimated coefficient on the dummy variable for the five Asian financial crisis countries for the period 1995–2000 is significantly negative, –0.023 (0.009), indicating that the five crisis countries grew during 1995–2000 at about 2.3 percentage points per year below the rate that would otherwise have been predicted by the set of explanatory variables.

Column 3 of Table 4.1 adds the dummy variable for the five other east Asian economies for the period 1995–2000. The estimated effect of the five Asian financial crisis countries remains similar to that in column l. For the five other east Asian economies, the estimated coefficient is insignificantly different from zero, –0.012 (0.009). Thus, only the five crisis-hit Asian economies experienced the significant shortfall of growth in the period

[11] The independent variable is the ratio of total trade, exports plus imports, to GDP filtered for the typical effect of country size on this trade measure. This last effect was estimated from a system in which the trade-GDP ratio over various periods was the dependent variable. Country size was represented by the logs of population and area. The trade variable was included in the instrument list.

1995–2000 from the rate that would have been predicted by the growth regression.

Column 4 of Table 4.1 includes two dummy variables for the five crisis-hit Asian economies — one for the period 1995–2000, and the other for the six other five-year periods (where the coefficient of the dummy for these six periods is constrained to be the same for each period). The estimated coefficient on the dummy for the period 1995–2000 is negative and marginally significant, −0.017 (0.010), whereas the estimated coefficient for the other six periods is significantly positive, 0.011 (0.006). Thus, the five Asian crisis countries had higher growth by about 1.1 percentage point per year in the intervals before 1995 whereas they had lower growth by about 1.7 percentage point per year during 1995–2000, compared to the rest of the sample in the corresponding period.

Column 5 adds the corresponding dummy variables — for the period 1995–2000 and for the six other five-year periods — for the five other Asian economies. With these variables included, the estimated effects of the five Asian crisis countries are similar to those in column 4; that is, significantly positive for the six other five-year periods and marginally significantly negative for the period 1995–2000. The estimated coefficient for the five other Asian economies for the period 1995–2000 is insignificant, −0.005 (0.010). The estimated coefficient for these economies for the other six periods was 0.011 (0.007) and is also statistically insignificantly different from zero.

Table 4.3, columns 1 and 2, details the growth shortfall during 1995–2000 for each of the east Asian economies. Column 1 contains the actual growth rates of per capita GDP. Column 2 shows the estimated values from the baseline system in column 1 of Table 4.1. Note that this system excludes all of the dummy variables for the east Asian economies. In most cases, the estimated values fall substantially short of the historical growth rates, which are shown for 1965–95 in column 3 of Table 4.3. The main reason for these shortfalls is that most of the economies have become much richer over time, and the convergence effect predicts a reduction in growth rates. This effect is partially offset by the generally favorable and, more pertinently, improving nature of the other explanatory variables that determine economic growth in the system shown in column 1 of Table 4.1 (The values of the explanatory variables for the east Asian economies are shown in Table 4.4). However, the net effect is to predict growth rates below the historical average for most of the east Asian economies. These lowered growth projections would also apply for future periods and would have applied even in the absence of the Asian financial crisis.

As an example, for South Korea, the model's estimated growth rate of per capita GDP for 1995–2000 is only 3.7 percent per year, compared with the 6.7 percent average growth rate experienced for 1965–95.[12] The model predicts similar retardations of growth for the other previously high growing east Asian economies: Hong Kong is 4.2 percent versus 5.4 percent, Singapore is 5.0 percent versus 6.6 percent, Taiwan is 2.6 percent versus 6.7 percent, and Thailand is 4.6 percent versus 5.4 percent. The cutback for Japan, 2.9 percent versus 4.1 percent, is also notable. The only economy in which a growth slowdown was not projected is the Philippines, which has 3.2 percent versus 1.0 percent. However, the main element in this case is the greatly disappointing growth performance during the 1965–95 period.

A comparison of the actual growth rates for 1995–2000 with the model's estimates shows that two of the east Asian countries actually exceeded expectations. These are China, for which the actual growth rate of 5.7 percent beat the model estimate of 4.2 percent, and Taiwan, for which the actual value of 4.8 percent was well above the estimate of 2.6 percent. The other eight countries showed shortfalls of varying sizes, including gaps of 4.3 percent per year for Thailand and 4.1 percent per year for Hong Kong.

4.3.2. *Investment Ratios*

Table 4.2 contains the results from cross-country estimation of the determinants of the ratio of real investment (public plus private) to real GDP. The dependent variables are the averages of the investment ratios over the seven five-year periods 1965–9, . . . 1995–9. The specification follows the

[12] This estimated growth rate for South Korea in 1995–2000 exceeds the average value in the sample (0.022) by 0.015. This deviation from the sample mean can be broken down into contributions from the ten explanatory variables shown in Tables 4.3 and 4.4. The results, all expressed as deviations from the sample mean, are as follows: −0.017 for the log of per capita GDP, 0.005 for schooling, 0.004 for government consumption, 0.001 for life expectancy, −0.002 for democracy, −0.001 for the terms of trade, 0.000 for the rule of law, 0.000 for openness, 0.007 for fertility, 0.001 for inflation, and 0.013 for investment.

Table 4.2. Cross-country panel regressions for investment ratios

Explanatory Variables	(1)	(2)	(3)	(4)	(5)
Lagged ratio to investment to GDP	0.711	0.712	0.712	0.721	0.072
	(0.002)	(0.023)	(0.023)	(0.021)	(0.021)
Log (per capita GDP)	−0.0082	−0.0086	−0.0086	−0.0062	−0.0049
	(0.0036)	(0.0037)	(0.0037)	(0.0034)	(0.0035)
Log (total fertility rate)	−0.0178	−0.0178	−0.0177	−0.0131	−0.0113
	(0.0058)	(0.0060)	(0.0059)	(0.0053)	(0.0054)
Male upper-level schooling	0.0028	0.0029	0.0028	0.0021	0.0018
	(0.0016)	(0.0017)	(0.0017)	(0.0015)	(0.0015)
Log (life expectancy)	0.065	0.064	0.064	0.067	0.064
	(0.020)	(0.020)	(0.020)	(0.019)	(0.019)
Government consumption/GDP	−0.062	−0.063	−0.063	−0.066	−0.061
	(0.027)	(0.027)	(0.027)	(0.025)	(0.025)
Rule-of-law index	0.0204	0.0202	0.0201	0.0208	0.0192
	(0.0082)	(0.0082)	(0.0082)	(0.0077)	(0.0077)
Inflation rate	0.0002	−0.0004	−0.0007	0.0040	0.0028
	(0.0097)	(0.0097)	(0.0097)	(0.0090)	(0.0089)
Democracy index	0.0259	0.0253	0.0254	0.0146	0.0143
	(0.0204)	(0.0206)	(0.0206)	(0.0200)	(0.0201)

Democracy index	−0.0240	−0.0229	−0.0226	−0.0140	−0.0123
Squared	(0.0190)	(0.0192)	(0.0192)	(0.0186)	(0.0188)
Openness measure	0.0189	0.0197	0.0195	0.0173	0.0151
	(0.0044)	(0.0045)	(0.0046)	(0.0040)	(0.0041)
Growth rate of terms of trade	0.076	0.077	0.076	0.077	0.074
	(0.032)	(0.032)	(0.032)	(0.032)	(0.032)
Group of 5 Asian financial crisis countries (dummy for 95–00)	—	−0.0137	−0.0131	−0.0210	−0.0186
		(0.0114)	(0.0115)	(0.0113)	(0.0115)
Group of 5 Other East Asian economies (dummy for 95–00)	—	—	−0.0035	—	0.0079
			(0.0118)		(0.0117)
Group of 5 Asian fin'l crisis countries (dummy for other periods)	—	—	—	0.0329	0.0345
				(0.0055)	(0.0055)
				—	
Group of 5 Other East Asian economies (dummy for other periods)	—	—	—	—	0.0071
					(0.0066)
Number of countries, observations	85	85	85	85	85
	535	535	535	535	535

Notes: The dependent variable is the ratio of real investment (private plus public) to real GDP. Data are from the World Tables 6.1. The measure used is the average of the ratio over the seven periods 1965–9, . . . , 1995–9. The lagged value of the investment ratio is the average of the ratio over the previous interval. See the notes to Table 4.1 for other information.

form of Table 4.1, except that the contemporaneous investment ratio is replaced in the group of explanatory variables by the lagged value of this ratio. Since the investment ratio displays a high degree of serial dependence, this lagged dependent variable has a lot of explanatory power. In the equations shown in Table 4.2, the estimated coefficient of this variable is in the neighborhood of 0.7 and is highly significant.[13] From the perspective of a partial-adjustment model, the investment ratio can be viewed as adjusting about 30 percent of the way over a five-year period to the target value determined by the other explanatory variables in the system.

The baseline model in column 1 of Table 4.2 shows a significantly negative effect on the investment ratio from the initial level of per capita GDP. The initial quantities of human capital in the forms of education and life expectancy have positive coefficients, though the one on education is marginally significant. The fertility rate has a significantly negative effect.

In terms of the policy variables, the main results are negative effects from government consumption and significantly positive effects from the rule of law and international openness. The inflation rate has an insignificant effect. The effect from democracy is non-linear: the estimated coefficient on the linear term is positive, and that on the square of democracy is negative. However, neither coefficient is statistically significant. Changes in the terms of trade have a significantly positive effect.

Columns 2–6 add dummy variables for the five Asian crisis countries and the five other east Asian countries. The results show that, for given values of the other explanatory variables, the investment ratios in the five Asian-crisis countries were significantly higher by about 3 percentage points than the rest of the sample in the intervals before 1995–9. However, these investment ratios became significantly lower by about 2 percentage points in the 1995–9 period. In contrast, for the five other east Asian economies, the investment ratios did not deviate significantly from those elsewhere in the periods before 1995–9 or in the 1995–9 period. Thus, the Asian-crisis countries differed from the other East Asian economies not only in terms of the adverse shocks to investment in the recent period but also in the sense of having abnormally high investment ratios at earlier times.

[13] In contrast, if a lagged dependent variable is added to the system for the growth rate in Table 4.1, column 1, the estimated coefficient differs insignificantly from zero.

Table 4.3 gives details about the actual and estimated investment ratios in the east Asian economies for the period 1995–9. Column 1 presents the actual investment ratios. Column 2 shows the estimated values from the baseline system in column 1 of Table 4.2. Among the five Asian-crisis countries, only Malaysia had an investment ratio above the estimated value (by one percentage point). For the other four crisis economies, the actual ratios fell short of the estimated ratios. Thailand showed the largest negative gap of five percentage points and the other crisis economies had negative gaps ranging from one to two percentage points. In contrast, for the five other east Asian economies, most of the gaps were positive, with the largest being plus two percentage points for Singapore.

4.3.3. *General Effects of Financial Crises*

The methodology employed thus far is useful for assessing the contemporaneous effects of the Asian financial crisis on growth and investment for the Asian-crisis countries and for other east Asian economies. When data for 2000–5 and beyond become available, the methodology could also be applied to assess whether effects from the Asian financial crisis persisted beyond the contemporaneous five-year interval.

Another approach, pursued by Park and Lee (2002) and Barro (2001), is to regard the Asian financial crisis of 1997–8 not as a unique event but rather as an example of a broader class of crises that have affected numerous countries. The cross-country regression framework can be used to assess the contemporaneous and persisting influences of the universe of currency crises on economic outcomes. The results from this exercise can then be extrapolated to the case of the Asian financial crisis. In this way, inferences can be made about the lasting economic effects of this crisis without waiting for additional data to materialize.

To get a broader international perspective on currency crises, we first need to define what a currency crisis is. A typical approach, following Frankel and Rose, (1996), is to identify the dates of crises with large nominal depreciations of a country's currency over a short period. However, severe speculative pressure does not always lead to large depreciations when the authorities successfully defend the currency by intervening in the foreign exchange market. Hence, Eichengreen, Rose, and Wyplosz

Table 4.3. Growth and investment in East Asian economies

Economy	(1) Growth Rate 1995–2000	(2) Estimated Growth Rate, 1995–2000	(3) Growth Rate 1960–95	(4) Investment Ratio 1995–99	(5) Estimated Investment Ratio, 1995–9	(6) Investment Ratio 1990–4
Indonesia	0.000	0.022	0.047	0.184	0.188	0.124
South Korea	0.032	0.037	0.067	0.346	0.353	0.287
Malaysia	0.026	0.033	0.042	0.283	0.271	0.199
Philippines	0.025	0.032	0.010	0.155	0.171	0.149
Thailand	0.003	0.046	0.054	0.305	0.357	0.310
China	0.057	0.042	0.043	0.219	0.209	0.157
Hong Kong	0.008	0.042	0.054	0.283	0.285	0.245
Japan	0.012	0.029	0.041	0.315	0.307	0.320
Singapore	0.029	0.047	0.066	0.421	0.406	0.440
Taiwan	0.048	0.026	0.067	0.217	0.216	0.179
Full sample (67 countries)	0.022	0.022	0.022	0.178	0.178	0.181

Notes: The growth rate refers to real per capita GDP. The estimated growth rate for 1995–2000 is from the panel regression shown in Table 4.1, column 1. The estimated value for the investment ratio for 1995–99 is from the panel regression shown in Table 4.2, column 1.

(1995) and Kaminsky and Reinhart (1999) use an alternative indicator of currency pressure by combining depreciation rates with additional variables such as foreign reserve losses and domestic interest rates. Then, a currency crisis is considered to have occurred if the composite indicator increased above a threshold level in terms of the country specific moments.

In our analysis, we combine the two approaches. We define a currency crisis as an episode identified by either the former or latter approach. For the former approach, as in Park and Lee (2002) and Barro (2001), we define a currency crisis as a circumstance in which the nominal depreciation of the currency was at least 25 percent during any quarter of the year and exceeded by at least 10 percentage points the depreciation of the currency in the previous quarter. In order to apply the criterion in the latter approach, we construct the indicator of currency pressure by a weighted average of monthly nominal depreciation rate and monthly percentage change of foreign reserve, with weights such that the two components of the indicator have an equal size in terms of sample volatilities. A currency crisis is then identified to have occurred in the specific year when the change in the indicator of currency pressure for any month of that year exceeded three standard deviations above the mean of the indicator over the sample period for each country, provided that either the monthly nominal depreciation rate or percentage change of reserve loss exceeds 10 percent.[14]

We apply a window of three years to isolate independent crises. That is, a currency crisis occurring in that year or three years following the initial crisis is counted as a continuation of the same crisis rather than a new episode. Applying this procedure, we identify 260 independent currency crises for 130 countries over the period from 1970 to 1999. According to these criteria, the five Asian-crisis countries all experienced currency crises in 1997.

We defined a currency-crisis dummy variable for each country during any five-year period to equal one if a crisis occurred during the period and

[14]We impose the condition of the monthly nominal depreciation rate or percentage change of reserve loss exceeding 10 percent. Otherwise, there might occur a potential problem such that the expected number of crises would be the same for all countries, if the form of the distribution were equally normal but the mean and standard deviations varied across countries.

Table 4.4. Explanatory variables for East Asian economies

Economy	(1) Log (Per Capita GDP) 1995	(2) Log (Total Fertility Rate) 1996	(3) Upper-level Schooling 1995	(4) Log (Life Expectancy) 1995	(5) Government Consumption/GDP 1995–99
Indonesia	8.20	0.98	1.5	4.18	0.10
South Korea	9.51	0.56	5.5	4.26	0.01
Malaysia	9.07	1.23	3.4	4.27	0.09
Philippines	8.02	1.31	2.3	4.22	0.11
Thailand	8.82	0.60	1.5	4.26	0.06
China	7.94	0.65	2.2	4.27	0.17
Hong Kong	10.15	0.21	4.8	4.36	0.03
Japan	10.05	0.35	4.3	4.37	0.03
Singapore	10.03	0.54	3.4	4.31	0.01
Taiwan	9.60	0.58	3.9	4.31	0.05
Full sample (74 countries)	8.79	0.96	2.6	4.25	0.08

Economy	(6) Rule of Law 1995–9	(7) Inflation Rate 1995–2000	(8) Democracy 1995–9	(9) Openness Measure 1995–9	(10) Growth of Terms of Trade 1995–2000
Indonesia	0.57	0.16	0.13	0.19	0.035
South Korea	0.73	0.04	0.83	0.02	−0.047
Malaysia	0.77	0.03	0.43	1.26	0.000
Philippines	0.67	0.07	0.83	0.37	0.052
Thailand	0.83	0.04	0.73	0.34	0.006
China	0.83	0.02	0.00	0.18	0.000
Hong Kong	0.90	0.01	0.37	1.68	0.004
Japan	1.00	0.00	1.00	−0.37	−0.018
Singapore	1.00	0.01	0.37	2.04	−0.004
Taiwan	0.73	0.01	0.80	0.13	0.009
Full sample (74 countries)	0.73	0.08	0.71	−0.02	−0.011

Notes: Per capita GDP is the PPP adjusted value in 1996 U.S. dollars. Upper-level schooling is the average years of attainment of males aged 25 and over in secondary and higher education. Life expectancy is at age 1. The total fertility rate is the number of live births for the average woman over her expected lifetime. The government consumption variable is the Summers–Heston ratio of real government consumption to GDP less the ratios for public spending on defense and education. The rule-of-law index, expressed on a zero-to-one scale, with one the most favorable, is based on the indicator from *International Country Risk Guide* for the maintenance of the rule of law. The inflation rate is the growth rate over each period of a consumer price index. The democracy index, expressed on a zero-to-one scale, with one the most favorable, is based on the indicator of political rights compiled by Freedom House. The openness variable is the ratio of exports plus imports to GDP less the estimated effect on this ratio from the logs of population and area. These effects were estimated in a panel system in which the dependent variable was the ratio of exports plus imports to GDP over various periods. The mean value of the openness variable was normalized to zero in each period. The terms-of-trade variable is the growth rate of the ratio of export to import prices.

to take on the value zero otherwise.[15] We considered the contemporaneous effects of this variable on economic growth and investment, and we also looked for effects from the presence of a currency crisis in the previous five-year period.

The Asian financial crises were not only currency crises but also involved severe distress for banking systems. To get a broad measure of banking crises, we followed the approach of Caprio and Klingebiel (1996) and Eichengreen and Rose (1998). These authors define a banking crisis as a situation in which bank failures or suspensions led to the exhaustion of much or all of bank capital. The data on banking crises are compiled from Caprio and Klingebiel (1996), Demirguc-Kunt and Detragiache (1997), and Glick and Hutchison (2001). The resulting data apply from 1970 to 1998. We also use a window of three years to isolate independent crises. According to these data, the five Asian-crisis countries all experienced banking crises during 1997–8.The variable we use is a dummy for whether a banking crisis occurred for each country during any five-year period. We again considered the contemporaneous and lagged effects of these crises on economic growth and investment.

The results from adding the currency crisis and banking crisis variables to the systems for economic growth are in Table 4.5. In column 1, a contemporaneous currency crisis (occurring sometime within the applicable five-year period) is associated with lower per capita growth — by 0.9 percent per year. This effect is statistically significant.

Column 2 adds a lagged effect of a currency crisis. The result shows that the contraction of growth does not persist into the next five-year period. The estimated contemporaneous effect is significantly negative and quantitatively similar to that in column 1. However, the lagged effect is positive. The estimated coefficient on the lagged currency crisis variable

[15]We used the interval 1970–4 for currency devaluation to correspond to growth for 1970-5 and to the average investment ratio for 1970–4 and similarly for the other periods. As an alternative procedure, we defined if the crisis occurred in the first year of the five year interval, 0.8 if the crisis occurred in the second year, and so on. This approach might be preferable if the effect of a currency crisis tended to persist at least for several years. However, this alternative approach generated a poorer fit to the data, especially on economic growth. This finding suggests that the effects of currency crises on economic outcomes are short lived.

Table 4.5. Impact of currency- and banking-crises on growth rates

Explanatory Variables	(1)	(2)	(3)	(4)	(5)	(6)
Log (per capita GDP)	−0.0287	−0.0276	−0.0270	−0.0274	−0.0290	−0.0281
	(0.0039)	(0.0039)	(0.0039)	(0.0039)	(0.0039)	(0.0039)
Log (total fertility rate)	−0.0159	−0.0161	−0.0177	−0.0171	−0.0164	−0.0159
	(0.0063)	(0.0062)	(0.0062)	(0.0062)	(0.0062)	(0.0062)
Male upper-level schooling	0.0035	0.0035	0.0026	0.0028	0.0033	0.0033
	(0.0018)	(0.0018)	(0.0018)	(0.0018)	(0.0018)	(0.0018)
Log (life expectancy)	0.0721	0.0634	0.0662	0.0666	0.0719	0.0641
	(0.0229)	(0.0231)	(0.0227)	(0.0226)	(0.0229)	(0.0229)
Government consumption/GDP	−0.010	−0.106	−0.093	−0.092	−0.100	−0.100
	(0.027)	(0.027)	(0.027)	(0.027)	(0.027)	(0.027)
Rule-of-law index	0.0171	0.0156	0.0172	0.0185	0.0175	0.0174
	(0.0082)	(0.0082)	(0.0082)	(0.0082)	(0.0082)	(0.0081)
Inflation rate	−0.0058	−0.0084	−0.0164	−0.0157	−0.0047	−0.0076
	(0.0084)	(0.0084)	(0.0082)	(0.0080)	(0.0082)	(0.0082)
Democracy index	0.0437	0.0420	0.0425	0.0439	0.0419	0.0427
	(0.0205)	(0.0202)	(0.0203)	(0.0202)	(0.0203)	(0.0199)
Democracy index	−0.0274	−0.0259	−0.0279	−0.0293	−0.0257	−0.0266
Squared	(0.0190)	(0.0187)	(0.0189)	(0.0188)	(0.0188)	(0.0184)
Openness measure	0.0120	0.0124	0.0104	0.0104	0.0116	0.0118
	(0.0048)	(0.0047)	(0.0047)	(0.0047)	(0.0047)	(0.0047)

(*Continued*)

Table 4.5. (*Continued*)

Explanatory Variables	(1)	(2)	(3)	(4)	(5)	(6)
Investment/GDP	0.058	0.064	0.071	0.074	0.068	0.076
	(0.032)	(0.032)	(0.032)	(0.032)	(0.032)	(0.032)
Growth rate of terms of trade	0.059	0.054	0.051	0.054	0.055	0.053
	(0.026)	(0.026)	(0.026)	(0.026)	(0.026)	(0.025)
Contemporaneous currency crisis	−0.0093	−0.0088	—	—	−0.0086	−0.0080
	(0.0031)	(0.0031)			(0.0031)	(0.0030)
Lagged currency crisis	—	0.0061	—	—	—	0.0057
		(0.0026)				(0.0025)
Contemporaneous Banking crisis	—	—	−0.0077	−0.0079	−0.0076	−0.0073
			(0.0024)	(0.0025)	(0.0024)	(0.0024)
Lagged banking crisis	—	—	—	0.0035	—	0.0031
				(0.0027)		(0.0027)
Number of countries,	85	85	85	85	85	85
observations	396	396	396	396	396	396

Notes: The dependent variable is the growth rate of real per capita GDP. The growth rate is the average for each of the five five-year periods 1975–1980, 1980–1985, …, 1995–2000. The earlier periods were deleted because of missing data on the currency-crisis and banking-crisis variables. The currency crisis is defined by combining two criteria. A currency crisis is judged to occur in the year when a country experienced a nominal currency depreciation of at least 25 percent in any quarter of a specific year and the depreciation rate exceeded that in the previous quarter by a margin of at least a 10 percent. A currency crisis is also identified at the month of a year when an indicator of currency pressure, a weighted average of monthly nominal exchange depreciation and monthly foreign reserve loss, exceeds three standard deviations above the mean of the indicator over the sample period for each country, provided that either the monthly nominal depreciation rate or percentage change of reserve loss exceeds 5 percent. A crisis that is not apart at least 3 years from the nearest crisis is counted as a continuation of the initial crisis rather than an independent crisis. The banking-crisis dummy variable equals one if at least one of the years in the five-year period features a banking crisis, as defined in Caprio and Klingebiel (1996). Data on banking crises are compiled from Caprio and Klingebiel (1996), Demirguc and Detragiache (1998), and Glick and Hutchison (2001). See the text for further details. See the notes to Table 4.1 for additional information.

is statistically significant: 0.006 (0.003). Hence, there is evidence that GDP growth rate tends to rebound by about 0.6 of a percentage point per year in the subsequent five-year period.

Column 3 shows that the corresponding effect for a banking crisis is a retardation of growth by 0.8 percent per year. This effect is statistically significant. In column 4, a lagged banking crisis variable is added. The result also shows that the contraction of growth does not persist into the next five-year period. The estimated coefficient here is again positive but statistically insignificant: 0.004 (0.003).[16]

Columns 5 and 6 of Table 4.6 include both currency and banking crises variables together. In column 5, the contemporaneous effects from currency and banking crises are negative and statistically significant. The difference between the two effects from currency and banking crises is not statistically significant — the *p*-value is 0.78. Thus, currency and banking crises seem to have quantitatively similar impacts on economic growth.

The broad cross-country analysis indicates that a combination of a currency and a banking crisis would be associated with reduced growth contemporaneously by about 2 percent per year. From this perspective, the recent economic contractions in the Asian-crisis countries look similar to the broader historical experience. In those cases, reflected in the dummy variables contained in Table 4.1, growth rates for 1995–2000 were reduced by about 2 percent per year. Table 4.5 presents the results from adding the currency-crisis and banking-crisis variables to the systems for the investment ratio. Column 1 of Table 4.6 shows that a currency crisis is associated with a statistically significant reduction by about 0.8 of a percentage point. In column 2, the estimated lagged effect of a currency crisis on investment is negative but statistically insignificant.

---

[16]Additional persistence would be implied through effects on the independent variables. For example, the reduced level of per capita GDP provides a channel whereby a currency or banking crisis would raise growth in the next period. These effects tend, however, to be small. Negative, but quantitatively even smaller, effects involve the persisting influences on investment. Other negative effects on subsequent growth would arise if, as examples, a currency or banking crisis reduces international trade or damages institutions that influence the rule of law. It is also possible that the occurrence of a currency or banking crisis alters the probability of a crisis in subsequent periods and thereby affects the expectation of future growth rates through those channels. These effects have not been investigated.

Table 4.6. Impact of currency- and banking-crises on investment ratios

Explanatory Variables	(1)	(2)	(3)	(4)	(5)	(6)
Lagged ratio to	0.631	0.626	0.622	0.607	0.626	0.610
Investment to GDP	(0.027)	(0.027)	(0.027)	(0.028)	(0.028)	(0.028)
Log (per capita GDP)	−0.0087	−0.0086	−0.0073	−0.0068	−0.0086	−0.0086
	(0.0046)	(0.0037)	(0.0046)	(0.0047)	(0.0047)	(0.0048)
Log (total fertility rate)	−0.0210	−0.0212	−0.0208	−0.0227	−0.0209	−0.0228
	(0.0070)	(0.0071)	(0.0071)	(0.0073)	(0.0071)	(0.0073)
Male upper-level schooling	0.0041	0.0039	0.0038	0.0034	0.0040	0.0037
	(0.0019)	(0.0019)	(0.0019)	(0.0020)	(0.0019)	(0.0020)
Log (life expectancy)	0.066	0.067	0.067	0.068	0.066	0.069
	(0.026)	(0.026)	(0.026)	(0.027)	(0.026)	(0.027)
Government consumption/GDP	−0.117	−0.119	−0.125	−0.132	−0.121	−0.129
	(0.033)	(0.033)	(0.033)	(0.034)	(0.033)	(0.034)
Rule-of-law index	0.0124	0.0112	0.0109	0.0101	0.0122	0.0113
	(0.0111)	(0.0106)	(0.0105)	(0.0105)	(0.0104)	(0.0106)
Inflation rate	0.0124	0.0114	0.0060	0.0051	0.0112	0.0128
	(0.0111)	(0.0112)	(0.0107)	(0.0105)	(0.0109)	(0.0109)
Democracy index	−0.0058	−0.0066	−0.0109	−0.0122	−0.0055	−0.0083
	(0.0249)	(0.0249)	(0.0250)	(0.0249)	(0.0248)	(0.0248)

Democracy index	0.0090	0.0103	0.0124	0.0140	0.0091	0.0125
Squared	(0.0231)	(0.0231)	(0.0233)	(0.0232)	(0.0231)	(0.0230)
Openness measure	0.0234	0.0235	0.0236	0.0241	0.0234	0.0240
	(0.0050)	(0.0050)	(0.0051)	(0.0052)	(0.0051)	(0.0051)
Growth rate of terms of trade	0.064	0.062	0.053	0.043	0.057	0.049
	(0.038)	(0.038)	(0.038)	(0.037)	(0.037)	(0.037)
Contemporaneous currency	–0.0083	–0.0079	—	—	–0.0073	–0.0075
crisis	(0.0041)	(0.0041)			(0.0041)	(0.0040)
Lagged currency crisis	—	–0.0021	—	—	—	–0.0026
		(0.0033)				(0.0033)
Contemporaneous	—	—	–0.0068	–0.0063	–0.0062	–0.0062
Banking crisis			(0.0032)	(0.0031)	(0.0031)	(0.0031)
Lagged banking crisis	—	—	—	–0.0078	—	–0.0077
				(0.0035)		(0.0035)
Number of countries,	85	85	85	85	85	85
observations	396	396	396	396	396	396

Notes: The dependent variable is the ratio of real investment (private plus public) to real GDP. The investment ratio is the average for each of the five five-year periods 1975–1979, 1980–1984, ..., 1995–1999. The earlier periods were deleted because of missing data on the currency-crisis and banking-crisis variables. See the text for further details. See the notes to Tables 4.2 and 4.5 for additional information.

Hence, the investment contraction due to a currency crisis does not seem to persist into the next five-year period.

Column 3 shows that a banking crisis is associated with a decrease in the investment ratio by 0.9 of a percentage point, and this result is statistically significant. Column 4 of Table 4.5 shows that the lagged effect from a banking crisis is a significantly negative 0.8 of a percentage point. This finding contrasts with the statistically insignificant effect from a currency crisis on the investment ratio. Hence, a banking crisis seems to have a persisting negative effect on investment, although such a crisis does not appear to have a persisting negative influence on economic growth (for given values of the investment ratio and other variables).

Column 5 shows that when currency and banking crises variables are included simultaneously, there are significant negative effects from currency and banking crises on investment in the contemporaneous period. The difference between the two contemporaneous effects from currency and banking crises is not statistically significant — the p-value is 0.84. Thus, currency and banking crises have quantitatively similar impacts on investment as well as economic growth.

From the perspective of the broad cross-country analysis, the sharp contractions of investment in the Asian-crisis countries in 1998 were not exceptional. In the Asian-crisis cases, reflected in the dummy variables in Table 4.2, average investment ratios for 1995–2000 decreased by about 2 percentage points. The broader analysis also suggests that a combined currency and banking crisis would typically have been accompanied by a contraction of the investment ratio by about 2 percentage points.

4.4. Concluding Remarks

The Asian financial crisis was associated with a sharp reduction of economic growth in east Asia, especially in the five countries that were most directly affected by the crisis. Investment ratios also fell sharply in these crisis countries, though not so much in other east Asian economies. Rates of economic growth in east Asia have rebounded in 1999–2002, but the permanence of this recovery is uncertain. The failure of investment ratios to rebound significantly in the crisis countries suggests that the crisis had a long-term adverse effect. This conclusion is reinforced by the observation that real stock-market prices in the crisis countries have failed to reattain their pre-crisis values.

A similar picture emerges from a broader study of currency and banking crises. This analysis documents the association of currency and banking crises with contemporaneously reduced values of economic growth and investment. The magnitude of the typical effect is quantitatively similar to that seen in the recent period in the Asian crisis countries. More importantly, the broader evidence does not indicate a persisting adverse influence of currency and banking crises on economic growth. Thus, if extrapolated to the Asian-crisis countries, the broad evidence predicts returns to the rates of economic growth that would have prevailed in the absence of the crisis. However, the broader international evidence shows some indication of a persisting adverse effect of a banking crisis on investment. Consequently, through the permanent depression of investment, the financial crisis would have a long-term adverse effect on growth in east Asia.

References

Barro. R. J. *Determinants of Economic Growth: A Cross-Country Empirical Study*, Cambridge MA: MIT Press, 1997.

Barro, R. J. Economic Growth in East Asia Before and After the Financial Crisis. *NBER Working Paper* No. 8330, June 2001.

Barro. R. J. and J. W. Lee. "Sources of Economic Growth." *Carnegie Rochester Conference Series on Public Policy* 40 (1994): 146.

Barro, R. J., and Sala-Martin, X. *Economic Growth.* 2nd Edition, Cambridge MA: MIT Press, 2004.

Caprio, G., and Klingebiel, D. Bank Insolvencies: Cross-Country Experience. *Policy Research Working Paper* Number 1620, Washington DC: The World Bank, 1996.

Demirguc-Kunt, A., and Detragiache, E. The Determinants of Banking Crises: Evidence from Developed and Developing Countries. Unpublished, International Monetary Fund, May 1997.

Eichengreen, Barry, Andrew K. Rose, and Wyplosz, Charles. "Exchange Market Mayhem: the Antecedents and Aftermath of Speculative Attacks." *Economic Policy*, 1995.

Frankel, J. A., and Rose, A. K. "Currency Crashes in Emerging Markets: An Empirical Treatment." *Journal of International Economics* 41 (No. 4 1996): 351–366.

Glick, R., and Hutchison, M. "Banking and Currency Crises: How Common Are Twins?" In Reuven Glick, Ramon Moreno, and Mark Spiegel (eds.), *Financial Crises in Emerging Markets.* NY: Cambridge University Press, 2001.

Heston, A., Summers. R., and Aten, B. *Penn World Tables Version 6.1.* Center for International Comparisons at the University of Pennsylvania (CICUP). October 2002.

Park, Y. C., and J. W. Lee. "Recovery and Sustainability in East Asia." In M. Dooley and J. Frankel (eds.). *Managing Currency crises in Emerging Markets.* The University of Chicago Press, 2002.

Kaminsky, Garciela, and Reinhart, Carmen. "The Twin Crises: The Causes of Banking and Balance-of-Payments Problems." *American Economic Review* 89 (No. 3 1999): 473–500.

Summers, R and Heston, A. "The Penn World Table (Mark 5): An Expanded Set of International Comparisons, 1950–1988." *Quarterly Journal of Economics* 106 (No. 2 1991): 327–368.

Part 2

Asian Financial Crises: Responses and Lessons

Chapter 5

Recovery and Sustainability in East Asia*

5.1. Introduction

Over the three years since the crisis broke out in 1997, the five Asian countries — Indonesia, Korea, Thailand, Malaysia, and the Philippines — managed impressive recoveries. The recoveries were faster than expected by anyone. The economies started to bottom out in the second half of 1998. The rebounding of the growth rate in 1999 was no less drastic than its free-fall. In Korea, for example, the growth rates showed a turnaround from –6.7 percent in 1998 to 10.7 percent in 1999.

The purpose of this paper is to make an assessment of this speedy adjustment from the crisis in East Asia. In particular, we analyze the macroeconomic adjustment process of the East Asian currency crisis in a broad international perspective. First, we assess the impacts of the crisis on gross domestic product (GDP) growth using a cross-country data set, which compiled all currency crisis episodes over the period from 1970 to 1995. From these cross-country data, we draw some stylized facts about the adjustment of key macroeconomic variables during the crisis. Then we investigate the critical factors that determine the adjustment process.

---

*This chapter is co-authored with Yung Chul Park and was originally published in Michael P. Dooley and Jeffrey A. Frankel eds., *Managing Currency Crises in Emerging Markets*, Chicago: University of Chicago Press, 2003, pp. 275–316;
The authors thank Robert Barro, Richard Portes, and conference participants for their helpful comments on an earlier draft. Si-Yeon Lee and Do-Won Kwak provided able research assistance.

Our analysis of cross-country patterns shows that GDP growth rates drop with the eruption of a crisis but then recover quickly to the precrisis level in two or three years, showing a V-pattern of adjustment. Thereafter, the GDP growth rates tend to rise slightly above the precrisis levels, but then they subside to a more sustainable level. We also compare the adjustment patterns of GDP growth rates between two subgroups of the currency crisis episodes, one with conditional financial assistance from the International Monetary Fund (IMF) and the other without. We find that the adjustment process was much sharper in the group of the crisis episodes with the IMF program compared to those without. That is, in the IMF-program countries, GDP growth rates start to fall precipitously even before the eruption of a crisis but then recover to their precrisis level more quickly in two years.

The macroeconomic adjustment process in East Asia is in general consistent with these stylized patterns. However, the degree of initial contraction and following recovery has been far greater in East Asia than what the cross-country evidence predicts. This paper tries to make an evaluation of what factors contributed to the sharper contraction and the quicker recovery in East Asia compared with the cross-country patterns.

As we will discuss in section 5.3, we believe that a large number of internal and external factors are responsible for the deeper crisis and the quicker recovery in East Asia. The origin and the nature of the shock, the initial conditions, the development of external environments, and the stabilization and structural adjustment policies taken must have a significant consequence on the adjustment path, as they did in the eruption of the crisis. From cross-country regressions based on the sample of previous crisis episodes, we find that depreciation of exchange rate, expansionary macroeconomic policies, and favorable global environments are the critical determinants of the postcrisis recovery. In the regression, the financial assistance from the IMF is found to have no independent impact on the recovery process.

We find that the quick recoveries in East Asia have been driven largely by the accommodating macroeconomic policies, favorable external environments, and more export-oriented structure. Korea, Malaysia, and Thailand shifted to a relaxation of monetary and fiscal policies by the second half of 1998, and then their economy took off. The sharp real depreciation of currency must have a bigger impact on more open Asian economies. Favorable external development also helped the quick improvement in East Asian exports. In this sense, the East Asian process of adjustment is not much different from the stylized pattern from the previous currency crisis episodes over the period from 1970 to 1995. However, the stylized pattern of adjustment cannot explain why the crisis was more severe and the recovery much faster than what was expected from the previous experiences of crisis. This paper argues that the sharper adjustment pattern in East Asia is due to the severe liquidity crisis that was triggered by investors' panic and then amplified by the weak corporate and bank balance sheet.

The stylized pattern of real GDP growth from the cross-country episodes displays that the crisis-hit countries can recover their precrisis or noncrisis average growth rate in three years after the crisis. Hence, it raises a question of whether the East Asian economies will be able to return to the precrisis trend rate of growth.

Although the financial crisis of 1997 abruptly brought a halt to Asia's period of robust growth, there was little in Asia's fundamentals that inevitably led to the crisis. This paper discusses the long-term prospects for growth in East Asia. From the cross-country regressions, we find that there is no evidence of a direct impact of a currency crisis on long-run growth. This suggests that, with a return to the core policies that resulted in rapid growth, the East Asian economies can again return to sustained growth.

The paper is organized as follows. Section 5.2 discusses the methodology for our cross-country analysis and presents central features in the macroeconomic adjustments of the crisis-hit countries. Then, using regression analysis based on the cross-country data, we assess the factors that can explain the behaviors of GDP growth rates during the crisis. Section 5.3 reviews the recent recoveries in East Asia and compares them with the stylized patterns from the cross-country analysis. We analyze the driving forces of the faster recovery in East Asia. Section 5.4 discusses the issue of the sustainability of the current recovery. Concluding remarks are found in the final section.

5.2. Cross-Country Patterns of Adjustment to Currency Crisis

5.2.1. *Data*

In order to assess the postcrisis adjustment of the crisis-hit countries, one needs first to define a currency crisis. Several alternative indicators and methods have been used in the literature to identify the year when a crisis erupted in each country. Frankel and Rose (1996) and Milesi-Ferreti and Razin (1998) used the nominal depreciation rate of the currency. Sachs, Tornell, and Velasco (1996), Radelet and Sachs (1998), and Kaminsky and Reinhart (1999) combined the depreciation rate with additional indicators such as losses in foreign reserves, increase in the interest rate, and reversal in capital accounts to identify the crisis.

Each definition still has its own limitations. A large-scale depreciation can occur in an orderly manner without a speculative attack. Identifying unsuccessful speculative attacks is a difficult task. Reliable data on reserves and interest rates in developing countries are often unavailable. Reserves or interest rates can change irrespective of an attack. Lee and Rhee (2002) suggested an alternative measure based on the initiation of an IMF stabilization program. However, countries often receive the IMF program after a crisis breaks out or without a currency crisis. Governments may sign an IMF agreement not necessarily because they need foreign exchange, but because they want austerity conditions to be imposed (Przeworski and Vreeland 2000).

Because the purpose of this paper is not to improve the measure of a currency crisis, we use the conventional nominal depreciation rate of the currency as a benchmark measure. However, in contrast to Frankel and Rose (1996), we use quarterly data, instead of annual data, to define a currency crisis. That is, based on quarterly data, a country is judged to have a currency crisis in the specific year when it has a nominal depreciation of currency of at least 25 percent in any quarter of the year and the depreciation rate exceeds the previous quarter's change in the exchange rate by a margin of at least 10 percent. Thus, our definition captures the incidences of currency crises that were severe but short-lived, perhaps due to successful interventions in the foreign exchange market. During the period from 1970 to 1997, the total number of currency crises was 260.

We use a window of plus/minus two years to identify an independent crisis. That is, if there was a precedent crisis within two years before a crisis, we count the latter as a consecutive crisis, not an independent one. This procedure yields a total of 192 currency crisis episodes.[1]

Then, we divide all crisis episodes into two groups based on whether the crisis-hit countries entered into an IMF program or not. We have compiled data on all types of IMF programs that include standby arrangements, Extended Fund Facility (EFF) arrangements, Structural Adjustment Facility (SAF), and Enhanced Structural Adjustment Facility (ESAF) over the period from 1970 to 1997.[2] The program is identified by the year when the loans are approved. Thus, if a country received financial assistance from the IMF during the year of, or one year after, the currency crisis, we consider it a case of a currency crisis with the IMF program. Note that the decision on participation in the IMF program following a currency crisis can be determined endogenously by various factors. A country may enter into agreements with the IMF when it faces a more severe foreign reserve crisis or a worse macroeconomic situation (Conway 1994). However, relying on the IMF conditionality may be just a way to impose domestically unpopular austerity policies (Przeworski and Vreeland 2000).

Table 5.1 shows a summary of data on currency crises based on our definition during the period from 1970 to 1997. There were 192 currency crisis episodes during this period. The number of crises was increasing over time, from forty in the 1970s, to sixty nine in the 1980s, to eighty three in the 1990s (1990–97). According to this data set, the number of countries that experienced at least one crisis was ninety nine.[3] Thus, on average each country had 1.86 crises over the period. Out of the 192 crisis episodes, 72 of them featured participation in an IMF program.

---

[1]Lee, Hong, and Rhee (2001) describe the data in more detail. The authors are grateful to Kiseok Hong and Changyong Rhee for sharing their cross-country data set.

[2]The data come from Lee and Rhee (2000), who compiled the information from the IMF Annual Report for each year.

[3]The sample does not include the former Soviet Union countries that experienced currency crises and subsequently received financial assistance from the IMF in the early 1990s.

Table 5.1. Incidence of currency crises and IMF program participation over the period 1970–97

		IMF Program Participation	
Period	Total Currency Crises	*Yes*	*No*
1970–1997	192	71	121
1970–1979	40	12	28
1980–1989	69	24	45
1990–1997	83	35	48

Notes: A currency crisis is defined as occurring in the year when a country has a nominal depreciation of currency of at least 25 percent in any quarter of a year and the depreciation rate exceeds the previous quarter's change in the exchange rate by a margin of at least 10 percent. If the country under a currency crisis received financial assistance from the IMF during the year of or one year after the currency crisis, it is classified as a case of a currency crisis with IMF program participation. Our sample does not include the former Soviet Union countries and counts only independent crises by imposing a plus/minus two years window.

5.2.2. *Macroeconomic Adjustment During the Currency Crisis*

On the basis of the currency crisis index, we investigate how the crisis-hit economies, on average, behave during the five years prior to and following the crisis. We first look at the movement of growth rates of real GDP and then investigate the sources of output changes by looking at the movements of GDP expenditure components and major macroeconomic policy variables in the typical crisis-hit country during the period before and after the crisis. We also construct a control group of tranquil observations. If a country was not subject to any crisis within a window of plus/minus two years surrounding a specific year, it is counted as a noncrisis country in that specific year.

The behavior of the macroeconomic variables between the two subgroups — one with conditional financial assistance from the IMF and the other without — is also compared.

We use the data for the period from 1970 to 1995. Thus, we attempt to draw the stylized pattern of macroeconomic adjustment from the crisis episodes that had occurred prior to the Asian crisis. There are

176 independent currency crises during this period, and in 64 episodes of them the countries participated in an IMF program.

Real Gross Domestic Product Growth

Figure 5.1 shows the movements of the average GDP growth rates during the five years prior to and following the crisis; that is, from $t-5$ to $t+5$, where t is the year of a currency crisis. For comparison, we include a straight line, which indicates the average GDP growth rate during the tranquil period, which did not experience a currency crisis or enter into an IMF program within a window of plus or minus two years.

In general, we find that the growth rates, on average, exhibit a V-type pattern of adjustment over the period before and following the crisis. The growth rates during the period three to five years prior to the crisis are slightly lower than the average during the tranquil period of 3.5 percent. The growth rate continues to decline over time, from 2.7 percent in $t-4$ to 1.1 percent in $t-1$, implying that economic conditions are aggravated prior to the eruption of a crisis.

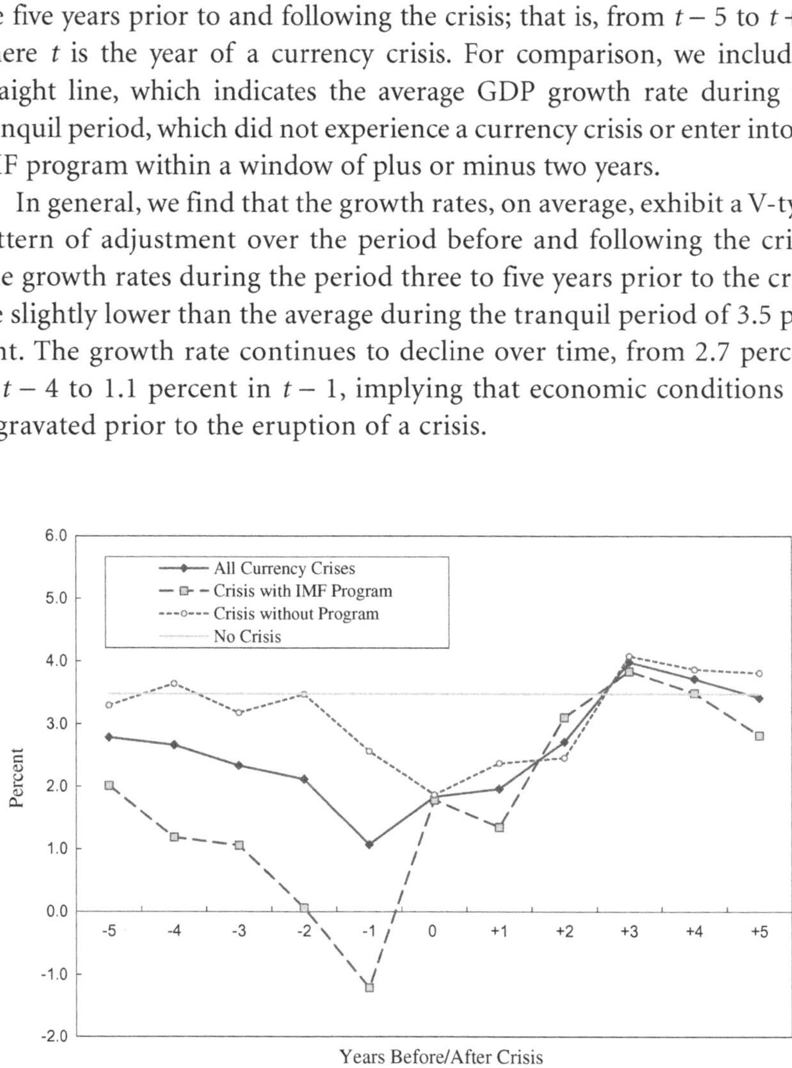

Figure 5.1 Changes in GDP growth during the currency crises

The growth rate increases slightly in the crisis year, which confirms that most currency crises have indeed been expansionary. As in Gupta, Mishra, and Sahay (2000), we also find that about 70 percent of the currency crises in our sample led to an output increase in the crisis year. The average GDP growth rate of the crisis-hit countries remains at about 1.9 percent over the crisis year and one year after. However, the GDP growth rate recovers its noncrisis level quickly, in three years after the crisis, reaching 4.0 percent in $t+3$ — that is, about 0.5 percentage points higher than the average of the noncrisis economies. Thus, the growth rate tends to exceed its precrisis or tranquil period average, indicating that after a crisis the country's level of GDP returns to the level of its precrisis growth path. Eventually, the growth rate tapers off and returns to the level of the tranquil period in four and five years after the crisis. This V-type pattern and the speed of recovery are broadly consistent with the findings in Hong and Tornell (1999) and Gupta, Mishra, and Sahay (2000).

Figure 5.1 compares the behavior of the GDP growth rates between the two subgroups, one with conditional financial assistance from the IMF and the other without. We find that the adjustment process shows a much sharper V-type pattern in the program countries than in the nonprogram countries. The program countries start with lower growth rates of around 1.2 percent in $t-4$ and continue to slow down. They reach the trough, where the growth rate is –1.2 percent, in one year prior to the initiation of the currency crisis.

This magnitude of decline in growth rates is much larger than that of the nonprogram countries. At the trough, the growth rate of the crisis-hit program countries is about 4.7 percentage points lower than that of the non-crisis economies. Thereafter, rebounding from the deeper trough, the program countries show a quicker recovery. The GDP growth rate begins to recover from the crisis year and reaches its precrisis level quickly, within two years after the onset of a crisis. The nonprogram countries also begin to recover a year after the crisis, and then their growth rates stabilize at the non-crisis level from $t+3$.

The fact that the program countries have much lower growth rates than the nonprogram countries confirms that only a very serious macro-economic situation forces a country to enter into agreements with the

IMF. Nevertheless, it is intriguing that the crisis-hit countries show a quicker recovery from a deeper recession with participation in the IMF program.

Gross Domestic Product Expenditure Components

Panels A to F of Fig. 5.2 show the movements of the components of GDP expenditure during the five years prior to and following the crisis.

Panel A shows that the share of private-consumption expenditure in GDP remains stable over the period. In other words, consumption moves closely with GDP. The adjustment pattern is similar in both program and nonprogram countries. For the overall period, the ratio of consumption to GDP in the crisis-hit economies exceeds the noncrisis tranquil period average, indicating that private consumption is high in the crisis-hit countries, and even after a crisis these countries' level of private saving does not increase to the level of the noncrisis countries.

Panel B of Fig. 5.2 shows that, in contrast to consumption, the investment (private plus public investment) ratio shows more fluctuations. The level is no higher in the crisis-hit economies than in the noncrisis countries. For four to five years prior to the crisis, the investment ratio remains at an average level of tranquil observations of 22.8 percent. Thus, a stylized fact is that the crisis-hit countries have had "overconsumption," but not necessarily "overinvestment," compared to the level of the noncrisis countries. In the crisis-hit countries, the investment rate tends to decline during the precrisis period, reaching 19.8 percent in the crisis year. After the crisis, the investment rate increases gradually but does not return to the level of the precrisis or tranquil period, remaining at 20.9 percent for five years following the crisis. A popular claim regarding the role of the IMF conditionality is that the austerity program has an adverse effect on investment. Panel B of Fig. 5.2 seems to support this claim. The IMF-program countries have experienced a more severe investment contraction than the other group in the precrisis period, as the investment ratio declines continuously from 21.4 percent in $t-5$ to 18.9 percent in t. In the postcrisis period of the crisis-hit countries in which an IMF program is introduced, the investment rate does not recover to the precrisis level, remaining at 19.7 percent in $t+4$ and 20.1 percent in $t+5$. In contrast, the investment

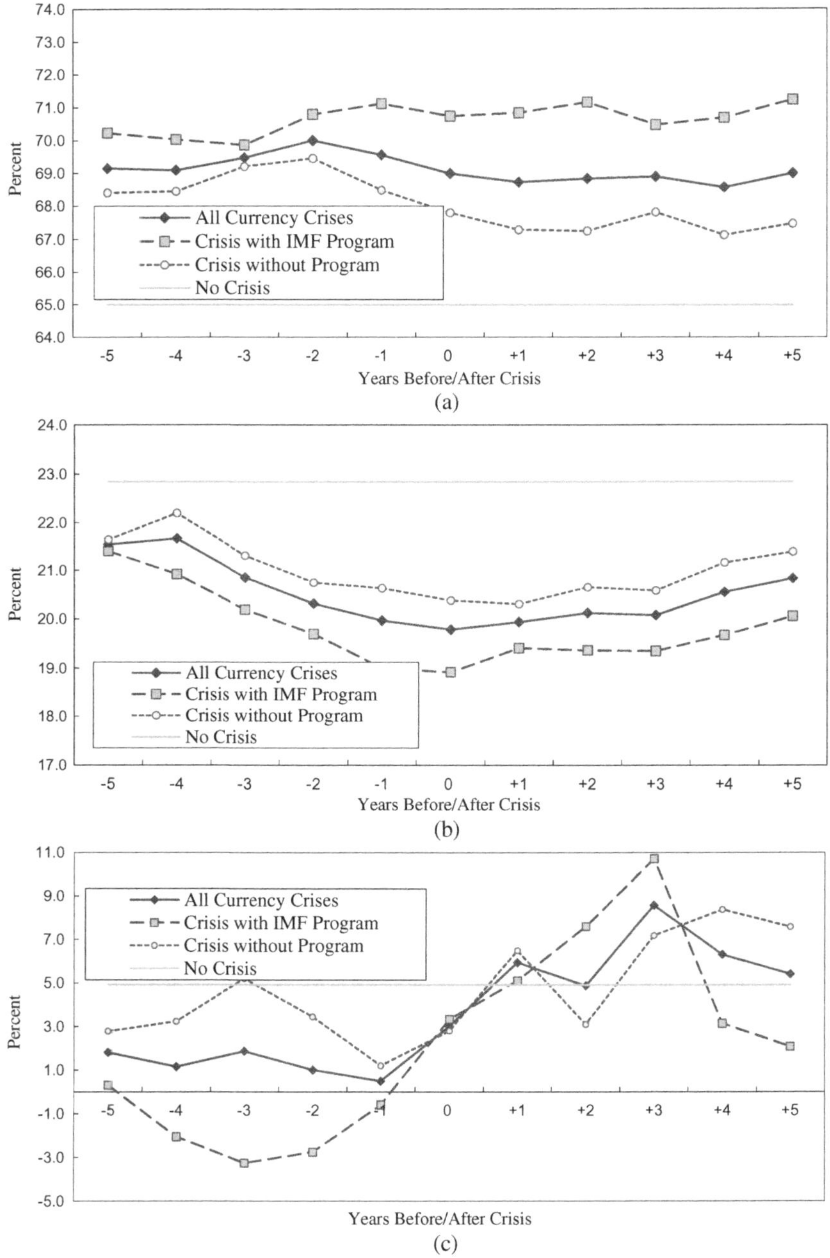

Figure 5.2 Changes in GDP expenditure components during the currency crises: *a*, private consumption in GDP; *b*, investment rate; *c*, real export growth rate; *d*, export share in GDP; *e*, real import growth rate; *f*, import share in GDP

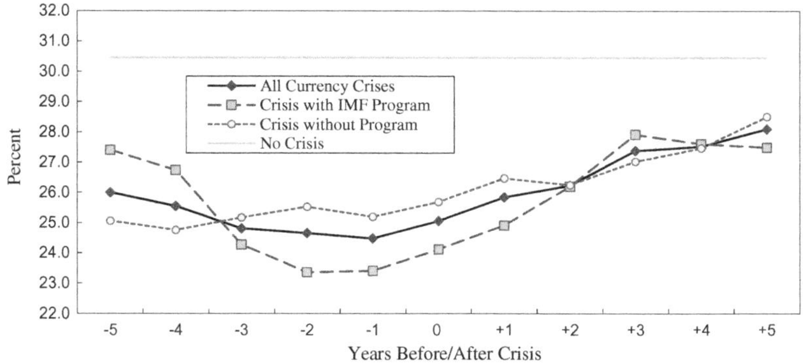

(d)

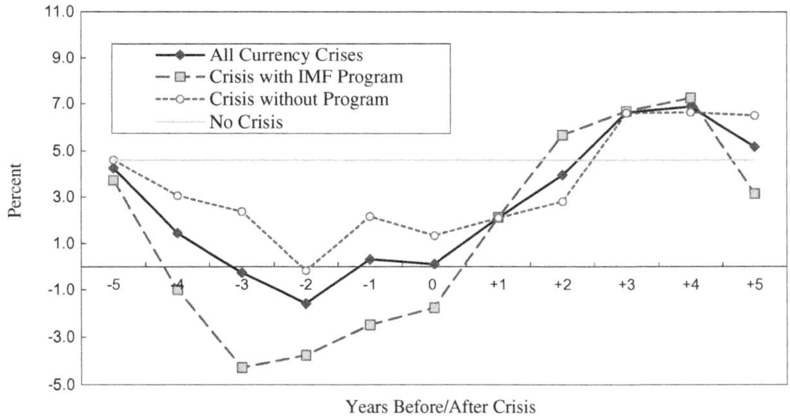

(e)

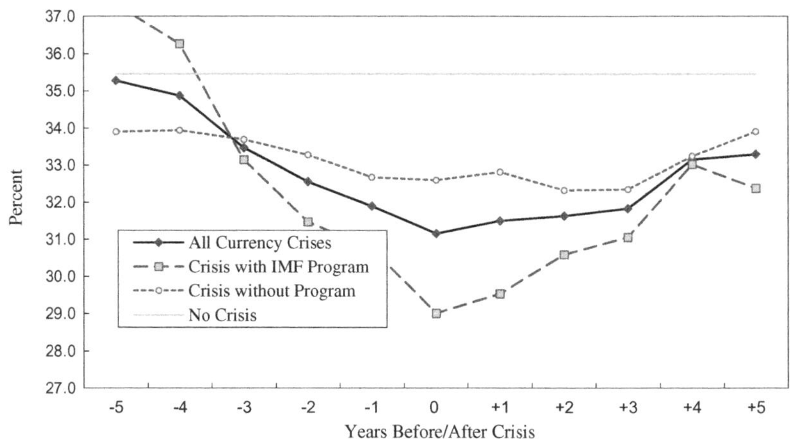

(f)

Figure 5.2 (*Continued*)

rate returns to the precrisis level in the nonprogram crisis-hit countries in five years after the crisis.

In the crisis-hit countries, domestic expenditure or demand either slowly recovers or remains permanently below the precrisis level. In contrast, export demand shows a quick recovery during the postcrisis period. Panel C shows that in the crisis-hit countries, real export growth rates jump from less than 1 percent in $t-1$ to 3.0 percent in the crisis year and to 5.9 percent in $t+1$, and then they remain at over 5 percent over the postcrisis period. For both program and nonprogram countries, export growth during the postcrisis period is faster than that of the precrisis or tranquil period and, thus, leads a strong recovery. Consequently, as shown in panel D of Fig. 5.2, after the currency crisis the export share increases permanently above the precrisis level. However, note that on average the export share in all crisis-hit countries is still lower than that of the noncrisis average.

During the early postcrisis period the quick recovery of export growth is accompanied by a contraction of import demand. The pattern of import reduction is more conspicuous in the program countries where import growth rates are negative in the precrisis period as well as the crisis year. Panels E and F of Fig. 5.2 show that although the growth rate of imports recovers to the precrisis and noncrisis average in two years following the crisis, its share in GDP remains below the noncrisis average of 35.5 percent. The growth of exports and imports shows that the ratio of current account to GDP improves quickly after the crisis. Thus, net exports tend to lead the recovery in the crisis-hit countries.

Macroeconomic Policy Indicators

Public consumption is an indicator of fiscal policy. Panels A and B of Fig. 5.3 show that public consumption growth rates tend to slow down slightly in the crisis year and then recover to the precrisis as well as noncrisis average. However, in the first year following the crisis, there is contrasting behavior between the program countries and nonprogram countries. Whereas the public consumption growth rate is over 5.0 percent for the nonprogram countries, it is −0.8 percent for the program countries in the year of $t+1$. This confirms that an agreement with the

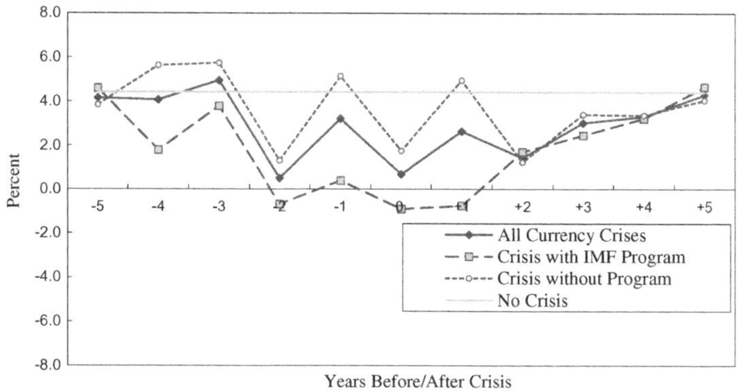

(a)

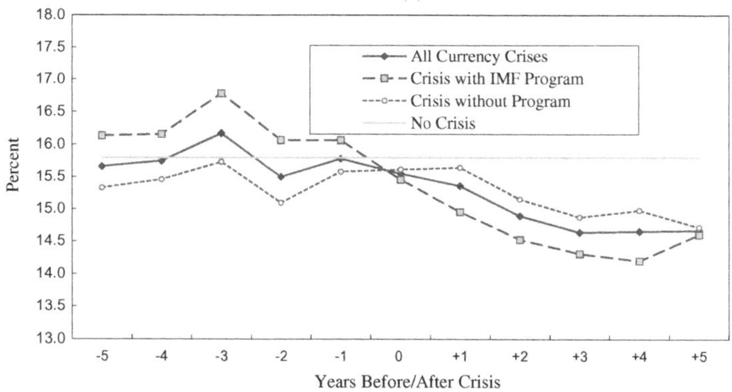

(b)

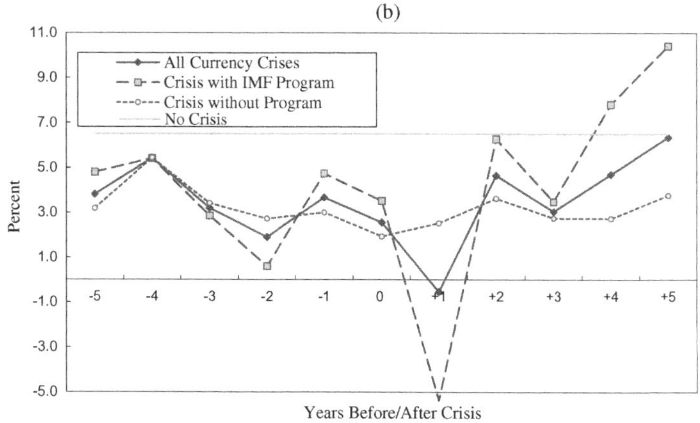

(c)

Figure 5.3 Macroeconomic policy indicators during the currency crises: *a*, real public consumption growth rate; *b*, public consumption in GDP; *c*, real money supply (M2) growth rate; *d*, real bank credit growth rate

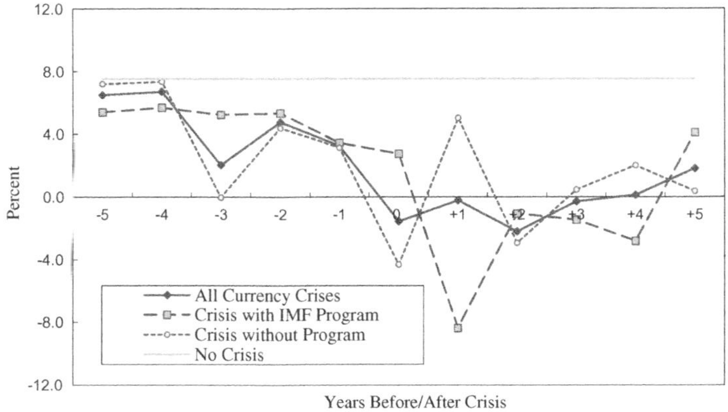

(d)

Figure 5.3 (*Continued*)

IMF introduces a contractionary fiscal policy in the program country. Reflecting this sharp contraction in public consumption expenditure, the ratio of public consumption to GDP declines quickly in $t + 1$ with the IMF program. The ratio remains at the level lower than the precrisis or noncrisis average in both program and nonprogram countries even five years after a crisis.

Like fiscal policy, monetary policy of the program countries contrasts sharply with that of the nonprogram countries. Panel C of Fig. 5.3 shows that the real money supply growth rate remains positive throughout the years following the crisis and increases over time to return to the precrisis level in five years after the crisis in the nonprogram countries. In contrast, in the sample of the crisis-hit countries with IMF program participation, money supply growth is negative. Thereafter, it returns to the precrisis average growth rate. The sharp reduction in money supply in the program countries implies that, as in fiscal policy, participation in an IMF program brings in tight monetary policy in the crisis-hit economy.

It is claimed that a currency crisis often develops into a banking crisis. As international lending declines suddenly, a weak banking sector is unable to play a proper intermediation role. Banks reduce the supply of credit to the private sector. Panel D shows that credit supply growth indeed slows down in the crisis-hit countries. For four to five years prior to the crisis,

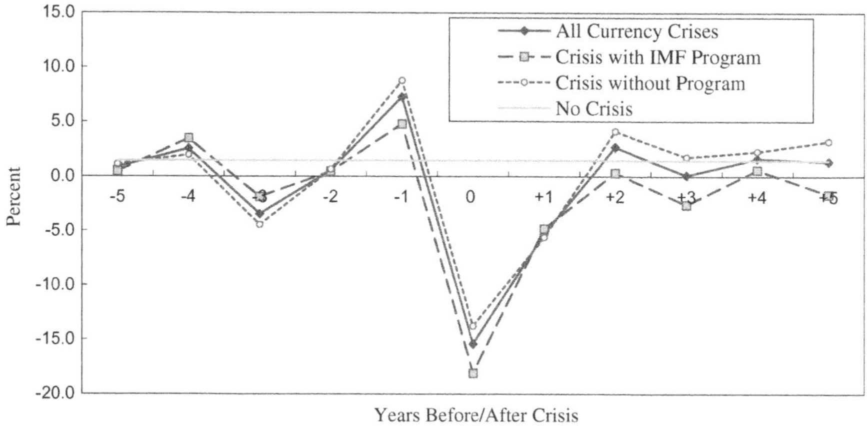

Figure 5.4 Change in real exchange rate during the currency crisis

the real credit growth rate is 7.4 percent. Thereafter, credit growth rates decline over time, reaching −1.6 percent in the crisis year. Even five years after the crisis, credit growth does not return to the level of the precrisis or tranquil period. The slowdown of real credit growth is more pronounced in the IMF-program countries. The supply of real credit declines by more than 8 percent in the year following the crisis and thereafter continues to slow down throughout the postcrisis period.

The robust growth of net exports during the postcrisis period is likely to be related to the real exchange depreciation associated with (or caused by) the currency crisis. Figure 5.4 shows that a currency crisis causes a sharp real depreciation of the exchange rate by about 15 percent in the crisis year. The real exchange rate also depreciates by 5.3 percent in the year following the crisis. Thereafter, it appreciates about 2 percent per year. Hence, the real exchange remains depreciated after the crisis. The pattern of adjustment in the real exchange rate is similar in the program and nonprogram countries.

5.2.3. *Determinants of the Postcrisis Recovery*

We believe there are a large number of factors that determine the stylized pattern of adjustment in real output growth in the crisis-hit countries. Broadly speaking, there are four major factors that influence the adjustment pattern: (a) the origin and nature of the shock; (b) initial conditions; (c) domestic policies; and (d) external environments.

Origin and Nature of the Shock

The origin and nature of the shock that has provoked a crisis can influence the evolution of the crisis. Many currency crises can be attributed to macroeconomic mismanagement — large budget deficits and consequent monetary expansion in a fixed exchange rate regime — as was the Latin America debt crisis in the early 1980s. In this case, real depreciation of the currency and contraction of domestic absorption help to restore internal and external balance, leading to improvement in the economy.

Investors' panic can intensify the effects of speculative attacks on currency. In particular, when the capital account is liberalized, a bad expectation by foreign investors can easily lead to a sudden reversal of foreign lending, thereby causing a significant contraction of the domestic economy. In particular, the adverse impact will be magnified if domestic corporations and financial institutions are heavily leveraged by large, unhedged, and short-term foreign currency debts. When a sharp and unexpected depreciation wreaks havoc with highly leveraged corporate and bank balance sheets, a sudden reversal of capital flows exacerbates the downturn in investment and the economy (Krugman 1999; Aghion, Bacchetta, and Banerjee 2000). However, once the investors' panic calms down and foreign capital resumes its inward flow, the economy can rebound quickly to its long-term trend.

Initial Conditions

Differences in initial conditions could result in different patterns of adjustment. For example, structural variables such as per capita output and openness could be important in determining the pattern of postcrisis recovery.

The level of initial per capita GDP can influence the growth rate in the postcrisis period. In growth theory, a country with a lower initial per capita GDP is in a more favorable position for future growth. The fundamental idea is that the gap in existing capital and technology between the current and steady-state levels offers a chance for rapid catching up, via high rates of capital accumulation as well as the diffusion of technology from more technically advanced economies. In addition, when a currency crisis leads an economy to a lower level of per capita income relative to that of its own trend, the subsequent growth rate of the economy that rebounds to its potential growth would be higher.

Openness can also influence the speed and extent of the postcrisis recovery. When the economy is more export-oriented, a quicker improvement in the current account follows a currency devaluation. Lee and Rhee (2000) argue that the quick recovery of the Korean economy may have been possible because of its openness and export orientation. An export-oriented economy benefits more from devaluation after the crisis, and a subsequent improvement in the current account could in turn help restore foreign investors' confidence and hence stability in the foreign exchange market.

Several studies also point out that the behavior of macroeconomic variables prior to the crisis can influence the degree of real output contraction. For example, a rapid expansion of bank credit or lending boom during the precrisis period is critical to the postcrisis recovery (Sachs, Tornell, and Velasco 1996; Hong and Tornell 1999). Gupta, Mishra, and Sahay (2000) find that the higher the size of short-term external debt and the amount of private capital flows in the years prior to the crisis, the more severe the contraction of output during the crisis period.

Policy Factors

Macroeconomic and structural reform policies implemented by the government for crisis management can play a key role in the postcrisis adjustment of real output. Fiscal policy has a direct impact on domestic demand. Monetary policy plays a critical role in determining domestic consumption and investment.

In addition to the macroeconomic stabilization policies, structural reform programs can have significant effects on the adjustment path. It is often argued that structural reforms introduced by the IMF play a catalytic role in resuming foreign trade and private capital inflows to a crisis-hit economy and thus contribute to its fast recovery, because the commitment to the reform program improves foreign investors' confidence in the economy. The critics of the IMF program, however, argue that the implementation of financial restructuring in conjunction with contractionary macroeconomic policies can make a credit crunch more severe than otherwise after the crisis.

For external demand, a larger depreciation of the exchange rate is expected to increase export earnings while cutting down import demand to improve the current account.

External Environments

A global economic environment is also critical to the postcrisis adjustment of crisis-hit countries. Business fluctuations of the world economy can influence postcrisis growth, because they have a substantial impact on the terms of trade and export earnings of the crisis-hit country.

To the extent that the relevant data are available, we carry out an empirical assessment of the factors determining the pattern of postcrisis recovery. The explanatory variables that we consider to explain the speed and the extent of postcrisis recovery include per capita real GDP in the crisis year; world economic growth, which is an average of per capita GDP growth rates of a crisis-hit country's trading partners weighted by its trade share; an interactive term of the real exchange depreciation rate with openness (trade-GDP ratio); real public consumption growth; and real money supply growth. We also include an investment rate.[4]

The regression also includes a dummy variable for the IMF-program countries to see if participation in an IMF program had any impact on the recovery process. Upon entering an agreement with the IMF, a member government subscribes to the IMF conditionality, which typically entails fiscal austerity, tight monetary policy, and currency devaluation. Because we include macroeconomic policies variables separately in the regression, the dummy variable may be able to capture the effect of the IMF program participation in postcrisis recovery.

---

[4] Investment ratio can be considered an endogenous variable. The regression results do not change qualitatively when we have excluded investment ratio from the regressions. Note that investment includes public investment in addition to private investment. The regressions for investment rate are presented in Table 5.3.

We also control the differences in country-specific factors that may influence the potential growth path, by including the average growth rate for three to five years prior to the crisis. However, we do not include the precrisis macroeconomic policy variables in the regressions, because the impact of these variables on the postcrisis recovery is extensively discussed in Hong and Tornell (1999) and Gupta, Mishra, and Sahay (2000). Also, we cannot incorporate any variables that measure structural vulnerabilities of the corporate and financial sectors due to the lack of broad cross-country data.

The dependent variable in the regression is the average growth rate of real GDP during the postcrisis period over k years.[5]

$$y_{i,t+k} = \frac{1}{k}\sum_{j=1}^{k}\left(\ln GDP_{i,t+j} - \ln GDP_{i,t+j-1}\right),\ I = 1,\ldots,N \tag{1}$$

where $GDP_{i,t+j}$ is real GDP for country i in the j years after the crisis year (t) and N is the number of crisis episodes in our sample. Then, $y_{i,t+k}$ represents the real GDP growth rate, averaged over the postcrisis period of k years. Because we are mostly interested in short-term recovery, we choose k from 1 to 5. In the previous literature, k was often chosen arbitrarily, and thus cross-section data in which each country had only one observation were used for empirical investigation. Our framework differs significantly in that we use panel data. Thus, we utilize both cross-section and time-dimension information. Our regression specification is as follows.

$$y_{i,t+k} = \beta' \mathrm{X}_{i,t+k} + \varepsilon_{i,t+k}, \quad i = 1,\ldots N, \quad k = 1,\ldots,5. \tag{2}$$

where X denotes the vector of the explanatory variables. Note that some independent variables, such as real GDP in the crisis year, precrisis average growth rate, and an IMF program dummy, are identical across all five equations. Fiscal policy variable is included as an average over the period from the crisis year t to the postcrisis year $t + k$, while monetary growth

---

[5]We have also estimated another specification by using the reversal of GDP growth rate between the crisis-hit (that is, $t - 1$ and t) and the postcrisis period, instead of postcrisis GDP growth, for the dependent variable in the regressions. We find the results do not change much.

and real exchange depreciation variables are included as an average over the period from the crisis year t to the postcrisis $t + k - 1$.

We estimate this system of the five equations by a seemingly unrelated regression (SUR) technique that corrects for heteroskedasticity in each equation and correlation of the errors across the equations.

Table 5.2 displays our estimates of the basic regression for postcrisis recovery at various horizons that was applied to a total of 101 previous crisis episodes during the period from 1970 to 1995.

We find a strong and statistically significant negative relation between the initial real per capita GDP and the postcrisis growth rate at all horizons, implying that countries with lower per capita income tend to have larger increases in GDP growth over the period after the crisis. The impact of initial GDP on the postcrisis recovery is much larger in the year following the crisis, but then it becomes smaller in the later years of the postcrisis period. The estimated coefficients imply that a 10 percentage point drop in per capita GDP in the crisis year is associated with a 0.2 percentage point [2.04 * ln(0.9)] increase in GDP growth in the first year after a crisis erupted, but with a 0.1 percentage point increase on average over five years after the crisis.

The world growth variable also has a significantly positive coefficient in most of the regressions. The estimated coefficient implies that a 1 percentage point increase in world per capita GDP growth is associated with about a 0.5 percentage point increase in GDP growth of the crisis-hit country in the postcrisis period.

The result also confirms the strong association between investment and GDP growth over the period of adjustment in the crisis-hit economies. The coefficients show that an increase of 10 percentage points in the ratio of investment to GDP is typically associated with an increase in the growth rate of about 1.3 percentage points per year.

Among the macroeconomic policy variables, the fiscal variable (measured by public consumption growth) turns out to be most significant for the recovery in all postcrisis periods except for the year of $t + 1$. The estimated coefficients imply that an increase of the public consumption growth rate by 10 percentage points leads to an increase in GDP growth rate by 0.5–0.9 percent.

Table 5.2. Determinants of the pace of recovery from the currency crises (a sample of 101 crisis episodes between 1970 and 1995)

	Dependent Variable: Average GDP Growth Rate from $t+1$ to $t+k$				
$(t+k=)$	t+1	t+2	t+3	t+4	t+5
Real GDP per capita at t	−2.037*	−1.240*	−1.028*	−0.817*	−0.816*
PPP-adjusted, log	(0.532)	(0.380)	(0.324)	(0.283)	(0.257)
Precrisis GDP growth average,	−0.137	−0.030	0.060	0.057	0.090
$t-3$ to $t-5$	(0.135)	(0.097)	(0.083)	(0.072)	(0.066)
World per capita GDP growth	0.445*	0.261	0.469*	0.580*	0.541*
average, $t+1$ to $t+k$	(0.225)	(0.175)	(0.155)	(0.166)	(0.198)
Investment ratio average,	0.133*	0.136*	0.123*	0.125*	0.104*
$t+1$ to $t+k$	(0.051)	(0.037)	(0.032)	(0.028)	(0.026)
Real exchange rate change × trade	0.032	0.004	−0.034**	−0.062*	−0.086*
share average, t to $t+k-1$	(0.023)	(0.020)	(0.019)	(0.023)	(0.029)
Public consumption growth	0.035	0.057*	0.072*	0.078*	0.086*
average, t to $t+k$	(0.032)	(0.025)	(0.021)	(0.019)	(0.024)
Real money supply growth	0.006	0.012	0.011	0.003	−0.0001
average, t to $t+k-1$	(0.015)	(0.011)	(0.010)	(0.009)	(0.010)
IMF program participation	−1.042	0.194	0.179	−0.215	−0.040
dummy	(0.968)	(0.699)	(0.589)	(0.515)	(0.468)
No. of crisis episodes	101	101	101	101	101
R^2	0.14	0.17	0.24	0.30	0.33

Notes: Standard errors reported in parentheses. The system has five equations, in which the dependent variables are the average real GDP growth rates over *k* years from the crisis year, *t*. The system is estimated by the seemingly unrelated regression (SUR) technique, which allows for different error variances in each equation and for correlation of these errors across equations. Each equation has a different constant term, which is not reported. An increase in real exchange rate indicates a real appreciation.

**Significant at the 90 percent level.

*Significant at the 95 percent level.

In contrast to the positive and significant contribution of fiscal policy, monetary policy turns out to be less important for postcrisis recovery. The average growth rates of real money supply are insignificant in all equations. One might argue that the weak effect of monetary policy on real output even in the short run is not credible. However, in our view, the real impact of monetary policy is ambiguous in the crisis-hit economies. Contractionary monetary policy, which is part of the IMF programs, can contribute to postcrisis growth as it helps stabilize prices and improve the current account.[6]

The test shows that the interactive term between trade share and exchange rate depreciation variables has a significant impact on the postcrisis GDP growth in only a few years following a crisis. The estimated coefficient shows that for the country with the average openness ratio of 0.6, a real exchange depreciation of 10 percent raises real GDP growth rate by about 0.4 percent per year over the four years after the crisis.

We also examined whether the agreements with the IMF had any impact on the postcrisis recovery. The estimated coefficient turns out to be statistically insignificant. Hence, there is no evidence that IMF programs had any significant impact on the recovery process after a currency crisis when other factors were controlled.[7]

Macroeconomic policies may have an additional impact on growth by influencing the level of investment. Table 5.3 shows the results of regressions for the investment rate. We find that both public investment and real money supply growth play a quite significant role in promoting investment from the beginning of the postcrisis period, whereas exchange rate depreciation is insignificant. The estimated coefficient for public investment suggests that an increase of 1 percentage point in the

---

[6] Goldfajn and Gupta (1999) find that the use of tight monetary policy is accompanied by a sharper recovery of output during the currency crises.

[7] A problem can occur in this regression when participation in the IMF program is endogenously determined. To avoid this simultaneous problem, we need to use an instrumental-variable technique. We do not implement this approach yet due to the lack of an ideal instrument.

Table 5.3. Regressions for investment rate in the post-crisis period

	Dependent Variable: Average Investment Ratio from $t+1$ to $t+k$		
$(t+k=)$	t + 1	t + 2	t + 3
GDP growth in the precrisis period average, $t-3$ to $t-5$	0.281** (0.152)	0.410* (0.141)	0.349* (0.156)
Real exchange rate change average, t to $t+k-1$	0.007 (0.040)	–0.012 (0.036)	0.011 (0.040)
Public investment-GDP ratio average, t to $t+k$	1.460* (0.231)	1.319* (0.131)	1.256* (0.111)
Real money supply growth average, t to $t+k-1$	0.010 (0.036)	0.085* (0.040)	0.133* (0.046)
IMF program participation dummy	1.002 (1.296)	1.748 (1.222)	1.798 (1.158)
No. of crisis episodes	81	81	81
R^2	0.60	0.65	0.68

Notes: Each equation is estimated by the least squares method. Robust standard errors reported in parentheses. Constant term is included, but not reported.
**Significant at the 90 percent level.
*Significant at the 95 percent level.

ratio of public investment to GDP contributes to an increase in the total investment ratio by more than 1 percentage point, between 1.3 and 1.5. Hence, public investment increases total investment more than one for one, implying that public investment does not crowd out an equal amount of private investment from domestic sources by competing in product markets or financial markets. Thus, public investment, perhaps by improving the condition of social infrastructure, stimulates private investment and thus contributes to the postcrisis recovery by augmenting capital accumulation. An increase in real money supply growth by about 10 percentage points leads to an increase in investment GDP ratio by about 0.9–1.3 percentage points per year over the two years following the crisis.

5.3. Assessments of the Recovery Process in East Asia

5.3.1. *Macroeconomic Adjustments in East Asia*

The economic turmoil that broke out in Thailand in July 1997 swept through East Asia, and its devastating impacts were much more severe than anyone had expected. The countries that fell victim to the crisis suffered a sharp reduction in real income. In 1998, the growth rate plunged from the precrisis average of 7.0 percent to −13.2 percent in Indonesia, −10.4 percent in Thailand, −7.5 percent in Malaysia, −6.7 percent in Korea, and −0.6 percent in the Philippines. However, since 1999 the five crisis-hit Asian countries have managed impressive recoveries, which have been faster than the similar previous episodes of recovery in other parts of the world. The rebounding of the growth rate in 1999 was no less drastic than its free-fall. Korea stood out as the best performer in that year by growing at 10.7 percent. For the other countries, the growth rate ranged from 5.4 percent in Malaysia to 0.2 percent in Indonesia.

With the passage of time, the recovery process has gained momentum. The growth outturn in 2000 is estimated to be higher than that of 1999 in four of the affected economies — Indonesia, Thailand, Malaysia, and the Philippines. In Korea, the growth rate slowed down from 10.7 percent to 8.3 percent.

Figure 5.5 shows the GDP growth rates of the five affected economies. The adjustment process in East Asia that can be inferred from changes in the growth rates seems to be in general consistent with the stylized V-pattern we observe from the previous crisis episodes. However, the East Asian experience is in marked contrast to the stylized pattern of adjustment in GDP growth in that the degree of initial contraction and subsequent recovery has been far greater than what can be predicted from the previous cross-country evidence.

The initial GDP contraction in 1998 was largely caused by the collapse of investment: the level of domestic capital formation plummeted in all five countries in 1998. The contraction amounted to more than 30 percent in Indonesia, Malaysia, and Thailand, 17 percent in Korea, and 9 percent in the Philippines (Table 5.4).

Compared to investment demand, private consumption fell to a lesser degree. The consumption-GDP ratio remained mostly stable in the crisis period, which is consistent with the cross-country stylized pattern.

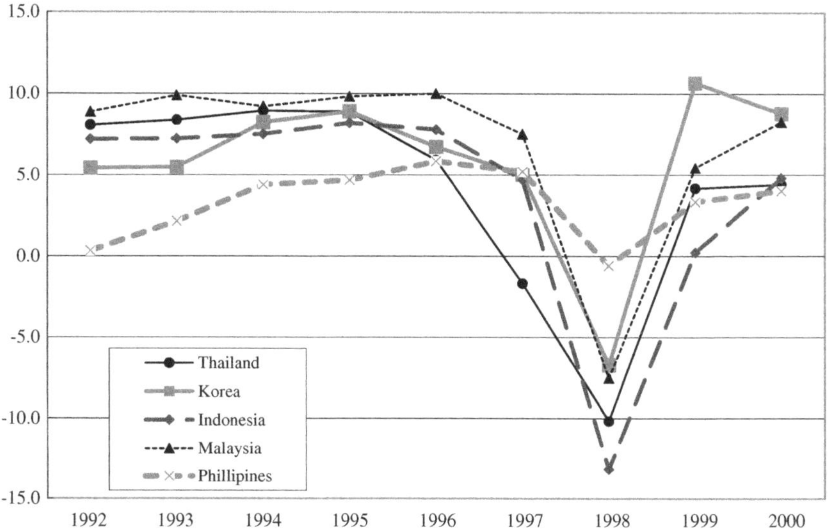

Figure 5.5 Adjustment of real GDP growth rate in East Asia

In contrast, the investment-GDP ratio dropped sharply. In Korea, for example, it fell from 33.4 percent in 1997 to 22.0 percent in 1998. Investment demand started to recover somewhat in 1999 in Korea and Malaysia, but it has continued to decline in the other countries.

While domestic demand was sluggish, a large increase in net export paved way for the initial recovery of the Asian economies. Import demand declined in all of the crisis-hit countries in 1998 by a substantial amount, ranging from 22 percent in Korea and Thailand to 5.3 percent in Indonesia, whereas exports continued to grow or remained unchanged in all countries except the Philippines.

It is therefore clear that net exports led the recovery in East Asia. Figures 5.6 and 5.7, based on quarterly data, demonstrate the pattern of adjustment in more detail. A close examination of the quarterly rates of GDP growth shows that both Korea and Thailand reached the trough as early as in the second quarter of 1998, and Indonesia, Malaysia, and the Philippines two quarters later (see fig. 5.6). Overall, the recession in East Asia bottomed out in the second half of 1998, less than a year after the crisis had broken out. As shown in Fig. 5.7, the subsequent recovery in 1999 was led mostly by a surge in net exports. Over the postcrisis period, the ratio of private consumption to GDP has remained stable in all countries

Table 5.4. Macroeconomic adjustment in East Asia, 1993–2000

	1993	1994	1995	1996	1997	1998	1999	2000
A. Indonesia								
GDP growth rate (%)	7.25	7.54	8.22	7.82	4.70	−13.20	0.23	4.8
Expenditure on GDP								
Private consumption growth rate	11.77	7.83	12.58	9.72	7.82	−3.32	1.48	3.6
Share in GDP, %	58.5	58.7	61.0	62.1	64.0	71.2	72.1	67.3
Government consumption growth rate	0.19	2.31	1.34	2.69	0.06	−15.37	0.69	6.5
Share in GDP, %	9.0	8.6	8.0	7.7	7.3	7.1	7.2	7.0
Gross domestic investment growth rate	4.88	10.83	11.01	11.97	6.89	−31.81	−15.85	8.9
Share in GDP, %	29.5	32.0	33.4	32.5	33.0	21.0	17.2	17.9
Exports of goods and services growth rate	6.81	9.94	7.72	7.56	7.80	11.18	−32.06	27.1
Share in GDP, %	26.8	27.4	27.2	27.2	28.0	35.8	24.3	26.9
Imports of goods and services growth rate	4.65	20.30	20.94	6.86	14.72	−5.29	−40.90	21.1
Share in GDP, %	23.8	26.6	29.7	29.5	32.3	35.2	20.8	23.3
Policy Indicators								
Government capital expenditure as % of inv.	27.0	23.3	19.7	17.8	14.8	24.1	n.a.	n.a.
Growth rate of real M2	10.5	11.5	17.8	19.2	19.0	5.0	−8.0	12.2
Annual real bank credit growth rate	13.9	12.2	12.5	14.5	17.2	−25.0	−56.5	9.8
Real effective exchange rate	n.a.	n.a.	100	109.5	104.5	52.7	74.5	59.1

B. Korea								
GDP growth rate (%)	5.49	8.25	8.92	6.75	5.01	−6.69	10.66	8.8
Expenditure on GDP								
Private consumption growth rate	5.60	8.19	9.60	7.07	3.50	−11.43	10.32	7.1
Share in GDP, %	54.4	54.4	54.7	54.9	54.1	51.3	51.2	57.3
Public consumption growth rate	4.58	1.90	0.81	8.17	1.45	−0.41	−0.60	1.3
Share in GDP, %	11.1	10.4	9.7	9.8	9.5	10.1	9.1	10.2
Gross domestic investment growth rate	5.87	8.55	9.37	7.50	−1.44	−16.68	2.90	8.0
Share in GDP, %	34.4	36.4	37.2	37.9	33.4	22.0	26.0	28.7
Exports of goods and services growth rate	11.30	16.08	24.59	11.21	21.44	13.25	16.35	19.9
Share in GDP, %	24.6	26.4	30.2	31.5	36.4	44.2	46.4	51.9
Imports of goods and services growth rate	6.21	21.58	22.36	14.25	3.18	−22.40	28.94	20.0
Share in GDP, %	25.1	28.2	31.7	33.9	33.3	27.7	32.3	35.7
Policy Indicators								
Government capital expenditure as % of inv.	6.0	6.7	8.6	10.0	11.0	21.6	18.8	17.3
Growth rate of real M2	11.8	12.4	11.2	10.9	9.7	19.5	26.6	23.1
Annual real bank credit growth rate	6.8	13.7	10.3	14.4	14.4	4.3	18.8	15.4
Real effective exchange rate	n.a.	n.a.	100	104.5	100.3	83.1	90.8	92.5

(*Continued*)

Table 5.4. (*Continued*)

	1993	1994	1995	1996	1997	1998	1999	2000
C. Malaysia								
GDP growth rate (%)	9.89	9.21	9.83	10.00	7.54	−7.50	5.42	8.3
Expenditure on GDP								
Private consumption growth rate	6.25	9.39	11.66	6.87	4.31	−10.80	2.53	12.2
Share in GDP, %	48.3	48.4	49.2	47.8	46.4	44.7	43.5	42.6
Government consumption growth rate	8.43	7.87	6.06	0.73	7.63	−7.84	20.08	1.7
Share in GDP, %	13.0	12.9	12.4	11.4	11.4	11.3	12.9	10.6
Gross domestic investment growth rate	15.41	14.14	19.04	6.71	8.87	−36.29	0.54	27.9
Share in GDP, %	41.7	44.9	49.2	47.3	48.9	30.2	26.9	26.8
Exports of goods and services growth rate	11.54	21.91	18.96	9.23	5.42	−0.21	13.76	16.1
Share in GDP, %	80.3	89.7	97.1	96.5	94.6	102.0	110.1	117.7
Imports of goods and services growth rate	15.04	25.64	223.7	4.89	5.74	−19.37	11.58	25.7
Share in GDP, %	83.3	95.9	108.0	102.9	101.2	88.2	93.4	106.5
Policy Indicators								
Government capital expenditure as % of inv.	13.5	12.4	12.9	12.0	11.9	23.8	n.a.	n.a.
Growth rate of real M2	23.0	7.9	16.8	20.8	14.7	−6.7	14.2	8.4
Annual real bank credit growth rate	7.1	10.2	26.5	16.9	19.9	−2.2	0.5	4.5
Real effective exchange rate	n.a.	n.a.	100.0	106.5	105.5	86.8	87.6	72.9

D. The Philippines								
GDP growth rate (%)	2.13	4.39	4.67	5.85	5.19	−0.59	3.32	4.0
Expenditure on GDP								
Private consumption growth rate	3.05	3.72	3.82	4.62	4.99	3.45	2.64	3.5
Share in GDP, %	78.8	78.3	77.7	76.8	76.6	79.7	79.2	70.7
Government consumption growth rate	6.15	6.13	5.62	4.10	4.67	−1.95	5.41	−1.1
Share in GDP, %	8.0	8.1	8.2	8.1	8.0	7.9	8.1	12.8
Gross domestic investment growth rate	8.00	7.14	4.94	9.94	9.77	−9.00	−0.11	2.3
Share in GDP, %	22.7	23.6	23.3	24.8	26.3	22.2	21.1	17.8
Exports of goods and services growth rate	6.26	19.77	12.04	15.40	17.15	−21.04	3.65	17.7
Share in GDP, %	34.9	40.1	42.9	46.8	52.1	41.4	41.5	46.9
Imports of goods and services growth rate	11.48	14.51	16.03	16.73	13.49	−14.71	−2.79	2.1
Share in GDP, %	43.9	48.2	53.4	58.9	63.6	54.5	51.3	51.3
Policy Indicators								
Government capital expenditure as % of inv.	15.0	13.7	13.4	8.1	8.0	8.0	11.0	n.a.
Growth rate of real M2	20.2	16.0	16.2	14.2	20.2	−1.2	9.4	0.5
Annual real bank credit growth rate	30.7	19.2	31.8	38.8	20.2	−15.4	−6.3	−1.2
Real effective exchange rate	n.a.	n.a.	100.0	110.4	111.0	94.0	100.8	69.0

(*Continued*)

Table 5.4. *(Continued)*

	1993	1994	1995	1996	1997	1998	1999	2000
E. Thailand								
GDP growth rate (%)	8.38	8.95	8.90	5.93	−1.68	−10.17	4.16	4.4
Expenditure on GDP								
Private consumption growth rate	8.43	7.87	7.55	6.83	−1.05	−12.33	3.49	4.6
Share in GDP, %	55.8	55.2	54.6	55.0	55.4	54.0	53.7	56.4
Government consumption growth rate	5.11	8.19	5.37	11.91	−3.03	1.94	2.82	6.5
Share in GDP, %	8.3	8.2	7.9	8.4	8.3	9.4	9.3	11.5
Gross domestic investment growth rate	8.55	10.83	10.04	8.08	−18.59	−35.17	−1.72	11.8
Share in GDP, %	40.9	41.6	42.7	43.0	33.7	19.0	20.5	22.7
Exports of goods and services growth rate	12.74	14.25	15.50	−5.53	8.41	6.72	8.86	19.5
Share in GDP, %	42.4	44.4	47.1	42.0	46.3	55.1	57.5	64.2
Imports of goods and services growth rate	11.78	15.75	19.87	−0.52	−11.38	−22.28	20.24	24.6
Share in GDP, %	44.9	47.7	52.5	49.3	44.4	38.4	44.4	47.5
Policy Indicators								
Government capital expenditure as % of inv.	12.9	13.4	12.0	16.6	23.4	29.3	23.1	17.7
Growth rate of real M2	15.1	7.7	11.3	6.8	10.9	1.6	5.1	−0.9
Annual real bank credit growth rate	18.6	24.6	15.1	9.4	13.6	−11.3	−6.0	−17.3
Real effective exchange rate	n.a.	n.a.	100.0	109.2	102.4	90.0	93.5	73.6

Notes: The share of expenditure components in GDP is constructed based on data in constant prices.
n.a. = not available.
Source: Asian Development Bank online country data, available at [http://www.adb.org/Statistics/country.asp]

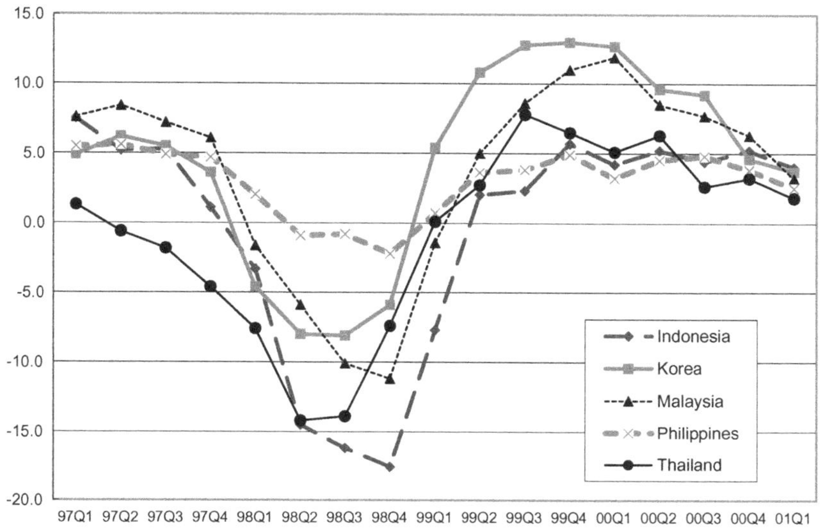

Figure 5.6 Quarterly changes of real GDP growth in East Asia (y-o-y, %)

except for Indonesia. In Indonesia, private consumption expenditure rose in 1998. In Korea and Malaysia, the investment rate started to increase from the latter half of 1998, whereas in the other countries the investment ratio has declined.

An increase in public investment appears to have contributed to the resurgence of total investment expenditure in Korea and Malaysia. Table 5.4 shows that in both countries the fraction of government capital expenditure in total investment jumped from 11 percent in 1997 to over 21 percent in 1998.

The large depreciation of currency has backed up the quick surge of net exports since 1998. Table 5.4 and Fig. 5.8 show that the level of real effective exchange rates in the five crisis-hit East Asian countries depreciated by 22 percent on average, ranging from 12 percent in Thailand to 50 percent in Indonesia in 1998.

5.3.2. *Factors Behind the Speedy Adjustment in East Asia*

A large number of internal and external factors are likely to have contributed to the pattern of macroeconomic adjustment to the crisis in East Asia.

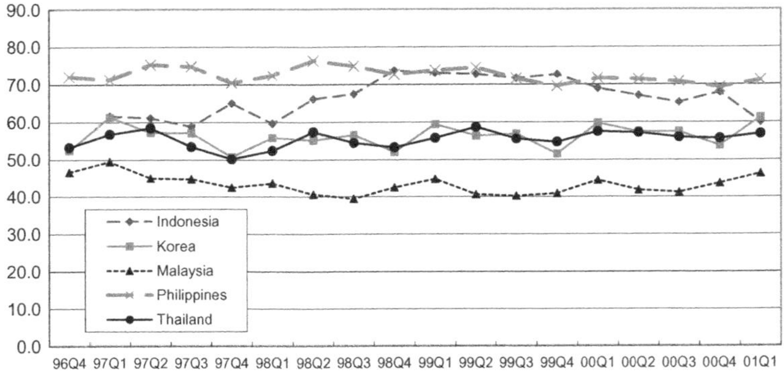

(a)

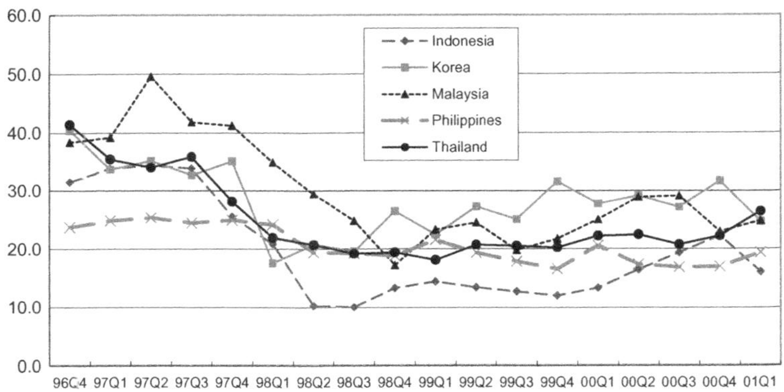

(b)

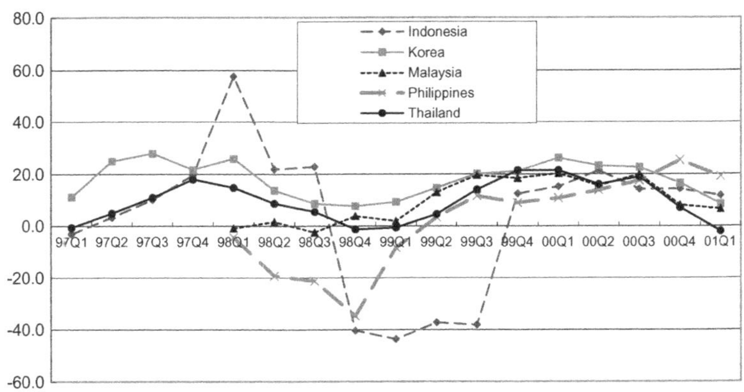

(c)

Figure 5.7 Quarterly movements of GDP components in East Asia: *a*, private consumption in GDP; *b*, investment rate; *c*, real export growth rate; *d*, real import growth rate

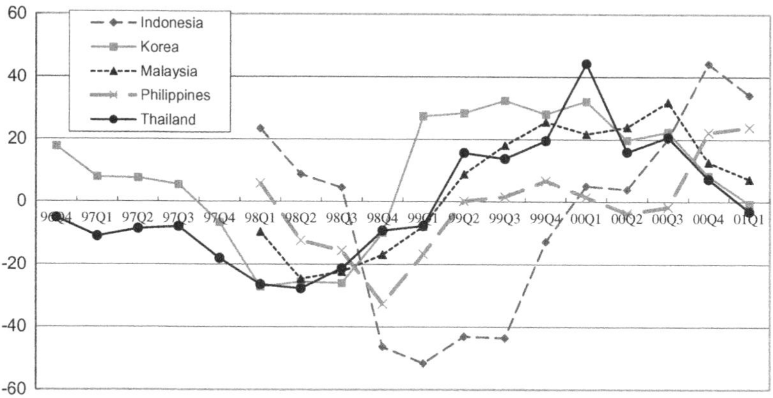

(d)

Figure 5.7 (*Continued*)

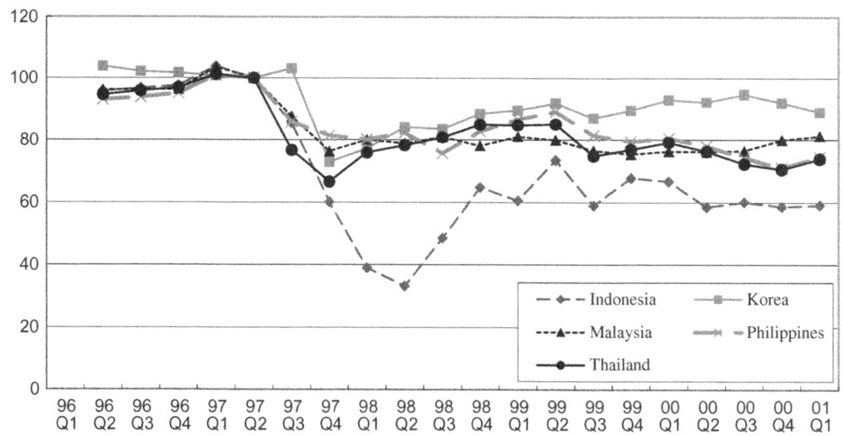

Figure 5.8 Real effective exchange rate in East Asia (1997:2 = 100)

On the basis of the cross-country evidence and available information on the pattern of macroeconomic adjustment in East Asia, we attempt to identify some of the factors that have engineered the postcrisis recovery.

Macroeconomic Factors

According to the empirical examination of the stylized pattern of adjustments from the previous 160 currency crisis episodes over the period from

1970 to 1995, which show a V-type adjustment of real GDP growth, a large real depreciation, expansionary monetary and fiscal policy, and an improvement in the global economic environment have been responsible for the upturn of the crisis-hit countries. In this sense, the East Asian process of adjustment is not much different from the stylized pattern. The same factors contributed to the quick postcrisis recovery of the East Asian economies.

Exchange Rate Depreciation and Openness. An important structural factor driving the speedy adjustment in East Asia may have been the region's higher level of openness. With a relatively large trade sector and export orientation, these economies benefited from a large depreciation of the real exchange rate. The level of openness in terms of the share of export and import in GDP ranges from 200 percent in Malaysia to 60 percent in Indonesia. Thus, compared to other crisis-hit economies before them, the depreciation is likely to have had a bigger impact on the more open East Asian economies. Note that the size of real exchange depreciation in the East Asian countries was comparable to the average depreciation rate in the previous crisis episodes.

One special feature of the East Asia crisis is that, compared to the cross-country evidence, the impact of depreciation on real depreciation on real output showed up as early as one year after the crisis. The large real exchange depreciation therefore restored external balance without much delay in East Asia. The flexibility in the labor market may have facilitated this swift adjustment, because the shift of resources from the nontradables to the tradables sector elicited by the massive real exchange rate depreciation requires flexible factor market.

Favorable External Environment. The quick improvement in East Asian exports has been supported by favorable external developments. The global economy was strong in 1999. The U.S. economy has been able to absorb a large amount of exports of the East Asian economies. The U.S. per capita GDP growth rates were 3.3–3.4 percent in 1998 and 1999 and jumped to 4.4 percent in 2000, which by far exceeded the average growth rate of 2.0 percent over the period from 1970 to 1995. As we saw from the cross-country regressions in section 5.2, global economic growth has a strong impact on the postcrisis recovery, in particular in the early years following the crisis. The deterioration in terms of trade that precipitated the crisis reversed in 1999. In particular, the increase in the prices of semiconductors helped to boost Korean, Malaysian, and Thai exports.

Macroeconomic Policy Adjustment. Concerning macroeconomic policy management, the swift change in policy stance toward expansion has supported a quick recovery of the crisis-hit economies. In Korea, relaxation of monetary and fiscal policy began around in April of 1998. A comparison of the turning points in the adjustment process measured by growth rates of the quarterly GDP with the timing of policy changes, broadly speaking, confirms that easing of monetary and fiscal policy has quickened the pace of recovery in both Thailand and Malaysia (Fig. 5.9). Thailand shifted to a modest relaxation of macroeconomic policy in June 1998, and its economy took off in the fourth quarter of the same year after zero growth in the preceding quarter. In particular, public consumption expenditure increased significantly in the latter half of 1998. It was not until the third quarter of 1998 — the end of August — that a relaxation of monetary and fiscal policy was announced in Malaysia, and its economy moved out of the trough one quarter later. In Indonesia, on the contrary, because of the continuing weakness of the rupiah, monetary policy remained contractionary until the second quarter of 1999. However, public consumption increased sharply in the third quarter of 1999. This expansion boosted output growth in 1999. In the Philippines, monetary policy was slightly contractionary over the post-crisis period, whereas public consumption expenditure has been growing since the first quarter of 1999.

The positive role of expansionary macroeconomic policies in postcrisis recovery raises the question of whether the initial tightening of monetary and fiscal policy was too harsh and maintained for too long and as a consequence deepened the crisis. In order to deal with the crisis itself — stopping bank runs, protecting the payment system, and stemming capital out-flows — the IMF prescribed tight monetary policy together with fiscal

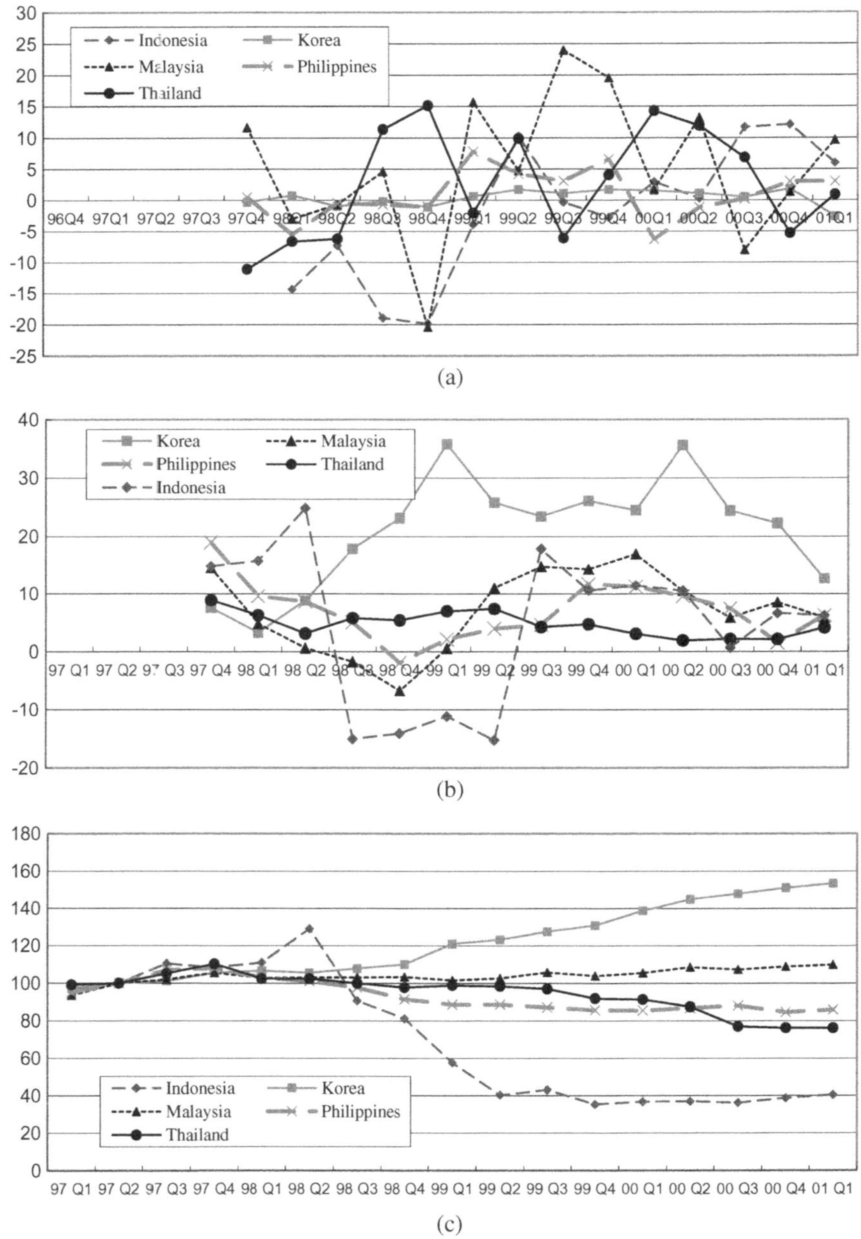

Figure 5.9 Policy indicators in East Asia: *a*, real public consumption growth; *b*, real money supply growth; *c*, real credit (1997:2 = 100)

austerity, which initially led to a sharp increase in interest rates. The contractionary monetary and fiscal policy has been criticized by many, including Radelet and Sachs (1998) and Feldstein (1998), as having been unnecessary because these countries were suffering from a liquidity problem. They imply that the traditional IMF prescriptions may have done more harm than good because they drove many highly leveraged but viable firms out of business, thereby deepening the downturn of the economy. The contribution of initial austerity from IMF programs remains controversial. On the other hand, it is quite clear that the swift change of macroeconomic policy stance toward an expansionary one helped these economies recover quickly. Fiscal policy had become contractionary immediately after the crisis, but it was reversed quickly to be expansionary. Change in monetary policy stance then followed. Once the depreciation of the currency was arrested and stability returned to the foreign exchange market, the authorities of the crisis countries were able to adjust gradually the interest rates downward and expand money supply.

Panic and Balance Sheet Effects

The contraction of real income in the East Asian countries that suffered the crisis was much larger, and the subsequent recovery of these countries has been much faster, than what can be predicted from the previous episodes of crisis elsewhere. There must be additional factors that have contributed to the deeper contraction and the quicker recovery in East Asia. We consider that the East Asian crisis has an aspect of a severe liquidity crisis caused by investors' panic. This nature of the crisis must have an important role in the macroeconomic adjustment during the crisis.

Panic and Spread of the Crisis. There is general agreement that a fixed peg to a currency basket dominated by the U.S. dollar when the current account was piling up deficits was one aspect of policy mismanagement that triggered the crisis in Thailand. In a recent paper, Williamson (2000) shows that had it been implementing a basket, band, and crawl (BBC) rule, Thailand might have staved off its crisis, because the country was suffering from a balance-of-payments crisis. However, the Thai crisis was contagious, as shown by Park and Song (2001a, b), and even a good exchange rate management using the BBC rule could not have saved other crisis victims like Indonesia and Korea from the contagion.

Although macroeconomic policies and economic fundamentals of Korea and Indonesia were regarded as being sound and credible, many foreign investors simply moved out of East Asian financial markets when they realized that most East Asian countries would suffer from macroeconomic and structural problems similar to those that were driving Thailand to the brink of debt default. With the withdrawal of foreign lenders and investors from the region, other East Asian countries experienced a sharp liquidity crisis and balance sheet problems associated with a large currency depreciation, causing a regionwide crisis explicable by a second- and third-generation model of the crisis. That is, the contagion of the Thai crisis set in motion a crisis characterized by self-fulfilling prophecy and balance sheet deterioration in other East Asian countries, which did not have a serious balance-of-payment problem. Once hit by contagion, the BBC system was simply unable to stave off the crisis because the band could not be maintained.

Why did foreign portfolio investors panic so much and exhibit herd behavior? They initially moved into East Asia with large sums of money to be invested in all types of local securities and real assets with the mistaken notion that rapid growth in the region would be sustained or that their investments would be protected by government guarantees. Most of the foreign investors paid little attention to the structural problems of the financial and corporate sections that began to haunt East Asia before moving in. When these problems came to light in the midst of currency depreciation and interest rate increases, they were startled. The ensuing fear of losing their investments then drove them to a state of panic, and every investor was scrambling to reach the exit.

Thus, one critical factor that could explain both the initial sharper contraction and the faster recovery is related to changes in the expectations of foreign investors and both domestic households and firms on economic prospects of the crisis countries. When foreign investors began to lose confidence in East Asian economies, capital flows abruptly reversed. As shown in Table 5.5, in 1997 private net capital flows reversed by $115 billion (from a $120 billion inflow in 1996 to a $5 billion outflow). It is no

Table 5.5. Capital flows to the five Asian economies (in US $billions)

	1996	1997	1998	1999	2000[a]
External financing, net (A + B)	118.6	39.5	−15.2	−4.9	−1.2
A. Private flows, net	119.5	4.9	−38.7	−5.2	−3.8
Equity investment	16.8	5.2	16.8	30.1	15.6
Direct equity	4.8	6.8	12.3	14.6	9.5
Portfolio equity	12.0	−1.7	4.5	15.4	6.1
Private creditors	102.7	−0.3	−55.5	−35.3	−19.3
Commercial banks	69.6	−17.4	−48.8	−29.3	−15.3
Nonbank private creditors	33.2	17.2	−6.7	−6.0	−4.1
B. Official flows, net	−0.9	34.6	23.5	0.2	2.6
International financial inst.	−1.9	22.7	19.7	−4.6	2.5
Bilateral Creditors	1.0	11.9	3.8	4.9	0.1

Note: The five countries include South Korea, Indonesia, Thailand, Malaysia, and the Philippines.
[a]Estimated.
Source: Institute for International Finance, January 2001.

wonder that this large-scale shift in financial inflows provoked deep contractions, huge depreciation, and financial embarrassment. The argument goes that once investors' panic calms down and foreign capital resumes inflow, the economy rebounds to its long-term trend.

Immediately after the crisis, there was rampant speculation that the crisis countries might not be able to avoid foreign debt default and hence might have to declare a debt moratorium. The international financial community, including international financial institutions, also did not hesitate to lay the blame on the East Asian countries for the crisis. With the emerging consensus that the crisis countries had profound problems that were more serious than had been realized before, the prospect for recovery in East Asia turned from bad to worse. Many were skeptical that these countries had the institutional capacity and political will to carry out the necessary structural reforms. Even if they had, the skeptics pointed out that these crisis countries would take many years to put their houses in order. Under these circumstances, it is quite possible that the households and firms as well as foreign investors came to believe that the crisis was a permanent shock that would lead to a new equilibrium lower in terms of output and employment than when the crisis was seen as a temporary shock. This perception of permanency may have induced domestic consumers and investors to cut down their spending much more than they otherwise would have during the first six months of the crisis. However, the extensive criticism of East Asia diminished and gradually gave way to a more optimistic outlook for the crisis economies, and the realization that the crisis might be a temporary phenomenon started sinking into the minds of consumers and investors, thereby encouraging their spending.

In restoring the confidence of foreign investors, large support packages from the IMF made some contribution. The funding helped to reduce the short-term liquidity constraints of the economies and provide resources to stem the exchange rate depreciation. There were other turning points. Korea, for example, reached an agreement with its creditor in February 1998 to lengthen the maturities of the short-term foreign currency loans (Radelet and Sachs 1998).[8] After the agreement was reached, at least some of foreign credit facilities, including trade credit, were restored. With this restoration of the credit linkage, the fear of the debt default abated considerably.

Balance Sheet Effects. A large decrease in aggregate investment demand during the crisis period suggests that corporate distress was one of the main factors responsible for the sharper contraction in output in East Asia. Structural weaknesses in the corporate and bank balance sheets were often pointed out as the main channel through which the effect of foreign disturbances was magnified in the East Asian crisis (Krugman 1999; Stone 2000).

The reversal of capital inflows combined with a sudden downward shift in expectation could lead to a sharp depreciation of the exchange rate. The large unexpected depreciation was much more disastrous in East Asia because most firms were highly leveraged. When the bulk of corporate

---

[8] They did not do so voluntarily, but at the urging of the Group of Seven governments and the IMF, and only when they were convinced that they would be repaid with handsome returns.

Table 5.6. Foreign exchange losses of the Korean corporate sector (in billion won %)

	1997	1998	1999
Gains on foreign exchange transactions (A)	−2,692	−784	203
Gains on foreign exchange valuation (B)	−14,571	−1,026	2,533
Total Gains (A + B)	−17,263	−1,810	2,736
% of total assets	−2.4	−0.2	0.3
% of GDP	−3.8	−0.4	0.6

Source: Authors' estimates based on the Bank of Korea Financial Statement Analysis.

debts is denominated in the U.S. dollar while revenues and assets are in local currency, the depreciation deteriorates the balance sheets of firms and inflicts large losses. Table 5.6 shows that foreign exchange losses of the Korean firms amounted to more than 17 trillion won, which was about 3.8 percent of GDP, in 1997.[9] These losses, together with the increase in foreign debt financing costs, result in a decline in the present value of the equity of the corporate sector. Gray (1999) estimates that a 50 percent depreciation reduces the equity value of Korean corporations by 9 percent and that of Indonesian corporations by 21 percent. The lower equity value leads to lower investment.

The balance sheets of the financial institutions were also very vulnerable to the currency depreciation. Because in East Asia banks had a large amount of foreign liabilities in their balance sheets, they suffered losses emanating from the currency mismatch.[10] In June 1997 the ratio of foreign liabilities to foreign assets of the banking sector ranged from 1.3 in Korea to 6.8 in Thailand (Table 5.7). Maturity mismatches also created vulnerability. Korean data show that short-term foreign liabilities were more than two times larger than short-term foreign assets (Table 5.8).

After banks and other nonbank financial institutions suffer a sharp decline in their profits and hence a substantial erosion of their capital base,

[9]According to Hahm and Mishkin (2000), the foreign liabilities accounted for about 16 percent in total corporate debt in 1997 in Korea.

[10]In 1997 the foreign liabilities accounted for about 55 percent of banks' total liabilities in Korea, 27 percent in Thailand, and 15 percent in Indonesia (Asia Development Bank [ADB] 2000).

Table 5.7. The ratio of foreign liabilities to foreign assets of the banking sector (%)

	Dec. 1996	Mar. 1997	June. 1997	Sept. 1997	Dec. 1997	Mar. 1998	June. 1998	Sept. 1998	Dec. 1998
Indonesia	1.4	1.7	1.8	1.8	1.5	1.2	1.0	0.8	0.8
Korea	1.3	1.3	1.3	1.3	0.9	0.8	0.8	0.8	0.9
Malaysia	2.6	2.5	2.8	2.3	2.1	1.6	1.4	1.3	1.7
The Philippines	1.8	1.7	1.9	2.0	1.7	1.8	1.7	1.6	1.4
Thailand	6.9	7.3	6.8	5.5	4.7	4.2	3.2	2.5	2.3

Note: Ratios calculated with grow foreign liabilities and assets of deposit money banks.
Source: Asian Development Bank, based on data from IMF, International Financial Statistics.

Table 5.8. Foreign assets and liabilities outstanding at financial institutions in Korea (in US $billions)

	Dec. 1996	Mar. 1997	Jun. 1997	Sept. 1997	Dec. 1997	Mar. 1998	Jun. 1998	Sep. 1998	Dec. 1998
Assets									
Total	67.2	70.4	72.1	72.0	72.0	70.5	71.2	68.1	63.9
Long-term	30.6	33.2	33.2	32.5	27.3	25.9	27.1	26.0	24.7
(% of total)	(46)	(47)	(46)	(45)	(38)	(37)	(38)	(38)	(39)
Short-term	36.6	37.2	38.9	39.5	44.7	44.6	44.1	42.1	39.2
(% of total)	(54)	(53)	(54)	(55)	(62)	(63)	(62)	(62)	(61)
Liabilities									
Total	116.5	126.2	129.4	127.1	89.9	83.8	79.8	74.0	70.9
Long-term	43.5	46.0	48.1	51.7	47.5	45.0	58.6	55.6	52.0
(% of total)	(37)	(36)	(37)	(41)	(53)	(54)	(73)	(75)	(73)
Short-term	73.0	80.2	81.3	75.4	42.4	38.8	21.2	18.4	18.9
(% of total)	(63)	(64)	(63)	(59)	(47)	(46)	(27)	(25)	(27)
Net Liabilities									
Total	49.3	55.8	57.3	55.1	17.9	13.3	8.6	5.9	7.0
Long-term	12.9	12.8	14.9	19.2	20.2	19.1	31.5	29.6	27.3
Short-term	36.4	43.0	42.4	35.9	−2.3	−5.8	−22.9	−23.7	−20.3
Long-term Asset/ Liabilities (%)	70.3	72.1	69	62.8	57.4	57.5	46.2	46.7	47.5
Short-term Asset/ Liabilities (%)	50.1	46.3	47.8	52.3	105.4	114.9	208	228.8	207.4

Source: Bank of Korea.

they are downgraded by the rating agencies and often denied access to international financial markets. As experienced by many money-losing financial institutions in East Asia, foreign banks and other institutional investors simply cut the lines of credit they had offered through the interbank loan market and refused the rollover of short-term loans when their client institutions were in trouble. This refusal created a serious liquidity problem as well as balance sheet loss problems at the East Asian financial institutions. Faced with the liquidity problem, many banks and nonbank financial institutions had to reduce their supply of loans in both local and foreign currencies drastically even to their viable loan customers.

The mounting losses caused by the bank balance sheet deterioration are bound to increase the country risk premium of the crisis-hit countries. A rise in the country risk premium, in turn, pushes up the cost of capital and lowers the present value of the equity of the corporate sector. Gray (1999) estimates that an 8 percent temporary rise in the country risk premium for a year leads to a drop of 7 percent in the present value of corporate equity in Korea and 2 percent in Indonesia.[11]

An increase in the interest rate and currency depreciation together with other shocks can reduce the equity value of the corporate sector below a threshold that triggers widespread default. The risk of default was higher in East Asia, where firms were highly leveraged with a large amount of short-term liabilities. The firms with a larger share of short-term debt faced more difficulties in financing and were unable to service their debts: bankruptcies soared, thereby magnifying the crisis.

In the recovery process, macroeconomic stability plays a crucial role for the normal operation of viable firms. Stabilization of the exchange rate and interest rate improves the equity value of the corporate sector and thus promotes investment. Improved confidence leads to an increase in spending. The restructuring of the corporate sector is necessary in order to reduce the vulnerability of the corporate sector and thus prevent the future crisis. However, in the short run, a quick recovery cannot be engineered unless there is resurgence of domestic demand.

---

[11]The high domestic interest rate, which aims at stemming rapid depreciation, has the same devastating effect on the value of corporate-sector equity and thus investment.

5.3.3. *Structural Reform and Recovery*[12]

At the beginning of the crisis, there was widespread belief that the crisis countries' commitment to structural reforms would be critical to the recovery in East Asia. The reforms were expected to help East Asia emerge from the crisis with more stable, transparent, and efficient financial and corporate sectors. This expectation of reform espousing a market-oriented system would then improve long-term growth prospects and, at the same time, restore market confidence, thereby inducing the return of foreign lenders and investors to the region.

Three years into the reform process, the crisis countries have accomplished a great deal in improving the soundness and profitability of financial institutions and alleviating corporate distress. The World Bank (2000) argues that "assertive structural adjustment helped restore credit flows and boosted consumer and investor confidence" (p. 7). However, it is not clear whether and to what extent financial and corporate restructuring has contributed to the ongoing recovery. Most of the serious structural problems that were identified as the major causes of the crisis in Indonesia, Korea, Malaysia, and Thailand could not have been resolved over a span of two years. In fact, banks are still holding in their balance sheets a large volume of nonperforming loans and remain undercapitalized in all four countries. Many corporations in the region are still unable to service their debts. As for institutional reform, new banking and accounting standards, disclosure requirements, and rules for corporate governance have been introduced, but they are not rigorously enforced. It will take many years for the new system to take root.

Because the crisis countries are not even halfway to restructuring their financial institutions and corporations, it would be presumptuous to argue that the reform efforts have established a foundation for sustainable growth in East Asia. Nor would it be correct to assert that the gain in efficiency through the restructuring, which is difficult to measure at this stage, has been one of the principal factors driving the recovery. The improvement in efficiency is likely to be realized and translated into high growth over a longer period of time, certainly longer than two years.

---

[12] See Park (2001a, b) for more details.

The available pieces of evidence also do not support the contention that the market-oriented reform has contributed to restoring market confidence in the East Asian crisis countries; it certainly did not appear to have done so during the first two years of the crisis. International credit rating agencies report that the reforms in the banking sector in the crisis countries have not gone through enough to ensure that these economies would be able to forestall another financial crisis. Only toward the end of 1999 did Moody's and Standard & Poor's upgrade the sovereign credit ratings of Korea and Malaysia to the lowest investment grade from the speculation grade. By that time, the recovery was in full swing in East Asia. Journalistic accounts have abounded with similar concerns and continued to raise doubts regarding the effectiveness of the reform in the crisis countries. Under these circumstances, most foreign investors would find it risky to return to the crisis countries, but they have. Many of the foreign investors appear to have been lured back by the rapid recovery and substantial improvements in external liquidity resulting from large surpluses on the current account.

Reflecting recovery rather than ratings improvement, capital inflows in East Asia have been rising. Because policy changes and structural reforms are subject to many uncertainties and require a long period of time to take effect, international banks and global institutional lenders do not seem to have either the patience or ability to monitor and assess the effects of structural reforms. This is particularly true when they are preoccupied with the short-term performance of their portfolios.

5.3.4. *Differences in Postcrisis Performance among the Asian Countries*

The five Asian countries most affected by the Asian financial crisis showed the speedy recovery that was faster than anyone had expected. However, the extent of the recovery from the crisis differed among the five countries. By the end of 1999 only Korea had surpassed its precrisis peak level of GDP. Malaysia and the Philippines did it later in 2000, whereas Thailand and Indonesia still need another year or so to recover to their pre-crisis output level.

Table 5.4 indicates that the difference in the postcrisis recovery in 1999 reflects mainly the difference in the performance of investment and export growth among the Asian countries. Although the annual growth rate of export in 1999 amounted to 16.4 percent in Korea, 13.8 percent in Malaysia, and 8.9 percent in Thailand, it was −32.1 percent in Indonesia. After investment ratios had dropped sharply in the five Asian countries in 1998 due to the crisis, they showed slow recovery in 1999 in both Korea and Malaysia. By contrast, in the other three Asian countries investment ratios contracted further in 1999.

The investment contractions reflect the significant distress in both the corporate and financial sectors. The financial crisis caused deterioration of the firms' balance sheets. Then the deterioration of the balance sheets of firms caused a massive accumulation of nonperforming loans at banks and other nonbank financial institutions. The accumulation of bad loans cut into profits and consequently decreased the equity value of the financial institutions. Decapitalized financial institutions, as a result of the mounting losses, were forced to curtail their lending to both viable and nonviable firms, thereby exacerbating the downturn of investment.

In the bank-oriented financial system that characterizes the financial structure of the crisis-hit countries in East Asia, the repercussion of the bank failure is much more pervasive and felt throughout the economy. Because of their dominance, therefore, banks are likely to bring down many viable firms when they are not able to function as intermediary.

Data show that the investment and output contractions in the Asian countries are closely associated with the sluggish bank lending. Although monetary supply began to expand in 1999 for the five Asian economies, the supply of bank credit in real terms continued to slow down in three of them — Indonesia, Thailand, and the Philippines (panels B and C of Fig. 5.9). In fact, more than three years after the crisis, real credit supply remains below the precrisis level yet in those three countries. The investment ratio recovered most quickly in Korea, where real credit increased at the highest rate over the postcrisis period.

5.4. Prospects for Long-Term Growth in East Asia

As the recovery continues in East Asia, there is a growing hope that these economies will be able to return to the precrisis level of robust growth. In this section, we make an assessment of the long-term growth prospects for East Asia.

5.4.1. *Impacts of a Currency Crisis on Long-term Growth*

In this section we investigate the impact of a currency crisis on long-run growth based on a cross-country regression framework. We control all important growth determinants and then examine whether a currency crisis has had any independent impact on GDP growth in the long run.

A wide variety of external environment and policy variables will affect growth prospects by changing the long-run potential income and the rate of productivity growth. Basing our calculations on the results from previous empirical research, we consider the following variables as the important determinants of long-run per capita income growth: (a) initial income; (b) human resources; (c) investment rate; (d) exogenous shock (terms of trade changes); and (d) institutions and policy variables (government consumption, rule of law, and openness).[13] For the measure of human capital stock, we use the average years of secondary and higher school education for the population aged 15 and over, available from Barro and Lee (2001). The rule-of-law index is a measure for the quality of institutions, which is based on the evaluation by international consulting firms that give advice to international investors. The openness measure is based on Sachs and Warner (1995). This index is calculated as the fraction of years during the period in which the country was considered to be open to trade and thus sufficiently integrated with the global economy. The evaluation of the country's openness is made on the basis of four dimensions of trade policy: average tariff rates, quotas and licensing, export taxes, and black market exchange rate premium.

Table 5.9 presents the results of regression for per capita real GDP growth rate using the explanatory variables just described. The data are a panel set of cross-country data over the two decades 1975–85 and 1985–95. The system of two equations is estimated by a SUR technique, which allows for the correlation of the errors across the equations.

The regressions show that most of the controlling variables are the significant determinants of long-term growth. For instance, the coefficient on the log value of initial GDP is highly significant. Thus, it provides strong evidence for conditional convergence: That is, a poor country with

[13] Our specification closely follows Barro (1997) in selecting the explanatory variables.

Table 5.9. Long-run impact of currency crisis on per capita growth rate

	Seemingly Unrelated Regression	
Estimation Method	**Equation (1)**	**Equation (2)**
Initial GDP per capita, log	−1.965	−1.975
	(0.360)	(0.365)
Years of schooling	0.350	0.357
	(0.246)	(0.247)
Investment rate	0.084	0.085
	(0.033)	(0.032)
Terms of trade change, % per annum	0.084	0.086
	(0.036)	(0.037)
Government consumption, % in GDP	−0.139	−0.140
	(0.032)	(0.032)
Rule-of-law index	1.212	1.195
	(0.830)	(0.829)
Openness, 1 = most open	2.726	2.708
	(0.482)	(0.485)
Currency Crisis, no. of crises in previous decade	0.043	0.211
	(0.033)	(0.436)
Currency Crisis with IMF Program, no. of crises in previous decade		−0.386
		(0.670)
R^2	0.54, 0.37	0.54, 0.37
N	84, 82	84, 82

Notes: The system has two equations, where the dependent variables are the growth rate of real per capita GDP for each of the two periods: 1975–85 and 1985–95. The estimations use the SUR (seemingly unrelated regression) estimation technique, which allows the error term to be correlated across the two periods and to have a different variance in each period. Each equation is allowed to have a different constant term (not reported). Standard errors are shown in parentheses. The R values and the number of observations apply to each period separately.

a lower initial income level grows faster when the variables influencing the steady-state level of income are controlled. Specifically, the coefficient in column (1) of Table 5.9 implies that a country at half the income level of another country grows by 1.4 percentage points [= 2.04% * ln(2)] faster than the richer country.

We add to the regression a variable that measures the occurrence of currency crises. The variable is constructed with the number of currency crises that each country experienced during the past decade. We have used the number of crises over the period 1970–75 for the first equation and the period 1975–85 for the second equation. Thus, we test whether an experience of a currency crisis can have an impact on growth in the next decade. The estimated coefficient turns out to be statistically insignificant, implying that there is no direct impact of currency crises on growth in the long run. In column (2) of the regression, we add another variable that represents the number of currency crises with the IMF program participation. We also found no significance for this variable.

Although there is no direct impact of a currency crisis on long-run growth, it would be possible that a currency crisis or IMF program can have an indirect impact on long-run growth by influencing the controlling variables. For instance, if the investment ratio becomes permanently lowered by the postcrisis stabilization program in the crisis-hit countries, it would have a negative impact on growth in the long run. On the contrary, if the IMF structural reform improves the quality of institutions, then a currency crisis with IMF program participation can have a positive impact on growth.

5.4.2. *Sustainability of East Asian Growth*

The quick turnaround of the Asian economy from the 1997 crisis has brightened the region's economic prospects. Despite the impressive record of the recovery, however, not everyone is sanguine about East Asia's future prospects. The World Bank and the IMF, for example, are not optimistic about the prospects of these countries' sustaining the ongoing recovery, largely because weaknesses of financial institutions and balance sheet problems of corporations still remain unresolved in the region.

The macroeconomic performance of the crisis countries in the next few years will provide important clues to the question of whether these countries will be able to return to the pre-crisis trend rate of growth. Up to the present, the pattern of recovery in East Asia has been quite similar to that of Mexico after its crisis in 1994.

Although the financial crisis of 1997 abruptly brought a halt to Asia's period of robust growth, there was little in Asia's fundamentals that inevitably led to the crisis. The key to the Asian crisis was too much short-term capital flowing into weak and undersupervised financial systems. This suggests that, with better financial management and a return to the core policies that resulted in rapid growth, the East Asian economies can again return to sustained growth (Radelet, Sachs, and Lee 2001). The major factors that brought the relatively high growth in East Asia were high rates of saving, good human resources, trade openness, and maintenance of good institutions. In terms of these fundamentals, East Asia still keeps strong potential for a sustained growth.

However, in the long term, the growth rate will be lower than the previous precrisis average of 7 percent. The convergence factor, which was found to be quite strong in the cross-country growth regression in the last section, implies that the faster growth in the last decades in itself will force the East Asian economies to grow at a slower pace in the next decade. That is, the East Asian countries now have a much smaller gap in reproducible (physical and human) capital and technical efficiency from their long-run potential levels than they had in the last decades. Hence, the East Asian economies will face a smaller chance for rapid catching up, via high rates of capital accumulation as well as the diffusion of technology from more technically advanced economies in the next decade, and will inevitably become adjusted to a lower growth path.

The coefficient in the cross-country growth regressions implies that the convergence factor alone makes the Asian economies grow by about 1.5 percentage points slower over the next decade, compared to the last decades, in which they had started with less than one half of the current income. Hence, unless the economies could achieve substantial improvements in other fundamental factors, such as quality of institutions, they would grow at the range of 5 percent per year in GDP.

5.5. Concluding Remarks

The contraction of real income in the East Asian countries that suffered the crisis that erupted in 1997 was much larger, and the subsequent recovery of these countries has been much faster, than what can be predicted from the previous episodes of crisis elsewhere. The purpose of this paper has been to identify some of the factors that may explain the severity of and rapid recovery from the crisis. According to our empirical examination of macroeconomic developments following the crisis in East Asia, including a V-type adjustment of real GDP growth, a large real depreciation, expansionary monetary and fiscal policy, and an improvement in the global economic environment have been responsible for the upturn of the crisis-hit countries. In this sense, the East Asian process of adjustment is not much different from the stylized pattern observed from the previous 176 currency crisis episodes over the period from 1970 to 1995. However, the stylized pattern of adjustment cannot explain why the crisis was more severe, and the recovery has been much faster, than what was expected from the previous experiences of crisis. This study argues that the East Asian financial upheaval was in large measure a liquidity crisis caused by investors' panic. Once the liquidity constraint was eased, as it was during the first half of 1998, domestic demand has since surged again, and the crisis countries have been able to move toward the precrisis path of growth.

References

Aghion, Philippe, Philippe Bacchetta, and Abhijit Banerjee. 2000. Currency crises and monetary policy in an economy with credit constraints. Harvard University, Department of Economics. Working Paper.

Asia Development Bank (ADB). 2000. Asian recovery report 2000. Manila, the Philippines: Asia Development Bank.

Barro, Robert. 1997. *Determinants of economic growth: A cross-country empirical study*. Cambridge: MIT Press.

Barro, Robert, and Jong-Wha Lee. 2001. International data on educational attainment: Updates and implications. *Oxford Economic Papers* 53(3): 241–63.

Conway, Patrick. 1994. IMF lending programs: Participation and impact. *Journal of Development Economics* 45: 365–91.

Feldstein, Martin. 1998. Refocusing the IMF. *Foreign Affairs* 77: 20–33.

Frankel, Jeffrey A., and Andrew K. Rose. 1996. Currency crashes in emerging markets: An empirical treatment. *Journal of International Economics* 41: 351–66.

Goldfajn, Ilan, and Poonam Gupta. 1999. Does monetary policy stabilize the exchange rate following currency crisis? *IMF Working Paper* no. WP/99/42. Washington, D.C.: International Monetary Fund.

Gray, Dale. 1999. Assessment of corporate sector value and vulnerability: Links to exchange rate and financial crises. *World Bank Technical Paper* no. 455. Washington, D.C.: World Bank.

Gupta, Poonam, Deepak Mishra, and Ratna Sahay. 2000. *Output response during currency crises.* Washington, D.C.: International Monetary Fund and World Bank. Mimeograph.

Hahm, Joon-Ho, and Frederic Mishkin. 2000. Causes of the Korean financial crisis: Lessons for policy. *NBER Working Paper* no. 7483. Cambridge, Mass.: National Bureau of Economic Research.

Haque, Nadeem Ul, and Mohsin S. Kahn. 1998. Do IMF-supported programs work? A survey of the cross-country empirical evidence. *IMF Working Paper* no. WP/98/169. Washington, D.C.: International Monetary Fund.

Hong, Kiseok, and Aaron Tornell. 1999. *Post-crisis development of Asia.* Korea Development Institute. Mimeograph.

Kaminsky, Graciela, and Carmen M. Reinhart. 1999. The twin crises: The causes of banking and balance-of-payments problems. *American Economic Review* 89(3): 473–500.

Krugman, Paul. 1999. Balance sheets, the transfer problem, and financial crises. In *International finance and financial crises: Essays in honor of Robert P. Flood, Jr.*, ed. Robert P. Flood, Andrew Rose, Assaf Razin, and Peter Isard, 31–56. Norwell, Mass.: Kluwer Academic.

Lee, Jong-Wha, Kiseok Hong, and Changyong Rhee. 2001. The macroeconomic adjustment during the currency crises. *Kyung Je Hak Yon Ku* 49(2): 227–53.

Lee, Jong-Wha, and Changyong Rhee. 2002. Macroeconomic impacts of the Korean financial crisis: Comparison with the cross-country patterns. *World Economy* 25(4): 539–62.

Milesi-Ferreti, Gian Maria, and Assaf Razin. 1998. Current account reversal and currency crises: Empirical regularities. *IMF Working Paper* no. WP/98/89. Washington, D.C.: International Monetary Fund.

Park, Yung Chul. 2001a. East Asian dilemma: Restructuring out or growing out? *Essay in International Economics* no. 223. Princeton, N.J.: Princeton University.

———. 2001b. *A post crisis paradigm of development for East Asia: Governance, markets, and institutions.* Korea University, Department of Economics. Mimeograph.

Park, Yung Chul, and Chi-Young Song. 2001a. Financial contagion in the East Asian crisis: With special reference to the Republic of Korea. In *International financial contagion*, ed. Stijn Classens and Kristin Forbes, 241–65. Norwell, Mass.: Kluwer Academic.

———. 2001b. Institutional investors, trade linkage, macroeconomic similarities, and the contagious Thai crisis. *The Journal of Japanese and International Economies* 15: 199–224.

Przeworski, Adam, and James R. Vreeland. 2000. The effect of IMF programs on economic growth. *Journal of Development Economics* 62: 385–421.

Radelet, Steven, and Jeffrey Sachs. 1998. The East Asian financial crisis: Diagnosis, remedies, prospects. *Brookings Papers on Economic Activity*, Issue no. 1: 1–74. Washington, D.C.: Brookings Institution.

Radelet, Steven, Jeffrey Sachs, and Jong-Wha Lee. 2001. Determinants and prospects of economic growth in Asia. *International Economic Journal* 15(3): 1–30.

Sachs, Jeffrey, Aron Tornell, and Andrei Velasco. 1996. The collapse of the Mexican peso: What have we learned? *Economic Policy* 22: 13–56.

Sachs, Jeffrey, and Andrew Warner. 1995. Economic reform and the process of global integration. *Brookings Papers on Economic Activity*, Issue no. 1: 1–118. Washington, D.C.: Brookings Institution.

Stone, Mark. 2000. The corporate sector dynamics of systemic financial crises. *IMF Working Paper* no. WP/00/114. Washington, D.C.: International Monetary Fund.

Williamson, John. 2000. Exchange-rate regimes for East Asia: Reviving the intermediate option. *Policy Analysis in International Economics*, no. 60. Washington, D.C.: Institute for International Economics.

Chapter 6

Crisis and Recovery: What We Have Learned from the South Korean Experience?*

6.1. Introduction

The sudden financial crisis was a devastating shock to the South Korean economy. The real gross domestic product (GDP) growth rate plunged to −6.7% in 1998 from the pre-crisis average of 7–8%. The sharp contraction in GDP was largely caused by the collapse in investment. The investment ratio dropped dramatically by more than 11 percentage points of GDP, from over 36% in the pre-crisis period to 25% of GDP in 1998.

The initial deep contraction of investment and output in the 1997 South Korean crisis is in general attributed to the severe liquidity crisis caused by investors' panic and weak balance sheet problems in the corporate and financial sector (Radelet & Sachs, 1998; Park & Lee, 2002). As in all emerging market financial crises, the South Korean crisis is also characterized by massive capital inflow and then sudden outflow by panicked

---

* This chapter is co-authored with Changyong Rhee and was originally published in *Asian Economic Policy Review*, Vol. 2, No. 1 (June 2007), pp. 146–164.

We are grateful to Yukiko Fukagawa, Colin McKenzie, Marcus Noland, and participants at the Asian Economic Policy Review Conference held in Tokyo on October 1, 2006, for helpful comments and discussions. Changyong Rhee is a participant in the BK21 program at Seoul National University. The views expressed in this paper are those of the authors and do not necessarily reflect the views of the Asian Development Bank.

foreign creditors holding short-term claims.[1] Prior to the crisis, the South Korean economy itself had some severe institutional weaknesses that made the economy unusually fragile to the sudden capital outflows (Corsetti *et al.*, 1999). The balance sheets of financial institutions were very vulnerable to the withdrawal of foreign credit. South Korean banks suffered from double mismatch problems — currency mismatch and maturity mismatch. The high leverage and excessive investment of South Korean firms, especially chaebol-affiliated firms, are also noted as causing some of the structural problems that made the economy extremely vulnerable to financial panic.

The recovery process from the crisis in South Korea has been no less drastic than its initial free-fall. South Korea managed an impressive recovery starting in 1999, only a year after the onset of the crisis. The GDP growth rates were 9.5% in 1999 and 8.5% in 2000. The V-shaped recovery in real GDP growth in South Korea follows the stylized pattern observed from the previous crisis episodes (Lee & Rhee, 2002; De Gregorio & Lee, 2004) as well as from the adjustment patterns in the other Asian crisis-hit economies (see Ito, 2007, Figure 1). The speedy recovery of the South Korean economy can be attributed to the early resolution of creditors panic. Large support packages from the International Monetary Fund (IMF) made some contribution. The first IMF program, signed on December 3, 1997, and the second IMF program, signed on December 24, 1997, helped reduce the short-term liquidity constraints in the economy and provided resources to stem speculative runs on international reserves.[2]

The quick improvement in the South Korean economy was also supported by the swift adjustment of macroeconomic policies. After the onset of the crisis, tight stabilization policies supported by the IMF were implemented, but starting in mid-1998, South Korea quickly changed its monetary and fiscal policy stance toward expansion. In addition to

[1] The amount of net private capital outflows in the last three months of 1997 was $US26.1 billion, which was equivalent to approximately 6% of the annual GDP in 1997. One reason that such a large amount of capital was able to leave so quickly was that a substantial portion had short-term maturity.

[2] See Radelet and Sachs (1998) and Blustein (2001) for the detailed description.

macroeconomic policies, structural reform programs also had significant effects on the recovery path. Immediately following the crisis, the South Korean government began to tackle non-performing loans (NPL) of financial sectors, as well as excess capacity, and over-leveraging problems of South Korean chaebols (conglomerates), which contributed to resolving early stage financial and corporate distress.

The purpose of this paper is to assess the role of macroeconomic policies and structural reforms in the recovery process of the South Korean economy and draw appropriate lessons.[3] Compared to the other crisis-hit Asian economies, South Korea managed to recover relatively quickly from the crisis (see Ito, 2007, Figures 1 and 2). With the external environments given, the government-led financial restructuring programs and macro-economic adjustment policies played an important role in the fast recovery of the South Korean economy. However, the fast recovery also generated unwelcome side-effects. Because of aggressive fiscal expansion through government-guaranteed bonds and public credit guarantee programs, sovereign liabilities increased greatly and the transparency of official fiscal stance deteriorated. Thanks to structural reform, corporate and financial sectors began to recognize the importance of micro risk management, but their risk aversion contributed to the slowdown of corporate investment and thereby reduced long-run growth perspective in South Korea.

The paper is organized as follows. Section 6.2 focuses on the role of macroeconomic policies, such as fiscal and monetary policies, in the speedy adjustment of the South Korean economy to the crisis. Section 6.3 analyzes the role of financial markets in mobilizing financial resources to the real sectors during the recovery process. We also analyze the role of financial and corporate reforms. Each section discusses the lessons from the South Korean experience. Section 6.4 concludes the paper.

---

[3] This paper does not focus on what lessons can be learned from examining the sources of the South Korean crisis. There has been a substantial volume of literature that analyzes the pre- and post-crisis development of the South Korean economy. See, for example, the papers in the edited books by Coe and Kim (2002) and Chung and Eichengreen (2004).

6.2. The Role of Macroeconomic Policies in the Recovery Process

6.2.1. *Fiscal Policy*

The section examines the role of fiscal policy in South Korea's financial crisis and recovery.

Re-evaluation of Fiscal Position Before and After the Crisis

Many believe that South Korea maintained a conservative fiscal stance prior to the crisis and a fiscal imbalance could not have been a cause of the financial crisis (Furman & Stiglitz, 1998; Radelet & Sachs, 1998). But some argue that the official budget deficits in South Korea do not correctly reflect the fiscal stance as there were large hidden contingent liabilities not captured in the official budget figures. Despite the officially reported conservative fiscal stance, large contingent liabilities could have contributed to self-fulfilling speculative attacks and helped to aggravate the financial crisis (Cho & Rhee, 1995; Burnside *et al.*, 2001; Corsetti & Mackowiak, 2005).

To address these questions, we reconstructed the consolidated budget deficits in South Korea by incorporating the quasi-fi activities of 55 public funds and 32 public enterprises, using their micro balance sheet data from 1972 to 2003. For detailed calculation, refer to Lee *et al.* (2006).

Figure 6.1 shows the reconstructed consolidated budget balance in South Korea that includes the public enterprises and public funds neglected in official budget figures. The solid line represents the ratio of the official consolidated budget deficit to GDP. The ratio of the reconstructed consolidated budget deficit to GDP when only public enterprises are included is shown by the thin dotted line. The thick dotted line shows the ratio of the reconstructed figures when both public enterprises and public funds are included.

Figure 6.1 shows many interesting features. First, we find that newly estimated budget deficits are significantly higher than the official figures throughout the sample period. This finding casts doubt on the view that the South Korean government had maintained a very sound fiscal position before the crisis and, therefore, a weak fiscal position cannot have been a cause of the financial crisis in South Korea.

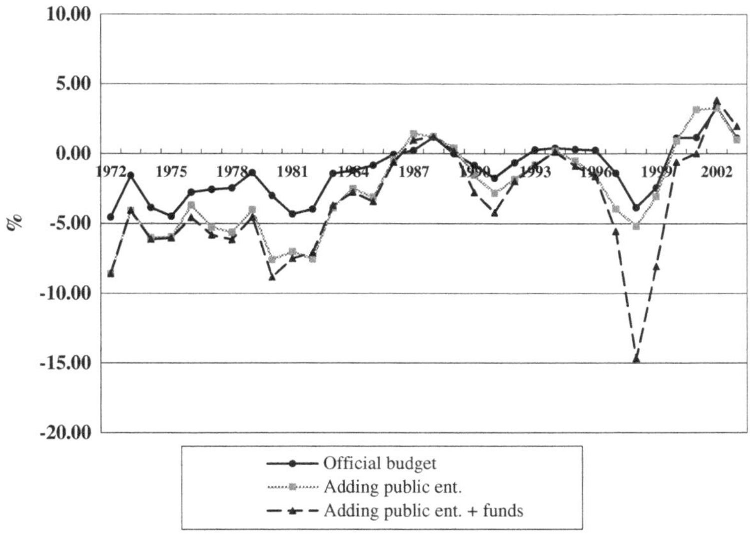

Figure 6.1 Official and reconstructed consolidated budget balance in South Korea

We also note, however, that the discrepancy between the official consolidated budget deficits and the newly estimated figures is distinct only throughout the 1970s and early 1980s. During the late 1980s and the 1990s, there is no significant difference. Even in the 1970s and early 1980s, the difference is mainly due to the social overhead capital expenditures of public enterprises, not hidden contingent liabilities. It is true that the official budget deficits have not correctly reflected the true fiscal stance as they do not include the quasifiscal activities of public funds and public enterprises. Nevertheless, the magnitude of the corrected fiscal deficit is not large enough to suggest that fiscal profligacy and hidden contingent liabilities were the main cause of the 1997 crisis in South Korea.

Interestingly, however, the discrepancy between the two measures dramatically increased after the crisis. The increase is largely due the issuance of a massive volume of government-guaranteed bonds by the Korea Deposit Insurance Corporation (KDIC) and the Korea Asset Management Corporation (KAMCO) to finance the public funds for financial restructuring after the crisis. This issuance of government-guaranteed bonds is not included in official budget deficit figures. In addition, to support financially distressed small- and medium-sized enterprises (SME), there was a significant increase in government loan guarantees during the crisis.

Countercyclical Fiscal Policy in South Korea

Before the crisis, fiscal policy was not used as a stabilization tool in South Korea in any significant way. The South Korean government emphasized fiscal discipline rather than the countercyclical stabilization role of fiscal policy. However, after the 1997 crisis, there was a remarkable shift in the perception of the role of fiscal policy. The credit crunch and financial market meltdown in the immediate aftermath of the crisis rendered monetary policy extremely ineffective. The fact that exchange rate stability became one of the major policy targets also served to limit the flexibility of monetary policy. It was clearly inevitable that fiscal policy should play a greater countercyclical role in stabilizing the economy.

In this respect, there is a widespread misunderstanding about the characteristics of the countercyclical fiscal aspects of the IMF program. As is widely known, the IMF stabilization program that was implemented in South Korea immediately after the crisis in 1997 called for tight fiscal policy. The initial IMF program announced in December 1997 prescribed a balanced budget or small budgetary surplus on the expectation that economic growth in 1998 would be around 3%. Criticisms were soon voiced against the tight fiscal policy to the effect that the IMF was applying a one-size-fits-all prescription to the crisis-hit countries in Asia without due consideration of their differences: the IMF did not distinguish between the Asian financial crisis and the financial crises in Latin America. The latter were mainly a result of large, unsustainable government deficits (Radelet & Sachs, 1998).

The fiscal policy in the IMF program may not have been adequately expansionary to counter the economic downturn, but one cannot claim that the IMF fiscal program was contractionary, even though it initially prescribed a balanced or small surplus budget. The misunderstanding is mainly due to the fact that the official consolidated budget figures do not include the quasifiscal activities of public finds. As explained, for financial restructuring, the KDIC and KAMCO issued huge volumes of government-guaranteed bonds immediately after the crisis. These public funds were used for financial restructuring such as deposit insurance claims as well as equity participation and NPL purchases from ailing financial institutions.

Ignoring the large volume of government-guaranteed bonds issued would seriously distort the true fiscal position of the IMF program. Government-guaranteed bonds issued by KAMCO and KDIC in 1998 totaled 39 trillion won, which amounted to 55% of the total government budget in 1998. If these government-guaranteed liabilities are included in the measurement of the official budget deficits, the ratio of the budget deficit to GDP in 1998 increased from 4 to 15%. The increase in the government-guaranteed bond issuance together with the tight monetary policy inevitably caused interest rates to rise. To lessen the pressure on interest rates and to secure long-term fiscal sustainability, the government and IMF agreed to pay the interest on these newly issued bonds from the government's general account. This is the reason the IMF initially prescribed a balanced or small surplus budget. In summary, the fact that the massive injection of government-guaranteed debt was not included in the measurement of the official budget shows that the IMF program in South Korea actually allowed considerable fiscal expansion, unlike IMF programs in Latin American countries.

Whether the proactive countercyclical fiscal policy in South Korea after the crisis has been effective is debatable. The positive view posits that consumption and investment expanded considerably as a result of the large injection of public money for structural adjustment. Theoretically also, the fiscal multiplier right after the crisis may have been larger than the conventional multiplier because the majority of fiscal expenditures during this period were injected into ailing banks and non-bank financial institutions. For this reason, government expenditures right after the crisis may have had two multiplier effects; one through the traditional effective aggregate demand channel and the other through relaxation of the credit crunch, which led to a larger monetary multiplier.[4]

[4] Lee *et al.* (2006) empirically analyze the effectiveness of fiscal policy in South Korea after the financial crisis.

Although the expansionary fiscal policy after the crisis successfully stimulated the economy and facilitated the development of the financial markets, it also generated unwelcome side-effects. First, sovereign liabilities increased sharply. As is readily apparent in Fig. 6.2, the ratio of sovereign liabilities to GDP increased from less than 6% before the crisis to 32% in 2004. The outstanding volume of treasury bonds accounted for 23% of GDP. Government-guaranteed bonds issued by KAMCO and the KDIC accounted for the bulk of the remaining sovereign liabilities. It is true that the sovereign liability to GDP ratio in South Korea is still below the average ratio of OECD countries, but South Korea can no longer be considered a country with a particularly low debt-to-GDP ratio. Second, the sharp increase in the volume of government-guaranteed bonds and contingent liabilities undermined fiscal transparency. In particular, after the collapse of the Daewoo Group in 1999, the government relied heavily on credit guarantee programs such as Primary-Collateral Bond Obligations (P-CBO) schemes, to deal with the credit crunch at the SME. However, a large proportion of the beneficiaries under the credit guarantee programs went bankrupt later, ultimately saddling the government with an even greater fiscal burden.

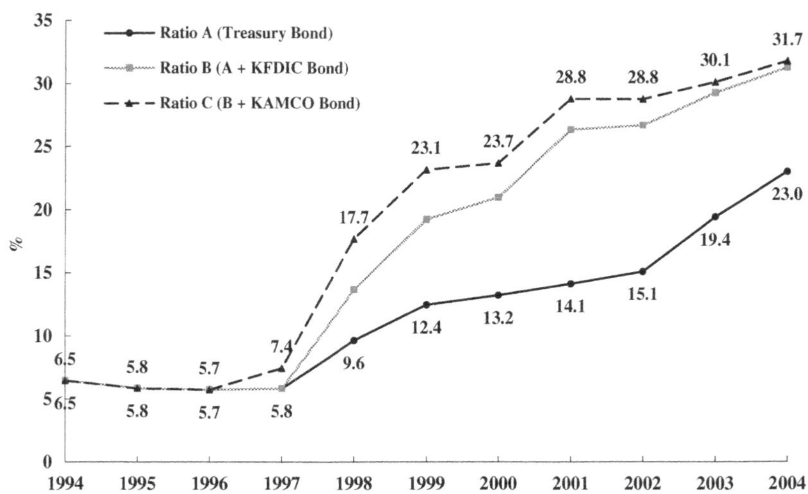

Figure 6.2 Ratio of public liabilities to gross domestic product in South Korea
Note: KAMCO, Korea Asset Management Corporation; KDIC, Korea Deposit Insurance Corporation.

Lessons from Fiscal Policies

Several lessons can be learned from the experience of fiscal policy in South Korea after the financial crisis.

First, sound fiscal stance in South Korea prior to the crisis was one of the critical elements contributing to the fast recovery from the crisis. The South Korean government had to rely heavily on fiscal resources in the process of financial market restructuring and building social safety nets. This massive injection of public funds was possible because the South Korean government had maintained fiscal discipline prior to the crisis.

Second, the aggressive fiscal policy during the recovery process raised questions about the credibility, transparency, and efficiency of many public credit guarantee programs. During the early stage of economic development, the government-led SME credit support programs were very effective in selecting and efficiently channeling funds to the most important investment projects. However, as South Korea became more developed, these government-led projects and programs naturally lost much of their effectiveness. Now that the domestic capital market has developed in tandem with the private sector, the recovery experience reminded the South Korean government of the importance of learning how to use the private capital market and induce private participation in risk-sharing to improve the efficiency of fiscal policy.

Third, the South Korean experience shows that countercyclical fiscal policy can be quite effective when combined with financial restructuring. The fiscal multiplier right after the crisis may have been larger than the conventional multiplier because the majority of the fiscal expenditures during this period were injected into ailing banks and non-bank financial institutions. For this reason, the government expenditures right after the crisis may have had two multiplier effects; the first through the traditional effective aggregate demand channel and the second through relaxation of the credit crunch, resulting in a larger monetary multiplier.

6.2.2. *Monetary Policy*

To deal with the crisis itself — stopping bank runs, protecting the payment system, and stemming capital outflows — the IMF prescribed tight monetary policy.

The overnight call rate rose from 12.5 to 21% on December 5, 1997, and reached 32% on December 26, 1997. This initial tight monetary policy was aimed at preventing large currency depreciation from initiating depreciation-inflation spirals. Theoretically, the increase in interest rates was expected to bring back foreign capital inflows. However, in reality, it failed to restore foreign investors' confidence in the midst of the crisis, but was effective in preventing sharp increase in demand for foreign currency by domestic firms and individuals and as such, partially contributed to restoring exchange rate stability. The severe recession induced by the tight monetary policy was also a main factor in reducing imports and rapidly improving current account balances. Without a significant current account surplus, restocking foreign reserves and restoring foreign investors' confidence would not have been possible.

Whether the initial tightening of monetary policy was too harsh, and consequently deepened the crisis, is debatable. The contractionary monetary policy was criticized as having been unnecessary because the economy was suffering from a liquidity problem. It is implied that the monetary tightening caused many highly leveraged but viable firms to encounter difficulties in obtaining credit to finance investment and production, thereby deepening the economic downturn. This is a widely prevailing "credit crunch" view.

Although the high interest rates were cited as evidence of a tight monetary stance in early 1998, it is not clear how tight the monetary policy stance was at that time.[5] Interest rates alone may not provide an adequate measure of the tightness of monetary conditions. Devaluation expectations must have pushed up the won interest rates. Higher interest rates also reflected an increase in perceived default risks. The behavior of monetary aggregates in 1998 depicted a mixed picture. In particular, broad money (M3) grew in 1998 at roughly the same rate as in previous years. In contrast, real domestic credit slowed down during the crisis. But it is not clear how significantly domestic credit conditions tightened. During the crisis period, both credit supply and demand decreased simultaneously. As pointed out by Borensztein and Lee (2002), weaknesses in financial institutions and corporate borrowers explain much of the credit

[5] See Borensztein and Lee (2005) for further discussion.

contraction during the crisis. Banks needed to increase capital ratios in line with Basel standards, and those institutions unable to increase equity had to decrease credit to their customers. Banks were also obligated to be more selective in choosing borrowers under the new financial sector regulations and environment. The corporate sector as well understood that, under the new conditions, it had to reduce their high leverage rates.

Regardless of whether money and credit supply was a constraining factor for the South Korean economy after the crisis, the monetary policy stance changed quickly toward expansion after mid-1998. The overnight rate started to decline rapidly after reaching a peak, and by July 1998 it was back at pre-crisis levels. Once the depreciation of the currency subdued and stability returned to the foreign exchange market, the monetary authority was able to adjust gradually the interest rates downward and expand money supply. The swift change to expansionary monetary policy stance supported a quicker recovery of the South Korean economy from the crisis, compared to the other crisis-hit Asian economies. Data show that the supply of real credit increased very rapidly since the fourth quarter of 1998 in South Korea, while it remained sluggish in the other crisis-hit Asian economies (Cho & Rhee, 1999; Park & Lee, 2002). In South Korea, the investment ratio recovered most quickly from 25 to 29.1% in 1999. In contrast, in other Asian economies, investment further contracted in 1999.

Lessons from Monetary and Exchange Rate Policy

First, to restore the confidence of international investors and stem capital outflows by both foreign and domestic investors, it seems hard to deny that a period of high interest rates was unavoidable. However, the contractionary monetary policy also amplified the pains from the credit crunch that accompanies structural reform. Therefore, the initial monetary contraction needs to be temporary only until the exchange market becomes stabilized.

Second, relaxed monetary policy during the recovery process was effective since structural reforms were simultaneously pursued. The South Korean experience emphasized that expansionary macroeconomic policy alone cannot have a large impact if structural problems remain unsolved. The reform progress reduced sovereign risk premium and inflation expectation by offsetting the initial worries that the government would monetize bailing out costs for troubled financial institutions. Because the origin of the crisis has to do little with macroeconomic imbalances, macroeconomic policy alone cannot solve the problems. Eventually the recovery must depend on the structural reform that tackles the roots of the problems that caused the crisis in the first place.

6.3. The Role of Financial Market Development and Structural Reforms

In adjustment to the crisis, capital markets, especially government and corporate bond markets, played an important role in mobilizing financial resources to the real sector. The fiscal and monetary policies have also had significant effects on the flow of funds in financial markets. South Korea has also made substantial progress in addressing structural weaknesses in financial and corporate sectors. This section analyzes the development of financial markets and the progress of financial and corporate reforms in the South Korean economy, and their implications to the recovery process.

6.3.1. *The Role of Financial Markets*

Development of Bond Markets

Before the crisis, bond markets in South Korea remained underdeveloped and did not play a significant role in the financial system. Because of its history of fiscal conservatism, the government issued only a small amount of South Korean treasury bonds (KTB) and these bonds were insufficient to support active secondary trading. As a result, unlike in other developed countries, the government bond market virtually did not exist in South Korea prior to the crisis and corporate bonds played a dominant role; 3-year maturity corporate bonds were the benchmark securities.

Despite its large nominal size, the corporate bond market was also inactive prior to the crisis. Corporate bonds were essentially disguised bank loans rather than capital market instruments. South Korean banks routinely guaranteed corporate bonds and held them to the maturity. Bond investment by banks was an alternative method to extend loans to a specific company when banks could not extend loans to the company due to loan exposure regulation. By investing in bonds, banks could escape regulation, which limited loan exposure per firm, as bond holding was classified as portfolio investment, not loans. These situations changed drastically with the crisis in both government and corporate bond markets.

After the financial crisis, issuances of KTB increased dramatically to help fund the cost of financial restructuring. To finance the cost of recapitalizing and restructuring the financial system, the government dramatically increased the size of KTB issuance from around 7 trillion won at the end of 1997 to 56 trillion won at the end of 2004. In addition, the government took steps to improve the market infrastructure and establish KTB as the benchmark bond. Institutional reforms played an important part in boosting the liquidity of the market and establishing the treasury bonds as the benchmark. Reforms included introducing a Dutch auction system to replace the compulsory underwriting in the primary market; primary dealer system; delivery versus payment (DVP) clearing and settlement; reopening and marked-to-market systems; and steps to develop the KTB futures market and the repurchase market for government bonds. As a result, within a relatively short period of time, the South Korean government bond market is now one of the most actively traded bond markets in Asia.[6]

Even though the government bond market developed steadily after the financial crisis in South Korea, corporate bond market development was a different story. When the crisis broke at the end of 1997, the South Korean banking system stopped lending in net terms (i.e. repayments were greater than new loans). However, almost immediately, a corporate bond market sprang to life, with firms able to obtain funding directly from households. In essence, the bond market acted as a "spare tire." The monthly average amount of corporate bonds issued was less than 3 trillion won prior to the crisis. However, this average increased to 7 trillion won in the second half of 1998. For all of 1998, the Bank of Korea reported net bond financing

---

[6] Kang *et al.* (2005) discuss details of the development of South Korean government bond market.

was 45.9 trillion won, about 9.5% of GDP, while there were net repayments to the financial intermediaries of 15.9 trillion won. This surge in bond issues was financed by household savings and the drawing down of bank deposits.

The flow of funds in this fashion, however, was highly concentrated. The Herfindahl index for gross loan flows was around 1 before the crisis. The Herfindahl index for gross bond flows was higher, and in 1998, was around 3. This suggests that the largest firms obtained disproportionately more funds from issuing bonds. Only after the government placed a limit on the amount of bonds that chaebols could issue on October 28, 1998, did the amount of corporate bonds issued start to decline.

By acting as a "spare tire," the corporate bond market played an important role in the fast recovery of the crisis in South Korea when the banking sector was hit hard. Unfortunately, however, this spare tire suffered from the inherent weakness in that it significantly reduced chaebol incentive to restructure. Some chaebols, especially Daewoo — the third largest chaebol at that time — kept pursuing expansionary strategies financed by bond issues. When the Daewoo Group collapsed in July 1999, the flow of funds from the banking sector to the capital market started a complete reverse, posing new challenges for the South Korean economy. As a large proportion of corporate bonds issued in 1998 became insolvent, the direction of financial flows after the collapse of the Daewoo Group turned exactly the opposite of what had happened before the Daewoo crisis. The flow of funds shifted from the corporate bond market to the banking sector, and even to postal savings institutions. The amount of corporate bonds issued was almost negligible after the Daewoo crisis, as investors became very sensitive to corporate credit risk. In summary, the corporate bond market in South Korea experienced roller-coaster movement. After a short period of booming, the corporate market became illiquid again and South Korea became a more bank-dependent economy.

Lessons

Several lessons can be learned from the South Korean experience. First, it suggests that the government and the corporate bond markets can develop rapidly even where all finance has previously run through the banking system. It also suggests that the switch to bond market finance acted as a "spare tire" and softened the blow from the banking crisis.

Second, the evidence suggests that while bond financing may add flexibility and be an important tool for the fast recovery of a crisis-hit and bank-dominated economy, such as South Korea, it may not necessarily be more efficient at allocating resources than the banking system. Only relatively large firms had access to direct financing via bond or equity markets. Funding from bonds was even more concentrated than bank lending before the crisis, despite the fact that the crisis was due in part to large firms over-expanding based on cheap credit.

Overall, there are two important functions of a financial market: to provide liquidity and to allocate credit efficiently. The South Korean environment demonstrates that bond markets can provide liquidity to relatively large firms in bank-dominated emerging economies, particularly during a banking crisis. However, capital markets have many prerequisites, such as reliable credit rating agencies, no "too big to fail" beliefs, and so on. In their absence, capital markets in emerging economies may allocate credit poorly, leading to subsequent crises.

Third, for financial restructuring after the crisis, the South Korean experience shows that more emphasis should be placed on debt-for-equity swaps rather than debt-to-debt swaps in order to end the vicious circle of credit crunch problems. In the beginning of the financial crisis, when banks refused to extend loans, corporations had to pay back loans by issuing bonds with higher interest rates. As the maturities of the bonds issued fell due, they had to issue new corporate bonds to roll over the previous bonds. As a result of this debt-to-debt swap, the total amount of corporate debt remained virtually unchanged in South Korea. The large amount of corporate debt is the main reason for high financial costs and low interest coverage ratios in the South Korean corporate sector. Regardless of how much taxpayers' money is injected into financial restructuring, the chance of another financial crisis is high if the total amount of corporate debt is not reduced. Hence, financial restructuring policy should focus on inducing corporations to engage in debt-for-equity swaps instead of rolling over existing debts.

Fourth, liquid government bond market is a prerequisite for developing well-functioning capital markets, and the case in South Korea is an ideal example of government-led efforts to foster the growth of financial market infrastructures. It has several implications for Asian countries that have tried to develop local bond markets after the financial crisis. In particular, the South Korean case demonstrates the benefits of a late-comer in developing government bond markets. Instead of being satisfied with developing an over-the-account market, South Korea has decided to introduce an electronic trading system for the government bond market. Rather than following the path of other countries, the South Korean government has decided to adopt the most advanced trading system in the world from the very beginning. This policy turned out to be successful and the electronic trading system has not only improved the transparency of the market but also increased the liquidity of the South Korean government bond market.

6.3.2. *Progress of Corporate and Financial Restructuring*

It is widely recognized that the financial crisis in South Korea in 1997 was largely the result of enormous accumulations of NPL at financial institutions. Therefore, the initial focus of recovery policy was naturally given to financial restructuring, in particular, of the banking sector. However, the corporate restructuring issue came to a head as it was soon recognized that financial restructuring alone could not revitalize the banking sector as long as underlying corporate sectors did not recover from the crisis. There can be no doubt that such banking and corporate sector restructuring vehicles were instrumental in South Korea's recovery from the crisis.

Financial Restructuring

During the period immediately after the outbreak of the crisis, the financial sector restructuring focused on the closure of troubled financial institutions and the disposal of NPL from these institutions. Two supervisory authorities, the Financial Supervisory Commission (FSC) and Financial Supervisory Services (FSS), were newly established by integrating four existing supervisory authorities for banks, security houses, insurance companies, and other financial institutions, leaving policy making to the

FSC. Together with the Ministry of Finance and Economy (MOFE), the FSC set the principles and developed the plans for the resolution of non-viable financial institutions in accordance with international standards and procedures.

A capital adequacy standard was the basis for identifying troubled financial institutions, and an evaluation committee reviewed the rehabilitation plans. If a rehabilitation plan was not approved, loan resolution was pursued. If the plan was accepted, the FSC provided support by disposing of NPL and by other means such as recapitalization. The FSC and MOFE also formulated policy schemes to facilitate the normalization of financial institutions. Major means to normalize troubled institutions include transfer of business units of nonviable financial institutions, purchase and assumption, mergers between non-viable banks, and mergers between sound banking and non-viable banks.

By June 2003, five banks had closed through purchase and assumption, and 10 banks had merged with other banks. In addition, 771 non-bank financial institutions were also closed, and 152 non-bank financial institutions had their licenses revoked; 150 merged, and 469 underwent restructuring through dissolution, business transfers, and sell-offs. In this process, the government had to inject a massive amount of public funds for deposit payments, recapitalization of banks, and purchases of NPL. The actual amount of public funds employed for financial restructuring totaled 160.5 trillion won. About 50% of public funds raised were injected into troubled financial institutions through the KDIC, to redeem insured deposits and for recapitalization. Another 25% was channeled through the KAMCO to purchase NPL.

This quick and government-financed financial restructuring inevitably weakened the government's budget position. But it surely contributed to the fast restoration of financial stability and sovereign credit rating of South Korea, and laid the foundation for rapid recovery from the crisis. Moreover, various improvements of financial infrastructures have been made in the last 10 years. For example, loan classification standards, provision requirements, and prompt corrective action procedures have been established. Lending practices and risk management systems have been improved significantly. Comprehensive disclosure standards for all types of financial institution have been introduced, and the deposit insurance system has been amended to prevent exposure to moral hazard on the part of depositors and financial institutions. The government has also made significant efforts to improve the corporate disclosure system, accounting standard, and credit evaluation system, and tried to bring its prudential regulations into conformity with international best practices. As a result, the soundness and efficiency of financial institutions in South Korea improved significantly after the crisis.

Corporate Restructuring

After the crisis, the initial focus of recovery policy was given to financial sector restructuring. However, the corporate restructuring issue came to a head as it was soon recognized that financial restructuring alone could not revitalize the banking sector as long as underlying corporate sectors could not recover from the crisis. To break the vicious cycle of financial and corporate distress, a wide array of corporate restructuring vehicles were quickly introduced by the government to help distressed firms as well as to help liquidate NPL in financial sectors. As for the disposal of NPL, since domestic restructuring vehicles were still at an incipient stage of development, public institutions such as KAMCO and the foreign restructuring vehicles played leading roles in the restructuring process. From the outbreak of the crisis in 1997 to October 2005, KAMCO purchased 110 trillion won (face value) in NPL, of which 72.9 trillion won (face value) worth have been disposed. Among them, 95 trillion won of NPL were purchased and 45 trillion won of NPL were disposed before the end of 2000. This clearly demonstrates the importance of KAMCO in financial and corporate restructuring in the early stage after the crisis. In 2000 and afterwards, however, the amount of NPL purchased and disposed of by KAMCO declined as the restructuring of banks and large corporations continued to decline.

As the restructuring of banking sector and large corporations progressed to some degree, attention moved towards restructuring of the non-banking financial sector and SME. An array of restructuring vehicles was introduced for corporate restructuring, including the corporate restructuring corporations (CRC), corporate restructuring vehicles (CRV), and corporate restructuring funds (CRF), to help turn around ailing financial and corporate institutions. A CRF, which is a paper company in the form of mutual funds (corporate-type investment trust), was established with the objective of providing financial support for SME saddled with excessive burdens of short-term debt, mainly by investing in their securities. The CRC are the main vehicle that has closely adhered to its corporate restructuring function, and have indeed played a major role in the corporate recovery process. The purpose of a CRC is to acquire majority stakes in companies, reshuffle management, or push other restructuring measures as necessary to raise the company's value, before reselling. The CRC have doggedly pursued the restructuring of distressed firms in their role as securities companies (i.e. as non-financial institutions). Compared to the CRV and CRF, which have focused mainly on the resolving and disposing of NPL, rather than taking on other corporate restructuring tasks, the CRC arguably have been the main instrument in the restoration and restructuring of distressed firms.

Lessons from Financial and Corporate Restructuring

First, early closure of troubled financial institutions and quick resolution of NPL consumed large amounts of public funds; yet, they were essential for fast restoration of financial stability and rapid recovery from the crisis in South Korea. However, it seems quick purchase of NPL from troubled financial institutions are more important than the quick disposal of NPL. In South Korea, the IMF requested disposal of at least 50% of NPL that KAMCO acquired through public funds within 3 years. The purpose of this restriction was understandable. IMF worried that KAMCO could help bail-outs of troubled financial institutions and wanted to secure repayment of its policy loans. To observe the restriction, however, KAMCO had to focus more on the expeditious disposal of NPL rather than maximizing the recovery ratio. As a result, there have been heated controversies over low selling prices of foreign capital since the crisis.

Second, it is important to develop domestic NPL markets prior to the crisis. There have been many critiques that the NPL resolution process in South Korea was excessively dominated by foreign capital. If we look at the winning bidders of KAMCO's activity such as auctions, establishment of joint asset management corporation, CRC, and asset backed securities

(ABS) issuance, they are overwhelmingly dominated by larger foreign players. Reliance on large foreign players was inevitable in South Korea since the total amount of NPL was too large to be resolved by South Korean capital only. Undeniably, capital injection from foreign players contributed significantly to fast recovery from the crisis. In retrospect, however, foreign restructuring vehicles have tended to seek out quick capital gains through the disposal of NPL, instead of trying to rejuvenate ailing companies through restructuring.

One of the main reasons for low domestic participation is also the lack of "track record" and "financial knowledge" of domestic financial institutions in the NPL field, rather than the lack of supply of risky capital itself. To provide opportunities at least for domestic capitals to compete with foreign players, policy effort has to be given in building domestic NPL markets so that domestic players can accumulate track records and financial knowledge in advance.

Third, standardizing NPL information and legal systems was helpful for the efficient resolution of NPL. Immediately after the crisis, KAMCO did not harmonize record keeping and IT standards in handling NPL from many financial institutions. Each institution had its own IT standard and KAMCO had to manually reclassify all NPL from scratch to determine purchase prices and resolution methods. It significantly delayed the NPL purchase process and KAMCO was heavily criticized for not moving fast enough when public funds were ready to be deployed. Only recently, KAMCO developed its own NPL management system, and the South Korean experience shows the importance of standardizing the NPL information system prior to the crisis across financial institutions.

In addition, before the crisis, there was no legal system prepared for efficient NPL disposition such as the ABS Law, Consolidated Bankruptcy Act, and Corporate Restructuring Promotion Act, and so on. Most importantly, before the establishment of the Public Fund Oversight Committee, there was no independent governing body with a responsibility for execution and collection of public funds. In retrospect, establishing legal systems and a central supervisory committee for monitoring and decision-making of the use of public funds were major steps in efficient disposition of NPL.

Fourth, the restructuring vehicles introduced immediately after the onset of the financial crisis have largely focused on addressing the problems of distressed or nonviable firms. But in the financial and corporate restructuring progress, there is increasing recognition of the need for ex ante restructuring, well before a firm becomes nonviable. To make a corporation more competitive, the restructuring markets need to give greater consideration to mergers and acquisition with healthy firms. Furthermore, the increasing difficulties of injecting public funds indicate that policy should be geared toward encouraging private capital to participate in restructuring markets. On this purpose, the South Korean government recently approved a bill that allows the establishment of private equity funds.

6.3.3. *Chaebol Reforms*

Large conglomerates (chaebols) had a dominating impact on the South Korean economy. In 1995, for instance, the valued added of the largest 30 groups (excluding the value added created by their financial affiliates) accounted for 16% of GNP and for 41% of value added in the manufacturing sector (Borensztein & Lee, 2005).

Chaebol is a conglomerate of many companies in diversified industries. Chaebol firms are governed by a parent company, which in turn is owned by one family. Thus, while the direct ownership of the controlling family in chaebol firms is typically very low, the controlling family effectively controls the entire chaebol group. Such weak corporate governance of chaebol firms is believed to have caused agency problems and promoted the so-called "empire-building" tendency in South Korea before the crisis.[7] At the same time, financial institutions believed that the government would protect the "too-big-to-fail" chaebol from bankruptcies, and financed many risky or unprofitable investments. Highly leveraged corporate firms were more vulnerable during financial crisis. Chaebol-affiliated

[7] Hong *et al.* (2006) show empirical evidence that before the 1997 crisis, chaebol firms, particularly ones with weak corporate governance structure, tended to invest relatively more that stand-alones.

firms had a higher debt–equity ratio prior to the crisis than non-chaebol firms. The median of the debt–equity ratio of chaebol firms was almost 400% in 1997.

While recognizing that over-diversification of business activities and duplicate investment in key sectors incurred the low profitability and high leverage of large conglomerates, the government urged the top five chaebols to focus on core businesses and exit non-viable businesses. In September 1998, the government and the top five chaebol leaders announced a framework for mergers and business swaps — referred to as "big deals." The "big deals" mergers were intended to help the economy by resolving two major problems in the corporate sectors (i.e. excess capacity and over-leveraging). However, the top chaebols agreed on the deals only reluctantly, and the swaps have not been particularly successful. The deals seem to be very hastily driven by government initiative without sufficient consideration of commercial factors.

There have also been various regulatory changes aimed at improvement in management transparency and corporate governance structure. They include the phased reduction of corporate leverage, elimination of cross-guarantees, consolidation of chaebol accounts, and improvement of the governance system. One of the most important and visible changes that occurred during the post-crisis period was the cut in the debt–equity ratio. After the crisis broke out, the South Korean government introduced a maximum debt–equity ratio of 200% for all firms, which was to be met by the end of 1999. Consequently, the debt–equity ratio of chaebol firms lowered substantially. Nevertheless, some argue that the reduction in the debt–equity ratio does not represent genuine improvement in capital structure because it was achieved mainly through increasing equity rather than reducing debt (see Haggard *et al.*, 2003).

In addition, the new government regulations posed a credible threat to chaebols and made them decrease investment expenditures perhaps too hastily. In particular, chaebol-affiliated firms with a higher debt–equity ratio were forced to reduce investment more aggressively (Hong *et al.*, 2006).

During the crisis and subsequent recovery process, South Korea has accomplished a great deal in alleviating the structural weaknesses of the corporate sector. There has been considerable progress in corporate debt and operational restructuring. It appears that in the post-crisis period, there is no more significant difference in terms of investment ratios between chaebols and non-chaebols. This indicates that over-investment by chaebols during the pre-crisis period, if existed, disappeared after the crisis. It is not clear, however, whether structural reforms of chaebol groups, particularly those with relatively poor governance structure, were fully successful. Although over the post-crisis period the volume of investment has declined substantially in chaebol groups, investment allocation may not necessarily become more inefficient.

Lessons

First, it is clear that chaebol restructuring was reasonably well executed in South Korea. No chaebol is "too-big-to-fail" anymore in South Korea. The successful improvement in management transparency and corporate governance structure must help to increase long-run profitability of chaebols and make the South Korean economy more resilient to external shocks. However, chaebol reforms should be intended to reinforce the market mechanism in the economy. Some government reform measures after the onset of the crisis were too hastily introduced without sufficient consideration of commercial factors, thereby resulting in unfavorable side-effects such as the undue decline in investment.

Second, the improvement in corporate governance and shareholder capitalism made the management of chaebols more transparent and is believed to have contributed to alleviate "Korean discount" in the South Korean stock market. In the last 20 years, the average rate of return from equity investment has been lower than that of corporate and government bonds even though its volatility was higher. In other words, risk premium in the Korean financial market had been negative. Lack of transparency in corporate governance and tunneling of profits from listed to non-listed companies were blamed as one of the reasons for this anomaly. However, the situation has changed significantly after the crisis. Owners of chaebols became sensitive in defending ownership from merger and acquisition threats and started to pay more attention to dividend payments and short-run changes in stock prices. These new movements contributed to the rapid growth of stock prices and the spread of shareholder capitalism after the crisis. However, on the other side of the coin, they are also making chaebols less enthusiastic about long-term investment and job creation. Until the South Korean business culture properly adapts to shareholder capitalism, the discrepancy between financial and real sector performances is expected to grow.

6.4. Conclusion

The quick turnaround of the South Korean economy was no less surprising than its sudden collapse after the financial crisis in 1997. The speedy recovery was supported by the fast restoration of financial stability due to early closure of non-viable financial institutions and quick resolution of NPL. The swift macroeconomic adjustment polices as well as the continuous structural reforms also helped strengthen the recovery process. Corporate and government bond markets also played an important role in expediting the macroeconomic adjustment process.

This paper analyzes these recovery processes of the South Korean economy from the 1997 financial crisis and summarizes some lessons from it. In particular, we emphasize that the fast recovery from the crisis was not without damage; it generated many unwelcome side-effects and new challenges to the South Korean economy. The aggressive fiscal expansion through government guaranteed bonds and public credit guarantee programs increased sovereign liabilities greatly, thereby deteriorating the transparency of official fiscal stance. The increase in perceived risk by corporate, financial and household sectors as well as the introduction of shareholder capitalism, which is new to the South Korean business culture, contributed to the slowdown of corporate investment, thereby reducing long-run growth perspective.

Despite the rebound of growth after the crisis, the average growth rates for the post-crisis period are much lower than the high growth rates of between 7% and 8% achieved in the decades before the crisis. From 2001 to 2005, the GDP growth averaged 4.5%. One of the main reasons for the drop of the GDP growth rates is the lower investment rates. Although real GDP growth rates in South Korea have rebounded quickly since 1999, the economy has not recovered to pre-crisis investment ratios. The investment ratio in 2004 remained at 30.2%, which is far lower than 36% level in the pre-crisis period. The permanent depression of investment ratios is also evident in the other crisis-hit Asian economies.

The lower investment rates might be attributed to the adjustment of excessive investment prior to the crisis. The existing excess capacity prior to the crisis must have held back new investment. Because the "catching-up" process is expected to slow down over time, the lower investment rates might indicate that the South Korean economy has adjusted to a new steady-state growth path (Lee, 2005). However, the lingering depression of corporate investment rates after the crisis appears to indicate that the investment rates have dropped below the optimal level.[8] How to revive long term investment as well as growth rates is an open question in South Korea, despite fast recovery from the crisis.

References

Blustein P., 2001. The Chastening: Inside the Crisis that Rocked the Global Financial System and Humbled the IMF. New York: Public Affairs.

Borensztein E., Lee J.W., 2002. Financial crisis and credit crunch in Korea: Evidence from firm-level data. *Journal of Monetary Economics* 49(4), 853–875.

Borensztein E., Lee J.W., 2005. Financial reform and the efficiency of credit allocation in Korea. *Journal of Policy Reform* 8(1), 55–68.

Burnside C., Eichenbaum M.E., Sergio R., 2001. Prospective deficits and the Asian currency crisis. *Journal of Political Economy* 109(6), 1155–1197.

Cho Y., Rhee C., 1995. A Study on Measurement and Management of Fiscal Policy Stance. Seoul: Korea Institute of Public Finance (in Korean).

Cho Y., Rhee C., 1999. Macroeconomic adjustments of the East Asian economies after the crisis: A comparative study. *Seoul Journal of Economics* 12(4), 347–390.

Chung D., Eichengreen B. (Eds.). 2004. The Korean Economy Beyond the Crisis. Cheltenham: Edward Elgar.

Coe D., Kim S. (Eds.). 2002. Korean Crisis and Recovery. Seoul: Korea Institute for International Economic Policy; Washington, DC: International Monetary Fund.

Corsetti G., Paolo P., Nouriel R., 1999. Paper tigers? A model of the Asian crisis. *European Economic Review* 43(7), 1211–1236.

[8]The IMF (2005) estimates that the current levels of investment in the majority of East Asian economies are below their long-run steady-state levels.

Corsetti G., Mackowiak B., 2005. Fiscal imbalances and the dynamics of currency crises. *European Economic Review* 50(5), 1317–1338.

De Gregorio J., Lee J.W., 2004. Growth and adjustment in East Asia and Latin America. *Economia* 5(1), 69–134.

Furman J., Stiglitz J., 1998. Economic crises: evidence and insights from East Asia. Brookings Papers on Economic Activity 2. Washington, DC: The Brookings Institution.

Haggard S., Lim W., Kim E., 2003. Wither the chaebol? In: Haggard S., Lim W., Kim E. (Eds.), Economic Crisis and Corporate Restructuring in Korea: Reforming the Chaebol. Cambridge, UK: Cambridge University Press, 307–336.

Hong K., Lee J.W., Lee Y.S., 2007. Investment by Korean chaebols before and after the crisis. Japan and the World Economy (forthcoming).

International Monetary Fund, Asia and Pacific Department (2005). Regional Outlook. September, Washington, DC: International Monetary Fund.

Ito T., 2007. Asian currency crisis and the International Monetary Fund, 10 years later: Overview. *Asian Economic Policy Review* 2(1), 16–49.

Kang K., Kim G., Rhee C., 2005. Developing the government bond market in South Korea: History, challenges, and implications for Asian countries. *Asia Economic Papers* 4(2), 91–113.

Lee J.W., 2005. Human capital and productivity for Korea's sustained economic growth. *Journal of Asian Economics* 16(4), 663–687.

Lee J.W., Rhee C., 2002. Macroeconomic impacts of the Korean financial crisis: Comparison with the cross-country patterns. World Economy 25(4), 539–562.

Lee Y., Rhee C., Sung T., 2006. Fiscal policy in Korea: Before and after the financial crisis. *International Tax and Public Finance* 13(4), 509–531.

Park Y.C., Lee J.W., 2002. Recovery and sustainability in East Asia. In: Dooley M., Frankel J. (Eds.), Managing Currency Crises in Emerging Markets. Chicago, IL: University of Chicago Press, 275–316.

Radelet S., Sachs J. 1998. The East Asian financial crisis: Diagnosis, remedies, prospects. Brookings Papers on Economic Activity 1. Washington, DC: The Brookings Institution.

Chapter 7

Financial Crisis and Credit Crunch in Korea: Evidence from Firm-Level Data*

7.1. Introduction

A financial crisis of unprecedented dimension developed after the exchange rate collapse of December 1997 in Korea. The real economy suffered a sharp, if short-lived, decline, with GDP plummeting by 6.7 percent in 1998, and fixed investment contracting by almost 40 percent. This constituted the worst economic contraction since the end of the Korean War in 1950. Average monthly bankruptcies surpassed 3000, more than double the volume for the same period of 1997.[1]

---

* Reprinted from *Journal of Monetary Economics*, Vol. 49, No. 4, Eduardo Borensztein and Jong-Wha Lee, Financial Crisis and Credit Crunch in Korea: Evidence from Firm-Level Data, pp. 835–875, Copyright (2002), with permission from Elsevier.

Part of this work was prepared while Jong-Wha Lee was visiting the Research Department of the International Monetary Fund and the Center for International Development at Harvard University. The authors are grateful to Andrew Berg, Ajai Chopra, Jason Furman, Jeanne Gobat, Cheng Hoon Lim, Steve Radelet, Andrew Warner, and seminar participants at the NBER Summer Institute and the Center for International Development for helpful comments on earlier versions of the paper. The views expressed are the authors' alone and should not be attributed to the organizations that the authors are affiliated with. The authors thank Nada Mora for excellent research assistance, and Young Soo Lee for assistance in collecting data.

[1] The term "credit crunch" typically denotes a situation in which an unusual sharp decline in the supply of credit generates an unsatisfied excess demand for credit at the prevailing interest rates. The term has also been used more loosely to describe a situation of tight credit conditions in general. See Ding *et al.* (1998) for the various concepts of credit crunch.

Financial distress, however, can result from different factors. Despite widespread criticism of tight monetary policies, citing the level of interest rates as evidence of such tightness, weaknesses in financial institutions and corporate borrowers may in fact explain much of the credit contraction.[2] For example, banks needed to increase their capital ratios in line with Basle standards, and those institutions unable to increase equity were not in a position to expand credit to their customers. Moreover, it is also the case that the financial reforms changed economic incentives for banks and corporations and affected both the demand for and the supply of credit. For example, the corporate sector understood that, under the new conditions, it was necessary to reduce their very high leverage rates (and was instructed to do so). Banks may (should) have become more selective in choosing borrowers, at a time when promising activities may not have been in abundance in Korea. Under those conditions, it is not clear that an easy monetary policy would have contributed much to expand credit to the corporate sector.

The purpose of this paper is to examine the nature of the credit crunch, as suggested by the pattern of the contraction (actually only a slowdown) in credit to the private sector in Korea in the months after the collapse of the won exchange rate in December 1997. In particular, the paper focuses on the following question: was there a general credit contraction or did the cutbacks affect only overindebted and probably non-viable firms? This question is better addressed using firm-level information rather than macroeconomic data. It should be noted that although there is anecdotal evidence indicating that many firms had difficulties in obtaining credit to finance investment and production, there has not been a systematic research into the characteristics of the firms that received less finance after the crisis in the Korean economy. This paper will start to fill this gap.[3]

---

[2] A selective reading list on these issues includes Berg (1999), Furman and Stigliz (1998), Lane *et al.* (1999), and Radelet and Sachs (1998).

[3] A notable exception is a study by Dollar and Hallward-Driemeier (1998) based on a survey of 1200 firms in the Thai manufacturing sector. It is noteworthy that the responses of the Thai firms in this survey, from the third quarter of 1997 to the first quarter of 1998, do not indicate that firms had problems obtaining financing for profitable projects but instead that unfavorable demand conditions led them to demand less credit.

Previous studies have approached the credit crunch question in different ways, mostly by examining aggregate data. Ding *et al.* (1998) and Domac and Ferri (1998) found evidence of a credit crunch in the sharp increases in the spread between bank lending rates and corporate bond yields, reflecting the tightening of bank loan market. Ferri and Kang (1999) found, based on individual bank data, that banks, in particular those with lower equity, raised lending rates and reduced their lending rapidly. Ghosh and Ghosh (1999), and Kim (1999) followed the approach of estimating equations for loan demand and supply and found opposite results. Kim found that the demand for bank loans exceeded the loan supply by a large margin after the financial crisis, but Ghosh and Ghosh failed to find an excess demand for credit in either Korea, Thailand or Indonesia.

Regardless of whether credit supply was the constraining factor or not for the economy as a whole, individual firms can face credit rationing, especially in a situation of financial crisis.[4] Using firm-level data enables us to analyze the differences in the determinants of the credit constraints faced by different firms. One of the crucial issues related to the credit crunch is the extent to which profitable and viable firms did or did not have access to finance. By looking at the characteristics of the firms that observed reductions in their bank credit volumes, we can assess the nature of the credit crunch in Korea in 1998. If the credit constraints affected all firms regardless of their financial situation, there would be evidence pointing to tight monetary policy as the cause for the credit crunch. If, on the contrary, there is evidence that profitable and viable firms were not affected by credit constraints, there would be evidence consistent with the structural corrections in the financial (and corporate) sectors being the main explanation for the credit crunch stories.

Our results indicate that, in contrast to evidence for the period before the crisis (Borensztein and Lee, 1998), there was a shift in the pattern of allocation of credit in the post-crisis period. Based on a

---

[4] Note that credit rationing, which describes a situation where credit demand exceeds supply and credit is allocated through non-price mechanisms, can occur without a contraction of the supply of credit; that is, there is no necessary connection between credit rationing and a credit crunch.

database of firm-level balance sheet records, we find evidence that, in the pre-crisis period, there was easier access to credit for firms connected with chaebols, while non-chaebol firms' access to bank credit was more influenced by market considerations. In 1998, the relative advantage of chaebol firms seems to disappear, and the track record of profitability appears as a significant determinant in the flow of credit to those firms. This changing pattern of credit allocation is at least consistent with the intended effect of the structural reforms in the financial sector.

7.2. Monetary Contraction and Credit Crunch

7.2.1. *What Credit Crunch?*

Monetary and financial indicators in Korea in 1998 depict a mixed picture, with interest rates increasing sharply in the first months after the currency crisis but monetary aggregates displaying a less clear pattern. Interest rates were sharply raised initially (at least in nominal terms) to defend the exchange rate and restore market confidence. The overnight call rate rose from 12.5 to 21 percent on December 5, 1997 and reached 32 percent on December 26, 1997.[5] The overnight rate started to decline rapidly after its peak, and by July it was back at pre-crisis levels. In fact, by August, the overnight rate was at its lowest level in the 1990s, in nominal terms. The 3-year corporate bond rate, a benchmark for the medium-term rate in Korea, displayed slightly less sharp changes, starting to decline a little earlier and more moderately (Fig. 7.1).[6]

It is hard to establish the behavior of real interest rates. One problem is that, as a consequence of the exchange rate depreciation, wholesale prices increased much faster than consumer prices, as the latter include a higher share of non-traded goods that did not rise in price to the same extent as traded goods. This means that there is no unique real interest rate measure; the relevant price index is not the same for an exporter than for a firm in the services sector, for example. Furthermore, inflationary expectations are particularly hard to approximate because the outlook for

[5] The call rate, the interest rate on the interbank market, is the commonly monitored indicator of liquidity conditions in the money market.

[6] A detailed analysis of monetary and financial market developments and reforms can be found in Balino and Ubide (1999).

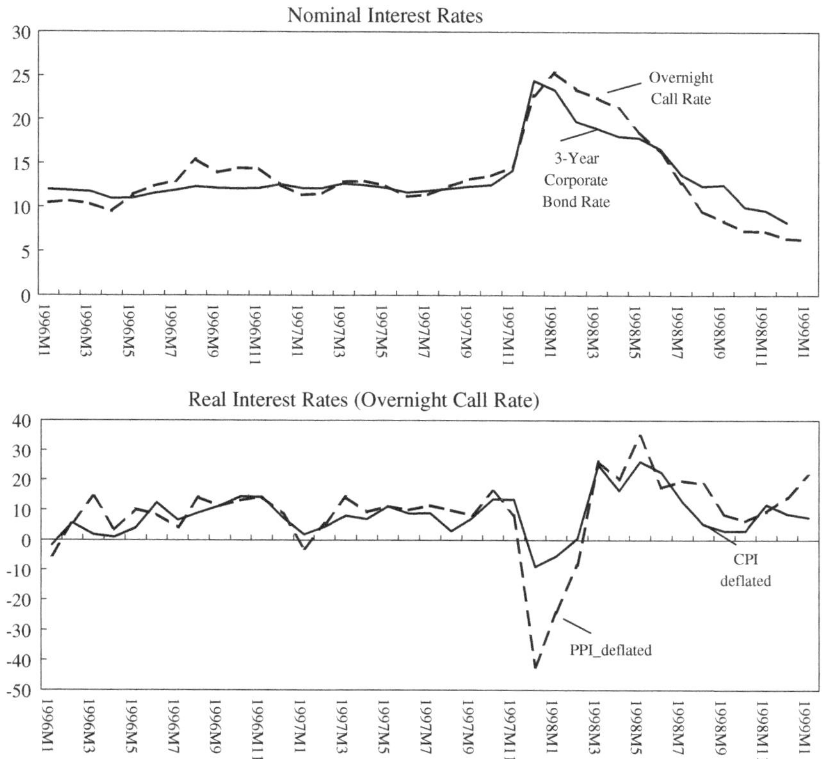

Figure 7.1 Nominal and real interest rates
Source: Bank of Korea

inflation depended heavily on expectations about the behavior of the highly volatile exchange rate. Ex-post short-term real interest rates can be calculated, for example, on the basis of (the monthly average of) overnight interest rates and price index movements over the same month. This measure of the real interest rate, while more erratic than nominal rates, also displays a significant increase in the first half of 1998. In addition, the ex-post real interest rate was highly negative in the period of passthrough of the devaluation, but tended to show some increase towards the end of 1998 on account of further declines in the rate of inflation (Fig. 7.1, bottom panel).

Although high interest rates suggest a tight monetary stance in the early part of 1998, interest rates alone may not provide an adequate measure of the tightness of monetary conditions. Devaluation expectations pushed up the whole structure of won interest rates, again of the stance of monetary policy; higher interest rates reflected also increased default risks (or at least an increase in perceived default risks).

The behavior of monetary aggregates is most surprising in light of the widely prevailing "credit crunch" view. In particular, it is surprising that broad money (M3) grew in 1998 at roughly the same rate as in previous years. Base money, by contrast, declined by 12.5 percent (measured in 12-month growth rates) by December 1998; the behavior of base money may be more indicative of the true stance of monetary policy, as it indicates that relatively tight liquidity prevailed, especially in the early part of 1998 (Fig. 7.2).[7] The implied behavior of the money multiplier is somewhat of a puzzle. Under conditions of financial uncertainty, one would expect that the banks' reluctance to extend loans, and perhaps the public's preference for saving vehicles outside the banking system, would have reduced the value of the money multiplier. In fact, there is some evidence in the United States that stricter capital requirements and financial difficulties in some depository institutions in the early 1990s were associated with a slowdown in monetary aggregates such as M2 (Lown *et al.*, 1999). In Korea, however, the sizable shift of deposits away from the troubled merchant banks was channeled to deposit money banks and this helped increase the growth rate in M2. The growth rate of M3 slowed down only slightly, helped by a number of factors.[8] Household demand for assets included in M3 was supported by the attractiveness of foreign currency deposits, higher interest rates, and the introduction of the deposit insurance scheme that extended coverage to deposits at non-bank financial institutions (including investment trust companies).[9]

---

[7] The behavior of the 12-month growth rate of base money was also affected by the reduction in reserve requirements in 1997.

[8] The financial sector definition in M3 in Korea is very broad, including deposit money banks, specialized banks, development banks, investment institutions and savings and insurance institutions.

[9] A part of the increase in foreign currency deposits came from the revaluation of their won value, but this effect was not significant. The increase in foreign currency deposits

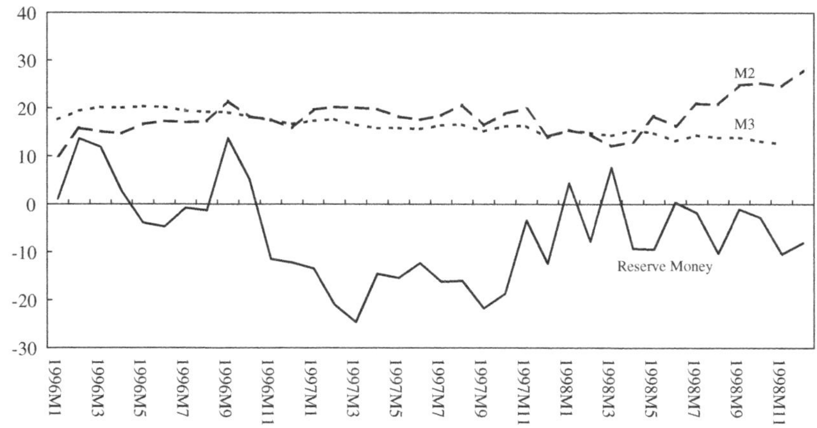

Figure 7.2 Growth of monetary aggregates (12-month percent change)
Source: Bank of Korea

And furthermore, the uncertain financial situation of the corporate sector made stocks and corporate bonds an unappealing alternative. The result was that the mass of financial resources at the disposal of financial institutions in 1998 increased roughly at the same pace as in "normal" times.

Financial institutions did cut back loans despite this relative abundance of resources. Deposit Money Banks used the increase in resources obtained from higher level of deposits and credit from the Bank of Korea to pay down foreign debts, increase credit to the public sector and moderately expand credit to the private sector (Table 7.1). On a broader basis, credit to the private sector from the financial sector as a whole was basically flat in real terms over the year (Fig. 7.3).

While the aggregate data indicates that real money and credit slowed down during the crisis, it is not clear on how significantly domestic credit conditions tightened.[10] In particular, considering that both credit supply

accounted for only 15 percent of the increase in M3 over the period November 1997–June 1998.

[10] In other financial crisis episodes, money and credit contracted sharply in real terms. In the case of Mexico, the growth rates of real money and real credit were −12.3 and −19.2 percent, respectively, in 1995. See Lane *et al.* (1999).

Table 7.1. Korea: Assets and liabilities of Deposit Money Banks (end of period, in trillion won)

	1995	1996	Nov-97	Jun-98	Nov-98	Nov-98 One-Year Change
Claims on public sector	21.1	23.3	21.3	37.4	42.1	20.8
Claims on private sector	200.8	240.9	294.0	299.4	307.4	13.4
Foreign assets	21.5	28.6	39.1	52.8	44.8	5.7
Deposits	137.8	163.0	190.3	206.1	241.5	51.3
Credit from Bank of Korea	28.4	24.5	22.9	55.2	44.7	21.9
Foreign liabilities	24.4	36.5	49.5	42.7	34.1	−15.4
Other items (net)[a]	51.9	69.0	91.8	85.7	74.0	−17.8

Note: [a]Sum of reserves (negative sign) and other liabilities (bonds, restricted deposits, government deposits and lending funds, capital accounts, and other net items).
Source: International Financial Statistics, IMF.

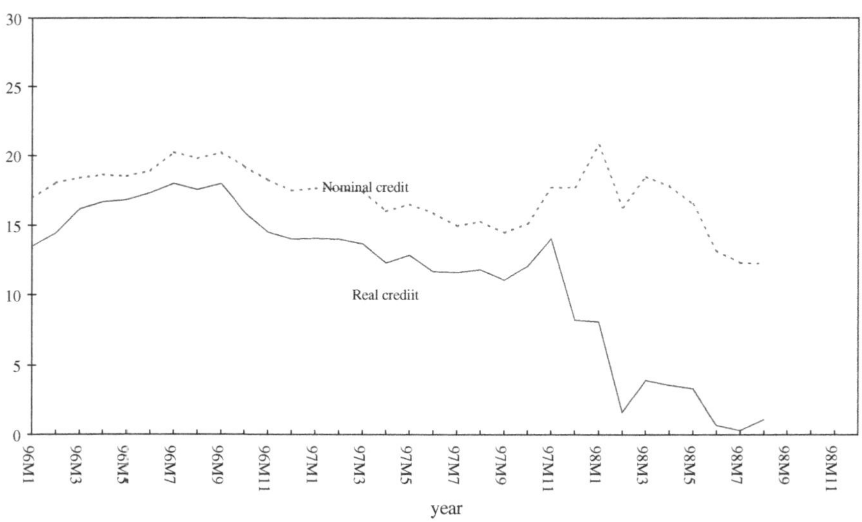

Figure 7.3 Growth of financial sector credit to the private sector (12-month percent change)

and demand felt simultaneously in the crisis period, it is not clear whether credit supply was really the binding constraint. Some studies have tried to avoid this simultaneous problem by looking at the changes in the interest spreads. Ding *et al.* (1998) and Domac and Ferri (1998) suggest that a credit crunch occurred because there were sharp increases in interest rate spreads, in particular, the spread between the bank overdraft lending rate and the corporate bond yield. They argue that the increase in the spread between bank loans and corporate bonds interest rates reflected the tightening credit conditions that affected bank-dependent borrowers more adversely. While this evidence is suggestive, a rise in interest rate spreads does not necessarily imply the existence of a general credit crunch. The increase in overdraft lending rates right after the crisis may have resulted from the fact that overdraft borrowers represented a higher default risk at a time of crisis than before.[11]

A look at monetary aggregates and interest rates data alone is insufficient to ascertain the existence of a credit crunch and, furthermore, it cannot explain why a credit crunch occurred. A fall in real credit and a rise in interest rates and spreads do not indicate necessarily that monetary contraction caused a credit crunch. The contraction of real lending can be caused not only by monetary contraction but by structural changes in the financial sector.

7.2.2. *The Causes for the Contraction in Lending*

The literature on the transmission mechanism of monetary policy may provide some insights on the response of banks and firms in 1998. The traditional view of the monetary transmission mechanism is that a shift in monetary policy affects real consumption and investment through an increase in interest rates. In contrast to this "interest rate channel", recent

---

[11]The bank overdraft lending rate soared to 37.5 percent in December 1997 from 17.1 in November 1997, while the interest rates of general bank loans increased more modestly to 15.3 percent from 12.3 percent over the same month.

literature has focused on a "bank lending channel". The lending view emphasizes the mechanism through which central bank actions have a direct effect on banks' loan supply and, in turn, real spending by bank borrowers.[12]

The operation of bank lending channel centers on two conditions. First, banks change the supply of loans in response to a shift in monetary policy by the central bank. This implies that, for instance, when reserves fall, banks will not keep their outstanding loans unchanged by simply drawing down their stock of government securities. Second, bank loans are not a perfect substitute for other sources of finance from the perspective of borrowers. This may generally be true for small- and medium-sized firms that cannot easily obtain funding by issuing securities directly to investors.

Empirical work on the bank lending channel has focused on identifying the relationship between bank lending and aggregate output.[13] However, when output and bank loans contract simultaneously, it is not obvious how to tell the causality between the bank lending and aggregate output. Essentially, the deceleration of bank credit may come from a shift in demand or supply. Kashyap *et al.* (1993), and Oliner and Rudebush (1995) attempted to avoid this identification problem by looking at the change of the ratio of bank borrowing to non-bank borrowing after a monetary contraction. The idea is that while output contraction or the usual interest rate channel is considered to shift the demand for bank loans and other types of finance altogether in the same direction, the contraction of loan supply will make bank loans lose their relative importance compared to other sources of finance. In their empirical work based on the US economy, Kashyap, Stein and Wilcox (1993) find that a monetary tightening induces a decline in the ratio of bank debt outstanding to the sum of bank debt plus commercial paper. By contrast,

[12] See Kashyap and Stein (1994) and Bernanke and Gertler (1995) for surveys of the bank lending view. Monetary tightening can also have an adverse effect on firms by the depressing effect on the firms' collaterals and internal funds — which is called separately as a "balance sheet channel".

[13] See, for example, Bernanke and Blinder (1988a, b, 1992), and Romer and Romer (1989, 1990).

Oliner and Rudebush do not find clear evidence that a monetary contraction induces a drop in the supply of bank debt relative to other forms of finance both for a sample of large firms and a sample of small firms in the US.

In the Korean context, the contraction in bank loans responded to both monetary conditions and structural changes in the financial sector. Several factors can explain the changes in the pattern of credit allocation. First, financial institutions became more reluctant to extend loans to enterprises because of the new financial sector regulations and environment. In particular, some banks did not meet capital adequacy ratios and could not raise equity capital easily; in that situation, exposure to highly leveraged or loss-making customers does not help.[14] In general, government securities or foreign assets (or a reduction in foreign debt) were more attractive options than loans to Korean borrowers. Second, the higher level of interest rates, by weakening the state of borrowers' balance sheets, may have reduced the demand for credit. Highly leveraged corporate firms were more vulnerable to the interest rate increases, and their investment demand declined substantially. Third is the traditional "crowding-out" effect. The fiscal deficit increased from a small surplus in 1997 to a deficit of almost 4 percent of GDP, without including the (non-interest) cost of financial restructuring in the deficit measure. As a result, the government had to tap domestic financial markets to a large extent in 1998. Fourth, as foreign lines of credit dried up, banks had no choice but to repay their short-term foreign debts, or later repay the emergency support that the Bank of Korea had provided on a temporary basis. Fifth, prudential regulations imposed by the new institutional framework including the establishment of a new independent financial supervisory

---

[14] Bernanke and Lown (1991) show that in the 1990–91 US recession period, banks with low capital ratio had slow lending growth. Peek and Rosengren (1997) show that banks that were targets of formal regulatory actions reduced their lending at a significantly faster rate than those that were not. Hall (1993) finds evidence that the introduction of the BIS risk-based capital standards induced US commercial banks to change the portfolio towards safer assets (e.g. Treasury securities) away from commercial loans, while Berger and Udell (1994) claim the effect of the risk-based capital regulations on lending was not quantitatively important. Ito and Sasaki (1998) confirm the effect of the risk-based capital standards on the lending behavior of Japanese banks in the period between 1990 and 1993.

agency may have prompted financial institutions to upgrade standards in project monitoring and risk evaluation.

In sum, to adapt themselves to the new regulations and the new incentives in the new financial environment, banks needed to change their lending practices. To be sure, a change in the composition of credit is not an unusual response by banks to any tightening in monetary conditions. In particular, a "flight to quality" may happen, whereby banks respond to a monetary tightening by shifting their loan portfolio toward more credit-worthier borrowers. Gertler and Gilchrist (1993, 1994), Lang and Nakamura (1995), and Oliner and Rudebush (1995) provide evidence of a broad reallocation of short-term bank lending away from small firms toward large firms after a monetary contraction. In the Korean context, however, a flight to quality in favor of more profitable and less leveraged firms is also consistent with the objectives of the financial sector reforms. Note that, in the distorted incentives circumstances of nearly bankrupt financial institutions, the opposite result could have been observed. That is, financial institutions could have channeled more resources to their weakest borrowers to keep them from going bankrupt and to maintain the appearance of a less troubled loan portfolio.

7.3. Credit Allocation During the Crisis: Empirical Evidence

In this section, we assess the allocation of credit by financial institutions after the start of the crisis. Traditionally, the Korean financial system had been used for industrial policy purposes, and banks did not need to attach importance to market principles in evaluating and monitoring projects. Furthermore, there was the expectation that troubled borrowers and lenders would benefit from government bailouts.[15] A break from those practices would be reflected in a significant redistribution of credit. To the extent that the financial reform started to have an impact, we would expect to see a redistribution of credit on stricter market basis.

[15] Borensztein and Lee (1998) provide some empirical evidence of inefficient credit allocations among Korean manufacturing sectors for the period from 1970 to 1996.

7.3.1. *The Firm-level Data*

The firm-level data used in this study come from the database constructed by the Korea Listed Companies Association, which provides comprehensive corporate and financial information on listed companies beginning in 1981. The company profiles and financial information data are compiled from the financial statements, business reports, and audit reports that every company is legally mandated to produce on a bi-annual basis. This is one of the most reliable data bases available on financial information on Korean firms.[16] We do not include financial service firms in our sample because their accounting practices are different from those of firms in other industries.

We then identified our sample firm's affiliation with business groups or "chaebols". Chaebols consist of many subsidiaries usually owned and controlled by a single family or by companies within the family's control.[17] In this study, we distinguish the top 30 chaebols from the non-chaebol firms on the basis of their asset size as of end-1996. The 30 largest chaebols produced about 16 percent of GDP and more than 40 percent of manufacturing output.[18] In 1996, the top 30 chaebols possessed on average some 22 subsidiaries (see Yoo, 1998, Table 4), while in our sample they have about four publicly listed companies on average.[19]

---

[16] Note that this database covers only listed companies which comprised 776 companies as of 1997. Another database compiled by the Korea Investors Service (KIS) contains financial information on much larger number of companies, including both listed and unlisted companies. The financial information on the unlisted firms can be considered as less reliable.

[17] The Korean Fair Trade Commission (KFTC) legally defines a business group as "a group of companies, more than 30 percent of whose shares are owned by some individuals or by companies controlled by those individuals". The KFTC identifies business groups and announces them every year.

[18] Among the 30 chaebols, the top 5 chaebols, comprising Hyundai, Samsung, Daewoo, LG, and SK, were the most powerful. The top five chaebols alone produced about 9 percent of GDP and accounted for 27 percent of manufacturing GDP in 1995. Daewoo went bankrupt in 1999.

[19] In 1996, total number of subsidiaries that belonged to the top 30 chaebols was 669. The listed companies accounted for 26 percent of the total (Yoo, 1998).

Table 7.2 provides summary statistics of the basic data for all sample firms over the period 1996 to June 1998. The table confirms that Korean firms went through difficult times in the crisis period of December 1997–June 1998. The year-on-year rate of growth of real sales for the average firm dropped from 4.3 percent in 1997 to –6.8 percent in the first half of 1998. The share of interest payments in total sales increased from 7.4 percent in 1997 to 11.6 percent in the first half of 1998. The profit rate started to decline in 1997, dropping from 1.59 percent in 1996 to –0.03 in 1997 and 0.05 percent in the first half of 1998.[20] The lower profit rates went hand in hand with higher leverage: the debt/capital ratio was 68.8 percent in December 1996 and increased to 71.8 percent in December 1997 and 72.1 percent in June 1998.

Both short- and long-term bank borrowing slowed down in real terms in the first half of 1998. The annualized growth rate of real short-term bank borrowing dropped for the average firm from 35.9 percent in the year 1997 to 20.6 percent in the first half of 1998. By contrast, the annualized growth rate of real total bank borrowing dropped more significantly from 30.5 percent in 1997 to 6.2 percent over the first 6 months of 1998. The higher growth rate of short-term borrowing, compared to that of total borrowing, may result from new short-term loans that were granted in order to capitalize interest on loans.

The firm-level data indicate that despite the financial crisis, there was no general credit contraction in the first half of 1998: both total and short-term real bank credit increased for the average firm. In fact, bank borrowing increased relative to other forms of finance over the period. The share of short-term bank borrowing in short-term debt slightly increased from 47.9 percent in December 1997 to 48.3 percent in July 1998. Over the same period, the share of total bank borrowing increased from 43.7 to 44.9 percent of total debt. This suggests that firms reduced their recourse to alternatives to bank lending, such as commercial paper and corporate bonds, relative to bank loans.

Table 7.2 also compares the performance of the top-30 chaebol firms with the other (non-chaebol) firms in the sample. The chaebol firms had

---

[20] The profit rate is defined as the ratio of ordinary income (net profit before income tax plus net extraordinary gains) to total assets.

Table 7.2. Summary statistics of Korean firm data (simple average, in percent)

	Total Firms ($N = 534$)			Top 30 Chaebols ($n_1 = 112$)			Non-chaebols ($n_2 = 442$)		
	1996	1997	June 1998	1996	1997	June 1998	1996	1997	June 1998
Profit rate	1.59	−0.03	0.05	0.57	−0.82	−1.34	1.85	0.17	0.41
Debt/asset	68.8	71.8	72.1	77.1	82.2	83.1	66.6	69.0	69.3
Short-term debt/total debt	62.1	63.3	65.5	61.4	60.3	61.3	62.3	64.1	66.6
Interest payments/sales	6.7	7.4	11.6	7.1	7.9	13.6	6.5	7.3	11.2
Real sales growth[a]	9.3	4.3	−6.8	12.1	11.6	−5.9	8.6	2.4	−7.0
Export/sales	27.2	28.9	34.5	29.1	34.4	40.0	26.8	27.5	33.1
Short-term bank credit[b]									
Real growth rate[a]	23.6	35.9	20.6	24.9	46.7	21.2	23.2	33.1	20.4
Ratio to short-term debt	45.2	47.9	48.3	47.2	47.7	51.2	44.6	47.1	47.5
Total bank credit[b]									
Real growth rate[a]	18.9	30.5	6.2	24.0	47.7	5.2	17.8	26.0	6.4
Ratio to total debt	40.2	43.7	44.9	41.4	45.5	45.7	39.9	43.2	44.7

Notes:

[a] The growth rate is per annum. The real sales growth in 1998 is the year-on-year change over June 1997–June 1998. The growth rate of bank credit in 1998 is an annualized rate of the growth rate over the 6 months from December 1997 to June 1998.

[b] Bank credit indicates firm's borrowings from all financial institutions including banks and non-bank financial institutions.

higher debt ratios and lower profit rates over the period. In June 1998, the financial situation was worse for the chaebol than for the non-chaebol firms: the average chaebol firm had a profit rate of −1.34 percent and the debt/capital ratio of 83.1 percent, while the average non-chaebol firm had a profit rate of 0.41 percent and a debt/capital ratio of 69.3 percent. Both the chaebol and the non-chaebol firms were hit hard by the crisis, however. The growth rate of sales for the average chaebol company dropped from 11.6 percent in 1997 to −5.9 percent in the first half of 1998, while it declined from 2.4 percent to −7.0 percent over the same period for the average non-chaebol firm. Bank lending slowed down both for chaebols and non-chaebols, but more sharply for chaebol firms. The annual growth rate of real short-term bank borrowing dropped on average from 46.7 percent in 1997 to 21.2 percent in June 1998 for chaebol firms, while it dropped from 33.1 to 20.4 over the same period for non-chaebols. The growth rate of real total bank borrowing dropped even further: from 47.7 percent in 1997 to 5.2 percent in the first half of 1998 for the chaebols and from 26.0 to 6.4 percent over the same period for the non-chaebols. Despite the slowdown in real bank borrowing, bank borrowing increased relative to other forms of finance in 1998 for both chaebols and non-chaebols. The share of short-term bank borrowing in short-term debt and the share of total bank borrowing in total debt both increased slightly in the first half of 1998 for both kinds of firms.

7.3.2. *The Pattern of Credit Allocation*

This section analyzes the determinants of credit across firms after the crisis erupted in end-1997. As noted earlier, we want to test whether there was a general contraction of bank lending to Korean firms or whether profitable and viable firms were largely not affected.

We first analyze how the supply of bank credit related to the firm's profit rate and leverage ratio in 1998. We divide all individual firms into five groups based on the quintile of firm's average profit rate over the 3 years from 1995 to 1997. For the five groups, we study the change in the supply of credit in the first half of 1998. The supply of credit is measured by the annualized growth rates of real short-term bank borrowing and of real total borrowing. In the spirit of the "credit channel" of monetary transmission, we also measure it by the changes in the ratio of short-term bank borrowing to short-term debt and the ratio of total bank borrowing to total debt.

Table 7.3 reports the relationship between firm's profitability and supply of credit. Comparing across the five groups, a clear pattern emerges, showing that credit was allocated to the more profitable firms. For instance, firms in the top quintile of the profit distribution observed an increase in real short-term borrowing of 38.8 percent per annum, while firms in the bottom quintile experienced a decline in real short-term bank credit of 6.8 percent. If the sample is divided into chaebols and non-chaebols, the relationship between profitability and bank credit is slightly weaker but still remains positive.

We also divide all individual firms into five groups based on the distribution of the average debt/capital ratio over the 3-year period from 1995 to 1997. We compare the change in the supply of credit in 1998 for the five quintiles of the distribution in Table 7.4. The relationship between finance availability and leverage is not monotonic. At lower levels of leverage (firms in the first to the third quintile) there is a positive association between credit growth and leverage but at higher levels of leverage (from the third to the fifth quintile) the relationship is negative. This pattern seems to be consistent with a redistribution of credit towards more creditworthy borrowers.

We formally test whether a firm's financial characteristics were a significant factor in the distribution of bank loans. Using the panel data set of 1583 firms over three periods (1996, 1997, and the first half of 1998), we estimate the following regression:[21]

$$\begin{aligned} \mathrm{D}(BL)_{jt} = a_0 + a_1 D(BL)_{j,t-1} + a_2 D98 + a_3 D98Profit_{j,t-1} \\ + a_4 D98Debt_{j,t-1} + a_5 D98Chaebol_{j,t-1} + \varepsilon_{j,t}, \qquad (1) \\ j = 1, \ldots, 527\,(\text{firms}),\ t = 1996, 1997, 1998, \end{aligned}$$

[21] We have used only the more recent years for the regression in order to maximize the number of firms included in the balanced panel. Since financial data are available for a much smaller number of firms in the earlier years than in the recent period, extending the data set into the earlier period would force many firms to drop out of the sample. The results reported below do not change qualitatively; however, when we use a balanced panel data set over the whole period from 1990 to 1998.

Table 7.3. Profit rates and credit allocation (in percent, p.a.)

	Profit Rate (Avg. 1997–97)		Rate of Change from December 1997 to June 1998			
	Range in Quintile	Average	ST Credit Growth Rate	Total Credit Growth Rate	ST Credit/ST Debt	Total Credit/ Total Debt
All firms	(1) 4.58–32.4	7.8	38.8	12.0	7.6	5.8
($N = 527$)	(2) 2.23–4.58	3.3	22.6	9.6	1.8	3.2
	(3) 0.77–2.23	1.5	31.6	15.4	2.2	2.6
	(4) −1.23–0.77	−0.1	16.2	4.8	−0.2	3.4
	(5) −25.8–1.23	−5.2	−6.8	−11.0	−4.6	−2.4
Chaebols	(1) 1.91–10.1	4.4	38.6	−6.2	2.8	−2.4
($n_1 = 106$)	(2) 1.12–1.91	1.5	70.8	40.2	8.8	5.6
	(3) 0.53–1.12	0.8	40.2	15.4	10.0	5.8
	(4) −1.61–0.53	−0.3	−6.6	−3.0	−2.4	0.2
	(5) −9.11–1.61	−4.3	−35.6	−20.8	−17.2	−6.8
Non-chaebols	(1) 5.16–32.4	8.4	25.6	5.8	6.4	5.4
($n_2 = 421$)	(2) 2.71–5.16	3.8	45.2	28.4	5.6	6.6
	(3) 1.08–2.71	1.9	15.2	2.8	−0.4	2.4
	(4) −1.10–1.08	0.1	14.6	2.4	−1.6	2.2
	(5) −25.8–1.10	−5.5	1.6	−7.0	−1.8	−1.2

Table 7.4. Debt ratio and credit allocation (in percent, p.a.)

	Debt Rate (Avg. 1995–97)		Rate of Change from December 1997 to June 1998			
	Range in Quintile	Average	ST Credit Growth Rate	Total Credit Growth Rate	ST Credit/ST Debt	Total Credit/ Total Debt
All Firms	(1) 23.0–55.4	45.0	19.6	2.0	4.2	3.6
($N = 527$)	(2) 55.4–65.1	60.2	19.8	4.4	1.6	3.0
	(3) 65.1–73.3	69.0	30.4	17.8	−1.2	3.4
	(4) 73.3–81.5	77.2	25.0	8.2	3.0	2.6
	(5) 81.5–310	97.6	7.6	−1.6	−0.8	0.2
Chaebols	(1) 54.1–70.1	64.2	45.0	16.6	1.6	3.0
($n_1 = 106$)	(2) 70.1–77.2	73.9	42.6	17.2	3.4	1.4
	(3) 77.2–81.7	79.2	31.6	2.0	7.8	2.0
	(4) 81.7–86.1	83.8	8.2	0.4	−3.6	−0.2
	(5) 86.1–120.9	93.9	−20.8	−9.8	−7.6	−4.0
Non-chaebols	(1) 23.0–52.3	43.5	21.8	4.4	3.6	3.6
($n_2 = 421$)	(2) 52.3–61.9	57.8	22.8	2.4	3.8	3.2
	(3) 61.9–70.0	65.8	11.8	3.6	−1.8	2.6
	(4) 70.0–78.3	73.6	38.0	25.4	1.4	5.0
	(5) 78.3–310	97.1	8.2	−3.2	1.0	0.8

where $D(BL)_{j,t}$ is the change in bank lending to firm j at time t. We use four different measures for D(BL): the growth rate of real short-term bank borrowing, the growth rate of real total borrowing, the change in the ratio of short-term bank borrowing to short-term debt, and the change in the ratio of total bank borrowing to total debt. We include a dummy variable for the crisis period, D98; which captures the average change of D(BL) in the first half of 1998. We expect the coefficient on D98 to be negative if the supply of credit was reduced on average in 1998. The effects of firms' profitability and debt size on the magnitude of credit contraction are captured by two multiplicative terms: the product of the previous period profit rate and D98, and the product of the debt ratio and D98. Hence, this specification allows us to detect the possible reallocation of bank lending among firms during the crisis period. We also include an interactive term between a chaebol dummy and the crisis dummy to see if bank loans were reallocated in favor of the chaebol group. The regression was estimated allowing for random effects, and controlling for each firm's previous year's dependent variable.[22]

Table 7.5 reports the results of regressions for the four different measures of credit contraction based on the total sample of 1583 firms. The results show that the profit rate variable always has a significantly positive coefficient, indicating that bank loans were indeed re-directed in favor of firms which had shown better profitability in the past.[23] In a typical case, the estimated coefficient implies that a one percentage point higher profit rate is associated with a 2.3 percentage points higher growth rate of real short-term bank credit. We also examined how bank lending was reallocated depending on the firms' leverage ratio. The debt-to-capital variable (again multiplied by the crisis dummy) resulted insignificant. This result casts some doubt on the extent to which leverage

[22] The results do not change qualitatively when the lagged dependent variable (which can be correlated to the unobserved firm-specific error term and thereby cause bias) is excluded. The main results also hold true when we allow for firm-specific fixed effect or when we include dummies for industry (total 24 dummies for 16 manufacturing and 8 non-manufacturing sectors) to control for industry effects.

[23] Ideally, we should test the effect of future profitability, rather than past profit rates, on credit growth. Unfortunately, we do not have an accurate measure of firm's future profitability such as Tobin's Q.

Table 7.5. Determination of credit allocation after the crisis (panel of three time periods: 1996, 1997, Jan–June 1998) Sample: Total firms (***N*** = 1583)

	Dependent Variable			
	ST Credit Growth Rate	**Total Credit Growth Rate**	***D* (ST Credit/ ST Debt)**	***D* (Total Credit/Total Debt)**
Lagged dependent variable	–0.073	0.017	–0.268	–0.155
	(0.030)**	(0.028)	(0.038)**	(0.036)**
*D*98 (dummy for crisis period)	–14.650	–27.070	–0.511	1.250
	(14.34)	(10.35)**	(3.189)	(2.275)
*D98**Profit rate ($t-1$)	2.297	1.717	0.536	0.462
	(0.563)**	(0.400)**	(0.125)**	(0.089)**
*D98**Debt rate ($t-1$)	0.072	0.126	0.011	0.009
	(0.194)	(0.140)	(0.043)	(0.031)
*D*98*Chaebol	2.821	–1.740	–0.325	–2.101
	(9.574)	(6.917)	(2.121)	(1.517)
Constant	31.730	24.010	1.445	1.382
	(2.914)**	(2.085)**	(0.608)**	(0.438)**
*R*2	0.02	0.03	0.05	0.03

Notes: The estimation is based on panel estimation with random effects.
Standard errors are reported in parentheses.
** Significant at 5 percent level.

was a relevant consideration in banks' decisions once one controls for profitability, although it may also be related to a non-linearity in the relationship between finance and leverage.

We also checked if the affiliation with chaebol groups had an impact on the allocation of bank loans during the crisis period. The estimated coefficient turns out to be statistically insignificant. Hence, there is no evidence that chaebol-connected firms were treated in a differential way in terms of access to bank after the financial crisis.[24]

7.3.3. *Comparing Credit Allocation Before and After the Crisis*

This section compares the determination of credit allocation in 1998 with that in 1996 and 1997. We estimate a specification that comprises the effect of the three variables that describe a firm's economic and financial situation (profitability, leverage and affiliation with a chaebol group) on the allocation of credit both before the currency crisis (the years 1996 and 1997) and after the currency crisis (the first half of 1998). That is, we estimate the following equation:

$$\begin{aligned} \mathrm{D}(BL)_{jt} &= a_0 + a_1 D(BL)_{j,t-1} + a_2 D98 + a_3 D98Profit_{j,t-1} \\ &+ a_4 D98Debt_{j,t-1} + a_5 D98Chaebol_{j,t-1} \\ &+ b_3 D96{\sim}97Profit_{j,t-1} + b_4 D96{\sim}97Debt_{j,t-1} \\ &+ b_5 D96{\sim}97Chaebol_{j,t-1} + \varepsilon_{j,t}, \\ j &= 1,\ldots,527(\text{firms}), t = 1996,1997,1998, \end{aligned} \tag{2}$$

where D96~97 represents a dummy variable that is equal to one for the observations corresponding to 1996 and 1997 and zero otherwise.

The results, summarized in Table 7.6, are quite interesting. They show that the main change in the aftermath of the crisis was experienced by chaebol firms. Before the crisis, affiliation with a chaebol group could

[24] The low value of the R^2 in the regressions is probably due to unobserved firm-specific error terms. We are, however, concerned mainly with the coefficients on the variables of our interest, rather than overall goodness of fit of the equation.

Table 7.6. Determination of credit allocation after the crisis (panel of three time periods: 1996, 1997, Jan–June 1998) Sample: Total firms ($N = 1583$)

	Dependent Variable			
	ST Credit Growth Rate	**Total Credit Growth Rate**	***D* (ST Credit/ ST Debt)**	***D* (Total Credit/Total Debt)**
Lagged dependent variable	−0.074	0.008	−0.265	−0.154
	(0.030)**	(0.028)	(0.038)**	(0.036)**
D98 (dummy for crisis period)	−17.730	−32.810	−1.684	2.801
	(16.87)	(12.18)**	(3.773)	(2.695)
*D98**Profit rate ($t-1$)	2.306	1.721	0.537	0.462
	(0.562)**	(0.404)**	(0.125)**	(0.089)**
*D98**Debt rate ($t-1$)	0.061	0.121	0.011	0.009
	(0.193)	(0.139)	(0.043)	(0.031)
*D98** Chaebol	3.392	−1.238	−0.332	−2.077
	(9.549)	(6.883)	(2.117)	(1.517)
*D96~97**Profit rate ($t-1$)	1.449	0.691	0.269	0.148
	(0.566)**	(0.406)	(0.125)**	(0.089)

(*Continued*)

Table 7.6. (*Continued*)

	Dependent Variable			
	ST Credit Growth Rate	**Total Credit Growth Rate**	***D* (ST Credit/ ST Debt)**	***D* (Total Credit/Total Debt)**
*D96~97**Debt rate ($t-1$)	−0.139	−0.164	−0.031	0.015
	(0.128)	(0.092)	(0.028)	(0.020)
*D*96~97* Chaebol	12.410	17.940	1.827	1.152
	(6.968)**	(4.985)**	(1.524)	(1.527)
Constant	35.560	30.270	2.600	−0.182
	(9.704)**	(6.952)**	(2.121)	(1.527)
R2	0.03	0.04	0.05	0.04

Notes: The estimation is based on panel estimation with random effects.
Standard errors are reported in parentheses.
** Significant at 5 percent level.

increase access to credit significantly. The coefficients on D96~97Chaebol are not only significant but quantitatively important in the regressions both for real short-term bank credit and real total bank credit growth: for instance, affiliation with a chaebol is associated with about an 18 percentage point higher growth rate of real total bank credit over the period from 1996 to 1997. In contrast, after the crisis, affiliation with a chaebol was not a significant determinant of credit allocation: the corresponding coefficients on D98Chaebol are not significantly different from zero and in fact negative in three of the four specifications. This suggests that the credit crunch was largely a chaebol problem.

To further investigate the chaebol/non-chaebol differences, we ran regression (2) on two separate samples: one constituted by firms affiliated with the top-30 chaebols and the other conformed by non-chaebol firms. The results, presented on Table 7.7, are revealing. For chaebol firms, profitability was not a significant determinant of the allocation of credit in the pre-crisis period. In 1998, profitability becomes an important determinant of credit growth.[25] For non-chaebol firms, by contrast, profitability was already a significant determinant for short-term bank credit in the pre-crisis period, while profitability became a significant variable for total bank credit only after the crisis.

7.3.4. *Credit Contraction and Output Decline*

This section investigates the extent to which the credit slowdown in 1998 impacted output. A credit contraction does not necessarily induce a fall in output in the short-run. Lower credit could be compensated by other sources: for example, (i) using up inventories, (ii) lowering employees' compensation, or (iii) obtaining alternative finance sources, including falling into arrears. Moreover, finding a positive association between credit and output is not sufficient to show that the decline in bank lending

---

[25] A recent study by Choi and Kang (1999) based on survey of 863 Korean firms also finds support for the result that firms belonging to chaebol groups became subject to tougher loan appraisal. The study shows that the proportion of large firms rejected for loans rose sharply from 21 percent in 1997 to 61 percent in the first half of 1998, far exceeding that of small and medium firms.

Table 7.7. Determination of credit allocation after the crisis for chaebol and non-chaebol firms (panel of three time periods: 1996, 1997, Jan–June 1998)

	ST Credit Growth Rate	Total Credit Growth Rate	*D* (ST Credit/ ST Debt)	*D* (Total Credit/Total Debt)
Chaebols ($n = 325$)	−0.061	0.124	−0.156	−0.009
Lagged dependent variable	(0.069)	(0.058)**	(0.087)	(0.094)
D98 (dummy for crisis period)	−51.590	−48.310	−47.220	−11.030
	(92.76)	(66.72)	(20.29)**	(15.65)
*D98**Profit rate ($t-1$)	12.690	5.533	3.265	1.006
	(2.803)**	(2.205)**	(0.613)**	(0.471)**
*D98**Debt rate ($t-1$)	1.100	0.352	0.523	0.104
	(1.026)	(0.740)	(0.223)**	(0.172)
*D96~97**Profit rate ($t-1$)	2.466	1.002	0.307	0.125
	(1.630)	(1.179)	(0.357)	(0.272)
*D96~97**Debt rate ($t-1$)	0.530	0.116	−0.074	−0.022
	(0.547)	(0.396)	(0.119)	(0.091)
Constant	−5.329	22.960	7.585	3.701
	(43.80)	(31.64)	(9.520)	(7.261)
R2	0.09	0.10	0.11	0.02

Non-chaebols ($n = 1258$)	−0.071	−0.016	−0.281	−0.180
Lagged dependent variable	(0.033)**	(0.031)	(0.042)**	(0.039)**
D98 (dummy for crisis period)	−19.630	−34.290	−0.550	3.105
	(17.30)	(12.55)**	(3.884)	(2.738)
*D98**Profit rate ($t-1$)	1.852	1.564	0.429	0.442
	(0.577)**	(0.415)**	(0.128)**	(0.091)**
*D98**Debt rate ($t-1$)	0.055	0.130	−0.002	0.007
	(0.198)	(0.142)	(0.044)	(0.031)
*D96~97**Profit rate ($t-1$)	1.399	0.665	0.263	0.144
	(0.608)**	(0.435)	(0.134)**	(0.098)
*D96~97**Debt rate ($t-1$)	−0.174	−0.178	−0.028	0.016
	(0.132)	(0.094)	(0.029)	(0.021)
Constant	37.890	37.739	2.427	−0.277
	(10.01)**	(7.140)**	(2.193)	(1.588)
R2	0.02	0.03	0.05	0.04

Note: See Table 7.6.

caused the output fall because the causality between credit and output can go in either direction. Credit could follow an output decline induced by other factors such as, for example, an adverse terms of trade shock.

To look more closely into the link between credit contraction and output decline after the Korean financial crisis, we run cross-section regressions using the firm-level data set. We regress proportional changes in real sales (in the first half of 1998 over the first half of 1997) against the change of bank credit in the first half of 1998. We use four different measures of bank credit.[26] Because the change in bank credit can itself be an endogenous variable, we applied a two-stage least squares method, using the independent variables that we used in the regressions of Table 7.5 — the lagged bank credit variable, the lagged profit rate, and the lagged debt ratio — as instruments for the supply of credit.[27]

The results from running this regression are displayed in Table 7.8. The test finds a strong association between credit contraction and output decline.[28] This implies that the allocation of bank credit indeed had an important impact on real output. This suggests that firms that saw their access to credit constrained adjusted, at least in part, via lower production and that higher-performing firms that found an increased level of credit availability were able to expand their level of production. The regression results also suggest that the export share in total sales was another important factor in the firms' sales performance. Export-oriented firms, which benefited from the effects of the exchange rate depreciation, experienced an increase in sales and could compensate the impact of any credit restrictions.[29] The results, however, should be treated with caution

[26] This regression is in the spirit of Calvo and Coricelli (1993) analysis of the output decline in the economies of Central and Eastern Europe at the outset of the reform process.

[27] Omitting the lagged debt ratio, which was not significant in the credit allocation regressions (Tables 7.5 and 7.6), from the list of instruments did not change the results significantly.

[28] The results do not change when we include dummies for industry to control for industry effects.

[29] Krueger and Tornell (1999) show that in the years after the Mexican financial crisis of 1994, tradable sector firms were subject to a less stringent credit crunch and experienced a faster recovery than firms in the non-tradable sector.

Table 7.8. Bank credit and real sales growth (Dec. 1997–June 1998) Sample: Total firms (**N** = 499)

Lagged dependent variable	0.206 (0.045)**	0.214 (0.046)**	0.204 (0.052)**	0.23 (0.052)**
Export/sales ($t-1$)	0.446 (0.057)**	0.466 (0.055)**	0.529 (0.064)**	0.567 (0.069)**
ST credit growth rate	0.201 (0.097)**			
Total credit growth rate		0.272 (0.135)**		
D (ST credit/ST debt)			0.91 (0.309)**	
D (total credit/total debt)				1.147 (0.443)**
Constant	−24.190 (2.510)**	−22.280 (2.279)**	−24.340 (2.724)**	−27.220 (3.248)**

Notes: The estimation is based on 2SLS regressions. Instruments for the credit variable are previous period bank credit variable, the lagged profit rate and the lagged debt ratio.
**Significant at 5 percent level.

as it is possible that the instrumental variable method may not completely overcome the endogeneity problem in this case.

7.4. Conclusions

This paper examined the nature of credit crunch in the aftermath of the Korean financial crisis. We used firm-level data to analyze changes in the allocation of credit in the post-crisis period. The evidence shows some significant changes in the determinant of credit allocation among borrowers. In particular, firms belonging to chaebol groups seem to have lost the preferential access to credit that they enjoyed in the pre-crisis period and seemed to be subject to more stringent profitability tests in order to obtain bank credit.

These results suggest that the "credit crunch" may have be the outcome of the structural changes in the financial sector rather than of a general monetary contraction. This implies that a more expansionary monetary policy would have done little to alleviate this kind of "credit crunch". In fact, one could even argue that an easier monetary stance would have allowed banks to get by without seriously restructuring their loan portfolios and thus slowed down the process of transformation.

Our findings do not directly address the "excess demand versus excess supply" controversy noted in the introduction. We think that the critical question is not whether there was excess demand or excess supply of bank credit in the aggregate but what type of firms were subject to a tightening in credit conditions. This is the critical question because, in a period when the financial institutions need to change their lending practices under the new regulations and the new incentives, some firms would necessarily find a more restricted access to the bank credit while the others would not, regardless of the aggregate credit market conditions.

We found that profitability was an important factor in maintaining access to credit and that firms connected with chaebols lost their previously easy access to credit. But we should note that while affiliation with the largest and most powerful groups became less of a consideration for obtaining bank credit and market viability gained in importance, this does not imply that non-chaebol firms were unaffected by the crisis. Although the volume of bank credit to the chaebol firms decreased by a larger magnitude than that to the non-chaebols firms, the non-chaebol firms could have been more affected by the credit decline because they lack access to other sources of finance. In the Korean economy, chaebols do have easier access to other sources of financing including bond financing than non-chaebols do.

It should be expected that a fundamental change in the behavior of financial institutions in terms of credit appraisal and loan allocation will certainly require a much longer period of learning and practice. Nonetheless, the results reported in this paper are moderately encouraging, although they comprise data on listed companies only. We could have seen an increasing volume of resources flowing to distressed corporation just to keep them alive. Instead, credit allocation seems to have improved by becoming more market-based. In the end, the process of financial reform and corporate restructuring, although triggered by a costly currency crisis, may provide the opportunity for long-term improvement in efficiency and soundness of the Korean financial system.

References

Balino, T., Ubide, A., 1999. The Korean financial crisis of 1997 — a strategy of financial sector reform. *International Monetary Fund Working Paper* WP/99/28.

Berg, A., 1999. The Asia crisis: causes, policy responses, and outcomes. *International Monetary Fund Working Paper* WP/99/138.

Berger, A.N., Udell, G.F., 1994. Did risk-based capital allocate bank credit and cause a credit crunch in the U.S.? *Journal of Money, Credit and Banking*, Part 2, 26(3), 585–628.

Bernanke, B., Blinder, A.S., 1988a. Credit, money and aggregate demand. *American Economic Association Papers and Proceedings* 78, 435–439.

Bernanke, B., Blinder, A.S., 1988b. The federal funds rate and the channels of monetary transmission. *American Economic Review* 82, 901–921.

Bernanke, B., Gertler, M., 1995. Inside the black box: the credit channel of monetary policy transmission. *Journal of Economic Perspectives* 9, 27–48.

Bernanke, B., Lown, C.S., 1991. The credit crunch. *Brookings Papers on Economic Activities* 2, 205–248.

Borensztein, E., Lee, J.-W., 1998. Credit allocation and financial crisis in Korea. *International Monetary Fund Working Paper* WP/99/20.

Calvo, G., Coricelli, F., 1993. Output collapse in Eastern Europe: the role of credit. In: Blejer, M., Calvo, G., Coricelli, F., Gelb, A. (Eds.), *Eastern Europe in Transition: From Recession to Growth.* IMF and World Bank.

Choi, N., Kang, D.-Y., 1999. A study on the crisis, recovery and industrial upgrading in Korea. Occasional Paper No. 30, Korea Institute for Industrial Economics and Trade.

Ding, W., Domac, I., Ferri, G., 1998. Is there a credit crunch in east Asia? *Asia Pacific Journal of Economics and Business* 2, 4–32.

Dollar, D., Hallward-Driemeier, 1998. Crisis, adjustment, and reform in Thai industry. Manuscript, World Bank.

Domac, I., Ferri, G., 1998. The real impact of financial shocks: Evidence from Korea. Working paper, World Bank.

Ferri, G., Kang, T.S., 1999. The credit channel at work: Lessons from the Republic of Korea's financial crisis. *World Bank Working Paper* 2190, World Bank.

Furman, J., Stigliz, J., 1998. Economic crises: Evidence and insights from East Asia. *Brookings Papers on Economic Activity*, pp. 1–123.

Gertler, M., Gilchrist, S., 1993. The role of credit market imperfections in the monetary transmission mechanism: Arguments and evidence. *Scandinavian Journal of Economics* 95, 43–64.

Gertler, M., Gilchrist, S., 1994. Monetary policy, business cycles and the behavior of small manufacturing firms. *Quarterly Journal of Economics* 109, 309–340.

Ghosh, S., Ghosh, A., 1999. East Asia in the aftermath: was there a crunch? *International Monetary Fund Working Paper* WP/99/38.

Hall, B.J., 1993. How has the Basel Accord affected bank portfolios? *Journal of the Japanese and International Economics* 7, 408–440.

Ito, T., Sasaki, Y.N., 1998. Impacts of the Basel capital standard on Japanese bank's behavior. *NBER Working Paper* No. 6730.

Kashyap, A.K., Stein, J.C., 1994. Monetary policy and bank lending. In: Gregory Mankiw, N. (Ed.), *Monetary Policy*. The University of Chicago Press, Chicago, pp. 221–261.

Kashyap, A.K., Stein, J.C., Wilcox, D.W., 1993. Monetary policy and credit conditions: Evidence from the composition of external finance. *American Economic Review* 83, 78–98.

Kim, H.E., 1999. A credit channel as the key transmission mechanism underlying the recent financial crisis in Korea. *World Bank Policy Research Paper Working Paper* 2103, World Bank.

Krueger, A., Tornell, A., 1999. The role of bank restructuring in recovering from crises: Mexico 1995–98. *NBER Working Paper* 7042.

Lane, T., Ghosh, A.R., Hamann, J., Phillips, S., Schultz-Ghattas, M., Tsikata, T., 1999. IMF-supported programs in Indonesia, Korea and Thailand: a preliminary assessment. *IMF Occasional Paper* 178, International Monetary Fund.

Lang, W.W., Nakamura, L.I., 1995. Flight to quality in banking and economic activity. *Journal of Monetary Economics* 36, 145–164.

Lown, C.S., Peristiani, S., Robinson, K.J., 1999. What was behind the M2 breakdown. Mimeo, Federal Reserve Bank of New York.

Oliner, S.D., Rudebush, G.D., 1995. Is there a bank lending channel for monetary policy? *Economic Review*, FRB of San Francisco 2, 1–20.

Peek, J., Rosengren, E., 1997. Bank regulation and the credit crunch. *Journal of Banking and Finance* 19, 679–692.

Radelet, S., Sachs, J.D., 1998. The onset of the East Asian financial crisis. Working Paper, Harvard Institute for International Development.

Romer, C.D., Romer, D.H., 1989. Does monetary policy matter? A new test in the spirit of Friedman and Schwartz. *NBER Macroeconomics Annual* 4, 121–170.

Romer, C.D., Romer, D.H., 1990. New evidence on the monetary transmission mechanism. *Brookings Papers on Economic Activity*, pp. 149–213.

Yoo, S.M., 1998. Corporate restructuring in Korea: Policy issues before and during the crisis. Manuscript, Korea Development Institute.

Chapter 8

IMF Programs: Who Is Chosen and What Are the Effects?*

8.1. Introduction

In recent decades, many countries have participated in loan programs of the International Monetary Fund. In fact, almost all developing countries have received IMF financial support at least once since 1970. The few exceptions include Botswana, Iraq, Malaysia, and Kuwait.

Given the broad reach of IMF loan programs, it is important to know the consequences of these programs for economic growth and other dimensions of economic performance. Do countries benefit from access to IMF loan programs or would countries be better off if these programs did not exist?

The main difficulty in answering this question is that IMF loans tend to be made in response to economic problems. This response, akin to a doctor administering to a sick patient, tends to generate a negative association between IMF loan programs and economic performance.

---

* Reprinted from *Journal of Monetary Economics*, Vol. 52, No. 7, Robert J. Barro and Jong-Wha Lee, IMF Programs: Who Is Chosen and What Are the Effects?, pp. 1245–1269, Copyright (2005), with permission from Elsevier.
This research has been supported in part by a grant from the National Science Foundation. We appreciate comments from Alberto Alesina, Eduardo Borensztein, Jeffrey Frankel, Jeffrey Frieden, Jinyoung Hahn, Simon Johnson, Mohsin Kahn, Robert King, Myoung-jae Lee, Greg Mankiw, Roberto Perrotti, and seminar participants at the Australian National University, Harvard University, the International Monetary Fund, the Korean Econometric Society Workshop, the State University of New York at Buffalo, the Study Center Gerzensee, and Tokyo University. Yunjong Eo provided valuable research assistance.

Obviously, it would be unfair to blame the IMF for these preexisting bad conditions. Thus, to assess the economic effects of the loan programs, one has to sort out the directions of causation, that is, distinguish the economic effects of the loans from the effects of economic conditions on the probability and size of the programs. Similar issues arise in evaluating foreign aid, debt relief, and other programs that respond to the economic health of a country.

To sort out the directions of causation, we would ideally observe experimental situations in which the IMF introduced a loan program without regard to a country's economic conditions. We try to approximate these sorts of experiments by taking a political/institutional approach to the IMF's decision-making. That is, we construct and use some political and institutional variables that, first, have substantial predictive value for IMF loan participation and, second, are exogenous with respect to economic performance. We then use these political and institutional variables to form instruments to isolate the effects of IMF loan programs on economic growth and other variables.

The key innovation of our analysis is that we model the IMF as a bureaucratic and political organization. Loans are more likely to be approved and are likely to be larger when countries are more influential at the IMF. We gauge this influence by the size of a country's quota at the IMF and by the number of the IMF's professional staff that come from the country. We also consider each country's political and economic connections to the most influential members of the IMF, the United States and the major countries of Western Europe. To measure these connections, we use voting patterns in the United Nations and the extent of bilateral trade linkages.

Our analysis shows that IMF loans are more likely to exist and to be larger in size when countries have larger quotas, more nationals on the IMF staff, and are more connected politically and economically to the United States and the major Western European countries. Considered as a whole, these political-economy variables have substantial explanatory power for IMF lending.

Our political-economy analysis of the determinants of IMF loan programs is of considerable interest for its own sake. However, most importantly, this analysis generates the instrumental variables that we use to study the effects of these programs. We can reasonably argue that our instrumental estimates isolate the effects of the loan programs on economic growth and other variables.

Overall, our results are not favorable for the economic role of the IMF. We find that, using our instrumental variables and holding fixed an array of other explanatory variables, greater IMF loan participation has a direct negative effect on economic growth. We also find that more participation and larger loans have small negative effects on democracy and the rule of law. The reduction in the rule of law provides another indirect channel whereby IMF loan programs lead to lower economic growth.

8.2. Characteristics of the IMF

The IMF has become an almost universal financial institution, with its membership rising from 44 states in 1946 to 184 at present. However, the members of the IMF do not have an equal voice. Each member contributes a quota subscription, as a sort of credit-union deposit to the IMF. Upon joining the Fund, a country pays 25% of its quota in the form of international currencies or SDRs and the remaining 75% in its own currency. The quota is the basis for determining voting power: each member has 250 basic votes plus one additional vote for each SDR 100,000 of quota. The initial quotas of the original members were determined at the Bretton Woods Conference in 1944. The allocations were based mainly on economic size, as measured by national income and external trade volume. Quotas of new members have been determined by similar principles.

The IMF charter calls for general quota reviews at intervals of no more than 5 years. These reviews allow for adjustments of quotas to reflect changes in economic power. There have been 12 general reviews since 1950, and 6 of these resulted in an increase in the total size of quotas. Most of these overall increases featured equi-proportional increases of quotas for the individual members (IMF, 1998).

The IMF's Board of Governors delegates most decision-making power to the Executive Board, which has 24 directors. Eight directors are appointed by the largest eight shareholders — the United States (37,149 million SDRs or 17.5% of the total IMF quotas), Japan (6.3%), Germany (6.1%), France (5.1%), the United Kingdom (5.1%), Saudi Arabia (3.3%), China (3.0%), and Russia (2.8%). The others are elected by 16 groupings of the remaining countries.

The major shareholders have strong influences on the IMF's decisions. Many important decisions require special voting majorities of 85%. Hence, the United States alone and a group of three major Western European countries have veto power. Although the managing director has traditionally been a European, the United States has exerted the strongest voice at the IMF and has sometimes openly wielded this power to influence decisions (Kahler, 1992; Stone, 2002).

On December 31, 2002, the IMF had a staff of 2681 — 763 assistant staff and 1918 professionals. About two-thirds of the professional staff were economists (IMF, 2003, p. 87).

The basic conception of the IMF's role, as envisioned at Bretton Woods in 1944, was to promote exchange stability and provide short-term finance to deal with temporary current-account deficits in advanced countries. Thus, with the breakdown of the "par adjustable peg system" in 1973, the IMF lost its major role as the "guarantor of fixed exchange rates" among advanced countries. Nevertheless, the IMF did not disappear, and its role expanded instead into many new areas. The IMF has now evolved into the "crisis manager" and "development financier" for developing countries.[1]

The primary role of the IMF is to provide credits to member countries in balance-of payments difficulties. Part of the credit is provided in relation to a country's quota. The first tranche, 25% of the quota, is available automatically, without entailing any discussion of policy. The use of IMF resources beyond the first tranche almost always requires an arrangement between the IMF and the member country. Under an IMF arrangement, the amount of resources committed is released in quarterly installments, subject to the observance of policy benchmarks and performance criteria. This process is often called conditionality.

[1] See Krueger (1998) and Bordo and James (2000) for discussions of the changing role of the IMF.

Stand-by Arrangements (SBA) and the Extended Fund Facility (EFF) are the main IMF programs designed to provide short-term balance-of-payments assistance to member countries.[2] The typical Stand-By Arrangement covers a period of 1–2 years, with repayments scheduled between $3\frac{1}{4}$ and 5 years from the date of the borrowing. The Extended Fund Facility program, introduced in 1974, was intended to provide somewhat longer-term financing in larger amounts. The EFF arrangement typically lasts up to 3 years, with repayments scheduled over a period of $4\frac{1}{2}$ –10 years.

The SBA and EFF programs did not cover very low-income countries. Confronted by increasing pressure, the IMF developed several new lending programs to provide long-term loans at subsidized interest rates for poor countries. The Fund established the Structural Adjustment Facility (SAF) in 1986 and the Enhanced Structural Adjustment Facility (ESAF) in 1987. The interest rate charged is 0.5%, and repayments are scheduled over 5–10 years after a 5-year grace period. Most ESAF cases were with sub-Saharan African countries and former planned economies. In 1999, the ESAF was replaced by the Poverty Reduction and Growth Facility (PRGF). Probably these activities should be viewed more as foreign aid, rather than lending or adjustment programs.

Table 8.1 shows the number and amounts approved for all types of IMF programs from 1970 to 2000.[3] Over this period, a total of 725 programs were approved. This total includes 594 short-and mid-term stabilization programs (SBA and EFF), which are the focus of our analysis. The number of these short-term programs peaked in the early 1980s with the Latin American debt crisis. Although the number declined

---

[2] A number of other short-term IMF arrangements have been introduced to supplement SBA and EFF. These arrangements include the Supplemental Reserve Facility (SRF), the Country Stabilization Fund (CSF), the Compensatory and Contingent Financing Facility (CCFF), and the Systematic Transformation Facility (STF). See IMF (1998) or the IMF website for details.

[3] The amount of loan approved was not always drawn by the member country. This situation can arise if the IMF terminated the arrangement because the borrower did not meet the conditionality, or if the country ended up not using its full allotment. Sometimes a country utilized an IMF program to build credibility and did not use the borrowing facility at all.

Table 8.1. Approval of IMF loan programs, 1970–2000 (cells show number of programs approved and amounts committed (in parentheses) in millions of SDRs)

	Stabilization Programs		Structural Programs		
Period	**SBA**	**EFF**	**SAF**	**ESAF/PRGF**	**Total**
1970–74	82				82
	(4913)				(4913)
1975–79	83	7			90
	(8091)	(1895)			(9945)
1980–84	116	26			142
	(20,520)	(22,692)			(43,213)
1985–89	90	3	29	7	129
	(14,117)	(1277)	(1455)	(955)	(17,804)
1990–94	79	12	8	27	126
	(14,974)	(14,479)	(130)	(3309)	(32,893)
1995–2000	72	24	1	59	156
	(83,250)	(36,659)	(182)	(6961)	(126,052)

Notes: An approval of an IMF program indicates that a new IMF financial arrangement was approved for a country in the fiscal year (from May of the previous year to April of the current year). SBA is Stand-by Arrangement, EFF is Extended Fund Facility, SAF is Structural Adjustment Facility, and ESAF is Enhanced Structural Adjustment Facility. The ESAF was replaced in 1999 by the Poverty Reduction and Growth Facility (PRGF).
Source: IMF (2000, Appendix Table II-1).

subsequently, the average size of the loans rose because of the financial crises experienced by larger countries, such as Mexico, South Korea, Russia, Brazil, Argentina, and Turkey.

8.3. Determination of IMF Loan Programs

Participation in an IMF program is a joint decision between a member country and the IMF. Countries that are experiencing economic difficulties come to the IMF for a financial arrangement. Then the IMF determines whether the country meets the Fund's criteria for approval. In this section, we estimate the economic and institutional variables that influence the size and frequency of IMF lending.

8.3.1. *IMF Loan Programs*

To capture the economic determinants of IMF lending, we use a number of standard variables that can be found in the previous literature, which is surveyed by Knight and Santaella (1997) and Bird and Rowlands (2001). Some of these factors can be viewed as influences on a country's demand for loans and others as effects on the IMF's willingness to supply loans.[4] The explanatory variables included for each country and time period are the level of international reserves in relation to imports, per capita GDP, total GDP, the lagged growth rate of per capita GDP, and a dummy variable for OECD membership.[5]

We extend the previous literature by including a number of institutional and political-economy variables as determinants of IMF lending. The first institutional variable is the country's share of IMF quotas. The quota measures a country's voting power at the IMF and also matters directly for a portion of the lending available to a member. Our hypothesis is that, for given economic conditions, a higher country quota raises the probability and size of an IMF loan.

In practice, quotas are persistent over time, with much of the allocations determined by the rules set out in 1944 at Bretton Woods. Basically, economically larger countries get larger quotas, but the concept of economically large involves the long ago past, rather than the present. For our purposes, we are most interested in countries that have unusually high or low current quotas, relative to their economic sizes. To get a sense of the outliers, we ran an OLS regression of IMF quota shares in 2000 on the levels of total and per capita GDP in 1995.[6] The residuals from this

---

[4] Knight and Santaella (1997) and Przeworski and Vreeland (2000) used a bi-variate probit model to estimate demand and supply functions for IMF loans. The estimation requires a number of identifying restrictions.

[5] The OECD dummy equals one for countries other than Turkey that have been members of the OECD since the 1960s. We found that, once these variables were considered, other measures of economic performance and political structure did not have significant explanatory power. See below for further discussion.

[6] The regressors were linear and squared terms in the levels and logs of total and per capita GDP.

regression show that the countries that were most over-weighted on quotas were the United Kingdom, France, Russia, and Venezuela. The most under-weighted were China, South Korea, Hong Kong, and Taiwan. (Hong Kong and Taiwan, as non-members, have zero quotas.)

The second institutional variable is the share of a country's nationals among the IMF professional staff of economists. Officially, to avoid conflicts of interest, the IMF does not allow staff members to have direct influence on lending decisions for their home countries.[7] However, from the standpoint of having good information, the IMF often seeks input from the nationals of a target country. Therefore, although own nationals cannot work directly as desk economists or mission team members for their home countries, these nationals are often sought out for comments on country programs. In addition, the presence of own nationals on the staff can help a country to get more access to inside information and, thereby, make it easier to negotiate with the IMF on the terms of a program. Our hypothesis is that, for given economic conditions, a larger national staff at the IMF raises the probability and size of a loan.[8]

We measured the staff for each country by the number of home-country nationals currently working for the Fund. Unfortunately, we lack the information to refine the staff data to consider ranks of positions. Also, it would be interesting to consider the number of ex IMF staff economists who currently work in the governments of their home countries. However, we lack the information to make this extension.

As with quotas, the number of nationals working at the IMF tends to reflect the economic sizes of countries (although the fit for staffs turns out

---

[7] Item 24 of the IMF *Code of Conduct for Staff* states: "The IMF will seek to avoid assigning nationals to work on policy issues relating specifically to IMF relations with their home country, unless needed for linguistic or other reasons."

[8] An example of this sort of influence is described by Mussa (2002), the head of the IMF's research department until summer 2001. He observed that, although the IMF anticipated the inevitable collapse of the Argentine economy in 2001, it did not halt its existing loan programs but instead provided increased financial support. He argued that this continuation of support arose because the IMF's economists became too close to their clients (see Mussa, 2002). Probably not coincidentally, in June 2002, the long-time head of the IMF's Latin America Department, an Argentine economist, was dismissed. He was replaced by an Indian economist (The Economist, 2002).

to be substantially poorer than that for quotas). For our purposes, we are most interested in countries that have surprisingly high or low staffs. To get a sense of these outliers, we ran another OLS regression, this time for IMF staff shares in 2000 on levels of total and per capita GDP in 1995. The residuals from this regression show that the countries that were most over-weighted on the IMF staff were the United Kingdom, France, India, Canada, and Peru. Those that were most under-weighted were China, Japan, Indonesia, Taiwan, and Hong Kong.

One concern is that the number of country nationals on the IMF staff is endogenously determined by the country's experience with IMF programs, rather than the reverse. However, a country's history of IMF program turns out not to have much impact on the hiring of that country's nationals — the lagged loan-participation rate lacks significant explanatory power for the size of the national staff.[9]

The IMF is also a political organization governed by its major shareholders. A common claim is that the IMF plays the roles best suited to the national interests of the United States. In the Cold War era, the IMF often supported countries — such as Argentina, Egypt, the Philippines, and Zaire — that were important to the United States for foreign policy reasons, despite the lack of effective reform programs (see Krueger, 1998; Bordo and James, 2000). This sort of political influence was clear in the 1994 Mexican crisis, where the IMF approved a loan of unprecedented scale, \$17.8 billion. The loan approval process featured intense lobbying by the U.S. government, including an incident where the Clinton Administration's pressure for rapid action was so strong that the usual minimal notice to executive directors was not given. In protest, some European directors abstained in the voting (Krueger, 1998). As another example of U.S. influence, in December 1997, the IMF approved a record-breaking loan to South Korea, \$21 billion. In this case, the U.S. Treasury and the IMF apparently collaborated to work out the form of the package (Blustein, 2001).

---

[9] In a regression with the log of the IMF staff share as the dependent variable, the significant explanatory variable, aside from the log of the lagged staff share, is the log of the IMF quota share. The estimated coefficient on the lagged IMF loan-participation rate is positive but statistically insignificant.

We use as a proxy for a country's political proximity to the United States the fraction of the votes that each country cast in the U.N. General Assembly along with the United States.[10] We construct analogous variables for France, Germany, and the United Kingdom. Our hypothesis is that greater political proximity to the United States and the major Western European countries raises the probability and size of IMF loan programs.

A study by Thacker (1999) used a different form of U.N. voting variable to investigate the U.S. influence over the IMF's lending decisions.[11] U.N. voting variables have also been used by Ball and Johnson (1996) and Alesina and Dollar (2000) to explain foreign-aid patterns.

We measure economic proximity to the United States by the ratio of the country's bilateral trade with the United States to the country's GDP. We construct analogous variables for the three Western European countries. Our hypothesis is that greater trade intensity with the United States and the European countries raises the probability and size of IMF loan programs.[12]

---

[10] We compiled data for 1975–85 on voting patterns in the United Nations from the Inter-University Consortium for Political and Social Research (1992). We then updated from on-line data available from the United Nations (unbisnet.un.org). The variable that measures the political proximity with the United States is the fraction of times that the United States and the country in question voted identically (either both voting yes, both voting no, or both voting abstention [or non-participation]) in all General Assembly plenary votes in a given year. Decisions adopted without votes and votes in which the country in question was not eligible to participate were excluded. Our results do not change qualitatively if we use some alternative measures, for example, if we exclude non-participation or abstention.

[11] Thacker used only "key" U.N. votes, as designated by the U.S. Treasury. He then constructed the fraction of the votes on these key issues that each country cast in the U.N. General Assembly along with the United States. One problem with this procedure is that the designation of which votes are key is subjective. In any event, we could not apply this approach in our setting, because the U.S. Treasury information is available only since 1983. Moreover, we lack analogous information for the European countries. Thacker found that the level of his U.N. voting variable was not significantly related to IMF lending. However, the first difference of his variable had a significantly positive effect. We do not find this pattern with our specification and sample period.

[12] Thacker (1999) and Bird and Rowlands (2001) used U.S. exports to each member country as an explanatory variable for IMF lending decision. They found unexpected *negative* coefficients.

8.3.2. *Empirical Framework for the Determination of IMF Loan Programs*

We have compiled data from 1975 to 2000. Although data are available for some variables and countries on an annual basis, we do not have annual observations for the national origin of the IMF staff, which we obtained at 5-year frequencies. Some of the other variables that we consider later (such as educational attainment, life expectancy, and fertility rates) are also available, at best, at 5-year frequencies. Since we think that little information can be gained from annual observations, we arranged all of the data at 5-year intervals. Hence, our panel covers 130 countries over the five 5-year periods 1975–79, 1980–84, 1985–89, 1990–94, and 1995–99. The panel is unbalanced with a total of 613 observations.[13]

We measured a country's involvement with IMF loan programs in several ways. The first measure considers approvals of new loans. Our dummy variable for program approval equals one if the IMF and the country made a new loan agreement at any time during a 5 year period. As mentioned before, we focus on the IMF's short-term stabilization programs (SBA and EFF). Hence, loan approval and our other measures of involvement with IMF loan programs consider only these kinds of loans. However, most of our results are similar if we use all types of IMF loans. In fact, our results on economic growth turn out to be stronger if we use overall IMF lending.

The second variable refers to participation in IMF loan programs. Our IMF loan-participation rate is the fraction of months during each 5-year period that a country operated under an IMF loan program. Thus, the participation rate varies almost continuously between zero and one. Note that participation in a 5-year period often reflects loan programs that were approved in the previous 5-year period. Moreover, the approval of a new program counts for participation only for the months contained within the current 5-year period.

Finally, we use a variable that takes account of the sizes of IMF loans. Our measure is the average for each 5-year period of the ratio of approved

[13] This sample excludes countries that lacked IMF membership during each 5-year period.

IMF loans to GDP.[14] This variable is analogous to our participation measure in that it includes loans that were approved in the previous 5-year period and counts newly approved loans only to the extent that they apply to the current 5-year period.

Since program approval is a binary-choice variable, we use a probit model to explain this variable:

$$I_{it*} = \alpha + \beta X_{it} + \gamma Z_{it} + \delta * time_t + u_{it} \tag{1}$$

$$\begin{aligned} I_{it} &= 1 \quad \text{if } I_{it*} > 0, \\ &= 0 \quad \text{if } I_{it*} \leq 0. \end{aligned} \tag{2}$$

The dependent variable, I_{it}, equals one if country i made at least one new loan agreement with the IMF during period t and equals zero otherwise. The vector X_{it} denotes country-specific economic factors that influence the existence and size of IMF loan programs. This vector includes the values at the beginning of the period of the ratio of foreign reserves to imports, per capita GDP, and total GDP. It also includes the growth rate of per capita GDP during the previous 5 years and the dummy for OECD membership. In addition, the regression includes time dummies to control for common effects of external factors such as world interest rates. The vector Z_{it} comprises the institutional and geopolitical factors that measure each country's political-economy connections to the IMF — the values at the beginning of the period of the share of IMF quotas and staff, the political proximity to the United States and the European countries (based on the U.N. voting patterns), and the intensity of trade with the United States and the European countries. The variable u_{it} is a random error term.

We use a Tobit model to explain IMF program participation. This specification takes account of the censoring of the dependent variable at zero. The model is

$$F_{it*} = \alpha + \beta X_{it} + \gamma Z_{it} + \delta * time_t + u_{it}, \tag{3}$$

---

[14] We measure GDP by the PPP-adjusted value from Penn-World Tables 6.1, as reported in Heston *et al.* (2002).

$$F_{it} = min\ [1, max\ (0, F_{it*})], \tag{4}$$

where X_{it}, Z_{it}, and time are defined as before. The dependent variable, F_{it}, is the fraction of time for which country i participated in an IMF loan program during period t.

The model for IMF loan size also requires a censored-regression framework. The Tobit specification is

$$L_{it*} = \alpha + \beta X_{it} + \gamma Z_{it} + \delta * time_t + u_{it}, \tag{5}$$

$$L_{it} = max\ [0, L_{it*}], \tag{6}$$

where L_{it} is the average for period t of the ratio of approved IMF loans to GDP for country i. $L_{it} = 0$ applies if the country had no loan outstanding during period t.

The specifications in Eqs. (1)–(6) can be viewed as reduced-form models that reflect the demand for and supply of IMF loans. We tried various functional forms for each model and selected the ones that delivered the best goodness-of-fit. Per capita GDP and the log of GDP each enter as quadratics. The IMF quota share, the IMF staff share, the U.N. voting variables, and the bilateral-trade-share variables enter as logs.[15]

The Tobit and probit models apply to panel data for 130 countries over the five 5-year periods from 1975 to 1999. To estimate these systems, we allow for within-country correlation of the error terms over time. Our reasoning is that a country that is favored by the IMF in one period — due to unexplained factors — is likely to be similarly favored in other periods.[16]

---

[15] To keep the zero observations when making the log transformations, we added 0.0009 to each observation of staff share, 0.0002 to each observation of quota share, and 0.0001 to each observation of bilateral trade share. These values are the minimum non-zero observations for staff share, quota share, and bilateral trade share, respectively, in the sample. The results are not sensitive to the specific values added for the log transformations.

[16] We get similar results if we estimate random-effects models, although the IMF staff share becomes less statistically significant. We do not emphasize these results because the conditions needed for the satisfactory implementation of random-effects Tobit or probit models seem unlikely to hold. In particular, these specifications require strict exogeneity of the explanatory variables. Fixed-effects Tobit or probit models cannot be implemented because

The summary statistics for all variables are in Table 8.2. Over the sample period, the average ratio of approved IMF loans to GDP (including the zeroes) was 0.003. For countries with positive loans, the average ratio to GDP was 0.007. Countries on average participated in an IMF financial arrangement 19% of the time, and 36% of the observations (for 5-year periods) featured at least one IMF program approval.

8.3.3 *Results on the Determinants of IMF Lending*

We begin with Tobit equations for the ratio of IMF loans to GDP, as shown in Eqs. (5) and (6). Consider first the results in columns 1–4 of Table 8.3. Column 1 excludes all political-economy variables. Column 2 includes the IMF staff share and the U.N. voting and trade intensity variables associated with the United States. Column 3 substitutes the IMF quota share for the IMF staff share. Column 4 includes all four of these political-economy variables.

The estimated coefficient of the lagged growth rate of per capita GDP is significantly negative in all of the specifications. The estimated coefficient in column 4 implies that, holding fixed the other explanatory variables, a decline in per capita GDP growth by 1% point per year would increase the ratio of IMF lending to GDP by 0.06% point.

The estimated coefficient of the ratio of international reserves to imports is significantly negative in all of the specifications. The estimated coefficient in column 4 implies that a decrease in reserves by 1 month of imports would raise the ratio of IMF lending to GDP by 0.13% point.

The ratio of IMF loans to GDP has a non-linear relationship with per capita GDP. In all specifications, the estimated coefficient on the level is significantly positive and the estimated coefficient on the square is significantly negative. (The two variables together are always jointly significant; the *p*-value is 0.05 or less.) Hence, the loan–GDP ratio initially increases with per capita GDP but later decreases.[17] The estimated

there does not exist a sufficient statistic allowing the fixed effects to be conditioned out of the likelihood. See Wooldridge (2002).

[17] If we replace IMF stabilization loans by total IMF loans as the dependent variable, the estimated coefficient on the level of per capita GDP becomes smaller in magnitude and

Table 8.2. Summary statistics for variables used in regressions

Variable	Mean	Median	σ
IMF loan–GDP ratio (EFF and SBA only)	0.0027	0	0.0094
IMF loan–GDP ratio (EFF and SBA only), sub-sample of positive loans	0.0066	0.0027	0.0139
IMF loan-participation rate (EFF and SBA only)	0.185	0	0.279
IMF loan approval frequency (EFF and SBA only)	0.364	0	0.481
Per capita GDP growth rate (lagged)	0.014	0.015	0.036
International reserves (months of imports)	3.300	2.651	2.85
GDP per capita (1996 U.S. thousand dollars)	6.745	4.100	6.729
Log (GDP) (1996 U.S. million dollars)	10.177	9.971	2.062
Group of advanced OECD countries	0.176	0	0.381
IMF quota share (log)	−5.822	−6.171	1.246
IMF staff share (log)	−5.663	−5.795	1.256
Political proximity to the United States (log)	−1.441	−1.423	0.478

(Continued)

Table 8.2. (*Continued*)

Variable	Mean	Median	σ
Political proximity to major Europe (log)	−0.882	−0.963	0.342
Intensity of trade with the United States (log)	−3.090	−3.082	1.448
Intensity of trade with major Europe (log)	−3.412	−3.332	1.006

Notes: The sample consists of the 613 observations for the 5-year periods from 1975 to 1999 that are used in the regressions in Tables 8.3–8.5. The IMF loan–GDP ratio is the average for each 5-year period. Participation is the fraction of time that a country was in an IMF loan program in each 5-year period. IMF loan approval takes on the value 1 if a loan is approved within a 5-year period. Only the EFF and SBA loans are included. The figures on GDP are the PPP-adjusted values, as discussed in Summers and Heston (1991) and Heston *et al.* (2002). The group of advanced OECD countries consists of countries other than Turkey that have been members of the OECD since the 1970s. The share of IMF staff nationals is the fraction of own nationals in IMF economists. The share of IMF quota is the fraction of each country's quota in the IMF total. Political proximity to the United States is the log value of the fraction of times out of all votes that each country voted in the U.N. General Assembly along with the United States. Political proximity to major Europe is the average value of the political proximity measures for France, Germany, and the United Kingdom. Trade intensity with the United States is the bilateral trade (exports and imports) between a country and the United States, expressed as a ratio to the country's GDP. Trade intensity with major Europe is the average value of the trade intensity measures for France, Germany, and the United Kingdom. All variables except the per capita GDP growth rate and the IMF loan variables are observed at the beginning of each 5-year period. The per capita GDP growth rate is the average over the previous 5-year period.

Table 8.3. Determinants of IMF loan-GDP ratio (cells show estimated coefficients with standard errors in parentheses)

	(1)	(2)	(3)	(4)	(5)	(6)
Per capita GDP growth rate	−0.086	−0.088	−0.054	−0.055	−0.054	−0.057
	(0.027)	(0.026)	(0.020)	(0.021)	(0.020)	(0.021)
International reserves	−0.0014	−0.0012	−0.0012	−0.0013	−0.0014	−0.0012
	(0.0005)	(0.0004)	(0.0004)	(0.0004)	(0.0005)	(0.0004)
GDP per capita	0.0025	0.0017	0.0017	0.0018	0.0024	0.0017
	(0.0010)	(0.0009)	(0.0009)	(0.0009)	(0.0011)	(0.0095)
GDP per capita squared	−0.00025	−0.00021	−0.00024	−0.00024	−0.00028	−0.00024
	(0.00009)	(0.00007)	(0.00009)	(0.00009)	(0.00010)	(0.00009)
Log (GDP)	0.0039	0.0024	0.0057	0.0056	0.0077	0.0056
	(0.0037)	(0.0033)	(0.0036)	(0.0036)	(0.0039)	(0.0036)
Log (GDP) squared	−0.00014	−0.00010	−0.00046	−0.00048	−0.00061	−0.00048
	(0.00018)	(0.00016)	(0.00023)	(0.00023)	(0.00026)	(0.00023)
Group of advanced OECD countries	−0.0025	−0.0047	−0.0026	−0.0040	−0.0074	−0.0061
	(0.0063)	(0.0067)	(0.0072)	(0.0076)	(0.0083)	(0.0079)
Log (IMF quota)			0.0100	0.0098	0.0105	0.0096
			(0.0039)	(0.0039)	(0.0040)	(0.0037)
Log (IMF staff)		0.0020		0.0017	0.0019	0.0017
		(0.0010)		(0.0009)	(0.0009)	(0.0009)

(*Continued*)

Table 8.3. (*Continued*)

	(1)	(2)	(3)	(4)	(5)	(6)
Political proximity to the US		0.0047	0.0051	0.0046		−0.0004
		(0.0028)	(0.0028)	(0.0028)		(0.0035)
Political proximity to major Europe					0.0083	0.0085
					(0.0036)	(0.0044)
Intensity of trade with the US		0.0021	0.0018	0.0018		0.0019
		(0.0008)	(0.0007)	(0.0007)		(0.0007)
Intensity of trade with major Europe					0.0003	0.0003
					(0.0008)	(0.0008)
p-value (a)		0.015	0.012	0.008	0.002	0.008
(b)		0.003	0.003	0.004	0.005	0.007
Number of obs.	613	613	613	613	613	613

Notes: The dependent variable is the average of the IMF loan–GDP ratio over the 5-year periods 1975–79, 1980–84, ..., 1995–99. A Tobit model was applied to the panel data for the five 5-year periods. The estimation allows for within-country correlation of the error terms over time. The summary statistics for all variables are shown in Table 8.2. See the notes to Table 8.2 for definitions of variables. Period dummies are included (not shown). Robust standard errors of the estimated coefficients are reported in parentheses. The *p*-value (a) indicates the significance level associated with a test of the joint hypothesis that the estimated coefficients of the included political-economy variables — IMF quota share, IMF staff share, U.N. voting variable(s), and trade intensity variable(s) — are all equal to zero. The *p*-value (b) applies to the same group of variables except for the trade intensity variable(s).

coefficients in column 4 imply that the switch occurs at a per capita GDP of $3750 (1996 U.S. dollars), which is below the sample median of $4150. The overall marginal effect of per capita GDP at the sample mean of $6745 is estimated to be negative. At that point, an increase in per capita GDP by $1000 is estimated to decrease the ratio of IMF lending to GDP by 0.14% point.

The positive relation between IMF lending and per capita GDP in the low range of per capita GDP likely reflects the Fund's reluctance to provide stabilization loans to countries that are not creditworthy. The negative effect in the upper range of per capita GDP likely signals the decreased demand for IMF loans among rich countries, which have other sources of credit.

We find that, after controlling for the log of per capita GDP and its square, the dummy for OECD membership has negative estimated coefficients in all of the specifications. The estimated value is not statistically significant in columns 1–4 but is marginally significant in some cases considered later.[18] The negative coefficient on the OECD dummy can be interpreted as another indicator of a low demand for IMF loans by advanced economies.

The log of total GDP enters as a level and its square. The estimated coefficients are, in each case, positive for the level of log(GDP) and negative for the square. The two coefficients are jointly marginally significant in some cases, with *p*-values ranging from 0.06 in column 4 to 0.62 in column 2. Thus, this scale variable appears not to be very important in the determination of the ratio of IMF loans to GDP. These variables turn out to be more important in some of the systems for IMF program participation and approval.

The results in columns 2–4 of Table 8.3 indicate that the political-economy variables are important overall for explaining IMF lending decisions. When considered jointly, the p-values for the statistical significance

---

statistically insignificantly different from zero, while the square term remains negative and statistically significant. Hence, per capita GDP has a monotonically decreasing effect on the ratio of total IMF loans to GDP.

[18] No substantial changes occur in the main results if we exclude the OECD dummy variable in the various systems.

of these variables range from 0.008 (column 4) to 0.015 (column 2) — see the line denoted *p*-value (a) in the table. If we consider the group of these variables exclusive of the bilateral trade share with the United States, the p-values are all less than 0.005 — see the line denoted *p*-value (b).

In column 4, the IMF staff share, the IMF quota share, and the economic proximity to the United States, as gauged by bilateral trade, each have individually significantly positive estimated effects at the 5% critical level. The estimated coefficient on the U.N. voting variable with the United States is also positive and individually significant at the 10% level.

The estimated coefficients in column 4 imply that an increase in the log of the IMF quota share by 1.25 (its standard deviation) raises the IMF loan size by 1.2% of GDP. An increase in the log of the IMF staff share by 1.26 (the variable's standard deviation) is estimated to raise IMF lending by 0.21% of GDP. A rise in the log of the U.N. voting variable for the United States by 0.48 (its standard deviation) is estimated to raise the ratio of IMF lending to GDP by 0.22% point. Similarly, an increase in the log of the intensity of trade with the United States by 1.4 (its standard deviation) is estimated to raise the ratio by 0.25% point.

Column 5 modifies the specification from column 4 to measure the U.N. voting and trade intensity variables in relation to the IMF's major European shareholders, rather than the United States. The U.N. voting and bilateral trade variables are now averages for France, Germany, and the United Kingdom. The estimated coefficient on the U.N. variable for Europe is positive and significant at the 5% level. The estimated effect of the European trade variable is not statistically significant.[19]

Column 6 includes U.N. voting and trade intensity variables for the United States along with those for the average of the European countries.

---

[19] We report here only the results when the U.N. voting and trade variables are averages for the three European countries. Since the U.N. voting variables for France, Germany, and the United Kingdom are highly correlated (correlations above 0.95), it is hard to disentangle the effects for the individual countries. The correlation between the U.N. voting variable for the United States and each of the European countries is much lower — ranging from 0.7 to 0.8. The trade intensity variables are substantially less correlated than the voting variables, ranging from 0.03 (between the United States and France) to 0.45 (between France and Germany).

In this setting, only the U.N. voting variable for Europe and the U.S. trade intensity variable are individually statistically significant at the 5% level. However, for our purposes, the most important result is the joint significance of the political-economy variables. This joint significance is clear — the p-value is 0.008 for all six variables and 0.007 for the four variables exclusive of the two trade intensity measures.

Table 8.4 presents estimates of the Tobit equations for the IMF loan-participation rate, as specified in Eqs. (3) and (4). The results are, in most respects, similar to those for loan size. For example, the *p*-values for joint significance of the political-economy variables are all below 0.003. The estimated coefficients on the IMF quota share, IMF staff share, and the U.N. voting and trade intensity variables with the United States are all positive and individually at least marginally statistically significant in columns 2–4. The estimated coefficient on the U.N. voting variable for Europe is significantly positive in columns 5 and 6.

Table 8.5 presents the estimates for the probit equations for the approval of IMF loan programs, as specified in Eqs. (1) and (2). The results are, in most respects, similar to those found for loan size and participation. However, the statistical significance of the IMF quota variable is less than that found before.

We have extended our analysis to consider other measures of economic and political variables as determinants of IMF lending. These variables include current-account balances, fiscal balances, inflation, and indicators of democracy and the rule of law. The estimation results, detailed in our working-paper version, show that these additional variables are statistically insignificant in most cases, whereas our political-economy variables remain significant when additional economic and political variables are included. Thus, from the standpoint of Staiger and Stock (1997), the instruments constructed from the set of political-economy variables will not be weak.

8.4. Economic Effects of IMF Loan Programs

Many previous studies have used cross-country data to assess the economic effects of IMF loan programs. This research, surveyed by Haque and Kahn (1998), yields conflicting results, depending on the sample and

Table 8.4. Determinants of IMF loan-participation rate (cells show estimated coefficients with standard errors in parentheses)

	(1)	(2)	(3)	(4)	(5)	(6)
Per capita GDP growth rate	–2.13	–2.17	–1.66	–1.69	–1.68	–1.75
	(0.70)	(0.67)	(0.72)	(0.72)	(0.71)	(0.71)
International reserves	–0.046	–0.041	–0.041	–0.042	–0.045	–0.041
	(0.013)	(0.012)	(0.012)	(0.012)	(0.012)	(0.012)
GDP per capita	0.101	0.080	0.077	0.083	0.094	0.078
	(0.029)	(0.028)	(0.029)	(0.029)	(0.030)	(0.030)
GDP per capita squared	–0.0097	–0.0089	–0.0092	–0.0094	–0.0100	–0.0092
	(0.0022)	(0.0021)	(0.0022)	(0.0022)	(0.0024)	(0.0023)
Log (GDP)	0.26	0.23	0.29	0.28	0.33	0.29
	(0.13)	(0.12)	(0.12)	(0.12)	(0.12)	(0.12)
Log (GDP) squared	–0.0090	–0.0091	–0.0141	–0.0149	–0.0179	–0.0151
	(0.0064)	(0.0060)	(0.0067)	(0.0067)	(0.0068)	(0.0068)
Group of advanced OECD countries	–0.14	–0.28	–0.22	–0.27	–0.39	–0.35
	(0.21)	(0.23)	(0.23)	(0.24)	(0.26)	(0.25)
Log (IMF quota)			0.155	0.146	0.164	0.150
			(0.082)	(0.080)	(0.081)	(0.080)

Log (IMF staff)		0.072		0.068	0.073	0.067
		(0.032)		(0.032)	(0.031)	(0.032)
Political proximity to the US		0.254	0.274	0.254		0.038
		(0.095)	(0.095)	(0.095)		(0.119)
Political proximity to major Europe					0.42	0.37
					(0.13)	(0.17)
Intensity of trade with the US		0.044	0.043	0.040		0.043
		(0.020)	(0.020)	(0.020)		(0.020)
Intensity of trade with major Europe					0.006	0.005
					(0.032)	(0.032)
p-value (a)		0.0009	0.0030	0.0011	0.0002	0.0016
(b)		0.0000	0.0003	0.0000	0.0001	0.0001
Number of obs.	613	613	613	613	613	613

Notes: The dependent variable is the fraction of time that a country participated in an IMF loan program during each 5-year period. Estimation was by the Tobit procedure, including allowance for within-country correlation of the error terms over time. See the notes to Tables 8.2 and 8.3 for additional information.

Table 8.5. Determinants of IMF loan approval (cells show estimated coefficients with standard errors in parentheses)

	(1)	(2)	(3)	(4)	(5)	(6)
Per capita GDP growth rate	−4.0	−4.2	−3.7	−3.8	−3.6	−3.8
	(1.8)	(1.8)	(1.8)	(1.8)	(1.8)	(1.8)
International reserves	−0.108	−0.101	−0.100	−0.102	−0.109	−0.102
	(0.029)	(0.028)	(0.028)	(0.028)	(0.029)	(0.028)
GDP per capita	0.194	0.157	0.148	0.158	0.187	0.157
	(0.068)	(0.071)	(0.071)	(0.072)	(0.071)	(0.073)
GDP per capita squared	−0.0185	−0.0174	−0.0173	−0.0178	−0.0192	−0.0178
	(0.0049)	(0.0049)	(0.0049)	(0.0051)	(0.0053)	(0.0052)
Log (GDP)	0.65	0.61	0.66	0.65	0.76	0.66
	(0.29)	(0.29)	(0.30)	(0.30)	(0.29)	(0.30)
Log (GDP) squared	−0.024	−0.023	−0.027	−0.028	−0.035	−0.030
	(0.014)	(0.014)	(0.016)	(0.016)	(0.016)	(0.016)
Group of advanced OECD countries	−0.49	−0.75	−0.62	−0.74	−0.96	−0.84
	(0.47)	(0.54)	(0.51)	(0.54)	(0.58)	(0.58)
Log (IMF quota)			0.14	0.12	0.17	0.14
			(0.18)	(0.18)	(0.18)	(0.18)

Log (IMF staff)		0.139		0.135	0.149	0.136
		(0.082)		(0.082)	(0.080)	(0.082)
Political proximity to the US		0.49	0.53	0.49		0.17
		(0.26)	(0.25)	(0.26)		(0.38)
Political proximity to major Europe					0.75	0.57
					(0.34)	(0.50)
Intensity of trade with the US		0.090	0.092	0.087		0.094
		(0.050)	(0.050)	(0.050)		(0.051)
Intensity of trade with major Europe					−0.016	−0.027
					(0.075)	(0.075)
p-value (a)		0.018	0.082	0.041	0.021	0.060
(b)		0.005	0.024	0.009	0.036	0.029
Number of obs.	613	613	613	613	613	613

Notes: The dependent variable is a dummy variable that equals one if a new IMF loan program was approved in any year of each of the 5-year periods. Estimation was by the probit procedure, including allowance for within-country correlation of the error terms over time. See the notes to Tables 8.2 and 8.3 for additional information.

methodology.[20] Our major concern with the various studies is their treatment of the endogeneity of IMF loan programs. The natural approach, as in program evaluation more generally, is to use instrumental variables (see Wooldridge, 2002). The problem, however, is that good instrumental variables have not previously been available for evaluations of IMF loan programs. Thus, our major contribution is to use an instrumental-variables approach, based on the political-economy determinants of IMF lending that we investigated in the previous section.

We view the Tobit models for IMF loans and participation as "first-stage" representations that we can use to generate predicted values of IMF loan–GDP ratios and IMF loan-participation rates. We then use these predicted values as instrumental variables in "second-stage" regressions for economic growth and other variables. We can base the predictions and, hence, the instruments either on the full set of first-stage regressors or on a sub-set of these regressors. Our preferred procedure is to base the predictions only on variations in the political-economy variables, that is, the variations that are plausibly exogenous with respect to economic growth. These variables are the IMF quota and staff shares and the measures of a country's political and economic proximity to the United States and the major Western European countries. The predicted values for IMF loans and participation come from the Tobit estimations in Tables 8.3 and 8.4, respectively, after holding fixed the other explanatory variables at their sample means.[21] We show later that our results for economic growth are robust to changes in the procedure for constructing the instrumental variables.

We focus on the determinants of economic growth, using an empirical framework that has been widely used in previous studies (see, for example, Barro and Sala-Martin, 2004, ch.12). We include in this analysis a representative set of the explanatory variables used in previous work. We begin by assessing the effects of IMF loan–GDP ratios and

---

[20]The studies include Goldstein and Montiel (1986); Conway (1994); Kahn (1990); Przeworski and Vreeland (2000); Dicks-Mireaux *et al.* (2000); and Hutchison (2002).

[21]We assigned predicted values of zero for non-member countries, which were ineligible for IMF loans. However, our sample for economic growth contains only three observations for non-member countries, and the results are similar if we exclude these observations.

loan-participation rates within a standard framework of cross-country growth regressions. Our first analysis does not consider the endogeneity of the IMF loan programs. Subsequently, we use our political-economy analysis of IMF lending to construct instrumental variables for the IMF loan programs.

8.4.1. *Basic Results*

Table 8.6 presents panel regression results for economic growth. The dependent variables are the 5-year growth rates of per capita GDP for 1975–80, 1980–85, 1985–90, 1990–95, and 1995–2000. The independent variables, detailed in the table, are, first, the log of per capita GDP at the start of each period; second, measures of human capital at the start of each period (educational attainment and life expectancy); third, the ratio of investment to GDP and the fertility rate; fourth, changes in the terms of trade; and, fifth, institutional and policy variables (government consumption, subjective indexes of the rule of law and democracy, international openness, and inflation).

We estimate the system of five equations by three-stage least squares, using mostly lagged values of the independent variables as instruments (see the notes to Table 8.6). The estimation allows for different error variances in each period and for correlation of these errors over time.[22]

To summarize briefly, the estimated coefficients on initial per capita GDP, fertility, government consumption, and inflation are significantly negative. The estimated coefficients on school attainment, life expectancy, international openness, the investment ratio, the rule-of-law index, and the growth rate of the terms of trade are significantly positive. The effect from democracy is non-linear: the estimated coefficient on the linear term is significantly positive, and the estimated coefficient of the square of democracy is negative and marginally significant.

---

[22] Some studies estimate panel growth regressions by fixed-effects or first-differenced GMM techniques, thereby allowing for an unobserved country-specific effect. However, these techniques eliminate information from time-persistent cross-section information. See Temple (1999) and Barro and Sala-i-Martin (2004, ch.12) for other statistical problems concerning the estimation of cross-country growth regressions.

Table 8.6. Regressions for per capita GDP growth (with instruments including IMF loan GDP ratios and loan participation rate)

	(1)	(2)	(3)	(4)	(5)	(6)
Log (per capita GDP)	−0.0271	−0.0260	−0.0290	−0.0293	−0.0283	−0.0277
	(0.0038)	(0.0038)	(0.0039)	(0.0040)	(0.0038)	(0.0039)
Male upper-level schooling	0.0037	0.0034	0.0039	0.0038	0.0039	0.0036
	(0.0018)	(0.0017)	(0.0018)	(0.0018)	(0.0017)	(0.0017)
Log (life expectancy)	0.064	0.063	0.073	0.074	0.069	0.068
	(0.023)	(0.023)	(0.023)	(0.023)	(0.023)	(0.022)
Log (total fertility rate)	−0.0149	−0.0151	−0.0143	−0.0152	−0.0146	−0.0154
	(0.0061)	(0.0060)	(0.0061)	(0.0061)	(0.0060)	(0.0060)
Investment/GDP	0.070	0.060	0.069	0.060	0.073	0.068
	(0.033)	(0.033)	(0.033)	(0.033)	(0.033)	(0.032)
Government consumption/GDP	−0.086	−0.083	−0.096	−0.091	−0.082	−0.077
	(0.027)	(0.027)	(0.027)	(0.027)	(0.026)	(0.026)
Inflation rate	−0.0154	−0.0190	−0.0154	−0.0190	−0.0149	−0.0186
	(0.0080)	(0.0079)	(0.0080)	(0.0079)	(0.0079)	(0.0077)
Openness measure	0.0109	0.0110	0.0097	0.0092	0.0098	0.0093
	(0.0049)	(0.0048)	(0.0049)	(0.0049)	(0.0048)	(0.0048)
Rule-of-law index	0.0168	0.0165	0.0191	0.0191	0.0166	0.0161
	(0.0081)	(0.0080)	(0.0081)	(0.0082)	(0.0080)	(0.0080)
Democracy index	0.044	0.046	0.045	0.050	0.047	0.052
	(0.021)	(0.021)	(0.021)	(0.021)	(0.021)	(0.021)
Democracy index squared	−0.030	−0.032	−0.032	−0.037	−0.034	−0.039
	(0.019)	(0.019)	(0.020)	(0.020)	(0.019)	(0.019)

Growth rate of terms of trade	0.068	0.068	0.074	0.074	0.071	0.070
	(0.028)	(0.028)	(0.028)	(0.028)	(0.028)	(0.028)
Contemporaneous IMF loan	−0.324	−0.309	—	—	−0.255	−0.251
	(0.099)	(0.102)			(0.110)	(0.111)
Lagged IMF loan	—	−0.075	—	—	—	−0.034
		(0.102)				(0.110)
Contemporaneous IMF participation	—	—	−0.0126	−0.0104	−0.0079	−0.0057
			(0.0045)	(0.0047)	(0.0049)	(0.0052)
Lagged IMF participation	—	—	—	−0.0054	—	−0.0042
				(0.0047)	(0.0050)	
p-value	0.001	0.004	0.005	0.012	0.001	0.005

Notes: The system has five equations, corresponding to 1975–80, 1980–85, 1985–90, 1990–95, and 1995–2000. The sample comprises 86 countries and 391 total observations. The dependent variables are the growth rates of per capita real GDP. Data on GDP are from Penn-World Tables version 6.1, as described in Summers and Heston (1991) and Heston *et al.* (2002).

The log of per capita GDP, the average years of male secondary and higher schooling, and the log of life expectancy at age one are measured at the beginning of each period. The ratios of government consumption (exclusive of spending on education and defense) and investment (private plus public) to GDP, the inflation rate, the total fertility rate, the growth rate of the terms of trade (export over import prices), and the democracy index are period averages. The rule-of-law index is the earliest value available (for 1982 or 1985) in the first equation and the period average for the other equations. The openness variable is the ratio of exports plus imports to GDP, filtered for the estimated effects on this measure from the logs of population and area. The IMF loan–GDP ratios and loan-participation rates are described in the notes to Tables 8.2–8.4.

Estimation is by three-stage least squares. Instruments are the actual values of the variables for schooling, life-expectancy, openness, and the terms of trade; dummy variables for Spanish or Portuguese colonies and other colonies (which have substantial explanatory power for inflation); lagged values of the log of per capita GDP, the government consumption ratio, and the investment ratio; and the initial values for each period of the rule-of-law and democracy indexes. In the first two equations, the rule-of-law indicator is for 1982 or 1985. The current and lagged values of the IMF loan–GDP ratios are used as instruments in columns 1 and 2, and the current and lagged values of the IMF loan-participation rates are used as instruments in columns 3 and 4. Columns 5 and 6 include as instruments the current and lagged values of the IMF loan–GDP ratios and IMF loan-participation rates.

Individual constants (not shown) are included for each period. The *p*-values indicate the significance level associated with a test of the hypothesis that the coefficients on the IMF variables included in each column are jointly zero.

Our primary interest is in the impact of IMF loan programs. We examine the effects of two measures: the IMF loan–GDP ratio and the IMF loan-participation rate (fraction of months in each 5-year period that a country participated in an IMF loan program). The participation variable picks up effects from involvement with an IMF program that are unrelated to the sizes of loans.

Column 1 of Table 8.6 includes as an independent variable the contemporaneous IMF loan–GDP ratio. Column 2 allows also for a lagged effect, that is, from the IMF loan–GDP ratio in the previous 5-year period. In these columns, the estimation includes as instruments the actual current and lagged IMF loan–GDP ratios. Thus, these results do not take account of the endogeneity of IMF lending. Columns 3 and 4 have a parallel treatment for the IMF loan-participation rate. Columns 5 and 6 include simultaneously the IMF loan–GDP ratios and loan-participation rates.

Column 1 shows that the estimated coefficient of the contemporaneous IMF loan–GDP ratio is significantly negative. The estimated coefficient (−0.32, s.e. = 0.10) implies, if viewed causally, that an increase in IMF lending by 1% of GDP (about one standard deviation, see Table 8.2) lowers the growth rate contemporaneously by 0.32% point per year. However, our conjecture is that this strong inverse relation between IMF lending and growth reflects the endogeneity of the lending.

Column 2 adds a lagged effect of IMF lending. The estimated contemporaneous effect is similar to that in column 1. The lagged effect is also negative, but the estimated coefficient is not statistically significant, −0.08 (0.10).

Columns 3 and 4 show a similar pattern of results for the IMF loan-participation rate. In column 3, the estimated coefficient, −0.013 (0.005), implies, if viewed causally, that an increase in IMF program participation by 0.3 (about one standard deviation) lowers the growth rate by 0.38% point per year. Column 4 shows that the estimated lagged effect is again negative but statistically insignificant, −0.005 (0.005).

Column 5 shows that loan size and loan participation each contributes to the negative relation with economic growth. The estimated coefficient of the contemporaneous IMF loan–GDP ratio is again significantly negative: −0.26 (0.11). The estimated coefficient of the loan-participation rate is negative and marginally significant: −0.0079 (0.0049). Thus, there may be a threshold effect, whereby participation in IMF lending of any positive amount is negatively related to growth. Then, in addition, the larger the loan the lower the growth rate. Column 6 shows that the lagged effects are still not important.

8.4.2. *Controlling for the Endogeneity of IMF Loan Programs*

Column 1 of Table 8.7 uses our instrumental variables to control for the endogeneity of IMF lending. In these estimates, the actual values of IMF loan–GDP ratios and IMF loan-participation rates are dropped from the instrument lists. Instead, we include predicted values based on variations in the political-economy variables from the first-stage Tobit models in Tables 8.3 and 8.4. The political-economy variables are the logs of the IMF quota and staff shares, the logs of the fractions of U.N. votes along with the United States and the European countries, and the logs of the intensity of trade with the United States and the European countries.

The results in column 1 of Table 8.7 should be compared to those in column 1 of Table 8.6. With the use of the instrumental variables, the estimated coefficient on the contemporaneous IMF loan–GDP ratio becomes much smaller in magnitude and is now statistically insignificantly different from zero (−0.15, s.e. = 0.20). We conclude that the main reason for the significantly negative coefficient in column 1 of Table 8.6 is the endogeneity of the IMF lending — that is, lower economic growth increases the likely size of IMF loans within the contemporaneous 5-year period.

In column 2 of Table 8.7, which adds the lagged IMF loan–GDP ratio, the estimated coefficient on the contemporaneous value is −0.23 (0.19) and that on the lagged value is −0.13 (0.20). These coefficients are individually and jointly statistically insignificantly different from zero — the p-value for joint significance is 0.39. Therefore, when we use the political-economy variables as instruments, we cannot reject the hypothesis that the IMF loan–GDP ratio has no effect on economic growth.

The results for the IMF loan-participation rate, shown in columns 3 and 4 of Table 8.7, provide a different picture. In column 3, the estimated coefficient of the contemporaneous loan-participation rate is negative and statistically significant: −0.0233 (0.0091). The magnitude of this point esti-

Table 8.7. Regressions for per capita GDP growth (instruments based on political economy determinants of IMF loans)

	(1)	(2)	(3)	(4)	(5)	(6)
Log (per capita GDP)	−0.0273	−0.0277	−0.0309	−0.0332	−0.0310	0.0332
	(0.0040)	(0.0038)	(0.0039)	(0.0041)	(0.0040)	(0.0042)
Male upper-level schooling	0.0037	0.0036	0.0042	0.0042	0.0042	0.0042
	(0.0018)	(0.0018)	(0.0018)	(0.0018)	(0.0018)	(0.0018)
Log (life expectancy)	0.066	0.066	0.076	0.085	0.081	0.087
	(0.023)	(0.023)	(0.028)	(0.023)	(0.024)	(0.024)
Log (total fertility rate)	−0.0147	−0.0152	−0.0140	−0.0160	−0.0140	−0.0159
	(0.0063)	(0.0062)	(0.0060)	(0.0062)	(0.0062)	(0.0063)
Investment/GDP	0.063	0.065	0.066	0.064	0.066	0.065
	(0.034)	(0.033)	(0.033)	(0.034)	(0.034)	(0.034)
Government consumption/GDP	−0.103	−0.091	−0.099	−0.097	−0.102	−0.090
	(0.030)	(0.031)	(0.027)	(0.028)	(0.031)	(0.030)
Inflation rate	−0.0143	−0.0154	−0.0142	−0.0140	−0.0127	−0.0145
	(0.0087)	(0.0088)	(0.0083)	(0.0081)	(0.0086)	(0.0084)
Openness measure	0.0117	0.0113	0.0092	0.0087	0.0093	0.0080
	(0.0050)	(0.0049)	(0.0050)	(0.0050)	(0.0050)	(0.0050)
Rule-of-law index	0.0191	0.0179	0.0169	0.0153	0.0173	0.0146
	(0.0085)	(0.0085)	(0.0082)	(0.0085)	(0.0085)	(0.0087)
Democracy index	0.041	0.046	0.049	0.057	0.047	0.059
	(0.021)	(0.021)	(0.022)	(0.023)	(0.022)	(0.023)

Democracy index squared	−0.027	−0.031	−0.036	−0.043	−0.034	−0.045
	(0.020)	(0.020)	(0.020)	(0.021)	(0.020)	(0.021)
Growth rate of terms of trade	0.069	0.073	0.076	0.079	0.077	0.081
	(0.028)	(0.028)	(0.028)	(0.028)	(0.029)	(0.029)
Contemporaneous IMF loan	−0.153	−0.227	—	—	0.057	−0.001
	(0.198)	(0.192)			(0.230)	(0.209)
Lagged IMF loan	—	−0.129	—	—	—	−0.043
		(0.197)				(0.229)
Contemporaneous IMF participation	—	—	−0.0233	−0.0228	−0.0237	−0.0269
			(0.0091)	(0.0086)	(0.0101)	(0.0097)
Lagged IMF participation	—	—	—	−0.0102	—	−0.0081
				(0.0091)		(0.0100)
p-value	0.44	0.39	0.011	0.009	0.038	0.008

Notes: The specifications of the regressions in Table 8.7 are the same to those in Table 8.6, except that the instrument lists delete actual IMF loan–GDP ratios and loan participation rates, and then instead add the IMF loan–GDP ratio or loan-participation rate predicted from the Tobit models in column 6 of Tables 8.3 and 8.4, respectively. These predictions are based only on variation in our political-economy variables — the IMF quota and staff shares and the measures of a country's political and economic proximity to the United States and the major European countries. The other explanatory variables used in Tables 8.3 and 8.4 are set at their sample means.

mate is larger than before (−0.0126 in column 3, Table 8.6). Thus, in contrast to the results for loan size, the use of instruments to control for endogeneity raises the estimated magnitude of the negative effect of IMF loan participation on economic growth. The point estimate of −0.0233 implies that an increase in the loan-participation rate by 0.3 (about one standard deviation) lowers the rate of economic growth within the contemporaneous 5-year period by 0.7% per year. In column 10, the estimated lagged effect is also negative but not statistically significant: −0.0102 (0.0091).

Columns 5 and 6 of Table 8.7 show that the same conclusions emerge when IMF loan size and participation are included simultaneously. The contemporaneous loan-participation rate is significantly negative in columns 5 and 6, lagged participation is insignificant in column 6, and the loan–GDP ratios are insignificant in columns 5 and 6.

To sum up, our main conclusion is that participation in IMF loan programs has a significantly negative effect on economic growth over the contemporaneous 5-year period. This result holds up (in column 3 of Table 8.7) when we use reasonable instruments for participation in IMF loan programs. Thus, we think that this estimate reflects the negative effect of program participation on growth, rather than the negative effect of growth on the participation rate. We also found a strong inverse relation between economic growth and the contemporaneous IMF loan–GDP ratio when we did not instrument (in column 1, Table 8.6), but this relation disappears when we use our instruments (in column 1, Table 8.7). Thus, the negative effect of IMF lending programs on growth seems to involve the fact, rather than the amount, of IMF lending.[23]

8.4.3 *Robustness of the Results*

To check the robustness of our findings, we begin by considering other ways of forming the instruments for IMF loan–GDP ratios and loan-participation rates. One possibility is to base the predictions for IMF

[23] Another possible explanation for the results is that the IMF loan-participation rate looks more important because it is measured more accurately than the IMF loan–GDP ratio. This interpretation still leaves the conclusion that IMF loan programs are bad for economic growth.

loans and participation on variation in all of the first-stage regressors contained in Tables 8.3 and 8.4. (We did not proceed this way in Table 8.7 because we thought that some of these variations would be endogenous with respect to economic growth.) If we allow for the variation in all of the first-stage regressors, we get only a small change in the estimated contemporaneous effect on growth from IMF loan participation. The coefficient changes from −0.0233, s.e. = 0.0091 in column 3 of Table 8.7 to −0.0202, s.e. = 0.0072. The other coefficients reported for the IMF variables also do not change greatly.

Going in the other direction, we can base the predictions for IMF loans and participation on a more restricted set of variables. In particular, we can exclude the variations in trade intensity with the United States and the major European countries because of a concern that these variations might be endogenous with respect to economic growth. In this case, the estimated contemporaneous effect from IMF loan participation is −0.0234, s.e. = 0.0091, almost identical to that shown in Table 8.7, column 3. Again, the other coefficients for the IMF variables do not change a lot.

We can also redo the analysis using total IMF loans rather than the sub-set of stabilization loans. In this case, we find more substantial negative effects from IMF loan participation on economic growth. Using the instrumental procedure applied in Table 8.7, column 3, we get an estimated coefficient for contemporaneous IMF loan participation (in all forms of IMF lending) of −0.0309, s.e. = 0.0095. Moreover, we find that lagged participation now has a significantly negative effect on growth. In the specification that parallels column 4 of Table 8.7, we get coefficients of −0.0283, s.e. = 0.0088 on contemporaneous participation and −0.0202, s.e. = 0.0092 on 5-year lagged participation. The p-value for joint significance is 0.0003. Thus, the use of total IMF lending provides stronger evidence that participation in IMF loan programs retards economic growth.[24]

As mentioned before, total IMF lending consists of stabilization loans — studied in our main analysis — plus longer term aid to poor countries. Thus, our findings on total lending suggest that the IMF's

---

[24]When we apply our instrumental procedure to total IMF loans, we still lack evidence of significant effects of IMF loan–GDP ratios on economic growth.

longer term assistance to poor countries has an especially negative and long-lasting effect on economic growth. In future research, we plan to study in more detail the effects of this form of lending. This study would bear on the economic effects of bilateral foreign aid and of loan programs by the World Bank. These forms of assistance are analogous to the IMF's loans to poor countries.

Finally, since some East Asian countries are particularly under-represented on IMF quotas and staff, there may be a concern that our instrumental variables pick up effects akin to an East Asian dummy variable. That is, East Asian countries have low quotas and staff and are therefore relatively unlikely to participate in IMF loan programs — a situation that our results characterize as positive for economic growth. To check out these possibilities, we entered an East Asian dummy variable, along with dummy variables for sub-Saharan Africa and Latin America, directly into the growth regressions. In this case, the estimated coefficient of contemporaneous IMF loan participation (parallel to column 3 of Table 8.7) becomes −0.0209, s.e. = 0.0084. This estimate is similar to the one that we found in the absence of the regional dummy variables. Thus, the estimated negative effect of IMF loan participation on growth does not involve a proxying for presence in East Asia.

8.4.4 *Effects of IMF Loan Programs on Other Variables*

The standard growth regressions assess the effects of IMF loan programs on economic growth, while holding constant the other explanatory variables. But, IMF loan programs may influence economic growth indirectly by affecting some of the explanatory variables that we held constant in the systems shown in Tables 8.6 and 8.7. We now check, using our instrumental variables, whether IMF loan programs influence the explanatory variables. The variables considered are the investment ratio, inflation rate, government consumption ratio, international openness, and rule of law. The specifications follow the form of Table 8.7. Instead of the rate of economic growth, the dependent variable is now the ratio of investment to GDP, the inflation rate, or one of the other variables. In each case, we include the 5-year lag of the dependent variable as an explanatory variable. Following this procedure, we can estimate influences of IMF loan programs on the explanatory variables in Table 8.7. Then we can use these results, along with those for economic growth in Table 8.7, to estimate further indirect effects of IMF loan programs on economic growth. We provide here only a sketch of these results. The details are available on request from the authors.

Our instrumental estimates do not reveal statistically significant effects of current and lagged IMF loan–GDP ratios or IMF loan-participation rates on several explanatory variables included in Table 8.7. These variables are the ratio of investment to GDP, the inflation rate, the ratio of government consumption to GDP, and the international openness measure. We find marginally significant negative effects of the IMF loan–GDP ratio on the democracy variable. However, given the non-linear way that democracy affects economic growth, this influence does not translate into significant indirect effects of IMF lending on growth (for the typical country).

The only statistically significant indirect effect on economic growth that we have isolated involves the rule-of-law variable. We find a significantly negative effect of IMF loan participation on the rule of law. The 5-year lagged participation rate has the strongest negative influence. Through this channel, we find marginally significant negative effects of IMF loan participation on economic growth. Compared with the direct effects shown in column 4 of Table 8.7, −0.0228 for contemporaneous participation and −0.0102 for lagged participation, we get indirect contributions through the rule-of-law variable of −0.0013 and −0.0019, respectively. Thus, these indirect effects reinforce, but only to a minor extent, the direct negative growth effects of IMF loan participation found in Table 8.7.

The findings on rule of law are consistent with those reported for foreign aid by Svensson (2000) and Alesina and Weder (2002). These studies found that an increase in foreign aid led to a rise in official corruption. The rationale was that foreign aid fostered rent-seeking activities by interest groups and government officials. Analogous possibilities might arise for IMF lending.

8.5. Concluding Observations

We began with a political-economy approach to the IMF's lending decisions. Holding fixed a set of standard economic variables, the probability and size of IMF loans were larger when a country had a bigger quota, more nationals working on the professional staff, and more political and economic proximity to the United States and the major Western European countries. We measured political proximity by voting patterns in the U.N. General Assembly and economic proximity by bilateral trading volume. The set of political-economy variables was statistically significant overall for explaining the size of IMF loans, the frequency of participation in IMF lending programs, and the probability of IMF loan approval.

This political-economy analysis of IMF lending practices is of substantial interest for its own sake. More importantly for present purposes, the results allow us to create instrumental variables to use to estimate the effects of IMF loan programs on economic outcomes. If we do not instrument, we find that the IMF loan–GDP ratio has a substantial inverse relation to economic growth in the contemporaneous 5-year period. However, the instrumental estimates indicate that the contemporaneous relation of the IMF loan–GDP ratio to economic growth is statistically insignificant. Thus, the apparent inverse relation likely reflects the endogenous response of IMF lending to weak economic conditions. In contrast, the instrumental estimates still show that the IMF loan-participation rate has a statistically significant negative influence on economic growth. Therefore, greater IMF program participation, rather than larger loans, seems to retard growth.

We also analyzed the effects of IMF loan programs on other economic and political variables — investment, inflation, government consumption, international openness, democracy, and the rule of law. The most important result was a negative effect of IMF loan participation on the rule of law. This channel implies a further, negative indirect effect of IMF loan participation on economic growth.

Our results do not explain what the direct negative effects of IMF loan participation on economic growth represent. We know that these effects do not derive from channels involving the explanatory variables that were held constant in the growth regressions shown in Table 8.7. However, the IMF may matter through channels involving additional variables.

As an example, the moral hazard created by the potential for IMF loans may cause governments to spend excessively on public investment or transfers, which were not included in our government consumption variable. The IMF programs may also encourage inefficient behavior on the part of government bureaucrats. IMF conditionality may harm economies in ways not captured by the inflation rate and the other variables considered. For example, there may be effects on tax structure and regulations. Finally, IMF loan programs may influence the size and structure of private credit markets. These possibilities constitute promising avenues for future research.

Finally, we end with something of a puzzle. Our results suggest that participation in IMF loan programs is bad for the economy, at least bad for economic growth. Why then do host governments choose to participate in IMF loan programs?[25] Or, to put it more strongly, why do countries in politically favored positions — because of large quotas, large IMF staffs, and political and economic proximity to the IMF's main shareholding countries — use their clout to obtain IMF loans when these loans apparently retard economic growth? We have several possible answers. First, IMF lending may be bad for the economy but good for the governments and individual politicians who arrange the lending. Second, the IMF lending may lower real GDP but raise a country's income, which is augmented by the subsidy element of an IMF program. Third, IMF lending may lower growth in the short run but raise growth in the long run. However, our analysis fails to find the higher long-run growth at least over a 5-year horizon. Finally, there may be a time-consistency issue. A country may be better off if it can commit in advance not to participate in IMF programs (or, possibly, in foreign aid, and so on). However, ex post, the country may be better off accepting the assistance. We plan to address these issues in future research.

References

Alesina, A., Dollar, D., 2000. Who gives foreign aid to whom and why? *Journal of Economic Growth* 5, 33–64.

Alesina, A., Weder, B., 2002. Do corrupt governments receive less foreign aid? *American Economic Review* 92, 1126–1137.

[25] We could ask, similarly, why countries accept foreign aid or debt relief when it seems likely that these programs are also bad for economic growth.

Ball, R., Johnson, C., 1996. Political, economic, and humanitarian motivations for PL 480 food aid: Evidence from Africa. *Economic Development and Cultural Change* 44, 515–547.

Barro, R.J., Sala-i-Martin, X., 2004. *Economic Growth*, second ed. MIT Press, Cambridge, MA.

Bird, G., Rowlands, D., 2001. IMF lending: How is it affected by economic, political and institutional factors. *Journal of Policy Reform* 4, 243–270.

Blustein, P., 2001. *The Chastening: Inside the Crisis that Rocked the Global Financial System and Humbled the IMF*. Public Affairs, New York.

Bordo, M., James, H., 2000. The International Monetary Fund: Its present role in historical perspective, *NBER Working Paper* 7724.

Conway, P., 1994. IMF lending programs: Participation and impact. *Journal of Development Economics* 45, 365–391.

Dicks-Mireaux, L., Mecagni, M., Schadler, S., 2000. Evaluating the effect of IMF lending to low-income countries. *Journal of Development Economics* 61, 495–526.

Economist, 2002. The IMF: Doubts inside the barricades, September 28, 2002, pp. 67–69.

Goldstein, M., Montiel, P., 1986. Evaluating fund stabilization programs with multi-country data: Some methodological pitfalls. *IMF Staff Papers* 33, 304–344.

Haque, N., Kahn, M.S., 1998. Do IMF-supported programs work? A survey of the cross-country empirical evidence. *IMF Working Paper*, WP/98/169.

Heston, A., Summers, R., Aten, B., 2002. Penn World Tables Version 6.1. Center for International Comparisons at the University of Pennsylvania.

Hutchison, M., 2002. A Cure worse than the disease? Currency crises and the output costs of IMF-supported stabilization program. In: Dooley, M., Frankel, J. (Eds.), *Managing Currency Crises in Emerging Markets*. The University of Chicago Press, Chicago, pp. 321–354.

IMF, 1998. Financial organization and operations of the IMF, pamphlet series no. 45. International Monetary Fund, Washington D.C.

IMF, 2003. Annual Report 2003. International Monetary Fund, Washington D.C. Inter-University Consortium for Political and Social Research, 1992. United Nations roll call data, 1946–1985, computer file. University of Michigan, Ann Arbor.

Kahler, M., 1992. The United States and the International Monetary Fund: Declining influence or declining interests? In: Mingst, K., Karns, M. (Eds.), *The United States and Multinational Institutions*. Routledge, Boston.

Kahn, M.S., 1990. The macroeconomic effects of Fund-supported adjustment programs. *IMF Staff Papers* 37, 195–231.

Knight, M., Santaella, J., 1997. Economic determinants of IMF financial arrangements. *Journal of Development Economics* 54, 495–526.

Krueger, A., 1998. Whither the World Bank and the IMF? *Journal of Economic Literature* 30, 1983–2000.

Mussa, M., 2002. *Argentina and the Fund: From Triumph to Tragedy.* Institute for International Economics, Washington DC.

Przeworski, A., Vreeland, J.R., 2000. The effect of IMF programs on economic growth. *Journal of Development Economics* 62, 385–421.

Staiger, D., Stock, J.H., 1997. Instrumental variables regression with weak instruments. *Econometrica* 65, 557–586.

Stone, R.W., 2002. *Lending Credibility: The International Monetary Fund and the Post Communist Transition.* Princeton University Press, Princeton NJ.

Summers, R., Heston, A., 1991. The Penn World Table (Mark 5): An expanded set of international comparisons, 1950–1988. *Quarterly Journal of Economics* 106, 327–368.

Svensson, J., 2000. Foreign aid and rent-seeking. *Journal of International Economics* 51, 437–461.

Temple, J., 1999. The new growth evidence. *Journal of Economic Literature* 37, 112–156.

Thacker, S.C., 1999. The high politics of IMF lending. *World Politics* 52, 38–75.

Wooldridge, J.M., 2002. *Econometric Analysis of Cross Section and Panel Data.* MIT Press, Cambridge MA.

Chapter 9

Exchange Rate Regime and Monetary Policy Independence in East Asia*

9.1. Introduction

The choice of an appropriate exchange rate regime is one of the most fundamental policy issues in an open economy. Each regime has advantages and disadvantages. Fixing the exchange rate helps to reduce transaction costs and exchange rate risks. It can also work as a credible nominal anchor for monetary policy. However, a floating exchange rate regime allows the domestic monetary authority to pursue an independent monetary policy.

The issue of monetary independence under floating exchange regimes, however, has been controversial. In theory, under a credible pegged exchange rate regime with perfect capital mobility, domestic interest rates cannot be set independently. The 'impossible trinity' says that countries can pursue two of three options — fixed exchange rates, domestic monetary autonomy and capital mobility. Thus, without restrictions on capital flows, the monetary authority that wishes to retain domestic interest rate as a policy instrument must adopt a flexible exchange rate arrangement. But, even if formally floating, countries may not allow exchange rates to

---

* This chapter is co-authored with Chang Jin Kim and was originally published in *Pacific Economic Review*, Vol. 13, No. 2 (May 2008), pp. 155–170.
This research is supported by the International Centre for the Study of East Asian Development (ICSEAD). We also thank two anonymous referees for thoughtful comments on the previous version of the paper.

fluctuate beyond the magnitude that they can tolerate. This 'fear of floating' view argues that the floating countries actually behave much as they would in a pegged system by keeping domestic interest rates close to the base rate (Calvo & Reinhart 2002).

The purpose of this paper is to examine empirically the independence of monetary policy in the context of eight East Asian economies including Hong Kong, Indonesia, Japan, Korea, Malaysia, the Philippines, Singapore and Thailand. In the wake of the financial crisis, most of the crisis affected East Asian economies such as Indonesia, Korea, the Philippines and Thailand shifted their exchange rate regimes from de facto US dollar pegs to floating ones. However, critics say that East Asian central banks have intervened heavily in foreign exchange rate markets in order to prevent the appreciation of their currencies for the pursuit of an export-led growth strategy (Dooley *et al.* 2003). McKinnon and Schnabl (2004) argue that most East Asian economies have returned to pre-crisis 'soft-pegging' to the dollar system in a sense that they moderate volatility of exchange rate vis-à-vis the US dollar on a daily or weekly basis. If so, the de jure free-floating system may not have enabled East Asian countries to retain their monetary autonomy.

Recent empirical studies — including Frankel (1999), Hausman *et al.* (1999), Borensztein *et al.* (2001), Frankel *et al.* (2004), and Shambaugh (2004) — formally investigate whether the choice of the currency regime affects monetary policy independence in practice. These studies estimate the sensitivity of local interest rates to changes in international interest rates, examining whether local rates are less sensitive to base interest rate changes under floating exchange rate regimes than under pegged regimes. In principle, under floating regimes, changes in the exchange rates would absorb the effects of international interest rate shocks and thereby provide 'insulation' for domestic interest rates. The existing studies provide somewhat contrasting results. For instance, Frankel *et al.* (2004) show that pegged exchange rate regimes do not increase the responsiveness of local interest rates to the base country's interest rates. In contrast, Shambaugh (2004) find countries with fixed regimes follow the base country's interest rates more closely than countries with floating regimes.

In the case of East Asian countries, the previous studies also provide inconclusive evidence. Borensztein *et al.* (2001) show that interest rates in

Hong Kong, which has a fixed exchange rate regime, react much more to US interest rates than do interest rates in Singapore, which has a floating exchange rate regime. This finding is consistent with the theoretical prediction. In contrast, Frankel *et al.* (2004) find that in the long run local interest rates are adjusted fully to international interest rates regardless of which exchange rate regime is in place for Hong Kong, Singapore, Thailand and the Philippines. But, the research does not consider the change of regimes after the crisis explicitly.

Our methodology for empirical investigation follows closely those in the previous literature, but improves on them in several important aspects. First, our empirical techniques based on Kim (2004) allow for the possibility that there is a structural break in the sensitivity of local interest rates to changes in international interest rates over the sample period. Moreover, we consider the possibility that the timing of the actual structural break in the degree of monetary independence and the timing of de jure exchange regime change may not coincide. We actually estimate the timing of the potential structural break in monetary autonomy. In addition, our model takes account of the endogeneity of international interest rate shocks.

Our empirical results show that in East Asian countries such as Korea and Thailand, the sensitivity of local interest rates to US rates declined after they adopted floating exchange rate regimes. We also find that a floater such as Japan has had more monetary autonomy than a pegged economy such as Hong Kong. These empirical findings suggest that the choice of exchange rate regime is an important factor for the independence of monetary policy. Floating regimes appear to provide some degree of monetary independence after the East Asian crisis.

The next section discusses the exchange rate regimes in East Asia. Section 9.3 explains the empirical framework and methodology. Section 9.4 discusses the empirical results and Section 9.5 discusses the implications of the results and concludes.

9.2. Exchange Rate Regimes in East Asia

Since the financial crisis in 1997, exchange rate regimes have changed significantly in many East Asian economies. Appendix Table 9.A reports the official IMF classifications of currency regimes for East Asian countries. The IMF classifications rely exclusively on each government's own declaration of its exchange rate regime. But, there are often contradictions between the de jure exchange rate regime and the way the de facto exchange rate policy is conducted. For example, a regime that is classified as floating (independently or managed) might be in effect a peg with which the country defends its exchange rate within a narrow margin around a fixed rate. Recent studies such as Reinhart and Rogoff (2004) and Levy-Yeyati and Sturzenegger (2005) highlight the contrast between countries' official declarations concerning their exchange rate regimes and the way they actually conduct exchange rate policy. The de facto classifications of exchange rate regimes for East Asian countries by Reinhart and Rogoff (2004) are reported in Appendix Table 9.B.

Before the 1997 currency crisis, most East Asian economies opted to adopt de facto US dollar peg systems for their exchange rate arrangements. The Hong Kong dollar was fixed to the US dollar. The Chinese yuan was also pegged to the US dollar, but with occasional adjustments. The Thai baht and the Malaysian ringgit were similarly stable against the dollar, although these monetary authorities officially adopted a multiple currency basket system. Singapore, Korea and the Philippines also targeted their currencies to the dollar rather loosely by combining discretion and market pressure with varying weights. Indonesia was on a de facto crawling peg to the US dollar by sliding the rupiah by several percent per year to offset the inflation gap between home and abroad.

Most of the crisis affected Asian economies have shifted their exchange rate regimes from de facto US dollar pegs to floating ones.[1] The dollar peg system they adopted before the crisis was thought to have contributed to the loss of confidence in their currencies in 1997. On 2 July 1997, Thailand adopted a managed floating exchange rate regime in which the value of the baht was determined by market forces and the Bank of Thailand would intervene in the market only when it was necessary to avoid excessive volatilities. In July 1998, Thailand moved to substantially greater exchange

[1] See Baig (2001) for a detailed description of exchange rate behaviour in East Asia after the crisis.

rate flexibility. Indonesia, Korea and the Philippines have also moved to floating exchange rate systems since the crisis. In contrast, Malaysia started pegging to the US dollar in September 1998. Hong Kong and China have also kept their currencies pegged to the US dollar.

Both the de jure and de facto definitions seem to have reflected these exchange regime changes in the post-crisis Asian countries. In fact, for the whole period of the 1990s, they render quite similar classifications of the exchange rate regime for each of the East Asian economies, at least in terms of three broad categories — fixed, intermediate and floating regimes. One exception is the Philippines. The IMF based classification defines the country's exchange rate regime as floating since October 1984, while the de facto one categorizes it as intermediate before August 1995, fixed between September 1995 and June 1997 and intermediate from December 1997 until the present.

9.3. Empirical Test of Monetary Policy Independence

9.3.1. *Empirical Specification of the Model*

The basic estimation model can be specified as follows,

$$\Delta r_t^{lc} = \alpha + \beta \Delta r_{t-1}^{lc} + e_t, e_t \sim N\left(0, \sigma_t^2\right)$$

Here r_t^{lc} represents the domestic nominal interest rate in the local currency of each country at time t, α is a constant term, r_t^* is the international interest rate and β is the sensitivity of the local interest rate to foreign rates. The specification is derived easily from uncovered interest parity conditions with open capital markets.[2] This specification also takes into account the dynamic adjustment of local interest rates to international interest rate shocks. The speed of adjustment towards the long-run equilibrium is defined by $1 - \rho$ and the total adjustment of local interest rates to international interest rate is measured by $\beta/(1 - \rho)$. Due to a failure to reject the

[2] See Shambaugh (2004) for the derivation of the specification and the discussion of how omitted variables such as expected changes in the exchange rate and risk premium affect the estimate of β coefficient.

null of a unit root for each of the interest rates under investigation we specify the model in the first differenced interest rates. We test if the local and US interest rates are cointegrated and cannot reject the null hypothesis of no cointegration.

We estimate the specification for each of the East Asian economies. By comparing the values of β across economies, we can assess whether the choice of the currency regime influences monetary policy independence across East Asian economies. According to the conventional view, more flexible exchange rate regimes allow countries additional room to pursue their independent monetary policies. Therefore, the sensitivity of local interest rates to international base rates should increase with the rigidity of the exchange rate regime. In other words, for a given degree of capital mobility, real integration and other factors, we would expect $\beta_{fixed} > \beta_{intermediate} > \beta_{floating}$. In fact, in a fixed exchange rate regime with full capital mobility, β_{fixed} equals 1. In countries with similar exchange rate regimes, the sensitivity of the local interest rate to the foreign rate increases with the degree of capital account liberalization.[3]

In the model, the parameter ρ captures the country heterogeneity in adjustment speed. The adjustment of domestic interest rates to the movement of the foreign base rate may not occur immediately (within a month). Differences in capital market openness and financial market development can cause heterogeneity in the adjustment dynamics among countries, even under the same exchange rate regimes. We expect that, all other factors being equal, the adjustment speed would be higher (i.e. a lower value of ρ) in fixed exchange rate regimes.

Some important issues occur in the estimation of the basic specification. Previous studies such as Frankel *et al.* (2004) assume that the changes in the US interest rates are exogenous and contemporaneously uncorrelated with the error term. This assumption can be justified in the sense that the

[3] During the sample period, as discussed later, the degree of capital account liberalization has remained unchanged or increased in most East Asian economies except Indonesia and Malaysia. While the increased capital opening would render an upward bias in the estimate of monetary independence, β, we find the estimate of β has decreased in some East Asian countries. This seems to imply that the change in the exchange rate regime has played an important role independently. Unfortunately, we do not have monthly data on capital account liberalization to formally test this.

financial markets of East Asian countries are relatively smaller than the US financial market.

However, as Borensztein *et al.* (2001) point out, this assumption is unlikely to be true. Common shocks that affect both US and domestic interest rates cause a potential endogeneity problem. Because East Asian economies are highly linked to the USA in trade, their business cycles tend to become synchronized. Hence, shocks to US activities are likely to affect the outputs of Asian economies, leading to co-movements of US and domestic interest rates. In general, any variables omitted from the specification, which are correlated with the US interest rates, can cause biased estimates of the sensitivity parameter, β.

Another issue is that the sensitivity of local to international interest rates can also change over time within an economy where the exchange rate regime has changed during the sample period. Furthermore, the timing of actual structural breaks in the degree of monetary independence and the timing of exchange regime change may not coincide.

This paper adopts an estimation technique that accounts for the endogeneity problem. This technique also allows for the possibility of a structural break at an unknown time and attempts to actually estimate the timing of the potential structural break in monetary autonomy.

9.3.2. *The Regime Switching Model with Endogenous Explanatory Variables*

For our empirical investigation of the issue, we employ a version of the regime switching model with endogenous explanatory variables as introduced by Kim (2004). For simplicity of exposition, we focus on the estimation of the following benchmark model in which the parameters undergo a structural break at an unknown break point and one of the regressors $\left(\Delta r_t^*\right)$ is correlated with the disturbance term (ν_t),

$$r_t = \alpha_{D_t} + \beta_{D_t} \Delta r_t^* + \rho_{D_t} \Delta r_{t-1} + v_t \qquad (1)$$

$$\Delta r_t^* = z_t' d + \varepsilon_t \qquad (2)$$

and

$$\begin{bmatrix} \varepsilon_t \\ \nu_t \end{bmatrix} \sim i.i.d.N\left(\begin{pmatrix} 0 \\ 0 \end{pmatrix}, \begin{pmatrix} \sigma_{\varepsilon}^2 & \sigma_{\varepsilon\nu,D_t} \\ \sigma_{\varepsilon\nu,D_t} & \sigma_{\nu,D_t}^2 \end{pmatrix}\right), \tag{3}$$

where r_t is the domestic interest rate and r_t^* is the foreign interest rate. Equation (3) suggests that (Δr_t^*) and ν_t are correlated and z_t is a vector of instrumental variables that are correlated with (Δr_t^*) but not with ν_t.

The subscript D_t indicates that the parameters of interest undergo a structural break at an unknown break point τ, in the following way,

$$\begin{aligned} &\theta_{D_t} = \theta_0(1 - D_t) + \theta_1 D_t \quad \theta = \alpha, \beta, \rho, \sigma_{\nu}^2, or\, \sigma_{\varepsilon,y} \\ &D_t = \begin{cases} 1, if\ t \leq \tau \\ 0, otherwise \end{cases} \end{aligned} \tag{4}$$

To complete the model, we specify the dynamics of the latent variable D_t as

$$\Pr[D_t = 1 \mid D_{t-1} = 0] = 1 - q, \ \Pr[D_t = 0 \mid D_{t-1} = 1] = 0, \tag{5}$$

which is designed to capture a one-time permanent structural break in the sample at an unknown point in time. The estimate of the transition probability q provides an estimate of the break date, as the expected duration of a regime before a structural break is given by $1/(1 - q)$.

In the absence of endogeneity in the explanatory variable, the above regime switching model can be consistently estimated using the approach proposed by Hamilton (1989). In the above specification, however, Hamilton's approach is invalid as one of the regressors in Equation (1) is correlated with the disturbance term. As Kim (2004) suggests, one way to solve the problem is to transform the model in Equation (1) so that all the explanatory variables and disturbances are uncorrelated. To this end, we note that we can rewrite ε_t and ν_t as functions of two independent standard normal random variables,

$$\varepsilon_t = \sigma_{\varepsilon,D_t w_{it}}, \qquad w_{it} \sim i.i.d.N(0,1), \tag{6}$$

and

$$\begin{aligned} v_t &= b_{21,D_t} w_{1t} + b_{22,D_t} w_{2t} = \frac{b_{21,D_t}}{\sigma_{\varepsilon,D_t}} \varepsilon_t + b_{22,D_t} w_{2t}, \\ w_{2t} &\sim i.i.d.\, N(0,1), \end{aligned} \tag{7}$$

where w_{1t} and w_{2t} are uncorrelated. From Equations (2), (6) and (7), we rewrite the disturbance term in Equation (1) in the following way,

$$v_t = \frac{b_{21,D_t}}{\sigma_{\varepsilon,D_t}} \left(\Delta r_t^* - z_t' d\right) + b_{22,D_t} w_{2t} \tag{8}$$

Then, by substituting Equation (8) into Equation (1), we get

$$\begin{aligned} \Delta r_t &= \alpha_{D_t} + \beta_{D_t} \Delta r_t^* + \rho_{D_t} \Delta r_{t-1} + \gamma_{D_t} \left(\Delta r_t^* - z_t' d\right) + w_t, \\ w_t &\sim N\left(0, b_{22,D_t}^2\right), \end{aligned} \tag{1'}$$

where $\gamma_D = b_{21,Dt}/\sigma_{\varepsilon,Dt}$.

Equation (1′) is our transformed model in which all the explanatory variables are uncorrelated with the new disturbance term. As the transformed model does not suffer from an endogeneity problem, we now can consistently estimate the parameters of our interest by employing the maximum likelihood estimation based on the Hamilton filter.

In addition, as the disturbance terms in Equations (2) and (1′) are uncorrelated, we can employ a simple two step procedure described below.

1st Step: Estimation of the Equation (2) using ordinary least-squares regression (OLS). Estimate Equation (2): $\Delta r_t^* = z_t' \hat{d} + \widehat{\varepsilon_t}$ and get the residuals $\widehat{\varepsilon_t}$.

2nd Step: A maximum likelihood estimation (MLE) founded on the Hamilton filter. After replacing the $(\Delta r_t^* - z_t' \hat{d})$ with $\hat{\varepsilon}$, estimate the following equation using the MLE proposed by Hamilton (1989),

$$\begin{aligned} \Delta r_t &= \alpha_{D_t} + \beta_{D_t} \Delta r_t^* + \rho_{D_t} \Delta r_{t-1} + \gamma_{D_t} \widehat{\varepsilon_t} + w_t, \\ w_t &\sim N\left(0, b_{22,D_t}^2\right), \end{aligned} \tag{1''}$$

Note that the above two-step procedure is further justified by the following decomposition of the log likelihood function,

$$\begin{aligned}&\ln L\left(\alpha_0,\alpha_1,\beta_0,\beta_1,\rho_0,\rho_1,\gamma_0,\gamma_1,b_{22,0},b_{22,1},q\right)\\&=\sum\nolimits_{t=1}^{T} ln\left[\sum\nolimits_{d_t=0}^{1} f\left(\Delta r_t \mid \Delta r_t^*, I_{t-1}, D_t = d_t\right)\right]\\&\quad Pr\left(D_t = d_t \mid I_{t-1}\right)+\sum\nolimits_{t=1}^{T} ln\left[\left(\Delta r_t^* \mid I_{t-1}\right)\right]\end{aligned} \tag{9}$$

9.3.3. *Data*

Our basic source of interest rate data is the International Monetary Fund (IMF). We work with monthly data on 90-day local money market rates. As the international interest rate, we use the 90-day US treasury bill rate. We focus on the sample period of January 1987 to April 2002. The vector of instrumental variables includes the four lags of domestic and US interest rates $\left(\Delta r_{t-1}^{lc}, \Delta r_{t-2}^{lc}, \Delta r_{t-3}^{lc}, \Delta r_{t-4}^{lc}, \Delta r_{t-1}^{*}, \Delta r_{t-2}^{*}, \Delta r_{t-3}^{*}, \Delta r_{t-4}^{*}\right)$.

We focus on eight East Asian economies: Hong Kong, Indonesia, Japan, Korea, Malaysia, the Philippines, Singapore and Thailand. Among them, five countries — Indonesia, Korea, Malaysia, the Philippines and Thailand — adopted new exchange rate arrangements after the 1997 Asian crisis.

9.4. Empirical Results

9.4.1. *Testing for Structural Breaks*

Before we apply the model introduced in Section 3, we employ a test of a structural break for each country. We then apply the regime switching model to the sample of the countries for which the null hypothesis of no structural break is rejected. For the other countries for which no structural break is detected, we estimate the model without imposing any structural break during the sample period.

When the break date is unknown, the break date is a nuisance parameter that exists only under the alternative hypothesis but not under the null. The appearance of such a nuisance parameter implies that the Wald tests of equality of the coefficients do not have the standard asymptotic properties. We employ the test developed by Andrews (1993) in order to deal with the problem of the nuisance parameter. The test is based on the following equations,

$$\Delta r_t = \alpha_{D_t} + \beta_{D_t} \Delta r_t^* + \rho_{D_t} \Delta r_{t-1} + \gamma_{D_t} \hat{\varepsilon}_t + w_t, \quad w_t \sim N\left(0, \sigma_t^2\right), \tag{10}$$

$$\hat{\varepsilon}_t = \Delta r_t^* - z_t' \hat{d} \tag{11}$$

and

$$D_t = \begin{cases} 1, \text{ if } t \leq \tau \\ 0, \text{ otherwise} \end{cases} \tag{12}$$

where τ is the break that needs to be estimated under the alternative hypothesis. We define the function $W_T(\tau)$ as the Wald statistic for the null hypothesis of no structural break in the coefficients, for each possible value of the break date τ. With T being the sample size, we assume that τ lies in a range $\tau_1 < \tau < \tau_2$, where $\tau_j < c_j T$, $0 < c_1 < c_2 < 1$. Andrews (1993) shows the asymptotic properties of the statistic $\sup_{\tau_1 < \tau < \tau_2} W_T = sup W_T(\tau)$ and reports the asymptotic critical values.

For each possible break date τ, we estimate Equation (10) using the OLS methodology. We then calculate the Wald statistic for test of no structural break for given break date, $W_T(\tau)$, using the heteroscedasticity consistent variance–covariance matrix for the estimated coefficients. The estimated break date is the value of τ that maximizes $W_T(\tau)$ and the value of the maximized $W_t(\tau)$ is the sup $W_t(\tau)$ test statistic.

The results of the Wald test are reported in Table 9.1. Among the eight East Asian economies under investigation, structural breaks were significant at a 5% significance level for the three crisis hit countries: Korea, Malaysia and Thailand. The test results show that structural breaks were not significant in the other five economies; these include Hong Kong, Japan and Singapore which did not experience a currency crisis; the final two, Indonesia and the Philippines, did experience a currency crisis.

9.4.2. *Estimation of the Model for Countries with and without a Structural Break*

Once structural breaks have been identified for Korea, Thailand and Malaysia, we investigate the nature of structural breaks in the interest rate equations for these countries. In order to account for high uncertainty

Table 9.1. Tests of structural breaks

	Sup-W Statistic	Break Date
Japan	7.87	—
Singapore	6.32	—
Korea	26.10*	1997:12
Thailand	25.51*	1998:08
Philippines	4.85	—
Malaysia	26.36*	1997:08
Indonesia	10.04	—
Hong Kong	9.91	—

Notes: * Significant at the 5% significance level. The test of the structural break: Andrews's (1993) test with an unknown breakpoint. Sample period: 1987:1-2002:4 (monthly data). Break dates were searched over the period 1993:1-1999:12.

$$\Delta i_t = \alpha_{D_t} + \beta_{D_t} \Delta i_t^* + \gamma_{D_t} \widehat{w_t} + \rho_{D_t} \Delta i_{t-1} + e_t, \quad e_t \sim N\left(0, \sigma_{et}^2\right)$$

$$\Delta i_t^* = z_t' \delta + w_t, \quad w_t \sim N\left(0, \sigma_{wt}^2\right)$$

$$D_t = 0 \ for\ t = 1, 2, \ldots, \tau; \ D_t = 1 \ for\ t = \tau + 1, \ldots, T$$

$$\tau: break\ point$$

where the $\hat{w}$ term is a bias correction term and z_t is a vector of instrumental variables.

during the period of the currency crisis, we apply a modified version of the model (Equation (1″)) such as[4]

$$\Delta r_t = \alpha_{D_t} + \beta_{D_t} \Delta r_t^* + \rho_{D_t} \Delta r_{t-1} + \gamma_{D_t} \hat{\varepsilon}_t + w_t, \quad w_t \sim N\left(0, \sigma_t^2\right),$$

$$\sigma_t^2 = \begin{cases} \sigma_1^2, if\ t < 1997:05 \\ \sigma_2^2, if\ 1997:05 \le t \le 1998:10 \\ \sigma_3^2, if\ t \ge 1998:10 \end{cases} \tag{13}$$

[4] Testing for endogeneity is easily done by testing the significance of the γ parameter in Equation (13). As Tables 9.2 and 9.3 suggest, this parameter is statistically significant for Thailand and the Philippines, suggesting the importance of the endogeneity problem. Thus, for these countries, ignoring endogeneity would result in a bias in the coefficient estimates. For the other countries, we estimated the model by imposing $\gamma = 0$ and the results were qualitatively the same as in Table 9.2 and 9.3.

where the variance of the disturbance term is assumed to have different values for three subsample periods: the pre-crisis period from January 1987 to April 1997; the crisis period from May 1997 to September 1998; and the post-crisis period from October 1998 to April 2002.

Estimation results are reported in Table 9.2. For the three countries under investigation, structural breaks occurred during the crisis period: August 1997 for Malaysia, December 1997 for Korea and August 1998 for Thailand. For Korea and Thailand, there is a discernable difference in the coefficients describing the response of domestic interest rates to foreign interest rates before and after the structural breaks. For the period before

Table 9.2. Estimation of the model for countries with significant structural break

			α	β	γ	ρ
Korea	Before	Break	0.080	2.946*	−0.518	−0.062
			(0.109)	(1.018)	(1.248)	(0.052)
	After	Break	−0.038	−0.290	0.568	0.752*
			(0.066)	(0.426)	(0.482)	(0.073)
	Break Date:	1997:08				
Thailand	Before	Break	−0.067	3.514*	−4.884*	−0.282*
			(0.173)	(1.633)	(1.954)	(0.090)
	After	Break	−0.060	0.392	−0.521	0.379
			(0.170)	(1.073)	(1.265)	(0.127)
	Break Date:	1998:08				
Malaysia	Before	Break	0.059	0.152	0.245	0.174
			(0.036)	(0.322)	(0.394)	(0.138)
	After	Break	−0.171	*−0.427	0.879	−0.074
			(0.074)	(0.501)	(0.590)	(0.155)
	Break Date: 1997:10					

Notes: * Significant at a 5% significance level. Standard errors are in the parentheses.

$$\Delta i_t = \alpha_{D_t} + \beta_{D_t} \Delta i_t^* + \gamma_{D_t} \widehat{w_t} + \rho_{D_t} \Delta i_{t-1} + e_t, \quad e_t \sim N\left(0, \sigma_{et}^2\right)$$

$$\Delta i_t^* = z_t' \delta + w_t, \quad w_t \sim N\left(0, \sigma_{wt}^2\right)$$

$$\Pr\left(D_t = 0 | D_{t-1} = 0\right) = q, \qquad Pr\left(D_t = 1 | D_{t-1} = 1\right) = 1$$

$$\frac{1}{1-q} : \textit{estimated break date}$$

the structural break, the estimated β coefficients are 2.95 (standard error = 1.01) and 3.51 (SE = 1.63) for Korea and Thailand, respectively. The estimates are statistically significant and large in magnitude. Note that they are not statistically different from 1. This confirms the theory; in the pre-crisis period when the countries adopted intermediate or de facto pegged regimes, domestic interest rates responded closely to foreign rates. In contrast, the estimates of β become smaller, close to zero, and statistically insignificant in the post-crisis period when the economies chose to float: 0.290 (SE = 0.426) for Korea and 0.392 (SE = 1.073) for Thailand. We also find that the speed of adjustment $(1 - \rho)$ became smaller with floating exchange rates after the structural break.

For Malaysia, the result shows that the estimated β coefficients indicating the response of domestic interest rates to foreign rates are statistically insignificant in both periods. That is, in contrast to the conventional theory, local interest rates did not become more sensitive to foreign rates in Malaysia after it changed its exchange rate regime from an intermediate regime in the pre-crisis period to a fixed one in the post-crisis period. This must be related to the tight capital controls adopted by the Malaysian government after the crisis. Even in pegged exchange rate regimes the monetary policy can be used independently by imposing capital control measures. Since capital controls permit domestic rates to react less to foreign interest rate shocks, the estimates of β become statistically insignificant in the post-crisis period.[5] Figure 9.1 shows a measure of financial openness constructed by Chinn and Ito (2006). This is a composite index that reflects the various categories of restrictions on external accounts. It clearly shows that Malaysia has switched its policy toward the strengthening of capital controls since the crisis, contrasting with the experience of Korea and Thailand. Therefore, the nature of the structural break for Malaysia is somewhat different from that for Korea or Thailand. For Malaysia, the structural break mainly occurred in the intercept term of the interest rate equation.

[5] Shambaugh (2004) shows that in a large sample of countries, the response of local rates to foreign interest rates is smaller in pegs with capital controls than in pegs with open capital markets.

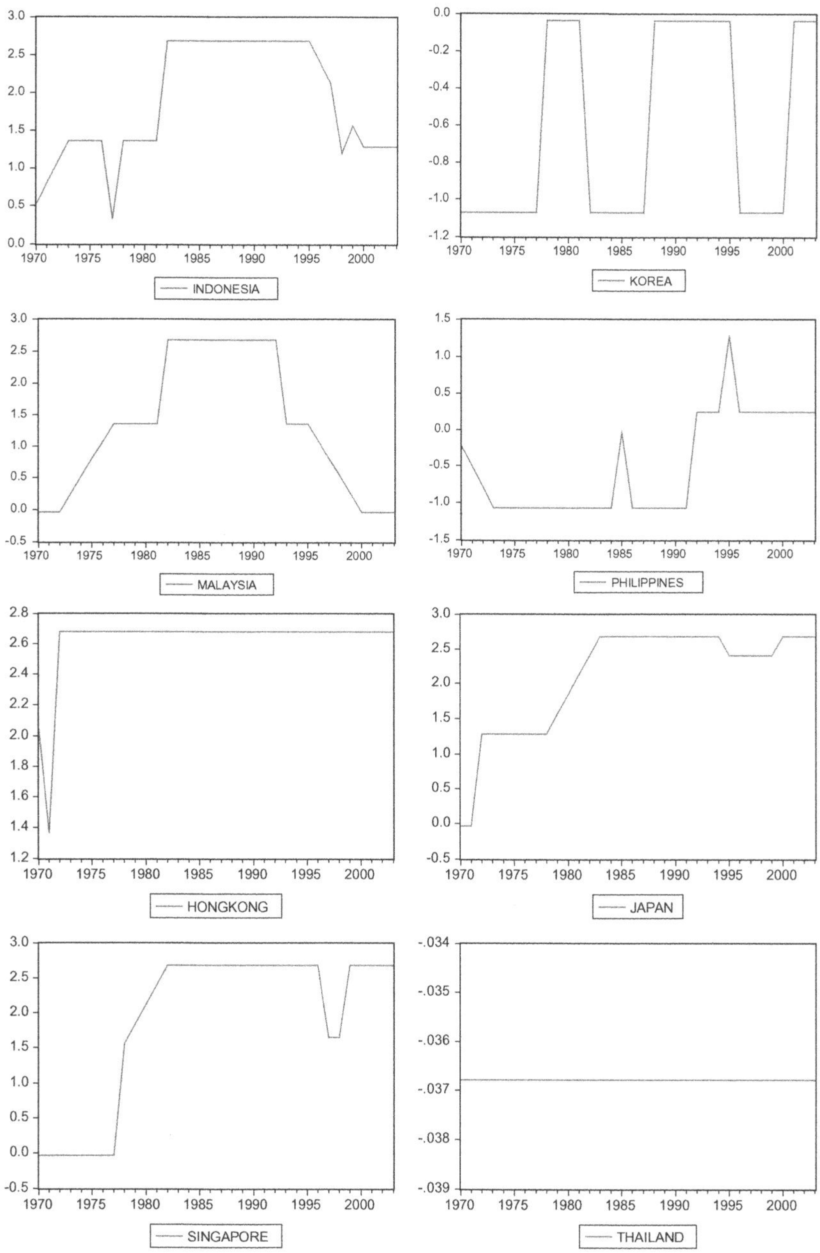

Figure 9.1 Capital market openness in East Asia

Note: The measure of capital market openness is a composite index that reflects various categories on the strictions on external accounts. A higher number indicates a higher level of openness.

Source: Chinn and Ito (2006).

Figure 9.1 shows that in most East Asian economies except Indonesia and Malaysia the process of capital account liberalization has remained unchanged or slightly accelerated over the 1990s (see also Kaminsky & Schmukler 2001). An increase in the degree of capital account liberalization would have reduced monetary independence, if the same exchange rate arrangements had been maintained before and after the structural break. Thus, the significant increase in monetary independence in Korea and Thailand after the structural break must have come from the adoption of more floating regimes, rather than the change in capital account liberalization.

Table 9.3 presents the estimation results for the other five countries — Hong Kong, Indonesia, Japan, Singapore and the Philippines — which did not have any structural break during the sample period. For this group, our main interest is in examining whether or not the β parameters have different values across the economies that adopted different exchange regimes.

The results are broadly consistent with conventional predictions: interest rates in Hong Kong, which has maintained a credible fixed exchange

Table 9.3. Estimation of the model for countries without significant structural break

	α	β	γ	ρ
Japan	−0.012	0.073	0.055	0.184*
	(0.013)	(0.113)	(0.131)	(0.072)
Singapore	−0.018	0.118	0.545	0.102
	(0.047)	(0.395)	(0.529)	(0.062)
Philippines	0.007	1.731*	−1.777*	0.215*
	(0.095)	(0.795)	(0.855)	(0.100)
Indonesia	0.003	0.043	0.357	−0.410
	(0.049)	(0.273)	(0.469)	(0.249)
Hong Kong	0.018	1.641*	−1.057	−0.326*
	(0.070)	(0.639)	(0.784)	(0.091)

Notes: * Significant at a 5% significance level. Standard errors are in the parentheses.

$$\Delta i_t = \alpha + \beta \Delta i_t^* + \gamma \widehat{w_t} + \rho \Delta i_{t-1} + e_t, \quad e_t \sim N\left(0, \sigma_{et}^2\right)$$

$$\Delta i_t^* = z_t' \delta + w_t, \quad w_t \sim N\left(0, \sigma_{wt}^2\right)$$

where the $\hat{w}$ term is a bias correction term and z_t is a vector of instrumental variables.

regime, were very responsive to US interest rates. The β estimate is positive and statistically significant (1.64, SE = 0.64). On the contrary, for Japan where the floating regime has been adopted, the domestic interest rates did not respond to US rates. The β estimate is 0.07 (SE = 0.11). The significant difference between Hong Kong and Japan — in the latter, capital market transactions were kept unrestricted over the sample period — indicates that exchange rate arrangement itself influences the degree of monetary independence significantly.

The estimates of the β coefficients vary a lot in intermediate regimes. In the Philippines, the local interest rates reacted closely to US rates. The β estimate is statistically significant (1.73, SE = 0.80). The Philippines has maintained de facto intermediate exchange rate regimes over the period except from September 1995 to June 1997 when the country kept a de facto fixed regime. For Singapore, the estimate of the response of local interest rates to US interest rates is small in magnitude and not statistically significantly different from zero (0.12, SE = 0.40). For Indonesia, which had adopted de facto intermediate exchange rate regimes before the crisis and then floated, the estimate of β is statistically insignificant too (0.043, SE = 0.273).

9.5. Conclusion

This paper examines whether the choice of an exchange rate arrangement influences monetary independence, focusing on the possible presence of structural breaks before and after the 1997 crisis in East Asian countries. For our empirical investigation of the issue, we employ a regime switching model with endogenous explanatory variables that allows for the endogeneity of foreign interest rate shocks and the possibility of a structural break in monetary autonomy at an unknown time.

We find that the sensitivity of local to international interest rates has declined in Korea and Thailand after they adopted floating exchange rate regimes. We also find that countries with established floating exchange rate regimes such as Japan had greater independence in monetary policy than pegged economies such as Hong Kong. These empirical findings suggest that greater exchange rate flexibility offers greater monetary independence for East Asian economies.

Our methodology assesses monetary autonomy based on the observed degree of co-movements of local and international interest rates. Thus, we do not specify the actual operation of monetary policy. The actual degree of monetary independence may differ from what is observed from the interest rates co-movements if the monetary authority's exercise of its monetary autonomy is influenced by other factors such as business cycle synchronization, exposure to international capital markets and political and institutional circumstances. Monetary policy would respond to local conditions such as output gap and inflation too. In subsequent research, we plan to include additional variables such as the domestic output gap, future expected inflation and measures of linkages with the base country in the domestic interest rate equation. Our estimation technique would be easily applicable to the extended model.

Appendix

Appendix Table 9. Exchange rate regimes in East Asia

A. De Jure Regime (Official Classification by the IMF)

	Period		Exchange Rate Regime Classification	
Country	**From**	**To**	**Narrow**	**Broad**
Philippines	Oct 81	Jun 82	Limited flexibility wrt US $	Intermediate
	Jul 82	Sep 84	Managed floating	
	Oct 84	Jan 02	Independently floating	Floating
Singapore	Jun 73	Jun 87	Limited flexibility wrt. a basket	Intermediate
	Jul 87	Jan 02	Managed floating	
Thailand	Jan 77	Feb 78	Peg to US$	Fixed
	Mar 78	Jun 81	Limited flexibility wrt a basket	Intermediate
	Jul 81	Mar 82	Managed floating	
	Apr 82	Oct 84	Limited flexibility wrt US$	
	Nov 84	Jun 97	Limited flexibility wrt a basket	
	Jul 97	Jun 98	Managed floating	
	Jul 98	Jan 02	Independently floating	Floating
Hong Kong	Jul 72	Oct 74	Peg to US$	Fixed
	Nov 74	Oct 83	Independently floating	Floating
	Oct 83	Jan 02	Peg to US$	Fixed
Indonesia	Nov 78	Jul 97	Managed floating	Intermediate
	Aug 97	Jan 02	Free floating	Floating
Japan	Dec 71	Jan 73	Peg to US$	Fixed
	Feb 73	Jan 02	Independently Floating	Floating
Korea	Aug 76	Jan 80	Peg to US$	Fixed
	Feb 80	Nov 97	Managed floating	Intermediate
	Dec 97	Jan 02	Independent floating	Floating

(*Continued*)

Appendix Table 9. (*Continued*)

A. De Jure Regime (Official Classification by the IMF)				
	Period		Exchange Rate Regime Classification	
Country	From	To	Narrow	Broad
Malaysia	Sep 75	Mar 93	Limited flexibility wrt US$	Intermediate
	Apr 93	Aug 98	Managed floating	
	Sep 98	Jan 02	Pegged to US$	Fixed
China	Mar 81	Jul 87	Pegged to a basket	Intermediate
	Aug 87	Aug 98	Managed floating	
	Sep 98	Jan 02	Limited flexibility wrt US$	Fixed

Notes: wrt, with respect to. This classification of exchange rate regimes is based on a quarterly database from the IMF which encompasses a total of ten regime categories, based on officially reported exchange arrangements.
Sources: Frankel *et al.* (2002) and IMF *Annual Report on Exchange Arrangements and Exchange Restriction.*

B. De Facto Regime				
	Period		Exchange Rate Regime Classification	
Country	From	To	Narrow	Broad
Philippines	Dec 72	Sep 83	De facto crawling band around US$	Intermediate
	Oct 83	Feb 85	Managed floating	
	Mar 85	Apr 92	De facto crawling peg to US$	
	May 92	Aug 95	De facto band around US$	
	Sep 95	Jun 97	De facto peg to US$	Fixed
	Jul 97	Dec 97	Freely floating/free falling*	Floating
	Dec 97	Dec 01	Managed floating	Intermediate
Singapore	Jun 72	Jun 73	Peg to US$	Fixed
	Jun 73	Nov 98	De facto moving band around US$	Intermediate
	Dec 98	Dec 01	Managed floating	

(*Continued*)

Appendix Table 9. (*Continued*)

B. De Facto Regime				
	Period		**Exchange Rate Regime Classification**	
Country	**From**	**To**	**Narrow**	**Broad**
Thailand	Oct 63	Mar 78	Peg to US$	Fixed
	Mar 78	Jul 97	De facto peg to US$	
	Jul 97	Jan 98	Freely floating/free falling*	Floating
	Jan 98	Dec 01	Managed floating	Intermediate
Hong Kong	Aug 62	Jul 72	Peg to pound sterling	Fixed
	Jul 72	Oct 83	De facto moving band around US$	Intermediate
	Oct 83	Dec 01	Currency board system/peg to US$	Fixed
Indonesia	Dec 70	Aug 71	Peg to US$	Fixed
	Aug 71	Oct 78	De facto crawling band to US$	Intermediate
	Nov 78	Jul 97	De facto crawling peg to US$	
	Aug 97	Jan 02	Freely floating/free falling*	Floating
	Apr 99	Dec 01	Freely floating	
Japan	Aug 71	Dec 71	Managed floating	Intermediate
	Dec 71	Jan 73	Bretton Woods basket peg	Fixed
	Feb 73	Nov 77	De facto moving band around US$	Intermediate
	Dec 77	Dec 01	Independently floating	Floating
Korea	May 74	Feb 80	Peg to US$	Fixed
	Feb 80	Nov 94	Pre-announced crawling band	Intermediate
	Nov 94	Nov 97	De facto crawling peg to US$	
	Dec 97	Jun 98	Freely falling*	Floating
	Jul 98	Dec 01	Freely floating	

(*Continued*)

Appendix Table 9. (*Continued*)

B. De Facto Regime

Country	Period		Exchange Rate Regime Classification	
	From	To	Narrow	Broad
Malaysia	Jun 67	Aug 75	Peg to pound sterling	Fixed
	Sep 75	Jul 97	Limited flexibility wrt US$	Intermediate
	Aug 97	Sep 98	Freely floating/free falling*	Floating
	Sep 98	Dec 01	Pegged arrangement	Fixed
China	Mar 81	Jul 92	Managed floating	Intermediate
	Aug 92	Jan 94	De facto crawling band around US$	
	Jan 94	Dec 01	De facto peg to US$	Fixed

Note: Free falling is a new separate category for countries whose 12-month rate of inflation is above 40%.
Source: Reinhart and Rogoff (2004).

References

Andrews, D.W.K., 1993. 'Tests for Parameter Instability and Structural Change with Unknown Change Point', *Econometrica* 61, 821–56.

Baig, T., 2001. 'Characterizing Exchange Rate Regimes in Post-crisis East Asia', *IMF Working Paper* No. 01/152.

Borensztein, E., Zettelmeyer J., Philippon T., 2001. 'Monetary Independence in Emerging Markets: Does the Exchange Rate Regime Make a Difference?', *IMF Working Paper* No. 01/1.

Calvo, G., Reinhart C., 2002. 'Fear of Floating', *Quarterly Journal of Economics* 117, 379–408.

Chinn, M., Ito H., 2006. 'What Matters for Financial Development? Capital Controls, Institutions, and Interactions', *Journal of Development Economics* 18, 163–92.

Dooley, M., Folkerts-Landau D., Garber P., 2003. 'An Essay on the Revived Bretton Woods System', NBER Working Paper no. 9971 (September).

Frankel, J.A., 1999. 'No Single Exchange Rate Regime Is Right for All Countries or at All Times', Graham Lecture, Princeton University, *Essays in International Finance* No. 215. Princeton: Princeton University Press.

Frankel, J.A., Schmukler S.L., Serven L., 2004. 'Global Transmission of Interest Rates: Monetary Independence and Currency Regime', *Journal of International Money and Finance* 23, 701–34.

Hamilton, J.D., 1989. 'A New Approach to the Economic Analysis of Nonstationary Time Series and the Business Cycle', *Econometrica* 57, 357–84.

Hausman, R., Panizza U., Stein E., 2001. 'Why Do Countries Float the Way They Float?', *Journal of Development Economics* 66, 387–414.

International Monetary Fund (various years) *Exchange Arrangements and Exchange Restrictions*. Washington: IMF.

Kaminsky, G., Schmukler S., 2008. 'Short-Run Pain, Long-Run Gain: Financial Liberalization and Stock Market Cycles,' forthcoming, Review of Finance.

Kim, C.-J., 2004. 'Markov-Switching Models with Endogenous Explanatory Variables', *Journal of Econometrics* 122, 127–36.

Levy-Yeyati, E., Sturzenegger F., 2005. 'Classifying Exchange Rate Regimes: Deeds and Words', *European Economic Review* 49, 1603–35.

McKinnon and Schnabl, 2004. 'The Return to Soft Dollar Pegging in East Asia: Mitigating Conflicted Virtue,' *International Finance*, Vol. 7, No. 2, 160–201.

Reinhart, C.M., Rogoff K.S., 2004. 'The Modern History of Exchange Rate Arrangements: A Reinterpretation', *Quarterly Journal of Economics* 119, 1–48.

Shambaugh, J.C., 2004. 'The Effect of Fixed Exchange Rates on Monetary Policy', *Quarterly Journal of Economics* 119, 301–52.

Part 3

Global Financial Crisis and Challenges to Asia's Sustained Growth

Chapter 10

Crises in Asia: Historical Perspectives and Implications*

10.1. Introduction

The global financial crisis that originated in the United States (US) subprime mortgage market is now pummeling the real economy. As household and corporate sectors cut spending on tightened credit and reduced wealth, global recession has become almost inevitable. Output in all major industrial countries is expected to fall in 2009. The recession will likely be deeper and more prolonged than originally expected, as it will take time for the global financial system to stabilize and government expansionary policies to take effect.

The global crisis has spread to Asia, affecting real economies and financial markets throughout the region. The global financial turmoil and economic slowdown have reversed capital flows and stunted export demand. Asia's output growth is decelerating given its close ties to the global economy through both trade and financial links. A more protracted recession and high volatility in G[1] financial markets would have severe spillover effects on Asia's economic outlook.

---

* Reprinted from *Journal of Asian Economics*, Vol. 21, No. 3, Kiseok Hong, Jong-Wha Lee and Hsiao Chink Tang, Crises in Asia: Historical Perspectives and Implications, pp. 265–279, Copyright (2010), with permission from Elsevier.

The authors are grateful to the participants in ADB–ADBI Joint Workshop on Global Imbalances and Crisis: Chartering Asia's Recovery held 16 February 2009 in Manila for helpful comments, and to Marthe Hinojales for able research assistance. The views expressed are the authors' and do not necessarily reflect the views and policies of ADB, its Board of Directors, or the governments ADB members represent.

[1] G3 includes European Union, Japan, and US.

The purpose of this paper is to empirically examine historical crisis episodes of Asian economies to derive implications of the current global crisis for Asia. We first investigate basic features of crisis episodes for 21 developing Asian economies during 1961–2007, providing stylized facts on movements of key macroeconomic and financial variables around crisis episodes. We then consider how Asia's crisis episodes link to global crises to derive implications of the current global crisis on Asia.

There have been several studies assessing how the current global crisis will compare with other past crises. Claessens, Kose, and Terrones (2008) provide extensive cross-country empirical analysis of past recessions that coincide with credit crunches, house price busts, and equity price busts. Lall, Cardarelli, and Elekdag (2008) also provide a similar analysis, but focus on the impacts of financial stress in banking, securities, and foreign exchange markets on economic activity. Reinhart and Rogoff (2008) focus on 18 bank-centered financial crises in industrialized countries since World War II. Barro and Ursua (2008) also look at long-term historical data to analyze major economic crises. We have not seen any systematic empirical research focusing on the stylized facts of economic and financial crises in developing Asian economies, and the links of these crises with global financial crises and recessions. The closest is a recent study by IMF (2009), which among others, also find recessions accompanied by financial stress (banking stress in particular) are often longer and deeper.

The paper is organized as follows: Section 10.2 describes the data and methodology in identifying crises; Section 10.3 provides various stylized facts on macroeconomic and financial crises in Asia; Section 10.4 examines impacts of the US/global crises on Asia, and Section 10.5 concludes the paper.

10.2. Data and Methodology

10.2.1. *Data*

In our analysis, we mainly investigate 21 developing Asian economies: the 10 Association of South East Asian Nations;[2] Bangladesh; People's

[2] Includes Brunei Darussalam, Cambodia, Indonesia, Lao People's Democratic Republic (Lao PDR), Malaysia, Myanmar, Philippines, Singapore, Thailand, and Viet Nam.

Republic of China (PRC); Hong Kong, China; India; Kazakhstan; Republic of Korea (Korea); Kyrgyz Republic; Pakistan; Papua New Guinea; Sri Lanka; and Uzbekistan. We exclude the Middle East and countries with low data availability. The sample period is from 1961 through 2007 at its longest and substantially shorter in many cases. For example, gross domestic product (GDP) growth rates for Cambodia are available for 19 years; 17 years for Kazakhstan; and 20 years for Uzbekistan. We use unbalanced panel data to include as many observations as possible.

To examine the impact of global shocks on Asian economies, we define the global economy as represented by 21 industrial, mostly Organisation for Economic Co-operation and Development (OECD) countries, including Australia, Austria, Belgium, Canada, Denmark, Finland, France, Germany, Greece, Ireland, Italy, Japan, Netherlands, New Zealand, Norway, Portugal, Spain, Sweden, Switzerland, United Kingdom, and US. This is the reference set for our comparative analysis with Asian economies.

Among key variables, GDP and other variables from national income accounts are considered at the annual frequency because, for most Asian economies in our sample, national income accounts data are available quarterly for only short periods of time. For prices and financial variables such as the consumer price index (CPI), domestic credit, and stock prices, we use quarterly series. When we need to combine the two sets of data, we annualize quarterly data. National income accounts data are mostly from the World Bank's World Development Indicators and most of our financial variables are from the International Monetary Fund's *International Financial Statistics.*

10.2.2. *Definition of Recession*

We define recessions based on "classical" business cycles, which dates turning points (peaks and troughs) in the level of economic activity to separate periods of relative prosperity and relative decline. The concept of "classical" business cycles was formalized by Burns and Mitchell (1946) and later implemented in algorithm by Bry and Boschan (1971) for monthly series and by Harding and Pagan (2002) for quarterly series. As our data are either annual or quarterly, we first need to consider the Harding and Pagan algorithm where for a quarterly series x, period t is defined as a trough if $x_t < x_{t+k}$, for k = −1, −2, 1, 2; and a peak if $x_t > x_{t+k}$, for k = −1, −2, 1, 2. A recession is naturally defined as the period immediately after a peak to the following trough. A censoring rule is also required to ensure that each cycle and each of its phases has a minimum duration. Harding and Pagan recommend setting the minimum duration for a single phase at two quarters and the minimum duration for a complete cycle at five quarters.

However, as mentioned above, we use annual, not quarterly, series for GDP and other national income account variables and thus modify Harding and Pagan's definition accordingly. When applied to annual series, their rule will imply that, for an annual series x, period t should be defined as a trough if $x_t < x_{t+k}$, for k = −1 and 1, and a peak if $x_t > x_{t+k}$, for k = −1 and 1. In other words, any period (year) of negative growth can be regarded as a recession. We apply this rule to our annual real GDP series to date recession periods. Watson (1994) uses the same reasoning in his analysis of annual data. It is clear that we do not need a separate censoring rule for annual series, because a complete cycle (from peak to peak) will always take at least 2 years, which is greater than five quarters.

We also follow Harding and Pagan in defining duration, amplitude, and cumulative loss of a recession. The duration is simply the length (number of years) of a recession, while the amplitude measures the peak-to-trough fall in the logarithmic value of the series. The cumulative loss is the sum of all losses from the peak value during the recession. Amplitude and cumulative loss both measure the severity of a recession. Fig. 10.1 provides an example. If the series in the figure represents the logarithm of GDP, the duration is given by 4 years (b), the amplitude 0.9 (a), and the cumulative loss 2.5 (= 0.4 + 0.5 + 0.7 + 0.9).

We follow Claessens *et al.* (2008) and define severe recessions as those with the amplitude belonging to the top quartile of the distribution.

10.2.3. *Definitions of Financial Downturns*

Downturns in the financial market, i.e., credit contractions and equity price declines, are defined the same way: we examine domestic credit and stock price levels to determine peaks and troughs in each series. Similar to

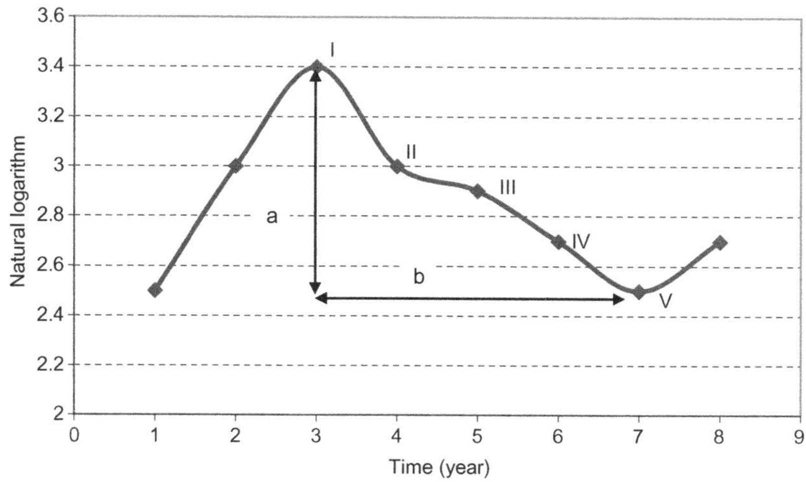

Figure 10.1 Definition of recession, duration, amplitude and cumulative losses
Note: Amplitude is the height of "a" and duration, the length of "b". Cumulative loss is the sum (on the y-axis) of I-II, I-III, I-IV and I-V.

recessions, credit contractions and stock price declines are defined as time periods between a peak and the following trough. We deflate both domestic credit and stock prices by the CPI before dating peaks and troughs. As both financial variables are available quarterly, we can directly use the Gauss algorithm provided by Harding and Pagan. Once peaks and troughs are dated, the duration, amplitude, and cumulative loss can be defined the same way as before. Also, we pick those severe downturns with the amplitude belonging to the top quartile of the distribution for each credit contraction and stock price decline, considering them as credit crunches and stock price busts, respectively.

When changing the frequency of our indicator series from quarterly to annual, we classify a whole year with any one or more quarters of contraction as a contractionary year. The duration, amplitude, and cumulative loss can be annualized in the same manner. We assign quarterly measures of the duration, amplitude, and cumulative loss to whichever year the quarter belongs. For example, if there is a trough in the second quarter of 1990, the duration, amplitude, and cumulative loss of that period are considered as the corresponding measures for all of 1990.

10.3. Stylized Facts of Economic Crises in Asia

10.3.1. *Descriptive Statistics on Recessions*

Using the above dating methodology, we identify recessions, credit contractions, and stock price declines. Table 10.1 offers some descriptive statistics on recession episodes for each Asian economy in our sample. Claessens *et al.* (2008) provide an almost identical table for OECD countries. The first column shows the proportion of time in recession that is defined as the number of recessionary years divided by the total number of years for which GDP data are available. The second column shows the average length (measured in number of years) of a recession episode. The third and the fourth columns indicate the severity of recessions. As shown in the table, Asian countries on average were in recession about 13% of the time, and each recession lasted about 1.6 years. The accumulated decrease in GDP during a recession (cumulative loss) was about 12%. These measures are lower for emerging Asian economies (including PRC, Hong Kong, China, India, Indonesia, Korea, Malaysia, Philippines, Singapore, and Thailand) than for the other developing Asian economies. Since there are a few outlier observations, we provide the median values as well, in parentheses. As expected, the median values for the frequency, duration and severity of recessions are smaller than the corresponding average values.

Also reported in the table are characteristics of severe recessions. According to the table, a severe recession lasts for about 2.3 years on average and is associated with cumulative GDP loss of about 35%. This result is roughly consistent with Barro and Ursua (2008) for GDP disasters based on much longer historical data. As Table 10.6 in Section 4 shows, the average duration of a GDP disaster is 2.9 years and the cumulative loss is about 25%.[3]

The same statistics are computed for OECD economies in order to provide a reference point for comparison. We do not simply cite the results from Claessens *et al.* (2008) because their results are derived from

[3]With wartime periods excluded from the Barro and Ursua (2008) sample, the duration is 2.35 years and the cumulative loss is 19.36%. When Central Asian countries (Kazakhstan, Kyrgyz Republic, and Uzbekistan) are excluded from our sample, the duration of severe recessions becomes 1.75 years and the cumulative loss 16.75%.

Table 10.1. Descriptive statistics on recessions

Country	All Recessions				Severe Recessions		
	Proportion of Time in Recession (%)	Duration (Years)	Amplitude (%)	Cumulative Loss (%)	Duration (Years)	Amplitude (%)	Cumulative Loss (%)
Bangladesh	10.64	1.25	6.47	7.84	2.0	19.45	24.93
Brunei Darussalam	23.33	1.4	7.44	9.14	2.0	26.82	33.82
Cambodia	—	—	—	—	—	—	—
People's Rep. of China	10.64	1.5	5.7	8.55	2.0	9.8	15.5
Hong Kong, China	2.13	1.0	6.03	6.03	—	—	—
India	8.51	1.33	2.74	3.55	—	—	—
Indonesia	4.26	1.0	7.69	7.69	1.0	13.13	13.13
Kazakhstan	35.29	1.0	1.9	1.9	—	—	—
Rep. of Korea	4.26	1.0	4.17	4.17	1.0	6.85	6.85
Kyrgyz Republic	33.33	2.33	20.97	62.33	5.0	62.71	186.78
Lao PDR	7.41	2.0	3.64	5.15	—	—	—
Malaysia	4.26	1.0	4.24	4.24	1.0	7.36	7.36
Myanmar	17.78	1.6	6.94	9.14	2.5	13.6	19.08
Pakistan	—	—	—	—	—	—	—
Papua New Guinea	27.66	1.86	3.63	5.57	2.0	7.67	11.58

(*Continued*)

Table 10.1. (*Continued*)

Country	All Recessions: Proportion of Time in Recession (%)	All Recessions: Duration (Years)	All Recessions: Amplitude (%)	All Recessions: Cumulative Loss (%)	Severe Recessions: Duration (Years)	Severe Recessions: Amplitude (%)	Severe Recessions: Cumulative Loss (%)
Philippines	8.51	1.33	5.26	7.7	2.0	14.63	21.95
Singapore	8.51	1.0	1.31	1.31	—	—	—
Sri Lanka	4.26	1.0	0.98	0.98	—	—	—
Thailand	4.26	2.0	11.88	13.25	2.0	11.88	13.25
Uzbekistan	25.0	5.0	20.09	65.46	5.0	20.09	65.46
Viet Nam	—	—	—	—	—	—	—
Emerging Asia	6.15	1.24	5.45	6.28	1.60	10.41	13.21
	(4.26)	(1.00)	(5.26)	(6.03)	(1.40)	(9.38)	(10.43)
Other Asia	20.52	1.94	8.01	18.61	2.98	25.34	56.75
	(23.33)	(1.60)	(6.45)	(7.84)	(2.25)	(23.14)	(29.38)
Asia	13.33	1.59	6.73	12.44	2.29	17.83	34.97
	(8.51)	(1.33)	(5.48)	(6.86)	(2.00)	(11.94)	(17.32)
United States	10.64	1.25	0.76	0.88	—	—	—
G7	7.29	1.13	1.28	1.46	1.50	3.01	4.04
OECD	8.52	1.32	1.73	2.58	2.07	4.83	8.77

Notes: — refers to nonavailability of data or such event. Median values are within parentheses; Severe recessions refer to recession episodes (including all economies) with the amplitude belonging to the top quartile of the distribution. The cutoff value of the amplitude in classifying severe recessions is 6.85. Emerging Asia refers to PRC, Hong Kong, China, India, Indonesia, Korea, Malaysia, Philippines, Singapore, and Thailand.

quarterly data and thus are not directly comparable to our results. When using annual data, some of the GDP fluctuations at the quarterly frequency are likely to be undetected or smoothed out. Indeed, a comparison between our statistics for OECD countries in Table 10.1 with the statistics by Claessens *et al.* (2008) confirms that our recessions are less frequent and less severe than recessions defined from quarterly data. The proportion of time in recession and the amplitude of a recession for OECD countries reported in Claessens *et al.* (2008) are 11% and 2.63%, respectively.

In our view, the most important pattern in Table 10.1 is the systematic difference between Asian economies and OECD countries in the duration and severity of recessions. While there is substantial diversity in Asia, the table shows that on average recessions are more often, longer lasting and more severe in Asian economies than in OECD countries. Clearly, Central Asian countries such as Kazakhstan, Kyrgyz Republic, and Uzbekistan exhibit extraordinary recession characteristics. The difference between Asia and OECD, however, is not solely driven by these countries. Even when these Central Asian economies are excluded from the sample, recessions still appear to be more severe in Asia: the duration is 1.35 years, the amplitude 5.21%, and the cumulative loss 6.29%. This suggests that Asian economies were more vulnerable to negative shocks. This pattern is consistent with previous findings on business cycles of developing economies. Mendoza (1995), Agenor *et al.* (1999), Neumeyer and Perry (2005), Aguiar and Gopinath (2007) commonly find that GDP volatility is greater in developing economies than in developed ones. One difference is that these studies consider not only recessions but also expansions. Our paper considers only recessions as we are concentrating on crisis episodes.

10.3.2. *Descriptive Statistics on Credit Contractions and Stock Price Busts*

We compute the same statistics for credit contractions and equity price declines for each economy, and report the results in Table 10.2. As credit contractions and equity price declines are identified from quarterly data, the duration here refers to the number of quarters between a peak and the following trough. As can be expected from the volatile nature of the financial variables, both credit and equity-price cycles exhibit a greater

Table 10.2. Descriptive statistics on financial downturns

	All Credit Contractions				Credit Crunches		
Country	Proportion of Time in Credit Contraction (%)	Duration (Quarter)	Amplitude (%)	Cumulative Loss (%)	Duration (Quarter)	Amplitude (%)	Cumulative Loss (%)
Bangladesh	17.05	5.0	5.66	17.36	—	—	—
Brunei Darussalam	62.07	9.0	72.46	340.93	9.0	72.46	340.93
Cambodia	19.64	5.5	18.07	51.68	7.0	22.05	67.94
People's Rep. of China	15.56	4.0	8.04	26.86	—	—	—
Hong Kong	40.00	5.33	11.38	40.29	7.0	26.10	100.34
India	16.15	3.5	7.61	17.37	—	—	—
Indonesia	21.29	4.13	36.79	82.20	3.67	77.14	154.82
Kazakhstan	—	—	—	—	—	—	—
Rep. of Korea	7.14	2.4	2.34	4.56			
Kyrgyz Republic	30.00	4.33	32.14	94.64	4.33	32.14	94.64
Lao PDR	46.15	4.50	29.50	71.67	5.67	43.48	114.10
Malaysia	16.67	3.00	5.38	12.77			
Myanmar	35.66	4.44	20.52	68.70	6.0	36.61	131.05
Pakistan	20.83	4.44	10.91	29.84	7.0	55.23	171.79
Papua New Guinea	43.80	9.33	27.79	230.52	12.75	38.18	339.98
Philippines	32.81	5.17	18.78	114.97	11.5	66.94	547.99

Singapore	22.62	3.45	11.78	29.42	2.0	35.51	52.95
Sri Lanka	22.40	3.58	11.52	26.68	4.0	31.20	52.56
Thailand	18.75	8.33	18.19	138.61	18.0	32.37	374.99
Uzbekistan	—	—	—	—	—	—	—
Viet Nam	7.69	2.0	2.01	3.5	—	—	—
Emerging Asia	21.22	4.36	13.36	51.90	8.43	47.61	246.22
	(18.75)	(4.00)	(11.38)	(29.42)	(7.00)	(35.51)	(154.82)
Other Asia	30.15	5.21	23.06	93.55	6.97	41.42	164.12
	(26.32)	(4.47)	(19.30)	(60.19)	(6.50)	(37.40)	(122.58)
Asia	26.12	4.81	18.47	73.82	7.53	43.80	195.70
	(21.84)	(4.44)	(11.78)	(40.29)	(7.00)	(36.61)	(131.05)
United States	21.35	6.83	4.02	22.49	—	—	—
G7	17.29	4.50	5.50	21.84	7.83	20.07	88.83
OECD	17.42	4.36	7.31	27.64	7.01	19.27	79.07

(*Continued*)

Table 10.2. *(Continued)*

	All Stock Price Declines				Stock Price Busts		
Country	Proportion of Time in Stock Price Decline (%)	Duration (Quarter)	Amplitude (%)	Cumulative Loss (%)	Duration (Quarter)	Amplitude (%)	Cumulative Loss (%)
Bangladesh	51.25	6.0	66.67	542.44	13.0	191.73	1987.53
Brunei Darussalam	—	—	—	—	—	—	—
Cambodia	—	—	—	—	—	—	—
People's Rep. of China	42.25	5.4	53.82	208.76	8.0	125.94	468.25
Hong Kong	32.14	4.33	43.38	126.65	4.0	70.16	190.97
India	47.40	7.0	37.60	214.51	17.0	74.56	784.91
Indonesia	40.00	5.0	61.07	227.11	7.0	128.15	461.08
Kazakhstan	—	—	—	—	—	—	—
Rep. of Korea	54.17	7.22	51.79	283.09	13.0	106.72	648.31
Kyrgyz Republic	—	—	—	—	—	—	—
Lao PDR	—	—	—	—	—	—	—
Malaysia	38.39	4.78	48.14	149.38	7.33	92.22	330.12
Myanmar	—						

Pakistan	49.47	7.0	39.39	230.57	19.0	153.24	1542.45
Papua New Guinea	35.71	2.33	12.89	26.03	—	—	—
Philippines	58.33	10.2	98.80	740.86	12.83	133.24	1088.41
Singapore	55.43	9.2	39.68	213.87	10.0	82.65	279.09
Sri Lanka	62.79	13.2	78.07	824.85	22.0	143.40	1610.69
Thailand	43.18	3.5	23.28	56.27	—	—	—
Uzbekistan	—	—	—	—	—	—	—
Viet Nam	57.14	4.0	13.76	38.49	—	—	—
Emerging Asia	45.70	6.29	50.84	246.72	9.90	101.70	531.39
	(43.18)	(5.40)	(48.14)	(213.87)	(9.00)	(99.47)	(464.66)
Other Asia	51.27	6.51	42.16	332.48	18.00	162.79	1713.56
	(51.25)	(6.00)	(39.39)	(230.57)	(19.00)	(153.24)	(1610.69)
Asia	47.69	6.37	47.74	277.35	12.11	118.36	853.8
	(48.43)	(5.70)	(45.76)	(214.19)	(12.83)	(125.94)	(648.31)
United States	38.54	5.21	24.22	84.27	8.0	65.20	215.17
G7	42.85	5.88	33.55	159.79	9.96	84.79	412.63
OECD	43.02	6.64	38.47	207.66	11.89	89.49	613.44

Notes: — refers to nonavailability of data or such event. Median values are within parentheses; Credit crunches refer to credit contractions (including all economies) with the amplitude belonging to the top quartile of the distribution. Similarly, stock price busts refer to stock price declines with the amplitude belonging to the top quartile of the distribution. The cutoff values of the amplitude in classifying credit crunches and stock price busts are 21.09 and 67.98, respectively. Emerging Asia refers to PRC, Hong Kong, China, India, Indonesia, Korea, Malaysia, the Philippines, Singapore, and Thailand.

probability of a downturn than the GDP cycle, although the duration, when translated to the annual frequency, is similar to that of GDP recessions. Also, the peak-to-trough amplitude and the cumulative loss are much greater than those from GDP series.

We examine severe financial downturns separately, though the same way we did for recessions in Table 10.1. Credit contractions and stock price declines with the amplitude belonging in the top quartile of the corresponding distributions are regarded as credit crunches and stock price busts, respectively. According to the last three columns in Table 10.2, credit crunches and stock price busts involve not only greater losses but also longer durations.

Similar to Table 10.1, Table 10.2 shows that there exist systematic differences between Asian developing countries and OECD countries. Downturns in the financial market are more frequent, longer lasting, and more severe among Asian countries. This suggests that not only the output market but also the financial market are more volatile in Asian economies than in OECD countries.

10.3.3. *Synchronization of Recessions, Credit Contractions, and Stock Price Busts*

Regional/global economic integration can make macroeconomic and financial fluctuations coincide across economies. One simple approach to considering synchronization of events is to examine their bunching in time. In Fig. 10.2, we plot the proportion of economies in recession, credit contraction, and stock price declines during 1960–2007, separately for developing Asia and OECD. A clear pattern that emerges from Fig. 10.2 is that recessions are less synchronized among Asian countries. For OECD, the proportion of countries in recession exceeds 50% in a couple of incidents and equals zero in many years. The high synchronization of recessions among OECD countries has been reported in Claessens *et al.* (2008) as well. For Asia, on the other hand, the proportion exhibits relatively small time-series variation, except during the 1997/1998 Asian financial crisis. Our results suggest that Asian countries are not as homogenous or interrelated as OECD countries. A similar difference is observed between the two regions for stock price declines. For OECD, the proportion of

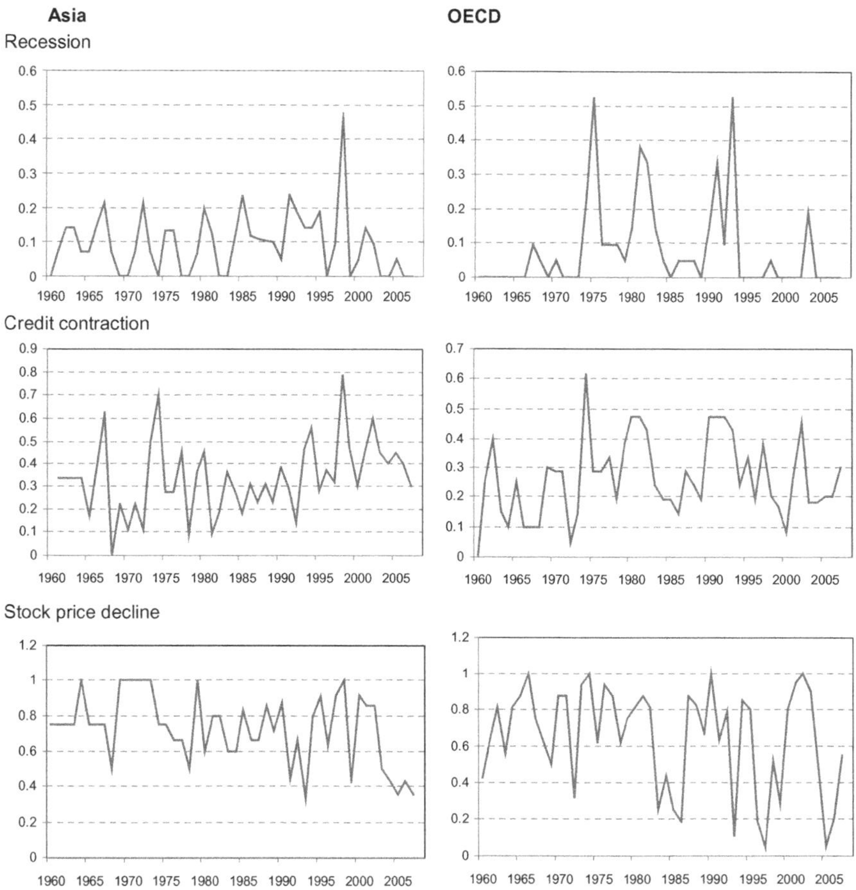

Figure 10.2 Proportion of economies in recession, credit contraction, and stock price decline

countries in stock price declines reaches as high as 100% on a few occasions and below 20% on several others. For Asia, the proportion reaches 100% only once during the Asian financial crisis since 1980 and never below 20% during the sample period. The high values of the series for earlier years are not reliable because the stock price data for that period are available only for a few economies. It is not clear whether the two regions can be similarly distinguished in terms of synchronization of credit contractions. The time-series variation in the proportion of countries in credit contractions (measured by standard deviation) is greater for Asia, partly due to the positive time trend apparent in the series since the 1990s.

Oftentimes a recession is accompanied or preceded by a financial downturn. For example, the Asian crisis in 1997 was triggered by turmoil in the foreign exchange market. The current US economic downturn was initiated by the subprime mortgage crisis. The synchronization of real downturns and financial downturns is clearly observed in our data set as well. In particular, we find that credit contractions and stock price declines tend to concur with recessions while stock price declines tend to precede credit contractions. As shown in Table 10.3, the correlation coefficient between recessions and credit contractions in Asia is 0.19 and the correlation between recessions and stock price declines is 0.18. Credit contractions and 1-year-lagged stock price declines are also positively correlated, with the correlation coefficient reaching 0.13. These correlations are all significant at the 5% level. In OECD countries, credit contractions tend to concur with GDP recessions while stock prices tend to precede GDP recessions. According to the lower panel of Table 10.3, the correlation between

Table 10.3. Correlations between recessions, credit contractions, and stock price declines

	Recession	**Credit Contraction**	**Stock Price Decline**
(A) **Asia**			
Credit Contraction	0.19**		
Stock Price Decline	0.18**	0.02	
Recession t – 1	0.30**	0.21**	–0.06
Credit Contraction t – 1	0.04	0.29**	–0.21**
Stock Price Decline t – 1	0.13**	0.12**	0.17**
(B) **OECD**			
Credit Contraction	0.24**		
Stock Price Decline	0.04	0.06*	
Recession t – 1	0.17**	0.14**	0.02
Credit Contraction t – 1	0.19**	0.38**	–0.05
Stock Price Decline t – 1	0.17**	0.07*	0.22**

Notes: Central Asian countries are included. *10% significance level. **5% significance level.

recessions and credit contractions in OECD is 0.24 and the correlation between recessions and 1-year-lagged stock price declines is 0.17. This suggests that stock prices are more forward-looking in OECD countries. Stock price declines and credit contractions are weakly correlated with each other, either contemporaneously or with a lag.

10.3.4. *Recessions Associated with Financial Crises*

When an economy is hit by combined recession and financial downturn, one may expect that the impact will intensify. This expectation is largely supported by Table 10.4, which compares recessions that are in association with financial crises and those that are not. Following Claessens *et al.* (2008, p. 13), "if a recession episode starts at the same time or after the beginning of an ongoing credit crunch or asset price bust", we consider the recession to be associated with a financial crisis. Since sample means of the recession characteristics are sensitive to outlier observations, Central Asian countries are excluded in Table 10.4. The last two columns of Table 10.4 indicate that the peak-to-trough drop in GDP and the associated cumulative loss in GDP tend to be greater when the recession is accompanied by a credit crunch or a stock price bust.[4] Similar patterns are observed for OECD countries.

Financial crises may increase not only the severity of a recession but also the likelihood of a recession. In order to examine this possibility, Table 10.5 counts the frequencies of recessions and financial downturns and their joint events, and computes various conditional probabilities. Severe credit contractions and severe stock price declines in the table are the same as credit crunches and stock price busts as defined above, respectively. The first row of Panel A of the table, for example, shows that the total number of credit contraction episodes in our sample is 115 and the total number of recession episodes is 32. For consistency with Table 10.4, the joint event is defined as a recession episode that starts at the same time or after the beginning of an ongoing credit contraction. The conditional probability, computed as the number of the joint events divided by the number of credit contractions, thus indicates there is about 19%

[4]When Central Asian countries are included, median values exhibit similar patterns.

Table 10.4. Descriptive statistics on combined recession and financial crises

	Proportion of Time Spent (%)	Duration (Years)	Amplitude (%)	Cumulative Loss (%)
(A) Asia				
Recession + Credit Crunch	9.32	1.31	7.36	8.65
Recession + No Credit Crunch	7.26	1.37	4.42	5.28
Recession + Stock Price Bust	6.24	1.19	5.00	5.76
Recession + No Stock Price Bust	12.37	1.60	4.01	5.31
(B) OECD				
Recession + Credit Crunch	3.65	1.63	3.22	4.79
Recession + No Credit Crunch	8.08	1.26	1.65	2.44
Recession + Stock Price Bust	4.92	1.33	1.48	2.31
Recession + No Stock Price Bust	4.92	1.13	1.28	1.62

Note: Central Asian countries are excluded because sample means are sensitive to outlier observations.

chance of a recession for a given credit contraction episode. Similarly, the conditional probability of 39% in the third row refers to the probability of a recession given that the economy currently has a severe credit contraction. From these two rows, it is clear that the probability of a recession increases when domestic credit decreases more severely. A similar pattern emerges from the second and the fourth rows. The probability of a severe recession increases from 3% to 9% as domestic credit decreases more severely. Panel B of the table repeats the computation for stock price declines. The total number of (severe) recessions in Panel B is smaller than that of Panel A because the number of observations with both GDP and stock price data is smaller than the number of observations with both GDP and domestic credit data. Panel B of Table 10.5 shows that the probability of a (severe) recession increases when the stock price decreases

Table 10.5. Frequencies of recessions and financial downturns

Asia				
		Frequency of		
(A) Credit Contraction	**Recession**	**Credit Contraction**	**Recession**	**Joint Event**
All	All	115	32	17
All	Severe	115	8	4
Severe	All	27	32	9
Severe	Severe	27	8	2
(B) Stock Price Decline		**Stock Price Decline**	**Recession**	**Joint Event**
All	All	98	19	18
All	Severe	98	5	5
Severe	All	23	19	12
Severe	Severe	23	5	4

(*Continued*)

Table 10.5. *(Continued)*

OECD				
		Frequency of		
(C) Credit Contraction	**Recession**	**Credit Contraction**	**Recession**	**Joint Event**
All	All	132	59	34
All	Severe	132	16	9
Severe	All	33	59	8
Severe	Severe	33	16	2
(D) Stock Price Decline		**Stock Price Decline**	**Recession**	**Joint Event**
All	All	221	47	34
All	Severe	221	8	4
Severe	All	57	47	23
Severe	Severe	57	8	2

Notes: Severe stock price declines are the same as stock price busts. Severe credit contractions are the same as credit crunches. Central Asian countries are included. The total number of recessions is not the same between Panels A and B and between Panels C and D because the number of observations with both GDP and stock price data is smaller than the number of observations with both GDP and domestic credit data.

more severely. The probability of a recession is 19% conditional on stock price decline, and jumps to 52% conditional on a stock market crash. Likewise, the probability of a severe recession is 5% conditional on stock price decline, and 17% conditional on a stock market crash.

OECD countries exhibit somewhat different patterns. As Panels C and D of Table 10.5 show, the conditional probability of a recession in OECD countries, while increasing with the severity of the stock price decline, is almost independent of the severity of the credit contraction. This, combined with Table 10.4 results, suggests that credit contractions in OECD increase the severity of a recession but not particularly the likelihood of a recession.

10.3.5. *Adjustments in Macroeconomic and Financial Variables*

Our discussion thus far has focused mainly on movements of GDP during a recession. In this subsection, we examine how various macroeconomic and financial variables change around a recession episode. Fig. 10.3 plots the growth rate of each variable for 3 years each before and after a peak. The peak year is denoted by 0. For variables that are available at quarterly frequencies (such as CPI, domestic credit, and the stock price), we use the year-on-year growth rate of the fourth quarter. In order to avoid influence of outlier values, Central Asian countries are excluded.

A prominent pattern in Fig. 10.3 is that all components of GDP tend to move in the same direction around a recession. For each component, the growth rate becomes negative in period 1 and resumes positive in period 2. Also, consistent with common expectation, fixed investment is most volatile, with the amplitude exceeding that of all the other components of GDP. It appears that fixed investment is the first thing to cut when things go bad. The least volatile component is consumption. Previous studies on business cycles of developing economies have often stressed that, unlike in developed countries, consumption is more volatile than GDP in developing economies. Aguiar and Gopinath (2007), for example, find that "smoothness" of consumption is not observed among 13 developing economies including Korea, Malaysia, Philippines, and Thailand. In order to explain the lack of consumption smoothness, they

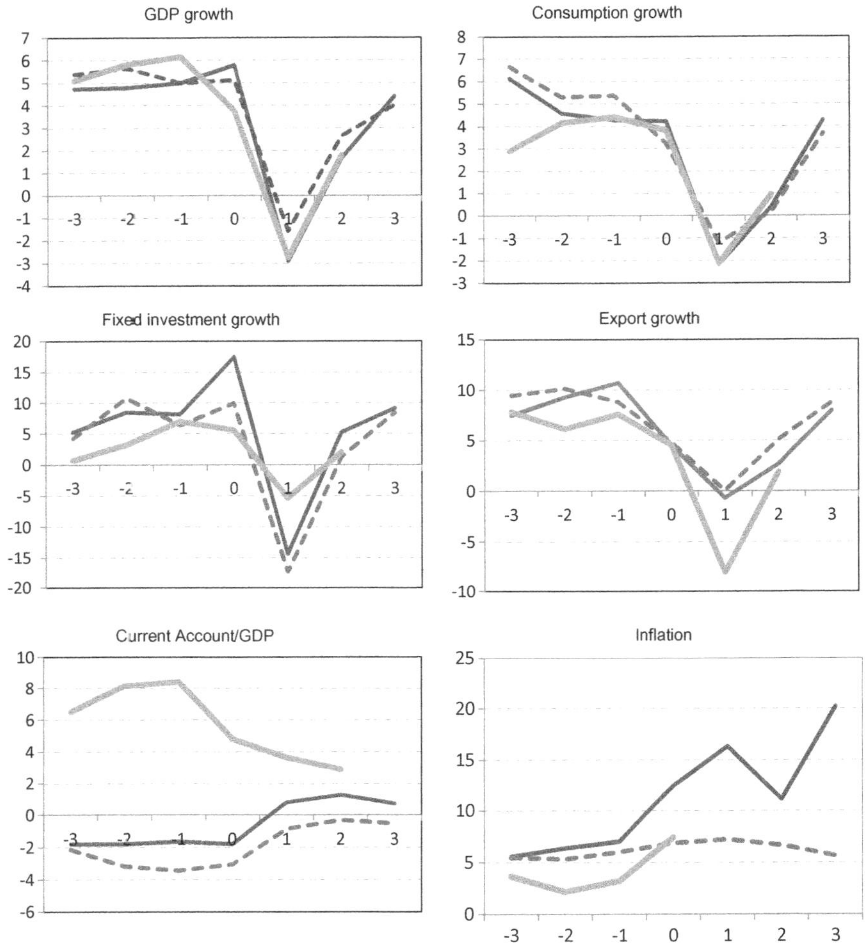

Figure 10.3 Adjustments in macroeconomic and financial variables around a recession (percent)

Note: "O" at the x-axis refers to peak.

develop a hypothesis on the nature of underlying productivity shocks. According to Fig. 10.3, however, the amplitude of the fall is smaller for consumption than for GDP. This suggests that, at least during GDP recessions, consumption smoothing is present even among Asian economies.

Also shown in Fig. 10.3 are adjustments in other macroeconomic variables and financial variables. As the figure illustrates, the current account/GDP ratio improves during a recession. On average, economies experience current account deficits prior to a peak and current account surpluses after a peak. In the next graph, we see the inflation rate tends to increase during a recession. The combination of high inflation and low growth suggests that recessions in developing Asia are mainly driven by supply shocks rather than demand shocks. As Claessens *et al.* (2008) report, OECD countries exhibit the opposite pattern, with the inflation rate decreasing during a recession.

The last two graphs in Fig. 10.3 show that recessions are likely to be associated with financial downturns. In particular, the growth rate of real credit falls substantially in period 1 and remains low even 3 years after the peak. This implies that adjustments in real credit are quite persistent. Stock prices seem to be forward-looking (at least on the way down), starting to fall even before the real economy peaks. Also, stock prices recover more quickly than domestic credit.

10.3.6. *Comparing the Current Recession with Past Recessions*

Using the patterns in Fig. 10.3, we can make a rough conjecture on how the current recession in Asia will evolve in the coming years. To compare the current recession with past recessions, the most recent changes and forecasts (where available) for Asian economies are plotted under the name "current recession." The economies considered are Hong Kong, China; Korea; Malaysia; Papua New Guinea; Philippines; Singapore; and Thailand, for which the Economist Intelligence Unit (EIU) forecasts negative GDP growth in 2009 (as of February). For these economies, period 0 refers to 2008. According to Fig. 10.3, recent developments in GDP and its components have been similar to the average during past recessions. This implies that, at the onset of the current recession, Asian economies were not particularly different from the norm. It is not clear, however, whether the peak-to-trough drop will also be typical. The EIU predicts that, while GDP and consumption will decrease by about the same percentages as before, the fall in fixed investment will be more modest and the fall in exports will be more severe. This prediction seems reasonable because fixed investment growth prior to the peak before this recession was not particularly high anyway, reducing the need for large adjustments in subsequent periods, and because export demand for Asian products will be hurt by the global recession.

The current account/GDP ratio is higher than usual because many Asian economies had current account surpluses in recent years. As a consequence of the sharper-than-usual decrease in exports, current accounts are expected to deteriorate rather than improve during the current recession. For the inflation rate and the financial variables, EIU forecasts are not available. Recent developments in these variables suggest that inflation may further pick up while domestic credit growth further decreases during the current recession. The sharper-than-usual adjustment in stock prices hints that the current recession will be a severe one. Above all, the sharper-than-usual fall in exports bodes ill for the many highly trade-dependent Asian economies.

10.4. The Global Crises and Asia

10.4.1. *The Impact of US/Global Crises in Asia*

As the ongoing global financial crisis continues to take its toll on the global real economy, two related questions are foremost on the minds of Asia's policymakers, researchers, and commentators. First, how deep will the global recession bite and for how long will it last, particularly as it relates to the US economy (which aside from being the world's largest economy, is the country where the crisis originated). Second, how bad will Asian economies be affected? The early view that the US would have seen the worst of the downturn heading into the second half of 2009 now looks increasingly optimistic.[5] Instead, the prevailing view is one of continued bearishness at least until the last quarter of the year.[6]

Thus far, the current US recession has behaved very much like previous episodes of recession cum financial crisis, which undoubtedly is more severe than the case without banking and housing crises

[5] For the earlier prediction see, among others, the US Federal Reserve Board (2008) and Reddy (2008).

[6] See the latest forecasting survey by the Wall Street Journal in Evans and Izzo (2009).

(see Reinhart & Rogoff, 2008, 2009; Claessens *et al.*, 2008; Lall *et al.*, 2008). There are reasons to believe the current downturn will be even more protracted. The build-up in the US housing price bubble was unparallelled (Reinhart & Rogoff, 2008) and the resulting pull-back in residential investment has been equally sharp (Claessens *et al.*, 2008). The bursting of the housing bubble has not only devastated traditional banking institutions, but more so the highly leveraged shadow banking institutions, with repercussions reaching every corner of the financial system. Amid these ongoing corrections, the stock market continues to slide downward. In essence, the US is experiencing a tri-factor of housing bust, stock market bust, and credit crunch simultaneously. With all major economies in crisis to differing degrees — and worse, all contracting at the same time — it will be a mammoth task for the US to simply export its way out of the slump. Based on Reinhart and Rogoff's (2009) historical comparison of crisis events, a typical peak-to-trough real GDP contraction is about 9.3% and lasts just under 2 years. This implies that if December 2007 was the start of recession, as indicated by the National Bureau of Economic Research, the US economy should stop contracting by end-2009. If, on the other hand, the collapse of Lehman Brothers in September 2008 is taken as the beginning of the current recession, the case for an early recovery in 2009 looks very unlikely. They also find real housing prices tend to fall 36% on average from peak-to-trough, lasting 5–6 years. Given the housing price peak of 2005, this implies current prices still have 8–10% to fall and will last well into 2011. In terms of equity prices, given that most stock prices peaked around mid-2007, any sustained rebound would be unlikely before 2010.

By and large, past US recessions were accompanied by recessions in other parts of the world, including emerging Asia (Table 10.6). Because emerging Asia's economies are more open, US recessions and Asian recessions seem to be more synchronized. During the past five US recessions since the early 1970s, US real GDP contracted, on average, 3.8% per year. GDP in other industrial countries fell by 2.0%; emerging Asia, 1.3%; Latin America, 1.7%; and emerging Europe, 3.6%. There were notable variations across recessions and regions. The 1972–1974 recession was unique because it was a common shock (oil price) that affected nearly all countries simultaneously. On the other hand, the 1982 recession, engineered to break the back of US inflation, was accompanied by continued positive

Table 10.6. US recessions and global growth

	Recession[a]					
	1974–75	**1980**	**1982**	**1991**	**2001**	
	Change in GDP Growth (Median for Region)					**Average**
US	−6.1	−3.4	−4.5	−2.1	2.9	−3.8
Other Industrial Countries	−5.4	−1.5	0.4	−1.3	−2.0	−2.0
Latin America	−3.2	−0.8	−3.9	1.1	−1.8	−1.7
Middle East and North Africa	1.2	−1.0	−3.3	0.8	−0.7	−0.6
Emerging Asia[b]	−3.5	−0.3	−1.5	−0.1	−1.1	−1.3
Sub-Saharan Africa	−0.5	—	1.0	—	0.6	0.2
Emerging Europe and CIS	...	...	...	−6.9	−0.3	−3.6

Notes: — means nonavailability of data; CIS = Commonwealth of Independent States.
[a]Year during which most of the impact on US growth was recorded — may not be the same as the dating by the National Bureau of Economic Research.
[b]Emerging Asia refers to People's Republic of China; India; Hong Kong, China; Republic of Korea; Singapore; Taipei, China; Indonesia; Malaysia; Philippines; Thailand; and Viet Nam.
Source: Based on Table 4.4 in *World Economic Outlook* (IMF 2007).

growth in other industrial countries, while significantly higher US interest rates and concern over debt sustainability brought large output contractions to Latin America and emerging Asia. The 1991 recession was more specific to the US due partly to the aftermath of the savings and loan crisis, where other industrial economies experienced only small declines in growth and many emerging economies continued to grow. And the 2001 US recession was special to emerging Asia as it affected them more widely than previous episodes.

The International Monetary Fund (IMF, 2008) provides a comprehensive study that attempts to analyze the impact of US spillovers on Asia both descriptively and quantitatively. The study finds Asia's trade and financial links with the US remain strong, and more importantly, that financial links have become stronger over time. Asia's export exposure to the US has in fact risen, despite prima facie evidence of decoupling, if one accounts for the PRC's role as final assembler of goods eventually shipped to industrial countries. Financial integration with the US has also increased markedly — given the huge rise in Asia's holdings of US securities bought from the large accumulation of international reserves since the Asian financial crisis. In addition, Asia's growth — particularly in the high-trade exposure economies of Malaysia; Singapore; and Taipei, China — were more correlated with the US growth cycle since 2000 than in the 1990s (see Kim, Lee, & Park, 2009). The same can be said about financial correlations in the form of stock market movements. As IMF (2007) noted, the correlations tended to be larger in falling markets. Besides trade openness and export exposure to the US, other initial economic conditions before an economy enters recession matter as well. Emerging economies with high current account deficits, net government debt, depreciated currencies, and larger negative output gaps tend to be more affected by US recessions than others.

In terms of the quantitative impact of US recessions, Table 10.7 summarizes the results of different methodologies used in the study, which range from a decline of 0.2% to 0.6% in Asia for every percentage point fall in US real GDP. Within Asia, different economies are affected differently with the more open ones being more vulnerable. For example, results from the vector autoregression model show the impact ranges from a decline of 0.0–0.9%. Among them, the high-trade exposure economies are most susceptible: Singapore declined by 0.9; Taipei, China 0.9; Hong Kong, China 0.8; and Malaysia 0.7.[7] Interestingly, though the results are not shown here, during 1996–2007, the impact of the US recession on Asian economies was larger than during the previous 1980–1995 period, reinforcing the importance of increased indirect trade exposure and financial linkages to the US. Finally, the study also examines several past US recessions (1980, 1981–1982, 1990–1991, and 2001) and finds that the 2001 recession was most severe. The burst of the information technology bubble in 2001 badly impeded electronics, a key export driver of Asian economies. As expected, economies that were most dependent on electronics

[7] This time around, the EIU and Consensus Forecasts have predicted all the newly industrialized economies (Hong Kong, China; Korea; Singapore; and Taipei, China) including Malaysia and Thailand would record negative growth for 2009.

Table 10.7. Summary results: Impact of a one percentage point US slowdown (in percentage points)

	Vector Autoregression	Cross-Country Regressions	2001 Recession[a]
Japan	0.2	0.3	0.7
Australia	0.5	0.7	0.4
New Zealand	0.3	0.9	0.0
People's Republic Rep. of China	0.0	0.1	0.2
Hong Kong, China	0.8	1.0	1.5
India	0.0	−0.2	−0.1
Indonesia	0.4	0.2	−0.3
Rep. of Korea	0.1	0.1	0.5
Malaysia	0.7	0.5	1.8
Philippines	0.4	0.6	0.6
Singapore	0.9	1.1	4.1
Taipei, China	0.9	1.2	2.9
Thailand	0.5	1.0	0.5
Asia[b]	0.2	0.3	0.6
Emerging Asia[b]	0.2	0.2	0.5
Emerging Asia[b] (ex. PRC and India)	0.5	0.5	1.1

Notes:
[a] Rescaled to the impact of a one percentage point US slowdown. The actual decline in output gap of the US in 2001 was 1.90. The size is measured as the average change in the output gap during the recession relative to the preceding four quarters. The potential output is derived from a Hodrick-Prescott filter.
[b] Weighted average using nominal GDP at market exchange rates.
Source: Based on IMF (2008, Table 2.11).

were most severely affected: Malaysia; Singapore; and Taipei, China. Moreover, the 2001 US recession occurred when many economies were still recuperating and undergoing reforms in the aftermath of the Asian financial crisis.

Based on the IMF forecast of a US real GDP decline of 2.5% for 2009, the overall estimates from Table 10.7 show Asia could contract by 0.5–1.5%. Individually, taking the extreme estimates of the 2001 US recession/technology burst, Singapore could be the worst hit, down by 10.2%; Taipei, China, 7.2%; Malaysia, 4.5%; and Hong Kong, China, 3.8%. Official forecasts are in the similar range: Singapore (−9 to −6%); Taipei, China (−4.3%); Malaysia (−5% to −4%); and Hong Kong, China (−6.5% to −5.5%).

Barro and Ursua's (2008) study on how Asia is affected by a US/global recession is also useful as it focuses on much longer historical time series; since 1870 including the Great Depression. From Table 10.8, of the five occasions where the US real GDP per capita contracted by more than a cumulative 10% from peak-to-trough, the 1929–1933 Great Depression

Table 10.8. US and Asian real GDP per capita disasters

Country	Peak	Trough	Duration	GDP Decline (%)
United States	1906	1908	2	10.5
	1913	1914	1	9.5
	1918	1921	3	11.8
	1929	1933	4	29.0
	1944	1947	3	16.5
Average			2.6	15.5
Indonesia	1930	1933	3	11.4
	1940	1945	5	54.5
	1997	1999	2	15.8
Malaysia	1902	1904	2	10.0
	1929	1935	6	19.3
	1936	1937	1	11.7
	1939	1941	2	23.5
	1942	1947	5	36.1
Philippines	1903	1904	1	15.8
	1913	1915	2	11.6
	1929	1935	6	13.4
	1939	1946	7	57.2
	1982	1985	3	18.7

(*Continued*)

Table 10.8. (*Continued*)

Country	Peak	Trough	Duration	GDP Decline (%)
Singapore	1902	1904	2	21.4
	1910	1913	3	33.7
	1915	1916	1	17.4
	1917	1920	3	23.5
	1925	1927	2	38.9
	1929	1933	4	41.2
	1937	1938	1	15.1
	1950	1952	2	34.5
	1956	1957	1	11.3
Rep. of Korea	1918	1919	1	11.1
	1938	1939	1	10.4
	1940	1945	5	48.0
	1949	1951	2	15.1
Taipei, China	1903	1905	2	21.4
	1910	1911	1	11.4
	1936	1945	9	66.2
Average (Asia)			2.9	24.8

Notes: The shaded rows for Asian economies refer closely to the corresponding US real GDP per capita disasters. Declines in real GDP per capita of 10% or greater are cumulative fractions from peak year to trough year. Barro and Ursua (2008) also include stock price, bill rates of returns, and inflation rate declines, but they are not shown here. Trough years in bold indicate a country is at war.
Source: Based on Barro and Ursua (2008, Table A2).

stands out. Then, US real GDP per capita contracted 29%; Indonesia 11.4%; Malaysia, 19.3%; Philippines, 13.4%; and Singapore, 41.2%. The biggest declines, however, were recorded during World War II, in the vicinity of 50% for most Asian economies, and lasted between 5 and 9 years, though not strictly triggered by the US recession.

10.4.2. *Synchronization of Global Crises and Asian Recessions*

In this subsection, we calculate various conditional probabilities to see how US financial crises (and global recessions) relate to Asian financial crises and recessions. The methodology is the same as in Table 10.5. We count the frequencies of foreign crises, Asian crises, and their joint events, and compute the probability of an Asian crisis conditional on a US crisis. Table 10.9, Panel A, last column, shows there is a 40% chance that Asia also experiences a credit contraction for a given US credit contraction. However, there is only an 8% chance that the Asian credit contraction will be a severe one. In the case of stock price declines (Panel B), there is a larger 51% chance that Asia also experiences a stock price decline when the US stock price drops. Similarly, the chances of that coinciding with a severe Asian stock price decline are also higher at 12% when compared with a credit contraction. This highlights the greater regularity of stock price declines (or volatility of stock price movements) in contrast to credit contractions. What is also salient is that in the severe cases of US credit contractions and severe US stock price declines, the probabilities of Asian credit contractions and stock price declines are even greater, at 63% and 88% respectively. This means that when a severe credit contraction (or severe stock price decline) happens in the US, the chances of an Asian credit contraction (or stock price decline) also increase.

Another interesting aspect to examine is the relationships between US credit contractions and stock price declines with Asian recessions. These results are presented in Table 10.10. What stands out is that for a given US credit contraction or US stock price decline, the chances of Asia being in recession are much less than Asia in credit contraction or having a stock price decline. Simply put, this means not all US financial downturns lead to an Asian recession. Still, if it is a US credit contraction, the chances of an Asian recession are higher (at 19%) than if it is a US stock price decline (13%). Although stock price declines happen more often than credit contractions, their impact on Asian economic activity is not as detrimental. Likewise as in Table 10.9, the severity of US financial downturns increases the chances of Asian recession. An even more interesting relationship to examine is between OECD (including US) recessions and Asian recessions. Table 10.11 shows a 14% chance of an Asian recession happens together with an OECD recession. In case of a severe OECD/US recession, the chances of an Asian recession increases further to 24%.[8]

[8] A severe OECD recession is where the proportion of OECD countries in recession is above 30% (see Fig. 10.2). Severe Asian recessions are defined as the usual top quartile events.

Table 10.9. Frequencies of US credit contractions/stock price declines and Asia credit contractions/stock price declines

		Frequency of			
(A) US Credit Contractions	**Asian Credit Contractions**	**US Credit Contractions**	**Asian Credit Contractions**	**Joint Event**	**Conditional Probability**
All	All	75	119	30	0.40
All	Severe	75	28	6	0.08
Severe	All	35	119	22	0.63
Severe	Severe	35	28	4	0.11
(B) US Stock Price Declines		**US Stock Price Declines**	**Asian Stock Price Declines**	**Joint Event**	
All	All	94	98	48	0.51
All	Severe	94	22	11	0.12
Severe	All	42	98	37	0.88
Severe	Severe	42	22	9	0.21

Notes: Severe US credit contractions refer to US credit contractions with the amplitude greater than the median. Severe US stock price declines refer to US stock price declines with the amplitude greater than the median. Severe Asian credit contractions and severe Asian stock price declines are the same as credit crunches and stock price busts defined above, respectively. Central Asian countries are included.

Table 10.10. Frequencies of US credit contractions/stock price declines and Asian recessions

		Frequency of			
A: US Credit Contractions	**Asian Recessions**	**US Credit Contractions**	**Asian Recessions**	**Joint Event**	**Conditional Probability**
All	All	85	51	16	0.19
All	Severe	85	13	3	0.04
Severe	All	44	51	14	0.32
Severe	Severe	44	13	3	0.07
B: US Stock Price Declines		**US Stock Price Declines**	**Asian Recessions**	**Joint Event**	
All	All	212	51	28	0.13
All	Severe	212	13	8	0.04
Severe	All	113	51	15	0.13
Severe	Severe	113	13	3	0.03

Notes: Severe US credit contractions refer to US credit contractions with the amplitude greater than the median. Severe US stock price declines refer to US stock price declines with the amplitude greater than the median. Severe Asian credit contractions and severe Asian stock price declines are the same as credit crunches and stock price busts defined above, respectively. Severe recessions are also the same as above. Central Asian countries are included.

Table 10.11. Frequencies of OECD recessions and Asian recessions

		Frequency of			
OECD Recessions	**Asian Recessions**	**OECD Recessions**	**Asian Recessions**	**Joint Event**	**Conditional Probability**
All	All	389	81	55	0.14
All	Severe	389	30	24	0.06
Severe	All	89	81	21	0.24
Severe	Severe	89	30	9	0.10

Notes: Severe Asian recessions are defined as before. For OECD, recessions are defined as the proportion of any one OECD country in recession in a given year — the same definition as in Figure 10.2. Severe recessions are those events where the proportion of OECD countries in recession is above 30%.

10.5. Concluding Remarks

Our analysis of historical crisis episodes in Asia shows that while there is substantial diversity, on average recessions and financial downturns are more frequent, longer lasting, and more severe in Asian economies than in OECD countries. We also find that the likelihood and severity of a recession tends to increase when it is associated with financial crises, such as credit crunches and stock market crashes. The probability of an Asian recession is 19% conditional on stock price decline, and jumps to 52% conditional on a stock market crash.

Our results also support the strong links between Asian economies and the global economy. Severe financial downturns or recessions in advanced economies are often associated with financial crises or recessions in Asia. Conditional on a stock market crash in the US, the probability of an Asian credit contraction is 63% and stock price decline is 88%. The probability of an Asian recession is 14% conditional on an OECD/US recession, and 24% on a severe OECD/US recession.

The financial turmoil that stemmed from the US subprime mortgage crisis in 2007 has blown up into a global economic crisis. Major industrialized economies have already entered recessions and despite policy measures taken, the probability of a deeper and more prolonged global recession is high. Emerging Asian economies have also been hit hard due to strong links between Asian economies and the global economy through trade and financial channels. A rapid reversal in capital flows due to risk repricing and deleveraging has led to a squeeze of external funding conditions and a collapse of asset prices. Asian export growth is slowing sharply as demand from major economies shrinks.

Given the severity of the current global crisis and financial downturns, the risk that many Asian economies will experience a deeper recession is high. The stylized facts of the movements of macroeconomic and financial variables from the historical recession episodes suggest that sharper declines in stock prices and export demand are associated with severe recession. However, considering that the current recession is unprecedented in many aspects, this episode may not entirely follow the stylized pattern previous recessions have taken.

In addition, the actual impact of the global crisis on Asian economies depends on the policies adopted in response to the crisis. Policymakers across the region have taken immediate actions to contain the spillover effects of global financial turmoil on domestic financial systems. However, the wide spread of the crisis on to the real sector has called for policy reactions to hold down economic deterioration. Asian countries have adopted a mix of policy tools including monetary, financial, fiscal, exchange rate, and structural. But it remains a question of what types of policies would be more effective in reducing the length and severity of the recession. For example, the current public debate focuses on calling for more active fiscal responses, considering that monetary policy may have less traction when financial conditions worsen. However, it is not clear whether and to what extent countercyclical fiscal policies can help limit the impact of the global crisis. This is where future research on the role of national policies in dealing with financial and macroeconomic crises in Asia will be useful.

References

Agenor, P., McDermott, C. J., & Prasad, E. S. (1999). Macroeconomic fluctuations in developing countries: Some stylized facts. *IMF Working Paper* 99/35.

Aguiar, M., & Gopinath, G. (2007). Emerging markets business cycles: The cycle is the trend. *Journal of Political Economy*, 115, 69–102.

Barro, R., & Ursua, J. (2008). Macroeconomic crises since 1870. *NBER Working Paper* 13940.

Bry, G., & Boschan, C. (1971). *Cyclical analysis of time series: Selected procedures and computer programs.* Massachusetts: National Bureau of Economic Research.

Burns, A. F., & Mitchell, W. C. (1946). *Measuring business cycles.* Massachusetts: National Bureau of Economic Research.

Claessens, S., Kose, A., & Terrones, M. (2008). What happens during recessions, crunches and busts? *IMF Working Paper* 08/274.

Evans, K., & Izzo, P. (2009). Outlook for US more bearish. *The Wall Street Journal* (Asia) 13–15 February.

Harding, D., & Pagan, A. (2002). Dissecting the cycle: A methodological investigation. *Journal of Monetary Economics*, 49, 365–381.

International Monetary Fund. (2007). Chapter 4: Decoupling the train? Spillovers and cycles in the global economy. *International Monetary Fund, World Economic Outlook*, Washington, D.C. IMF.

International Monetary Fund. (2008). *Regional economic outlook: Asia and Pacific* (April). Washington, D.C. IMF.

International Monetary Fund. (2009). Chapter II. Recessions and recoveries in Asia: What can the past teach us about the present recession? *International Monetary Fund, regional economic outlook: Asia and Pacific* (May), Washington, D.C. IMF.

Kim, S., Lee, J. W., & Park, C. Y. (2009). Emerging Asia: Decoupling or recoupling. Asian Development Bank and Korea University, Mimeo.

Lall, S., Cardarelli, R., & Elekdag, S. (2008). Chapter 4: Financial stress and economic downturns. *International Monetary Fund, World Economic Outlook* (September), Washington, D.C. IMF.

Mendoza, E. G. (1995). The terms of trade, the real exchange rate, and economic fluctuations. *International Economic Review*, 36(1), 101–137.

Neumeyer, P. A., & Perry, F. (2005). Business cycles in emerging economies: The role of interest rates. *Journal of Monetary Economics*, 52(2), 345–380.

Reddy, S. (2008). Recession dating, when in doubt, wait for a crisis. *Wall Street Journal* (Asia), 1 December.

Reinhart, C., & Rogoff, K. (2008). Is the 2007 US sub-prime financial crisis so different? An international comparison. *NBER Working Paper* 13761.

Reinhart, C., & Rogoff, K. (2009). The aftermath of financial crises. *American Economic Review*, 99(2), 466–472.

US Federal Reserve Board (2008). Minutes of the Federal Open Market Committee 28–29 October. Washington, D.C.

Watson, M. W. (1994). Business cycle durations and postwar stabilization of the U.S. economy. *American Economic Review*, 84(1), 24–46.

Chapter 11

Global Financial Turmoil: Impact and Challenges for Asia's Financial Systems*

11.1. Introduction[1]

The global financial turmoil originating from the U.S. sub-prime mortgage market is deepening and broadening. Conditions in global financial markets remain distressed, despite sizable liquidity injections and other emergency measures by the world's major central banks. Markets for short-term funding in the major countries have periodically seized up — with interbank borrowing rates rising to high levels — and financial firms continue to hoard liquidity. However, spillover to the Asian financial markets has been relatively limited so far, and manifested mainly through equity and U.S. dollar debt markets. The region's banks have been affected minimally, and short-term credit markets show few signs of stress. Domestic funding conditions have been generally positive and capital inflows to the region remain strong.

---

*Jong-Wha Lee, Cyn-Young Park, 'Global Financial Turmoil: Impact and Challenges for Asia's Financial Systems', Asian Economic Papers, 8:1 (Winter, 2009), pp. 9–40.

We thank Yung Chul Park, Doo Yong Yang, and other participants in the Asian Economic Panel Meeting, Seoul, Korea, 25–26 April 2008 for helpful comments. The views expressed in this paper are the authors' and do not necessarily reflect the views and policies of the Asian Development Bank (ADB), its board of directors, or the governments that ADB's members represent.

[1] Data used for this article are of May 2008.

Looking forward, Asian financial markets and systems will most likely continue to weather the current financial turmoil. A few important factors help explain this resilience. First, the region's financial institutions have relatively small direct exposure to U.S. sub-prime mortgages and structured credit products. Second, strong growth prospects and sound external positions have continued to support investor confidence in the regional economies. Third, improved policies and the continued exercise of prudence in most emerging economies are helping to mitigate the impact of external shocks.

However, these positive factors do not guarantee the complete insulation of the region's financial markets and systems from global financial turbulence, especially if it exacerbates. Uncertainty in the external environment is growing and unsettled conditions will likely continue. Of particular concern, sub-prime-related losses are still growing worldwide, with investors requiring increasingly higher risk premiums on their holdings of mortgage-based and complex derivative securities. Growing concerns about counterparty credit risk have intensified the strain on funding and market liquidity, although coordinated actions by the world's major central banks have eased some of them. Massive write-downs in several major global financial institutions have resulted, such as the nationalization of Northern Rock in the United Kingdom, the assistance of the U.S. Federal Reserve (the Fed) in the fire sale of Bear Stearns, and the liquidation of some well-known investment funds, including Carlyle Capital.

Further global instability could transmit to the region's financial markets and affect regional economies through several important channels. Heightened risk perception and declining investor confidence could trigger a sudden reversal of financial flows from the region's capital markets, pushing down asset prices in the region and intensifying financial market volatility. A swing in market sentiment and a sudden change in liquidity conditions could also affect local financial markets and institutions more directly. Although the region's banking systems reportedly have small direct exposure to the sub-prime and related credit derivatives, there are signs of stress related to increased volatility in asset prices and to rising risk premiums in offshore funding markets. Contagion might affect the region's financial markets more seriously if tightening credit conditions and financial instability weigh on broader economic activity.

This paper will examine the evolution of the U.S. sub-prime-generated turmoil and its spillover onto Asia's emerging financial markets. It assesses the strengths and vulnerabilities of the region's financial systems in the face of rapidly changing global financial market conditions, and sheds light on the challenges the region's policymakers may face. Section 11.2 briefly summarizes recent events surrounding the U.S. sub-prime turmoil and its background. Section 11.3 examines the impact so far on regional financial markets and the various channels of further contagion. Section 11.4 discusses the challenges posed by new trends in financial innovation and globalization to the region's financial systems, which could increase financial vulnerability. Section 11.5 suggests some policy options.

11.2. The Recent Turmoil and Background

The genesis of the U.S. sub-prime meltdown in mid-2007 can be traced back to the housing boom of 2001–05. As housing markets thrived amid historically low interest rates, U.S. residential mortgage lending soared, with an increasing portion made to borrowers with less-than-perfect (that is, sub-prime) credit histories.[2] Several factors — including the deregulation of the housing finance system in the 1980s,[3] the introduction of the

[2] Assessment of the borrower's ability to afford repayments on a mortgage is typically based on the borrower's credit history, credit score, debt-to-income (DTI) ratio, and the mortgage loan-to-value (LTV) ratio. Lending guidelines by Fannie Mae provide benchmarks for what it considers "prime" borrowers on conforming loans in the United States. Prime borrowers have a credit score above 620 (credit scores are between 350 and 850 with a median in the United States of 678 and a mean of 723), a DTI ratio no greater than 75 percent (meaning that no more than 75 percent of net income pays for housing and other debt), and an LTV ratio of 90 percent, meaning that the borrower is paying a 10-percent down payment. Accordingly, borrowers who do not meet these criteria are sub-prime borrowers by Fannie Mae standards.

[3] U.S. federal policy to promote home ownership resulted in some important changes to federal legislation in the 1980s. Key legislation includes the Depository Institutions Deregulatory and Monetary Control Act of 1980, which eliminated all usury controls on first-lien mortgage rates, and the St. Germain Depository Institutions Act of 1982, which allowed adjustable rate mortgages and removed interest rate ceilings for savings and loan banks. The Tax Reform Act of 1986 also made the interest payment on mortgage loans tax deductible.

automated underwriting system, and the growing use of securitization — also encouraged the rapid development of the sub-prime mortgage market. Together with increased competition among mortgage lenders that led to lax lending criteria, a proliferation of new types of mortgages (e.g., "affordability products" that require little or no down payment and initially carry very low "teaser" rates) allowed sub-prime borrowers to gain easier access to credit. As a result, the sub-prime mortgage market grew rapidly after 2003 — according to some estimates, it accounted for as much as one-fifth of new mortgages by 2006.

Typically, sub-prime borrowers are charged higher interest rates than prime borrowers to compensate for a higher default risk, and their mortgages are often at adjustable rather than fixed rates. As the Fed began to raise interest rates in July 2004, these sub-prime mortgage borrowers naturally faced larger interest payments. The subsequent cooling in the housing market also made it difficult for them to refinance their mortgages into loans with better terms or to pay off the mortgages by selling homes. Consequently, delinquencies on sub-prime mortgages picked up significantly from mid-2005 (Fig. 11.1).

Defaults on U.S. sub-prime mortgages quickly spilled over onto the balance sheets of hedge funds and other investment funds. They also

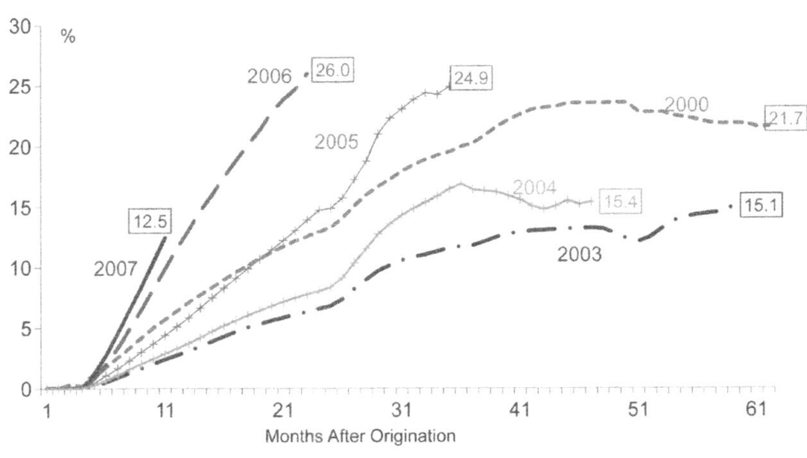

Figure 11.1 U.S sub-prime delinquencies by vintage year
Source: Global Financial Stability Report (*April 2008*), International Monetary Fund.

affected a number of banks through their off-balance sheet financial "conduits," which invested heavily in related mortgage derivatives and credit products. The proliferation of structured credit products, which helped bundle, repackage, and sell sub-prime mortgages to a broad spectrum of global investor groups, provided the link for financial contagion. These new credit risk transfer instruments have gained popularity among international financial institutions as a way of boosting profits in an environment of relatively low interest rates, while helping to manage risk exposure. In particular, banks set up structured investment vehicles (SIVs) to invest in these higher-yielding or more risky long-term assets, while keeping them off their balance sheets and thus avoiding the need to set aside large regulatory capital. However, when asset values declined sharply and liquidity dried up suddenly in the market, SIVs were brought back onto banks' balance sheets.

Uncertainty about the valuation, the disclosure of structured products, and rising risk aversion have since spread the contagion.[4] As financial institutions have become concerned about counterparty risk and unknown exposure to the sub-prime mortgages and related credit derivatives, this added pressure on the assessment of risk drove financial institutions to become cautious and hoard liquidity. Consequently, strains in short-term funding markets in the United States and elsewhere — notably interbank and asset-backed commercial paper markets — have intensified (Fig. 11.2). Major financial firms' credit default swaps widened sharply as risk perception stayed high. Banks' profits have suffered from large write-downs of sub-prime products and their absorption of SIVs formerly involved in sub-prime markets. Higher levels of financial leverage and significant maturity mismatches implied by the funding of SIVs in sub-prime-related long-term investments through short-term borrowing remain a major source of vulnerability.

The sub-prime mortgage mess has revealed key structural weaknesses in the evolution of modern credit markets. First, the "originate-to-distribute" model of financing made popular by greater availability of credit transfer instruments has weakened the link between the lender and

---

[4] See IMF (2008) for a detailed explanation of issues related to structured finance and market illiquidity.

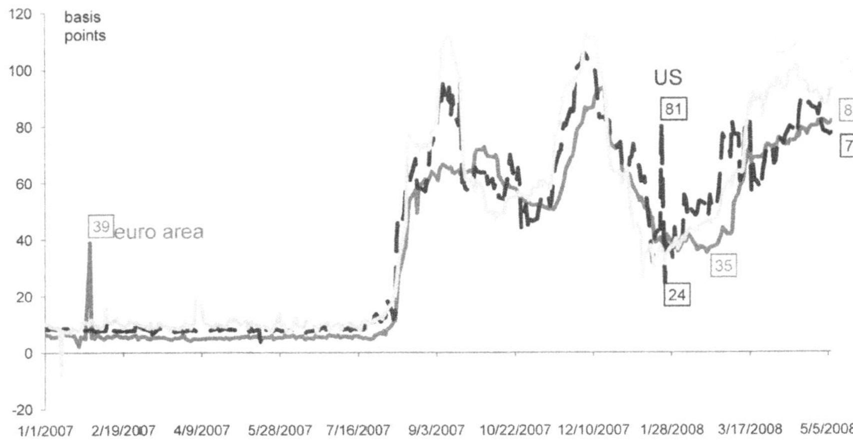

Figure 11.2 Three-month London Inter-Bank Offered Rate (LIBOR) to three-month Overnight Index Swap (OIS) spreads (basis points)

Note: Euro area or EU12 = Austria, Belgium, Finland, France, Germany, Greece, Ireland, Italy, Luxembourg, the Netherlands, Portugal, and Spain.

Source: Bloomberg.

the borrower. This has diluted incentives to assess rigorously the creditworthiness of the borrower and to monitor the obligor's financial state. Second, the growing use of complex structured credit products has increased uncertainty about the valuation of financial assets. The high leverage embedded in these products tends to blur the size of commitment in each layer of securitization, obscuring the degree of risk exposure. Thin-trading of these sophisticated products also makes market-based valuation especially difficult in times of financial distress when market liquidity suddenly dries up. Third, a rise in leverage in the overall financial system has increased vulnerability to a shift in risk perception and changes in liquidity conditions. Increasing reliance on market-driven financial intermediation tends to generate a false sense of liquidity in times of relative market calm. However, in a time of distress, elevated uncertainty may lead to a collective failure of liquidity provision in the market. In particular, a sharp decline in asset values forces regulated financial institutions to liquidate positions during market distress, adding to the liquidity crisis.

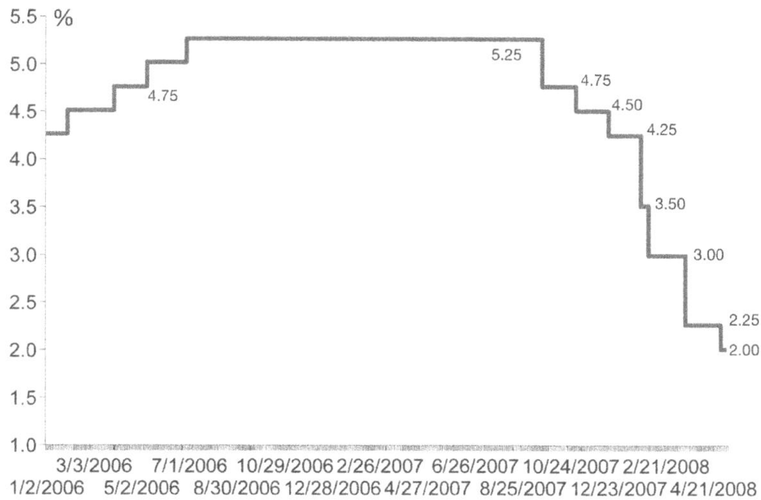

Figure 11.3 U.S. Fed funds rate (percent)
Source: Bloomberg.

Major central banks have taken several measures to restore normal market functioning: These include the injection of large amounts of liquidity, a relaxation of rules to include a broader range of collateral, an extension of maturity on discount lending, and a widened range of counterparties to provide liquidity support (including investment banks in the United States). The Fed also set up a new lending facility using Treasury securities. Authorities in the United States and Europe have also bailed out high-profile financial institutions with public funds, such as American International Group (AIG), Bear Stearns, and Northern Rock. Consequently, central banks' balance sheets now reflect much higher levels of sub-prime-related risk.

On monetary policy, the Fed has slashed its target federal funds rate (Fig. 11.3). Other major central banks have also largely held back from the previous tightening stances and adopted a "watch-and-see" strategy. Alongside the still-large U.S. current account imbalance, this has seen the U.S. dollar weaken sharply, in particular against the euro and the Japanese yen.

11.3. Impact on Asian Financial Markets and Further Potential Spillover

11.3.1. *Impact*

So far, Asia's financial markets have suffered only minimally (largely through equity and offshore bond markets) from the sub-prime-related troubles. Heightened anxiety over increasing sub-prime losses, deteriorating credit quality, and a slowing global economy have prompted large sell-offs in the region's stock markets (Fig. 11.4). Share prices have tracked losses on the major markets since early in 2007 — particularly in countries where equities were already quite high. Further, significant losses are still possible in some markets where the price-earnings ratio remains high (Fig. 11.5). In response, local and foreign firms have postponed plans for new issuance in the equity markets.

Offshore bond markets for emerging Asian issuers have also experienced a significant re-pricing of credit and liquidity risk since the turmoil erupted last year. Reflecting generally heightened risk aversion, credit

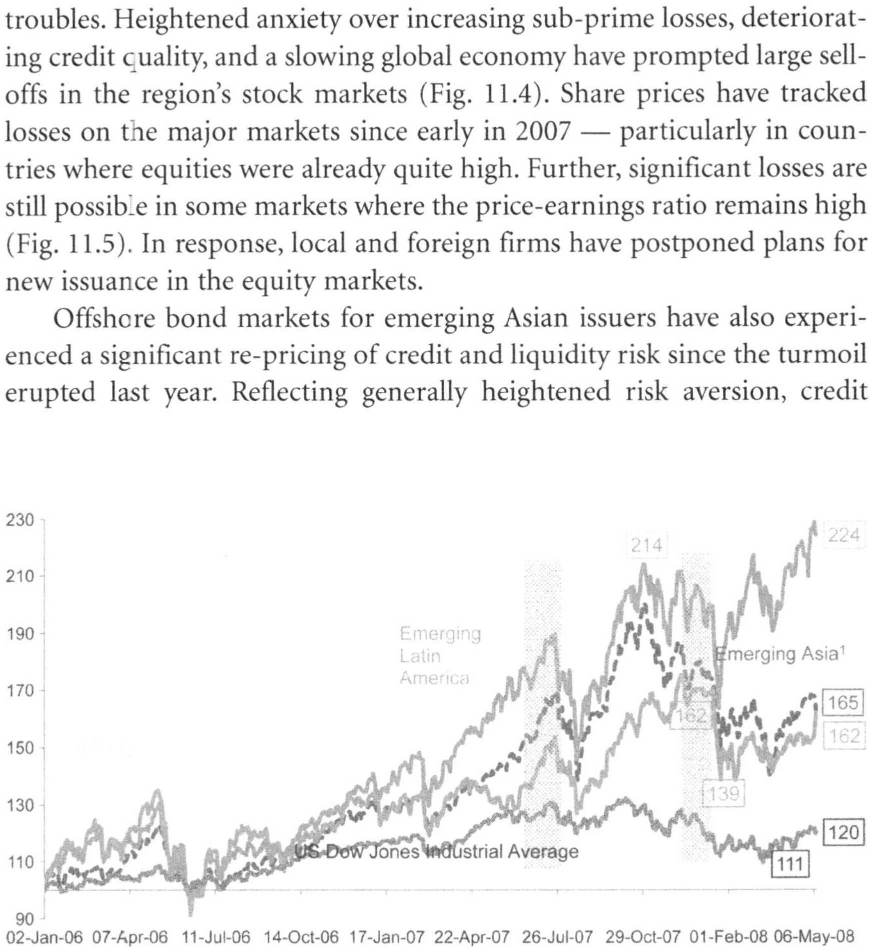

Figure 11.4 Morgan Stanley Capital International (MSCI) indexes (2 January 2006 = 100)
Notes: Shaded areas indicate the periods 15 Jul to 20 Sep 2007 and 14 Jan to 28 Feb 2008.
[1] Includes People's Republic of China, India, Indonesia, the Republic of Korea, Malaysia, Pakistan, Philippines, Taipei, China, and Thailand.
Source: Morgan Stanley Capital International (MSCI) Barra and Bloomberg.

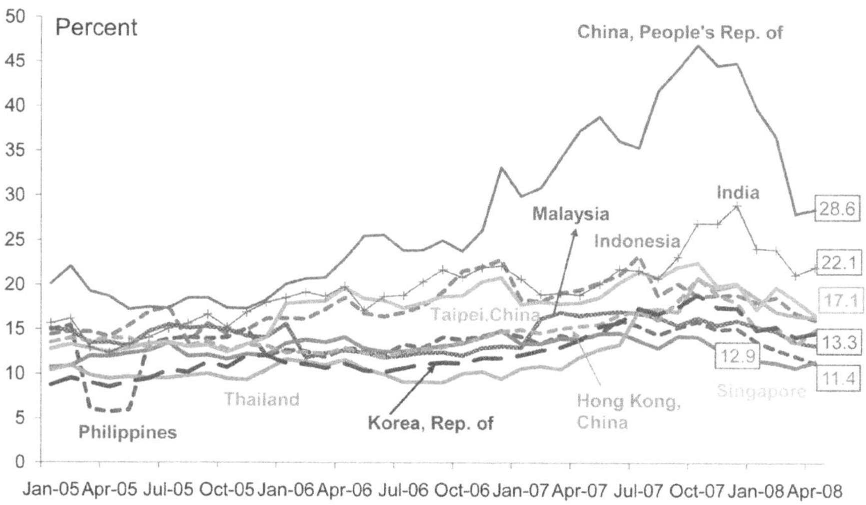

Figure 11.5 Price earnings ratio
Source: Bloomberg.

spreads on high-risk borrowers, including emerging Asian market borrowers, have widened sharply (Fig. 11.6). Indonesian and Pakistan bonds have been among the worst hit, but the adverse effects throughout the region have been broad. Offshore bond issuance by emerging Asian issuers has also generally dropped (Fig. 11.7). However, so far the deterioration in external debt financing conditions appears to have had little impact on the region's local currency debt markets.

The region's banking systems entered this period of financial turbulence in relatively good health, their financial resilience underpinned by limited exposure at the origins of the problem.[5] Tables 11.1a–c report the

[5] Regional banking systems have reported relatively small direct exposure to sub-prime-related losses compared to their western counterparts, but it is on the rise. According to Japan's financial regulator, the Financial Services Agency, its financial institutions' losses from the U.S. sub-prime crisis nearly tripled the initial estimate, amounting to a total of US$ 4.1 billion in the final quarter of 2007. Japan's two biggest banks — Mizuho Financial Group Inc. and Mitsubishi UFJ Financial Group, Inc. — reported much larger losses. Fairly substantial exposure to the sub-prime debt has also been unveiled in some large People's Republic of China banks, including Bank of China, which recently reported a holding of about US$ 5.0 billion worth of sub-prime-related assets. The Industrial and Commercial

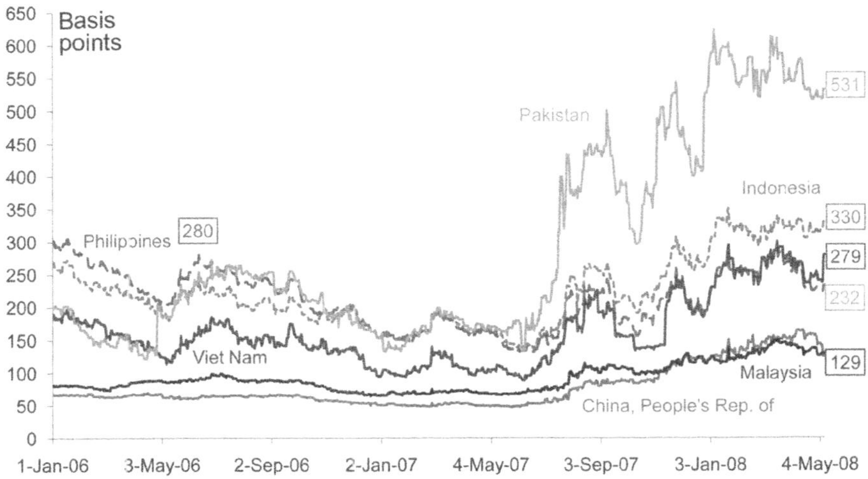

Figure 11.6 JP Morgan Emerging Markets Bond Index (EMBI) sovereign stripped spreads
Source: Bloomberg.

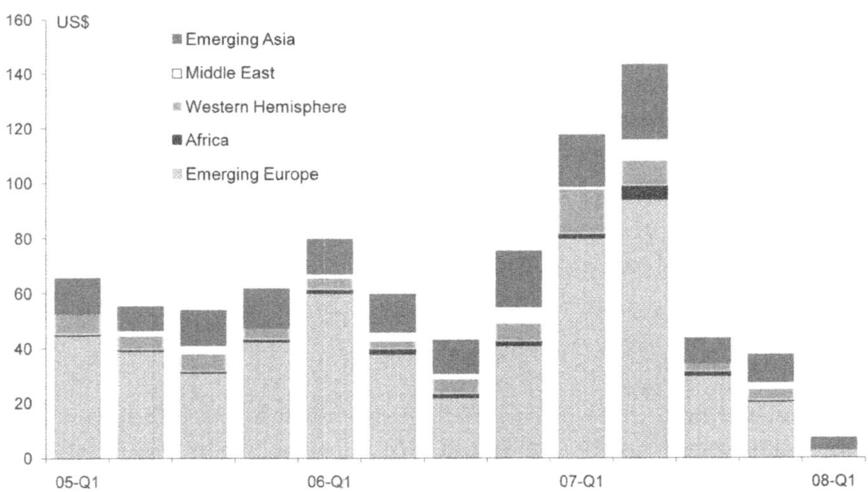

Figure 11.7 Private sector gross external bond issuance (US$ billion)
Source: International Monetary Fund.

Table 11.1a. Nonperforming loans (percent of commercial bank loans)

	1998	2003	2004	2005	2006	2007[a]
China, People's Rep. of[b]	28.5[c]	17.8	13.2	8.6	7.1	6.2
Hong Kong, China[d]	5.3	3.9	2.3	1.4	1.1	0.9
India	14.4	9.1	7.2	4.9	3.5	2.7
Indonesia	49.2	8.2	5.7	8.3	7.0	4.6
Korea, Rep. of	7.6	2.2	1.7	1.1	0.8	0.7
Malaysia[d]	10.3	8.3	6.8	5.6	4.8	3.2
Philippines[d]	10.4	14.1	12.7	8.2	5.7	4.5
Singapore	5.3[c]	6.7	5	3.8	2.8	1.8
Thailand	42.9	12.8	10.9	8.3	4.1	3.9
Memo						
Germany	3.0	5.2	4.9	4.0	3.4	n.a.
Japan[e]	5.4	5.2	2.9	1.8	1.5	1.5
U.S.	1.0	1.1	0.8	0.7	0.8	1.1

Notes: n.a. = not available.

[a] Data for Hong Kong, China; Rep. of Korea; Japan, Singapore, and the United States as of September 2007.

[b] 1999–2001 data are for state-owned commercial banks only.

[c] Figure refers to 1999 data.

[d] Reported nonperforming loans are gross classified loan ratio of retail banks.

[e] End of fiscal year, (March of the following calendar year).

Source: National sources; CEIC; and Global Financial Stability Report, International Monetary Fund.

overall improvements of the region's banking systems in their profitability, operational efficiency, and financial soundness. Banks' balance sheets appear healthy and little affected by the unsettled conditions in major financial markets. Nonperforming assets have declined dramatically across the region since the 1997–98 Asian financial crisis. Risk-weighted capital adequacy ratios are higher. Post-crisis reforms and restructuring of banks

Bank of China reportedly wrote off sub-prime-related losses amounting to 30 percent of its US$ 1.2 billion asset holdings, whereas China Construction Bank set aside reserves equal to 40 percent of its $1 billion in sub-prime holdings to cover possible losses. Woori Bank of Korea also reported a loss of $445 million out of $491 million in assets linked to sub-prime loans and collateralized debt obligations.

Table 11.1b. Risk-weighted capital adequacy ratios (percent-of-risk-weighted assets)

	1998	2003	2004	2005	2006	2007[a]
Hong Kong, China[a]	18.5	15.3	15.4	14.9	14.9	13.6[b]
India	11.6	12.7	12.9	12.3	12.3	12.6
Indonesia	−13.0	19.4	19.4	20.5	20.5	19.3
Korea, Rep. of	8.2	11.2	12.1	12.7	12.7	12.9
Malaysia	11.8	14.0	14.3	13.1	13.1	12.6
Philippines	17.7	17.4	18.7	18.5	18.5	19.4
Singapore	18.1	17.9	16.2	15.4	15.4	14.0
Thailand	10.9	14.0	13.0	14.5	14.5	14.8
Memo						
Germany	10.5	13.4	13.2	12.2	12.5	n.a.
Japan[c]	9.6	11.1	11.6	12.2	13.1	12.9
U.S.[d]	11.6	13.0	13.2	12.9	13.0	12.8

Notes:
[a] Data for Japan, Rep. of Korea, Singapore, and the United States as of September 2007; the Philippines as of June 2007.
[b] Based on Basel II calculations. The previous years' calculations based on Basel I.
[c] Major banks; end of fiscal year (March of the following calendar year).
[d] U.S banks with assets greater than US$1 billion.
Sources: National sources and *Global Financial Stability Report*, International Monetary Fund.

and once-highly-leveraged firms resulted in visible improvements in banks' balance sheet structures. Banks have reduced short-term external borrowings, which had previously exposed them to risks stemming from currency and maturity mismatches. In addition, banks have now broadened income sources by diversifying into new, more profitable lines of business such as consumer lending and real estate, new types of financial services, and stronger fee structures.

11.3.2. *Channels of Further Financial Contagion*

The limited spillover so far, nonetheless, partly reflects underlying weaknesses in the region's banking systems: Financial institutions remain largely unsophisticated, with risk management systems challenged by still weak institutional and systemic support. In addition, in the absence of

Table 11.1c. Rate of return on commercial bank assets (percent per annum)

	1998	2003	2004	2005	2006	2007[a]
China, People's Rep. of	0.1[b]	0.3	0.8	0.8	0.9	n.a.
Hong Kong, China	0.4	1.4	1.5	1.6	1.5	1.7
India	0.8	1.0	1.1	0.9	1.0	1.1
Indonesia	−19.9	2.6	3.5	2.6	2.6	2.8
Korea, Rep. of	−3.3	0.2	0.9	1.3	1.1	n.a.
Malaysia	1.1[b]	1.3	1.4	1.3	1.3	n.a.
Philippines	0.8	1.2	1	1.1	1.3	1.4
Singapore	0.4	1.0	1.2	1.2	1.4	1.4
Thailand	−5.1	0.7	1.3	1.4	0.8	0.1
Memo						
Germany	0.3	−0.1	0.1	0.3	0.3	n.a.
Japan[c]	−0.6	−0.1	0.2	0.5	0.4	0.2
U.S.	1.1	1.4	1.3	1.3	1.3	1.1

Notes: n.a. = not available.

[a] Data for Japan, Singapore, and the United States as of September 2007; Hong Kong, China, as of March 2007.

[b] Figure refers to 1999 data.

[c] End of fiscal year (March of the following calendar year).

Sources: CEIC, national sources, and *Global Financial Stability Report*, International Monetary Fund.

active risk management, bank lending to the private sector has become more conservative since the 1997–98 Asian financial crisis, although it has risen recently (Table 11.2). In order to boost profitability, banks moved into consumer lending and securities investment, exposing them to potential bubbles in local real estate and equity markets. In some countries, banks are relying increasingly on capital markets for financing rather than retail deposits.

Potential spillover could occur as the move into such new lines of business broadens exposure to new types of market risk. Although lending to the corporate sector remains large, the share of housing and consumer credits in assets is expanding rapidly. Where the data are available, the share of household lending in total loans — which includes both mortgage-related and consumer financing — has nearly doubled since the crisis and in India, the Republic of Korea (Korea), and Malaysia since 2000

Table 11.2. Growth of bank credit to private sector (y-o-y, percent)

	Average (1992–96)	2003	2004	2005	2006	2007
China, People's Rep. of	27.7	20.8	11.2	9.2	14.3	19.3
Hong Kong, China	15.4	−2.8	3.7	6.0	1.8	9.8
India	15.7	9.7	30.6	26.2	27.5	23.7
Indonesia	20.4	21.1	33.0	24.8	12.5	26.4
Korea, Rep. of	16.2	8.9	1.3	7.4	14.5	12.5
Malaysia	29.8	6.8	6.6	9.2	6.9	9.4
Pakistan	18.3	24.3	35.2	14.9	18.1	17.9
Philippines	37.2	1.1	9.3	−2.2	7.4	4.5
Singapore	15.2	5.4	4.4	2.0	4.9	17.6
Thailand	25.0	−1.3	11.3	7.7	4.0	3.9
Viet Nam	n.a.	28.4	41.6	31.6	25.5	39.2
Memo						
Euro Area	n.a.	5.7	6.5	9.9	11.4	12.9
Japan	2.3	−4.3	−2.3	3.0	−0.3	−0.1
U.S.	4.4	7.2	10.6	10.6	9.5	9.5

Note: n.a. = not available. Euro area or EU12 = Austria, Belgium, Finland, France, Germany, Greece, Ireland, Italy, Luxembourg, the Netherlands, Portugal, and Spain.
Source: International Financial Statistics, *International Monetary Fund*.

(Table 11.3). Mortgage-related lending, in particular, has increased visibly with recent housing booms across the region. Signs of stress have emerged in the household sector, as shown in high levels of household indebtedness in some countries (Table 11.4). In most, the level of household debt remains largely manageable when considering rapid GDP growth, household income, and financial wealth. However, this does not preclude potentially disruptive adjustment to recent housing price inflation and its economic impact on some countries.

An increase in the share of banks' securities holdings and their investment banking-type activities also implies greater market risk. Regional banks are actively participating in securities-related transactions such as underwriting, dealing, and brokerage, and foreign exchange transactions, leasing, and insurance activities. With government efforts to develop local

Table 11.3. Composition of bank lending (as percent of total domestic credit)

	Housing Loans			Consumer Loans			Loans to Enterprise		
	1995	**2000**	**2007**	**1995**	**2000**	**2007**	**1995**	**2000**	**2007**
Hong Kong, China	3.40	4.86	2.57	1.45	2.61	3.17	n.a.	n.a.	n.a.
India[a]	n.a.	4.03	12.03	n.a.	7.20	11.30	n.a.	n.a.	n.a.
Indonesia	n.a.	n.a.	9.47	n.a.	n.a.	28.33	n.a.	n.a.	53.20
Korea, Rep. of (commercial banks)	n.a.	11.29	7.86	n.a.	27.66	43.03	n.a.	56.47	47.31
Korea, Rep. of (all banks)	n.a.	17.77	29.36	n.a.	20.12	18.81	n.a.	62.11	51.83
Malaysia	n.a.	13.01	22.17	n.a.	0.88	0.44	n.a.		28.71
Philippines	n.a.	1.86	2.14	n.a.	n.a.	10.11	65.39	64.16	48.56
Singapore	16.04	25.03	31.33			13.92			54.75
Taipei, China	n.a.	19.94	27.30	n.a.	14.22	13.27	n.a.	40.71	40.78
Thailand	n.a.	n.a.	12.25	n.a.	0.00	12.25	n.a.	n.a.	n.a.
Memo									
Euro area	n.a.	27.08	30.87	n.a.	6.86	5.55	n.a.	n.a.	n.a.
Japan	11.02	15.54	24.27	3.27	2.43	1.97	n.a.	76.98	68.14
U.S.	3.23	3.35	7.12	18.79	13.96	11.93	27.49	27.91	21.08

Notes: Banks include all banks for Hong Kong, China and Taipei, China; scheduled commercial banks for India; commercial banks for Indonesia, Malaysia, the Philippines, Thailand, and the United States; domestic licensed banks for Japan; domestic banking units for Singapore; and monetary financial institutions for Euro area.

n.a. = not available. Euro area or EU12 = Austria, Belgium, Finland, France, Germany, Greece, Ireland, Italy, Luxembourg, the Netherlands, Portugal, and Spain

[a] Latest data is for 2006

Source: CEIC, Bank of Korea, and Financial Supervisory Service (Korea).

currency bond markets, banks are also often encouraged to take part in the development of the local bond market as issuers, underwriters, investors, and guarantors, given their dominant role in domestic financial markets. The broader scope of bank activities exposes them to new risks. Figure 11.8 illustrates an increase in banks' securities holdings, although much of the increase is due to a rise in government security holdings. In any case, a sharp pickup in interest rates could depress bond prices, hurting the banks' profits from bond holdings.

Table 11.4. Household indebtedness (percent of GDP)

	1998	2003	2004	2005	2006	2007[a]
Hong Kong, China	54.8	60.2	58.1	55.5	52.0	49.9
India[b]	2.7[f]	4.6	6.4	8.1	9.7	n.a.
Indonesia	4.3[f]	6.7	8.2	9.1	8.5	8.3
Korea, Rep. of	15.0	34.9	35.3	37.6	40.8	40.8
Malaysia	37.3	49.2	50.0	52.5	53.1	50.8
Philippines	8.9	4.8	5.2	4.7	4.2	4.0
Singapore[c]	n.a.	n.a.	51.0	49.4	46.4	46.5
Thailand	n.a.	n.a.	24.5	24.6	23.6	23.3
Memo						
Euro area[d]	42.1	47.1	49.0	52.0	53.8	54.2
Japan	19.1[f]	21.8	21.3	21.9	21.5	21.5
U.S.[e]	n.a.	16.2	18.4	18.6	18.6	17.8

Notes: n.a. = not available. Euro area or EU12 = Austria, Belgium, Finland, France, Germany, Greece, Ireland, Italy, Luxembourg, the Netherlands, Portugal, and Spain

[a] As of 30 September 2007 for Hong Kong, China; Japan; the Republic of Korea; and the Philippines.

[b] Refers to personal housing loans (outstanding credit).

[c] Sum of loans for personal uses, credit cards, purchase of consumer durable goods, and purchase of passenger cars for commercial banks, merchant banks, and finance companies; 2006, only data from commercial banks and merchant banks are available.

[d] Refers to loans extended by monetary financial institutions (MFIs).

[e] Refers to outstanding consumer credit.

[f] Earliest data available for Indonesia are as of 2001; India and Japan as of 2000.

Source: National sources and *CEIC*.

The region also remains open to broader contagion from global financial market turbulence. In a climate of heightened uncertainty, a sudden shift in the direction and magnitude of financial flows is a significant concern. Financial inflows to the region remain strong, but may fluctuate more amid the re-pricing of financial assets due to greater risk sensitivity among investors. A sharp reversal in risk appetite could also trigger a sudden reversal of capital flows, and involve a potential unwinding of "carry trades," which are of particular concern. This poses a potentially greater risk to the countries that have experienced rapid growth in portfolio investment flows and asset price inflation. Growing foreign participation

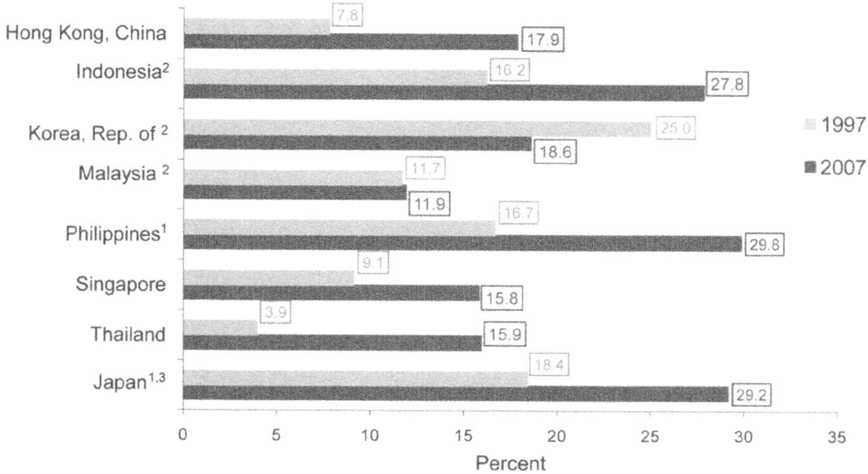

Figure 11.8 Securities investment to total bank assets of commercial banks (percent)
Notes: For Indonesia, claims rather than securities data are used.
[1] Data for the Philippines as of Oct 2007; Japan as of March 2007.
[2] Earliest data available for Malaysia is as of 1999; Korea as of 2000; and Indonesia as of 2001.
[3] End of fiscal year (March of the following calendar year).
Sources: CEIC, Hong Kong Monetary Authority, Bank Indonesia, and Bangko Sentral ng Pilipinas.

in local capital markets makes the region's financial markets vulnerable to changes in global financial market conditions such as sudden swings in investor sentiment (Table 11.5). International institutional investors also tend to unwind their positions in emerging markets when liquidity conditions deteriorate in their home countries.

Figure 11.9 shows that gross capital flows to emerging Asian economies reached record highs in recent years. Large capital inflows, strong credit expansion, and adverse macroeconomic consequences are not new to emerging market economies.[6] Many past episodes of financial turbulence came after large excesses of the asset market bubble, including the overvaluation of many stocks and rapid credit expansion. In recent years, the changing composition of capital inflows has been worrisome. Short-term foreign capital inflows have been strong in many of the region's economies, with "other investment" inflows picking up faster. The sharp

[6] See ADB (2007a).

Table 11.5. Total portfolio investment liabilities (US$ billion)

Economy	Total Foreign Portfolio Investment Liabilities			Domestic Capital Market			Ratio of Foreign Portfolio Investment to Domestic Capital Market (%)		
	2001	2004	2006	2001	2004	2006	2001	2004	2006
China, People's Rep. of	20.3	67.1	281.6	764.2	1,769.2	1,632.6	2.7	3.8	17.2
Hong Kong, China	96.7	123.7	233.7	558.2	924.4	1,781.0	17.3	13.4	13.1
India	15.4	71.4	179.7	n.a.	n.a.	n.a.	n.a.	n.a.	n.a.
Indonesia	5.5	25.4	38.9	72.2	134.5	226.5	7.6	18.9	17.2
Korea, Rep. of	76.8	166.0	280.5	633.2	1,149.8	1,844.8	12.1	14.4	15.2
Malaysia	22.6	51.6	59.4	201.8	292.3	382.5	11.2	17.7	15.5
Pakistan	0.5	0.7	2.2	n.a.	n.a.	n.a.	n.a.	n.a.	n.a.
Philippines	12.7	17.0	30.3	44.8	64.2	112.7	28.4	26.5	26.9
Singapore	50.7	68.4	126.1	168.7	290.2	470.9	30.0	23.6	26.8
Thailand	12.0	25.7	37.8	73.1	183.4	251.6	16.4	14.0	15.0
Memo									
Japan	542.3	948.6	1,434.9	7,774.5	12,502.7	13,106.2	7.0	7.6	10.9
EU15[a]	6,308.9	7,260.1	9,995.9	13,093.5	20,412.1	25,738.8	48.2	35.6	38.8
U.S.	3,101.2	4,843.6	6,254.2	28,886.2	35,400.2	42,189.6	10.7	13.7	14.8

Notes: n.a. = not available.

[a]Domestic capital market data excludes Luxembourg, as data are unavailable. The EU15 refers to the 15 members of the European Union prior to its May 2004 expansion to 25 countries. The 15 members include Austria, Belgium, Denmark, Finland, France, Germany, Greece, Ireland, Italy, Luxembourg, the Netherlands, Portugal, Spain, Sweden, and the United Kingdom.

Sources: *Asian Bonds Online and Coordinated Portfolio Investment Survey*, International Monetary Fund.

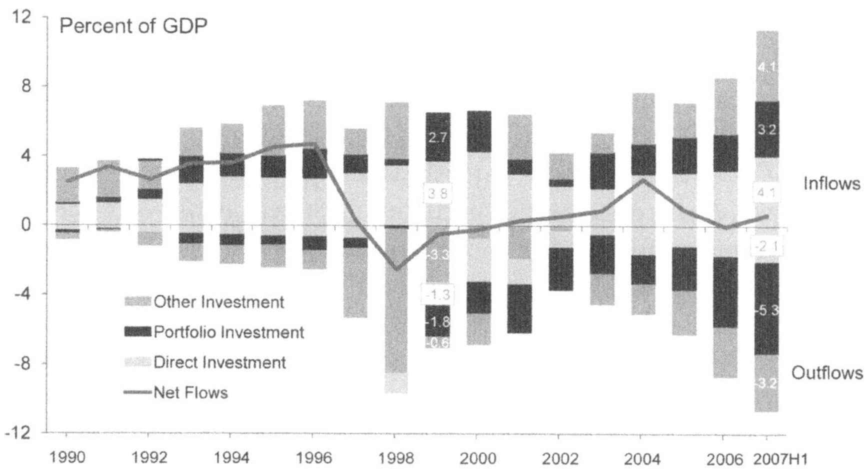

Figure 11.9 Financial account (percent of GDP)

Notes: Figures include China, People's Rep. of; Hong Kong, China; India; Indonesia; Korea, Rep. of; Malaysia; Philippines; Taipei, China; Thailand; and Singapore. Due to data unavailability, figures for 1990–97 do not include Hong Kong, China and Taipei, China;1998–99 figures do not include Taipei, China; 2007H1 figures do not include India and Malaysia.

Sources: OREI staff calculations based on data sourced from the International Financial Statistics, International Monetary Fund, and country sources.

increase in the short-term investment component of capital inflows in the mid-1990s, which was immediately withdrawn at onset of the 1997–98 Asian financial crisis, has often been blamed as a prime reason for the crisis. In particular, large swings in the "other investment" category between pre-and post-crisis periods reinforced the region's awareness of risks inherent in volatile short-term financial flows.

Named as "other investments," such non-FDI, non-portfolio inflows often represent short-term borrowing of the region's banking systems and trade credits. Substantial increases in other investment inflows may also reflect increased "carry trade" activities and "hot money" driven by interest rate differentials. Although country-specific factors can partly explain recent increases — such as a sharp rise in overseas borrowing by banks in Korea to help local shipbuilders hedge future dollar receipts — this cannot be the full story given the magnitude of the regional pattern. To the extent that the "other investment" component of short-term capital inflows is extremely volatile and highly interest-rate sensitive, the region's financial markets are subject to the vagaries of foreign investor sentiment.

Despite generally conservative banking activity in the region, largely unregulated non-bank financial institutions are already taking increasingly risky investment opportunities for higher returns. Local institutional investors started to increase their overseas investments and diversified their holdings into riskier and more sophisticated equity, credit, and currency derivatives. A sharp increase in portfolio investment outflows in the past few years (mainly foreign debt securities purchased by the People's Republic of China [China] and Korea) suggests that the exposure of the Asian economy to mortgage-related securities might be bigger than currently estimated. Higher cross-border holdings of financial assets also raise vulnerability to sharp adjustments in the valuation of global financial assets.

In globalized finance, a swing in market sentiment could also hurt local companies' funding conditions and hence investment decisions. Tighter credit conditions — together with elevated funding costs — and increased financial market volatility could squeeze funding for corporate investment, particularly where the business environment remains less friendly. So far, domestic funding conditions remain generally healthy, and the region's relatively strong banking sectors, which dominate its financial systems, provide a positive backdrop. Bank lending rates remain relatively low (Fig. 11.10)

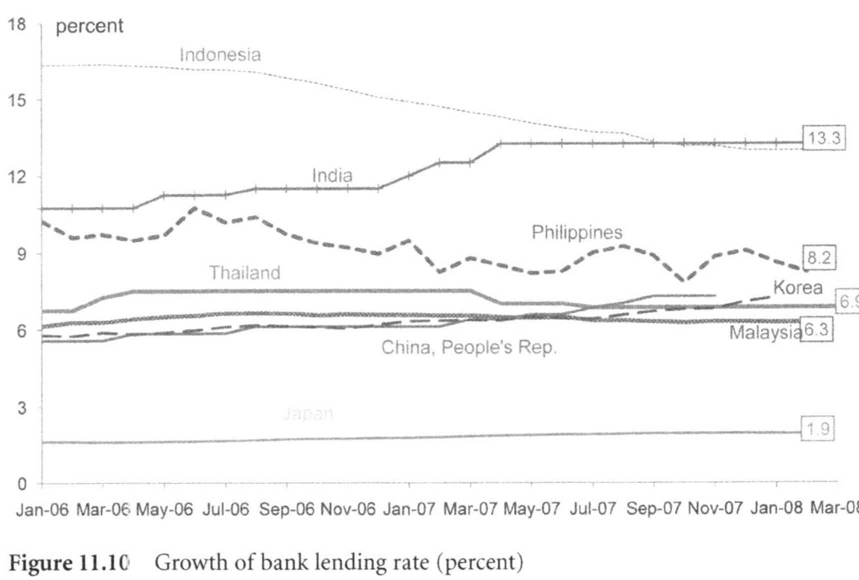

Figure 11.10 Growth of bank lending rate (percent)
Source: International Financial Statistics, International Monetary Fund.

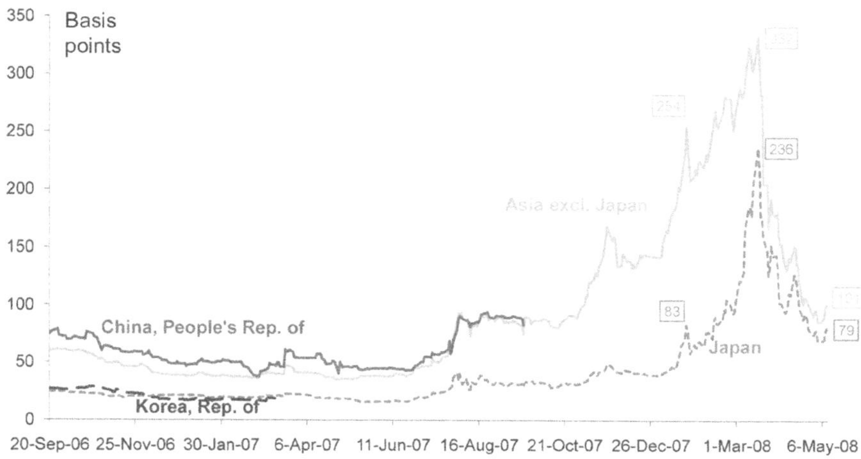

Figure 11.11 iTraxx Credit Default Swap spreads (in basis points)
Note: iTraxx is the brand name for the family of credit default swap index products covering regions of Europe, Japan, and non-Japan Asia which form a large sector of the overall credit derivative market.
Source: Thomson Datastream.

and credits to the private sector have been strong (see Table 11.2). Nevertheless, heightened credit concerns are reflected in the rising costs of protecting against corporate default in emerging Asia (Fig. 11.11). A worsening of credit conditions, potentially leading to a credit crunch, could dampen broader economic activity and, in turn, corporate profits.

11.4. Challenges from the Changing Financial Landscape

11.4.1. *Financial Innovation and Asian Financial Systems*

The relative strength of regional financial systems reflects a number of factors. Regional banking systems — still dominant in financial intermediation — are stronger than before: Balance sheets are healthy, risk management practices are generally better, and prudential oversight has been strengthened. Prudent macroeconomic management provides a backdrop for currency and financial stability, with inflation targeting introduced, fiscal budgets consolidated, and exchange rate regimes made more flexible. Meanwhile, ongoing efforts to develop capital markets continue to broaden corporate financing sources, increasing the resilience of the overall financial system. However, pockets of weakness remain in the region's banking and financial systems, and new challenges are emerging.

The pace of financial innovation has gathered momentum in recent years, and has been driven by the introduction of new information and communication technologies, the evolution of consumer needs, and the removal of regulatory barriers. The result has been the introduction of new innovative financial instruments and technologies, such as securitization. Since the 1980s, securitization has become a powerful and widely used tool in both developed and emerging markets across the globe.[7] The process usually uses pooled assets or income, configured to provide yield that investors find acceptable over extended periods of time and from institutions with credible credit ratings. A much wider range of instruments has meant more freedom for both savers and investors to customize their financial positions and best fit their risk profile. This allows more scope for providing or acquiring funds. Markets have also grown in importance as providers of financial services, relative to banks and other traditional providers. Technology advances have also spurred the globalization of finance by making it easier to invest savings around the globe and lowered the cost of financial intermediation and funding costs.

However, such innovation and competition have lagged in many Asian financial systems. In Asia, in the wake of the 1997–98 Asian financial crisis, securitization has been used increasingly as a means to address loan losses by financial intermediaries or as a device to help bring about market-based systemic reform (Fig. 11.12). Despite its growth, however, Asia's use of securitization is currently far more modest than in Europe and North America. The development of auxiliary markets such as derivatives and swap markets also lags, hampering hedging activities in the market.

Non-bank financial institutions — such as private investment funds, mutual and pension funds, insurance and leasing companies, and venture capital firms — although growing rapidly in recent years,[8] remain

---

[7] See ADB (2007b).

[8] The size of managed assets of mutual funds and private pension funds in the newly industrialized economies (Hong Kong, China; Republic of Korea; Taipei, China) is rising rapidly

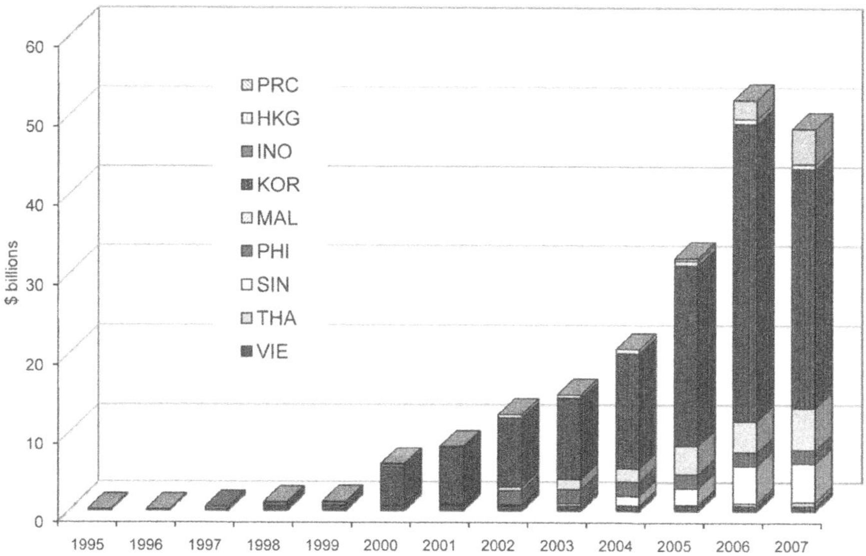

Figure 11.12 Total outstanding securitization (emerging East Asia)
Sources: AsiaBondsOnline, Bloomberg, Chinabond.

underdeveloped. The size of managed assets of institutional investors remains much lower than in the United States and Europe, reflecting largely unsophisticated financial institutions in the emerging Asian region (Table 11.6).

The rapid penetration of financial innovation into some parts of largely underdeveloped domestic financial systems is another concern in Asia. Despite its potential to create more efficient and resilient financial markets, financial innovation entails significant uncertainty by making changes in financial intermediation and market functioning. Some major financial disturbances in the past decade have occurred after some innovations — imbued with overly optimistic views about benefits — challenged market participants' and regulators' understanding of risk. A lack of institutional capacity among both financial institutions and regulators is

at about 25.4 percent on average over the past 5 years, based on estimates by the Organization for Economic Co-operation and Development and the Investment Company Institute.

Table 11.6. Size of markets for institutional investors in selected Asian economies (2006)

	Pension Funds	Mutual Funds	Life Insurance	Pension Funds	Mutual Funds	Life Insurance
	US$ billion			% of GDP		
China, People's Rep. of	34.8	131.9	44.3	1.3	5.0	1.7
India	20.7	58.2	37.2	2.4	6.6	4.2
Korea, Rep. of	191.3	12.9	58.8	21.5	1.5	6.6
Hong Kong, China	49.5	713.0	15.3	26.1	375.3	8.1
Singapore	81.1	18.9	7.1	59.4	13.8	5.2
Indonesia	7.3	5.7	2.9	2.0	1.6	0.8
Malaysia	66.6	21.3	5.0	42.7	13.6	3.2
Philippines	0.4	1.2	0.9	0.3	1.0	0.8
Taipei, China	170.3	65.0	41.3	46.6	17.8	11.3
Thailand	10.3	29.0	3.5	5.0	14.0	1.7
Emerging Asia	**632.3**	**1,057.1**	**216.3**	**10.6**	**17.8**	**3.6**
Memo						
EU15	3,433.2	7,445.8	887.9	25.4	55.2	6.6
Japan	1,439.2	578.9	378.5	32.9	13.2	8.6
U.S.	9,721.1	10,413.6	533.6	73.6	78.9	4.0

Note: EU15 refers to members EU12 plus Denmark, Sweden, and United Kingdom.

Sources: *Country Finance 2006 and 2007 Reports*, Economist Intelligence Unit; *World Economic Outlook Database* (April 2008), International Monetary Fund; *Stigma April 2007*, Swiss Re; *2007 Investment Company Factbook*, Investment Company Institute; *Pension Markets in Focus*, OECD November 2007, Issue 4.

another factor that can hamper effective risk monitoring and control, let alone the onslaught of evolving financial technology. This has led to disproportionately large damage in less developed financial systems. For example, the 1997–98 Asian financial crisis was caused partly by reckless overseas borrowing by banks using then-modern techniques. New innovative investment strategies also incurred large losses at Long-Term Capital Management (LTCM) and similar institutions in 1998; and together with the Russian debt default,[9] the collapse of these investment strategies rippled through the global financial system.

Some of more advanced regional economies need to remain vigilant against further revelation of their banking systems' risk exposure to the current turmoil. They must also continue to guard against spillover, while accelerating reforms to keep up with global financial market trends and developments. The region's banking and financial systems may not be as advanced as their counterparts in industrialized countries. However, these systems continue to ride the wave of financial liberalization and globalization brought on by factors including the increasing presence of foreign investors, tightening global networks alongside the information and communications revolution, and the introduction of increasingly sophisticated financial products and services.

In this environment, prudent risk management requires the skill to assess the full magnitude and details of risk under stressful times and prepare for an extreme, yet plausible market event. Testing various stress scenarios can be helpful to gauge portfolio risks and assess potential losses under stressful market conditions. The current market turmoil presents ample evidence of just what sorts of events are plausible models for stress testing, although the underlying portfolio will determine what would be the appropriate stress test for its risk management.

11.4.2. *Global Financial Integration and Spillover*

After the 1997–98 Asian financial crisis, Asian economies took various steps to improve domestic financial systems and promote capital account liberalization. The region also used the crisis as an opportunity to deepen financial cooperation and integration at the regional level — in part as a

---

[9] On 17 August 1998, the Russian government devalued the ruble, defaulted on sovereign debt, and declared a suspension of payment to foreign creditors. The sharp decline in the price of oil and other raw materials in the aftermath of the Asian financial crisis had severe consequences for the Russian economy, which relied heavily on commodity exports. The Russian crisis unsettled global financial markets and the related market volatility brought down LTCM and similar sorts through their exposures to the Russian market and the use of leverage.

safeguard against the spillover of global market instability, but also as a platform for regional financial development. There have been several important regional initiatives, such as the ASEAN Surveillance Process, the Chiang Mai Initiative, the Asian Bond Markets Initiative, and the Asian Bond Fund.[10] Despite these efforts, regional financial integration remains limited. A number of studies find that the financial markets in Asia are integrated more financially with the global economy than with each other.[11] Their increasing integration at the global rather than regional level, along with the rapid expansion of global capital markets, suggests that the potential for the financial transmission of global shocks has likely increased. However, direct evidence on this point is patchy.

We test the extent of financial integration of the region's equity and bond markets with the global markets (see the Appendix for the description of data, empirical methodology, and specification issues).[12] If equity or bond markets in the region are fully integrated with global markets and no country-specific disturbances occur, stock prices or bond yields should only react to news common to all markets. The empirical results show that Asian equity markets track the U.S. markets closely. Tighter global integration translates into increased spillover from a global shock on returns and volatilities of regional equities. In contrast to the equity market, the results suggest Asian bond markets remain generally segmented from the U.S. bond market.

It is assumed that an unexpected component of individual stock market returns can be decomposed into a purely local shock (an intercept or α_i) and a reaction to global news (proxied by an unexpected component of U.S. market returns). If the local stock markets are integrated globally, a global shock will dominate in explaining the unexpected component of an individual market return. That is, country-specific sensitivity (β_i) in the reaction to a U.S. market shock will increase. On the other hand, the relative importance of local market shocks (α_i) will decrease. Under the assumption of complete global integration, α is close to zero and β close to 1.

---

[10] See ADB (2008) for details.

[11] Kim, Lee, and Shin (2007) and Kim and Lee (2008).

[12] The empirical methodology is drawn largely from a European Central Bank (ECB) report on financial integration (ECB, 2008) for financial integration indicators.

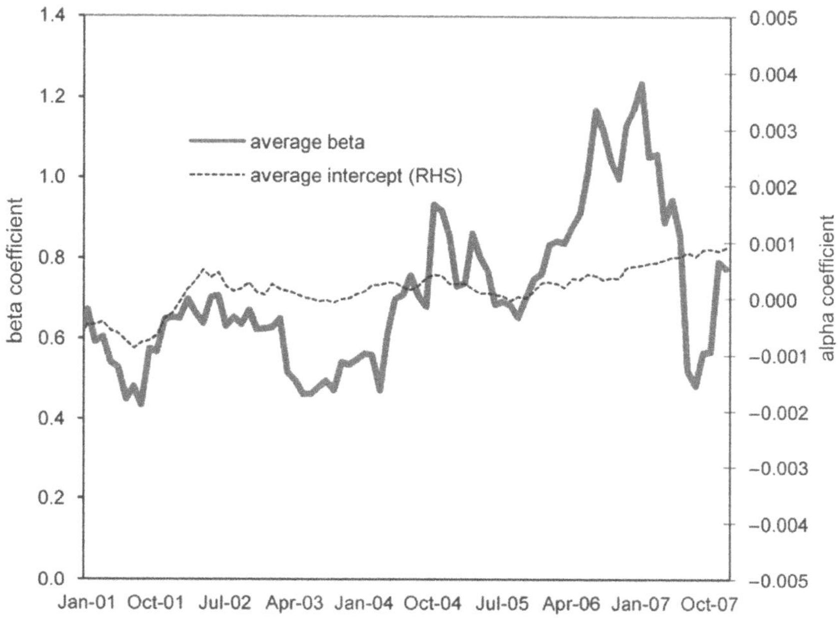

Figure 11.13 U.S. shock spillover intensity in Asian equity markets

Figure 11.13 presents the regional stock market's α and β (un-weighted average of α_i and β_i from individual stock markets). This generally confirms increasing spillover of a global shock to Asian stock market returns and the limited influence of purely local news in explaining the returns.

Figure 11.14 shows the proportion of the total domestic equity market volatility explained by U.S. shocks for the period 2001–07. In many emerging Asian markets, a U.S. shock is an important force behind the domestic equity volatility movements. Equity markets in Hong Kong, Korea, Singapore, and, to a more modest degree, Taipei, China, are relatively more sensitive to volatility spillover from the U.S. market, while comparatively less developed markets in China, Indonesia, and the Philippines show lower sensitivity. In Thailand, the spillover from the U.S. market is modest. However, the Thai market experienced a spike in volatility in late 2006 and early 2007, largely due to the effect of the coup d'état in September 2006. Excluding these rather unusual observations, the portion of variance that can be explained by U.S. shocks is higher. Overall, the rising incidence of

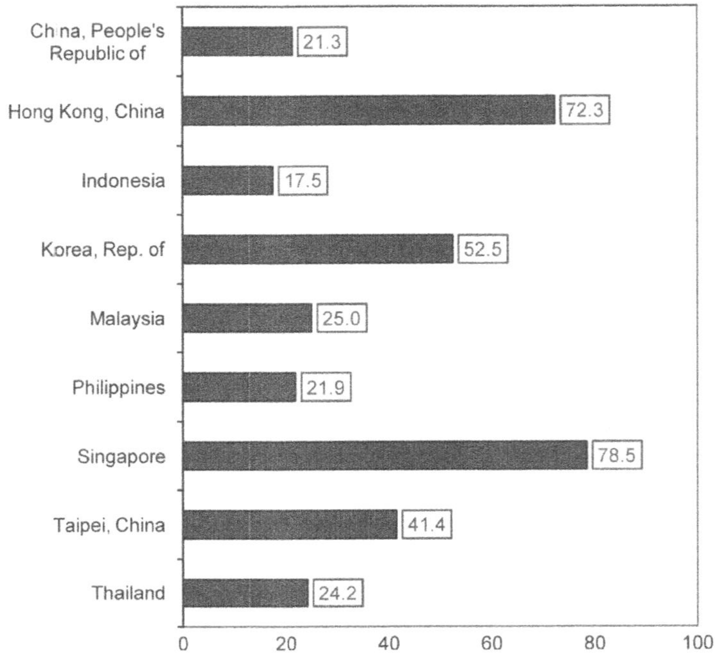

Figure 11.14 Share of variance in local equity returns explained by U.S. shocks (2001–07)

spillover of global shocks on Asian market returns and volatility are supportive of greater global integration of relatively more advanced markets in emerging Asia.

Evidence is less clear for Asian bond markets. A model for bond yields can be constructed, similar to the equity return spillover. If Asian bond markets are fully integrated with the global bond market, changes in local bond yields will simply reflect the changes in the global bond yields. Figure 11.15 reports the average alpha/beta from estimated individual alpha/beta for 10-year local government bond markets. The local bond markets can be said to be globally integrated if the average α is close to zero and β close to 1. The results of relatively low β show no clear sign of global integration for 10-year Asian government bond markets during the period 2001–07.

Again, in terms of volatility, local bond markets are generally not much influenced by global bond volatility. In Fig. 11.16, the proportion of

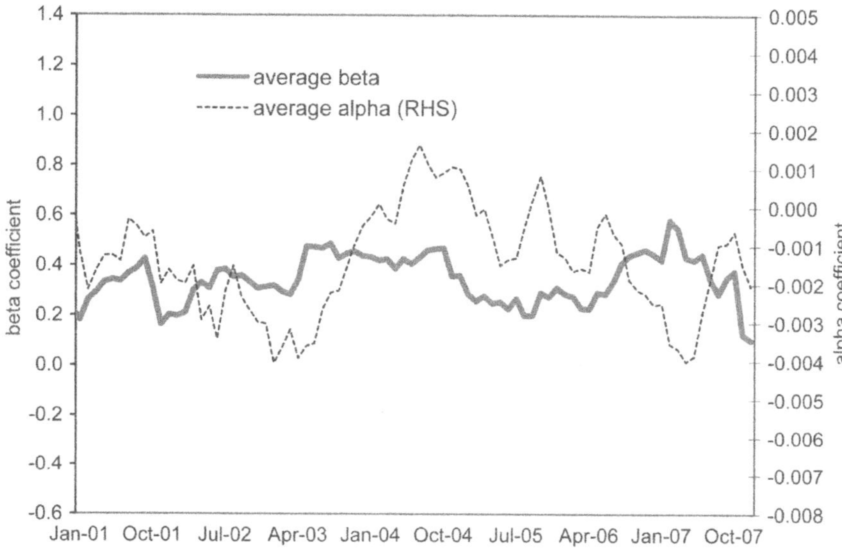

Figure 11.15 U.S. shock spillover intensity in Asian bond markets

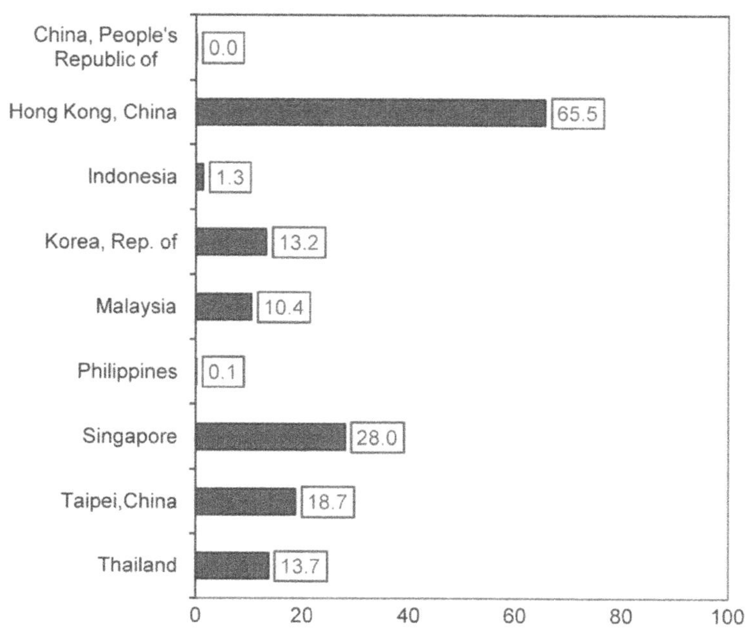

Figure 11.16 Share of variance in 10-year local government bond yields explained by U.S. shocks (2001–07)

the variance of local bond yields that can be explained by global volatility is relatively small, with the notable exception of Hong Kong, China, whose monetary policy is tied to the United States due to its dollar peg. In addition, this share generally decreased in the latter period during which the recent credit turmoil likely increased the U.S. market volatility. This empirical result is consistent with other evidence that shows relative resilience of local bond markets to financial turmoil that has affected global credit markets.

11.5. Policy Implications

The 1997–98 Asian financial crisis was due to the confluence of many factors including over-reliance on bank financing and inadequate financial regulatory and supervisory frameworks. In its aftermath, a number of crucial banking reforms were undertaken to make banking systems in the region more resilient. However, more needs to be done given the increasing financial uncertainty and potential instability in global markets. Policy priorities include (i) enhancing transparency and governance; (ii) improving risk assessment and management of financial institutions; (iii) strengthening regulation and supervision; and (iv) deepening and broadening financial systems, especially by developing corporate bond markets.[13]

A lack of market transparency and governance infrastructure impairs investor confidence and hampers the development of domestic financial sectors. Credit risk managers in emerging markets have a difficult task: The necessary information on credit ratings and traded security prices, for example, can be sparse. Many regional economies also have limited default history data and provide little support to infrastructure, such as credit

[13] Recently, the Financial Stability Forum (FSF), which has undertaken an analysis of the causes of the current global turmoil for the G7 ministers and central bank governors, published a report that contains recommendations for increasing the resilience of financial markets and institutions. The report (FSF, 2008) proposes concrete action in the five areas: (i) strengthening prudential oversight of capital, liquidity, and risk management; (ii) enhancing transparency and valuation; (iii) implementing changes in the role and uses of credit ratings; (iv) strengthening the authorities' responsiveness to risks; and (v) applying robust arrangements for dealing with stress in the financial system.

information bureaus. Even where data are available, drastic changes in the economic environment in which banks operate, across Asia since the 1990s, make it difficult to gauge default probability or exposure to defaults in the current economic climate. Building information and governance infrastructure such as credit information systems, accounting and disclosure rules, and internal and external auditing systems are essential to provide certainty and foster investor confidence in the domestic financial systems, let alone an important precondition for financial liberalization without undermining financial stability.

In light of the current turmoil in the global financial markets and the structural weaknesses of regional banking systems, it is important to strengthen the banking sector and build institutional and systemic support for effective risk management.

Special attention is needed for some recent and notable changes in the region's banking, such as rising household lending and securities transactions. Rapid expansion by financial institutions into unfamiliar areas inevitably entails new types of risk. Recent trends in the global financial system — importantly, the growing presence of non-bank financial institutions and the proliferation of new instruments for risk transfer — will also become increasingly relevant in the region.

Regulators need to renew efforts to test the capacity of their regulated institutions to manage the risks they assume, and to explore the dynamics and sensitivities of the assets they hold. They need to better understand the collateral's character and the tranching structure, particularly if instruments are difficult to value or have illiquid secondary markets. Regulators should also be better able to audit the risk management systems used by these institutions, to verify that they are appropriately tailored to individual risks.

The expansion of the services of credit rating agencies into the region's markets, for example, can help investors make sound investment decisions on adequate and fair information, and this is an important element of the necessary infrastructure for financial market stability. The increasingly complex product structures of modern financial assets, however, increase challenges facing credit rating agencies. Furthermore, as the issuers of these complex securities are often the clients for the credit rating agencies, there is potential for conflicts of interest. The agencies must remain independent of political or client pressure. This requires having financial independence based on adequate capital and diverse income sources.

Strengthening regulatory and supervisory frameworks is particularly important for emerging Asian markets, which face relatively weak financial market infrastructure for credit risk assessment and effective risk management. It is critical that the minimum capital requirements are met for regulated financial institutions. However, more importantly, the implementation of a rigorous supervisory review process needs to ensure that banks maintain sound balance sheets and exercise due vigilance in their risk management practices. Adequate institutional reforms need to ensure that systemic supports, such as credit information and credit rating systems, are in place.

This is the approach taken by the Basel Committee[14] — to steer the supervisory focus onto better risk management. As supervisory authorities embrace a more risk-focused approach in the way financial institutions deploy their own resources, firms will be given greater incentives to invest in more sophisticated risk management systems. In addition, enhanced transparency can encourage market discipline in monitoring the banks' risk-taking behavior. It should enable markets to reward financial institutions that take responsible approaches to risk management and penalize those that do not. A well-established governance structure for clear accountability is particularly important for those with more advanced financial systems, where the increasing complexity of financial services and products further complicates regulatory tasks.

A lack of institutional capacity in both financial institutions and regulators is another factor that hampers proper risk monitoring and controls, let alone dealing with evolving financial technology. The region's financial institutions should recognize that complex operations require well-established and refined internal risk management and control processes.

[14] The Basel Committee on Banking Supervision was created in 1974 by the central bank governors of the Group of Ten nations, including Belgium, Canada, France, Germany, Italy, Japan, the Netherlands, Sweden, Switzerland, the United Kingdom and the United States. The Basel Committee's recommendations on banking laws and regulations have been issued as "Basel Accord" and the second set of this is referred to as "Basel II," which incorporates three pillars (minimum capital requirements, supervisory review, and market discipline) to promote greater stability in the financial system.

It is also important to have knowledgeable staff to monitor risk exposure by setting effective risk limits and clearly communicating with executive management and boards of directors. Capacity building in the regulatory and supervisory bodies is essential to enable effective monitoring of risk exposure and safeguarding systemic stability against a rapidly changing financial environment.

Finally, broadening financial sectors and deepening the markets remain important long-term agenda items for creating more efficient and resilient domestic financial systems. One of the most valuable lessons of the 1997–98 Asian financial crisis was the need to deepen and diversify financial systems and markets. Prior to the crisis, the region's financial system concentrated on the banking sector, which relied heavily on short-term foreign currency debt to finance long-term investment projects in domestic currency. This exposed the financial system to systemic risk. However, despite considerable progress since the 1997–98 Asian financial crisis, Asian financial systems remain bank-dominated. Many domestic banking systems still tend to dominate in the composition of domestic financing. The development of liquid and well-functioning capital markets offers an alternative financing source to bank loans, provides long-term domestic currency funding for investment, and helps foster financial stability.

Whereas some Asian stock markets are as large as, or larger than comparable regional emerging markets, other segments of financial markets are much less developed. Money and bond markets in much of the region are illiquid and fragmented and, with the exception of Japan and Korea, local currency bond markets largely account for a much smaller share of GDP than in major economies. The growth in size of the region's local currency bond markets has been phenomenal, but the growth of the corporate bond markets has been slower than government bond markets, suggesting much remains to be done. Many markets require a broad range of reforms to increase liquidity and efficiency of local currency bond markets. Priorities include: (i) improving the legal and regulatory frameworks to ensure transparency and investor protection; (ii) removing impediments to market entry and investment, particularly those on capital and exchange controls; and (iii) broadening and diversifying the investor base.

Regional cooperation can support national initiatives to strengthen Asia's financial markets and overcome their fragmentation. Efforts to enhance the efficiency and stability of Asian capital markets need to be made at the regional and national levels, while fostering the integration of national financial markets. Strengthening regional cooperation in information sharing, monitoring and surveillance, and local-currency bond market development will also help promote regional financial stability.

Appendix A

A.1. Data Description

The empirical analysis was conducted for a sample set of countries from emerging Asia, which includes People's Republic of China; Hong Kong, China; Indonesia; Korea; Malaysia; the Philippines; Singapore; Taipei, China; and Thailand; and the United States as a proxy for the global market.

We employed the national stock market indexes[15] in computing equity returns and 10-year government bond indexes for bond yields, both obtained from Bloomberg LP. Both equity returns and bond yields are measured in local currency[16] with daily frequency from 1 January 2001 to 31 December 2007 for five trading days in a week. For the equity returns,

---

[15] Regional stock market indexes are: Shanghai Composite Index (SHCI) for China; Hang Seng Index for Hong Kong, China; Jakarta Composite Index for Indonesia; Korea Composite Stock Price Index (KOSPI) for Korea; Kuala Lumpur Composite Index (KLCI) for Malaysia; Philippine Composite Index (PCI) for the Philippines; FTSE Straits Times Index (FSSTI) for Singapore; Taiwan Stock Exchange (TWSE) Index for Taipei, China; and SET Index, Thailand. For the U.S. market, S&P 500 was used.

[16] Asset returns are often expressed in terms of the U.S. dollar or any single currency in financial integration studies in light of the "law of one price." In this analysis, however, the main interest is to assess the spillover of U.S. shocks to local markets and the impact on returns to local investors, rather than global investors. This is of particular interest to local policymakers in the wake of global financial turmoil. Nonetheless, the impact of daily exchange rate volatility is little on the trend of financial integration or on the degree of spillovers. We used the equity returns in the dollar terms to measure spillover intensity and variance ratios in the preliminary analysis. The results from the preliminary analysis produce nearly the same trends over time, whereas the actual levels are only slightly different.

we calculated the continuously compounded total returns, measured by the log differences of daily closing price levels such that, $R_{c,t} = \mathrm{In}(P_{c,t}) - \mathrm{In}(P_{c,t-1})$ for market c on day t. For the bond yields, end-of-day values for yields-to-maturity have been collected.

A.2. Empirical Methodology

A.2.1. *Equity Markets*

The returns of individual equity markets are modeled as having an expected component and an unexpected one, $\varepsilon_{c,t}$. Following the ECB (2008) approach, the expected return is obtained by relating individual market returns to a constant term and to the returns in the previous period. The error terms from the regression constitute the unexpected component of the return, or innovation.[17] The unexpected component is then decomposed into a purely local shock ($\alpha_{c,t}$) and a reaction to global (U.S.) news ($\varepsilon_{us,t}$):

$$\varepsilon_{c,t} = \alpha_{c,t} + \beta_{c,t}^{us} \varepsilon_{us,t} \tag{1}$$

where β represents the country-specific sensitivity to U.S. market shocks (of the unexpected component of equity returns).

It is assumed that innovation of local returns that is not explained by the common global factor is entirely due to local news. If equity markets are fully integrated globally and there is no country-specific disturbance, all innovation will be global. That is, an unexpected component of the returns of any individual market should react exclusively to common global news, which is reflected by an unexpected component of the returns in the global (U.S.) market. Hence, under the assumption of complete financial integration, $\alpha_{c,t} = 0$ and $\beta_{c,t}^{us} = 1$.

In order to investigate the development of the country-specific betas over time, time-varying betas of individual markets have been calculated

[17] The conditional variance of the error terms is assumed to follow a standard asymmetric GARCH(1,1) process.

for the period 2001–07. The time-varying betas are derived by running the given regression in an 18-month rolling window. That is, the first $\beta^{us}_{c,t}$ is estimated, using the monthly averages of equity returns for the first 18 months. Subsequently, the data window is moved one month ahead and the equation is re-estimated until the last observation is reached.

Figure 11.13 reports the unweighted average of $\beta^{us}_{c,t}$, for all *c*, as spillover intensity by which a U.S. shock is transmitted to local equity markets, as well as the unweighted average of $e_{c,t}$, for all *c*, as an influence of purely local disturbance.

Figure 11.14 reports the variance ratios for individual market returns. This is to estimate the proportion of total domestic equity volatility explained by the global (U.S.) shock. The conditional variance is estimated by the GARCH (1,1) model for individual country-specific returns. Total volatility is then given by

$$\sigma^2_{c,t} = h_{c,t} + \left(\beta^{us}_{c,t}\right)^2 \sigma^2_{us,t} \tag{2}$$

where $h_{c,t}$ is the variance of the local shock component.

The variance ratio for an individual market is then obtained by

$$VR^{us}_{c,t} = \frac{\left(\beta^{us}_{c,t}\right)^2 \sigma^2_{us,t}}{\sigma^2_{c,t}} \tag{3}$$

The variance ratio will be close to 1 if the beta approaches 1 and when the volatilities of the local and the U.S. market returns are of a similar magnitude. The variance ratio is derived by assuming that local shocks are not correlated with the U.S. returns.

A.2.2. *Bond Markets*

Similarly, if bond markets are fully integrated globally and no country-specific disturbance affects credit risk, bond yields should respond only to common global markets. That is, changes in the bond yields of individual countries should react exclusively to common global news, which is reflected by a change in the global benchmark bond yield (10-year U.S.

Treasury note). To separate common from local influences, the following regression is run:

$$\Delta R_{c,t} = \alpha_{c,t} + \beta_{c,t}\Delta R_{us,t} + \varepsilon_{c,t} \tag{4}$$

where α denotes a time-varying and country-dependent intercept; β is a country-specific and time-varying beta with respect to the benchmark (U.S.) bond yield; ΔR is the change in the bond yield; and ε is a country-specific shock.

A time series is obtained for α and β, respectively, using the same 18-month rolling regression as for the previous equity returns.

Figure 11.15 reports the unweighted average of $\beta_{c,t}$ for all c as well as the unweighted average of $\alpha_{c,t}$ for all c, respectively, for the magnitude of influence of the U.S. and local market disturbance.

Again, Fig. 11.16 shows the share of the variance of local (country-specific) bond yields that can be explained by the variance of the global benchmark yields (or 10-year U.S. Treasury note yields). The total variance of local bond yields is given by

$$\mathrm{Var}\left(\Delta R_{c,t}\right) = \beta_{c,t}^2 Var\left(\Delta R_{us,t}\right) + Var\left(\varepsilon_{c,t}\right) \tag{5}$$

and the variance ratio by

$$VR_{c,t} = \frac{\beta_{c,t}^2 Var\left(\Delta R_{us,t}\right)}{Var\left(\Delta R_{c,t}\right)} \tag{6}$$

A.3. Specification Issues

Some important caveats should be kept in mind when interpreting the empirical results. First, the econometric methodology is subject to potential specification problems. We consider the simplest possible equations where changes in equity returns or bond yields are determined only by local and global news. Thus, many other factors that may influence the rate of return to equity or bond are not specified. The omission of such factors may cause bias of parameter estimates in these parsimonious equations.

Second, the empirical results depend on the selection of the most appropriate benchmark equity returns or bond yields. Here, we have employed the U.S. market as a proxy for the global market. But the U.S. market is not necessarily the global benchmark. Third, the assumption of the benchmark case of perfect market integration is unrealistic in that common factors cannot fully explain changes in local equity returns or bond yields. Earlier financial literature[18] shows evidence of partial segmentation or time-varying integration. It is thus unlikely that reactions to local and global news can be completely separated and uncorrelated. Finally, multiple facets of financial market integration make it difficult for any single measure to provide a comprehensive assessment of market integration. It is worth noting that the methodology applied in this paper is just one among many indicators and unlikely to give a definite picture of market integration. Given the significant specification problems and technical difficulties, the empirical results should be interpreted with caution and taken illustratively.

References

Asian Development Bank. 2007a. *Asian Economic Monitor (July)*. Available at http://aric.adb.org.

———— 2007b. *Asia Bond Monitor (November)*. Available at http://www.adb.org/publications/asia-bond-monitor-november-2007.

———— 2008. *Emerging Asian Regionalism: A Partnership for Shared Prosperity.* Manila: ADB.

European Central Bank. 2008. *Financial Integration in Europe (April)*. Frankfurt: ECB.

Financial Stability Forum. 2008. *Report of the Financial Stability Forum on Enhancing Market and Institutional Resilience.* Available at http://www.financialstabilityboard.org/wp-content/uploads/r_0804.pdf.

International Monetary Fund. 2008. *Global Financial Stability Report.* Washington, DC: International Monetary Fund.

Kearney, Colm, and Brian M. Lucey. 2004. International Equity Market Integration: Theory, Evidence and Implications. *International Review of Financial Analysis* 13 (5):571–583.

[18] For literature survey on international capital market integration, see Kearney and Lucey (2004).

Kim, Soyoung, and Jong-Wha Lee. 2008. Real and Financial Integration in East Asia. *ADB Working Paper Series on Regional Economic Integration* 17. Manila: ADB.

Kim, Soyoung, Jong-Wha Lee, and Kwanho Shin. 2007. Regional and Global Financial Integration in East Asia. In: *China, Asia and the New World Economy,* edited by Barry Eichengreen, Charles Wyplosz, and Yung Chul Park, pp. 168–200. London: Oxford University Press.

Chapter 12

Real and Financial Integration in East Asia*

12.1. Introduction

After the 1997/98 financial crisis, the East Asian economies took various steps toward economic integration. As economies recovered dramatically from the crisis, the region took the opportunity to deepen market-led integration and policy-induced cooperation. On the real side, outward-oriented economic policies, such as lowering trade barriers and forming free trade agreements, continued to propel the region's rapid expansion in international trade. The private sector driven vertical integration of production networks across countries has also contributed to greater trade integration, both at regional and global levels. On the financial side, governments have promoted cross-border financial transactions through financial market deregulation and capital account liberalization.[1]

Increasing economic integration in East Asia has far-reaching implications for the region and for the global economy. For example, it is often

---

*This chapter is co-authored with Soyoung Kim and was originally published in *Review of International Economics*, Vol. 20, No. 2 (May 2012), pp. 332–349.

The authors are grateful to Yoonbai Kim and participants at the AEA/KAEA session, 2007 American Economic Association annual meeting for helpful comments and Fidelis Sadicon, Marshall Mays, and Junyup Kim for data assistance. This work was supported by the National Research Foundation of Korea Grant funded by the Korean Government (NRF-2010-327-B00088).

[1] The Asian crisis prompted policy dialogue and initiatives to strengthen regional financial and monetary integration such as the Chiang Mai Initiative (CMI) and the Asian Bond Markets Initiative (ABMI).

pointed out that increasing integration at the regional rather than global level can help the region "decouple" from the global economy and better sustain fast growth, independently of the USA or the European economies. Asia's fast-rising share of global trade and finance has also been linked with the region's rising political power in the global community.

The purpose of this paper is to empirically investigate the degree of economic integration for East Asian economies. While rapid integration into regional and global markets has been a salient feature of the East Asian economies since the 1990s, the extent, nature, and consequences of East Asian integration have not been clearly assessed yet. Empirical evidence on the extent of real and financial integration and implied macroeconomic interdependence/consequences in East Asia has been scattered, limited, and inconclusive. This paper fills the gap by documenting the extent and macroeconomic consequences of integration for East Asian countries in a comprehensive way.

The paper documents various aspects of economic integration for East Asia, contrary to most past studies that document only a few aspects of economic integration. The focus is on the following three comparisons of the extent of economic integration: (i) real vs financial market integration; (ii) regional (within East Asia) vs global (with the rest of the world or major industrial countries) integration, and (iii) for the period before vs after the Asian financial crisis.

With these comparisons, the analysis will address various issues, scatteredly raised in past studies. First, studies such as Asian Development Bank (ADB) (2007) and International Monetary Fund (IMF) (2007) found that the degree of real integration (as measured by output co-movement) among the region has been increasing, in part as a result of an increase in intra-regional trade (in addition to common regional shocks and common policies). It is not evident that Asian economies have decoupled from or have even become less interdependent with the global economy. Empirical studies differ on the extent to which Asian economies have become more autonomous (IMF, 2007). Second, several studies showed evidence of limited extent of financial market integration in the region as a whole (Kim *et al.*, 2006; Cavoli *et al.*, 2004). Lee (2008) pointed out that the degree of regional financial integration lags real (trade) integration in East Asia. In contrast, *Kim et al.* (2008) documented that regional financial integration has deepened in the 2000s. Third, some studies such as

Eichengreen and Park (2004), and Kim *et al.* (2008) suggested that the East Asian financial markets are integrated relatively more with global markets than with each other, while Asdrubali and Kim (2011), and Kim *et al.* (2004a) showed mixed results on global vs regional risk sharing.

To analyze these issues, various measures were adopted (price, quantity, and macro consequences) to gauge the extent of real and financial integration, contrary to most past studies that document only a few measures. Based on various measures, some interesting insights are drawn, for example, whether the results based on various measures provide a similar conclusion, if it is not, how and why the results are different. Further, some measures are newly developed in this paper.

Fully integrated real markets can be defined as a situation in which goods can move freely within an area; while fully integrated financial markets can be defined as a situation in which traders can transact financial assets freely within an area. Related to such definitions, first this paper briefly reviews the price measures (such as cross-country interest differentials and correlations of financial asset returns) since in fully integrated markets, prices across countries should be equalized. Second, volume measures, such as the size of trade volume and cross-border financial assets, are considered to provide more direct evidence on real and financial integration.

Macroeconomic measures such as cross-country output and consumption relation are also examined to infer the macroeconomic consequences of real and financial integration. The output relation can capture the inter-dependence of the real side of the economy as a consequence of real economic integration. Real and trade integration can increase the inter-dependence of output across countries. Although both trade volume and structure are important in determining the influence of real and trade integration on the co-movement of output, empirical literature has suggested that real and trade integration tend to increase the co-movement of output (Canova and Dellas, 1993; Frankel and Rose, 1998). In contrast, a vast literature on international risk sharing (Backus *et al.*, 1992; Obstfeld, 1995) has suggested that international risk sharing, often achieved through international financial markets, also tends to increase the co-movement of consumption across countries.

Contrary to past studies using a correlation approach, this paper develops dynamic measures for real and financial macroeconomic interdependences, based on the impulse responses from the panel vector autoregression (VAR) model. Interestingly, the measures for real and financial interdependence are directly comparable. This method has some advantages over a simple correlation approach and other methods adopted. First, differently from a correlation approach, the VAR approach can disentangle the nature of shocks, for example, by regional and global shocks.[2] Second, one can separate the size of shocks and the effects given the size of the shock. Finally, although most past studies used static measures, this paper uses dynamic measures.[3]

12.2. Price and Quantity Measures of Integration

12.2.1. *Real Integration*

Quantity measures show that East Asian economies have been more integrated in goods and services trade, both globally and regionally.[4] Trade openness in the nine emerging East Asian economies[5] — measured by the ratio of total trade in gross domestic product (GDP) — reached 95% in 2005, from 71% in 1990, and 21% in 1970. The share of East Asian trade in world GDP has grown more than four-fold since the 1970s, currently exceeding over 20% of world trade volume.

Intraregional trade among these nine East Asian economies increased steadily to 40.9% of total trade in 2006, from 30.0% in 1990, although it declined to 35% in 2009 owing to the global financial crisis (Table 12.1).

[2] The approach is especially useful when one compares regional vs global integration. By identifying regional vs global shocks, one can clearly infer how an individual economy responds to each shock.

[3] Asdrubali and Kim (2004) developed a dynamic measure, but did not separate regional vs global risk sharing.

[4] The law of one price is widely recognized as a measure of the extent of goods market integration; however, there has been no study to test the extent of goods market integration among Asian economies owing to a lack of data. Therefore, only quantity measures are reported.

[5] Throughout the paper, the ten East Asian economies are: the People's Republic of China; Hong Kong (China), Indonesia, the Republic of Korea, Malaysia, Philippines, Singapore, Taipei (China); Thailand, and Japan. The nine East Asian economies exclude Japan from the ten East Asian economies.

Table 12.1. Trade with selected economies in East Asia (as percentage of total trade)

	East Asia 9				**Japan**				**USA**			
Year	**1990**	**2000**	**2006**	**2009**	**1990**	**2000**	**2006**	**2009**	**1990**	**2000**	**2006**	**2009**
China, People's Rep. of	42.3	26.3	29.8	23.5	14.5	17.5	11.8	10.4	10.2	15.7	14.9	13.6
Hong Kong, China	47.6	50.2	64.9	60.6	10.9	8.8	7.7	6.7	16.1	14.8	9.8	8.3
Indonesia	23.5	31.0	48.7	42.8	34.3	20.7	14.6	13.3	12.3	12.4	8.0	8.4
Korea, Rep. of	11.8	23.6	34.4	32.4	21.9	15.7	12.3	10.2	25.6	20.1	12.2	9.6
Malaysia	35.6	35.5	45.6	44.7	19.7	16.7	10.8	11.0	16.9	18.8	16.0	11.1
Philippines	22.0	27.0	43.9	38.4	19.0	16.7	15.0	14.2	26.6	24.5	17.3	14.5
Singapore	31.7	37.7	50.1	46.7	14.8	12.3	6.8	6.0	18.5	16.2	11.3	9.1
Taipei, China	19.2	32.6	43.6	45.0	20.0	19.0	14.7	13.4	28.2	20.8	12.9	11.0
Thailand	22.4	26.3	35.0	33.3	25.0	19.5	16.4	14.3	15.7	16.8	10.9	8.8
East Asia 9	**30.0**	**33.5**	**40.9**	**35.0**	**18.2**	**14.8**	**11.4**	**9.9**	**19.0**	**16.8**	**12.9**	**11.2**
Japan	28.3	33.4	43.5	41.9	...	...	...	...	27.5	25.2	17.7	13.7
East Asia 10 (including Japan)	**40.6**	**33.5**	**50.5**	**36.3**	...	...	...	...	**22.3**	**19.4**	**13.9**	**11.7**
Other Regions												
EU 25	65.4	65.1	65.4	65.1	3.2	2.6	1.7	1.4	7.1	8.5	6.1	5.5
NAFTA	37.2	46.8	42.0	39.4	13.1	8.3	5.9	4.8	17.8	24.0	20.7	19.0

Note: The average of export and import is reported.

Source: *Direction of Trade Statistics*, International Monetary Fund.

The level is only slightly lower than the North American Free Trade Agreement (NAFTA) economies (39.4% in 2009) but significantly lower than the 25 EU economies (65.1% in 2009). If measured by share of GDP, the share of intra-East Asian trade reached 19.3% in 2006 and 11.2% in 2009, from 10.3% in 1990, only slightly lower than the EU economies (20.8% in 2006 and 18.3% in 2009) and substantially higher than NAFTA (5.8% in 2006 and 4.6% in 2009). The share of intra-regional trade is also substantial among the 10 East Asian economies (including Japan), increasing to 50.5% in 2006, from 40.6% in 1990, but it declined to 36.3% in 2009. The share of intraregional trade-to-GDP ratio has also increased, to 16.1% in 2006 from 6.5%, but it declined to 8.6% in 2009.[6]

The share of the US economy in trade in the nine East Asian economies has been declining, but remains substantial at 12.9% in 2006 and 11.2% in 2009, from 19.0% in 1990. The ratio of US trade to East Asian GDP, declined to 6.1% in 2006 and 3.6% in 2009, from 6.5% in 1990. The importance of trade with industrial economies, including the USA, remains strong considering the global production network with which Asian economies are becoming increasingly intertwined. A substantial part of intraregional trade is driven by trade of intermediate goods among the emerging Asian economies, with final production destined for export outside the region. In this context, intra-regional trade dynamics remain sensitive to changes in external demand in industrialized economies (see ADB, 2007).

12.2.2. *Financial Market Integration*

The law of one price in financial markets implies that in fully integrated markets arbitrage equalizes the price or return of similar assets. This paper first examines cross-country differences in yields in bond and money markets. The cross-country standard deviation of government bond yield spreads from benchmark bonds (US treasury bonds) for 5- and 10-year maturities are calculated on the basis of daily data. The data are smoothed by calculating a 61-(business) day centred moving average of the standard

[6] See Kim and Lee (2008) for detailed statistics relative to GDP.

deviation, transformed into monthly figures. Similarly, the cross-country standard deviation of overnight interbank offer rates from benchmark rates is constructed.[7]

Figure 12.1(a) shows that cross-country standard deviation in government bond yield spreads has increasingly converged in the East Asian economies since the Asian financial crisis. Substantial divergence remains in East Asia compared with the EU economies, in which the dispersion of yield and overnight bank rate differentials converged to zero with the introduction of the euro (European Central Bank (ECB), 2007). Similarly, the cross-sectional dispersion of overnight interbank rates has declined over time, but remains sizable (Figure 12.1(b)).

The convergence of bond yields and overnight bank rates is indicative of financial market integration with regional markets, which can be attributed to continuous capital market opening in the East Asian economies, but it is also significantly influenced by changes in cross-country differences in exchange rate risk, perceived credit risks, financial market infrastructure, and other factors.

Another, possibly more appropriate, price measure of financial integration examines whether the rates of return of comparable financial assets across countries are equalized after taking care of exchange rate risk. In this regard, Table 12.2 reports the mean of the covered interest differential for 2000–04 and 2005–10 for each of the 10 East Asian economies using daily observations of 3-month interbank rates, spot exchange rates, and the corresponding forward rates.[8] Absolute differentials compared with the equivalent US and Japanese interbank rates, are presented to gauge the extent of Asian financial market integration with the USA and among the Asian countries. The period average of the absolute magnitude shows that the differential compared with the US rate has been smaller

[7] The European Central Bank (ECB) adopts this definition of financial integration (ECB, 2007).

[8] Any deviation from the covered interest parity can be generated from capital controls that restrict cross-border capital movements. Although other factors, such as differences in investment risks on default and temporary liquidity problems, can also generate non-zero interest differential, the covered interest differential can be regarded as an indicator to show the degree of financial market integration in general.

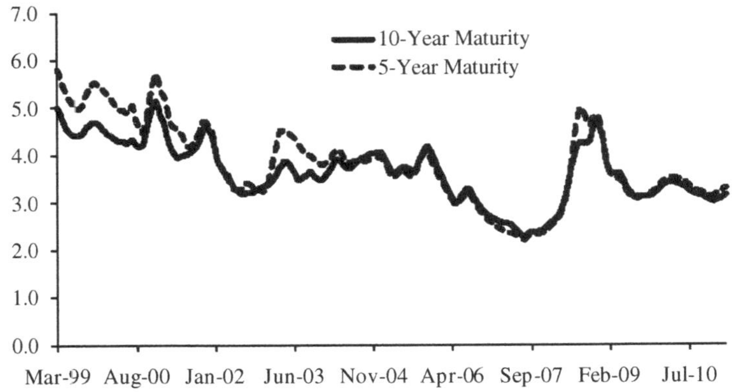

(a) Government Bond Yield Spread

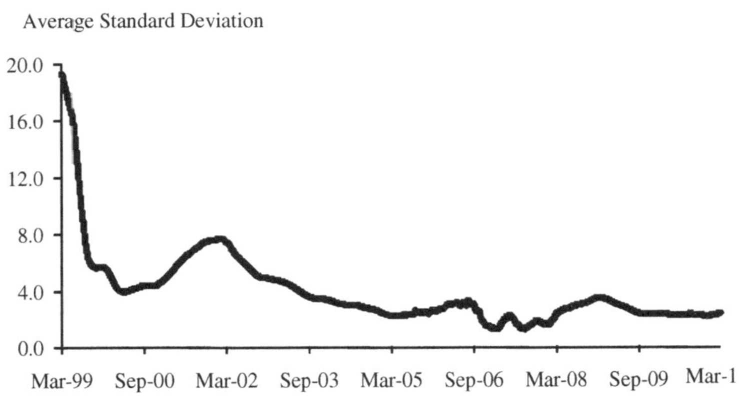

(b) Overnight Interbank Rates

Figure 12.1 Cross-country average standard deviation

Note: Countries include People's Republic of China; Hong Kong, China; India; Indonesia; Republic of Korea; Malaysia; Philippines; Singapore; Taipei, China; Thailand; and Viet Nam. Values refer to 61-day average of daily standard deviation.

Source: Bloomberg.

than that compared with the Japanese interbank rate over the period, indicating that the degree of integration with global financial markets has been larger than the extent of regional financial integration. This has been a common feature of most Asian economies. The averages for the subperiods of 2000–04 and 2005–10 can be compared for four Asian economies which have complete data. Both differentials tend to be higher in the

Table 12.2. Deviation from covered interest parity

	Vis-à-vis US$ IBOR		Vis-à-vis JP¥ IBOR	
Economy	**Average, 2000–04**	**Average, 2005–10**	**Average, 2000–04**	**Average, 2005–10**
China, People's Rep. of	0.021	0.017	0.027	0.348
Hong Kong, China	0.003	0.051	0.019	0.268
Indonesia	—	0.047	—	0.374
Korea, Rep. of	—	0.021	—	0.337
Malaysia	—	0.138	—	0.457
Philippines	0.296	0.135	0.313	0.473
Singapore	0.004	0.071	0.025	0.176
Taipei, China	—	0.017	—	0.344
Thailand	—	0.201	—	0.692
Japan	0.02	0.134	—	—

Notes: The figures indicate the period average of absolute daily values of covered interest differentials, that is, interest differential less forward discount, based on 3-month interbank offer rates vis-à-vis corresponding US or Japanese rates. —, implies that data is not available.

Source: Authors' calculation based on Bloomberg data.

later period, which reflects financial turmoil during the recent global financial crisis.

Considering more diverse asset characteristics in the equity markets, the literature on stock market integration uses the co-movement of stock prices. If financial markets are more integrated, market movements may be more closely associated with each other. Table 12.3 shows cross-country correlation of the quarterly increase in the stock price index (in US dollars) for two sub-periods: pre-crisis period (1990Q2–1996Q4) and post-crisis period (2000Q1–2007Q2). The average of correlation coefficients for East Asian stock markets with the regional market (represented as EA10 including Japan) has increased after the Asian financial crisis in all countries, regardless of whether the period of global financial crisis is included. The correlation with the US stock market has also increased in East Asia. On average, the correlation coefficient of the regional aggregate stock price (EA10) with the US stock price increased from 0.18 in the pre-crisis period

Table 12.3. Correlation for stock prices in East Asia

	PRC	HKG	INO	KOR	MAL	PHI	SNG	TAP	THA	JPN	USA
(a) 1990:Q2–1996:Q4											
PRC	1.00	−0.04	−0.10	0.25	0.19	−0.06	0.08	−0.04	0.25	0.06	−0.05
HKG	−0.04	1.00	0.62	−0.02	0.70	0.60	0.60	0.19	0.52	−0.07	0.41
INO	−0.10	0.62	1.00	−0.10	0.70	0.47	0.58	0.21	0.57	−0.01	0.45
KOR	0.25	−0.02	−0.10	1.00	0.10	0.10	0.31	0.37	0.18	0.45	−0.13
MAL	0.19	0.70	0.70	0.10	1.00	0.62	0.76	0.34	0.71	0.30	0.33
PHI	−0.06	0.60	0.47	0.10	0.62	1.00	0.72	0.63	0.64	0.15	0.35
SIN	0.08	0.60	0.58	0.31	0.76	0.72	1.00	0.42	0.81	0.34	0.37
TAP	−0.04	0.19	0.21	0.37	0.34	0.63	0.42	1.00	0.23	0.33	0.32
THA	0.25	0.52	0.57	0.18	0.71	0.64	0.81	0.23	1.00	0.05	0.30
JPN	0.06	−0.07	−0.01	0.45	0.30	0.15	0.34	0.33	0.05	1.00	0.00
Average	0.07	0.34	0.33	0.18	0.49	0.43	0.51	0.30	0.44	0.18	0.24
(b) 2000:Q1–2010:Q4											
PRC	1.00	0.85	0.64	0.74	0.49	0.64	0.80	0.68	0.65	0.69	0.73
HKG	0.85	1.00	0.72	0.81	0.72	0.73	0.89	0.85	0.79	0.68	0.82
INO	0.64	0.72	1.00	0.74	0.75	0.75	0.81	0.66	0.83	0.57	0.65
KOR	0.74	0.81	0.74	1.00	0.67	0.70	0.83	0.88	0.83	0.68	0.77
MAL	0.49	0.72	0.75	0.67	1.00	0.65	0.74	0.74	0.74	0.53	0.62
PHI	0.64	0.73	0.75	0.70	0.65	1.00	0.79	0.67	0.77	0.51	0.64
SIN	0.80	0.89	0.81	0.83	0.74	0.79	1.00	0.81	0.79	0.68	0.85
TAP	0.68	0.85	0.66	0.88	0.74	0.67	0.81	1.00	0.84	0.66	0.77
THA	0.65	0.79	0.83	0.83	0.74	0.77	0.79	0.84	1.00	0.61	0.67
JPN	0.69	0.68	0.57	0.68	0.53	0.51	0.68	0.66	0.61	1.00	0.72
Average	0.53	0.64	0.65	0.61	0.66	0.58	0.62	0.71	0.67	0.67	0.55

Notes: The figures indicate pairwise correlation coefficients of quarterly increase in stock prices in US dollar terms over the period. Average is the simple average of correlations with nine East Asian economies (excluding own economy). People's Republic of China (PRC); Hong Kong, China (HKG); Indonesia (INO); the Republic of Korea (KOR); Malaysia (MAL); Philippines (PHI); Singapore (SIN); Taipei, China (TAP); Thailand (THA); and Japan (JPN).

Source: Authors' calculations based on Bloomberg data.

to 0.55 (including the period of global financial crisis) in the post-crisis period. In sum, cross-country correlations of stock price indices show that East Asian stock prices have moved more closely with each other and with the US market since the Asian financial crisis.[9]

As quantitative measures of financial integration, Table 12.4 shows cross-border holdings of total international portfolio assets and liabilities including equity portfolio and long-, and short-term debt securities in East Asia.[10] The total recorded level of portfolio asset holdings of seven East Asian economies (excluding Japan, the PRC and Taipei, China) is about US$324.8 billion in 2001. It increased about three-fold to US$941.6 billion in 2006 and further to US$1320.33 billion in 2009. For eight East Asian economies, including Japan, the amount has increased from US$1.61 trillion in 2001 to US$3.29 trillion in 2006 and US$4.16 trillion in 2009.

Intraregional financial integration has been increasing. East Asian assets constituted 14.8% of total holdings for seven East Asian economies in 2001 but 24.3% in 2006 and 24.9% in 2009. In comparison, the US share declined to 14.5% in 2006 and 15.3% in 2009, from 19.6% in 2001. The seven East Asian economies are, therefore, now integrated more with each other than they are with the USA. Because Japan holds a very small investment in East Asian assets and invests more in the USA, the share of intra-regional asset holdings in total asset holdings of eight East Asian economies is much lower (only 8.4% in 2006 and 9.4% in 2009) than the

---

[9] When the correlation is estimated for the period of 2000:1–2007:2 by dropping the period of global financial crisis, correlations are still higher than the pre-crisis period (Kim and Lee, 2008). The correlation per se, however, cannot identify the source of shocks — such as national, regional, and global common factors. Chai and Rhee (2005) examined the extent to which the error variance of the stock market of each East Asian country is explained by local, regional, and global factors. They found that the importance of regional common factors had increased significantly since the Asian crisis but the US market remained an important force for East Asian stock markets: it turns out that East Asian financial markets have closer ties with the US market than with each other.

[10] Data on international capital flows may also be regarded as quantitative measures of financial market integration. See Kim *et al.* (2004b), Kumhof (2001), Mandilaras and Popper (2009) as examples of studies on international capital flows in East Asian economies.

Table 12.4. Total portfolio investment in East Asia (US$ billion)

Year	Economy	Assets in				Liabilities from			
		East Asia 9	Japan	US	Total	East Asia 9	Japan	US	Total
2001	China, People's Rep. of	—	—	—	—	10.03	1.67	3.00	20.26
	Hong Kong, China	23.10	9.25	39.25	205.60	5.49	6.12	32.05	96.69
	Indonesia	0.15	0.00	0.25	0.72	1.01	0.16	1.84	5.55
	Korea, Rep. of	1.54	0.18	3.76	8.03	8.33	5.83	34.47	76.78
	Malaysia	0.78	0.02	0.21	2.28	9.77	2.54	4.26	22.59
	Philippines	0.12	0.01	1.84	2.13	2.63	1.56	4.02	12.73
	Singapore	22.03	10.55	18.01	105.24	3.52	2.13	22.82	50.70
	Taipei, China	—	—	—	—	3.46	0.48	19.86	41.09
	Thailand	0.25	0.00	0.29	0.83	3.72	1.04	2.70	12.01
	East Asia 9	**47.97**	**20.01**	**63.62**	**324.83**	**47.97**	**21.52**	**125.02**	**338.39**
	as % of total	***14.8%***	***6.2%***	***19.6%***	***100.0%***	***14.2%***	***6.4%***	***36.9%***	***100.0%***
	Japan	21.52	—	490.20	1289.75	20.01	—	197.84	542.31
	East Asia 10	**69.49**	—	**553.82**	**1,614.59**	**67.98**	—	**322.86**	**880.69**
	as % of total	***4.3%***	—	***34.3%***	***100.0%***	***7.7%***	—	***36.7%***	***100.0%***
2006	China, People's Rep of	—	—	—	—	115.7	10.27	75.31	281.64
	Hong Kong, China	139.80	18.84	64.87	592.48	28.91	11.72	87.52	233.68
	Indonesia	0.29	0.00	0.11	1.51	5.74	0.92	14.07	38.91
	Korea, Rep. of	9.78	2.62	30.41	83.52	32.76	9.11	123.88	280.52
	Malaysia	2.67	0.25	0.82	7.19	18.30	1.55	15.40	59.38
	Philippines	1.32	0.01	3.09	7.16	1.99	1.60	10.99	30.25
	Singapore	74.27	6.50	37.09	244.58	12.48	7.50	52.73	126.08

	Taipei, China	—	—	—	—	7.35	2.66	74.45	145.09
	Thailand	0.96	0.01	0.36	5.14	5.86	1.19	13.05	37.80
	East Asia 9	**229.09**	**28.23**	**136.75**	**941.58**	**229.09**	**46.52**	**467.40**	**1233.37**
	as % of total	***24.3%***	***3.0%***	***14.5%***	***100.0%***	***18.6%***	***3.8%***	***37.9%***	***100.0%***
	Japan	46.52	—	797.61	2343.48	28.23	—	585.57	1434.92
	East Asia 10	**275.61**	—	**934.36**	**3285.06**	**257.32**	—	**1052.96**	**2668.29**
	as % of total	***8.4%***	—	***28.4%***	***100.0%***	***9.6%***	—	***39.5%***	***100.0%***
2009	China, People's Rep. of	—	—	—	—	181.57	13.12	102.30	406.99
	Hong Kong, China	189.15	17.98	92.40	810.78	26.66	16.46	92.89	254.68
	Indonesia	0.65	0.15	0.47	4.70	11.37	2.46	22.74	71.52
	Korea, Rep. of	22.25	2.79	32.77	102.37	58.97	12.99	104.83	309.03
	Malaysia	9.18	0.11	6.01	27.05	17.11	3.10	18.92	69.53
	Philippines	0.34	0.11	2.32	5.00	3.38	1.64	9.33	28.98
	Singapore	91.10	22.92	65.63	347.03	12.32	10.05	52.10	132.84
	Taipei, China	—	—	—	—	2.84	34.27	75.74	463.09
	Thailand	16.08	0.10	2.00	23.41	6.06	1.77	14.22	49.24
	East Asia 9	**328.75**	**44.16**	**201.59**	**1320.33**	**328.75**	**64.49**	**494.18**	**1479.18**
	as % of total	***24.9%***	***3.34%***	***15.27%***	***100.0%***	***22.23%***	***4.36%***	***33.41%***	***100.0%***
	Japan	64.49	—	919.35	2845.89	44.16	—	405.12	1197.56
	East Asia 10	**393.24**	—	**1120.93**	**4166.23**	**372.91**	—	**899.30**	**2676.74**
	as % of total	***9.44%***	—	***26.9%***	***100.0%***	***13.93%***	—	***33.6%***	***100.0%***

Note: —, implies that data is not available.
Source: Coordinated Portfolio Investment Survey (CPIS), International Monetary Fund.

US share (28.4% in 2006 and 26.9% in 2009) even in the post crisis period. In addition, the size of asset holdings of the USA in East Asia, even excluding Japan, increased both in level terms and as a ratio to GDP, which may imply that the degree of integration with the USA indeed increased.[11]

Table 12.4 also presents the geographical distribution of the total portfolio liabilities for East Asia, which shows a similar pattern to that of assets. Although regional financial integration among the East Asian economies has been increasing, it remains limited, falling behind that of integration with global financial markets, especially when accounting for the small regional investment by Japan.

12.3. Empirical Model for Macroeconomic Consequences

A simple correlation approach does not provide a precise inference of real and financial integration, so a VAR approach is developed.[12] VAR models can identify relevant structural shocks, such as global and regional shocks, and analyze the effects of each shock on an individual variable in a more systematic way. This paper uses panel structure to increase the degree of freedom because sample periods under consideration are short. The individual fixed effect is introduced to control for the country specific factors that are not included in the model. The reduced form panel VAR model is estimated first. Then, the structural form with a recursive structure (Sims, 1980) is recovered. See Asdrubali and Kim (2004) and Kim and Lee (2008) for details.

---

[11] See Kim and Lee (2008) for details on the numbers relative to GDP.

[12] First, an examination was made of the cross-country output and consumption correlation. It was found that not only the average of pairwise correlation coefficients between individual GDP and regional aggregate GDP for the 10 East Asian economies but also the average of pairwise correlation coefficients between individual East Asian economies and US GDP increased substantially. This evidence supports the growing regional as well as global output interdependence of East Asian economies, which can be a result of increasing real integration — both regionally and globally — of East Asian economies. The results are similar for consumption correlation, which supports the growing regional and global consumption risk sharing of East Asian economics. The details are reported in Kim and Lee (2008).

To measure the extent of the real integration or real inter-dependence, this paper examines how aggregate world output shocks and aggregate East Asian output shocks affect individual output of East Asian economies. For that purpose, a three-variable panel VAR model is constructed. The data vector is $[\Delta \log Y_{W,t}\ \Delta \log Y_{A,t}\ \Delta \log Y_{i,t}]'$, where the contemporaneously exogenous variables are ordered first, Y_W is the world aggregate output, Y_A is the East Asian aggregate output, and Y_i is an individual output of East Asian economies.[13] The first two variables are included to identify the world aggregate output shocks and the East Asian aggregate output shocks. The last variable is included to examine the effects of these two shocks on the individual output of East Asian economies. The ordering of the variables can be regarded as a natural one since individual country (or the regional aggregate) output is far smaller than the regional (or the world) aggregate output.

From the estimated VAR model, two ratios are calculated in order to infer the degree of inter-dependence: (1) the ratio of cumulative impulse responses of individual output to those of world aggregate output in the presence of world aggregate output shocks; and (2) the ratio of cumulative impulse responses of individual output to those of Asian aggregate output in the presence of Asian aggregate output shocks. In this way, one can infer by what percentage domestic output changes when world (or Asian) aggregate output changes by 1% in the presence of world (or Asian) aggregate output shocks at various horizons after the shock. The first and the second ratios show how individual East Asian economies are influenced by the global and regional economy, respectively.

To measure the extent of financial integration, this paper uses international consumption risk sharing theory. In a simple model of risk sharing, one country's consumption growth rate depends more on aggregate consumption growth rate if there is more risk sharing across countries. This

---

[13] The panel unit root test by Im *et al.* (2003) shows that the null hypothesis of unit root in (log of) each variable is not rejected at the 5% level. To be consistent with these results, this paper uses the variables in (log) difference form. In contrast, the panel co-integration test by Pedroni (1999) does not reject the null hypothesis of co-integration among these variables in some cases. An estimation was made of the vector error correction model in which the estimated co-integration relation among these variables is imposed. The main conclusion does not change. See Kim and Lee (2008) for some results.

idea can be expressed as the following equation, which appeared in previous studies such as Obstfeld (1995) and Crucini and Hess (2000).

$$\Delta \log(C_{i,t}) = \alpha + \lambda\,\Delta \log(C_{w,t}) + (1-\lambda)\Delta \log(Y_{i,t}) + e_{i,t},\ \ i = 1,2,\ldots, R \quad (1)$$

where C_i is the consumption of the country i, Y_i is the income of the country i, C_w is the consumption of the world, the constant term, α, may reflect the difference in the discount factor across countries, the error term, e_i, may reflect the preference shocks, λ represents the degree of risk sharing, and Δ indicates a change from the previous period. To the extent that the risk sharing arrangements are established (λ), its consumption growth rate follows the aggregate consumption growth rate since the country-specific risks are shared. However, the rest (fraction $1-\lambda$) of the consumption growth rate follows its own income growth rate because that is what is domestically available.[14]

The theory is extended to a case in which risk sharing with both the Asian region and the world can be considered as follows. To the extent that one country established risk sharing arrangements within the Asian region (λ_A), the consumption growth rate of the country follows the consumption growth rate of the aggregate consumption of Asia. Similarly, to the extent that one country established risk sharing arrangements with the world (λ_W), the consumption growth rate of the country follows the consumption growth rate of the aggregate consumption of the world. The rest of the consumption growth rate of the country follows its income growth rate ($1-\lambda_A-\lambda_W$). This idea can be expressed as the following equation.

$$\Delta \log(C_{i,t}) = \alpha + \lambda_W\,\Delta \log(C_{W,t}) + \lambda_A\,\Delta \log(C_{A,t}) + (1-\lambda_W-\lambda_A)\,\Delta \log(Y_{i,t}) + e_{i,t} \quad (2)$$

By rearranging the equation, the following equation can be obtained:

$$(\Delta \log(C_{i,t}) - \Delta \log(Y_{i,t})) = \alpha + \lambda_W\,(\Delta \log(C_{W,t}) - \Delta \log(Y_{i,t})) + \lambda_A(\Delta \log(C_{A,t}) - \Delta \log(Y_{i,t})) + e_{i,t} \quad (3)$$

[14] See Crucini (1999) and Asdrubali and Kim (2008, 2009) for more recent empirical methods that explicitly consider intertemporal consumption smoothing.

Equation (3) can be estimated using a static regression, but here a VAR model is constructed to examine the dynamic properties of consumption risk sharing in the spirit of Asdrubali and Kim (2004). A three-variable VAR model is constructed in which the data vector is $[(\Delta \log C_{w,t} - \Delta \log Y_{i,t})\ (\Delta \log C_{A,t} - \Delta \log Y_{i,t})\ (\Delta \log C_{i,t} - \Delta \log Y_{i,t})]'$. As in the previous model, the ordering is natural.[15]

From Equation (3), one can infer the degrees of global (or regional) risk sharing λ_W (or λ_A) by comparing the relative ratio of changes in $\log(C_{i,t}) - \log(Y_{i,t})$ to changes in $\log(C_{w,t}) - \log(Y_{i,t})$ (or $\log(C_{A,t}) - \log(Y_{i,t})$) from the previous period when $\log(C_{w,t}) - \log(Y_{i,t})$ (or $\log(C_{A,t}) - \log(Y_{i,t})$) changes exogenously. From the estimated VAR model, one can infer the degrees of global (or regional) risk sharing by calculating the ratios of cumulative impulse responses of of $\Delta\log(C_{i,t}) - \Delta\log(Y_{i,t})$ to $\Delta\log(C_{W,t}) - \Delta\log(Y_{i,t})$ (or $\Delta\log(C_{A,t}) - \Delta\log(Y_{i,t})$) over a certain horizon when there are shocks to (or $\Delta\log(C_{A,t}) - \Delta\log(Y_{i,t})$).[16]

Note that the measures for real and financial inter-dependence are directly comparable. To obtain both measures, three variable VAR models are constructed that include individual, regional, and global indicators. Real GDPs are included at various levels for the real measure but real consumptions are included at various levels (net of individual real GDP) for the financial measure. Similar ratios of global (or regional) to individual cumulative responses in the presence of global (or regional) shocks are also exploited.

The study uses quarterly data and estimates the model for three sample periods: (1) the period before the Asian financial crisis (1990Q2–1996Q4); (2) the period after the Asian financial crisis, excluding

[15] Panel unit root tests by Im *et al.* (2003) showed that the null hypothesis of unit roots in the log of each variable is not rejected at the 5% level. In addition, the panel co-integration test by Pedroni (1999) rejects the null hypothesis of co-integration among these variables at the 5% level in most cases. To be consistent with these results, variables in (log) difference form were used.

[16] This is because cumulative impulse responses of $\Delta\log(C_{i,t}) - \Delta\log(Y_{i,t})$ and $\Delta\log(C_{w,t}) - \Delta\log(Y_{i,t})$ (or $\Delta\log(C_{A,t}) - \Delta\log(Y_{i,t})$) over a certain horizon show the changes in $\log(C_{i,t}) - \log(Y_{i,t})$ and $\log(C_{w,t}) - \log(Y_{i,t})$ (or $\log(C_{A,t}) - \log(Y_{i,t})$) over a certain horizon and a shock to $\Delta\log(C_{W,t}) - \Delta\log(Y_{i,t})$ (or $\Delta\log(C_{A,t}) - \Delta\log(Y_{i,t})$) represents an exogenous force to change $\log(C_{w,t}) - \log(Y_{i,t})$ (or $\log(C_{A,t}) - \log(Y_{i,t})$).

global financial crisis (2000Q2–2007Q2); and (3) the period after the Asian financial crisis, including global financial crisis (2000Q2–2010Q4). A constant term and four lags are assumed. The world aggregate is constructed as the aggregate of G7 countries, excluding Japan. The Asian aggregate is constructed as the aggregate of 10 Asian countries excluding own economy.

12.4. Results for Macroeconomic Consequences

Figures 12.2(a) and 12.2(b) report the cumulative impulse responses to global and regional output shocks for 16 quarters with 90% probability bands for the periods of 1990–96 and 2000–10, respectively.[17] Cumulative impulse responses are constructed in order to easily see the effects on (log) level of each variable over various horizons. The responding variables are denoted at the far left of each row of graphs while the names of shocks are denoted at the top of each column of graphs. "Y_G6," "Y_A10," and "Y" stand for $\log Y_{w,t}$, $\log Y_{A,t}$, and $\log Y_{i,t}$, respectively.

For the period before the Asian financial crisis, world aggregate output shocks do not have much effect on domestic output. Positive Asian aggregate output shocks even have a negative effect on domestic output. For the period after the Asian financial crisis, however, positive world aggregate output shocks and the Asian aggregate output shock have significant positive effects on the domestic output. This result suggests that real interdependence of Asian countries within the Asian region and with the world increased substantially after the financial crisis.

Figure 12.2(c) reports the relative cumulative impulse responses for 16 quarters with 90% probability bands. The first (or the second) row of the panel shows the ratio of cumulative impulse responses of individual output to cumulative impulse responses of the world (or Asian) aggregate output in the presence of world (or Asian) aggregate output shocks. Each column of panels shows the results for three sample periods.

---

[17] The results on impulse responses in output and consumption VAR models for the period of 2000–2007:2 are reported in Kim and Lee (2008); they are similar to those for the period of 2000–10.

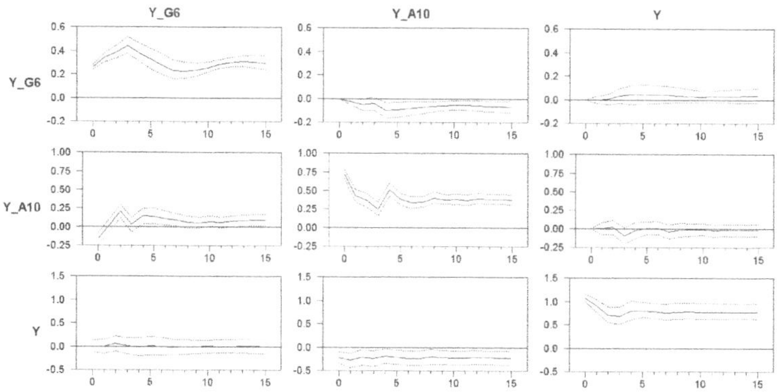

(a) 1990–1996

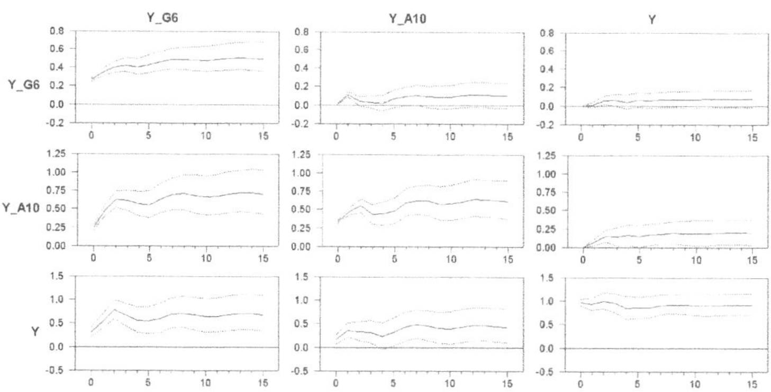

(b) 2000–2010

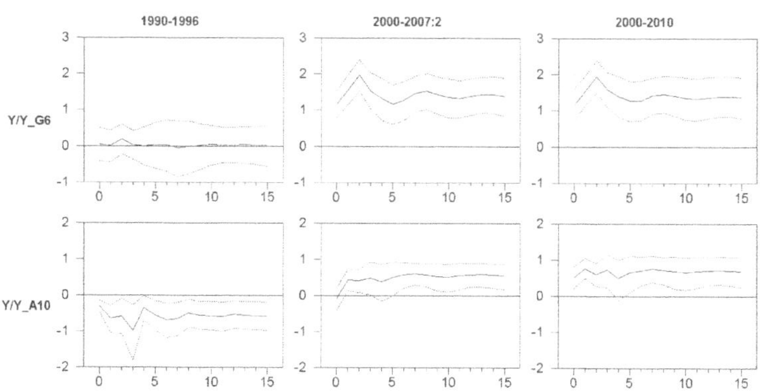

(c) Relative Cumulative Impulse Responses

Figure 12.2 Cumulative impulse responses to world and regional output shocks for 10 East Asian economies

The results show that the positive co-movement (or dependence) of individual output with the regional and world aggregate output increased substantially after the Asian financial crisis and that the increase in the degree of dependence with regional aggregate output is as large as that with the world aggregate output. For two sub-sample periods after the Asian financial crisis, domestic output increases by about 50% of the size of the Asian aggregate output increase in the presence of the Asian aggregate output shocks for the long-horizon while domestic output increases by over 100% of the size of the world aggregate output increase in the presence of world aggregate output shocks for the long-horizon.

Figures 12.3(a) and 12.3(b) report the cumulative impulse responses to world and regional consumption (net of domestic output) shocks for the periods of 1990–96 and 2000–10. Cumulative impulse responses are constructed in order to easily see the changes in the level of each variable over various horizons. The responding variables are denoted at the far left of each row of graphs while the name of shocks are denoted at the top of each column of graphs. "C_G6," "C_A10," and "C" stand for $\log(C_{W,t}) - \log(Y_{i,t})$, $\log(C_{A,t}) - \log(Y_{i,t})$, and $\log(C_{i,t}) - \log(Y_{i,t})$.

In both sample periods, world consumption shocks have a significant positive effect on individual consumption but regional consumption shocks do not have much effect on individual consumption. This suggests that the degree of regional financial integration is very small.

Figure 12.3(c) reports the relative cumulative impulse responses. The results are similar in all sample periods. The individual consumption does not change much in response to regional aggregate consumption shocks. In response to world aggregate consumption shocks, however, individual consumption changes by about 30–50% of the world aggregate consumption changes. This result confirms that risk sharing within Asia is very small but risk sharing with the world is far larger.

12.5. Conclusion

An examination is made of the degree of real vs financial integration, the degree of global vs regional integration (within Asia), and the degree of integration before vs after the Asian crisis. For this purpose, various

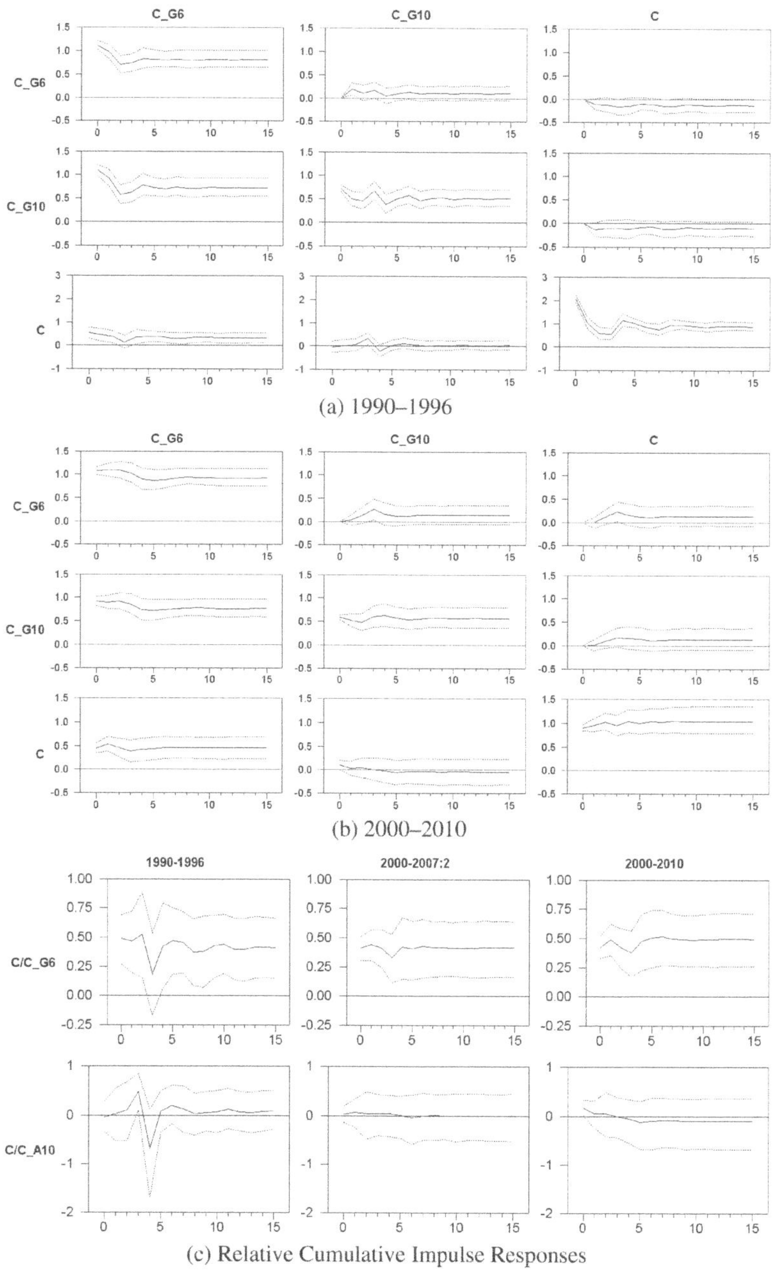

Figure 12.3 Cumulative impulse responses to world and regional consumption (net of domestic output) shocks

measures of integration are analyzed, including price, quantity, and macroeconomic aggregate measures.

It is found that real integration in the region has been accelerating, as evidenced by increasing intraregional trade among East Asian economies. Yet, the share of global markets in Asian trade remains substantial, although it has been decreasing. The price measures of financial integration from cross-country government bond yields, overnight interbank rates, and stock prices show that the degree of integration of financial markets of East Asian economies increased substantially after the Asian crisis. However, the data on the covered interest differentials and cross-border financial asset holdings suggest that the extent of regional integration remains limited, falling behind that of integration with global financial markets.

Findings from the panel VAR models suggest that the extent of real integration based on output linkage increased substantially both regionally and globally after the Asian crisis. The increase in the degree of regional dependence seems as large as that in the degree of global dependence. On the contrary, the extent of financial integration based on consumption linkage shows that the degree of financial integration does not change much and that global integration is substantial but regional integration is nil.

These results also suggest some answers and reconcilements of the questions and debates raised in the past studies. The degree of trade and real integration within Asian regions increased substantially, but Asian economies are not decoupled from global economy, and still depend much on global economy. The volume of cross-border financial assets within Asia increased substantially, which may imply a substantial increase in the degree of financial integration. However, international risk sharing within Asia is very far from complete, showing a discrepancy between inferences based on the volume measure and consumption-based measure of international risk sharing. This may explain some discrepancies in the results of some past studies.

Overall, it is found that the degree of regional financial integration lags behind the extent of real integration in East Asia, and that the financial markets in East Asia are integrated relatively more with global markets than with each other. There is strong skepticism as to whether Asian regionalism can move forward successfully from trade (real) to financial and monetary integration, as occurred in the European integration. It is often argued that Asia's wide diversity of economic development and political interest and lack of formal institutional arrangements will further hinder successful integration in the region. Since the Asian crisis, East Asian economies have made major financial cooperation initiatives such as (i) the economic review and policy dialogue, (ii) the regional reserve pooling arrangement (Chiang Mai Initiative), and (iii) the development of local-currency bond markets (the Asian Bond Markets Initiative and the Asian Bond Fund). To enhance regional financial development and integration, financial cooperation efforts must be strengthened. Future research on the role and prospect of regional cooperation in promoting financial and monetary integration in the region would be of great interest.

References

Asian Development Bank, "Uncoupling Asia: Myth and Reality," *Asian Development Outlook 2007* (2007):66–81.

Asdrubali, Pierfederico and Soyoung Kim, "Dynamic Risksharing in the U.S. and Europe," *Journal of Monetary Economics* 51 (2004):789–836.

———, "Incomplete Risksharing and Incomplete Intertemporal Consumption Smoothing," *Journal of Money, Credit and Banking* 40 (2008):1521–31.

———, "On the Empirics of International Smoothing," *Journal of Banking and Finance* 33 (2009):2293–300.

———, "Global vs. Regional Risk Sharing in East Asia," in Michael Devereux, Phillip Lane, Cyn-Young Park, and Shang-Jin Wei (eds.) *The Dynamics of Asian Financial Integration: Facts and Analytics*, Abingdon, UK: Routledge–ADB (2011):77–92.

Backus, David, Patrick J. Kehoe, and Finn Kydland, "International Real Business Cycles," *Journal of Political Economy* 100 (1992):745–75.

Chai, Hee-Yul and Yeongseop Rhee, "Financial Integration and Financial Efficiency in East Asia," Paper presented at the Claremont-KIEP international conference on the Political Economy of Regional Integration, 18 November 2005, Claremont, CA (2005).

Canova, Fabio and Harris Dellas, "Trade Interdependence and the International Business Cycle," *Journal of International Economics* 34 (1993):23–47.

Cavoli, Tony, Ramkishen S. Rajan, and Reza Siregar, "A Survey of Financial Integration in East Asia; How Far? How Much Further to Go?" *Centre for*

International Economic Studies discussion paper 0401, University of Adelaide (2004).
Crucini, Mario J. "On International and National Dimensions of Risk Sharing," *Review of Economics and Statistics* 81 (1999):73–84.
Crucini, Mario J. and Gregory D. Hess, "International and Intranational Risk Sharing," in Gregory D. Hess and Eric van Wincoop (eds.), *Intranational Macroeconomics*, Cambridge: Cambridge University Press (2000):37–59.
Eichengreen, Barry and Yung Chul Park, "Why Has There Been Less Financial Integration in Asia Than in Europe?" *MAS Staff Paper*, Monetary Authority of Singapore (2004):1–21.
European Central Bank, *Financial Integration in Europe*, Frankfurt am Main, ECB (March 2007).
Frankel, Jeffrey and Andrew Rose, "The Endogeneity of the Optimum Currency Area Criteria," *Economic Journal* 108 (1998):1009–25.
Im, Kung So, M. Hashem Pesaran, and Yongcheol Shin, "Testing for Unit Roots in Heterogeneous Panels," *Journal of Econometrics* 115 (2003):53–74.
International Monetary Fund, *World Economic Outlook — Spillovers and Cycles in the Global Economy*, Washington, DC: IMF (April 2007).
Kim, Soyoung and Jong-Wha Lee, "Real and Financial Integration in East Asia," *Working papers on Regional Economic Integration* 17, Asian Development Bank, Manila (2008).
Kim, Soyoung, Sunghyun H. Kim, and Yunjong Wang, "Global vs. Regional Risksharing in East Asia," *Asian Economic Papers* 3 (2004a):182–201.
———, "Macroeconomic Effects of Capital Account Liberalization: the Case of Korea," *Review of Development Economics* 8 (2004b):624–39.
———, "Financial Integration and Consumption Risksharing in East Asia," *Japan and the World Economy* 18 (2006):143–57.
Kim, Soyoung, Jong-Wha Lee, and Kwanho Shin, "Regional and Global Financial Integration in East Asia," in Barry Eichengreen, Charles Wyplosz, and Yung Chul Park (eds.), *China, Asia and the New World Economy*, Oxford: Oxford University Press (2008):168–200.
Kumhof, Michael, "International Capital Mobility in Emerging Markets: New Evidence from Daily Data," *Review of International Economics* 9 (2001):626–40.
Lee, Jong-Wha, "Patterns and Determinants for Cross-Border Financial Asset Holdings in East Asia," *ADB working paper series on Regional Economic Integration* 13, Asian Development Bank, Manila (2008).

Mandilaras, Alex and Helen Popper, "Capital Flows, Capitalization, and Openness in Emerging East Asian Economies," *Review of International Economics* 17 (2009):734–50.

Obstfeld, Maurice, "International Capital Mobility in the 1990s," in Peter Kenen (ed.), *Understanding Interdependence: The Macroeconomics of the Open Economy*, Princeton, NJ: Princeton University Press (1995):201–61.

Pedroni, Peter, "Critical Values for Cointegration Tests in Heterogeneous Panels with Multiple Regressors," *Oxford Bulletin of Economics and Statistics* 61 (1999):635–70.

Sims, Christopher A., "Macroeconomics and Reality," *Econometrica* 48 (1980):1–48.

Chapter 13

Emerging Asia: Decoupling or Recoupling*

13.1. Introduction

The economies of emerging Asia, especially East Asia, are becoming increasingly interdependent.[1] Foremost among the drivers of regional integration is intra-regional trade. The share of intra-regional trade as a percentage of emerging East Asia's total trade increased significantly over the last decade. Emerging East Asian economies are also increasingly integrated through direct investment, financial flows and other forms of economic interaction.

* This chapter is co-authored with Soyoung Kim and Cyn-Young Park and was originally published in The World Economy, Vol. 34, No. 1 (January 2011), pp. 23–53. © 2011 Blackwell Publishing Ltd., 9600 Garsington Road, Oxford, OX4 2DQ, UK and 350 Main Street, Malden, MA 02148, USA.

This paper was prepared for the Conference on International Linkages held in Tokyo, Japan, on 2–3 October 2008. We are grateful to seminar participants for useful suggestions and to Zhai Fan, Fidelis Sadicon, Rogelio Mercado and Mara Claire Tayag for data assistance. We are also grateful to two anonymous referees for their comments. We thank Kevin Donahue for edits and Ma. Theresa Anna Robles provided excellent secretarial assistance. The views expressed in this paper are ours and do not necessarily reflect the views and policies of the Asian Development Bank (ADB), its Board of Directors, or the governments of ADB members.

[1] Throughout this paper, emerging East Asia refers to nine selected economies in East and South East Asia. The nine Asian economies include China; Hong Kong, SAR; Indonesia; Korea, Republic of (Korea); Malaysia; the Philippines; Singapore; Taipei, China; and Thailand.

Against this backdrop of intensifying regional integration, the hypothesis of 'decoupling' has attracted much attention in recent years.[2] The issue of decoupling is highly contentious. In a narrow scope, it is a question of whether emerging East Asia can weather a US slowdown or recession. But in a broader sense, it is relevant to the changing nature of macroeconomic interdependence between emerging East Asia and the rest of the world as the region's economic prowess grows and its integration progresses.

The rise of East Asia is changing the landscape of the world economy. On the back of strong growth and rapidly integrating regional trade and production linkages, emerging market economies in East Asia as a group have become a key player in the global economy. The region now exerts significant influence in global markets as a producer of manufacturing goods and consumer of many primary commodities. Rapid financial globalisation is another force behind ever-rising economic interdependence between emerging East Asia and the world. The growing influence of emerging East Asia, especially China; tightening intra- and inter-regional trade linkages; and the globalisation of financial markets are making fundamental changes to the nature of macroeconomic interdependence and economic spillovers between emerging East Asia and major industrial countries.

Emerging East Asia accounted for 18 per cent of total world gross domestic product (GDP) in 2007 (on a purchasing power parity basis), compared to 9 per cent in 1990. Over the past several decades, emerging East Asia has shown remarkable economic progress and has had a profound impact on the world economy. In the aftermath of the 1997/98 Asian financial crisis, emerging market economies in East Asia maintained an average annual growth rate of 7.5 per cent over the period 2000–07. Underpinning this performance has been dynamic growth in China, which has contributed more than four percentage points per annum to East Asian growth during the same period.

The emergence of China has been one of the most important features reshaping the world economy. China is now the third largest economy in the world (at market exchange rates) and the largest global trader. The Chinese economy has accounted for about one-fifth of incremental

[2] See the survey in Section 2.

demand in the world economy in recent years. Given the prominent economic role played by emerging East Asia, especially China, the impact of emerging East Asian economies on the global business cycle is of particular interest.

The purpose of this paper is to investigate the evolution and nature of macroeconomic interdependence between emerging East Asia and major industrial countries such as the Group of Seven (G7) economies.[3] With increasing economic integration and the growing influence of emerging East Asia in the world economy, the pattern of global macroeconomic interdependence is evolving. The macroeconomic interdependence and growth spillovers between emerging East Asia and G7 countries appear to have become 'bi-directional', rather than 'uni-directional'. In addition, if emerging East Asian shocks are positively transmitted to major industrial economies, they can be another source of positive co-movement between emerging East Asia and G7 countries. In other words, emerging East Asia and G7 countries can be 'recoupling', with positive spillovers from emerging East Asia to G7 countries. It would be interesting to investigate whether the direction and magnitude of growth spillovers between emerging East Asia and G7 countries would reflect these changes.

To shed light on such issues, we first document changes in inter-regional and intra-regional economic linkages, such as trade and financial market linkages, and report various business cycle co-movement statistics between emerging East Asia and G7 countries. To assess the evolution of macroeconomic interdependence and to measure bi-directional macroeconomic impacts between emerging East Asia and G7 countries, we employ a panel vector autoregression (VAR) model. To the best of our knowledge, there has been no systematic empirical research addressing the level of bi-directional macroeconomic interdependence between emerging East Asia and G7 countries.

This paper is organised as follows. Section 13.2 presents a concise literature survey on the issues of decoupling and global business cycle synchronisation. Section 13.3 examines the evolution of global macroeconomic interdependence through changing trade and financial linkages at both

[3] The G7 economies comprise Canada, France, Germany, Italy, Japan, United Kingdom and the United States.

regional and global levels, and investigates the role of emerging East Asia in shaping these changes and the rapidly changing global financial landscape that is being driven by financial technology and innovation. Section 13.4 employs a VAR model to evaluate the impact of ongoing changes in bi-directional linkages between emerging East Asia and G7 countries in terms of growth spillovers and business cycle synchronisation. Concluding remarks follow in Section 13.5.

13.2. Economic Integration and the Decoupling of Asia: Literature Survey

13.2.1. *Economic Integration and Business Cycle Synchronisation*

Theoretically, the effect of economic integration on business cycle co-movement is ambiguous. In the literature on international business cycles, trade is emphasised as an important channel of output co-movement. Greater trade integration stimulates the spillover of aggregate demand shocks, thereby increasing output co-movement (Frankel and Rose, 1998). The spread of technology shocks through trade can also make business cycles more correlated across countries (Canova and Dellas, 1993). In addition, spillovers can occur through a change in relative prices of factors and products. As much as countries trade freely, a positive shock in one country that raises the relative price of labour-intensive goods may lead to higher wages and employment throughout the world (Kraay and Ventura, 2002).

On the other hand, as Krugman (1993) and Kose and Yi (2002) argue, more trade may encourage greater specialisation of production, resulting in less synchronisation of business cycles.[4] In this context, not just the

[4] Several studies emphasise the similarity of production structures as an important determinant of co-movement of output. Industry-specific shocks can cause more business cycle synchronisation among countries with similar production structures. Clark and van Wincoop (2001) and Imbs (2004) provide evidence that greater similarity in industry structure is associated with higher co-movement of output and employment. Imbs emphasises that the effect of trade on business cycle synchronisation is largely driven by intra-industry trade reflecting similar production structures.

magnitude of trade among countries, but also the similarity of production structures, is considered to be important in explaining output co-fluctuations. Some studies found that when bilateral trade concentrates more on intra-industry trade, rather than inter-industry trade, the tendency of synchronising output fluctuations strengthens (Imbs, 2004; Shin and Wang, 2004).

While the theoretical predictions remain varied and conflicting, most empirical studies find that business cycles are more synchronised as trade integration deepens (Frankel and Rose, 1998; and Baxter and Kouparitsas, 2005).

The link between financial integration and output co-movement is also not unambiguous. Kalemli-Ozcan *et al.* (2001) argue that better income insurance attained through greater capital market integration may lead to higher specialisation of production and, hence, less symmetric output fluctuations. Financial integration can also facilitate the transfer of resources across countries, for example, by moving capital from a country with a negative shock to one with a positive shock, implying a negative output correlation. On the other hand, if capital flows are correlated internationally, closer financial integration leads to greater output synchronisation (Imbs, 2004). With imperfect information and/or liquidity constraints, investors' herd behaviour can cause them to withdraw capital from many countries simultaneously, contributing to positive output correlations, as observed during the 1997/98 Asian financial crisis. In fact, Kim *et al.* (2007) showed that shocks to capital flows generated positive business cycle correlations for Asia-Pacific countries.

Empirical evidence of the link between financial integration and business cycle co-movement is also conflicting. Several studies — including Kalemli-Ozcan *et al.* (2001) and Heathcote and Perri (2002) — present evidence that higher financial integration leads to a decline in the correlation of output. However, Imbs (2004, 2006) finds that the business cycles of countries with strong financial links are significantly more synchronised, even though they also tend to be more specialised.

The effect of economic integration on business cycle co-movement also hinges on the broad macroeconomic policy environment. In an integrated region, policymakers can no longer pursue an optimal policy without taking account of neighbour countries' actions. For example, with a tightly integrated capital market and a hard peg exchange rate regime, a small open economy must delegate its monetary policy to an anchor country's central bank. In general, deeper integration necessitates further macroeconomic policy cooperation among policymakers in the integrated region in order to manage increasing macroeconomic interdependence more effectively.

It is, however, an open question whether increased macroeconomic policy cooperation would increase or decrease the extent of output co-movement. For example, when national autonomy over monetary policy is sacrificed for the sake of a fixed exchange rate regime, pegging countries are subject to common monetary policy shocks. And with a pegged regime, real shocks to an economy are transmitted across countries to a larger extent without being mitigated by exchange rate movements. In this context, closer exchange and monetary policy cooperation can contribute to greater co-movement of output. However, arguments also run in the opposite direction. Outputs might move more asymmetrically in a financially integrated region with a fixed exchange rate regime if idiosyncratic domestic shocks are not dampened by independent monetary policy.

13.2.2. *Empirical Studies on Output Co-movement in Asia*

Empirical studies differ on the extent and nature of business cycle co-movement among Asian economies. It appears that the choice of empirical methodology and sample has a major impact on the analytical results.

While they vary, most empirical studies find that the degree of business cycle synchronisation among Asian economies has been increasing, partly due to deepened trade integration. But, it is not conclusive whether the output of Asian economies has decoupled from, or become less interdependent with, the global economy.

ADB (2007, 2008) reports that the correlation coefficients of Asian business cycles, among emerging Asian economies and with Group of Three (G3) economies,[5] increased after the Asian financial crisis and have remained high. The high synchronicity between Asian business cycles and

[5] The G3 economies comprise the European Union, Japan and the United States.

the G3 cycle is interpreted as evidence refuting the view of Asia decoupling. But, the increased correlation is only indicative since correlation can be spurious without clearly distinguishing regional shocks from global shocks.

Several studies adopt dynamic factor models that can deconstruct an economy's output fluctuations into contributions by different factors, including global, regional and country-specific factors. Moneta and Ruffer (2006) estimate various specifications of a dynamic factor model for the output of 10 East Asian economies and find a significant common factor in their business cycles. Specifically, a considerable part of the common factor is the result of co-movement in exports, which, in turn, is attributed to a number of exogenous factors such as the price of oil and the JPY/USD exchange rate. However, Moneta and Ruffer (2006) find Asian output is only weakly affected by developments in industrial countries.

The International Monetary Fund (IMF) (2007) and Kose *et al.* (2008) find that global and regional common shocks have accounted for a sizeable percentage of business cycle fluctuations in both industrial countries and emerging market economies (including emerging Asia), but the relative importance of the global factors has decreased, while that of regional factors has increased. The result supports the theory of decoupling, or divergence, between the business cycles of industrialised countries and emerging Asian economies. But, since the analyses of the IMF (2007) and Kose *et al.* (2008), as well as Moneta and Ruffer (2006), focus on the patterns in Asia's business cycles over the past two decades, the 1997/98 Asian financial crisis must have increased the influence of common regional shocks.

Several studies adopt the VAR approach to disentangle the nature of shocks, and analyse output interdependence for East Asian economies. Kim and Lee (2008) find that the extent of output linkage increased substantially, both regionally and globally, after the 1997/98 Asian financial crisis. The increase in the degree of regional dependence is similar in magnitude to the increase in the degree of global dependence. ADB (2008) and Takagi and Kozuru (2008) also provide similar evidence that Asia's output is responding significantly to both regional and global output shocks in the post-crisis period.

13.3. Evolution and Nature of Macroeconomic Interdependence

13.3.1. *Trends and Stylised Facts about Asian Business Cycles*

Regional integration has gained momentum in recent decades through advances in trade, finance and macroeconomic links (ADB, 2008). The effect of strengthened trade and financial linkages on business cycle co-movements remains inconclusive on the theoretical and empirical fronts. However, the process of regional integration continues to reshape the dynamics of regional economies, both among themselves and with the rest of the world. The evolution of emerging East Asia's business cycles will reflect these changes in intra- and inter-regional macroeconomic interdependence.

Figure 13.1 illustrates the movement of real GDP for emerging East Asia and G7 economies in terms of their growth rates. Judging from the patterns of growth fluctuations, emerging East Asia's business cycles appear to have changed quite significantly after the 1997/98 financial

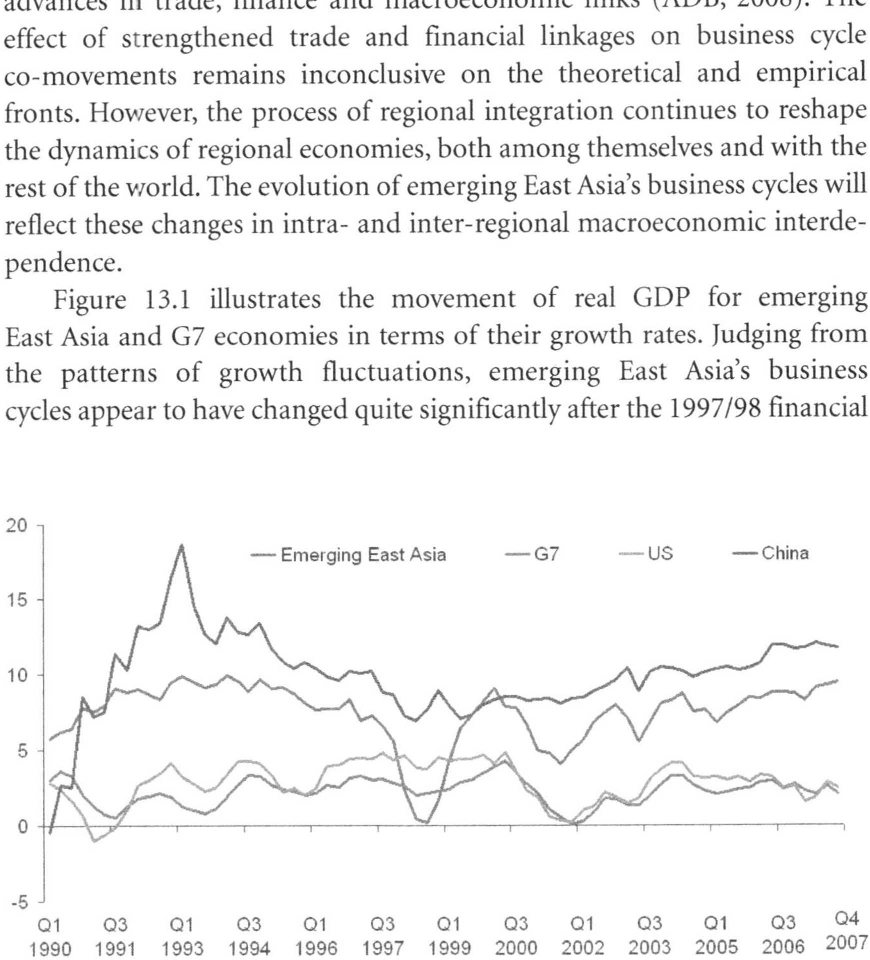

Figure 13.1 GDP growth (%)

Note: Emerging East Asia comprises China; Hong Kong SAR; Indonesia; Korea; Malaysia; Philippines; Singapore; Taipei, China; and Thailand.

Source: Oxford Economics, *Quarterly Model*, August 2008.

Table 13.1. Intra- and inter-regional business cycle correlations[a]

	Pre-crisis[b]	Post-crisis[c]
Intra-regional business cycle correlations		
Emerging East Asia	0.000	0.448
Emerging East Asia excluding China	0.007	0.446
Inter-regional business cycle correlations		
Emerging East Asia-G7	0.084	0.611
Emerging East Asia-US	0.233	0.715
Emerging East Asia-Japan	−0.618	0.647
Emerging East Asia excluding China-G7	0.619	0.537
Emerging East Asia excluding China–US	−0.345	0.724
Emerging East Asia excluding China–US	0.033	0.659

Notes: Emerging East Asia comprises China; Hong Kong, SAR; Indonesia; Korea; Malaysia; Philippines; Singapore; Taipei, China; and Thailand.

[a]GDP cyclical component, calculated by applying the Hodrick-Prescott filter method on the natural log of real GDP in local currency, was used to compute the business cycle correlations.

[b]Pre-crisis period = 1999Q1–1996Q4.

[c]Post-crisis period = 2000Q1–2007Q2.

Source: Oxford Economics, *Quarterly Model*, August 2008.

crisis. In the post-crisis period, the cyclical movements of these economies have become more distinctive. The behaviour of post-crisis emerging East Asian business cycles also resembles more closely that of the G7 cycles, in that they became more periodic in terms of upturns and downturns. A notable exception to this new pattern is China. The Chinese economy appears to beat the business cycle with continued robust growth regardless of the ups and downs of the regional and international economy.

Table 13.1 reports the correlation coefficients of emerging East Asia's business cycles with each other and with the global economy for the pre-crisis (1990–96) and post-crisis (2000–07) periods. The crisis period is omitted intentionally. The 1997/98 Asian financial crisis was perhaps the most significant common shock for Asian economies, leading to positive correlations during the crisis period. But the same event is likely to have dampened the correlation between Asian and G7 business cycles. In order to assess the synchronicity of Asian business cycles without the crisis effect, the correlations for the pre-crisis and post-crisis periods are reported separately.

Evidence based on the correlation analysis of business cycles suggests that there may be higher degrees of both regional and international business cycle synchronisation in the post-crisis period. The correlation analysis of the cyclical components shows that the correlations of emerging East Asian business cycles have increased markedly, both with each other and with the G7 cycles, when comparing the pre-crisis and the post-crisis periods.

The first two rows in Table 13.1 present the average of the bilateral correlations between all the possible pairings of nine emerging East Asian economies in the sample over the pre-crisis and post-crisis periods. If their business cycles co-move, then the average of the bilateral correlations would be high. A similar approach is taken to calculate the average correlations for the emerging East Asian economies excluding China (AXC). For both emerging East Asia and AXC, the average correlations rose substantially from the pre-crisis to the post-crisis period. This increased business cycle synchronisation may reflect greater intra-regional integration.

The bottom six rows in Table 13.1 report the correlations between emerging East Asian business cycles and the cycles of the G7, the United States (US) and Japan. The correlation coefficients are generally much higher in the post-crisis period than in the pre-crisis period. The only exception is the correlation between AXC and the G7, which decreased slightly from a relatively high pre-crisis level. The result also shows that business cycle co-movements between emerging East Asia and Japan have increased substantially more than the co-movements between emerging East Asia and the US, suggesting that Japan's integration with the regional economy is an important driver behind the increase in inter-regional business cycle correlations. Given its geographical proximity, Japan is expected to be more integrated with the rest of Asia than any other G7 economy. But the result suggests that emerging East Asia may be less integrated with Japan than with the US. Nonetheless, in the last decade, Japan has significantly increased its level of integration with the rest of Asia, particularly with China.

The correlations of China's business cycles with the cycles of the rest of Asia, the G7, Japan and the US are shown separately in Table 13.2, given

Table 13.2. Business cycle correlation with China[a]

	Pre-crisis[b]	Post-crisis[c]
Emerging East Asia excluding China	−0.379	0.549
G7	−0.304	0.58
US	0.49	0.517
Japan	−0.633	0.477

Notes: Emerging East Asia comprises China; Hong Kong, SAR; Indonesia; Korea; Malaysia; Philippines; Singapore; Taipei, China; and Thailand.
[a] GDP cyclical component, calculated by applying the Hodrick-Prescott filter method on the natural log of real GDP in local currency, was used to compute the business cycle correlations.
[b] Pre-crisis period = 1999Q1–1996Q4.
[c] Post-crisis period = 2000Q1–2007Q2.
Source: Oxford Economics, *Quarterly Model*, August 2008.

the significant differences between emerging East Asian and AXC business cycles. This confirms that China's cyclical behaviour is quite different from both the regional and G7 business cycles. The correlations of China's cycles with both regional and G7 cycles are relatively low, although they have increased significantly in the post-crisis period. The results also suggest that the Chinese economy is increasingly integrated with the rest of the region and Japan. The post-crisis correlations for the rest of emerging East Asia and Japan with China are significantly higher than the pre-crisis correlations, while the increases in these correlations are greater than the increases in the correlations for the G7 and US with China.

13.3.2. *Trade Linkages*

Emerging East Asia is generally more open than other groupings of countries in the world and trade linkages within the region have been growing much more strongly in recent years. Total exports of emerging East Asian economies grew from US$419 billion in 1990 to US$2,995 billion in 2007. The region's export-to-GDP ratio reached 50 per cent in 2007, which was up from 34 per cent in 1990. Total trade as a percentage of GDP also grew from 69 per cent to 95 per cent over the same period, while the share of intra-regional trade in total GDP increased from

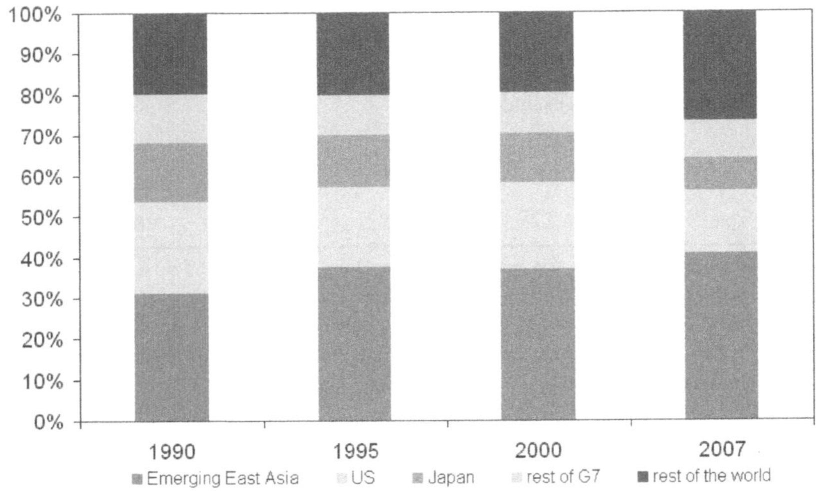

Figure 13.2 Destination of emerging East Asia's export (% of total exports)
Note: Emerging East Asia comprises China; Hong Kong SAR, China; Indonesia; Korea; Malaysia; Philippines; Singapore; Taipei, China; and Thailand.
Sources: International Monetary Fund (IMF) *Direction of Trade Statistics*, and CEIC for Taipei, China.

21 per cent to 38 per cent, reflecting an increasing level of Asian economic and trade integration.

Emerging East Asia's increasing trade openness has been accompanied by significant progress in the diversification of its export base. Figure 13.2 shows the composition of emerging East Asian exports by destination. The geographical composition of its export market has become much more diversified. The share of exports to G7 markets has declined significantly, accounting for only 32 per cent of emerging East Asia's total exports in 2007, which is down from 49 per cent in 1990. The share of exports to the US — emerging Asia's single largest market — fell to 15 per cent from 22 per cent over the same period. Meanwhile, the share of intra-regional trade in total exports rose from about 31 per cent in 1990 to 41 per cent in 2007.

The popular hypothesis of decoupling has drawn on the very idea that strengthening regional ties might help cushion emerging East Asia against a slowdown in the US and other major industrial economies. There is little doubt that emerging East Asian economies are increasingly integrated

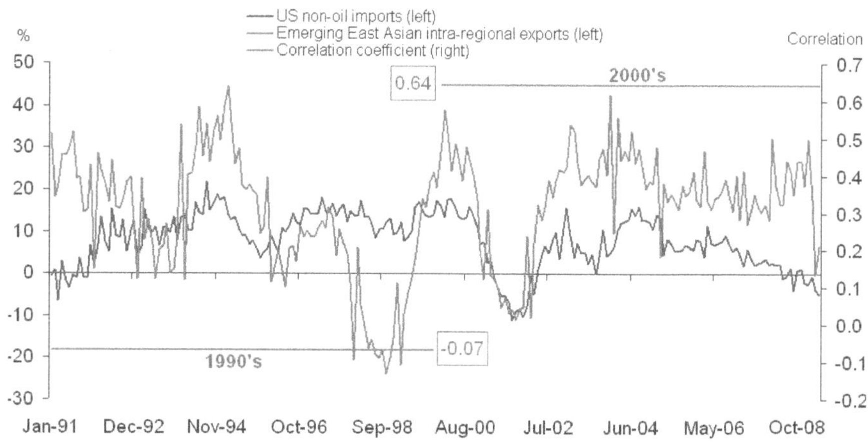

Figure 13.3 Correlation between growth in emerging East Asia's intra-regional exports and US non-oil imports

Note: Emerging East Asia comprises China; Hong Kong SAR, China; Indonesia; Korea; Malaysia; Philippines; Singapore; and Thailand.

Sources: IMF *Direction of Trade Statistics and Datastream.*

through growing intra-regional trade, investment and financial linkages. The rapid expansion of intra-regional trade suggests that the emerging East Asian economy has strengthened its regional economic ties. At the same time, the relative decline in its trade with the rest of the world suggests Asia's reliance on external trading partners might be diminishing.

However, changing demand conditions in the world's major economies, particularly the US, appear to represent a dominant factor behind Asia's export growth. Figure 13.3 demonstrates the tight relationship between US non-oil imports and emerging East Asia's export growth. Although the share of the US market in terms of emerging East Asia's total exports is on the decline, Figure 13.3 indicates that the relationship has strengthened over time. The pre- and post-crisis correlations between the growth rates of US non-oil imports and emerging East Asian exports confirm that this linkage is significant and has even tightened in the post-crisis period.

Underlying this strong linkage is the nature of intra-regional trade, a marked feature of which is that it is driven by vertical integration of production chains whose final output is exported outside the region.

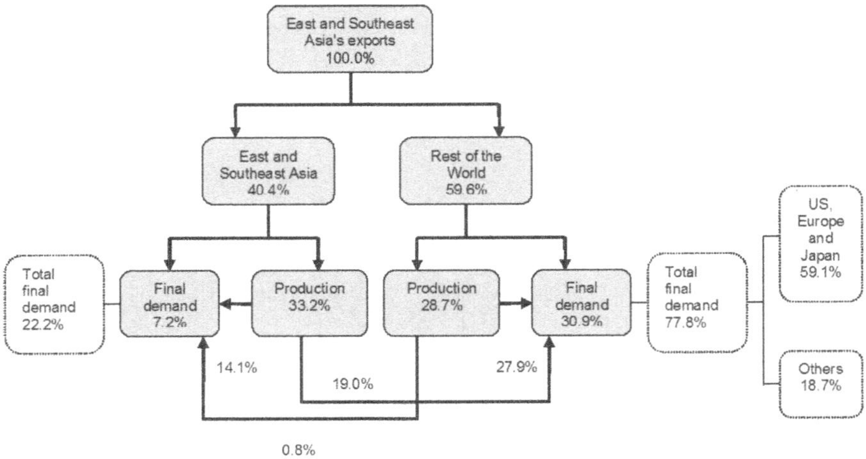

Figure 13.4 Breakdown of emerging East Asia's exports
Source: Data sourced from Global Trade Analysis Project (GTAP) version 7.

Figure 13.4 shows a breakdown of emerging East Asian exports between those destined for other countries within the region and those that leave the region. The information for Figure 13.4 was taken from the Global Trade Analysis Project (GTAP) database.[6] Intra-regional trade within emerging East Asia is then factored into the region's final demand, as well as what is used in the production process. A similar deconstruction is made for trade among the rest of the world. At both ends of Figure 13.4, total final demand by different regions is reported, taking into account the trade of intermediate goods in the production process. Based on this analysis, about 60 per cent of all emerging East Asia's exports are eventually consumed by the US, Europe and Japan (instead of about 32 per cent of total exports listed above). The results suggest that the world's major industrial countries still remain the main export destination for final goods departing from the region's ports when taking into account the

[6] The GTAP database (version 7) corresponds to the world economy in 2004. The database provides 'detailed bilateral trade characterizing economic linkages among regions, together with individual country input–output databases, which account for inter-sectoral linkages within regions' (Hertel, 1998, p. 2). This version disaggregates the world economy into 113 countries and regions (including all nine economies in East and Southeast Asia under this study) and 57 sectors.

share of intermediate goods that are traded for assembly and production within the region before being shipped out of the region.

This export dynamic is also confirmed by other sources. The Monetary Authority of Singapore (MAS) (2003) estimated that only about 22 per cent of total emerging East Asian exports are eventually absorbed by the region's domestic demand, based on the 1995 Asian input–output table (AIO table).[7] Meng *et al.* (2006) showed that the dependence of emerging East Asian production on overseas markets has strengthened rather than weakened between 1995 and 2000, based on the comparison of the 2000 AIO table with the 1995 AIO table. Using the country-level update of the AIO table for 2006, Pula and Peltonen (2009) also concluded that intra-regional trade (including Chinese markets) is responsible for only 7 per cent of the region's overall GDP, while G7 countries account for about 16 per cent.

Given that intra-regional trade has been significantly bolstered by demand from outside the region, the growth of intra-regional trade's share in total exports does not automatically lead to emerging East Asia's independence from the effects of an external demand shock. Contrarily, to the extent that intra-regional trade is dictated by intra-industry processing and assembly through vertically-integrated production chains, the regional economy can be highly sensitive to an external shock, particularly an industry-specific one that emanates from major demand destinations. The US slowdown in 2001/02 originated within the information technology (IT) industry and its ripple effects through the global IT industry, including Asian manufacturers, was a vivid example of such sensitivity.

13.3.3. *Financial Spillovers*

The recent US subprime turmoil and its ripple effects in global financial markets illustrates the advanced nature of financial globalisation. Rapid financial innovation has also contributed to cross-border financial integration in recent years, which has gathered pace since the early 1990s along with financial deregulation and capital account liberalisation.

[7] Citigroup (2006) updated the result based on the newly released 2000 AIO table and reported that only 11 per cent of Asian exports are destined for regional demand.

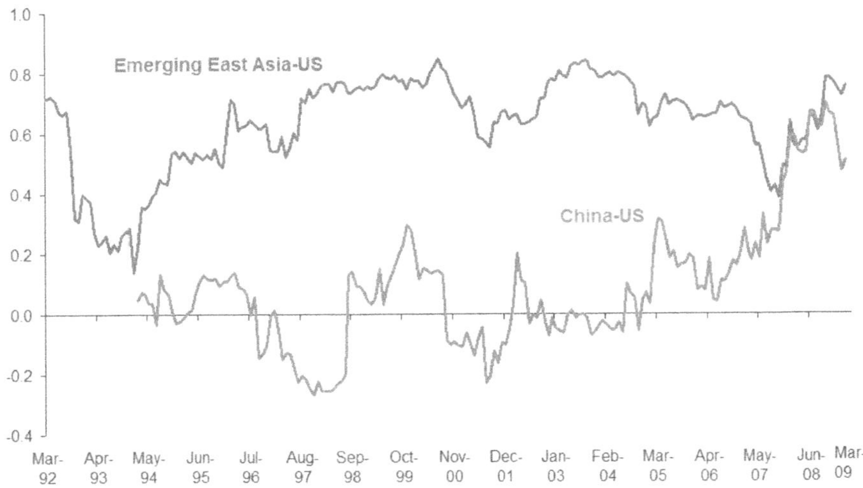

Figure 13.5 Stock returns correlation (two-year rolling)

Notes: Emerging East Asia comprises China, Hong Kong, SAR China; Indonesia; Rep. of Korea; Malaysia; Philippines; Singapore; Taipei, China; and Thailand. Stock returns are computed as long difference of grouped and individual country index.

Sources: Morgan Stanley Capital International (MSCI) Berra and Bloomberg.

Financial market co-movement has increased globally in recent years. Figure 13.5 shows stock market correlations for emerging East Asia and China with the US. Stock market correlations between emerging East Asia and the US reached very high levels in the late 1990s through to the mid-2000s. Given the predominant influence of the US stock market in the global financial system, emerging East Asia's stock markets tend to track very closely with changes in the US market. On the other hand, stock market correlations between China and the US were low until the mid-2000s before rising sharply in the past few years.

The strong rise in stock market correlations can be attributed to greater financial openness since the 1990s. Capital flows to and from the region reached record highs in recent years (Figure 13.6). With the volume of cross-border capital flows on the rise, cross-border holdings of financial assets also increased sharply. The region's gross external assets and liabilities as a share of GDP reached 215 per cent in 2006, up from 158 per cent in 1990 (Lane and Milesi-Ferretti, 2006). The region's portfolio investment

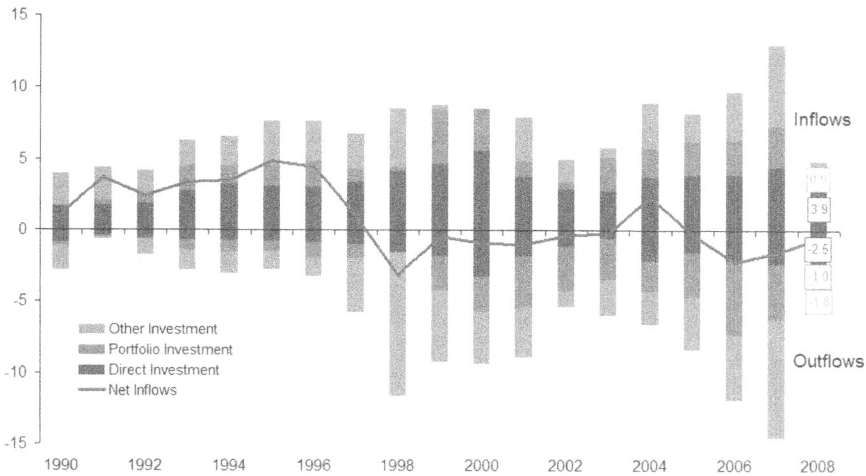

Figure 13.6 Emerging East Asia's financial account (% of GDP)

Notes: Emerging East Asia comprises China; Hong Kong, SAR China; Indonesia; Rep. of Korea; Malaysia; Philippines; Taipei, China; Thailand, and Singapore. Other Investment includes financial derivatives.

Sources: Data sourced from the *International Financial Statistics*, International Monetary Fund and national sources.

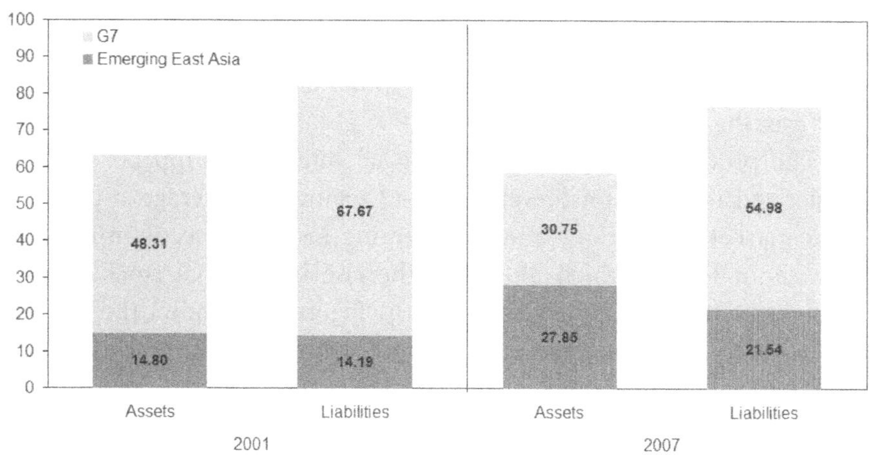

Figure 13.7 Emerging East Asia's portfolio investment (% of total foreign assets and liabilities)

Notes: Emerging East Asia comprises China; Hong Kong, SAR China; Indonesia; Rep of Korea; Malaysia; Philippines; Singapore; Taipei, China; and Thailand.

Source: International Monetary Fund, Coordinated Portfolio Investment Survey.

Figure 13.8 Average pairwise correlation of stock returns (two-year rolling)
Notes: Emerging East Asia comprises China; Hong Kong, SAR China; Indonesia; Rep. of Korea; Malaysia; Philippines; Singapore; Taipei, China; and Thailand. Data for China begin 1992. Data represent average pairwise correlations of stock returns. Stock returns are computed as log difference of individual country index.
Source: Bloomberg.

in regional assets also rose significantly from about 15 per cent of total assets in 2001 to about 28 per cent in 2007, while G7 economies' account of the region's liabilities declined from about 68 per cent to about 55 per cent over the same period (Figure 13.7).

The process of cross-border financial integration appears to have accelerated at the regional level. Figure 13.8 shows the average of pairwise stock market correlations among emerging East Asian economies with or without China, which illustrates the rise in regional stock market co-movements in recent years. Similarly, Figure 13.9 shows the average standard deviation of government bond yields, indicating convergence among regional bond yields.

There is little doubt that global financial turbulence, particularly from the US market, travels rapidly around the globe. In globalised finance, a swing in market sentiment could also hurt local companies' funding conditions and, hence, investment decisions. Growing foreign participation in local capital markets makes the region's financial markets vulnerable to changes in global financial market conditions, including sudden swings in

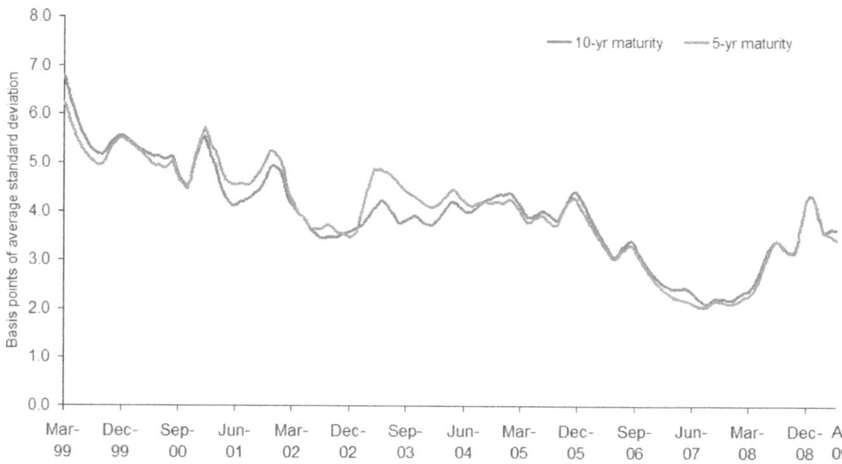

Figure 13.9 Average standard deviation of emerging East Asian government bond yield spreads over US treasuries

Note: Average standard deviation (61-day) of government bond spreads with US treasuries of nine economies including China; Hong Kong, SAR China; Indonesia; Rep. of Korea; Malaysia; Philippines; Singapore; Taipei, China and Thailand.

Source: Bloomberg.

investor sentiment. For example, a sharp reversal in risk appetite could trigger a sudden reversal of capital flows and, of particular concern, involve a potential unwinding of carry trades (Lee and Park, 2009). Higher cross-border holdings of financial assets can also raise the level of vulnerability to sharp adjustments in the valuation of global financial assets.

It is plausible to expect that generally stronger global financial market integration could drive global, rather than regional, business cycle co-movements. Nevertheless, the considerable differences in the degree of financial integration and asset and liability positions at the regional and global levels imply that the effects of financial transmission on regional and global business cycle synchronisation remain dubious.

13.3.4. *The Rise of Asia and Its Impact on the World*

With emerging East Asia's share of world output growing rapidly, the region plays an increasingly important role in global trade, finance and

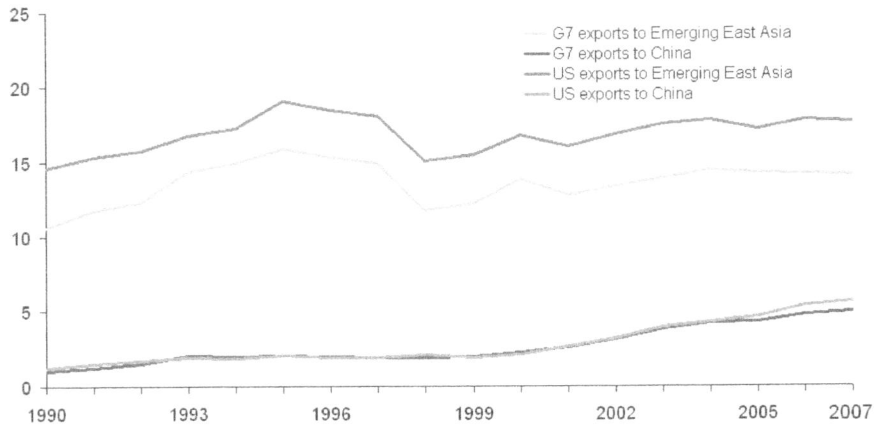

Figure 13.10 G7 exports to emerging East Asia (% of total exports)
Note: Emerging East Asia comprises China; Hong Kong, SAR China; Indonesia; Korea; Malaysia; Philippines; Singapore, Taipei, China; and Thailand.
Source: International Monetary Fund, *Direction of Trade Statistics* and CEIC for Taipei, China.

economic output. Emerging East Asia's rapid economic and structural transformation will also likely spur competition in world trade and investment. As trade and financial flows are important factors for macroeconomic interdependence, changes in the direction and magnitude of these flows will affect business cycle co-movements.

Figure 13.10 illustrates the growing importance of emerging East Asian economies, particularly China, as destinations for G7 and US exports. The share of G7 exports destined for China has visibly increased since 2000. As such, fast-growing Asian economies, with their potentially large spending power, can provide additional sources of global demand. Per capita income is an important variable for demand in global markets. Proponents of the theory of decoupling have also argued that these new sources of demand coming from emerging East Asia may help the global economy weather the adverse consequences of a US slowdown.

Emerging East Asia also plays an increasingly important role in the global financial system based on high levels of regional savings. Since the 1997/98 Asian financial crisis, emerging East Asia has accumulated massive foreign exchange reserves valued at over US$3 trillion. And on the back of such large reserve holdings, some countries in the region have

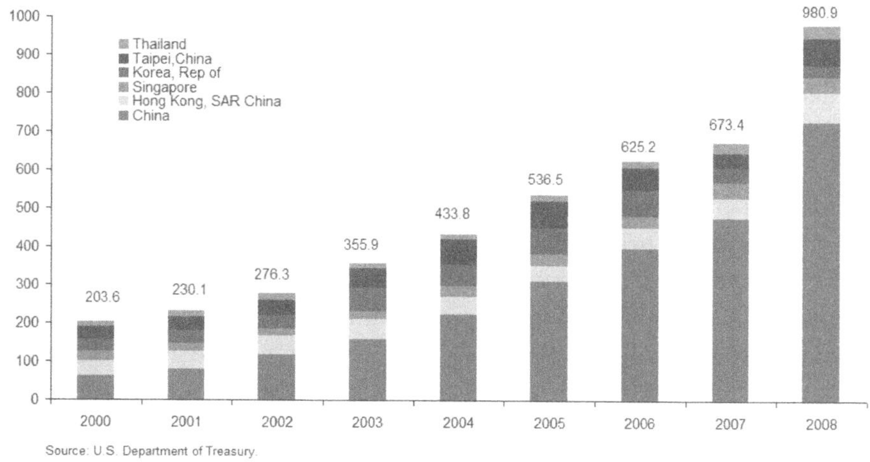

Figure 13.11 Emerging East Asia's US Treasuries holdings ($ billion)
Source: US Department of Treasury.

established, or more actively managed, sovereign wealth funds in recent years. The pattern of global payment imbalances also suggests that emerging East Asia finances a significant share of US current account deficits. Figure 13.11, for example, shows a substantial rise in emerging Asia's holdings of US Treasuries.

There are also signs that emerging Asia exerts increasing influence on key prices in G7 economies, such as imported goods, wages, exchange rates and interest rates. Shocks from emerging Asia can be transmitted to G7 economies through price changes, leading to the synchronisation of business cycles between emerging Asia and G7 economies. For example, a positive supply shock in China can lower the price of imported goods in G7 economies, leading to higher real wages and employment among the G7.

Technological advances and productivity growth, along with the industrialisation process, are often important factors in business cycle patterns. Technological advances in an emerging economy can arise from innovation or from the imitation of existing technologies found elsewhere. For emerging East Asian economies, the imitation and adaptation of advanced technologies developed in G7 countries traditionally played a major role in technology growth. However, in recent years emerging East Asian economies have realised productivity gains through the creation of indigenous new technologies.[8] As a result, the vibrant and integrated Asian region is increasingly contributing to global productivity growth.

Another important factor is the changing role of emerging East Asian economies in global commodity markets (Park and Zhai, 2007). In the past, commodity price fluctuations were dictated primarily by demand from industrialised countries, which then caused spillover effects on the economic performance of developing countries. Driven by rapid income growth and economic development, however, emerging Asia has surfaced as a major demand force behind the price dynamics of primary commodities. The region is exerting considerable and increasing influence on international commodity markets and prices.

Figure 13.12 illustrates evolving correlations between GDP growth rates of both G7 and emerging Asian economies, and commodity price fluctuations. While the linkage between G7 growth and the global commodity price cycle gradually weakened during the period under review, the linkage between developing Asia's growth and global commodity price fluctuations jumped beginning in the early 1990s. It can be inferred that strong growth in emerging Asia's demand was a major driver behind an upswing in commodity markets through the mid-1990s prior to the 1997/98 Asian financial crisis, while the crisis itself led to a slump in commodity markets in 1998/99.

At least in theory, in terms of global business cycle co-movements, the overall effect of higher correlations between emerging East Asian business cycles and global commodity prices remains ambiguous. For example, a boom in Asian economies will lead to higher commodity prices, which could slow economic activity globally. Again, deciphering the effect of growing Asian influence on the global business cycle is ultimately an empirical question.

---

[8] The available US patent ownership data, which is often used for international comparisons of innovative outputs, shows that emerging Asian economies, especially Korea and Taipei, China, have substantially increased their share of global patents. See USPTO, 'Patents Counts by Country/State and Year – Utility Patents' at http://www.uspto.gov/go/oeip/catalog/products/tafstat1.htm.

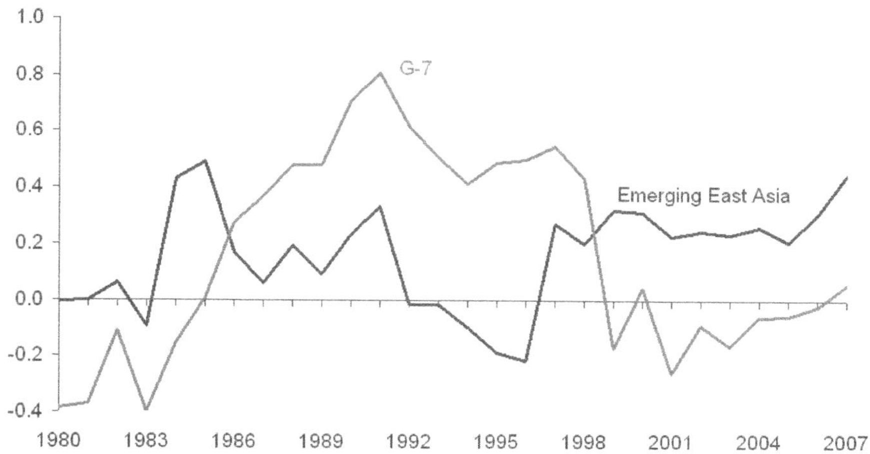

Figure 13.12 Correlation between real commodity price inflation and GDP growth
Notes: Emerging East Asia comprises China; Hong Kong, SAR China; Indonesia; Korea; Malaysia; Philippines; Singapore; and Thailand.
Sources: Bloomberg, CEIC, IMF *International Financial Statistics Online*, and World Bank *World Development Indicators* database.

13.4. Empirical Analysis

13.4.1. *Panel VAR Model*

To examine the issue, we use VAR models. VAR models can identify the relevant structural shocks, such as G7 and East Asian regional shocks, and analyse the effects of each shock on an individual variable in a systematic way. We use a panel structure to increase the degree of freedom because the sample periods under consideration are relatively short.

Let us assume that an economy, i (i = 1, 2,..., 10), is described by the following structural form equation:

$$G(L)y_t^i = d^i + e_t^i \tag{1}$$

where G(L) is a matrix polynomial in the lag operator L, y_t^i is an m × 1 data vector, d^i is an m × 1 constant matrix, m is the number of variables in the model, and e_t^i denotes a vector of structural disturbances. By assuming that structural disturbances are mutually uncorrelated, var(e_t^i) can be denoted by Λ, which is a diagonal matrix where diagonal elements are the variances of structural disturbances. The individual fixed effect, d^i, is introduced to control for the country-specific factors that are not included in the model. We are interested in examining the time-series relationship. Therefore, by including the individual fixed effect, we exclude the cross-sectional information in the estimation.

We pooled the data and estimated the following reduced-form panel VAR with the individual fixed effects:

$$Y_t^i = c^i + B(L)y_{t-1}^i + u_t^i, \tag{2}$$

where c^i is an m × 1 constant matrix, *B(L)* is a matrix polynomial in the lag operator *L*, and $\text{var}(u_t^i) = \Sigma$.

There are several ways of recovering the parameters in the structural-form equation from the estimated parameters in the reduced-form equation. The identification schemes under consideration impose recursive zero restrictions on contemporaneous structural parameters by applying Cholesky decomposition to the reduced-form residuals, Λ, as in Sims (1980).

13.4.2. *Empirical Model*

To examine the relationship between major industrial countries such as G7 economies and Asian regional output, and their effects on the output of individual East Asian economies, we constructed a three-variable VAR model [log *RY_W*, log *RY_A*, log *RYi*], where the contemporaneously exogenous variables are ordered first: RY_W is the G7 aggregate output, *RY_A* is the East Asian aggregate output, and *RYi* is an individual output of an East Asian economy. The first two variables are included to examine the relationship between G7 output and East Asian regional output. The last variable is included to examine the effects of G7 and East Asian regional output shocks on the output of individual East Asian economies.

The ordering of the variables can be regarded as a natural one. G7 aggregate output is treated as contemporaneously exogenous to East Asian aggregate output and individual country output as the size of G7 economies is far larger than the size of East Asian economies. East Asian aggregate output is treated as contemporaneously exogenous to individual country output as aggregate size of East Asian economies is far larger than the size of an individual East Asian economy.

The East Asian aggregate is constructed as the aggregate of nine emerging East Asian economies (China; Hong Kong, SAR; Indonesia; Korea; Malaysia; Philippines; Singapore; Taipei, China; and Thailand), while excluding each country's own economy. The log of individual output of nine emerging East Asian countries is included as log *RYi*.

We also construct a three-variable system in order to examine the role of China. The variables are log *RY_W*, log *RY_C* and log *RYi*. The contemporaneously exogenous variables are ordered first and *RY_C* is the Chinese output. Again, the ordering of the variables can be regarded as a natural one. G7 aggregate output is treated as contemporaneously exogenous to Chinese output and individual country output. Chinese output is treated as contemporaneously exogenous to other individual country outputs since the Chinese economy is far larger than other emerging East Asian economies. The East Asian aggregate is constructed as the aggregate of eight emerging East Asian economies (excluding China). The log of individual output of eight East Asian countries (excluding China) is included as log *RYi*.

We use quarterly data and estimate the model for two sample periods: the period before the 1997/98 Asian financial crisis (1st quarter 1990–4th quarter 1996) and the period after the crisis (1st quarter 2000–2nd quarter 2007). A constant term and two lags are assumed. As the measure of output, real GDP is used. Since we are interested in business cycle phenomenon, we exclude the trend from data by applying an HP filter for each sub-period.

13.4.3. *Results*

Figures 13.13 and 13.14 report the impulse responses for 16 quarters — for the pre-crisis and post-crisis periods, respectively — in the case of the [log *RY_W*, log *RY_A*, log *RYi*] model. There are nine graphs in each figure. Each graph shows the impulse response of each variable to shocks to each variable. The responding variables are denoted at the far left of each row of graphs, while the names of shocks are denoted at the top of each column of graphs. For example, the graph in the third row and the second

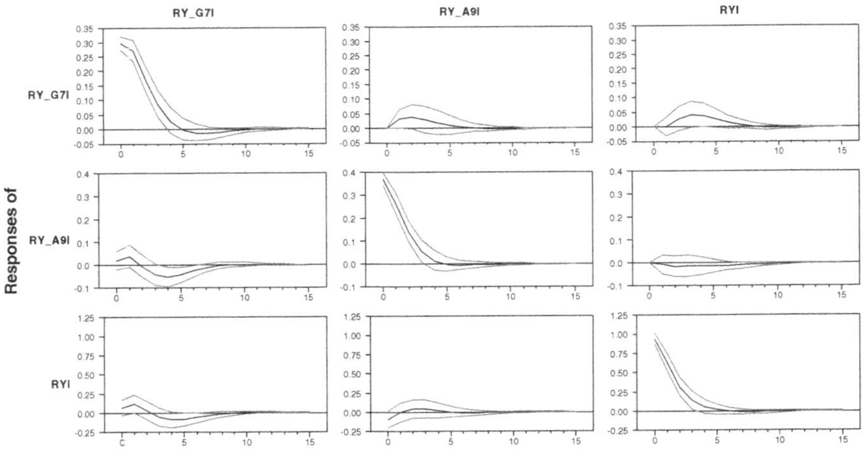

Figure 13.13 Impulse responses, the model with Asian aggregate (1990–96)
Notes: RY_G7I = aggregate output of G7 (Canada, France, Germany, Italy, Japan, United Kingdom, and United States); RY_A9I = aggregate output of nine emerging Asian economies (China; Hong Kong, China; Indonesia; Korea; Malaysia; Philippines; Singapore; Taipei, China; and Thailand); RYI = output of individual emerging Asian economies.

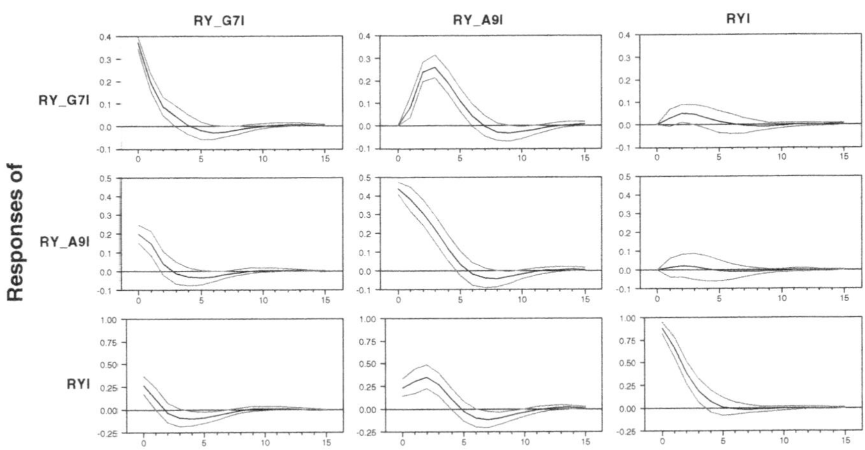

Figure 13.14 Impulse responses, the model with Asian aggregate (2000–2H2007)
Notes: RY_G7I = aggregate output of G7 (Canada, France, Germany, Italy, Japan, United Kingdom, and United States); RY_A9I = aggregate output of nine emerging Asian economies (China; Hong Kong, China; Indonesia; Korea; Malaysia; Philippines; Singapore; Taipei, China; and Thailand); RYI = output of individual emerging Asian economies.

column shows the impulse responses of log RY_RY_i to shocks to log RY_A. The solid line in each graph shows the point estimate while the dotted lines show 90 per cent probability bands. The numbers show percentage changes.

Impulse responses show that the effects of G7 shocks on the East Asian aggregate and individual economies increased substantially in the 2000s. While the effects are minor in the 1990s, the effects become significantly stronger in the 2000s. In the 2000s, in response to G7 shocks, G7 output increases about 0.35 per cent on impact, decreases over time, and returns to the initial level in three years. This reveals the nature of G7 shocks. In response to G7 shocks, the East Asian aggregate output and individual outputs increase 0.2–0.3 per cent on impact, decrease over time, and return to the initial levels in two to three years.

The effects of East Asian shocks on G7 economies also increased substantially in the 2000s. While the effects are small and much delayed in the 1990s, the effects are far larger in the 2000s when, in response to East Asian aggregate shocks, the East Asian aggregate increases about 0.4 per cent on impact, decreases over time, and returns to the initial level in five years. Compared to the G7 shocks, East Asian aggregate shocks are larger and more persistent. In response to East Asian aggregate shocks, G7 output increases over time. The peak increase of about 0.3 per cent is realised in two years before returning to the initial level in seven years. Individual output increases about 0.2 per cent on impact and decreases back to the initial level in five years. It is particularly interesting that East Asian aggregate shocks have such strong effects on G7 economies in the 2000s.

To infer the role of G7 and East Asian regional shocks in output fluctuations, forecast error variance decomposition is reported in Figures 13.15 and 13.16. The graphs in each row show the percentage contribution of three shocks to fluctuations in each variable. The point estimate and 90 per cent error bands are reported. From the graphs, we can infer that the role of G7 shocks in explaining East Asian aggregate output and individual country output increased substantially in the 2000s, as did the role of East Asian aggregate shocks in explaining G7 and individual output. The contribution of G7 shocks to Asian aggregate output fluctuations increases from less than 10 per cent in the 1990s to about 20 per cent in the 2000s. The contribution of G7 shocks in explaining individual East Asian output

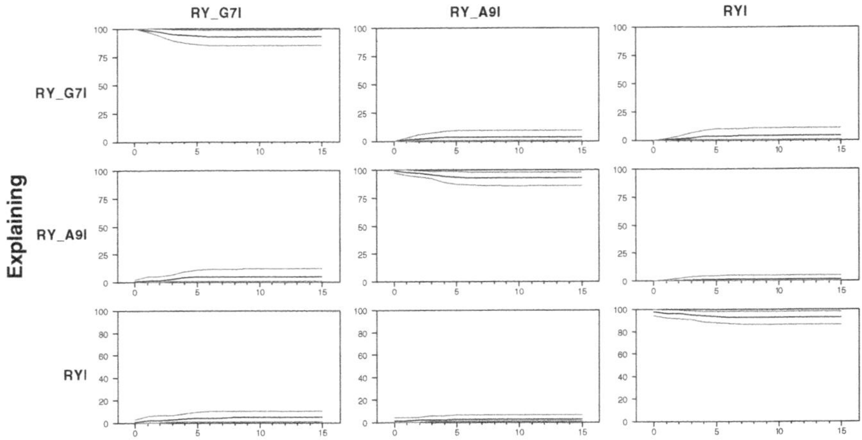

Figure 13.15 Forecast error variance decomposition, the model with Asian aggregate (1990–96)

Note: RY_G7I = aggregate output of G7 (Canada, France, Germany, Italy, Japan, United Kingdom, and United States); RY_A9I = aggregate output of nine emerging Asian economies (China; Hong Kong, China; Indonesia; Korea; Malaysia; Philippines; Singapore; Taipei, China; and Thailand); RYI = output of individual emerging Asian economies.

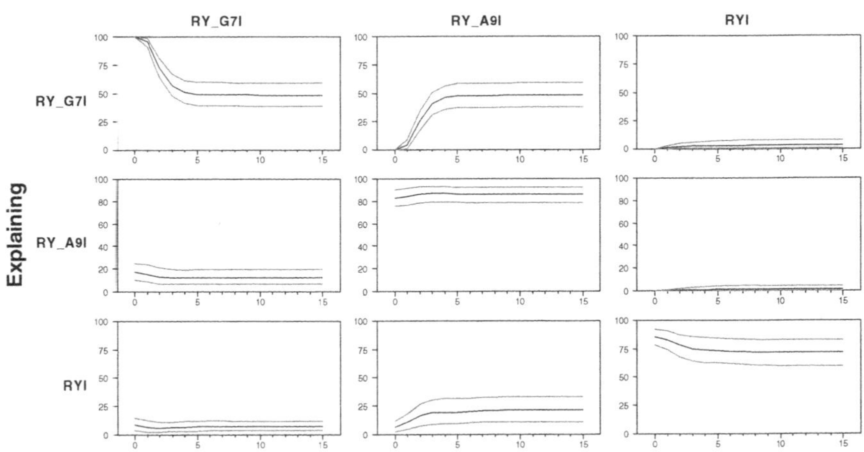

Figure 13.16 Forecast error variance decomposition, the model with Asian aggregate (2000–2H2007)

Notes: RY_G7I = aggregate output of G7 (Canada, France, Germany, Italy, Japan, United Kingdom, and United States); RY_A9I = aggregate output of nine emerging Asian economies (China; Hong Kong, China; Indonesia; Korea; Malaysia; Philippines; Singapore; Taipei, China; and Thailand); RYI = output of individual emerging Asian economies.

was less than 5 per cent in the 1990s, but over 10 per cent in the 2000s. The contribution of East Asian aggregate shocks in explaining G7 output fluctuations (at medium- and long-term horizons) increases from less than 20 per cent in the 1990s to about 50 per cent in the 2000s. The contribution of East Asian aggregate shocks in explaining individual output fluctuations also increases from less than 5 per cent to over 20 per cent during the same period.

It is quite striking that the proportion of East Asian aggregate output shocks in explaining G7 output fluctuations is huge (about 50 per cent) in the 2000s, which is far larger than the proportion of G7 shocks in explaining East Asian aggregate output fluctuations (about 20 per cent). Also, the proportion of East Asian aggregate output shocks in explaining individual country output fluctuations is larger than that of G7 shocks. However, this does not necessarily imply that the East Asian economy influences the G7 economy far more than the other way around. From the impulse responses, we can see that the size and persistence of East Asian aggregate shocks are larger than those of G7 shocks. If the nature of the G7 shocks and East Asian aggregate shocks are the same, the effect of East Asian aggregate shocks on the G7 economy may not be far larger than the effect of G7 shocks on the East Asian economy. To some extent, the fact that East Asian aggregate shocks were larger and more persistent than global shocks may explain the finding that the contribution of East Asian aggregate shocks to G7 and individual output fluctuations is far larger than that of G7 shocks to East Asian aggregate and individual output fluctuations. Even after considering this difference in the nature of shocks, the huge effect of East Asian aggregate shocks on the G7 economy is still quite interesting.

In the model in which Chinese output, instead of East Asian aggregate output, is included, the results are qualitatively similar to the previous model with East Asian aggregate shocks in that the positive effects of G7 shocks on Chinese and individual East Asian economies, and the positive effects of Chinese shocks on G7 and individual East Asian economies, are larger in the 2000s than in the 1990s. Also, Chinese shocks are larger and more persistent than G7 shocks. In addition, the contribution of G7 shocks on China and individual East Asian economies, and the contribution of Chinese shocks on G7 and individual Asian economies, are far

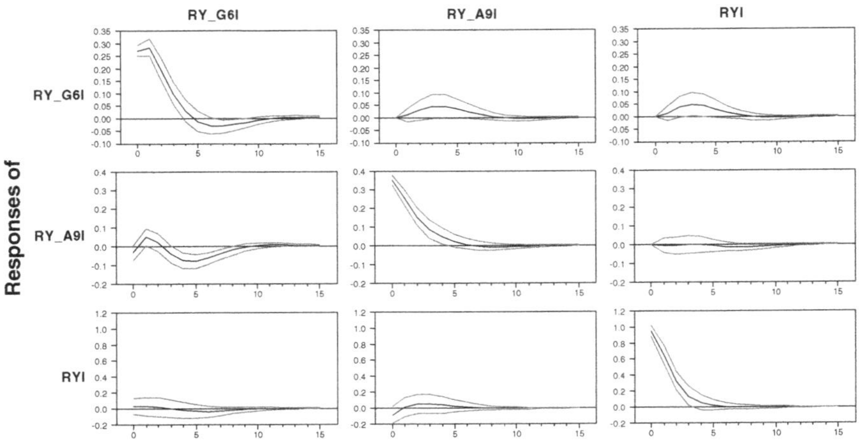

Figure 13.17 Impulse responses, the model with Asian aggregate and the G6 (1990–96)
Notes: RY_G6I = aggregate output of G6 (Canada, France, Germany, Italy, United Kingdom, and United States); RY_A9I = aggregate output of nine emerging Asian economies (China; Hong Kong, China; Indonesia; Korea; Malaysia; Philippines; Singapore; Taipei, China; and Thailand); RYI = output of individual emerging Asian economies.

larger in the 2000s than in the 1990s. Detailed results are reported in Kim *et al.* (2009).

Our empirical finding of the huge effects of China and East Asian economies on the G7 economy may depend on how to construct the global aggregate. Especially interesting is whether to include Japan in the global aggregate because China and East Asian economies may have a relatively stronger effect on Japan than other major industrial countries. To examine such a possibility, we also construct the model with a 'G6' aggregate (i.e. the G7 countries excluding Japan).

Figures 13.17 and 13.18 show impulse responses for the 1990s and the 2000s using the G6 aggregate. As in the model with the G7 aggregate, the (positive) effects of global shocks on the Asian aggregate are larger in the 2000s than in the 1990s. In addition, the (positive) effects of the East Asian aggregate on major industrial economies tend to be larger in the 2000s than in the 1990s.

From impulse responses in the 2000s, the (positive) effect of G6 shocks on East Asian aggregate output is larger in this model than in the model with the G7 aggregate. But the effect of East Asian aggregate shocks

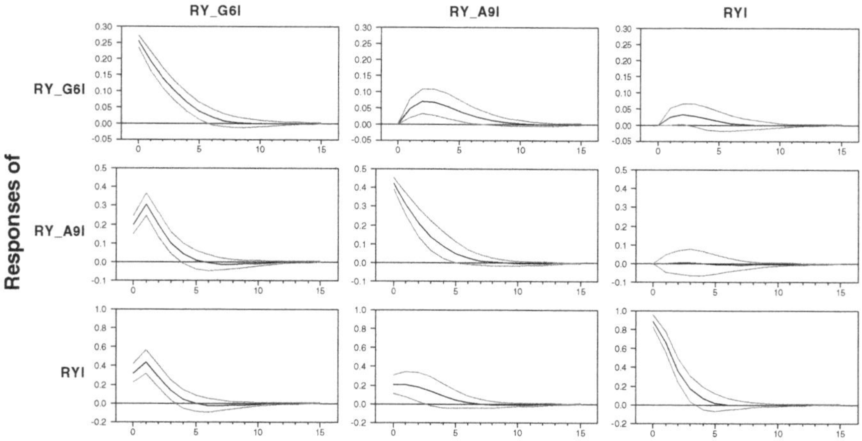

Figure 13.18 Impulse responses, the model with Asian aggregate and the G6 (2000–2H2007)

Notes: RY_G6I = aggregate output of G6 (Canada, France, Germany, Italy, United Kingdom, and United States); RY_A9I = aggregate output of nine emerging Asian economies (China; Hong Kong, China; Indonesia; Korea; Malaysia; Philippines; Singapore; Taipei, China; and Thailand); RYI = output of individual emerging Asian economies.

on G7 output is smaller in the 2000s. As a result, in this model the variance decomposition for the 2000s shows a larger role for G6 shocks in explaining East Asian output fluctuations than in the model with the G7 aggregate, and a smaller role for East Asian output shocks in explaining G6 output fluctuations (Figures 13.19 and 13.20). In this model, G6 shocks explain a large degree of East Asian aggregate output, but East Asian aggregate shocks explain only a small degree of G6 output fluctuations (less than 10 per cent).

We also experiment with the model in which G6 aggregate is used, but Chinese output is included instead of East Asian aggregate output. The results are qualitatively similar to the model in which G6 aggregate and East Asian aggregate output are used. Detailed results are found in Kim *et al.* (2009).

To summarise, the effects of G7 shocks on China and emerging East Asian economies increased substantially in the 2000s to the point that G7 shocks explain a substantial part of fluctuations in the Chinese and East Asian economies during this period, ranging from 20 per cent to 40 per

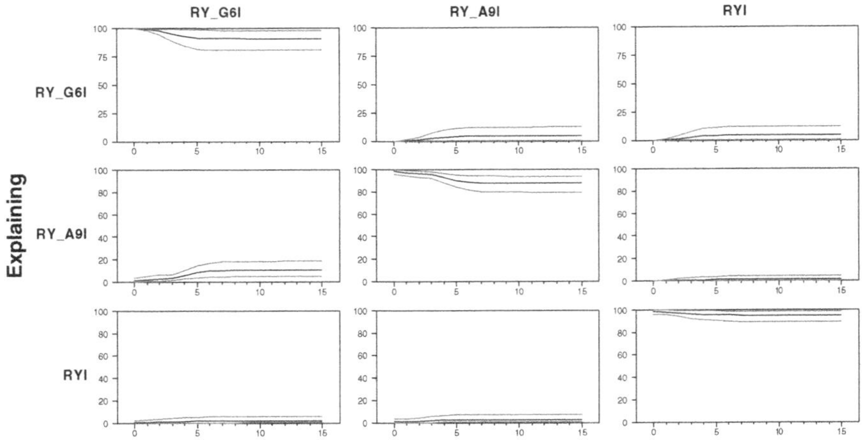

Figure 13.19 Forecast error variance decomposition, the model with Asian aggregate and the G6 (1990–96)

Notes: RY_G6I = aggregate output of G6 (Canada, France, Germany, Italy, United Kingdom, and United States); RY_A9I = aggregate output of nine emerging Asian economies (China; Hong Kong, China; Indonesia; Korea; Malaysia; Philippines; Singapore; Taipei, China; and Thailand); RYI = output of individual emerging Asian economies.

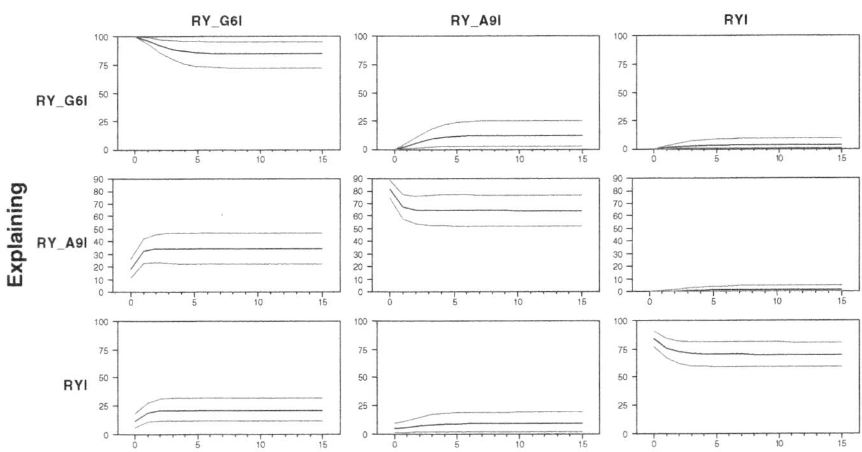

Figure 13.20 Forecast error variance decomposition, the model with Asian aggregate and the G6 (2000–2H2007)

Notes: RY_G6I = aggregate output of G6 (Canada, France, Germany, Italy, United Kingdom, and United States); RY_A9I = aggregate output of nine emerging Asian economies (China; Hong Kong, China; Indonesia; Korea; Malaysia; Philippines; Singapore; Taipei, China; and Thailand); RYI = output of individual emerging Asian economies.

cent, depending on the model specifications. The effects of the Chinese and emerging East Asian economies on the G7 economy also increased in the 2000s. The exact effect depends largely on whether Japan is included as a part of the G7 economy. With Japan, the effects are huge, surpassing the effects of G7 shocks on the Chinese and emerging East Asian economies. Without Japan, the effects become smaller than the effects of G7 shocks on the Chinese and emerging East Asian economies.

13.5. Concluding Remarks

Traditionally, the macroeconomic relationship between developing and developed countries was characterised by uni-directional dependence — often dubbed the 'North–South relationship' — with cyclical fluctuations and growth in the South (developing countries) being determined primarily by the developments in the North (developed countries). But, with the growing influence of emerging East Asia in the world economy, the North–South relationship between emerging East Asia and industrialised countries is likely to take on a new pattern of bi-directional interdependence (Akin and Kose, 2008). Heated debates on decoupling also centre on the notion that on the back of the rapidly growing regional economy emerging Asia, especially East Asia, should be able to provide a new engine of global growth and challenge the old paradigm of the North–South relationship.

This paper has explored the nature and evolution of macroeconomic interdependence between emerging East Asian and G7 economies. We have found that while the effects of G7 shocks on emerging East Asian and Chinese economies increased substantially, the effects of the Chinese and emerging East Asian economies on the G7 economy also increased in the 2000s.

It is undeniable that emerging East Asia has made remarkable progress in regional economic, trade and financial integration. But the process of economic integration within emerging East Asia is also tightly linked to global integration, rather than signalling a departure from it. The analysis of business cycle co-movements, both within emerging East Asia and between emerging East Asia and G7 countries, generally affirms the global nature of the regionalisation of economic activities in emerging East Asia.

As shocks from emerging East Asian economies have a greater positive influence on global economies, emerging East Asia and G7 economies have been recoupling, rather than decoupling, with each other. The growing influence of emerging East Asia and China, tightening intra- and inter-regional trade linkages, and the globalisation of financial markets are combining to make fundamental changes to the nature of macroeconomic interdependence and growth spillovers between emerging East Asia and the industrial countries of the G7.

Increasing macroeconomic interdependence between emerging East Asian and major industrial economies has far-reaching implications for the region as well as the global economy. Greater economic interdependence and tighter trade linkages among emerging East Asian economies, as well as between emerging East Asia and the world, require greater cooperation in trade, finance and exchange rate policies at both the regional and global levels.

As economic and financial shocks travel rapidly from a country to its trading partners through increased trade and financial linkages at the regional level, it is in the common interest of all Asian countries to maintain sound macroeconomic conditions and prudent economic management at the national level. Synchronisation of real growth and inflation in the region should also generate regional common interests to ensure close cooperation in macroeconomic and exchange rate policies.

Greater global integration also necessitates closer policy cooperation at the global level to respond more effectively to shocks and crises in global and regional markets. The growing influence of China and emerging East Asia necessitates an amplification of Asia's voice in global forums and institutions. Asia will likely exercise increasing leadership in global decision making, while also being asked to be a cooperative and responsible partner in the global community.

References

ADB (2007), 'Uncoupling Asia: Myth and Reality', in *Asian Development Outlook* (Manila: Asian Development Bank).

ADB (2008), *Emerging Asian Regionalism: A Partnership for Shared Prosperity* (Manila: Asian Development Bank).

Akin, C. and M.A. Kose (2008), 'Changing Nature of North–South Linkages: Stylized Facts and Explanations', *Journal of Asian Economics*, 19, 1–28.

Baxter, M. and M.A. Kouparitsas (2005), 'Determinants of Business Cycle Co-movement: A Robust Analysis', *Journal of Monetary Economics*, 52, 113–57.

Canova, F. and H. Dellas (1993), 'Trade Interdependence and the International Business Cycle', *Journal of International Economics*, 34, 23–47.

Citigroup (2006), *Asia Macro Views*, 4 September.

Clark, T. E. and E. van Wincoop (2001), 'Borders and Business Cycles', *Journal of International Economics*, 55, 59–85.

Frankel, J. and A. Rose (1998), 'The Endogeneity of the Optimum Currency Area Criteria', *Economic Journal*, 108, 1009–25.

Heathcote, J. and F. Perri (2002), 'Financial Globalization and Real Regionalization', *NBER Working Paper* No. 9292 (Cambridge, MA: NBER).

Hertel, T. (1998), 'Introduction to the GTAP Data Base', in R.A. McDougall, A. Elbehri and T.P. Truong (eds.), *Global Trade Assistance and Protection: The GTAP 4 Data Base* (Center for Global Trade Analysis, Purdue University).

Imbs, J. (2004), 'Trade, Finance, Specialization, and Synchronization', *Review of Economics and Statistics*, 86, 723–34.

Imbs, J. (2006), 'The Real Effects of Financial Integration', *Journal of International Economics*, 68, 2, 296–324.

IMF (2007), 'Decoupling the Train? Spillovers and Cycles in the Global Economy', in *World Economic Outlook* (Washington, DC: International Monetary Fund).

Kalemli-Ozcan, S., B. Sorensen and O. Yosha (2001), 'Economic Integration, Industrial Specialization, and the Asymmetry of Macroeconomic Fluctuations', *Journal of International Economics*, 33, 107–37.

Kim, S. and J.-W. Lee (2008), 'Real and Financial Integration in East Asia', *ADB Working Paper Series on Regional Economic Integration* No. 17 (Manila: Asian Development Bank).

Kim, S., S.H. Kim and Y. Wang (2007), 'International Capital Flows and Boom–Bust Cycles in the Asia Pacific Region', Working Paper (Korea University).

Kim, S., J.-W. Lee and C.-Y. Park (2009), 'Emerging Asia: Recoupling or Decoupling?', *ADB Working Paper Series on Regional Economic Integration* No. 31 (Manila: Asian Development Bank).

Kose, M.A. and K.-M. Yi (2002), 'The Trade Co-movement Problem in International Macroeconomics', *Federal Reserve Bank of New York Staff Report* No. 155 (Federal Reserve Bank of New York).

Kose, M.A., C. Otrok and E. Prasad (2008), 'Global Business Cycles: Convergence or Decoupling?', *International Monetary Working Fund Working Paper* No. 08/143 (Washington, DC: International Monetary Fund).

Kraay, A. and J. Ventura (2002), 'Product Prices and the OECD Cycle', *Advances in Macroeconomics*, 2, Issue 1, Article 1.

Krugman, P. (1993), 'Lessons of Massachusetts for EMU', in F. Giavazzi and F. Torres (eds.), *The Transition to Economic and Monetary Union in Europe* (New York: Cambridge University Press).

Lane, P. and G.M. Milesi-Ferretti (2006), 'The External Wealth of Nations Mark II', *International Monetary Fund Working Paper* No. 06/69 (Washington, DC: International Monetary Fund).

Lee, J.-W. and C.-Y. Park (2009), 'Global Financial Turmoil: Impact and Challenges for Asia's Financial Systems', *Asian Economic Papers*, 8, 9–40.

Meng, B., H. Sato, J. Nakamura, N. Okamoto, H. Kuwamori and S. Inomata (2006), 'Inter-industrial Structure in the Asia-Pacific Region: Growth and Integration, by using 2000 AIO Table', *Institute of Developing Economies–Japan External Trade Association IDE Discussion Paper* No. 50 (Institute of Developing Economies–Japan External Trade Organization).

Moneta, F. and R. Ruffer (2006), 'Business Cycle Synchronization in East Asia', Working Paper No. 671 (European Central Bank).

Monetary Authority of Singapore (2003), *Macroeconomic Review*, January.

Park, C.-Y. and F. Zhai (2007), 'Asia's Imprint on Global Commodity Markets', *Minerals and Energy – Raw Materials Report*, 22, 18–47.

Pula, G. and T. Peltonen (2009), 'Has Emerging Asia Decoupled? An Analysis of Production and Trade Linkages using the Asian International Input–Output Table', Working Paper No. 993 (European Central Bank).

Shin, K. and Y. Wang (2004), 'Trade Integration and Business Cycle Co-movements: The Case of Korea with Other Asian Countries', *Japan and the World Economy*, 16, 213–30.

Sims, C.A. (1980), 'Macroeconomics and Reality', *Econometrica*, 8, 1–48.

Takagi, S. and I. Kozuru (2008), 'Output and Price Linkages in Asia's Post-crisis Macroeconomic Interdependence', manuscript. Presented at the 'Symposium on Asian Economic Integration', Nanyang Technological University, 4–5 September.

Chapter 14

Financial Integration in Emerging Asia: Challenges and Prospects*

14.1. Introduction

The 1997–1998 Asian financial crisis motivated the drive toward regional financial integration in Asia. The rationale behind the drive was based on the region's shared understanding that the absence of regional capital markets and largely underdeveloped domestic financial systems were the major hurdles to channeling the region's savings into investments within emerging Asia. Since then, Asian policymakers have undertaken various reforms to develop more efficient and stable financial systems, including a number of collective initiatives to promote integration. These important initiatives include regional economic surveillance processes in the Association of Southeast Asian Nations (ASEAN) and ASEAN+3 (ASEAN plus China, Japan, and South Korea), the Chiang Mai Initiative, the Asian Bond Markets Initiatives, and the Asian Bond Fund Initiative.

Despite the efforts and progress made thus far, regional financial market development and integration seems insufficient. Past studies find that the region's financial integration lags substantially behind its trade and real economic integration (see Jang, 2011, for a literature survey on financial integration in East Asia). Several studies also suggest relatively weak intraregional link among Asian financial markets compared with their

*This chapter was published in *Asian Economic Policy Review*, Vol. 6, No. 2 (December 2011), pp. 176–198.

The authors would like to thank Roger Mercado for his excellent research assistance and Kevin Donahue for editing.

global links (ADB, 2008; Kim *et al.*, 2008). This may be attributed to a lack of an anchor country or financial centers that can mediate financial transactions in emerging Asia (Kim *et al.*, 2008). Although Hong Kong, Special Administrative Region (SAR) and Singapore have acted as two important regional financial centers in East Asia, they have served the clients of major international capital markets rather than local capital markets, helping the region's financial markets to become more globally integrated rather than integrating regionally.

Discrepancy between real and financial sector development and integration across emerging economies in Asia breeds significant financial imbalances. Many economies in Asia run current-account surplus, generating aggregate excess savings for the region. However, much of the excess savings are invested outside the region, notably in major advanced economies. A growing literature is also attributing global imbalances to insufficient financial development and integration in emerging economies. Mendoza *et al.* (2009) argue financial integration among countries with different stages of financial sector development may lead to global financial imbalances. This is partly driven by the desire of emerging economies seeking to increase investment in less risky assets along with strong growth in their income and wealth. To this end, Gourinchas and Rey (2007) find that emerging economies have reduced net holdings of risky assets and increased holdings of riskless assets amid globalization of capital markets. Emerging Asia is a good example. Lack of financial depth and liquidity associated with market fragmentation and limited availability of regional financial products hampers efficient resource allocation across the region. Meanwhile, financial globalization allows the regional economies to invest their excess savings in global safe assets, contributing to global imbalances.

Understanding the degree and dynamics of financial integration in emerging Asia is important for shaping the region's policies, not only for economic growth and development, but also for financial stability. Financial integration, in theory, offers many benefits, such as better consumption smoothing through international risk sharing, more efficient allocation of capital for investment, and enhanced macroeconomic and financial discipline. However, tighter financial linkages also generate a higher risk of cross-border financial contagion in practice.

The purpose of this paper is to assess the progress of financial integration in emerging Asia over the past two decades covering the impact of two financial crises, namely the 1997/1998 Asian financial crisis and the 2008/2009 global economic crisis, and to shed light on policymakers' strategy for future Asian financial integration. Section 14.2 assesses varying degrees of progress toward regional and global integration across different sub-groupings within the region using both quantity- and price-based measures. Section 14.3 analyzes the degree of regional versus global financial integration and estimates the potential contagion effects from regional and global shocks in both regional equity and bond markets. Conclusions and policy implications follow in Section 14.4.

14.2. Financial Integration Trends in Asia

In this section, we assess the progress of financial integration in Asia since the 1990s, using both price and quantity measures. Typically, increased international financial flows, cross-border asset holdings, and convergence in asset prices suggest a higher degree of financial integration. Here we estimate the degrees of financial integration of Asian economies at both the regional and global levels.

14.2.1. *The Pattern of Financial Flows*

The wave of financial deregulation and capital account liberalization since the 1990s has led to a surge in capital flows to emerging market economies. Asia has been at the forefront of this trend, attracting about 57% of total financial inflows to emerging market economies during the period 1990 and 2009.

Recent studies suggest that the composition of capital flows matters significantly in terms of financial volatility. Empirical evidence suggests short-term capital flows such as bank lending and portfolio investments tend to be more volatile than long-term flows such as foreign direct investment (FDI). Wei and Wu (2001), Wei and Ju (2006), Levchenko and Mauro (2007), and Tong and Wei (2009) also find that the economy is more vulnerable to a financial crisis if the composition of capital flows is skewed toward short-term flows that are more likely to be reversed than FDI in times of financial stress. Emerging Asia has been able to attract relatively stable FDI inflows since the Asian financial crisis, accounting for more than 50% of total FDI inflows to emerging market economies in the 2000s. Portfolio investment inflows to the region also increased sharply in the 2000s, taking up a lion's share of 79% of total portfolio investment inflows to emerging market economies. On the other hand, the region's share of total other investment inflows to emerging market economies is 44%, reflecting the tighter prudential oversight on cross-border banking flows in the aftermath of the 1997/1998 crisis.

However, the region-wide picture masks significant differences across individual economies. Figure 14.1a–c illustrates the geographic distribution of financial inflows in the form of FDI, portfolio investment, and other investment flows in emerging Asia. The figure shows that China has been the dominant recipient of FDI inflows to the region, receiving 46% of the region's FDI in the 2000s. Newly industrialized economies (NIEs) of Hong Kong, SAR; South Korea; Singapore; and Taipei, China also attract a substantial share of FDI inflows to emerging Asia. Meanwhile, the share of ASEAN-5 (Indonesia, Malaysia, the Philippines, Thailand, and Viet Nam) of FDI inflows lags behind, although a slight increase in the mid-2000s was detected. The emergence of India as a recipient of FDI inflows is also noticeable in recent years.

Portfolio investment flows are a source of volatility in emerging Asia, given the risk of a sudden stop and withdrawal. Portfolio investment inflows substantially increased from 2003 to 2007, averaging 2.1% of the region's gross domestic product (GDP) over this period, compared with 1.2% from 1995 to 2002. NIEs dominate the portfolio investment flows in and out of the region, reflecting the openness of their markets and their role as globalized financial centers.

Other investment flows, which consist mainly of short-term banking flows, have been consistently more volatile and tend to be more susceptible to external shocks and currency instability compared with FDI and portfolio investment flows. These short-term flows tend to reverse sharply in the wake of a crisis. During the recent global financial crisis, large outflows in other investment once again instigated currency and financial market instability in the region. Both the 1997/1998 and 2008/2009 crisis periods saw a sharp increase in other investment outflows, turning the net flows significantly negative. Meanwhile, NIEs comprised the majority of other investment flows in both directions.

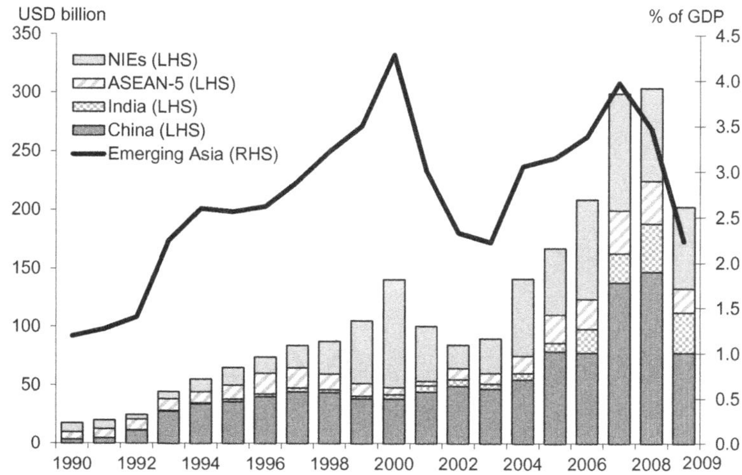

(a) Foreign direct investment inflows[1]

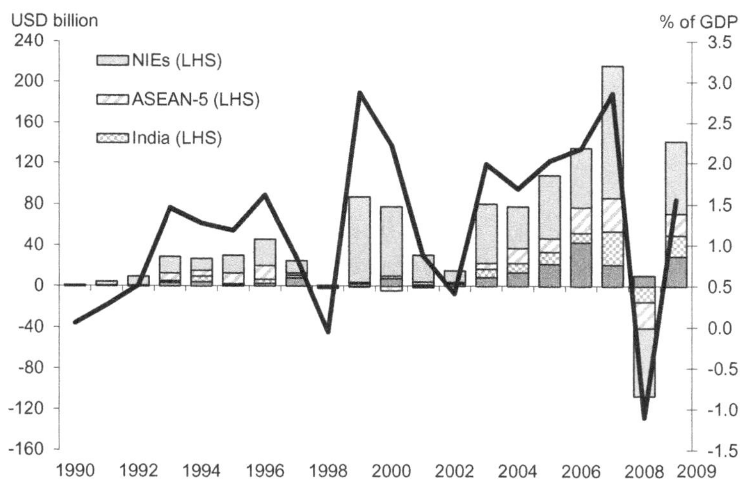

(b) Foreign portfolio investment inflows[2]

Figure 14.1 (a–c) Financial inflows — emerging Asia

Notes: ASEAN, Association of Southeast Asian Nations; GDP, gross domestic product; LHS, left-hand scale; NIE, newly industrialized economy; RHS, right-hand scale.

[1] Data refer to foreign direct investment in reporting country.

[2] Data refer to foreign portfolio investment liabilities.

[3] Data refer to other investment and financial derivative liabilities.

Sources: International Financial Statistics and World Economic Outlook Database, International Monetary Fund.

Figure 14.1 (a-c) (*Continued*)

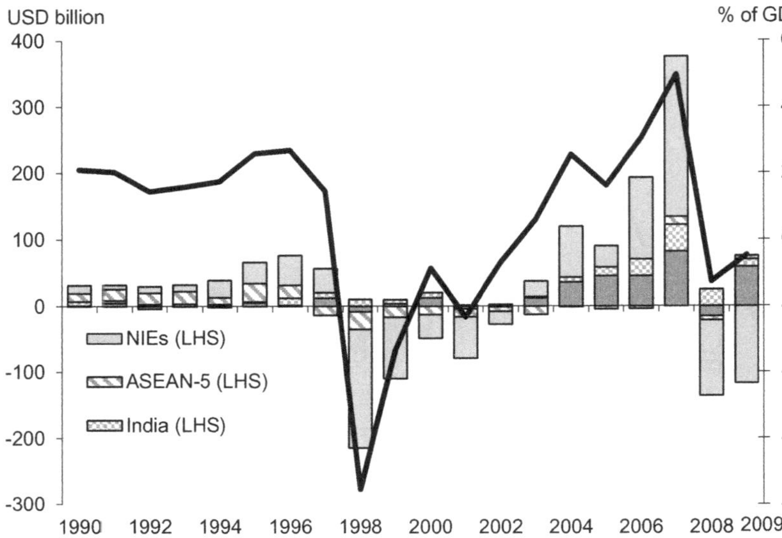

(c) Other investment inflows[3]

14.2.2. *The Pattern of Cross-border Financial Asset Holdings*

In line with increased international capital mobility, the share of international portfolio assets and liabilities held by Asian economies is increasing over time. The International Monetary Fund's (IMF, 2011) Coordinated Portfolio Investment Survey (CPIS) reports data on international portfolio asset holdings by providing a breakdown of a country's stock of portfolio investment assets by the issuer's country of residency.[1] First conducted in 1998 with data from 1997, the CPIS have been available annually since 2001.

[1] Throughout this paper, emerging Asia refers to 11 emerging economies from Asia, including China; Hong Kong, SAR; India; Indonesia; South Korea; Malaysia; the Philippines; Singapore; Taipei, China; Thailand; and Viet Nam, unless specified otherwise.

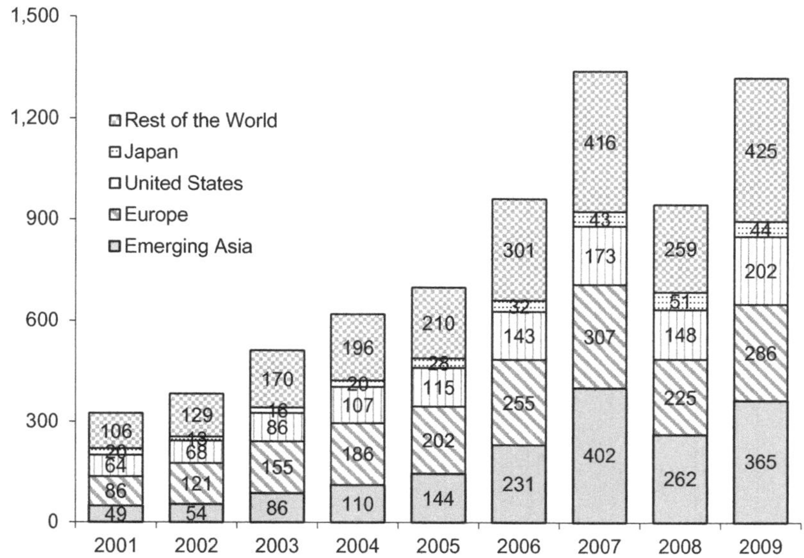

Figure 14.2 Cross-border portfolio asset holdings — emerging Asia (US$ billion)
Sources: Coordinated Portfolio Investment Survey, International Monetary Fund. Data for China; Taipei, China; and Vietnam are not available in Coordinated Portfolio Investment Survey.

Using the CPIS, Figures 14.2 and 14.3 show the trend of the cross-border portfolio asset holdings of eight emerging Asian economies by region since 2001 in terms of US dollar value and percent of GDP, respectively (data for China; Taipei, China; and Viet Nam are not available). The value of emerging Asian economies' foreign portfolio asset holdings surged from $324.8 billion in 2001 (2.6% of world total foreign portfolio assets) to $1.3 trillion (3.6%) in 2009. When the value is scaled by GDP, the size of emerging Asia's foreign asset holdings increased from 19.2% of GDP in 2001 to 36.5% in 2009.

Hong Kong, SAR; South Korea; and Singapore are the three largest investors among these eight emerging Asian economies. Hong Kong, SAR held international portfolio assets of approximately $810 billion, or 2.2% of world total international portfolio assets in 2009. Singapore held $347 billion, and South Korea held $102 billion. On average, however, each of

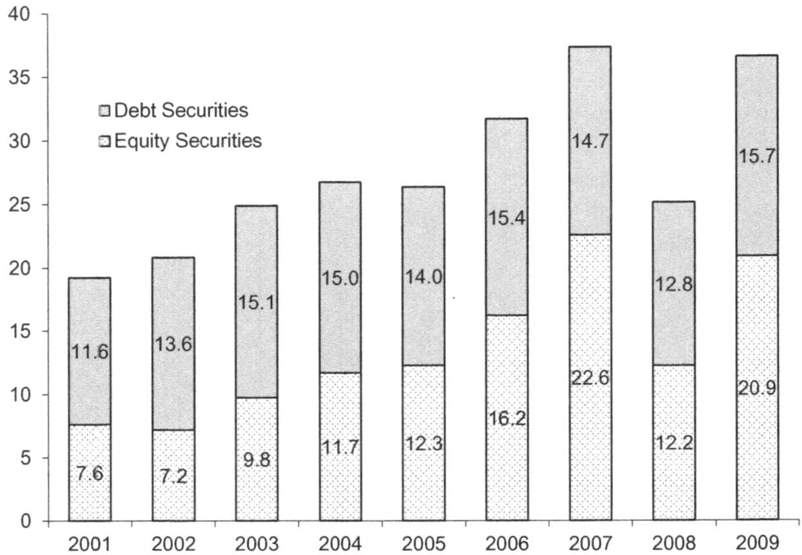

Figure 14.3 Cross cross-border portfolio asset holdings — emerging Asia (% of GDP)
Note: GDP, gross domestic product.
Source: Coordinated Portfolio Investment Survey, *International Monetary Fund*.

the eight economies held foreign portfolio assets worth $165 billion in 2009, which is much lower than the $1.0 trillion average for individual European economies. The European economies reviewed include the 17 members of the eurozone plus the United Kingdom.

Figure 14.2 suggests that emerging Asia's foreign portfolio asset holdings became more balanced in terms of geographic distribution between 2001 and 2009. First, although advanced economies still account for a major share of emerging Asia's foreign portfolio assets, the share of advanced economies as a percentage of emerging Asia's total foreign assets has dropped significantly. The combined share of the USA and Europe in eight emerging Asian economies' total foreign portfolio assets stood at 36.9% in 2009 compared with 46.2% in 2001.

Second, emerging Asia's foreign portfolio assets are increasingly being invested in the region, with intraregional asset holdings rising from 15.0% of the region's total foreign asset holdings in 2001 to 27.6% in 2009. This suggests a higher share of financial assets may be traded within the region and held by regional investors, pointing to increased integration of the region's financial markets since 2001.

Third, the share of the rest of the world remained relatively stable in terms of investment destination — 32.7% in 2001 and 32.1% in 2009.

When we include Japan, however, the picture is quite different. Japan holds very few Asian assets (2.4% of its total foreign assets in 2009) and invests heavily in the USA (32.3% in 2009). Including Japan, Asian economies still hold a sizable share of foreign assets in the form of US assets. However, only 10.4% of Asian foreign assets were held within the region in 2009, which is actually up from a mere 4.4% in 2001.

In terms of asset classification, the foreign portfolio investments of emerging Asian economies are increasingly skewed toward equities (Figure 14.3). In 2001, foreign debt securities exceeded foreign equities in emerging Asia's holdings of foreign portfolio assets.

Over time, the growth rate of emerging Asia's foreign equity investments has accelerated, while investment in foreign debt securities made a relatively steady increase. In 2009, emerging Asia's foreign equity holdings were 33.3% more than their foreign debt security holdings.

Figure 14.4 shows the amount of foreign equities held by emerging Asia. The value of emerging Asian foreign equity holdings reached $755.1 billion in 2009, up from $128.8 billion in 2001. The share of equities in the region's foreign portfolio asset holdings has also been steadily on the rise, except for a rather sharp drop in 2008, reflecting the impact of the global financial crisis. Equities accounted for 57.1% of emerging Asia's total foreign portfolio assets in 2009, up from 39.6% in 2001.

Emerging Asia's foreign equity holdings have also become more geographically dispersed. The share of the advanced economies (the USA and Europe) in emerging Asia's foreign equity holdings fell sharply from 40.7% of the region's total foreign equity holdings in 2001 to 24.7% in 2009, while those of the region and the rest of the world have increased. In fact, emerging Asia's share of foreign equity holdings within the region rose to 33.0% in 2009 from 20.0% in 2001.

If Japan is included, the situation is once again different. Japan's holding of Asian equities amounted to 8.1% of its total foreign assets in 2009, yet this share is much lower than the share of US equities in its holding of

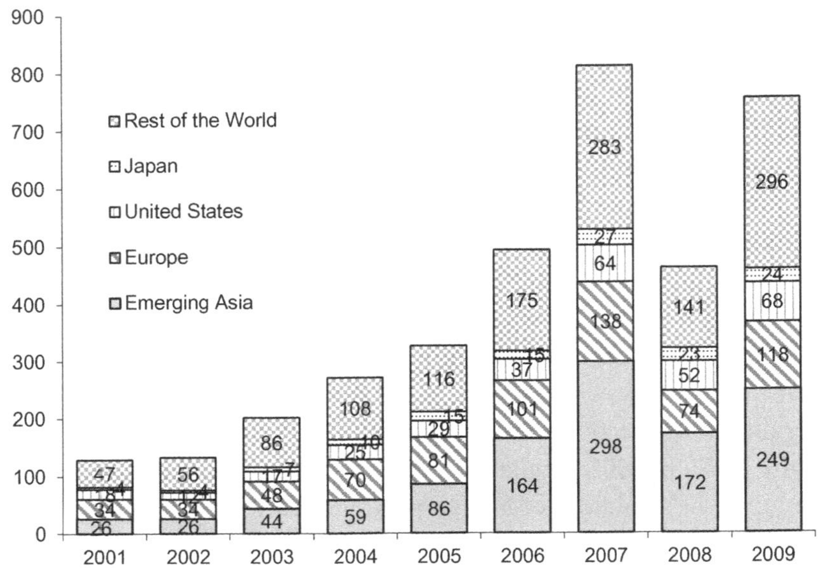

Figure 14.4 Foreign equity holdings — emerging Asia (US$ billion)
Source: Coordinated Portfolio Investment Survey, *International Monetary Fund*.

foreign equities at 38.8%. Including Japan, Asian equities held within the region rose to 22.0% in 2009 from 9.6% in 2001.

The share of foreign debt securities in the region's total foreign portfolio assets has been on the decline. The value of emerging Asian foreign debt securities, however, reached $566.6 billion in 2009, up from $196.1 billion in 2001. Similar to the pattern of increased regional holdings in equities, emerging Asian holdings of regional debt securities have increased from 11.6% of their total foreign debt securities in 2001 to 20.5% in 2009 (Figure 14.5). Meanwhile, debt securities of advanced economies (particularly the USA and Europe) have maintained a fairly steady share of the region's foreign debt security holdings — from 49.8% of the region's total foreign equity holdings in 2001 to 53.2% in 2009. This reflects the fact that demand for safe assets continues to support demand for debt securities of advanced economies rather than emerging markets' debt securities.

The sharp increase in emerging Asia's international portfolio asset holdings suggests a greater degree of the region's financial openness and integration. The pace of financial integration in emerging Asia still lags

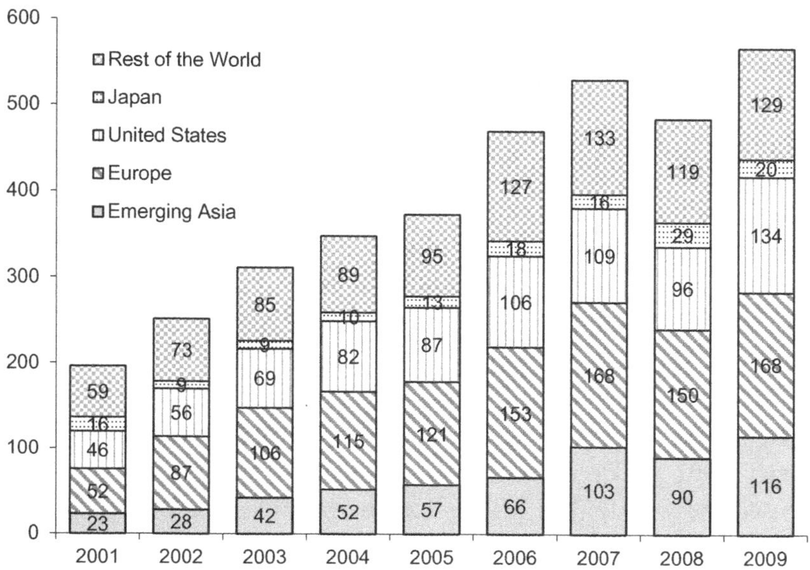

Figure 14.5 Foreign debt securities — emerging Asia (US$ billion)
Source: Coordinated Portfolio Investment Survey, *International Monetary Fund*.

behind that in Europe. The international portfolio asset holdings of an average emerging Asian economy in 2009 amounted to 54.6% of its GDP, while the comparable figure for an average European country was 120.9%. Moreover, the share of emerging Asian portfolio assets (both equities and debt securities) in total international portfolio asset holdings of emerging Asia in 2009 was much lower (27.6%) than that of European asset holdings of European economies (63.2%). However, financial integration of emerging Asia is far ahead of that of Latin America. The international portfolio asset holdings of an average Latin American country stand at 27.6% of its GDP. Intraregional asset holdings of Latin American economies also amount to mere 7.7% of their total international asset holdings.

14.2.3. *The Convergence of Equity Premia and Bond Returns*

If financial markets are fully integrated, assets with similar risk characteristics should be priced similarly (after adjusting for risks). In other words, greater financial integration should be accompanied by the closer co-movement of prices.

The data used to measure the degree of co-movement of financial asset returns comprise benchmark stock price and bond total return indexes from 10 emerging Asian economies (data for Viet Nam were not available), all sourced from Bloomberg LP. In addition, the USA, Japan, and Europe are included as advanced economies. For stock market returns, we calculate the weekly log differences of benchmark stock price indexes to get the continuously compounded weekly total returns from January 1993 to December 2010. For bond returns, the total return indexes of HSBC Asian local currency bond indexes are used. Bond returns, estimated by the weekly log differences of the total return indexes from January 2001 to December 2010, are also continuously compounded. We used the weekly data for the returns (sampled on Wednesdays each week) — as opposed to daily — to avoid the potential problem of nonsynchronous data.[2] Both equity and bond returns are in local currency.[3]

Table 14.1 reports simple averages of cross-country stock return correlations among different groups of regional and global economies over four different time periods. The increased correlations of Asian equity markets within and beyond regional markets suggest Asian equity markets are becoming more integrated both regionally and globally. Intraregional correlations are generally higher than the correlations of Asian markets with global markets such as the USA and Europe in recent years. Especially noticeable is the sharp increase in the regional markets' correlations with Japan. Regional integration with the Japanese market seems to have accelerated during the sample period from a very low level.

The results also point to different patterns of integration among emerging Asian economies, arguably depending on the degree of their financial openness. First, ASEAN-4 (Indonesia, Malaysia, the Philippines, and Thailand) equity markets appear to be more correlated with regional markets than with the US and European markets. Second, more open

[2] Refer to the IMF (2011) website at http://www.imf.org/external/np/sta/pi/cpis.htm for details.

[3] Burns *et al.* (1998) and Lo and MacKinlay (1990) study the effects of nonsynchronous trading across international markets in different time zones.

Table 14.1. Average simple correlation of stock price index weekly returns

	Emerging Asia				Japan				United States				Europe			
Economy	**1993–1995**	**1996–2000**	**2001–2005**	**2006–2010**	**1993–1995**	**1996–2000**	**2001–2005**	**2006–2010**	**1993–1995**	**1996–2000**	**2001–2005**	**2006–2010**	**1993–1995**	**1996–2000**	**2001–2005**	**2006–2010**
Emerging																
Asia	**0.24**	**0.08**	**0.32**	**0.60**	**0.08**	**0.25**	**0.33**	**0.62**	**0.13**	**0.24**	**0.28**	**0.45**	**0.23**	**0.28**	**0.32**	**0.59**
ASEAN–4	**0.32**	**0.05**	**0.30**	**0.61**	**0.05**	**0.25**	**0.24**	**0.61**	**0.18**	**0.26**	**0.20**	**0.42**	**0.27**	**0.29**	**0.21**	**0.58**
NIEs	**0.24**	**0.12**	**0.38**	**0.65**	**0.12**	**0.33**	**0.47**	**0.71**	**0.14**	**0.34**	**0.43**	**0.51**	**0.28**	**0.40**	**0.53**	**0.65**
China	**0.05**	**0.07**	**0.08**	**0.35**	**0.07**	**0.06**	**0.06**	**0.26**	**0.02**	**−0.09**	**0.06**	**0.24**	**0.04**	**−0.06**	**−0.01**	**0.33**
India	**0.08**	**0.03**	**0.35**	**0.61**	**0.03**	**0.11**	**0.40**	**0.61**	**−0.01**	**0.11**	**0.24**	**0.53**	**0.06**	**0.11**	**0.29**	**0.68**
Japan	0.08	1.00	0.33	0.62	1.00	1.00	1.00	1.00	0.20	0.37	0.36	0.60	0.24	0.40	0.51	0.72
United States	0.13	0.20	0.28	0.45	0.20	0.37	0.36	0.60	1.00	1.00	1.00	1.00	0.54	0.65	0.76	0.81
Europe	0.23	0.24	0.32	0.59	0.24	0.40	0.51	0.72	0.54	0.65	0.76	0.81	1.00	1.00	1.00	1.00

Notes: Values refer to the average pair-wise correlations. Stock price indexes for each country are in local currency value. Weekly returns are computed as the natural log difference of a stock price index for Wednesday closing price to the previous week's Wednesday closing value. Data for Europe refers to MSCI Europe index.

Source: Authors' calculations using data accessed from Bloomberg.

economies such as Hong Kong, SAR; Korea; and Singapore show higher stock market correlations with other regional markets as well as the US and European markets than ASEAN-4. Third, the Chinese market is by far the least correlated with other markets in the sample, although its correlations with both regional and global markets have increased significantly in 2006–2010. The Chinese market is also more correlated with the regional markets than with the US and European markets. Fourth, the Indian market's correlations with both regional and global markets have also increased sharply since 2000 from the very low levels in the 1990s.

A substantial body of literature has documented that correlations among international stock returns are time varying, with evidence pointing to an increase in correlations across international stock markets at times of stress and market downturns (King & Wadhwani, 1990; Longin & Solnik, 1995; Karolyi & Stulz, 1996; Forbes & Rigobon, 2002). In our sample, two subperiods (1996–2000 and 2006–2010) include one financial crisis each. There is a concern that the different extent of crisis effects on the co-movement of cross-border asset prices may influence the cross-country correlations upward. Indeed, the global crisis of 2008/2009 appears to have exerted strong influence on both regional and global correlations of emerging Asian markets. Nevertheless, the consistent increases in both regional and global correlations over the four subperiods and across different groupings of regional and global economies suggest regional and global stock market integration.

Table 14.2 reports the cross-country correlations of local currency bond returns in 2001–2010. Correlations of Asian local currency bond returns increased over this decade, albeit from very low levels. The results also point to different patterns of integration across subgroups of emerging Asian economies similar to the case of stock market integration by subgroups of the regional economies. First, ASEAN-4 bond markets show limited degrees of integration with the global markets. Second, the relatively more open and developed bond markets of NIEs such as Hong Kong, SAR; South Korea; and Singapore show greater bond market correlations with both other regional economies and the global market than ASEAN-4. Third, China, India, and the Philippine markets are the least correlated with the global market, while China, Indonesia, the Philippines, and Taipei, China have the lowest correlations with the other regional

Table 14.2. Average simple correlation of government bond weekly returns

	Emerging Asia		Global	
Economy	**2001–2005**	**2006–2010**	**2001–2005**	**2006–2010**
Emerging Asia	0.09	0.17	0.19	0.21
ASEAN–4	0.05	0.17	0.08	0.17
NIEs	0.15	0.18	0.38	0.29
China	0.05	0.12	0.05	0.05
India	0.01	0.19	–0.05	0.10
Global	0.19	0.21	1.00	1.00

Notes: Weekly returns are computed as Wednesday-on-Wednesday difference of the natural log values of HSBC Asia Local Bond Index. The HSBC Asia Local Bond Index tracks the total return performance of a bond portfolio which consists of local-currency denominated, government bonds in Asia ex-Japan. Data refers to government bonds. Global bond returns refers to Citigroup World Government Bond Index in local currency.
Source: Authors' calculations using HSBC Asia Local Bond Index and Citigroup World Government Bond Index data accessed from Bloomberg.

markets in the sample. Finally, the bond market correlations of Hong Kong, SAR and Singapore with the global market are noticeably higher than those of other bond markets in the region. The high correlations reflect these economies' more open and globally integrated bond markets. Yet, this may also reflect the effect of their rigid exchange rate regimes and the associated strong influence of the US monetary policy on their bond yields.

Figures 14.6 and 14.7 show the trend of convergence in cross-country stock and bond returns among different groupings of regional economies. For various subgroups of regional economies, the cross-market dispersions of weekly equity returns have become smaller over time, suggesting increasing regional market integration (Figure 14.6). The cross-market dispersion of weekly equity returns also declines when we include the global markets. For bond markets, the cross-market dispersions of weekly returns have narrowed modestly in the years leading up to the recent crisis. But the crisis saw an uptick in the dispersions, especially when we consider the group including global bond markets, with the dispersion increasing sharply in recent months, perhaps reflecting the increased volatility in European bond markets (Figure 14.7).

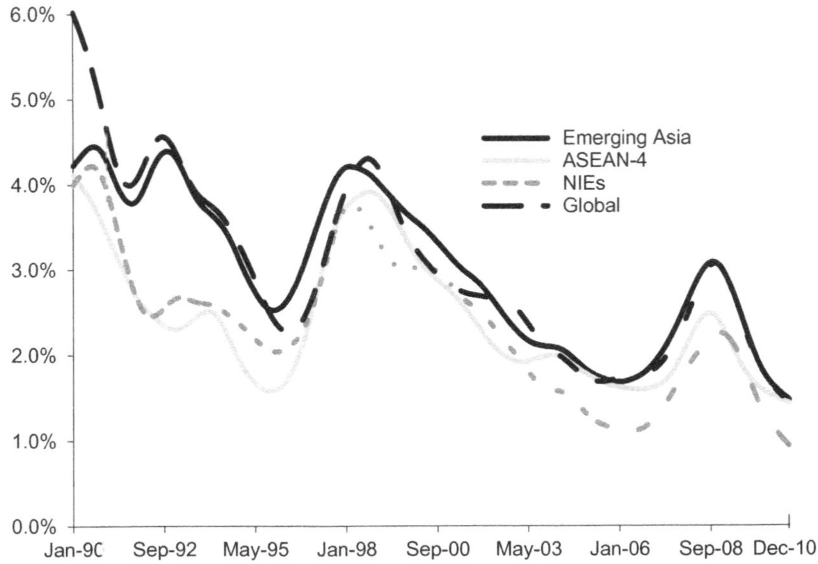

Figure 14.6 Cross-market convergence of weekly equity returns[a]

Notes:

(a) Values were smoothened using Hodrick-Prescott filter method. Stock price indexed for each country are in local currency units. Global includes 25 advanced and emerging economies including those from Asia. Data for Vietnam are not available.

(b) ASEAN. Association of Southeast Asian Nations; NIE, newly industrialized economy.

Source: Author's calculations using data accessed from Bloomberg. Accessed January 2011.

The figures illustrate an uptick in cross-market dispersions during the crisis periods, reflecting the crisis impact on individual markets and volatility. For stock markets, the cross-market dispersions increased during both the 1997/1998 Asian financial crisis and the 2008/2009 global financial crisis. For bond markets, while the data are available only from 2000, the recent global financial crisis also led to a peak.

14.3. Financial Integration and Risk of Contagion

Financial integration in emerging Asia, either regionally or globally, may increase the potential for the financial transmission of external shocks. But direct evidence on this point is patchy. In this section, we examine the

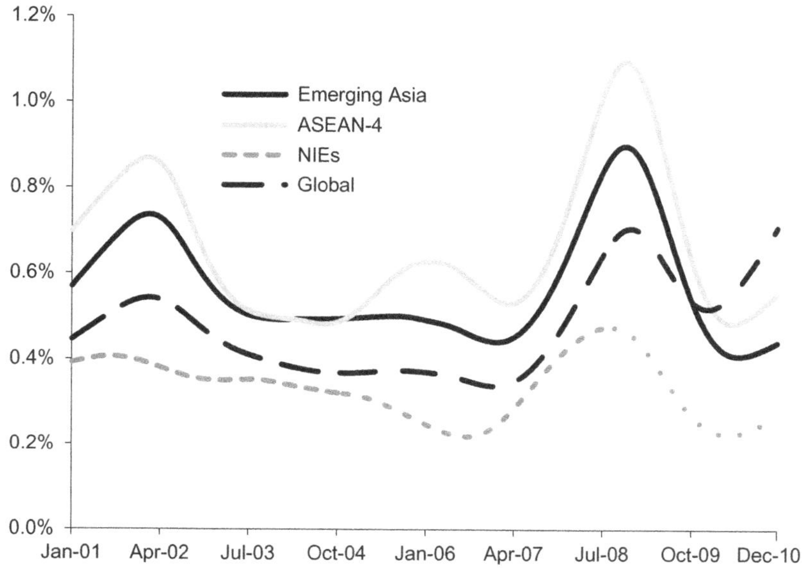

Figure 14.7 Cross-market convergence of weekly government bond[a]

Notes:

(a) Values are computed as the standard deviation of individual country weekly returns, smoothened using Hodrick-Prescott filter. Data for Asia refer to HSBC Asia Local Bond Index which tracks the total return performance of a bond portfolio consisting of local-currency denominated government bonds. Global government bond returns are computed as the standard deviation of weekly returns, smoothen using Hodrick-Prescott filter, for 20 advanced and 10 emerging Asian economies. Data for advanced economies refer to Citigroup government bond index total returns in local currency. Data for Vietnam are not available.

(b) ASEAN. Association of Southeast Asian Nations; NIE, newly industrialized economy.

Source: Author's calculations using data accessed from Bloomberg. Accessed January 2011.

extent of financial integration of individual equity and bond markets in emerging Asia by analyzing the reaction of these markets to regional and global shocks.

14.3.1. *Data Description*

We use the same returns from the national stock price indexes and bond total return indexes in section 14.2.3 to examine the degree of integration of a regional equity or bond market with the rest of the regional markets and the global markets. In addition to the equity and bond markets of 10 emerging Asian economies either individually or regionally, MSCI All Country (AC) World Index was used as a proxy for the global stock market and Citigroup World Government Bond Index Returns for the global bond market.

Regional returns are computed as the weighted sum of individual country returns, excluding the country returns for which the analysis is conducted, using GDP in US dollars as weights. For example, for the analysis of China's integration with the regional market, the regional market is the aggregate of the other nine emerging Asian markets in the sample.

14.3.2. *Empirical Methodology*

We model that the returns of individual equity (bond) markets have an expected component and an unexpected one. Following the approach taken by Lee and Park (2009), the expected returns are obtained by relating individual market returns to a constant term and to returns in the previous period. The error terms from this regression, $\varepsilon_{c,t}$ will constitute the unexpected component of the returns, or innovation.[4] Similarly, $\varepsilon_{EA,t}$ and $\varepsilon_{G,t}$ are estimated as the unexpected components of the regional and the global market returns, respectively. $\varepsilon_{c,t}$ is then decomposed into a purely local shock (an intercept or $\alpha_{c,t}$), a reaction to regional news ($\beta_{c,t}^{EA}\,\varepsilon_{EA,t}$), and a reaction to global news ($\beta_{c,t}^{G}\,\varepsilon_{G,t}$):

$$\varepsilon_{c,t} = \alpha_{c,t} + \beta_{c,t}^{EA}\varepsilon_{EA,t} + \beta_{c,t}^{G}\varepsilon_{G,t} \tag{1}$$

Where $\beta_{c,t}^{EA}$ and $\beta_{c,t}^{G}$ represent the country-specific sensitivity to a regional and a global market shock, respectively.

If the local stock (bond) markets are integrated regionally or globally, a regional or global shock will be a dominating factor in explaining the

[4] We used local currency returns here to focus on the asset market factors for integration, rather than the impact of exchange rate variations on the spillovers. Especially for bond markets, the magnitude of changes in weekly returns is generally small compared to the exchange rate fluctuations. While some studies on financial market integration examine the returns in US dollar terms, the impact of exchange rate fluctuations remains a source of debate. Although we do not report here due to space constraints, we conducted the same analysis for stock returns in US dollar terms and found the results to be broadly consistent with the ones reported in the paper.

unexpected component of an individual market return. That is, country-specific sensitivity to a regional ($\beta^{EA}_{c,t}$) or a global shock ($\beta^{G}_{c,t}$) will increase. Meanwhile, the relative importance of local market shocks ($\alpha_{c,t}$) will decrease. It is important to note that the value of α cannot be directly compared with the value of βs (sensitivity to regional or global shock). The appropriate counterparts to α would be the averages of $\beta^{EA}_{c,t}\varepsilon_{EA,t}$ or $\beta^{G}_{c,t}\varepsilon_{G,t}$.

It is assumed that innovation in local returns that is not explained by common regional and global factors is entirely due to local news. If the individual equity (bond) market is fully integrated globally and there is no country- or region-specific disturbance, all innovation will be global. That is, an unexpected component of the returns of any individual market should react exclusively to common global news and, therefore, be reflected by an unexpected component of the global market returns. Hence, under the assumption of complete global integration, $\alpha_{c,t}$ and $\beta^{EA}_{c,t}$ are close to zero, and $\beta^{G}_{c,t}$ is close to 1.

In order to investigate the development of the country-specific betas over time, time-varying betas of individual markets have been calculated using the returns. The time-varying betas are derived by running the above regression in an 18-month (78 weeks) rolling window. Subsequently, the data window is moved 1 week ahead and the equation is re-estimated until the last observation is reached.

We also calculated the variance ratios for individual market returns to estimate the proportion of total domestic equity (bond) market volatility explained by either regional or global volatility. For the volatilities, the conditional variances are estimated using the Generalized Auto-Regressive Conditional Heteroskedasticity (GARCH) (1,1) model for individual, regional, and global market returns.[5]

Two variance ratios were derived for each individual market. First, the regional variance ratio was computed as:

$$VR^{EA}_{c,t} = \frac{(\beta^{EA}_{c,t})^2 \sigma^2_{EA,t}}{\sigma^2_{c,t}} \tag{2}$$

[5] That is, the conditional variance of the error terms is assumed to follow a standard asymmetric GARCH (1,1) process.

Second, the global variance ratio was calculated as:

$$VR_{c,t}^{G} = \frac{(\beta_{c,t}^{G})^2 \sigma_{G,t}^{2}}{\sigma_{c,t}^{2}} \tag{3}$$

where $\sigma_{EA,t}^{2}$, $\sigma_{G,t}^{2}$, $\sigma_{c,t}^{2}$, are regional, global, and individual market volatilities, respectively.

The variance ratios are derived under the assumption that local shocks are neither correlated with the regional nor the global market returns, and that the regional and global shocks are uncorrelated. The sum of two variance ratios will be close to one if $\beta_{c,t}^{EA}$ is close to zero and $\beta_{c,t}^{G}$ is close to 1 (assuming the perfect global integration), and when the volatilities of individual, regional, and global markets are of a similar magnitude. In perfect market segmentation, individual market volatility in its entirety would be explained by purely local market volatility.

14.3.3. *Empirical Findings*

The empirical results suggest a strong global influence on Asian equity markets. Tighter global integration translates into increased spillovers from a global shock that impact the returns and volatilities of regional equities. In contrast to equity markets, there is limited impact from global and regional shocks on Asian local currency bond markets.

Figure 14.8 presents the regional stock market's α and βs — unweighted average of $\alpha_{c,t}$, $\beta_{c,t}^{EA}$, and $\beta_{c,t}^{G}$ — from individual stock markets. The figure shows fairly consistently higher β^{G} than β^{EA} during the sample period. During the 1997/1998 crisis, emerging Asian stock markets' sensitivity to a regional shock rose sharply, suggesting the effects of financial contagion across regional markets. Asian stock markets have made progress in regional integration since the 1997/1998 crisis, as suggested by regional markets' increased sensitivity to a regional shock compared with the precrisis period. Their global integration also appears to have accelerated in the mid-2000s, leading up to the global financial crisis of 2008/2009. Reflecting the relative resilience of the region's equity markets compared with other parts of the world, their sensitivity to a global shock declined during the crisis as suggested by a sharp drop in β^{G}. Interestingly,

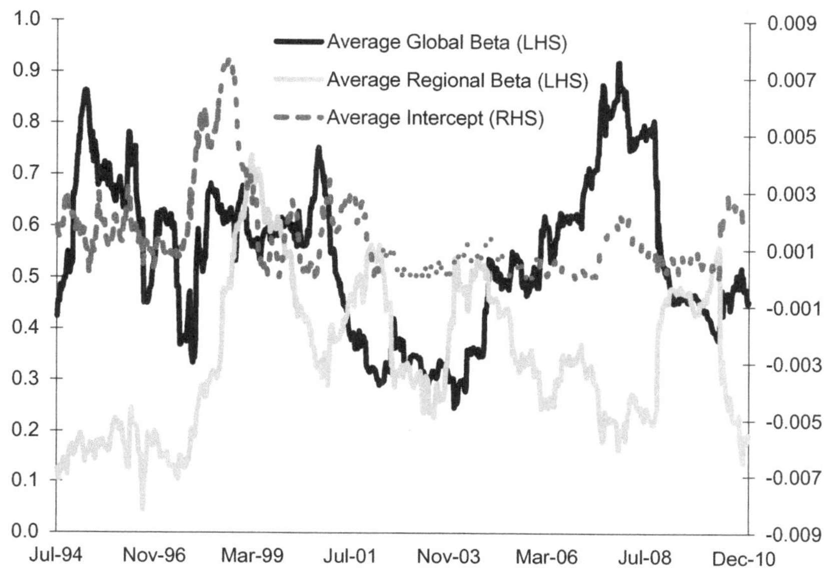

Figure 14.8 Global and regional spillover intensity in emerging Asian equity markets
Notes: LHS, left-hand scale; RHS, right-hand scale.
Source: Author's calculations.

however, during the recent crisis period, β^{EA} picks up again. This increased sensitivity of the regional markets to a regional shock may suggest that international investors' risk sensitivity to a regional shock increases during a period of market turbulence. The regional factor seems to exert strong influence on co-movements of regional equity markets during the crisis, given the similar risk characteristics shared by regional economies.

On the other hand, the share of an unexpected return explained by a purely local shock (α) had made a modest but steady decline since the peak during the 1997/1998 Asian financial crisis before the outbreak of the recent crisis.

Figure 14.9 shows the proportion of total domestic equity market volatility explained by global and regional shocks for the period 1994–2010. In most emerging Asian markets, a global shock is a major driver behind domestic equity market volatility. Equity markets in Hong Kong, SAR; Singapore; and South Korea are more sensitive to volatility spillovers from global markets than the region's other markets. Regional influence,

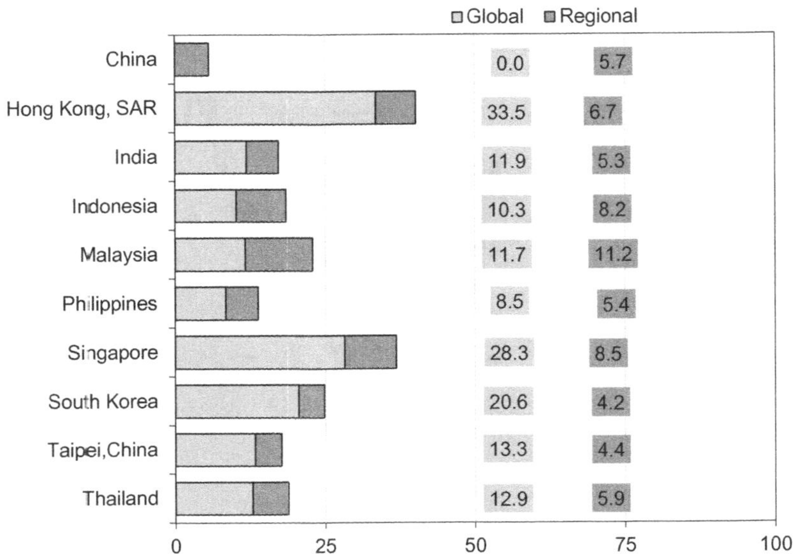

Figure 14.9 Share of variance in local equity returns explained by global and regional shocks, 1994–2010

Source: Author's calculations.

though still smaller than global influence, is relatively strong in ASEAN stock markets, particularly in Indonesia, Malaysia, the Philippines, and Thailand. China is the only exception where the impact of a regional shock is greater than that of a global shock, although the influences of both shocks remain weak. The rest of the total market volatility would be the maximum share of the purely local market volatility. Overall, the evidence is supportive of the contention that the region's stock market integration is more global than regional.

Evidence of integration is much more muted for Asian local currency bond markets. Figure 14.10 reports the average α and β from estimated individual $\alpha_{c,t}$ and $\beta_{c,t}$ for Asian local government bond returns. The relatively low $\beta^{G}_{c,t}$ suggests no clear sign of global integration for Asian local currency government bond returns in 2001–2010. On the other hand, $\beta^{EA}_{c,t}$ climbed high in the mid- to late-2000s before dropping in the wake of the recent crisis. The average α for the bond market, albeit very small, made very marginal decline as well.

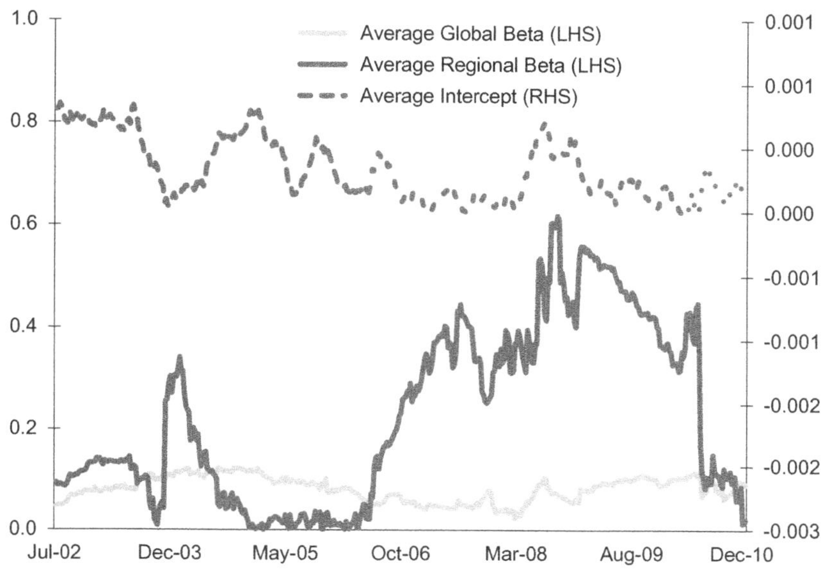

Figure 14.10 Global and regional spillover intensity in emerging Asian bond returns
Notes: LHS, left-hand scale; RHS, right-hand scale.
Source: Author's calculations.

Again, in terms of volatility, global and regional shocks have limited influence on Asian local currency bond returns in individual markets. The majority of the market volatility remains the local market-specific volatility. Figure 14.11 shows the proportions of the variance of local currency bond returns that can be explained by global and regional volatilities. Global volatility accounts for a small share of total volatility of Asian local currency bond returns. The notable exceptions are Hong Kong, SAR and Singapore. The bond markets of South Korea and Taipei, China also show a modest degree of global integration. Regional factors also have limited influence on Asian local currency bond returns as well, suggested by the small fractions of regional volatility in explaining total volatility across the region. These empirical results are generally consistent with other evidence pointing to local currency bond markets that are relatively segmented from regional and global bond markets.

Some important caveats should be kept in mind when interpreting the empirical results. First, the econometric methodology is subject to major

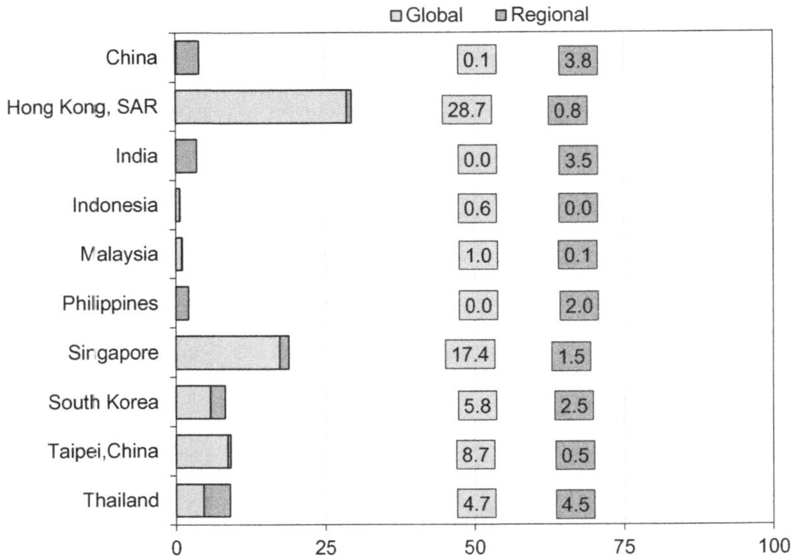

Figure 14.11 Share of variance in local bond returns explained by global and regional shocks, 1994–2010
Source: Author's calculations.

specification problems. We consider the simplest possible equation where changes in equity and bond returns are driven only by local, regional, and global news. However, there are many other factors — often fundamental economic and policy changes — that require a proper structural model to capture causality, interdependence, and spillovers among these variables. The omission of such factors may lead to an overestimation of parameters in these parsimonious equations. Second, the strong assumption of perfect market integration is unrealistic. Earlier financial literature (Bekaert & Harvey, 1995; Fratzscher, 2001; de Jong & de Roon, 2005; Abada *et al.*, 2011) finds evidence of partial segmentation or time-varying integration. It is thus unlikely that reactions to local and global news can be completely separated and uncorrelated. Finally, financial market integration is a complex process with multiple dimensions, which is unlikely captured by any single indicator. Given the significant specification problems and other caveats, the empirical results should be interpreted with caution and taken as only illustrative.

14.4. Conclusions and Policy Implications

The degree of regional and global financial market integration is an important issue for Asian policymakers. On the one hand, it implies the potential benefits of consumption smoothing and risk sharing across borders. On the other hand, it is an important element in assessing the potential risk from financial contagion. In this paper, we contribute to the existing literature on financial market integration in emerging Asia by (i) empirically investigating how the degree of integration has evolved over time in emerging Asian financial markets using both quantity- and price-based measures, and (ii) assessing the impact of a regional relative to a global shock on both local equity and bond markets in emerging Asia.

The empirical findings of this paper suggest that emerging Asian equity markets are increasingly integrated both regionally and globally. Both quantity- and price-based measures of integration suggest an increasing degree of financial openness and integration of emerging Asian equity markets. Capital flows in and out of emerging Asia have consistently increased, driven particularly by strong portfolio investment flows over the past decade. Emerging Asia's foreign asset holdings are increasingly skewed toward equities compared to debt securities, reflecting relatively more open and integrated equity markets. Cross-border equity prices have also converged over time both within and beyond regional economies. The results from cross-border equity holdings and cross-country equity return correlations also indicate a noticeable progress in equity market integration between emerging Asia and Japan. However, emerging Asia's equity markets remain more globally integrated than regionally integrated, despite the overall progress of regional integration. Regional integration in emerging Asia also compares poorly with the European regional integration, based on cross-border financial asset holdings and correlations of asset returns.

Our findings also confirm that global shock is an important driver for Asian equity market returns and volatilities. The degree of intraregional integration, though increasing, continues to lag behind that of the region's global integration. The extent to which an individual equity market responds to a regional shock remains rather limited compared with its sensitivity to a global shock. Interestingly, however, the region's sensitivity to a regional shock increases during crisis periods. This may reflect international investors' heightened risk aversion to emerging market assets and concerns about the possibility of financial contagion.

Emerging Asian equity markets, particularly those with tight financial linkages to global markets, have demonstrated vulnerabilities to an abrupt swing in global investor sentiment and a reversal in foreign portfolio investment flows. Volatile capital flows with their potential of abrupt reversal present considerable policy challenge to emerging economies in Asia. Effectively managing capital flows requires a comprehensive policy framework, including maintaining a sound macroeconomic environment and ensuring efficient and resilient economic and financial systems through extensive structural reforms (ADB, 2010).

On the other hand, the region's local currency bond markets remain largely segmented from each other as well as from the global markets. The limited integration of the region's local currency bond markets also reflects their relatively low degree of development. Similarly, Eichengreen and Park (2005), by looking specifically at cross-border bank lending markets in both East Asia and Europe, suggest that a lower level of capital market liberalization and the underdevelopment of financial markets and institutions may have contributed to relatively lower regional integration in East Asia compared with Europe.

In emerging Asia, where financial systems have been traditionally bank dominated, the financial infrastructure and legal framework for debt securities have struggled to develop. Auditing and accounting standards remain subpar in many emerging market economies, with low levels of transparency and weak governance further hampering the development of local currency bond markets. For many emerging Asian economies, local currency bond markets remain much smaller than domestic equity markets. Local currency bond markets in emerging Asia also lack liquidity and remain largely fragmented.

Developing vibrant local currency bond markets is essential to efficiently channeling the region's vast resources and reducing reliance on foreign currency debt and its concomitant currency mismatches. The development of local currency bond markets also has the potential to mitigate the global shortage of sound and liquid financial assets; lessen the probability that a currency depreciation will morph into a full-blown financial crisis; lower the incentives of holding excessive foreign exchange reserves; and hence reduce massive inflows into US debt securities, helping begin to unwind global imbalances.

A case can be made for supporting regional integration of financial markets. Financial integration at the regional level allows for the region's economies to benefit from allocation efficiency and risk diversification. Of course, these benefits may increase further if the integration is global as global markets are deeper, more liquid, and more diversified. However, the limited degree of regional integration, when compared with global integration, may also help contain the risk of unfettered financial flows. Investors may be more familiar with regional financial assets, given similar economic structures and cultures, and find it easier to assess the related risks. At the same time, the availability of regional financial products and services — for example, through long-term local currency bond markets — could help improve the region's financial resilience to external shocks by channeling the region's own savings to meet its need for investment. Finally, regional integration and cooperation could facilitate deeper trade integration among geographically close economies, improve information sharing, and add peer pressure to promote financial development and stability.

References

Abada P., Chuliáb H. & Gómez-Puigc M. (2011). Time-varying integration in European government bond markets. Unpublished paper presented at the European Financial Management Association meeting. Accessed 5 August 2011. Available from URL: http://www.efmaefm.org/0EFMAMEETINGS/EFMA%20ANNUAL%20MEETINGS/2011-Braga/papers/0078.pdf.

Asian Development Bank (ADB) (2008). *Emerging Asian Regionalism: A Partnership for Shared Prosperity*. Manila: Asian Development Bank.

Asian Development Bank (ADB) (2010). Managing capital flows: Issues and policy challenges for emerging Asia. *Asia Capital Markets* Monitor. Manila: Asian Development Bank.

Bekaert H. & Harvey C.R. (1995). Time-varying world market integration. *Journal of Finance*, 50(June), 403–444.

Burns P., Engle R. & Mezrich J. (1998). Correlations and volatilities of asynchronous data. *Journal of Derivatives*, 5(4), 7–18.

Eichengreen B. & Park Y.-C. (2005). *Financial liberalization and capital market integration in East Asia.* The EU Center of the University of California, Berkeley and the Ford Foundation.

Forbes K. & Rigobon R. (2002). No contagion, only interdependence: Measuring stock market co-movements. *Journal of Finance*, 57(5), 2223–2261.

Fratzscher M. (2001). Financial market integration in Europe: On the effects of EMU on stock markets. ECB Working Paper no. 48. Frankfurt: European Central Bank.

Gourinchas P.O. & Rey H. (2007). From world banker to world venture capitalist: US external adjustment and the exorbitant privilege. In: Clarida R.H. (ed.), *G7 Current Account Imbalances: Sustainability and Adjustment.* Chicago: University of Chicago Press, 11–66.

International Monetary Fund (2011). *Coordinated Portfolio Investment Survey.* Accessed June 2011. Available from URL: http://www.imf.org/external/np/sta/pi/cpis.htm.

Jang H.B. (2011). Financial integration and cooperation in East Asia: Assessment of recent developments and their implications. IMES Discussion Paper no. 2011-E-5. Tokyo: Institute for Monetary and Economic Studies.

de Jong F.C.J.M. & de Roon F.A. (2005). Time-varying market integration and expected returns in emerging markets. *Journal of Financial Economics*, 78(3), 583–613.

Karolyi G.A. & Stulz R. (1996). Why do markets move together? An investigation of US-Japan stock returns co-movements. *Journal of Finance*, 51(3), 951–986.

Kim S., Lee J.-W. & Shin K. (2008). Regional and global financial integration in East Asia. In: Eichengreen B., Park Y.C. & Wyplosz C. (eds), *China, Asia, and the New World Economy.* Oxford: Oxford University Press, 168–200.

King M. & Wadhwani S. (1990). Transmission of volatility between stock markets. *Review of Financial Studies*, 3(1), 5–33.

Lee J-W. & Park C-Y. (2009). Global Financial Turmoil: Impact and Challenges for Asia's Financial Systems. *Asian Economic Papers*, 8(1), 9–40.

Levchenko A. & Mauro P. (2007). Do some forms of financial flows help protect from sudden stops? IMF Working Paper no. 06/202. Washington DC: International Monetary Fund.

Lo A.W. & MacKinlay A.C. (1990). Data-snooping biases in tests of financial asset pricing models. *Review of Financial Studies*, 3(3), 431–467.

Longin F. & Solnik B. (1995). Is the correlation in international equity returns constant: 1960–1990? *Journal of International Money and Finance*, 14(1), 3–23.

Mendoza E., Quadrini V. & Ríos-Rull J.-V. (2009). Financial integration, financial development, and global imbalances. *Journal of Political Economy*, 117(3), 371–415.

Tong H. & Wei S.-J. (2009). The composition matters: Capital inflows and liquidity crunch during a global economic crisis. NBER Working Paper no. 15207. Cambridge MA: National Bureau of Economic Research.

Wei S.-J. & Ju J. (2006). A solution to two paradoxes of international capital flows. NBER Working Paper no. 12668. Cambridge MA: National Bureau of Economic Research.

Wei S.-J. & Wu Y. (2001). Negative alchemy? Corruption, composition of capital flows, and currency crises. NBER Working Paper no. 8187. Cambridge MA: National Bureau of Economic Research.

Chapter 15

Will the Renminbi Emerge as an International Reserve Currency?*

15.1. Introduction

The global crisis in 2008 and 2009 revealed inherent weaknesses in the current international monetary system that contributed to global financial instability and a weak world economy. For emerging economies, which depend heavily on international trade and capital flows for growth and development, the failure of the current global reserve system in ensuring sufficient international liquidity caused them to suffer from the spillovers of global shocks.

After the collapse of Lehman Brothers in September 2008, emerging economies were hit hard by the speed and severity of financial shock spillovers from the global economy. As the global credit shortage intensified, economic and financial systems came under increased pressure. Despite the large build-up of foreign exchange reserves over the past decade, severe dollar shortages tested the resilience of emerging market financial systems. With access to international interbank markets limited, the cost of borrowing dollars increased sharply. The combination of the rapid financial shock spillover and deteriorating global economic situation made a slowdown of economic growth in emerging countries inevitable.

---

* Reprinted from *The World Economy*, Vol. 37, No. 1, Jong-Wha Lee, Will the Renminbi Emerge as an International Reserve Currency?, pp. 42–62, Copyright (2014), with permission from Elsevier.

The author is grateful to Dong He, Sabyasachi Mitra, Donghyun Park, Lei Lei Song, Akiko Terada-Hagiwara, and Shang Jin Wei for helpful comments and suggestions, and Ruth Francisco, Hanol Lee and Lea Sumulong for able research assistance.

The use of a dominant currency such as the US dollar as an international reserve currency heightens the so-called Triffin dilemma (Triffin, 1960). The world's demand for international reserve assets increases with international income and trade. The reserve-issuing country must continue to run balance-of-payments deficits to meet the growing demand, while surplus countries accumulate reserves, seemingly indefinitely (Bergsten, 2009). The outstanding external debt of the reserve-issuing country would rise without limit, causing investors at some point to lose confidence in the value of reserve assets. There is no ready mechanism forcing surplus countries or the reserve issuer to make an adjustment to fix this unsustainable systemic imbalance.

In principle, floating exchange rates and well-functioning international capital markets help reduce the need for reserves. Despite the increasing trend of adopting floating exchange rate systems and capital mobility, the demand for reserves has not declined.[1] A sharp rise in the demand for reserves in recent years reflects emerging economies' desire to self-ensure against capital account crises, when they cannot borrow at going interest rates if needed. Furthermore, high capital mobility can be an additional source of disturbance, heightening the need for reserves. During balance-of-payments crises, reserves play an important role in lessening output loss (Becker *et al.*, 2007). Yet, hoarding international reserves — mostly in the form of low-yielding short-term US Treasury securities — is expensive and less efficient in the absence of assertive external debt management policies (Rodrik, 2006).

This paper argues that alternative currencies can play a greater role in strengthening the global reserve system.[2] A gradual evolution to a multicurrency system is desirable because it reduces the ever-growing balance-of-payments deficit pressure on a single reserve currency issuer as described by

---

[1] Total foreign exchange reserves, excluding gold, increased from just special drawing right (SDR) 811.3 billion in 1994 to SDR 6.26 trillion at the end of 2010 (International Monetary Fund, 2000, 2011).

[2] Introduction of alternative insurance arrangements would also be important to strengthen the global reserve system, because it helps to reduce demand for a single reserve currency. These arrangements include bilateral swaps, private sector insurance, regional financing facilities, and capital controls (see Mateos y Lago *et al.*, 2009).

the Triffin dilemma.[3] A multicurrency reserve system provides alternatives for countries to diversify their foreign exchange currency holdings. If dollar liabilities increase and confidence declines, for example, central banks can switch to the other reserve currencies.[4]

This paper focuses on the role an Asian currency can play in the global reserve system and argues that the Chinese renminbi has great potential to become a new international reserve currency. The euro has emerged as a serious rival to the US dollar because its international use has grown rapidly over time (Chinn and Frankel, 2007; Eichengreen, 2007; European Central Bank (ECB), various years). The euro is increasingly being used in trade invoicing, for international debt securities, and as a medium of exchange globally. Once China develops and removes exchange and capital controls, it will become a strong candidate to join the euro as an alternative international reserve currency.

The emergence of Asia — and in particular China — has been one of the most important features reshaping the world economy. The fast-growing economies of developing Asia are providing an important source of global production and demand. Asia's emerging and developing economies maintained an average annual growth rate of 6.8 per cent over 2000–10. In 2010, Asia (including Japan) accounted for about 27 per cent of global GDP, up from a mere 12 per cent in 1960. By comparison, in 2010, the United States contributed 23.1 per cent and the European Union (EU) 25.8 per cent to world GDP (Table 15.1). In addition, Asia controlled 51.5 per cent of global foreign exchange reserves in 2010, a figure that has grown in tandem with its economic clout. Seven of the world's top 10 reserve holding countries are in Asia — China, Japan, Taiwan, Republic of Korea (Korea), India, Hong Kong, Singapore.

Underpinning this remarkable performance has been China's dynamic growth. It is now the world's second largest economy. It is the second largest

---

[3] The Triffin dilemma would remain even in a multi-currency reserve system if the demand for safe reserve assets strained the ability of the issuers to supply sufficient amounts (see Obstfeld, 2011).

[4] Portfolio shifts between different currencies by central banks can alter exchange rates and bond prices and thus destabilise a multi-currency reserve system. However, central banks would not make frequent, large adjustments to reserve portfolios (Eichengreen, 2011).

Table 15.1. Comparison of Asia, Europe, and the United States: Selected indicators

	GDP (US$ billion), 2010	GDP (PPP billion), 2010	Foreign Trade (US$ billion), 2010	Stock Market Capitalization (US$ billion), December 2010	Government Bond Outstanding (US$ billion), December 2010	Foreign Exchange Turnover by Country (Total = 100%), April 2010	Foreign Exchange Turnover by Currency (Total = 200%), April 2010	Reserve Asset Share (%), December 2010
Developing Asia								
China	5,927	9,122	2,974	4,763	1,623	0.4	0.3	31.1
Hong Kong, China	224	295	823	1,080	87	4.7	2.4	2.9
India	1,727	3,763	570	1,616	608	0.5	0.9	3.0
Indonesia	707	931	293	360	91	0.1	0.2	1.0
Korea	1,014	1,321	892	1,089	475	0.9	1.5	3.2
Malaysia	238	375	364	411	141	0.1	0.3	1.1
Philippines	200	332	110	157	62	0.1	0.2	0.6
Singapore	209	264	663	370	103	5.3	1.4	2.4
Taiwan, China	423	811	526	726	157	0.4	0.5	4.1
Thailand	319	530	380	278	167	0.1	0.2	1.8

Other								
European Union	16,241	13,877	3,792	10,504	9,055	50.0	56.2	7.7
Euro Area	12,149	9,890	1,462	6,277	7,166	9.5	39.1	3.3
Japan	5,459	3,897	1,462	4,100	11,632	6.2	19.0	11.5
United Kingdom	2,262	2,021	972	3,107	1,326	36.7	12.9	0.7
United States	14,587	13,085	3,246	17,139	11,839	17.9	84.9	1.3

Notes:

(a) European Union comprises 27 countries (Austria, Belgium, Bulgaria, Cyprus, the Czech Republic, Denmark, Estonia, Finland, France, Germany, Greece, Hungary, Ireland, Italy, Latvia, Lithuania, Luxembourg, Malta, the Netherlands, Poland, Portugal, Romania, Slovakia, Slovenia, Spain, Sweden and the United Kingdom).

(b) Reserve asset share refers to international reserves as per cent of world total.

Sources: *Asian Development Outlook database*; Bank for International Settlements, *Triennial Survey* (2010); CEIC Data Company Ltd.; European Central Bank, available: http://sdw.ecb.europa.eu; Eurostat, http://epp.eurostat.ec.europa.eu; International Monetary Fund, *International Financial Statistics* online and *World Economic Outlook* database; author's calculations.

global trader and holds the largest amount of foreign exchange reserves (see Table 15.1). In recent years, the Chinese economy accounted for about one-fifth of incremental demand worldwide.

In fact, while the global financial crisis harmed the Chinese economy, there has been a lively debate on the possibility that the crisis could place China at global centre stage. Although its leaders have been quite guarded, many Chinese scholars, policymakers, and particularly the local media, aspire for a world economic and financial order less dominated by the United States — and one where China plays a more influential role. They suggest China should actively involve itself in the process of establishing a new world financial order. One proposal is to strengthen the position of the renminbi in bilateral trade and capital flows as a prelude to its future internationalisation.

In March 2009, the People's Bank of China (PBOC) released a statement by its governor, Zhou Xiaochuan, calling for reform of the international monetary system (Zhou, 2009). Specifically, Zhou promotes the creation of an international reserve currency detached from individual country economic conditions and able to maintain stability in the long run. He advocates wider use of special drawing right (SDRs),[5] especially in international trade, commodity pricing, investment and corporate bookkeeping. Zhou argues that a super-sovereign currency will not hold the inherent risks caused by using credit-based national currencies. The Stiglitz Commission (United Nations, 2009) also argued for the creation of a new global reserve system based on the SDR. It suggested its global role should be increased, both through new SDR issues, especially during world recessions, and a bigger role for SDRs in International Monetary Fund (IMF) lending to countries requiring short-term finance. However, a key challenge would be how to make a super-sovereign currency like the SDR commercially viable. The share of SDRs in private markets is negligible. Central banks would hold only a fraction of reserves in SDRs

[5] The special drawing right (SDR) was created in 1969 to provide additional liquidity to the global financial system. Its value is based on a basket of four international currencies including the euro, yen, pound sterling and US dollar. During the 2008/09 global crisis, allocations were made to avoid a liquidity shortage: a general SDR allocation was implemented on 28 August 2009, and a special allocation on 9 September 2009, raising the amount of SDRs from SDR 21.4 billion to SDR 204.1 billion.

unless deep and liquid SDR markets existed. With no national constituency to back up its intrinsic value, the SDR is an unlikely international reserve candidate (Eichengreen, 2011). Chinese policymakers appear to support a partial or total switch to a multicurrency reserve system, with greater use of SDRs and the gradual internationalisation of the renminbi (Chin and Yong, 2010). Internationalising the renminbi is regarded as beneficial for Chinese banks and firms and as a way of rebalancing the Chinese economy (Gao and Yu, 2009).

The remainder of this paper is organised as follows. The next section discusses characteristics of an international reserve currency and the prospects of a shift to a multicurrency reserve system. Section 15.3 investigates empirically the determinants of reserve currency status and predicts the renminbi's share of international reserves in the coming decades. Section 15.4 assesses the current monetary cooperation in Asia and explores the possibility of an Asian currency. Concluding remarks follow in Section 15.5.

15.2. From a Single to Multicurrency Reserve System

15.2.1. *Fall and Rise of International Currencies*

The question of using the renminbi as an international currency is directly linked to the future of the US dollar. As the US-originated global financial crisis spread, the debate intensified over whether the US dollar could lose its international pre-eminence as international reserve currency. The consensus for the moment appears to be that the US dollar will remain the dominant international currency for the time being (Posen, 2008; Eichengreen, 2011).

According to the literature, an international currency must satisfy three major criteria. It must be a (i) unit of account; (ii) medium of exchange; and (iii) store of value. These roles have uses for both private and official purposes. Officially, an international currency may be used as the reference currency for determining exchange rates, the vehicle currency for foreign exchange intervention and the currency for holding international reserves. In addition, private entities may use an international currency for invoicing and settlement of trade and financial transactions and for holding international assets.

The dollar remains the dominant reserve currency for the world's central banks and governments. And the US Treasuries market is the most liquid financial market in the world — making Treasuries an attractive investment for holding central bank reserves. The dollar remains the dominant currency for invoicing trade and is used in denominating most foreign debt securities.

Examining the long history of reserve currencies shows a tendency for one currency to dominate, with any change in status often reflecting a shift or rebalancing of economic and political power. The theory of network externalities backs this view of a dominant single international currency at any given point in time. The argument is that there are strong incentives to choose the currency that others use for international transactions as it helps lower transaction costs (Krugman, 1980; Rey, 2001; Mileva and Siegfried, 2007). From the perspective of a central bank, it is best to hold reserves in the most liquid asset market — one where most others invest reserves as well. The concept of network externalities explains why an incumbent international currency has a natural advantage in maintaining the status quo.

The network externalities theory does not mean, however, that currency ranks cannot change. Over time, a dominant currency can lose its hegemony to a competing currency. History supports this view. The British pound sterling was the leading international currency prior to 1914. While historical statistics are scarce and less reliable than those available today, estimates indicate that between 1860 and 1914, about 60 per cent of world trade was invoiced and settled in pounds sterling, as was a similar share of holdings in global foreign exchange reserves (Eichengreen, 2007). The United Kingdom's great imperial power and London's deep and liquid financial markets encouraged the use of the pound in British colonies and beyond. It took decades — until the end of the Second World War — for the US dollar to become the dominant international currency by replacing the sterling atop the currency pyramid. Since then, the dollar has held hegemony as leading international currency.[6]

---

[6] Schenk (2010) argues that the transition process was much longer than popular perception because there was collective global interest in the continuation of the preeminent role of the sterling as an international reserve currency.

As the sterling fell from its pedestal, so too could the US dollar. Its reserve currency status is attributed to the vibrant US economy, financial market liquidity and stability in US monetary policy (Eichengreen, 2011). The United States also has a strong interest in maintaining reserve currency seignorage and prestige. Arguably, there are quantifiable gains to the socalled 'exorbitant privilege' of issuing an international currency.[7] Nonetheless, the threat to the dollar's dominance is apparent. Current account and fiscal deficits, external indebtedness, overseas military commitments and currency weakness all affected the British pound following the Second World War. Today, similar trends are pressuring those holding US Treasuries to search for alternatives. With the global financial crisis emanating from Wall Street, its attraction for both foreign companies and governments to raise funds would not remain the same as before, despite being the deepest and most liquid financial market in the United States.

For the time being, the dollar remains the dominant currency of choice for international trade. Although the US trade share in the global economy is declining, exporters still choose an invoicing currency that keeps ex post prices of goods similar to competitors' prices and provides hedging benefits (Goldberg and Tille, 2008). Safe-haven demand for the dollar remains unscathed by recent events. Even after Standard and Poor's downgraded the US credit rating in August 2011, the safe-haven instinct of the market was to rush to the dollar. Nonetheless, it is doubtful whether over time central banks and governments will continue to buy and hold US securities in large amounts. The US economy faces unsustainable structural problems. The key question is whether economies with surplus savings will continue to finance US current account and fiscal deficits as confidence in the US financial system weakens. As emerging Asian economies shift away from export-led growth and reduce foreign exchange

[7] Gourinchas and Rey (2007) show that the US earns a significant average excess return on its net foreign asset position and that the excess return can be divided into a composition effect resulting from an asymmetric structure of the external balance sheet of the United States -assets are riskier and less liquid than liabilities — and a return effect — an excess return within class of assets. Habib (2010) shows that the excess return on net foreign assets of the United States was indeed exorbitant, amounting to more than 330 basis points per year between 1981 and 2007 which is accounted for by a positive yield differential from investment income and capital gains.

intervention, it is likely Asian authorities will look elsewhere to invest their accumulated reserves.

The US dollar maintained currency hegemony for 60 years mainly because no alternative asset was as attractive. But times have changed — and continue to change. The eurozone provides as large, as deep and as liquid a market as the United States. The eurozone economy is roughly the same size as the United States and accounts for a larger share of world trade. In the eurozone, for the most part, macroeconomic stability has improved as its members adhere to the stability and growth pact, a rule-based framework for coordinating national fiscal policies, and as the ECB pursues its anti-inflationary monetary policy.

The euro has grown to become an international currency from being a simple consolidation of fragmented national currencies. It has emerged as a useful second reserve currency held by many of the world's central banks (Figure 15.1). At the end of the 2010, the euro's share of global foreign exchange reserves was 26.0 per cent compared with 61.8 per cent for the US dollar (Table 15.2).

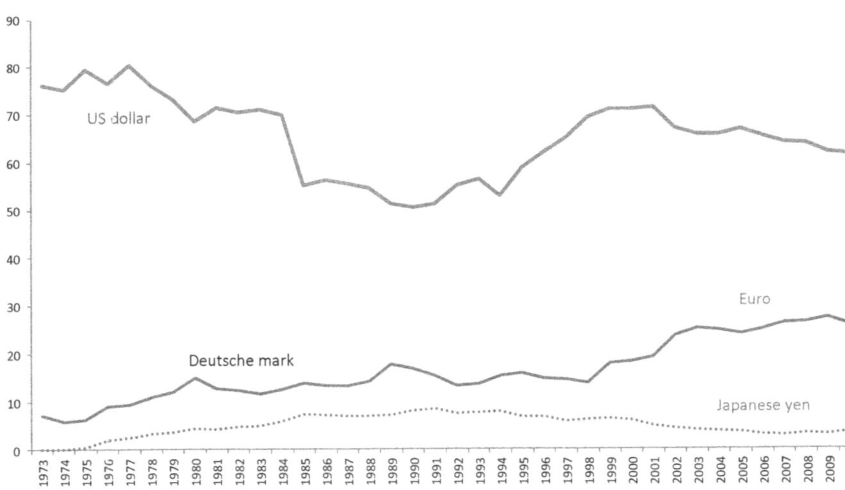

Figure 15.1 Reserves held by central banks as share of total — major currencies, 1973–2010

Source: *IMF Annual Report*, various years; International Monetary Fund, *Currency Composition of Foreign Exchange Reserves Database.*

Table 15.2. Currency composition of foreign exchange reserves (%)

	US Dollar	Japanese Yen	Pound Sterling	Swiss Franc	Euro	Deutsche Mark	French Franc	Netherlands Guilder	ECU	Other Currencies
1975	79.4	0.5	3.9	1.6	—	6.3	1.2	0.6	—	6.5
1980	68.6	4.4	2.9	3.2	—	14.9	1.7	1.3	—	3
1985	55.3	7.3	2.7	2.1	—	13.9	0.8	0.9	11.6	5.4
1990	50.6	8	3	1.2	—	16.8	2.4	1.1	9.7	7.1
1995	59	6.8	2.1	0.3	—	15.8	2.4	0.3	8.5	4.8
1999	71	6.4	2.9	0.2	17.9	—	—	—	—	1.6
2000	71.1	6.1	2.8	0.3	18.3	—	—	—	—	1.5
2001	71.5	5	2.7	0.3	19.2	—	—	—	—	1.3
2002	67.1	4.4	2.8	0.4	23.8	—	—	—	—	1.6
2003	65.9	3.9	2.8	0.2	25.2	—	—	—	—	2
2004	65.9	3.8	3.4	0.2	24.8	—	—	—	—	1.9
2005	66.9	3.6	3.6	0.1	24	—	—	—	—	1.7

(Continued)

Table 15.2. (*Continued*)

	US Dollar	Japanese Yen	Pound Sterling	Swiss Franc	Euro	Deutsche Mark	French Franc	Netherlands Guilder	ECU	Other Currencies
2006	65.5	3.1	4.4	0.2	25.1	—	—	—	—	1.8
2007	64.1	2.9	4.7	0.2	26.3	—	—	—	—	1.8
2008	64.1	3.1	4	0.1	26.4	—	—	—	—	2.2
2009	62.1	3	4.3	0.1	27.4	—	—	—	—	3.1
2010	61.8	3.7	3.9	0.1	26	—	—	—	—	4.4

Notes:
(a) Data cover only countries that report their currency composition to the International Monetary Fund (IMF).
(b) There was a large change in 1979–80 from the 1978 figure because of the substitution of European Currency Units (ECUs) for US dollars in the reserves of members of the European Monetary System.
Sources: IMF, *Annual Report* (various years); Currency Composition of Official Foreign Exchange Reserves (COFER), available:http://www.imf.org/external/np/sta/cofer/eng/index.htm, downloaded 3 July 2012; author's calculation.

As these figures indicate, there is no evidence that the euro is replacing the dollar as the dominant international currency. The share of the euro in foreign exchange market turnover has remained stable, but far below that of the US dollar (Table 15.3). And while the euro's role in trade invoicing and foreign exchange transactions has been increasing, it is mostly with neighbouring countries. The US dollar continues its pre-eminence in Asian currency trades — it was used on one side of about 93 per cent of transactions in Asian foreign exchange markets in 2010.

As many scholars point out, there can be more than one international currency competing at any given point in time (Eichengreen, 2007; Cohen, 2008). The coexistence of the US dollar and pound sterling as reserve currencies during the interwar period supports the idea that there is room for more than one major reserve currency. While the theory of network externalities emphasises a dominant single international currency, it may hold

Table 15.3. Currency composition of global foreign exchange market turnover (percentage shares of average daily turnover)

	1995	1998	2001	2004	2007	2010
US dollar	84.1	88.5	91.9	90.4	88.2	86.1
Euro	—		37.5	36.5	36.1	38.7
Yen	23.1	19.6	22.3	19.7	16.3	17.6
Pound sterling	9.4	11.0	13.4	17.0	14.9	13.3
Swiss franc	7.2	6.8	6.0	6.0	6.7	6.5
Canadian dollar	3.4	3.6	4.4	4.1	4.2	5.4
Deutsche mark	36.3	31.0	—	—	—	—
French franc	8.0	5.1	—	—	—	—
Chinese renminbi	—	—	0.0	0.1	0.6	0.8
Other currencies	28.6	34.3	24.6	26.1	33	31.5
All currencies	200.0	200.0	200.0	200.0	200	200

Notes:

(a) Reporting dealers and other financial institutions are used to proxy private transactions in the foreign exchange market. Nonfinancial customers in the Bank for International Settlements data are excluded as they cover government firms, in addition to corporate firms.

(b) Because two currencies are involved in each transaction, the sum of the percentage shares of individual currencies totals 200% instead of 100%.

Source: Bank for International Settlements, Triennial Survey (various years).

in trade invoicing or in denominating foreign debt securities. It becomes less valid, however, when it comes to denominating reserves. Several liquid financial markets can exist side by side as risk diversification motivates central banks to accumulate reserves in an array of assets denominated in several currencies. With the euro now providing a deep and liquid financial market, it offers significant benefits for central banks seeking greater diversification.

In the short term, the US dollar and the euro will likely remain the main reserve currencies, and any relative shift between their respective shares will be gradual (Galati and Wooldridge, 2006; Chinn and Frankel, 2007). The biggest threat to the reserve currency status of the euro in the long term is the perceived lack of economic dynamism in the eurozone (Posen, 2008). There is a widespread perception that the eurozone's future economic prospects lag behind those of the United States and Asia. The ongoing debt crisis in the eurozone adds credence to this perception. Also, with its separate national governments, the EU cannot offer a universal euro-denominated financial instrument that can match US Treasury bills. In addition, the future of the euro as the world's next primary reserve currency — replacing a troubled US dollar — has been compounded by the worsening financial crisis in the eurozone recently. The eurozone needs to strengthen coordination to enforce fiscal discipline and harmonise regulation and supervision of the financial system for a well-functioning monetary union.

15.2.2. *The Rising Renminbi — Towards a Tripolar System*

Is there room for a new major international currency to join the US dollar and euro, shifting the current bipolar structure to a tripolar international monetary system?

History tells us that there have often been more than two currencies vying to become dominant international reserve currency. At the end of 1913, pound sterling balances accounted for less than half of total official foreign exchange holdings, while the French franc made up about a third and the German mark about one-sixth (Eichengreen, 2007). In the 1920s and 1930s, it was again three currencies, although the US dollar had replaced the German mark as a reserve currency. During the 1970s and 1980s — after the post-war recovery had transformed Japan into the second largest world economy — the use of the yen internationally accelerated significantly (see Table 15.2). This led to a brief tripolar period involving the US dollar, the mark and the yen. However, the yen's appeal as international currency eroded quickly as Japan's economic bubble burst at the end of the 1980s. At the end of the 2010, the yen's share of global foreign exchange reserves was merely 3.7 per cent, far below 61.8 per cent for the US dollar and 21.0 per cent for the euro.

An obvious candidate to become a new international currency is the renminbi. With China's growing weight relative to the world economy, it is often argued that the renminbi will become the key currency in Asia and holds promise to become a new international reserve currency over the long run. In the light of China's large and growing influence in the global economy, some say it is only natural to ask when the renminbi will become a reserve currency (see, for example, Li and Liu, 2010).

If it continues to maintain rapid economic growth, China will likely overtake the United States as the world's largest economy within a few decades. Its economy is highly dependent on trade, with both exports and imports expected to continue to grow rapidly. The fact that China exports a diverse mix of manufactured goods to virtually all countries reinforces the renminbi's potential role as an international medium of exchange. And Chinese investments overseas are accelerating, further increasing its influence on the world economy. In addition, China has achieved macroeconomic stability in recent years. Inflation has been low and stable, averaging 2.0 per cent during 2000–10. Its fiscal balance has been healthy, with a deficit averaging 1.7 per cent of GDP over the same period. The government places high priority on macroeconomic stability, and this bodes well for the renminbi as a store of value.

However, internationalising the renminbi has its obvious limitations given China's relatively undeveloped financial system and limited convertibility of its capital account (Prasad and Ye, 2012).[8] Over the past decade, there has been important progress in reforming and restructuring the financial system, such as interest rate liberalisation, reforms of governance

[8] Eichengreen (2012) points out that China's current political system can be an obstacle to renminbi internationalisation considering financial development requires rule of law and political stability.

structure in state owned commercial banks and improvement in financial infrastructure and regulatory system.[9] Despite the efforts introduced so far, Chinese financial system's efficiency and transparency lag far behind major international financial centres. The financial system is subject to extensive government guidance and control and dominated by banks. Despite rapid growth in recent years, Chinese capital markets remain relatively underdeveloped. For the renminbi, the main lesson from the yen's failure to become a reserve currency is that open and efficient financial markets are an indispensable precondition for reserve currency status. Like today's China, Japan in the 1970s and 1980s enjoyed rapid growth in output and trade, rising overseas investments, macroeconomic stability and a concomitant growing influence on the world economy. What was missing among the preconditions for internationalisation was the existence of open and efficient financial markets — as Japanese markets lagged the United States and many European markets. The same is true for today's China, only to a much greater extent. It is a critical question whether China can continue to make successful progress of financial liberalisation and opening, so that it can promote successfully not only the renminbi (RMB) internationalisation but, more importantly, stable and sustainable economic growth over the next decades (The World Bank and DRCSC, 2012).

There is a fairly firm consensus that strict capital controls preventing the free flow of funds between China and the rest of the world constrain the use of the renminbi as an international currency. Over the past decade, China has reformed the financial sector and lifted or eased some capital controls. The Qualified Foreign Institutional Investors in 2002 and Qualified Domestic Institutional Investors programmes in 2006 were designed to gradually allow crossborder capital movements. China appears increasingly ready to remove remaining controls. However, it could take years after first introducing greater exchange rate flexibility before the renminbi can become a freely convertible currency for capital account transactions.

[9] See The World Bank and Development Research Center of the State Council (DRCSC) (2012, Part II, chapter 3) for the progress and challenges of China's financial system development.

Chinese authorities have — and are likely to continue — to proceed cautiously, striving to minimise potential risks from rapid currency internationalisation. Holding reserve currency status carries several benefits — including convenience and seignorage (Hai and Yao, 2010). International reserve currency status can also give political prestige, although causality here runs in both directions. Britain's rise and fall of international currency status have occurred with its rise and fall of political and military pre-eminence. In addition, currency internationalisation facilitates domestic currency denominated borrowing from abroad, which helps dampen the impact of financial shock when a sudden stop in foreign lending occurs. The need to accumulate 'excessive' international reserves will also decline. But holding reserve currency also entails costs. Once capital account is completely open and international demand for the renminbi fluctuates, the Chinese monetary authority cannot target a specific level of money stock or interest rate, especially when exchange rate is not allowed to move flexibly. Upward pressure on the renminbi's exchange rate due to stronger demand can be a powerful deterrent against the currency internationalisation. Capital account liberalisation and currency convertibility are expected to lead to strong capital inflows, and, with increased foreign demand for the renminbi as international reserves, the Chinese currency will be appreciated. In the 1970s, the Japanese authority was discouraged from pushing yen internationalisation because it was worried about the possibility that yen internationalisation would lead to currency appreciation and loss of the export competitiveness in the international markets. For China, it is not at all clear whether benefits outweigh costs — and this uncertainty can deter attempts to internationalise the renminbi. However, somewhat surprisingly, China appears more enthusiastic about internationalising the renminbi than Japan did with the yen prior to the 1990s (Cohen, 2008; Frankel, 2011).

Renminbi use in the settlement of cross-border trade is now increasing.[10] In June 2010, the Chinese authorities expanded the RMB cross-border trade settlement scheme to 20 Mainland Chinese provinces and

[10] The first half of 2011, the accumulated business amount of RMB settlement on cross-border trade was 958 billion yuan, 13.3 times more than the previous year. In 2011, RMB trade settlements amounted to about 9 per cent of China's total trade in goods and services.

cities and allowed Mainland Designated Enterprise exporters in these provinces to settle trade transactions in RMB with any part of the world, while Chinese importers had no restrictions in using RMB to pay overseas vendor. Subsequently, the authorities took steps to remove obstacles in the RMB cross-border settlement of capital account items. The steady stream of liberalisation measures has driven rapid growth in the offshore renminbi market, most evident in the expansion of RMB deposits in Hong Kong, China.[11]

Hong Kong, being an international financial centre, could become a conduit for promoting the internationalisation of the renminbi in trading and financial transactions. As argued by He and McCauley (2010), the development of offshore markets can help increase the recognition and acceptance of the currency. China is fortunate to have the special administrative region of Hong Kong, giving it the opportunity to develop a renminbi market without disturbing the mainland's domestic financial system. Shanghai will also develop into an international financial centre in the near future.

As the 2008/09 global financial crisis played out, China actively pursued cooperative agreements with its neighbours, particularly in providing mutual liquidity assistance. Between December 2008 and July 2010, the PBOC signed eight bilateral currency swap arrangements with the central banks of Korea, Hong Kong, Malaysia, Belarus, Indonesia, Argentina, Iceland and Singapore totalling RMB 800 billion.

In short, the renminbi faces a daunting array of difficult challenges it must overcome before it can become a serious candidate for international reserve currency status. Not surprisingly, the internationalisation of the renminbi to date has been insignificant, although China is taking steps to raise the renminbi profile, at least regionally. Once China actively engages in regional financial and economic cooperation and ensures exchange rate and monetary stability, the renminbi can evolve into a dominant currency for regional trade and financial transactions, for example.[12] It will take

---

[11] Renminbi deposit taking was introduced in Hong Kong on 25 February 2004. From just RMB 895 million in February 2004, renminbi deposits increased to RMB 600 billion in October 2011, which made up more than 8 per cent of total deposits in Hong Kong.

[12] By the end of 2007, seven of the 14 countries sharing borders with China (Russian Federation, Mongolia, the Democratic People's Republic of Korea, Kazakhstan, Vietnam,

time before the government removes restrictions on currency conversion by non-residents through the capital account. Building an open and strong renminbi bond market and integrating that with the domestic monetary system will be a big challenge. In China, appropriate monitoring and managing of massive borrowings of local governments is also important for the stability of the monetary system and the internationalisation of the renminbi. It is most likely that the evolution of the renminbi towards reserve currency status will be a gradual, drawn-out process that takes place over several decades — rather than a sudden, quick shift over a few years. The slow, deliberate and gradual emergence of the renminbi as a new reserve currency is consistent with historical patterns.

15.3. Empirical Investigation of Reserve Currency Shares

This section explains the factors that determine the use of international reserve currencies and applies the estimated relationships to forecast the shares of renminbi in the coming decades. This quantitative assessment is for illustrative purposes and relies unavoidably on a number of simplifying assumptions (see, for example, Truman, 2007).

For the dependent variable, we have constructed currency shares of global reserve holdings using IMF annual data on official foreign exchange reserves.[13] According to the literature, there are four major factors that determine the suitability of a currency for international currency status (Chinn and Frankel, 2008).

15.3.1. *Size of Output and Trade*

The relative size of a country's output and trade gives it a distinct advantage in having its currency used internationally. The United States is the largest economy in the world in terms of output. But the combined

---

Myanmar, and Nepal) had established renminbi settlement accounts with banks in Chinese border trade areas. Currently, about 95 per cent of cross-border trade settlements with Vietnam, Laos, Cambodia and Myanmar are in renminbi.

[13] IMF data on currency composition of foreign exchange reserves are based on information collected from member central banks. The currency composition has changed gradually over time both due to valuation changes and quantity changes.

economic size of the 16 countries in the eurozone has increased to match the United States in output and surpass it in trade volume. China's share in world GDP has also increased rapidly over the past decades, from 3.0 per cent in 1973 to 9.4 per cent in 2010 at market exchange rates. It is now the world's second largest economy in terms of GDP, the world's largest merchandise exporter (10.5 per cent of the world total) and second in merchandise imports (9.2 per cent share).

15.3.2. *Financial Markets*

A country's financial market must be open, unrestricted, deep and developed for its currency to attain international currency status. We use the foreign exchange turnover data from Chinn and Frankel (2008) to measure the size, depth and development of financial centres. Since 1998, foreign exchange turnover in China has been rising. From a daily average of US$211 million, foreign exchange turnover increased to US$19.8 billion in 2010. However, the daily turnover in China still dwarfs those in the more developed and open financial centres of the United Kingdom (US$1.9 trillion) and the United States (US$904 billion). In addition, we use the index of capital account liberalisation generated by Chinn and Ito (2008) to measure the degree of a country's openness to global financial markets. The index ranges from −1.81 to 2.54. While China has maintained a higher index since the early 1990s (−1.13) from only −1.81 in the late 1980s, it remains far below index values of the United States and the eurozone (2.54 and 1.73, respectively), implying China's greater use of restrictive policies.

15.3.3. *Confidence in the Value of the Currency*

A key requirement for an international currency is stability in value. An international currency is more attractive to hold if there is assurance that its future value will not be depleted. We use a country's inflation rate as a confidence measure of currency. In the past 10 years, the mean of China's inflation rate was below that for advanced economies. Its standard deviation, however, is much higher, as the change in consumer prices ranged from −2.0 to 8.7 during the period. In recent years, China has seen gradual rising inflation in both goods and real assets. Increasing price instability works against the renminbi evolving into an international reserve currency.

15.3.4. *Network Externalities*

There is a bias due to inertia in favour of currencies already used as international currencies. Thus, a currency that is more widely used internationally has higher value. This suggests that changes in the determinants of reserve currency status are unlikely to lead to parallel changes in reserve currency share holdings in the short run. In other words, the switch in dominance from one international currency to another will happen only gradually. We include the lagged reserve currency share as an additional variable to account for inertia in capturing network externalities.[14]

We constructed variables for these determinants for the empirical investigation.[15] For all variables, Germany and eurozone data are spliced to come up with a complete series from 1975 to 2010. Following Chinn and Frankel (2008), we estimate the following international reserve currency demand function[16]:

$$\begin{aligned} \textit{Logit (currency share)}_{it} = \beta_0 &+ \beta_1 \textit{ (GDP share)}_{it} \\ &+ \beta_2 \textit{ (Inflation difference)}_{it} + \beta_3 \textit{ (FX turnover)}_{it} \\ &+ \beta_4 \textit{ (KA openness)}_{it} + \beta_5 \textit{ (lag logit of currency} \\ &\quad \textit{share)}_{it} + \gamma_{it} \end{aligned} \tag{1}$$

[14] The network effects, though not directly measurable, come from various factors such as trade invoicing, the denomination of foreign debt securities and the choice of currency peg. See the discussion in Section 2 and Truman (2007).

[15] The dataset with the note on the definition and source of the variables are available upon request from the author.

[16] Since trade and output are highly correlated, we use only output shares in our estimation. When the regression includes the orthogonal component of trade share — the residual from a regression of trade share on output share — this additional trade variable is also statistically significant. This implies that rising China's trade size will also contribute to the international use of renminbi. We have also used exchange rate volatility, measured by standard deviation of the log first difference of the monthly SDR value of each currency. It is not statistically significant in the regression.

The data set has a feature of panel structure consisting of 216 annual observations for six country groups (United States, eurozone (Germany), Japan, China, UK and Switzerland) from 1975 to 2010. The specification uses the logit transformation of currency share, log (share/(1 - share)), to consider the nonlinear relationship between currency share and its determinants or a 'tipping point phenomenon'. The non-linear relation indicates that a regime switch can occur in the holding of reserve currency when the use of a new international vehicle currency exceeds a threshold value (Rey, 2001; Terada-Hagiwara, 2011). The threshold value can be a 'tipping point', after which demand for the reserve currency accelerates over time. Figure 15.2 displays the scatter plot between currency shares and GDP shares from the sample of 216 annual observations for six country groups.[17] The upper panel of Figure 15.2 shows that the slope of curve between currency share and GDP share switches in the middle, supporting the non-linear relationship or a 'tipping point phenomenon'. In the lower panel, the logit transformation of currency share is plotted against currency share.

Table 15.4 presents the regression results for the determination of currency shares. The model is estimated by adopting random-effects panel estimation procedure. Specification (1) excludes renminbi shares in the sample, while specification (2) includes them.

The results are similar for the samples without and with renminbi — column (1) versus column (2). The relative size of the home country and the lagged dependent variable are shown to have statistically significantly positive effects on currency shares, with and without the renminbi. Foreign exchange turnover or the relative depth of the home financial centre enters statistically significantly in column (1), but becomes less significant in column (2). Inflation enters negatively in both specifications but is not statistically significant. The estimated coefficient on GDP share is lower in column (2) with the renminbi (1.46) than in column (1) without the renminbi (1.77).

The coefficient of the index of capital account liberalisation is positive and significant only in specification (2). This explains that the renminbi's

[17] To keep China's zero observations, when making the logit transformations, we added 0.001 across all currencies.

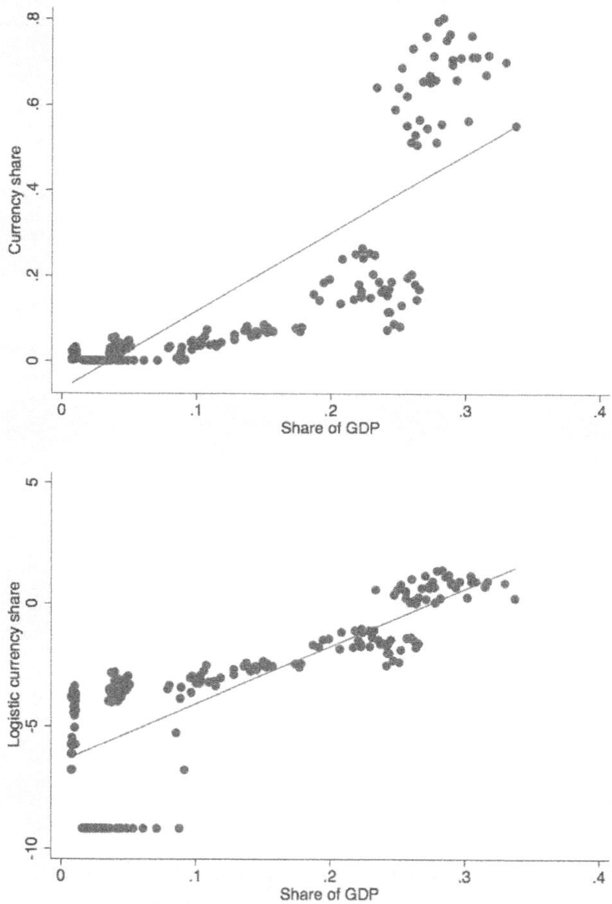

Figure 15.2 Scatter plots of GDP share and currency share, 1973–2010

Notes:

(a) Each panel shows a scatter plot between shares in world GDP and world currency reserve holdings by six country groups including United States, Eurozone (Germany), Japan, China, UK, and Switzerland from 1975 to 2010.

(b) In the lower panel, the logit transformation of currency share, Log [share/(1-share)], is used to consider the nonlinear relationship between currency share and GDP share.

Sources: World Bank, *World Development Indicators*; IMF *Annual Reports*, various years; International Monetary Fund, *Currency Composition of Foreign Exchange Reserves Database*.

Table 15.4. Panel regression results for the determination of currency shares

	w/o China	w/China
Explanatory Variable	(1)	(2)
GDP share	2.2708 (4.91)***	1.8109 (4.51)***
Inflation difference	−0.8977 (0.99)	−0.2947 (0.57)
Foreign exchange turnover	0.3341 (1.99)**	0.2921 (2.00)**
Index of capital account liberalisation	−0.0259 (0.73)	0.0485 (2.94)***
Lag of logit currency share	0.8716 (34.38)***	0.8975 (40.98)***
Constant	−0.6291 (3.71)***	−0.6656 (4.50)***
Observations	180	216
Number of currencies	5	6
R^2	0.99	0.99

Notes:
(a) Estimated using OLS random-effects model.
(b) *significant at 10%; **significant at 5%; ***significant at 1%.
(c) Absolute value of z-statistics in brackets.
(d) Dependent variable: Logit of proportion of currency reserve holdings, logit (share/(1 − share)).
(e) Sample: 1975–2010.
Source: Author's calculations.

lowest standing in the rank of an international currency is strongly related to its capital account restrictions.

We can use the estimation result to project the shares of the US dollar, euro and renminbi in the coming decades. First, the change in GDP shares will influence the long-run shares of the currencies. We make projections under two growth scenarios for China: (i) high growth path, in which the historical real GDP growth rate of 9.5 per cent for 1999–2008 (excluding the global crisis period) and real exchange rate appreciation rate of about 3.4 per cent[18] are maintained through 2035; and (ii) low growth path, applying a 6.0 per cent real GDP growth rate with the same real exchange rate appreciation rate.[19] Lee and Hong (2012) project that, based on the

[18] Real exchange rate appreciation for China is estimated as the difference between the growth in GDP deflator in US dollar terms between China and the US (5.88 – 2.49 = 3.39).
[19] If real appreciation is positively related to labour productivity growth, the slower GDP growth in China will lead to smaller appreciation. According to the estimates of Rogoff

model of conditional convergence, China's GDP growth will decrease to between 5.5 and 6.6 per cent over the next two decades, which is consistently lower than the historical average.

In both scenarios, we assume that the United States, eurozone and the rest of the world maintain nominal GDP growth at historical rates.[20] We construct the projected economic sizes for the United States, eurozone and China under the two scenarios. Assuming that China continues on the high growth path, it is forecast to reach 34.6 per cent of world GDP by 2035, surpassing the United States (13.0 per cent) and eurozone (11.8 per cent). Meanwhile, if China follows a low growth path, it will reach 19.3 per cent of world GDP, slightly higher than that of the United States (16 per cent of world GDP) and the eurozone (14.6 per cent).

In Figure 15.3, we present our currency share projections for the renminbi under the two scenarios. We use the coefficient estimates in column (2) along with our economic size projections to examine how renminbi shares will change as China's share in world GDP increases over time. In this simulation, we assume that China gradually improves its foreign exchange turnover and capital account openness from 2011 to 2020 to reach the averages of the United States.[21]

Under the moderate growth scenario, the renminbi share is expected to increase marginally to 2.7 per cent by 2035. It could reach up to 12.4 per cent if the Chinese economy grows at its faster historical rate. The estimation results show that once China gains full renminbi convertibility and operates a stable and prudent financial system, the renminbi would eventually become an international currency within the region and beyond — sharing from about 3 to 12 per cent of global central bank reserve holdings in 2035.[22] This would exceed that of the yen or pound

(1996), a 1 per cent increase in real per capita GDP is associated with about a 0.37 per cent real appreciation.

[20] Real GDP growth rates for the US, eurozone, and the rest of the world are assumed at 2.1, 1.7, and 4.0 per cent, respectively.

[21] The simulations, which are not reported here, show that without capital account convertibility and financial sector reform, the renminbi's share will be insignificant by 2035 despite the significant portion of China's output in world GDP.

[22] Emergence of the renminbi as a fully convertible reserve currency will enable China to reduce its (self-insurance) demand for international reserve and switch into a supplier of

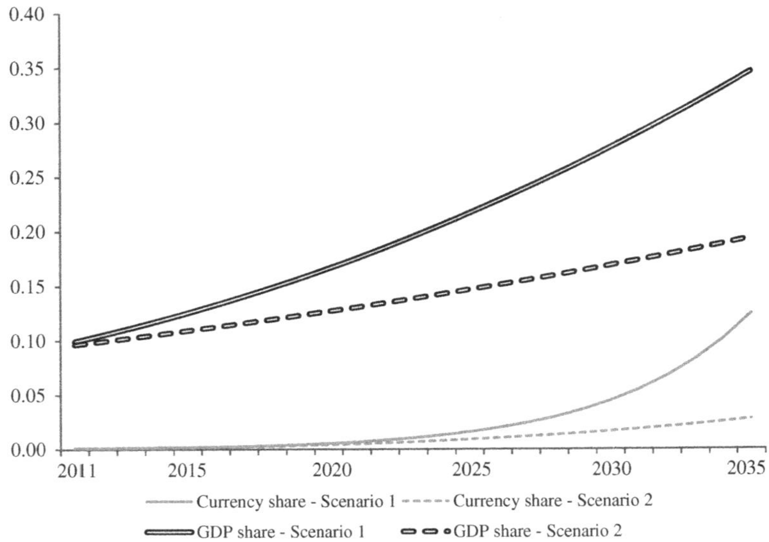

Figure 15.3 Projected gross domestic product (GDP) and currency shares of the People's Republic of China (PRC), 2011–35

Notes:

(a) Scenario 1 denotes a high growth path for the PRC; Scenario 2 denotes a low growth path for the PRC.

(b) The high growth path assumes that the historical real GDP growth rate of 9.5 per cent for 1999–2008 and real exchange rate appreciation rate of about 3.4% are maintained through 2035; and the low growth path assumes a 6.0 per cent real GDP growth rate.

(c) In both scenarios, we also assume that the PRC will achieve the same daily foreign exchange turnover and capital account openness as in the US from 2011 to 2020.

(d) The estimates of GDP shares are in current US dollar.

Source: Author's calculations.

sterling. But the simulation exercises also demonstrate that, despite the substantial increase in China's GDP share, the renminbi's reserve currency share does not increase in parallel. This reflects the strong influence of network externalities.[23] The strong, positive coefficient of the lagged

---

reserve assets. Accordingly, China's share in global reserves is expected to decline gradually from the current level — about 30 per cent of global reserves, while other central banks will increase holdings of the RMB as a reserve currency.

[23] The rise of the renminbi to international currency status would occur much faster along with GDP if the network externality effect were not considered. Li and Liu (2010) estimate

dependent variable (with its value close to one) implies that the renminbi's rise to international currency status would occur only gradually. With a small initial currency share, the increase of the renminbi's share in international reserve currency holdings in response to the GDP share increase is smaller.[24] On the other hand, the non-linear relationship implies that with the rise of China's share of GDP and the strong effect of the lagged currency share term, a 'tipping point' appears in which the renminbi's reserve currency share immediately jumps to a higher level, after which the increase accelerates over time. As other major currencies stagger, the moment the renminbi becomes an international currency may happen more quickly.

15.4. Monetary Cooperation and an Asian Common Currency

The failure of yen internationalisation during the 1970s and 1980s provides important lessons for the internationalisation of the renminbi. As mentioned earlier, the lack of open and efficient financial markets — compared with United States and European markets — hindered the yen from completing the internationalisation process. Because Japanese authorities were not eager to internationalise the yen, it failed to take root

---

that the renminbi will account for between 15 and 21 per cent of international reserves in 2020 by using an empirical specification similar to (1) without the lagged dependent variable.

[24] In the logit specification, the coefficient does not correspond to the marginal effect of the independent variable on currency share. The elasticity can be calculated by using estimates and the values of the variables. The elasticity of currency share to GDP share at the mean values $\xi = (\partial \textit{currency share} \, \partial \textit{ GDP share})(\textit{GDP share/currency share})$ are approximated as b′1 GDP share (1 – *currency share*). This implies that the elasticity with respect to GDP share increases with GDP share and decreases with currency share. For China, this ranges from around 0.18 to 0.34 under the low growth scenario; 0.18–0.55 under the high growth scenario, holding all else constant. These imply that a 1 per cent increase in China's shares in world GDP leads to a rise of around 18 to 34 per cent increase in the renminbi's share of global central bank reserve holdings under the low growth scenario and 18 to 55 per cent under the high growth scenario. The long-run elasticity of currency share with respect to any explanatory variable is much higher because of the strong persistence of currency share.

as a reserve currency. Another important reason was that the yen failed to establish itself as a regional currency first. For historical and geopolitical reasons, most Asian countries were reluctant to use the yen for trade or financial transactions. The emergence of a yen bloc in East Asia would have helped consolidate the region's fragmented currencies and would have boosted the yen's chances of reaching reserve status.

China may face similar problems. Despite its growing economic and financial influence, it is doubtful whether other Asian countries are prepared or willing to submit to regional hegemony. Whether they do or not could depend on how the Chinese political system and regional geopolitics evolve over time.

In East Asia, members of Association of South East Asian Nations (ASEAN)–3[25] used the 1997/98 Asian financial crisis as an opportunity to bolster regional financial and monetary cooperation. There has been substantial progress in information sharing, economic surveillance, strengthening regional bond markets and reserve pooling. In 2001, ASEAN+3 finance ministers agreed to establish a network of bilateral swap arrangements, known as the Chiang Mai Initiative (CMI), which can provide emergency liquidity lending for troubled members. The global crisis in 2008/09 gave ASEAN+3 new momentum to upgrade its bilateral system of swap agreements into a multilateral pooled fund of US$120 billion. In May 2009, the ASEAN+3 Finance Ministers agreed on the details of CMI multilateralisation (CMIM) including governance structure, voting rights and financial contributions. The CMIM has been in effect since March 2010. China's contribution (including contributions from Hong Kong) is 32 per cent of the US$120 billion or US$38.4 billion.

Nonetheless, monetary cooperation in Asia remains weak. Formal regional institutions are underdeveloped in the region, especially compared with Europe. The successful regional cooperation on the CMIM is a promising first step for future rules-based regional institutions. Enhanced economic cooperation may help for neighbouring countries in accepting the increasing role of the Chinese economy as well as its currency.

---

[25] ASEAN+3 consists of the 10 countries of the Association of South East Asian Nations (ASEAN) plus China, Japan, and Korea.

Perhaps an option in promoting regional monetary cooperation is building an Asian Monetary System (AMS), in which each currency is pegged to a common basket currency — for example, an Asian Currency Unit (ACU). The value of the ACU could be based on a basket of weighted amounts of ASEAN+3 currencies, with its bilateral exchange rate allowed to fluctuate within a limited band around a central exchange rate. The ACU could become a basis for trade or other financial transactions within the region. Asian governments could issue ACU-denominated bonds. Of course, this is fraught with political considerations on currency weightings and how they should evolve over time. There are plenty of sensitivities between China, Japan, Korea, the 10 ASEAN members and India as well. The AMS would face the sensitive N-1 problem: when N currencies are linked to each other, there are N-1 restrictions and one exchange rate must be determined exogenously. This is how the European Monetary System (EMS) evolved to become a Deutsche mark-led arrangement (Wyploz, 2010).

Moving towards an AMS is likely to require a lengthy period of preparation and negotiation for necessary institutional arrangements in the region. Exchange rate coordination typically requires coordination in other macroeconomic policies such as monetary and fiscal policies, which would be a formidable challenge to Asian countries with diverse economic conditions. Nevertheless, over time, East Asian economies undoubtedly will improve exchange rate and monetary policy coordination. Enhanced regional cooperation in regional liquidity provision, economic surveillance and capital market development might lead to the adoption of an ACU (Kawai, 2010). Eichengreen (2006) argues that that the circulation of ACU as a parallel currency alongside national currencies would be an advantage for East Asian economies. This parallel currency system would not conflict with the gradual emergence of the renminbi as a credible regional currency. Gao and Yu (2009) argue that, no matter whether China's final goal is to create a regional currency or make the renminbi a core international reserve currency, China must pursue the internationalisation of the renminbi, at least in its initial stage.

On the other hand, a currency union in East Asia is unlikely in the immediate future. Barro and Lee (2011) show that, judging from optimum currency area (OCA) criteria — including the symmetry of output and price shocks across countries, commitment to price stability, trade and financial integration, as well as the degree of political proximity — East Asia does not appear to have very favourable economic conditions for a currency union. This is particularly true when compared with the eurozone. They envision, nevertheless, that the prospect for an East Asian currency union will hinge on future developments of economic and political conditions, rather than current environments. However it develops, China — and the renminbi — will play a major role in any new Asian currency arrangement.

15.5. Concluding Remarks

The world economy is already tripolar — comprising the United States, EU and Asia. And Asia's relative economic and financial weight is set to rise even further in the light of its faster output growth. So, it is somewhat of an anomaly that only two currencies of this tripolar world — the US dollar and the euro — hold reserve currency status. Asia is left out. A more natural reserve currency arrangement in a tripolar world would be for each pole, including Asia, to have its own reserve currency. Given China's continuing strong growth and expanding economic influence globally, the renminbi has great potential to emerge as a new international reserve currency. Nevertheless, internationalising the renminbi has its obvious limitations given China's relatively undeveloped financial system and limited capital account convertibility. Despite important progress in financial reform and opening over the past decades, the Chinese financial system is still far from an open, sound and efficient one. It is a critical question whether China can continue to do financial liberalisation and opening with adequate pace and sequencing.

The global financial crisis and ongoing recovery have hampered the long-term prospects of both the US dollar and the euro as reserve currencies. The crisis has compromised both currencies as safe-haven stores of value. The renminbi is not a significant international currency yet. Our simulation shows that renminbi internationalisation will be a gradual and drawn-out process. Once the currency is more convertible, the renminbi can gradually grow to become an international currency within the region and beyond — sharing from about 3 to 12 per cent of international reserves by 2035. If markets actively seek a new currency for trade, investment and as a store of value, however, the renminbi may rise more quickly as an international currency than many currently anticipate.

Creating a more efficient, stable and equitable global reserve system is a vital priority for emerging economies, which rely heavily on international trade and capital flows. The internationalisation of the renminbi will offer an alternative to the US dollar and euro. The wellfunctioning multicurrency system with an expanded role for the renminbi can contribute to global financial stability by reducing the negative externalities inherent in self-insurance through large-scale reserve accumulation in nonreserve countries.

References

Barro, R. J. and J.-W. Lee (2011), 'East Asia Currency Union', in R. J. Barro and J.-W. Lee (eds.), Costs and Benefits of Economic Integration in Asia (New York: Oxford University Press and Asian Development Bank), 10–52.

Becker, T. I., O. Jeanne, P. Mauro, J. D. Ostry and R. Ranciere (2007), 'Country Insurance: The Role of Domestic Policies', Occasional Paper No. 254 (Washington, DC: International Monetary Fund).

Bergsten, C. F. (2009), 'The Dollar and the Deficits: How Washington Can Prevent the Next Crisis', Foreign Affairs, 88, 6, 20–38.

Chin, G. and W. Yong (2010), 'Debating the International Currency System: What's in a Speech?' China Security, 6, 1, 3–20.

Chinn, M. and J. A. Frankel (2007), 'Will the Euro Eventually Surpass the Dollar as Leading International Reserve Currency?', in R. H. Clarida (ed.), G7 Current Account Imbalances: Sustainability and Adjustment (Chicago, IL: University of Chicago Press), 283–335.

Chinn, M. and J. A. Frankel (2008), 'Why the Euro will Rival the Dollar', International Finance, 11, 1, 49–73.

Chinn, M. and H. Ito (2008), 'A New Measure of Financial Openness', Journal of Comparative Policy Analysis, 10, 3, 309–22.

Cohen, B. J. (2008), 'Toward a Leaderless Currency System', Paper 49 (Santa Barbara, CA: Orfalea Center for Global and International Studies).

Eichengreen, B. (2006), 'The Parallel Currency Approach to Asian Monetary Integration', American Economic Review, Papers and Proceedings, 96, 2, 432–36.

Eichengreen, B. (2007), Global Imbalances and the Lessons of Bretton Woods (Cambridge, MA: MIT Press).

Eichengreen, B. (2011), Exorbitant Privilege: The Rise and Fall of the Dollar and the Future of the International Monetary System (New York: Oxford University Press).

Eichengreen, B. (2012), 'Number One Country, Number One Currency?', Paper presented at the CEPII-GEP-IFO Conference, 6–7 September. European Central Bank (various years), The International Role of the Euro (Frankfurt am Main: European Central Bank).

Frankel, J. (2011), 'Historical Precedents for the Internationalization of the RMB', Paper presented at a workshop in Beijing organized by the Council on Foreign Relations and the China Development Research Foundation.

Galati, G. and P. Wooldridge (2006), 'The Euro as a Reserve Currency: a Challenge to the Pre-Eminence of the US dollar?', Working Papers 218 (Basel: Bank for International Settlements).

Gao, H. and Y. Yu (2009), 'Internationalization of the RMB', Research Paper (Basel: Bank for International Settlements).

Goldberg, L. and C. Tille (2008), 'Vehicle Currency Use in International Trade', Journal of International Economics, 76, 2, 177–92.

Gourinchas, P.-O. and H. Rey (2007), 'From World Banker to World Venture Capitalist: US External Adjustment and The Exorbitant Privilege', in R. Clarida (ed.), G-7 Current Account Imbalances: Sustainability and Adjustment (Chicago, IL: University of Chicago Press), 11–55.

Habib, M. M. (2010), 'Excess Returns on Net Foreign Assets: the Exorbitant Privilege from a Global Perspective', Working Papers 1158 (Frankfurt am Main: European Central Bank).

Hai, W. and H. Yao (2010), 'Pros and Cons of International Use of the RMB for China', in W. Peng and C. Shu (eds.), Currency Internationalisation: Global Experiences and Implications for the Renminbi (London: Palgrave/Macmillan), 139–66.

He, D. and R. N. McCauley (2010), 'Offshore Markets for the Domestic Currency: Monetary and Financial Stability Issues', Working Paper 02/2010 (Hong Kong: Hong Kong Monetary Authority).

International Monetary Fund (2000), Annual Report 2000 (Washington, DC: International Monetary Fund).

International Monetary Fund (2011), Annual Report 2011 (Washington, DC: International Monetary Fund).

Kawai, M. (2010), 'Quest for a Regional Monetary Framework in East Asia', Paper presented at the Conference on Diversification of Reserve Currencies and

Development of Regional Financial Markets in Asia, Asian Development Bank Institute.

Krugman, P. (1980), 'Vehicle Currencies and the Structure of International Exchange', Journal of Money, Credit and Banking, 12, 3, 513–26.

Lee, J.-W. and K. Hong (2012), Economic Growth in Asia: Determinants and Prospects', Japan and the World Economy, 24, 2, 101–13.

Li, D. D. and L. Liu (2010), 'RMB Internationalization: Empirical and Policy Analysis', in W. Peng and C. Shu (eds.), Currency Internationalisation: Global Experiences and Implications for the Renminbi (London: Palgrave/ Macmillan), 167–85.

Mateos y Lago, I., R. Duttagupta and R. Goyal (2009), 'The Debate on the International Monetary System', Staff Position Note SPN/09/26 (Washington, DC: International Monetary Fund).

Mileva, E. and N. Siegfried (2007), 'Oil Market Structure, Network Effects and the Choice of Currency for Oil Invoicing', ECB Occasional Paper 77 (Frankfurt am Main: European Central Bank).

Obstfeld, M. (2011), 'The International Monetary System: Living with Asymmetry', Working Paper 17641 (Cambridge, MA: National Bureau of Economic Research, Inc).

Posen, A. S. (2008), 'Why the Euro will Not Rival the Dollar', International Finance, 11, 1, 75–100.

Prasad, E. and L. Ye (2012), The Renminbi's Role in the Global Monetary System (Washington DC: The Brookings Institutions).

Rey, H. (2001), 'International Trade and Currency Exchange', Review of Economic Studies, 68, 2, 443–64.

Rodrik, D. (2006), 'The Social Cost of Foreign Exchange Reserves', International Economic Journal, 20, 3, 253–66.

Rogoff, K. (1996), 'The Purchasing Power Parity Puzzle', Journal of Economic Literature, 34, 2, 647–68.

Schenk, C. R. (2010), The Decline of Sterling: Managing the Retreat of an International Currency 1945–1992 (Cambridge: Cambridge University Press).

Terada-Hagiwara, A. (2011), 'Asian Holdings of US Treasury Securities: Trade Integration as a Threshold', Journal of the Japanese and International Economics, 25, 3, 321–35.

The World Bank and Development Research Center of the State Council, the People's Republic of China (2012), China 2030: Building a Modern, Harmonious, and Creative High-Income Society (Washington, DC: The World Bank).

Triffin, R. (1960), Gold and the Dollar Crisis: The Future of Convertibility (New Haven, CT: Yale University Press).

Truman, E. M. (2007), 'Comment on Will the Euro Eventually Surpass the Dollar?', in R. H. Clarida (ed.), G7 Current Account Imbalances: Sustainability and Adjustment (Chicago, IL: University of Chicago Press), 322–35.

United Nations (2009), Recommendations by the Commission of Experts of the President of the General Assembly on Reforms of the International Monetary and Financial System (Stiglitz Commission). (New York: United Nations).

Wyploz, C. (2010), 'An Asian Monetary Unit?', Paper presented at the conference on 'The Future Global Reserve System — An Asian Perspective', ADB Institute, March 16–18.

Zhou, X. (2009), 'Reform the International Monetary System', speech, March 23, available at: http:// www.bis.org/review/r090402c.pdf (accessed 6 June 2013).

Chapter 16

Economic Growth in Asia: Determinants and Prospects*

16.1. Introduction

Developing Asia weathered the global economic crisis of 2008/ 09 well. It was the first region to emerge from the turmoil, helped by decisive and large-scale fiscal and monetary policy measures. Domestic demand has been resilient, especially in the region's larger economies, and the economic cycle clearly suggests that economies have bottomed and begun to recover. A number of Asian economies even posted double-digit gross domestic product (GDP) growth in the first half of 2010.

Now, as the recovery takes firm hold, the region faces a more crucial challenge for its sustained growth in the long run. The question is whether the economies in the region can return to the rapid growth of the past few decades.

Developing Asian economies[1] have grown impressively over a period of nearly 30 years. The region's real GDP in purchasing power parity (PPP)

---

* Reprinted from *Japan and the World Economy*, Vol. 24, No. 2, Jong-Wha Lee and Kiseok Hong, Economic Growth in Asia: Determinants and Prospects, pp. 101–113, Copyright (2012), with permission from Elsevier.

This paper was prepared for the Asian Development Bank's TA7470-REG: "Long-term Projections of Asian GDP and Trade." We thank the participants in the workshops in Seoul and Hong Kong, China for helpful comments and Lea Sumulong for excellent research assistance. The views expressed in this paper are those of the authors and do not necessarily reflect the views or policies of the Asian Development Bank or its Board of Governors or the governments they represent.

[1] Developing Asia here includes the People's Republic of China; Hong Kong, China; India; Indonesia; the Republic of Korea; Malaysia; Pakistan; the Philippines; Singapore; Taipei,

terms climbed from about $3.3 trillion in 1980 to an estimated $24.5 trillion in 2009. That is an increase of 7.5 times, compared with just three times for the world economy during the same period. Real per capita GDP expanded in excess of four times during the period, while average global income registered less than a two-fold increase. Such robust, prolonged growth has clearly raised incomes, lifted millions out of poverty, and expanded developing Asia's global economic influence.

Per capita GDP in developing Asia remains below the global average, but is rapidly catching up. In 1980, the income of the average Asian was just over a quarter of the world average; by 2009, it had risen to nearly two thirds.

Several factors were responsible. While Asia's economic growth had been considered a "miracle" in the 1990s (World Bank, 1993; Lucas, 1993), a number of empirical studies were able to explain the determinants. They highlight the role of investment, human resources, fertility, and institutional and policy variables. For example, Sachs *et al.* (2001) find that East Asia's rapid growth was due to its (i) large potential for catching up; (ii) favorable geography and structural characteristics; (iii) demographic dividend; and (iv) economic policies and strategy that were conducive to growth. The empirical studies show that the role of economic policies, particularly those relating to openness, played a highly significant role in the region's sustained growth.

The standard growth model, such as the extended version of the neoclassical growth model as described by Barro and Sala-i-Martin (2003), predicts the conditional convergence of income, in which a country with a low level of initial income relative to its long-run or steady-state level of potential income will tend to grow faster than a country that is already nearing its potential. Controlling for the factors that influence the long-run or steady-state income level, this implies that a poorer country is expected to grow faster than a higher income country. This is because in poorer countries, levels of physical and human capital and technological progress are farther from their long-run levels, and thus can accumulate capital and learn existing technology more quickly than more advanced

China; Thailand; and Viet Nam. These economies account for about 95% of emerging Asia's GDP, and are thus representative of regional trends.

economies. In other words, the greater potential for catching up among poorer countries allows them to grow more quickly.

Across developing Asia, growth rates in per capita income have varied in the past three decades. The People's Republic of China (PRC), with the lowest initial level of income per capita in 1980, grew fastest at 8.2% between 1981 and 2007, allowing it to develop from an economically desolate country into a global powerhouse. In Hong Kong, China; the Republic of Korea; Singapore; and Taipei, China, with relatively higher levels of initial income per capita, average growth rates declined during the three decades. This generally supports the conditional convergence hypothesis in which poorer countries tend to grow faster and richer countries slower.

However, the more important question now is whether this rapid economic growth can continue in the next two decades. Does convergence imply that as income levels in Asian economies increase they can no longer achieve high rates of growth? We believe this is not necessarily the case. The conditional convergence theory predicts that, through appropriate policies and institutional changes, an economy can shift its growth path higher and expand the long-run or steady-state level of potential income, thereby continuing to enable the long-run target level of potential income to remain in excess of the current income. Other growth theories, such as the various models of endogenous growth, also predict that policies can have permanent impact on an economy's rate of growth.

Measures are thus needed to ensure developing Asia's sustained growth in the coming decades. In considering the variations in the initial levels of income per capita across developing Asia, the challenge for the region ranges from closing the gap with the steady-state or long-run levels of potential income for low-income economies, to expanding the steady-state or long-run potential income levels for high-income economies. Lower-income economies have more opportunity for factor accumulation, and can thus focus on policies that encourage increases in human and physical capital, such as improvements in the quality and quantity of education and in the investment climate. Indeed, physical capital accumulation accounted for most of GDP growth in the less mature Asian economies until 2007. More mature economies with larger capital stocks, meanwhile, will be subject to diminishing returns to capital and must progressively rely on productivity increases to drive growth. Improvements in total factor productivity were actually significant contributors to GDP growth in Hong Kong, China; the Republic of Korea; Singapore; and Taipei, China from 1981 to 2007.

But why is it important for Asia to sustain its growth beyond the crisis? Despite its remarkable growth in recent decades, developing Asia still remains as a relatively poor region and is home to two thirds of the world's poor. Long run growth is essential to reduce poverty in the region on a sustainable basis. Also, just as the last 30 years of growth in developing Asian economies brought large changes to the global and regional economies, Asia's performance in the coming decades is also expected to substantially influence the global and regional landscape. Knowing how the region will evolve in the next few decades is crucial to how Asian policymakers prepare for their future role in the global community.

Today more than ever, Asia's influence in the global economy has deepened dramatically as the region helps pull the global economy out of recession. Nonetheless, while it is generally expected that Asia's economic expansion will carry on, it is unlikely that the economies that achieved very strong growth in recent years, such as the PRC, Viet Nam, and India will maintain such rapid growth rates in, say, the next 20 years. It would thus be interesting to know how Asia's economic environment will be transformed in the two decades ahead.

In particular, we would like to find answers to the following questions: How will Asia's growth likely pan out? Will a different group of economies take the helm in driving regional growth prospects? If so, what would be the impact on the global and regional economies? What will be the contribution of labor, human capital, physical capital, and technology diffusion to Asia's future growth? How will Asia fare relative to the industrialized economies of the United States (US), Japan, and the European Union? What would be the impact of Asia's continued growth in the global balance of power in the coming decades?

While our study is clearly not the first attempt to address these questions, we can be differentiated for having a focus specifically on developing Asia. Also, we explicitly incorporate growth regression analysis into the conventional growth accounting approach to produce long-run GDP forecasts. In most GDP projections based only on growth accounting, each component of GDP growth is forecast independently of the others with no attention paid to possible inconsistencies between them. By estimating a simultaneous equation system of GDP growth components and incorporating it into growth accounting, we can increase internal consistency among the forecasts. These differences of our paper will hopefully lead to more plausible and valid description about the future of developing Asia.

Section 16.2 briefly describes developing Asia's performance from 1981 to 2007. Section 16.3 lays out the sources of growth for the 12 Asian economies using a growth accounting framework. Section 16.4 analyzes the determinants of developing Asia's growth using a system of equations. Section 16.5 presents the estimation results and projects GDP growth through 2030 for the developing Asian economies. Section 16.6 concludes.

16.2. Sources of Growth, 1981–2007

The aggregate production function is used, and the level of output per labor is produced by combining productive inputs and total factor productivity (TFP). We assume a Cobb–Douglas production function as,[2]

$$Y = AK^{\alpha}(hL)^{1-\alpha} \tag{1}$$

where K denotes the stock of physical capital, h represents the amount of human capital per labor, L represents the number of laborers, and A denotes a measure of TFP. The production function can be rewritten in terms of output per labor, $y = \frac{Y}{L}$, i.e.,

$$y = Ak^{\alpha}h^{1-\alpha}, \tag{1'}$$

where k is physical capital per labor.

Following the pioneering work of Solow (1957), the growth accounting method has long been used to break down the growth rate of aggregate output into contributions from the growth of inputs as well as the growth of productivity.

This method is applied to the Cobb–Douglas production function in Eq. (1):

$$\Delta \ln Y = \Delta \ln A + \alpha \cdot \Delta \ln K + (1 - \alpha) \cdot \Delta \ln h + (1 - \alpha) \cdot \Delta \ln L \tag{2}$$

---

[2]Note that by assuming neutral technological progress, rather than labor-augmenting progress, our framework considers the role of productivity more important.

This equation can be rewritten in per labor terms as:

$$\Delta \ln y = \Delta \ln A + \alpha \cdot \Delta \ln k + (1 - \alpha) \cdot \Delta \ln h \tag{2'}$$

Following the above formula, the growth of output per labor is decomposed into growth rates of physical and human capital per labor and the total factor productivity. This equation allows us to decompose the differences in GDP per labor across countries into the differences in the capital–labor ratio, the differences in human capital, as well as the differences in TFP.

To conduct the decomposition of output, the output per labor is measured by the level of GDP per labor force. GDP data is taken from the Penn-World Tables (PWT) 6.3 of Heston *et al.* (2009). The labor force is from the ILO Laborsta database. We do not have reliable data on the number of work hours for most countries.

Physical capital stock data is constructed using the perpetual inventory method, which is based on aggregate investment data in the PWT 6.3.[3] Specifically, the capital stock in time t is computed as follows: $K_{i,t} = K_{i,t-1}(1 - \delta) + I_{i,t}$. The data comes from Barro and Lee (2010).

Regarding the capital share parameter, it is assumed that α is 0.4 and constant across countries.

Human capital per labor is assumed to have a relation to the number of years of schooling as follows[4]:

$$h = e^{\phi(s)} \tag{3}$$

[3] In computing initial capital stock, most researchers follow Harberger's approach (1978), which assumes that the economy is initially in a steady state. Recall that in the steady state, the growth rates of capital and output are the same ($dK/K = dY/Y$). Since $(K_t - K_{t-1})/K_{t-1} = (I_t/K_{t-1}) - \delta$), then $(I_t/K_{t-1}) - \delta = g$, where K is capital stock, I is capital flow or investment, δ is the depreciation rate, and g is the growth rate of output. Rearranging terms yields, $K_{t-1} = I_t/(g + \delta)$. To control for short-term fluctuations in output, Harberger suggested the use of average growth rate of output centered around, say, a three-year period. Nehru and Dhareshwar (1993), King and Levine (1994), Bernanke and Gurkaynak (2001), and Barro and Lee (2010) employed a modified version of this approach in computing for an initial capital stock estimate. The annual depreciation rate of physical capital is assumed to be constant at 0.06. We exclude the first 5 years of available capital stock observations generated by the perpetual inventory method.

[4] See Barro and Lee (2010).

In this equation, $\phi(s)$ measures the efficiency of a unit of labor, with s years of education being relative to one without any schooling. We further assume that $\phi(s)$ is linear,

$$h = e^{\theta s} \tag{3'}$$

In this equation, θ measures the average marginal return to an additional year of schooling. Barro and Lee (2010) find that, after controlling for the simultaneous determination of human capital and output, by using the 10-year lag of parents' education as an instrumental variable (IV) for the current level of education, the estimated rate-of-return to an additional year of schooling is close to the typical Mincerian return estimates found in the labor literature. We assume $\theta = 8\%$.[5]

Following convention, TFP growth is measured as Solow residual:

$$\Delta \ln A = \Delta \ln y + \alpha \cdot \Delta \ln k + (1 - \alpha) \cdot \Delta \ln h. \tag{4}$$

This is a standard methodology in growth accounting, although not free from shortcomings.[6] Alternative approaches to measuring TFP, such as the time trend method (e.g., Kim and Lau, 1996) and the frontier analysis (e.g., Fare *et al.*, 1994) have their own drawbacks. See Wei and Hao (2011) for more discussions on the measurement of TFP.

Table 16.1 reports the growth rates of output, factor inputs, and TFP for each of the three decades under review, i.e., 1981–90, 1991–2000, and 2001–07 and also for 1981–2007. Three countries stand out as having their GDP per labor rates steadily rising over the three decades — the PRC, Viet Nam, and the Philippines. GDP per labor in the PRC has increased, from

[5] Bernanke and Gurkaynak (2001) and Bosworth and Collins (2003) assume that the average marginal return to an additional year of schooling is 8%.

[6] As is well known, the Solow residual has business cycle effects mixed with productivity growth effects. Also, it does not distinguish between two different sources of TFP growth, i.e., technical efficiency change and technological progress. However, a frontier analysis by Koop *et al.* (2000) reports that, for Asia over the 1965–1990 period, TFP growth was driven almost entirely by technological progress: of 3.6 percent TFP growth, 3.5 percent was attributable to technological progress and 0.1 to technical efficiency change. This provides some support to the traditional approach to TFP.

Table 16.1. Basic growth accounts, 1981–2030 (annual average growth rates)

	Actual				Projections	
	1981–1990	**1991–2000**	**2001–2007**	**1981–2007**	**2011–2020**	**2021–2030**
China, People's Rep. of						
GDP	8.34	9.09	11.15	9.35	6.09	4.98
GDP per labor	5.81	7.91	10.22	7.73	5.75	5.06
Labor input	2.53	1.18	0.93	1.61	0.34	−0.08
Education	0.70	1.19	0.83	0.91	0.65	0.15
Capital per labor	5.93	8.72	9.16	7.80	7.50	7.02
Total factor productivity	3.02	3.72	6.06	4.07	2.36	2.17
Hong Kong, China						
GDP	6.24	3.85	4.67	4.95	4.40	2.83
GDP per labor	4.59	2.16	3.33	3.36	3.88	3.44
Labor input	1.65	1.69	1.34	1.58	0.52	−0.61
Education	1.11	−0.08	0.92	0.62	0.72	0.48
Capital per labor	5.62	4.71	1.79	4.29	5.62	4.86
Total factor productivity	1.67	0.33	2.06	1.27	1.20	1.21
India						
GDP	5.39	4.74	6.76	5.51	4.67	4.28
GDP per labor	3.04	2.69	4.73	3.35	2.94	2.90
Labor input	2.35	2.06	2.03	2.16	1.73	1.38
Education	1.10	0.60	0.74	0.82	0.58	0.28
Capital per labor	2.70	3.45	5.78	3.78	3.56	3.68
Total factor productivity	1.30	0.95	1.97	1.34	1.16	1.26
Indonesia						
GDP	5.68	4.11	4.51	4.80	4.66	4.12
GDP per labor	2.64	1.53	2.58	2.21	3.16	3.08
Labor input	3.04	2.58	1.93	2.58	1.50	1.04
Education	0.09	0.80	0.79	0.54	0.46	0.28
Capital per labor	5.69	3.11	−0.04	3.25	3.79	3.84
Total factor productivity	0.31	−0.19	2.12	0.59	1.37	1.37

(*Continued*)

Table 16.1. *(Continued)*

	Actual				Projections	
	1981–1990	1991–2000	2001–2007	1981–2007	2011–2020	2021–2030
Korea, Rep. of						
GDP	8.96	5.33	3.97	6.32	4.39	3.42
GDP per labor	6.34	3.80	2.91	4.51	3.97	3.66
Labor input	2.63	1.53	1.06	1.81	0.42	−0.24
Education	0.85	1.37	0.64	0.99	0.33	0.29
Capital per labor	7.52	7.32	3.61	6.43	4.08	3.93
Total factor productivity	2.82	0.05	1.08	1.35	2.14	1.91
Malaysia						
GDP	5.85	7.40	5.14	6.24	5.51	4.79
GDP per labor	2.43	4.12	2.78	3.15	3.59	3.41
Labor input	3.42	3.28	2.36	3.09	1.92	1.38
Education	1.39	1.38	0.94	1.27	0.52	0.27
Capital per labor	4.67	5.83	1.15	4.19	4.02	4.16
Total factor productivity	−0.27	0.96	1.76	0.71	1.67	1.58
Pakistan						
GDP	5.96	3.51	6.16	5.10	6.76	6.33
GDP per labor	2.71	0.55	2.43	1.84	2.70	2.83
Labor input	3.25	2.96	3.73	3.27	4.06	3.50
Education	0.62	0.76	1.49	0.90	0.88	0.49
Capital per labor	2.30	1.10	0.11	1.29	2.85	3.38
Total factor productivity	1.42	−0.35	1.49	0.78	1.04	1.19
Philippines, The						
GDP	2.02	3.76	4.81	3.39	5.96	5.53
GDP per labor	−1.00	1.10	2.57	0.70	3.84	3.71
Labor input	3.02	2.66	2.24	2.69	2.12	1.82
Education	0.67	0.67	0.53	0.63	0.38	0.30
Capital per labor	0.07	0.69	0.18	0.33	3.50	3.74
Total factor productivity	−1.43	0.42	2.18	0.19	2.21	2.03

(Continued)

Table 16.1. *(Continued)*

	Actual				Projections	
	1981–1990	1991–2000	2001–2007	1981–2007	2011–2020	2021–2030
Singapore						
GDP	7.00	7.84	4.86	6.76	5.24	3.28
GDP per labor	3.80	4.93	2.71	3.94	3.65	3.34
Labor input	3.20	2.91	2.15	2.82	1.59	−0.06
Education	1.32	1.15	0.77	1.11	0.63	0.48
Capital per labor	3.99	4.13	0.84	3.23	5.26	4.71
Total factor productivity	1.42	2.59	1.92	1.98	1.17	1.17
Taipei, China						
GDP	7.61	6.40	3.66	6.14	3.68	2.48
GDP per labor	5.22	4.90	2.36	4.36	3.78	3.44
Labor input	2.40	1.50	1.30	1.78	−0.09	−0.96
Education	0.89	0.97	1.27	1.02	0.47	0.30
Capital per labor	5.52	7.42	2.98	5.56	4.93	4.45
Total factor productivity	2.48	1.35	0.41	1.52	1.52	1.48
Thailand						
GDP	7.54	3.71	4.85	5.42	4.01	3.58
GDP per labor	4.30	3.05	3.34	3.59	3.87	3.64
Labor input	3.24	0.65	1.51	1.84	0.15	−0.06
Education	0.81	0.70	0.91	0.80	0.76	0.52
Capital per labor	3.89	6.42	0.76	4.02	4.16	4.01
Total factor productivity	2.26	0.06	2.48	1.50	1.74	1.72
Vietnam						
GDP	5.69	6.50	7.41	6.44	4.86	3.74
GDP per labor	3.02	4.40	5.12	4.08	3.73	3.37
Labor input	2.67	2.10	2.29	2.36	1.14	0.36
Education	−0.92	0.78	1.02	0.21	0.49	0.12
Capital per labor	1.50	9.13	8.29	6.08	2.91	3.08
Total factor productivity	2.98	0.29	1.19	1.52	2.27	2.07

Note: GDP = gross domestic product. The projections are based on the estimation results in column (2) of Table 16.2.

Sources: Calculations from Heston, Summers, and Aten (2009); ILO (2010); Barro and Lee (2010).

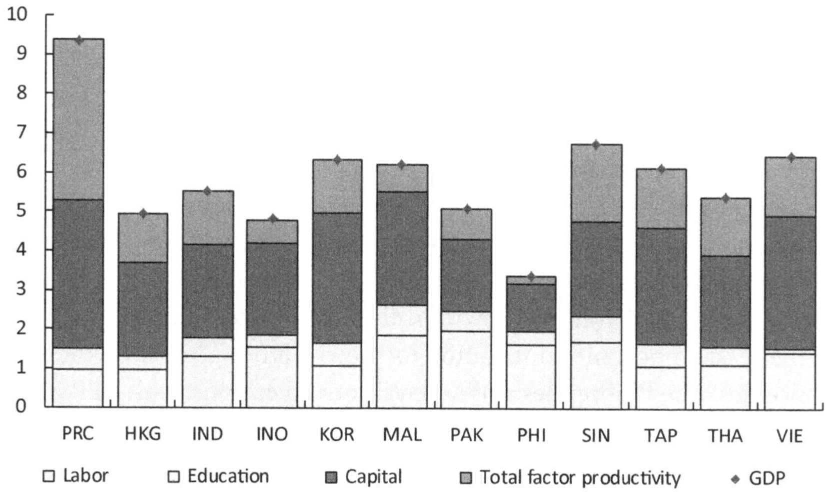

Figure 16.1 Contributions to GDP growth, 1981–2008 (percentage points)
Notes: GDP = gross domestic product; PRC = People's Republic of China; HKG = Hong Kong, China; IND = India; INO = Indonesia; KOR = Republic of Korea; MAL = Malaysia; PAK = Pakistan; PHI = Philippines; SIN = Singapore; TAP = Taipei, China; THA = Thailand; and VIE = Viet Nam.
Sources: Calculations from Heston, Summers, and Aten (2009); ILO (2010); Barro and Lee (2010).

just 5.8% in the first period, to 7.9% in the second, and 10.2% in the third.[7] Viet Nam's performance has been more modest, starting at 3.0% in the 1980s, rising to 4.4% in the 1990s, and then to 5.1% in the 2000s. The Philippines case is even more moderate, beginning with a 1.0% contraction in GDP per labor during 1981–90, followed by a small 1.1% increase in 1991–2000, and a 2.6% rise in 2001–07. The Republic of Korea and Taipei China recorded gradual declines in growth of GDP per labor over the three decades.

Figure 16.1 shows the contributions of the growth of each factor to the growth of output for the 12 Asian economies. We can see from Fig. 16.1 that among the 12 economies in our sample, it is only in the PRC where TFP growth contributed the most to GDP growth between 1981 and 2007.

[7]The Chinese numbers need to be taken with cautions. Summers and Heston (1994) explain in PWT 5.6 that, since "it is widely felt that (China's) growth rates are too high," they arbitrarily lowered the reported consumption growth and investment growth during 1980–1993 by 30 percent and 40 percent, respectively.

Specifically, TFP in the PRC grew by an average of 4.1% from 1981 to 2007.[8,9] Singapore recorded the second fastest growth in TFP, at about 2.0% during the same period. In the majority of the other economies, growth in physical capital accounted for the large part of the growth in GDP. In the PRC, capital stock per labor increased by an average 7.8% per year in 1981–2007. Growth in capital stock per labor was also rapid in the Republic of Korea and Viet Nam, at 6.4% and 6.1%, respectively. The Philippines and Pakistan are exceptions, as GDP growth in these economies was mainly driven by growth in the labor force. Education seems to be the least important contributor to growth among most of the Asian economies. The Philippines and Malaysia are exceptions, with TFP growth the smallest contributor to GDP growth. While the PRC stands out as the country with the highest growth rate, the Philippines's growth is conspicuously slow. From Fig. 16.1, we can see that it has the least commonality with the other economies in the region. We now go to a decadal view of the growth contributors for each economy.

In the 1980s and 1990s, capital was the main source of GDP growth in the PRC. This changed in the 2000s, when TFP growth began to account for more than half of the growth in output. Since the 1980s, labor's contribution to GDP growth has been on a declining trend. Meanwhile, as in previous studies including Bosworth and Collins (2008), the contribution of education is estimated to be small. This result, however, does not necessarily imply that human capital does not matter, for a couple of reasons.

---

[8] There are widely different views on the contribution of TFP growth to China's GDP growth. Young (2003) argues that, after correcting for measurement errors in deflators and labor inputs, TFP growth in the nonagricultural economy of China during 1978–1998 was only 1.4 percent per year. Similarly, Woo (1998) reports TFP growth of 1.1–1.3 percent per year for 1979–1993. On the other hand, World Bank (1997) reports that TFP in China grew at 4.3 percent per year during 1978–1995. Islam and Dai (2007) use standard growth accounting called "primary approach" and obtain a similarly high estimate of TFP growth (4.57 percent per year) for 1991– 2002.

[9] The particularly high TFP growth of China during 2001–2007 may partly reflect business cycle effects, as TFP is measured as a residual. While a measurement problem as to physical capital and human capital may also be accountable for the exceptional TFP growth, we find that our estimates of physical and human capital growth and TFP growth for China are similar to those of Bosworth and Collins (2008) for corresponding years in 1978–2004.

First, our measure of human capital is a function simply of the number of schooling years and thus does not incorporate quality of education. Second, as Benhabib and Spiegel (1994) suggest, human capital may affect TFP indirectly through the adoption and implementation of new technologies.

The major sources of growth for Hong Kong, China follow the patterns recorded in the PRC — capital in the first two decades, and TFP in the third — albeit with differing magnitudes. No definitive trends in labor and education are evident during the three periods reviewed.

In India, growth in capital stock was consistently the main growth driver in the 1980s, 1990s, and 2000s. In the first period, growth in labor and TFP accounted for almost the same rates of contribution to GDP growth, at about 25% each. In the second, the contribution of TFP growth declined to about 20%, allowing labor to shore up a greater share of GDP growth. In the final period, the situation was reversed, with TFP growth explaining a significantly larger share of growth in GDP (about 30%) than labor growth (about 18%). Across all three periods, education was the smallest contributor to growth.

Growth in capital stock explained more than half of the GDP growth in Indonesia in the 1980s and 1990s. By the 2000s, capital fell to third place as a growth contributor. Meanwhile, growth in labor input consistently maintained its rank as the second most important donor to GDP growth. From being an almost non-contributor in the 1980s, education has emerged as a consistent source of GDP growth, accounting for more than 10% of total growth during the 1990s and 2000s.

In the Republic of Korea, capital has been the primary growth source for the last three decades. The share of labor was likewise been consistent, at about 16–18% of GDP growth during the periods in review. The contributions of TFP growth and education, however, were unstable, ranging from 1 to 31% and 6–15%, respectively.

For Malaysia, labor and education were relatively stable sources of growth during the 1980s, 1990s, and 2000s. The share of labor has hovered between 27% and 35%, while that for education has ranged from 11 to 14%. Growth of capital stock has contributed steadily less to GDP growth over the three decades, while TFP growth has progressively explained a larger share of output growth.

Growth in capital stock and in labor has remained the top two GDP growth contributors in Pakistan in the three review periods. However, while capital stock growth dominated in the 1980s, growth in labor prevailed during the 1990s and 2000s. The share of education has been rising over the three decades, starting from just about 6% in the 1980s to about 15% in the 2000s. TFP growth contributed about 24% of GDP growth in the 1980s and 2000s, but subtracted about 10% in the 1990s.

GDP growth in the 1980s in the Philippines was largely explained by growth in labor and capital. Education also contributed positively, but its share was relatively small. During that decade, TFP growth subtracted from growth. In the 1990s, labor and capital were still the top sources of GDP growth, jointly accounting for more than three quarters of the total. Education and TFP growth, meanwhile, each contributed about 11%. By the 2000s, TFP growth had gained the top spot among the sources of GDP growth, with a share of about 45%. Labor growth was still number two, contributing 28% to the total. Capital was a close third, accounting for about 20%. Education barely contributed during the decade.

In Singapore, the share of capital stock growth in GDP growth has been steadily declining over the three growth periods, while the share of TFP growth has been steadily rising. The shares of labor and education have generally been stable at about 22–27% and 9–11%, respectively. In the 1980s and 1990s, the ranking of the sources of GDP growth in Taipei, China was the same — capital stock, TFP, labor, and education.

In the 2000s, capital stock growth was still the largest growth contributor, but labor and education tied for the number two spot. TFP growth fell to fourth place.

There is no evident pattern in the contributors to GDP growth in Thailand. In the 1980s, capital stock, TFP, and labor contributed from 26 to 38% of total growth. The share of education was just about 6%. In the 1990s, growth in capital stock explained more than three fourths of GDP growth. The shares of labor and education were about 11% each, while TFP growth was a measly 2%. By the 2000s, there was a drastic change in the ranking of the growth sources. TFP growth contributed more than half of GDP growth, while capital and labor shares were at 19% each. The share of education remained at 11%.

In Viet Nam, TFP growth was the primary contributor to GDP growth in the 1980s, with a share of about 52%. Growth of capital stock and labor were similar, at about 28–29%. At that time, education subtracted from growth. In the two succeeding decades, capital stock growth was the major contributor to GDP growth. The shares of labor and education were similar during the last two periods, at 19% and 8%, respectively. The share of TFP growth, meanwhile, sharply increased from about 4% in the 1990s to 16% in the 2000s.

16.3. Determinants of Growth

Asia's rapid growth path can be explained by an extended version of the neoclassical growth model that incorporates the role of human capital and technology catch-up (see Barro and Sala-i-Martin, 2003; Sachs *et al.*, 2001). This model predicts 'conditional convergence' of income (output) per capita: a country with low initial income per capita relative to its own long-run (or steady-state) potential level of income per capita will grow faster than a country that is already closer to its long-run potential level of output per capita. The farther an economy is located from its steady-state output level, the greater is the gap of reproducible (physical and human) capital and technical efficiency from their long-run levels. The gap of existing capital from the steady-state level encourages high rates of capital accumulation, by providing higher rates of return to capital. The greater technology gap offers the chance for rapid technology "catch-up" via the diffusion of technology from more technologically advanced economies. Hence, the lower the initial level of per capita output relative to the steady state, the higher subsequent growth tends to be. This framework presumably helps to explain why an industrialized economy such as Japan, with its relatively large capital stock and with it already operating near the world's technological frontier, grows more slowly than emerging Asian countries that are catching up with the leaders.

The 'conditional convergence' framework implies that each country has its own steady-state levels of output per labor and productivity to which it is converging. Crucially, the long-term levels depend on various external environmental and policy variables. Countries with favorable economic policies and economic structure tend to have a higher steady-state level of income, and therefore faster growth at any given initial level of income.

The basic model is summarized in the following system of equations:

$$\Delta \ln A_t = \beta_A \left[\ln(A^{ss}) - \ln(A_{t-1}) \right] \tag{5}$$

$$\Delta \ln k_t = \beta_k \left[\ln(k^{ss}) - \ln(k_{t-1}) \right] \tag{6}$$

$$\Delta \ln h_t = \beta_h \left[\ln(h^{ss}) - \ln(h_{t-1}) \right] \tag{7}$$

$$\Delta \ln y_t = \Delta \ln A_t + \alpha \cdot \Delta \ln k_t + (1-\alpha) \cdot \Delta \ln h_t \tag{8}$$

$$\Delta \ln y_t = \beta_A \left[\ln(A^{ss}) - \ln(A_{t-1}) \right] + \alpha \cdot \beta_k \left[\ln(k^{ss}) - \ln(k_{t-1}) \right] + (1-\alpha) \cdot \beta_h \left[\ln(h^{ss}) - \ln(h_{t-1}) \right]$$

where the growth of each component of GDP (i.e., A, k, and h) is explained by its convergence from the initial level at time t-1 to the steady-state level (denoted by superscript *ss*). β_A, β_k, and β_h denote the coefficients of the adjustment speed of components A, k, and h, respectively.

Figure 16.2 supports the convergence hypothesis. The PRC, which had the lowest initial level of GDP per labor, grew the fastest from 1981 to 2007. Singapore and Hong Kong, China, with significantly higher GDP per labor in 1980, registered relatively lower rates of growth. The Philippines tends to be the outlier, with relatively low initial GDP per labor level, yet recording the lowest growth rate during the three-decade period. Convergence is more apparent in capital stock per labor and TFP, as shown by the steeper fitted lines in the figures. Note that this relationship holds without controlling for the determinants of the steady-state levels.

Considering the determinants of the steady-state levels of A, k, and h, the equations can be rewritten as (see the companion papers by Park (2010), Shioji and Vu (2010), and Lee and Francisco (2010)):

$$\Delta \ln A_t = f(\ln A_{t-1}, \ln life\_ex_{t-1}, h_t, \ln pop_{t-1}, \Delta \ln RND_t) \tag{5'}$$

$$\Delta \ln k_t = f\left(\ln k_{t-1}, \Delta \ln A_t, \ln A_{t-1}, \left(\frac{S}{Y}\right)_t, \Delta \ln pop_t, open_t, prop\_right_t\right) \tag{6'}$$

$$\Delta \ln h_t = f(\Delta enrol_{t,t}, sh\_pop_t^{15-24}) \tag{7'}$$

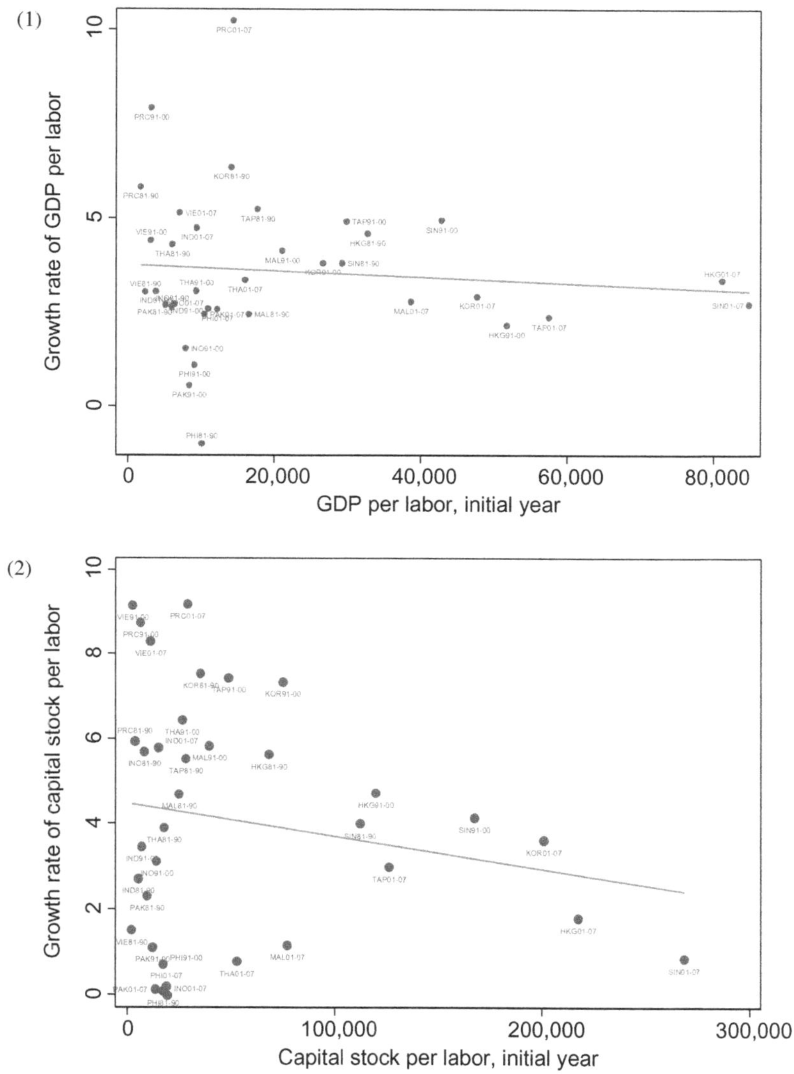

Figure 16.2 Convergence in GDP per labor and its factors, 3 decades
(1) Convergence in GDP per Labor
(2) Convergence in Capital Stock per Labor
(3) Convergence in TFP

Notes: GDP = gross domestic product; TFP = total factor productivity; PRC = People's Republic of China; HKG = Hong Kong, China; IND = India; INO = Indonesia; KOR = Republic of Korea; MAL = Malaysia; PAK = Pakistan; PHI = Philippines; SIN = Singapore; TAP = Taipei, China; THA = Thailand; and VIE = Viet Nam.

Sources: Calculations from Heston, Summers, and Aten (2009); ILO (2010); Barro and Lee (2010).

(3)

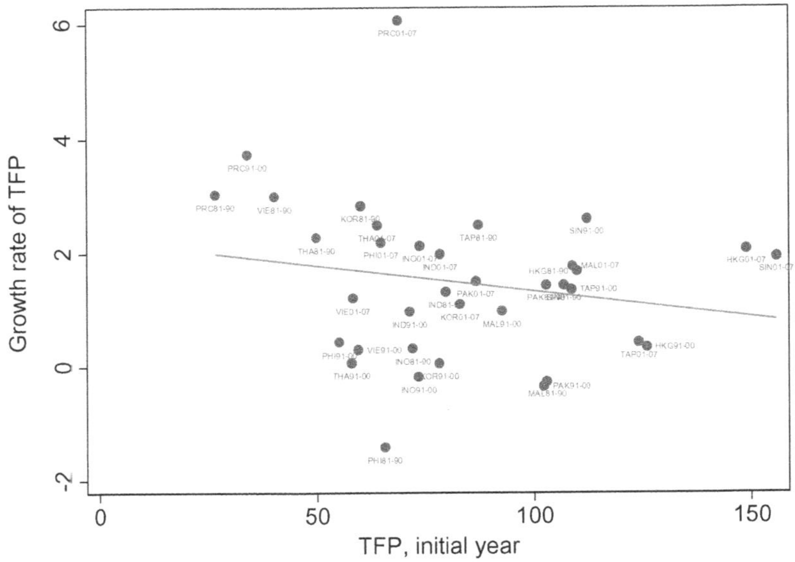

Figure 16.2 (*Continued*)

where $\ln A_{t-1}$ denotes the log of the initial level of TFP, $\ln life\_ex_{t-1}$ the log of the initial life expectancy at birth, $\ln popt_{-1}$ the log of initial population, $\Delta\ln RND_t$ the growth rate of R&D capital stock, $\ln k_{t-1}$ the log of the initial capital stock per worker, $\ln A_{t-1}$ the log of the initial level of TFP, $(S/Y)_t$ the saving rate, $\Delta\ln pop_t$ the growth rate of population, $open_t$ a measure of openness defined as (exports + imports)/GDP, and $prop\_right_t$ the Heritage Foundation's "Property Rights" index, $\Delta enrol_{j,t}$ the change in enrolment rate for level j = primary, secondary, and tertiary, and $sh\_popt_t^{15-24}$ the share of population 15–24 years old to total population.[10]

As dictated by the convergence hypothesis, the growth of each component of GDP is specified as a function of the component's initial level.

[10] The initial levels of TFP and life expectancy at birth can alternatively be defined as relative to levels in the United States, as in Park (2010). We obtain the same results regardless of how the initial levels are defined, because year dummies are included in all regressions.

Also, cross influences between the components are allowed, with the initial level and/or the growth rate of one component affecting the growth rate of another. For example, the initial level of educational attainment is related to TFP growth, and TFP growth is related to the growth rate of capital stock per worker. As additional determinants, initial life expectancy (due to its correlation with people's overall health), population size (due to the non-rivalrous nature of technological innovation), and research and development (R&D) investment (for obvious reasons) are considered for TFP growth. Population growth is expected to have a negative impact on capital accumulation as in the Solow model, while openness and the protection of property rights have a positive impact on capital accumulation. The accumulation of human capital is determined by the relative size and school enrolment of the young-age population.

$\left(\frac{S}{Y}\right)_t$, is also endogenously determined as follows (see the companion paper by Horioka and Terada-Hagiwara (2010)):

$$\left(\frac{S}{Y}\right)_t = f(life\_ex_t, dep\_young_t, dep\_old_t, \ln y_t, \Delta \ln y_t, labor\_part65), \tag{9}$$

where $life\_ex_t$ denotes life expectancy at birth; dep_young_t the youth dependency ratio that is defined as population aged 14 and below divided by population aged 15–64; dep_old_t the old dependency ratio defined as population aged 65 and above divided by population aged 15–64; and labor_part65, the labor force participation rate of elderly people. A longer lifespan is expected to increase savings because people may want to save more in preparation for longer post-retirement spans. Dependency ratios and the GDP growth rate are standard determinants of savings, according to the Life-Cycle Hypothesis. In addition to the GDP growth rate, the level of per capita GDP may also be important for savings, according to the Keynesian consumption theory. Finally, a greater labor participation rate among the elderly may increase aggregate savings by lowering the proportion of dependents among the elderly.

16.4. Estimation Results

Eqs. (5′), (6′), (9), and (8) provide a simultaneous equation system with three endogenous variables — $\Delta\ln A_t$, $\Delta\ln k_t$, $(S/Y)_t$ — and one accounting identity about $\Delta\ln y_t$. All other variables are either exogenous or predetermined. We assume that $\Delta\ln h_t$ is exogenously determined because both its determinants, the enrolment rate and the age structure of population, are exogenous to our specification. Following the convention in the literature, we will assume that all equations are linear.

Since some of the equations contain endogenous variables among the explanatory variables, we need to use instrumental variables (IV) estimation to produce consistent estimates. Also, there may be contemporaneous correlation of errors across equations which should be taken into account to improve efficiency. For these reasons, we estimate the equation system using 3SLS (Three-Stage Least Squares). While system methods are more sensitive to specification error than single equation methods, we find that our system estimation results are largely similar to equation-by-equation IV estimation results.

Our sample is an unbalanced panel that covers both developing and developed economies in 1981–1990, 1991–2000, and 2001–2007. For each period, the first year of the period corresponds to the initial year t – 1 from the above equations. From our initial data set with about 200 countries, we first excluded obvious outlier observations in some of the key variables.[11] We then picked those countries that have no missing values in any of the variables used for at least two out of the three periods. This leaves us with 159 observations from 61 countries. We take the period average for all contemporaneous conditions and the beginning period values for all initial conditions. To control for possible time-fixed effects, period dummy variables are included in all regressions.

In addition to time-fixed effects, we control for Asia-fixed effects and PRC-fixed effects. In particular, we include the Asia dummy in each of Eqs. (5′), (6′), and (9) and include the PRC dummy in Eq. (6′). This is intended to represent the view that developing Asia's economic growth,

[11] Specifically, we excluded the growth rate of R&D stock greater than 0.4, the growth rate of capital-per-worker greater than 0.1 or lower than 0.07, the population growth rate greater than 0.07, and the saving rate lower than 0.5.

particularly in the PRC, has been higher than can be explained by other economies' experiences and that the PRC has been most outstanding in its capital accumulation. We do not control for all country-fixed effects because, while the fit of the model can improve greatly by the inclusion of individual country dummy variables, the issue of cross-country differences in growth will be largely unaddressed.[12]

Our estimation results are provided in Table 16.2. For a robustness check, we estimate the system both with and without the Asia and the PRC dummies. As columns (1) and (2) show, we obtain similar results in both specifications and the results are largely consistent with theoretical expectations. First, regardless of the specification used, convergence is strongly supported by the data. For both $\Delta \ln A_t$ and $\Delta \ln k_t$, the coefficient on the corresponding initial level is significantly negative. Second, there seem to be substantial interactions among endogenous variables. For example, in column (1), the saving rate in the $\Delta \ln k_t$ equation and the GDP growth rate in the $(S/Y)_t$ equation each has a significantly positive coefficient. The coefficients remain positive in column (2), even if less significant and smaller than in column (1). Note that this is not caused by endogeneity biases because we used 3SLS in our estimation. Third, among other results, the positive effect of the level of TFP on $\Delta \ln k_t$ and the positive effect of per-capita GDP on $(S/Y)_t$ are particularly robust. Fourth, the Asia dummy and the PRC dummy are always positive, indicating that Asia in general and the PRC in particular have shown extraordinary performance in all the components that cannot be explained by the variables in the regression. The dummy variables are also statistically significant for the saving rate equation and the $\Delta \ln k_t$ equation. Barro (2001) similarly finds that a dummy variable for five crisis-hit Asian countries enters his investment equation with a significantly positive coefficient.[13] Fifth, although not reported in that table, we find that the overall fit of the regression

[12] Similar problems exist with time-fixed effects. All cross-period differences in growth are controlled away by period dummy variables. This problem can be particularly critical in making forecasts for future periods. See footnote 10.

[13] Although it is unclear what cultural or economic influences the dummy variables represent, inclusion of the variables clearly improves the fit of the regression.

Table 16.2. Estimation results

		(1)	(2)
TFP Growth			
	Log(TFP)	−0.0204	−0.0189
		(−6.24)	(−5.34)
	Log(Life_expect)	0.0449	0.0340
		(3.17)	(2.19)
	Years of schooling	0.0006	0.0012
		(1.07)	(1.96)
	Log(Population)	0.0019	0.0007
		(3.18)	(0.99)
	R&D stock growth	0.0498	0.0409
		(2.61)	(1.85)
	Asia dummy		0.0044
			(1.29)
K/L Growth			
	Log(K/L)	−0.0250	−0.0179
		(−6.52)	(−4.4)
	Log(TFP)	0.0316	0.0222
		(3.73)	(3.00)
	TFP growth	1.2077	0.3274
		(4.42)	(1.21)
	Population growth	−0.2696	−0.6857
		(−1.05)	(−2.79)
	Saving rate	0.1414	0.0578
		(4.97)	(1.79)
	Openness	0.0049	0.0037
		(1.19)	(0.97)
	Property right	0.0004	0.0005
		(4.77)	(5.84)
	Asia dummy		0.0149
			(2.89)
	PRC dummy		0.0420
			(3.27)

(*Continued*)

Table 16.2. (*Continued*)

		(1)	(2)
Saving Rate			
	Life expectancy	0.0029	0.0029
		(1.41)	(1.41)
	Old dependency	−0.3876	−0.4597
		(−2.31)	(−2.65)
	Young dependency	−0.1262	−0.2440
		(−1.08)	(−2.09)
	Elderly participation	0.2663	0.2977
		(3.97)	(4.3)
	GDP growth	3.0528	1.3071
		(3.45)	(1.33)
	Log(GDP per capita)	0.1137	0.1062
		(5.23)	(5.13)
	Asia dummy		0.0560
			(2.25)
Number of countries		61	61
Observations		159	159

Notes: TFP = total factor productivity, R&D = research and development, K = physical capital, L = labor, GDP = gross domestic product. Z-ratios are in parentheses. The system of equations is estimated by the 3SLS (Three-Stage Least Squares) method. Column (1) shows results with the no dummy variable specification. Column (2) shows results for the specification with an Asia dummy for all equations and a PRC dummy for the K/L equation.

Source: Authors' calculations.

among the Asian economies is relatively low for $\Delta \ln k_t$ and high for $(S/Y)_t$.

16.5. Growth Projections, 2011–2030

16.5.1. *Baseline Projections*

Once the equations are estimated, we can solve out the system to derive reduced form equations for the endogenous variables where only exogenous and/or predetermined variables appear on the right hand side.[14] This is straightforward because of the linearity of our system.

Using the reduced form equations in addition to the forecasts of exogenous variables, we can produce forecast series of the endogenous variables. Since historical data for the endogenous variables are currently available only up to 2007, while our projection period starts from 2010, we first need to fill in the gaps by assuming arbitrary numbers. We assume that, for each endogenous variable, the 2001–2007 historical average will hold for 2008 and 2009. We have alternatively used the 2001–2007 fitted values instead of the historical average and found that our results change only marginally. For exogenous variables, we take the forecasts provided by other sources — projections of L are from Kim (2010), while h forecasts are from Lee and Francisco (2010). Exceptions are the following: (i) we assume that R&D stock growth, openness, and property rights will remain constant in each country at their respective 2001–2007 average values for the next two decades; (ii) Viet Nam's R&D stock growth is given by the average of the other Asian countries excluding the four newly industrialized economies of Hong Kong, China, the Republic of Korea, Singapore, and Taipei, China; and (iii) property rights in Taipei, China are assumed to be of the same level as in the Republic of Korea.

We use the estimation results in column (2) of Table 16.2 for our baseline projections. Although not reported here, similar results are obtained with column (1) of Table 16.2,[15] our baseline forecasts are provided in the last two columns of Table 16.1. The main results are as follows. Firstly, the forecasts of GDP growth are consistently lower than the historical averages over 1981–2007 across countries. In particular, forecasts for the PRC's growth at 6.09% for 2011–2020 and 4.98% for 2021–2030, are substantially lower than the historical average of 9.35%. Only for Pakistan and the Philippines do the forecasts exceed the historical average. Secondly, the forecasts closely track the historical cross-country variation in GDP growth. The correlation between 2001–2007 average GDP growth

[14] In each estimated equation, the coefficients on year dummies do not exhibit a clear trend. Thus, we simply take the average of the coefficients on three period dummies and add it to the constant term.

[15] The results are available upon request.

and 2011–2020 average GDP growth as shown in Table 16.1 is 0.5. For GDP per labor growth, the correlation between the historical average and our forecast is 0.76. Thirdly, in all 12 economies, the GDP growth rate is projected to decrease between 2011–2020 and 2021–2030. This result is driven by the "convergence" in both factor accumulation and TFP growth.

In general, the projected performance of the 12 Asian economies explains the cross-country catch-up phenomenon. The low-income economies of the region are generally expected to grow faster than the high-income economies. The model predicts that those that experienced fast growth over the last three decades would tend to grow slower in the future. These countries include Hong Kong, China; the Republic of Korea; Singapore; and Taipei, China. Meanwhile, the PRC, India, and Viet Nam, which have generally recorded rising growth rates over the past three decades, are projected to register slowing growth in the next two decades. However, countries that might have grown below their potential growth rates over the past decades would tend to expand more rapidly than their historical performance. Pakistan and the Philippines belong to this group.[16]

Figure 16.3 shows the sources of growth for developing Asia as a whole and selected individual economies from the 1980s through 2030. On the whole, the contribution of labor is declining as a result of fertility decline and population ageing. It is only in those countries which have not yet fully reaped the demographic dividend, such as ASEAN5, India, and Pakistan, where labor is expected to continue accounting for a substantial share in GDP growth. The contribution of education to GDP growth is also forecast to decline.

In many emerging Asian economies, TFP growth is projected to contribute more to GDP growth in the next two decades than in the past 30 years. This is especially true for Indonesia, the Republic of Korea,

[16] Pakistan and the Philippines have had low growth largely due to institutional weakness and governance failures. These structural problems may well persist for decades to come, preventing the catch-up effect to materialize. Our model does not fully address these problems. Thus, our projections for Pakistan and the Philippines are best interpreted as an estimate of the potential growth rate that these economies can achieve when their capacity is fully utilized.

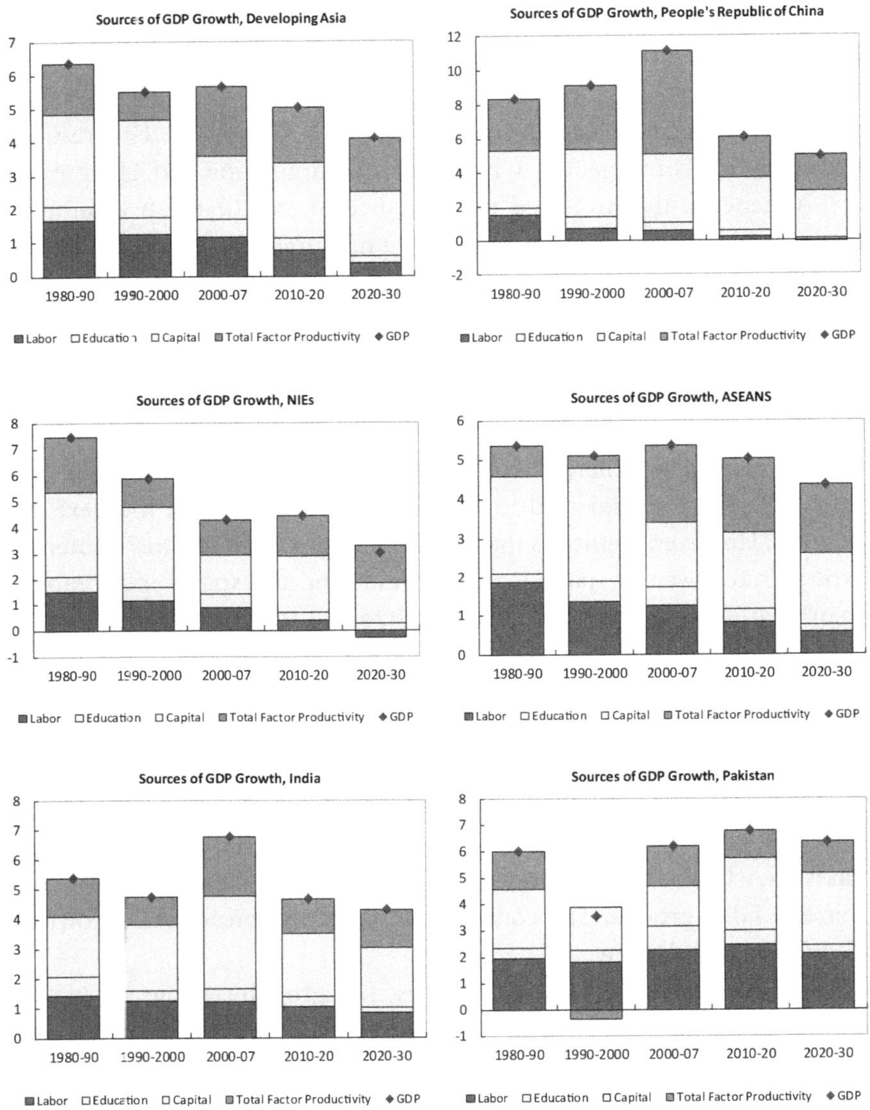

Figure 16.3 Sources of GDP growth, 1981–2030 (percentage points)

Notes: GDP = gross domestic product. Developing Asia comprises all 12 countries considered in the paper. The NIEs comprise Hong Kong, China; Republic of Korea; Singapore; and Taipei, China. ASEAN5 comprise Indonesia, Malaysia, Philippines, Thailand, and Viet Nam.

Sources: Authors' calculations from Heston, Summers, and Aten (2009); ILO (2010); Barro and Lee (2010); and own projections.

Malaysia, Pakistan, the Philippines, Thailand, and Viet Nam. In the PRC, the portion of GDP growth explained by TFP growth is projected to decline over the next 20 years. Nevertheless, TFP growth will remain an important source of the PRC's future GDP growth. TFP growth in Hong Kong, China and Taipei, China are forecast to remain at about the same rates recorded in the last three decades.

For most economies in developing Asia, the contribution of growth in capital stock over the next 20 years is set to decline. This is because in the earlier years of our sample, capital had been a major source of growth for these countries, and as the marginal productivity of capital declines, the contribution of growth in capital stock to GDP growth tends to fall. The exceptions are Pakistan and the Philippines, where growth in capital stock accounted for a smaller share of GDP growth between 1981 and 2007. From 2011 through 2030, this situation is set to improve as growth in capital stock contributes more significantly to GDP growth for Pakistan and the Philippines.

16.5.2. *Reform Scenario*

As mentioned above, our baseline projection assumes that R&D stock growth and property rights will remain constant at their historical means for the next two decades. Changes in the average years of schooling are based on the assumption that for the younger population (15–19 and 20–24 years old), primary, secondary, and tertiary enrolment rates continue to grow over time according to their respective historic trends and follow a similar logistic growth path towards the maximum enrolment rate.[17] Population is assumed to grow according to the United Nation's medium variant fertility rate assumption. The distribution of educational attainment among the older age groups (25 years and above[18]) is assumed

[17] The enrolment rate at time t for level j = primary, secondary, and tertiary is $enrol_{j,t} \frac{enrol_j^{max}}{(1+e^{-a-b_j.time})}$, where $enrol_j^{max}$ is the maximum enrolment rate (that is, 100); a and b are parameters of the logistic growth curve.

[18] For the population 65 years and over, educational attainment is adjusted following the assumption that mortality rate is higher for less educated.

to be the same as that of the age group five years younger five years ago. However, these variables may improve over time, particularly in countries with currently unfavorable conditions, because there is so much room for government policy reforms.

In order to examine the potential impacts of policy reforms on GDP growth, we consider a scenario where all three policy oriented variables — years of schooling, R&D stock growth, and property rights — improve at the same time over the baseline case. These are the same three key variables that determine productivity growth in the endogenous growth model of Aghion and Howitt (2005).[19] First, the growth rate of R&D stock per worker is adjusted upward in proportion to the deviation of each country from the per-worker R&D level of the US. In particular, we assume that the R&D growth rate in country i increases by following a formula such as 0.02 × (log of per worker $R\&D_{US}$ — log of per worker $R\&D_i$). Our scenario assumes that R&D growth accelerates in each economy in a pattern consistent with Park (2010).[20] For reforms in property rights, we consider full convergence by 2020 of the property rights index in each economy to 90, the 2009 level of the US; Hong Kong, China; and Singapore. For example, the PRC's property rights index gains 6.1 points every year to increase from 29 in 2010 to 90 in 2020.[21] The index remains constant after 2020. An education policy reform is assumed such that primary, secondary, and tertiary enrolment rates across all emerging Asian economies will continue to grow logistically over time and by 2030, con-

[19] In Aghion and Howitt (2005), countries with productive R&D, high education, and good property right protection will converge to the growth rate at the technology frontier, while countries with low R&D, poor education, and low property rights will stop growing.

[20] Park (2010) reports that, among OECD economies and the newly industrialized economies of Hong Kong, China, the Republic of Korea, Singapore, and Taipei, China, the R&D growth rate is negatively correlated with the log of initial R&D stock relative to that of the US. When the R&D gap between US and country *i* is negative, the R&D growth rate is set equal to the historical average.

[21] If the PRC remains as a communist country, the level of PRC's property right index may not increase as much as assumed in the scenario by 2020. When the PRC's property right is alternatively assumed to increase by 3 points every year to reach 90 by 2030, the GDP growth rate forecast decreases slightly to be 6.4 percent for 2011–2020 and 6.0 percent for 2021–2030.

verge to the best prevailing enrolment rates among them. The same reform will also result in convergence in primary, secondary, and tertiary completion rates among emerging Asian countries by 2030 to the best prevailing completion rates among them, also following a logistic growth time trend.

GDP growth projections under the reform scenario are reported in Table 16.3. As expected, gains from the policy reforms are most evident among less developed economies with low initial values of the policy variables. The increase in the GDP growth rate ranges from 1.2 to 1.8 percentage points in India, Indonesia, Pakistan, the Philippines, and Viet Nam, and the gain typically accelerates between 2011–2020 and 2021–2030. For the four newly industrialized economies of Hong Kong, China; the Republic of Korea; Singapore; and Taipei, China, the increases are much smaller, with an average of 0.2 percentage points for 2011–2020 and 0.16 percentage points for 2021–2030. For the PRC, the GDP growth rate increases by about 1 percentage point in each decade.

The increases in GDP growth rates arising from policy reforms can be decomposed into the contributions of the resulting improvements in years of schooling, capital per labor, and TFP. Results from our reform scenario show that increases in TFP growth can contribute to GDP growth in developing Asian economies ranging from 0.02 to 0.49 percentage points. India, Indonesia, Pakistan, the Philippines, and Viet Nam are the major beneficiaries of higher TFP growth, raising their average GDP growth per year from 2011 to 2030 by at least 0.34 percentage points.

The extent of the contribution of education to GDP growth is very similar to that of TFP. GDP is forecast to grow by an additional 0.02–0.50 percentage points annually on account of higher years of schooling in the 12 Asian economies. The contribution of education to GDP growth is especially large for India, Pakistan, and Viet Nam, averaging 0.39 percentage points from 2011 to 2030.

The impact of increases in growth in capital per labor on GDP growth is more diverse across emerging Asian economies. Its contribution to GDP growth ranges from 0.01 to 1.14 percentage points per year over the next 20 years. The largest contribution is recorded in Viet Nam, with GDP growing by an additional 1.14 percentage points annually in 2011–2030. In the PRC, India, Indonesia, Pakistan, and the Philippines,

Table 16.3. GDP projections–alternative specifications

	Baseline Projections		Reform Scenario Projections	
	2011–2020	2021–2030	2011–2020	2021–2030
China, People's Rep. of				
GDP	6.09	4.98	7.00	6.23
GDP per labor	5.75	5.06	6.66	6.31
Labor input	0.34	−0.08	0.34	−0.08
Education	0.65	0.15	0.85	0.30
Capital per labor	7.50	7.02	8.93	9.75
Total factor productivity	2.36	2.17	2.58	2.23
Hong Kong, China				
GDP	4.40	2.83	4.62	2.92
GDP per labor	3.88	3.44	4.10	3.53
Labor input	0.52	−0.61	0.52	−0.61
Education	0.72	0.48	0.86	0.55
Capital per labor	5.62	4.86	5.68	4.90
Total factor productivity	1.20	1.21	1.32	1.24
India				
GDP	4.67	4.28	6.13	5.78
GDP per labor	2.94	2.90	4.39	4.40
Labor input	1.73	1.38	1.73	1.38
Education	0.58	0.28	1.77	0.76
Capital per labor	3.56	3.68	4.65	5.74
Total factor productivity	1.16	1.26	1.47	1.65
Indonesia				
GDP	4.66	4.12	6.16	5.82
GDP per labor	3.16	3.08	4.66	4.78
Labor input	1.50	1.04	1.50	1.04
Education	0.46	0.28	1.14	0.54
Capital per labor	3.79	3.84	5.26	6.55
Total factor productivity	1.37	1.37	1.88	1.83

(*Continued*)

Table 16.3. (*Continued*)

	Baseline Projections		Reform Scenario Projections	
	2011–2020	2021–2030	2011–2020	2021–2030
Korea, Rep. of				
GDP	4.39	3.42	4.65	3.70
GDP per labor	3.97	3.66	4.23	3.94
Labor input	0.42	−0.24	0.42	−0.24
Education	0.33	0.29	0.52	0.39
Capital per labor	4.08	3.93	4.33	4.40
Total factor productivity	2.14	1.91	2.19	1.94
Malaysia				
GDP	5.51	4.79	6.24	5.59
GDP per labor	3.59	3.41	4.32	4.21
Labor input	1.92	1.38	1.92	1.38
Education	0.52	0.27	0.92	0.45
Capital per labor	4.02	4.16	4.86	5.72
Total factor productivity	1.67	1.58	1.83	1.65
Pakistan				
GDP	6.76	6.33	8.42	7.97
GDP per labor	2.70	2.83	4.36	4.47
Labor input	4.06	3.50	4.06	3.50
Education	0.88	0.49	2.03	0.62
Capital per labor	2.85	3.38	4.36	6.22
Total factor productivity	1.04	1.19	1.40	1.61
Philippines, The				
GDP	5.96	5.53	7.09	6.81
GDP per labor	3.84	3.71	4.98	4.99
Labor input	2.12	1.82	2.12	1.82
Education	0.38	0.30	0.79	0.41
Capital per labor	3.50	3.74	4.65	5.85
Total factor productivity	2.21	2.03	2.64	2.40

(*Continued*)

Table 16.3. (*Continued*)

	Baseline Projections		Reform Scenario Projections	
	2011–2020	2021–2030	2011–2020	2021–2030
Singapore				
GDP	5.24	3.28	5.35	3.29
GDP per labor	3.65	3.34	3.76	3.35
Labor input	1.59	−0.06	1.59	−0.06
Education	0.63	0.48	0.76	0.46
Capital per labor	5.26	4.71	5.28	4.73
Total factor productivity	1.17	1.17	1.19	1.18
Taipei, China				
GDP	3.68	2.48	3.89	2.73
GDP per labor	3.78	3.44	3.98	3.69
Labor input	−0.09	−0.96	−0.09	−0.96
Education	0.47	0.30	0.59	0.39
Capital per labor	4.93	4.45	5.17	4.90
Total factor productivity	1.52	1.48	1.56	1.50
Thailand				
GDP	4.01	3.58	4.75	4.25
GDP per labor	3.87	3.64	4.60	4.31
Labor input	0.15	−0.06	0.15	−0.06
Education	0.76	0.52	0.94	0.42
Capital per labor	4.16	4.01	4.94	5.39
Total factor productivity	1.74	1.72	2.06	1.91
Vietnam				
GDP	4.86	3.74	6.43	5.73
GDP per labor	3.73	3.37	5.30	5.36
Labor input	1.14	0.36	1.14	0.36
Education	0.49	0.12	1.20	0.40
Capital per labor	2.91	3.08	4.86	6.83
Total factor productivity	2.27	2.07	2.63	2.39

Note: GDP = gross domestic product.
Source: Authors' calculations.

higher growth in capital per labor contributes at least 0.60 percentage points to GDP growth.

These results suggest that through policy reforms, developing Asia can substantially increase its growth performance and partly offset the slowdown in growth caused by the convergence phenomenon.

16.5.3. *Comparison and Discussion of GDP Projections*

Our study's growth projections are comparable to those of earlier studies. Table 16.4 presents our forecasts for GDP growth relative to the forecasts of three other sources, i.e., Maddison (2007), Fogel (2007), and Goldman Sachs (Wilson and Stupnytska, 2007).

Table 16.4. Comparison of projections of GDP growth

	GDP Growth				
	Lee and Hong: Baseline 2011–2030	**Lee and Hong: Reform 2011–2030**	**Maddison: 2004–2030**	**Fogel: 2001–2040**	**Goldman Sachs: 2008–30**
China, People's Rep. of	5.5	6.6	5.0	8.4	5.8
Hong Kong, China	3.6	3.8			
India	4.5	6.0	5.7	7.1	6.2
Indonesia	4.4	6.0	3.5		4.8
Korea, Rep. of	3.9	4.2	2.6		3.2
Malaysia	5.2	5.9			
Pakistan	6.5	8.2			5.0
Philippines, The	5.7	7.0			5.2
Singapore	4.3	4.3			
Taipei, China	3.1	3.3	2.8		
Thailand	3.8	4.5	2.9		
Vietnam	4.3	6.1			7.0

Note: GDP = gross domestic product.
Sources: Authors' calculations from Maddison (2007); Fogel (2007); Wilson and Stupnytska (2007); and own projections.

We find that our GDP growth forecasts are generally higher than Maddison's projected GDP growth rates. Apart from the difference in the average level, however, our forecasts are highly correlated with Maddison's: the correlation coefficient is 0.73 with our baseline projection and 0.80 with our reform scenario projection. Fogel's GDP growth projections for the PRC and India are more optimistic than the results from both our baseline and reform scenarios. In contrast, GDP growth projections by Goldman Sachs are on average in between our baseline results and reform scenario results. The correlation between our forecasts and Goldman Sachs is not particularly high: the correlation coefficient is 0.1 for the baseline specification and 0.4 for the reform scenario specification.

Table 16.5 presents our forecasts for the levels of per capita GDP and GDP in 2030, both under the baseline and reform scenario, along with the actual values in 2007. The PWT 6.3 provides per capita GDP series in PPP-converted US dollars using 2005 as the base year, for 1950–2007. By combining the per capita GDP value for 2007 with our growth forecasts, we extend the per capita GDP series up to 2030. Total GDP forecasts are simply per capita GDP forecasts multiplied by total population forecasts.

Under our baseline specification, GDP is forecast to increase between 2007 and 2030 by 2.7 times, on average, among the 12 developing Asian economies. In particular, GDP in the PRC is forecast to grow 3.9 times, from $11.25 trillion in 2007 to $44.3 trillion in 2030.

The expansion in per capita GDP levels across the region is likewise substantial. Per capital GDP is projected to increase 2.2 times on average among the 12 countries, and 3.6 times in the PRC.

Using our baseline projections, we estimate the share of the Asian economies in world GDP through 2030. For historical data from 1980 to 2007, we use real GDP in 2005 PPP terms from Heston *et al.* (2009). From 2008 to 2010, we use GDP growth rates from IMF (2010). From 2010 onwards, we apply the projected GDP growth rates under our baseline specification for developing Asian economies, while we use Maddison's forecasts for GDP growth for the world, the US, the European Union, and Japan.[22]

---

[22] A similar analysis has been done in a series of papers by Goldman Sachs. However, our results are not directly comparable with those of Goldman Sachs because Goldman Sachs uses the market exchange rate instead of the PPP exchange rate in converting each country's

Table 16.5. GDP and per capita GDP projections

	GDP ($ 2005 PPP billion)			Per Capita GDP ($ 2005 PPP)		
	2007 Actual	2030 Baseline	2030 Reform	2007 Actual	2030 Baseline	2030 Reform
China, People's Rep. of	11,250	44,300	54,984	8,511	30,291	37,596
Hong Kong, China	301	587	606	43,121	71,756	73,978
India	4,322	12,801	17,206	3,826	8,622	11,590
Indonesia	1,217	3,025	4,166	5,186	11,142	15,346
Korea, Rep. of	1,151	2,707	2,856	23,850	55,082	58,117
Malaysia	444	1,346	1,568	17,891	38,149	44,442
Pakistan	608	2,573	3,577	3,588	9,683	13,463
Philippines, The	451	1,168	1,487	4,791	9,388	11,953
Singapore	203	417	422	44,619	76,308	77,235
Taipei, China	617	1,087	1,138	27,005	45,698	47,866
Thailand	612	1,463	1,684	9,406	19,910	22,918
Vietnam	319	874	1,247	3,743	8,288	11,828

Notes: GDP = gross domestic product, PPP = purchasing power parity.
Source: Authors' calculations.

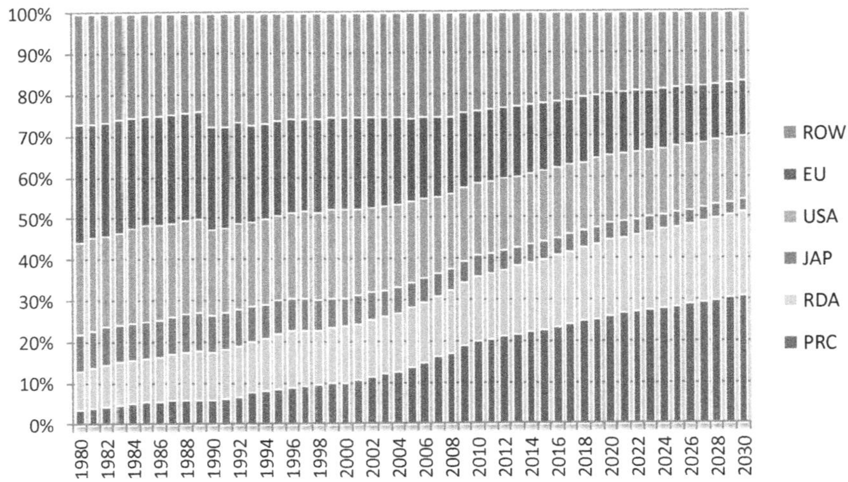

Figure 16.4 Share of world GDP (percent, in 2005 PPP terms)
Notes: GDP = gross domestic product; PRC = People's Republic of China; RDA = Rest of developing Asia; JAP = Japan; USA = United States; EU = European Union; ROW = Rest of the world.
Sources: Authors' calculations from Heston *et al.* (2009); IMF (2010); and own projections.

From Fig. 16.4, we see that as of 2009 the PRC has become the largest economy in the world in 2005 PPP terms. In 2009, the PRC's share in global output at 18.8% has surpassed the 17.7% share of the US and the 18.3% share of the European Union. As the PRC continues to grow at about 5.5% per year in the next two decades, it will remain the world's largest economy, with its share in global GDP rising to 30.8% by 2030. In contrast, the shares of the US and the European Union will decline to 15.4% and 13.3%, respectively.

GDP into common currency units. The discrepancy between the market exchange rate and the PPP exchange rate can be substantial. In the case of the PRC, the PPP exchange rate is about one fourth of the market exchange rate. Also, according to the Balassa–Samuelson effect, the discrepancy between the two exchange rates is negatively correlated with the income level. For example, Frankel (2005) shows that a one percent relative increase in real per capita GDP is associated with about 0.35% real appreciation of the market exchange rate. This implies that, when the market exchange rate is used for international comparisons of GDP, one needs to make adjustments for the real appreciation in accordance with income growth. Since our forecasts are based on constant PPP terms, there is no effect of real appreciation on the movement of the GDP share of each economy.

As a whole, Developing Asia will account for roughly a half (50.6%) of the world economy in 2030. This is almost double the 34.3% share of the region in 2009. India's share will also grow, but at a much more modest rate — from 6.9% in 2009 to 9.1% in 2030. Similarly, Pakistan will account for a larger share of world output in 2030. From 0.9% in 2009, Pakistan's share will grow to 1.6% in 2030.

If, instead, the GDP growth forecasts under our reform scenario specification prevail in the next 20 years, then the PRC's share in 2030 will rise to 37.8% of world GDP. India's share will grow to 12.1% and Pakistan's share will increase to 2.2%. Developing Asia will account for a total of 63.5%.

16.6. Conclusion

The developing Asian region has grown strongly over the past three decades, but the pace clipped twice: in the 1997/98 Asian financial crisis and the 2008/09 global financial crisis. Nevertheless, the region managed to rebound quickly from both.

Using a growth accounting framework, we examine the factors that contributed to developing Asia's rapid economic performance from 1981 to 2007. We find that the region's economic expansion has generally been marked by robust growth in capital accumulation. While labor input, education, and total factor productivity have on the whole been positive as well, their contributions to GDP growth have been much more moderate.

We then generated baseline projections of GDP growth for our sample economies for 2011–2020 and 2021–2030, by combining the growth accounting framework with regression results for key components of GDP growth. We find that GDP growth projections for the next two decades tend to be lower than the historical performance of the 12 developing Asian economies. Only in Pakistan and the Philippines did GDP growth projections turn out to be higher than past figures. Forecasts for 2011–2020 also tend to be higher than those for 2021–2030, driven largely by the "convergence" phenomenon.

For Asia to continue growing strongly, economies should either increase their rates of factor accumulation or raise productivity. Authorities can implement various reforms to achieve these. However, the demographic dividend is likely to wane for most economies in the coming years, so there is not much room for reform in the area of labor inputs. Education was a small contributor to GDP growth between 1981 and 2007, particularly in economies where enrolment and completion rates have fallen short of best practice rates in the region and in the world. Reforms to lift enrolment and completion rates could thus raise the contribution of education to GDP growth in the next 20 years.

The majority of the 12 developing Asian economies have already registered high rates of capital accumulation in the past three decades, and the marginal productivity of capital is set to decline. But if the investment climate is kept attractive, such as through improvements in property rights protection, capital could continue to flow into the regional economies. In addition, improvements in productivity, such as through greater spending on research and development, could increase GDP growth in 2011–2030. Our simulation results confirm that improvements in government policy relating to education, property rights, and research and development can increase our projected GDP growth significantly.

Our reform scenario results also show that considerable gains could be achieved by less developed Asian economies with low initial values of the three policy variables. For instance, GDP growth will increase by more than 1 percentage point in the PRC, India, Indonesia, Pakistan, the Philippines, and Viet Nam. This suggests that policy reforms can substantially increase developing Asia's growth performance and partly offset the slowdown in growth caused by the convergence phenomenon. If Asia adopts growth-friendly policies, it can continue to expand at robust rates in the next 20 years.

References

Aghion, P., Howitt, P., 2005. Growth with quality-improving innovations: an integrated framework. In: Aghion, P., Durlauf, S. (Eds.), *Handbook of Economic Growth*. North Holland, pp. 67–110.

Barro, R.J., 2001. Economic Growth in East Asia Before and After the Financial Crisis. *NBER Working Paper* No. 8330. National Bureau of Economic Research, Cambridge, Massachusetts.

Barro, R., Lee, J.-W., 2010. A New Data Set of Educational Attainment in the World, 1950–2010. *NBER Working Paper* No. 15902. National Bureau of Economic Research, Massachusetts.

Barro, R., Sala-i-Martin, X., 2003. *Economic Growth.* The MIT Press, Massachusetts.

Benhabib, J., Spiegel, M.M., 1994. The role of human capital in economic development: evidence from aggregate cross-country data. *Journal of Monetary Economics* 34(2), 143–173.

Bernanke, B., Gurkaynak, R., 2001. Is Growth Exogenous? Taking Mankiw, Romer and Weil Seriously. *NBER Working Paper* No. W8365. National Bureau of Economic Research, Massachusetts.

Bosworth, B., Collins, S.M., 2003. The empirics of growth: an update. *Brookings Papers on Economic Activity* 34(2), 113–206.

Bosworth, B., Collins, S.M., 2008. Accounting for growth: comparing China and India. *Journal of Economic Perspectives* 22(1), 45–66.

Fare, R., Grosskopf, S., Noriss, M., Zahang, Z., 1994. Productivity growth, technical progress, and efficiency change in industrialized countries. *American Economic Review* 84(1), 66–83.

Fogel, R., 2007. Capitalism and Democracy in 2040: Forecasts and Speculations. *NBER Working Paper* No. 13184. National Bureau of Economic Research, Massachusetts. Available from: www.nber.org/papers/w13184.

Frankel, J., 2005. On the Renminbi: The Choice between Adjustment under a Fixed Exchange Rate and Adjustment under a Flexible Rate. *NBER Working Paper* No. 11274. National Bureau of Economic Research, Cambridge, Massachusetts.

Harberger, A., 1978. Perspectives on capital and technology in less developed countries. In: Artis, M.J., Nobay, A.R. (Eds.), *Contemporary Economic Analysis.* Croom Helm, London.

Heston, A., Summers, R., Aten, B., 2009. *Penn World Table Version 6.3.* Center for International Comparisons of Production, Income, and Prices at the University of Pennsylvania (August).

Horioka, C.Y., Terada-Hagiwara, A., 2010. Saving Projections. *ADB Economics Working Paper.* Asian Development Bank, Manila (forthcoming).

International Labour Office, 2010. Laborsta Database. Available from: http://laborsta. ilo.org/ (accessed 21.06.10).

IMF, 2010. *World Economic Outlook* (April Database). International Monetary Fund, Washington, DC Available from: imf.org/ (accessed 30.06.10).

Islam, N., Dai, E., 2007. Alternative Estimates of TFP Growth in China: Evidence from Application of the Dual Approach. *ICSEAD Working Paper Series*, vol. 2007-03.

Kim, J., 2010. Past and Future of the Labor Force in Emerging Asian Countries. *ADB Economics Working Paper*. Asian Development Bank, Manila (forthcoming).

Kim, J.-I., Lau, L.J., 1996. The source of Asia Pacific economic growth. *Canadian Journal of Economics* 29(2), S448–S454.

King, R.G., Levine, R., 1994. Capital fundamentalism, and economic development, and economic growth. *Carnegie-Rochester Conference Series on Public Policy* 40(1), 259–292.

Koop, G., Osiewalski, J., Steel, M.F.J., 2000. Modeling the sources of growth in a panel of countries. *Journal of Business and Economic Statistics* 18(3), 284–299.

Lee, J.-W., Francisco, R., 2010. Human Capital Accumulation in Emerging Asia 1970–2030. *ADB Economics Working Paper*. Asian Development Bank, Manila (forthcoming).

Lucas, R.E., 1993. Making a miracle. *Econometrica* 61(2), 251–272.

Maddison, A., 2007. *Contours of the World Economy, 1-2030 AD*. Oxford University Press, New York.

Nehru, V., Dhareshwar, A., 1993. A new database on physical capital stock: sources, methodology, and results. *Rivista de Analisis Economico* 8, 37–59.

Park, J., 2010. Projection of Long-term TFP Growth for 12 Asian Economies. *ADB Economics Working Paper*. Asian Development Bank, Manila (forthcoming).

Sachs, J., Radelet, S., Lee, J.-W., 2001. Determinants and prospects of economic growth in Asia. *International Economic Journal* 15(3), 1–29.

Shioji, E., Vu, T.K., 2010. Projection of Investment and Capital Stock for Asia. *ADB Economics Working Paper*. Asian Development Bank, Manila (forthcoming).

Solow, R., 1957. Technical change and the aggregate production function. *Review of Economics and Statistics* 39(3), 312–320.

Summers, R., Heston, A., 1994. Append 5.6: Appendix Table of Contents for a Space-Time System of National Accounts Aka Penn World Table 5.6., In: http:// www.nber.org/pub/pwt56/ascii/append.56.

Wei, Z., Hao, R., 2011. The role of human capital in China's total factor productivity growth: a cross-province analysis. *The Developing Economies* 49(1), 1–35.

Wilson, D., Stupnytska, A., 2007. The N-11: More Than an Acronym. *Global Economics Paper* No. 153. Goldman Sachs Economic Research, New York. Available from: www2.goldmansachs.com/ideas/global-economic-outlook/n-11-acronym-doc.pdf?bcsi_scan_7823DFCE46415F3E=yfE2dnU3ULgbeYezHeQ5ygEAAA BZgooA&bcsi_scan_filename=n-11-acronym-doc.pdf.

World Bank, 1993. *The East Asian Miracle: Economic Growth and Public Policy*. Oxford University Press, New York.

World Bank, 1997. *China 2020: Development Challenges in the New Century.* World Bank, Washington, DC.

Woo, W.T., 1998. Chinese economic growth: sources and prospects. In: Fouquin, M., Lemoine, F. (Eds.), *The Chinese Economy: Highlights and Opportunities.* Economia, London.

Young, A., 2003. Gold into base metals: productivity growth in the People's Republic of China during the reform period. *Journal of Political Economy* 111(6), 1220–1261.

Index

Lightning Source UK Ltd.
Milton Keynes UK
UKOW06n1555240516

274908UK00002B/3/P

9 789814 749633